Lecture Notes in Computer Science 13066

More information about this subseries at http://www.springer.com/series/7410

Daniel Dougherty · José Meseguer ·
Sebastian Alexander Mödersheim ·
Paul Rowe (Eds.)

Protocols, Strands, and Logic

Essays Dedicated to Joshua Guttman
on the Occasion of his 66.66th Birthday

 Springer

Editors
Daniel Dougherty
Department of Computer Science
Worcester Polytechnic Institute
Worcester, MA, USA

José Meseguer
Th.M. Siebel Center for Computer Science
University of Illinois Urbana-Champaign
Urbana, IL, USA

Sebastian Alexander Mödersheim ⓘ
Institute of Mathematics and Computer
Science
Technical University of Denmark
Kongens Lyngby, Denmark

Paul Rowe
J83K
The MITRE Corporation
Bedford, MA, USA

ISSN 0302-9743   ISSN 1611-3349   (electronic)
Lecture Notes in Computer Science
ISBN 978-3-030-91630-5   ISBN 978-3-030-91631-2   (eBook)
https://doi.org/10.1007/978-3-030-91631-2

LNCS Sublibrary: SL4 – Security and Cryptology

Joshua D. Guttman

Preface

This volume contains papers written in honor of Dr. Joshua Guttman on the occasion of his 66.66th birthday, in recognition of his seminal contributions to the foundations of computer security and in celebration of the generosity of spirit that his friends and colleagues have enjoyed over many years.

Joshua, as Research Professor at Worcester Polytechnic Institute and Senior Principal Researcher at The MITRE Corporation, has been for many years a leader in the field of formal methods for security. He has generated foundational notions and results and has led the development of several tools for the analysis of systems. Through this entire time he has been a vital presence in the global community, forming collaborations, facilitating the creation and maintenance of conferences and workshops, and mentoring young researchers.

Computer security has become a rich and varied field, with an ever-expanding array of problems and techniques for their solution. Security protocols, sometimes called cryptographic protocols, are communication protocols designed to achieve goals such as authentication, confidentiality, and integrity. The problem of reasoning about security protocols has received considerable attention over the past 30 years and various algorithms and tools for checking security properties have been developed. A notable aspect of research in security is that it features the interaction between sophisticated mathematical theories and powerful software tools.

Perhaps Joshua's most influential and enduring contribution to the field has been the development of the strand space formalism for analyzing cryptographic protocols. It is one of several "symbolic approaches" to security protocol analysis in which the underlying details of cryptographic primitives are abstracted away, allowing a focus on potential flaws in the communication patterns between participants. In the strand space formalism, the history of individual protocol participants is organized into patterns of message transmissions and receptions called "strands." A network adversary's capabilities are naturally represented by strands as well. The strand space formalism lies at the foundation of at least three separate automated protocol analysis tools (CPSA, Maude-NPA, and Scyther).

The characteristic feature of Joshua's research approach is the recognition of the core principles involved in a research question and the consequent emphasis on understanding these key elements. This has resulted in research contributions to a variety of domains beyond the confines of cryptographic protocol analysis, including such topics as policy analysis for Security Enhanced Linux and Software Defined Networks, information flow, and remote attestation.

His attention to the underlying logic of strand spaces has also allowed him to merge domain-specific reasoning about protocols with general purpose, first-order logical theories. This enables analyses that explore the protocol in the base theory of strand spaces, but also reason about higher-level system processes (e.g. policies based on the protocols) in the more generic logic.

Indeed, this has led to recent work that weaves many of the threads of research described above into a single approach for analyzing Intel's SGX attestation mechanism. The power of Joshua's clarity of thought is exemplified by this combination of protocol analysis, remote attestation, and policy analysis ideas into a single approach.

The identification of clear principles in a domain paves the way to automated reasoning, and Joshua has been a leader in the development and distribution of several tools for security analysis.

Joshua is a principal architect of the Cryptographic Protocol Shapes Analyzer (CPSA). The crucial aspect of CPSA is that it provides users with the ability to play "what if?" with protocols. Users not trained in formal logic can explore the expected—and unexpected—behaviors of a protocol without necessarily having to specify formal properties they hope to be true.

In the mid 2000's Dr. Guttman, with coworkers at MITRE, designed the Cryptographic Protocol Programming Language (CPPL), a domain-specific programming language for expressing cryptographic protocols. The key innovation of CPPL is the ability to associate trust management assertions with protocol actions, so that the actions of each agent are compatible with its own trust policy.

The Security-Enhanced Linux Analysis Tool (SLAT), he developed with colleagues in the early 2000's, is a tool for verifying information-flow properties of access-control policies in the highly-influential SELinux operating system.

In the early 1990's Joshua, with colleagues William Farmer and F. Javier Thayer, developed the Interactive Mathematical Proof System (IMPS). IMPS was a novel approach to interactive theorem proving, based on higher-order classical logic, an interesting treatment of partiality, and proof tactics.

Alongside Joshua's research contributions stands the equally important impact he has had through his service and personal relationships with members of the community. Joshua was one of the founders of the Computer Security Foundations Workshop (now Symposium), and of the Principles of Security and Trust workshop. As a faculty member at Worcester Polytechnic Institute he has advised undergraduate and graduate students, at MITRE he has worked with a stream of summer interns and beginning researchers, and he routinely serves as an external committee member on international PhD committees.

We are honored to consider Joshua a colleague and friend, and it has been a pleasure to edit this volume celebrating his achievements. We thank all the authors who contributed articles and also those who helped us review them.

December 2021

Daniel Dougherty
José Meseguer
Sebastian Mödersheim
Paul Rowe

Contents

Securing Node-RED Applications

Mohammad M. Ahmadpanah[1(✉)], Musard Balliu[2], Daniel Hedin[1,3],
Lars Eric Olsson[1], and Andrei Sabelfeld[1]

[1] Chalmers University of Technology, Gothenburg, Sweden
mohammad.ahmadpanah@chalmers.se
[2] KTH Royal Institute of Technology, Stockholm, Sweden
[3] Mälardalen University, Västerås, Sweden

Abstract. Trigger-Action Platforms (TAPs) play a vital role in fulfilling the promise of the Internet of Things (IoT) by seamlessly connecting otherwise unconnected devices and services. While enabling novel and exciting applications across a variety of services, security and privacy issues must be taken into consideration because TAPs essentially act as persons-in-the-middle between trigger and action services. The issue is further aggravated since the triggers and actions on TAPs are mostly provided by third parties extending the trust beyond the platform providers.

Node-RED, an open-source JavaScript-driven TAP, provides the opportunity for users to effortlessly employ and link *nodes* via a graphical user interface. Being built upon Node.js, third-party developers can extend the platform's functionality through publishing nodes and their wirings, known as *flows*.

This paper proposes an essential model for Node-RED, suitable to reason about nodes and flows, be they benign, vulnerable, or malicious. We expand on attacks discovered in recent work, ranging from exfiltrating data from unsuspecting users to taking over the entire platform by misusing sensitive APIs within nodes. We present a formalization of a runtime monitoring framework for a core language that soundly and transparently enforces fine-grained allowlist policies at module-, API-, value-, and context-level. We introduce the monitoring framework for Node-RED that isolates nodes while permitting them to communicate via well-defined API calls complying with the policy specified for each node.

1 Introduction

Trigger-Action Platforms (TAPs) play a vital role in fulfilling the promise of the Internet of Things (IoT). TAPs empower users by seamlessly connecting otherwise unconnected *trigger* and *action* services. Popular TAPs like IFTTT [24] and Zapier [57], as well as open-source alternatives like Node-RED [36], offer users the ability to operate simple trigger-action *applications* (or, for short, *apps*) such as "Tweet your Instagrams as native photos on Twitter" ☗, "Get emails via Gmail with new files added to Dropbox" ☗, and "Covid-19 live Ticker via Twitter" ☗.

© Springer Nature Switzerland AG 2021
D. Dougherty et al. (Eds.): Guttman Festschrift, LNCS 13066, pp. 1–21, 2021.
https://doi.org/10.1007/978-3-030-91631-2_1

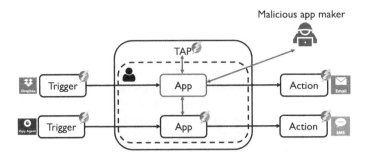

Fig. 1. Threat model of a malicious app deployed on a single-user TAP [3].

A TAP is effectively a "person-in-the-middle" between trigger and action services. While greatly benefiting from the possibility of apps to run third-party code, TAPs are subject to critical security and privacy concerns. Attacks by third-party app makers on the platform may lead to compromising the integrated trigger and action services. Figure 1 illustrates how a malicious app deployed by a user on a TAP like Node-RED can compromise the associated trigger and action services, another installed app, and the platform [3]. Depending on the security configuration of the TAP's deployment, the attacker may also compromise the underlying system.

In contrast to proprietary centralized platforms such as IFTTT and Zapier, Node-RED can be entirely run on a user's own server. Node-RED is an open-source platform built on top of Node.js, enabling users to inspect and customize the source code of the platform and the apps as desired. Moreover, Node-RED relies on JavaScript packages from third parties to facilitate the integration of new functionalities. In fact, Node.js *nodes* are the basic building blocks of Node-RED apps (also named as *flows*), freely available on the Node Package Manager (NPM) [43] and automatically added to the Node-RED Library [41]. Node-RED is inspectable and thus can be verified by users in terms of the platform's correctness and security. Third-party apps integrated into the underlying platform, however, can still threaten the security of the users and the entire system.

The starting point of this paper is the recently identified attacks on Node-RED by malicious nodes, ranging from exfiltrating users' sensitive data to taking over the platform and the host system [3]. A Node-RED flow is technically a static representation of how nodes are wired together; therefore, a malicious node controlled by an attacker can be employed in any user-defined or third-party flows, resulting in malicious behaviors.

This observation motivates the need for controlling APIs invoked in nodes to ensure the security of the platform and the users. Although the enforcement mechanism must guarantee security, it also should restrict access only if it is against the node's policy, according to the *least privilege principle* [47]. Only the APIs which are necessary for the intended functionality should be accessible in a node; thus, if none of the APIs of a module are required, loading of the module must be denied. In some cases, the interaction through APIs needs to be

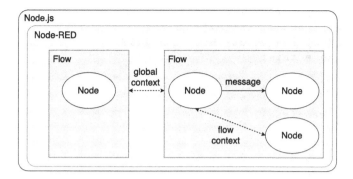

Fig. 2. Node-RED architecture [3].

value-sensitive when an API call should be permitted only with a list of defined arguments, for instance, when it comes to allowing a node to make an HTTPS request to a specific trusted domain. Furthermore, Node-RED makes use of both message passing and the shared context [40] to exchange information between nodes and flows, and both types of exchange need to be secured. Previous work proposes SandTrap [3], a runtime monitor for JavaScript-driven TAPs. However, SandTrap's security guarantees are argued only informally.

Motivated by SandTrap, this work is a step toward formally understanding how to monitor Node-RED apps. We present a sound and transparent monitoring framework for Node-RED for enforcing fine-grained allowlist policies at module-, API-, value-, and context-level. In the following, we discuss Node-RED along with overviewing platform- and app-level vulnerabilities and attacks (Sect. 2); propose an essential model for Node-RED, suitable to reason about nodes and flows, be they benign, vulnerable, or malicious; and present a monitoring framework to express and enforce fine-grained security policies, proving its soundness and transparency (Sect. 3).

2   Node-RED Vulnerabilities

Node-RED is "a programming tool for wiring together hardware devices, APIs and online services", which provides a way of "low-code programming for event-driven applications" [36]. As an open-source platform, Node-RED is mainly targeted for deployment as a single-user platform, although it is also available on the IBM Cloud platform [23]. We overview the architecture of Node-RED (Sect. 2.1) and explain two types of vulnerabilities with respect to our attacker model, i.e., malicious app makers: (i) *platform-level isolation vulnerabilities* (Sect. 2.2) and (ii) *application-level context vulnerabilities* (Sect. 2.3). Our discussion expands the condensed presentation of these vulnerabilities from previous work [3].

```
module.exports = function(RED){
  function NodeName(config){
    RED.nodes.createNode(this, config);
    var node = this;
    // register a callback when a message is received...
    node.on("input", function(msg){
      ... // functionality of node
      node.send(msg); // or an array of messages for multiple
                      outputs
    });
  }
  RED.nodes.registerType("type-name", NodeName);
}
```

Fig. 3. Node-RED node structure.

2.1   Node-RED Platform

Figure 2 illustrates the Node-RED architecture, consisting of a collection of apps, known as *flows*, linking components called *nodes*. The Node-RED runtime is built on the Node.js environment and can run multiple flows simultaneously. It supports inter-node and inter-flow communication via direct messages through the wiring between nodes in a flow, while the *flow* and the *global* contexts [40] are alternative communication channels between the nodes of a flow and across the nodes of different flows, respectively.

A node is a reactive Node.js application triggered by receiving messages on at most one input port (dubbed *source*) and sending the results of (side-effectful) computations on output ports (dubbed *sinks*), which can be potentially multiple, unlike the input port. Figure 3 illustrates the code structure of a Node-RED node. A special type of node without sources and sinks, called *configuration* node, is used for sharing configuration data, such as login credentials, between multiple nodes.

A flow is a representation of nodes connected together. End users can either create their own flows on the platform's environment or deploy existing flows provided by the official Node-RED catalog [33] and by third parties [41]. As shown in Fig. 4, flows are JSON files wiring node sinks to node sources in a graph of nodes where messages, represented by JavaScript objects, are passed between. Multiple messages can be sent by any given node, although instances of a single message can be repeatedly sent to multiple nodes as well. To facilitate end-user programming [55], flows can be shown visually via a graphical user interface and deployed in a push-button fashion. As an example, Fig. 5 demonstrates a flow that retrieves earthquake data for logging and notifying the user whenever the magnitude exceeds a threshold. Specifically, the flow retrieves data of the recent quakes (either periodically or by clicking on the button), parses the given CSV file, and shows the data (stored in `msg.payload`) to the user. For each magnitude value exceeding the specified threshold, it also branches and the payload triggers an alarm notification.

```
[                           // list of nodes
  {                         // node 0
    /* parameters of interest in every node */
    id: NODE0,              // unique ID of node, string
    type: function         // type of node, string
    wires: [                // array of array of strings
      [ NODE1 ],            // first output port to node 1
      [ NODE2, NODE3 ]     // second output port to nodes 2 and 3
    ],
    ...                     // other parameters
  },
  ...                       // other nodes
]
```

Fig. 4. Node-RED flow structure.

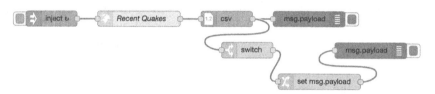

Fig. 5. Earthquake notification and logging ☑.

In Node-RED, *contexts* provide a shared communication channel between different nodes without using the explicit messages that pass through a flow [40]. Therefore the node wiring visible in the user interface reflects only a part of the information flows that are possible in the flow. It introduces an implicit channel that is not visible to the user via the graphical interface of a flow. Node-RED defines three scope levels for the contexts: (i) *Node*, only visible to the node that sets the value, (ii) *Flow*, visible to all nodes on the same flow, and (iii) *Global*, visible to all nodes on any flow. For instance, a sensor node may regularly update new values in one flow, while another flow may return the most recent value via HTTP. By storing the sensor reading in the global shared context, the data is accessible for the HTTP flow to return.

Node-RED security relies on the platform running on a trusted network, ensuring that users' sensitive data is processed in an environment controlled by the users. The official documentation [37] also includes programming patterns for securing Node-RED apps. These patterns include basic authentication mechanisms to control access to nodes and wires. The official node Function ☑ runs user-provided code in a vm sandbox [42], suggesting that it may protect the user from unauthorized access. However, the vm's sandbox "is not a security mechanism" [42], and there are known breakouts [26].

TAPs generally lack the means to specify user's security policies [9]. Fortunately, Node-RED's user-centric setting enables us to *interpret* intended security policies. In fact, Node-RED's GUI for flows provides an intuitive way to inter-

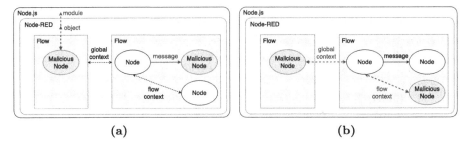

Fig. 6. Node-RED vulnerabilities: (a) Isolation vulnerabilities; (b) Context vulnerabilities [3].

pret top-level user policies; it is reasonable to consider that the user endorses the flow of information between the nodes connected by the graph that depicts a flow in the GUI. For instance, the Earthquake notification flow in Fig. 5 implies a policy where notification data may only flow to the notification message. Only the Inject node can trigger updates. The policy allows no other node (from any flow) to tamper with the Recent Quakes node, preventing any malicious node from corrupting the source of quake information. Such an interpretation provides us with a *baseline* security policy. For more fine-grained policies, e.g., the list of permitted URLs to retrieve the recent quakes, it is reasonably presumed that the node developer designs these *advanced* policies since they know the precise specification of the node. The provided policies can later be vetted by the platform and the user, before deploying the node. SandTrap [3] offers a policy generation mechanism to aid developers in designing the policies, enabling both baseline and advanced policies customized by developers or users to express fine-grained app-specific security goals.

In the following, we discuss Node-RED attacks and vulnerabilities that motivate enriching the policy mechanism with different granularity levels. These policies will further be formalized in Sect. 3.

2.2   Platform-Level Isolation Vulnerabilities

While facilitating the integration and automation of different services and devices, due to imposing insufficient restrictions on nodes, Node-RED is exploitable by malicious node makers. All APIs provided by the underlying runtimes, Node-RED and Node.js, are accessible for node developers, as well as the incoming messages within a flow. As shown in Fig. 6a, there are various attack scenarios for malicious nodes [3]. At the Node.js level, an attacker can create a malicious Node-RED node including powerful Node.js libraries like child_process, allowing the attacker to execute arbitrary shell commands with exec, e.g., taking full control of the user's system [44]. Restricting library access is laborious in Node-RED; while access to a sensitive library like child_process is required for the functionality of Node-RED, attackers can exploit trust propagation due to transitive dependencies in Node.js [45,58]. A malicious node enables the attacker to compromise the confidentiality and integrity of sensitive data and libraries stored by other flows in the global context. A malicious node within a sensitive flow may also indirectly read and modify sensitive data by manipulating the flow context.

At the platform level, the main object in the Node-RED structure, named RED [39], is also vulnerable. There are different ways for a malicious node to misuse the RED object, such as aborting the server (e.g., by RED.server._events = null) or introducing a covert channel shared between multiple instances of the node in different flows by modifying existing properties or adding new properties to the RED object (like RED.dummy). Therefore, *access control at the level of modules and shared objects* is necessary for Node-RED nodes.

On the other hand, a malicious node can directly manipulate incoming messages resulting in accessing or tampering with the sensitive data. As a subtle example of this scenario to invade users' privacy, the official Node-RED email 🗗 can be modified to send the email body to the original recipient and also forward a copy of the message to an attacker's address. The benign code sets the sending options sendopts.to to contain only the address of the intended recipient:

```
sendopts.to = node.name || msg.to; // comma separated list
    of addresses
```

It can be modified to the following by a malicious node maker to include the attacker's address as well:

```
sendopts.to = (node.name || msg.to) + ", me@attacker.com";
```

In this example, we demonstrate that an attacker can alter the value that is placed as the argument of an API call, which is necessary for the functionality of the node, to steal sensitive information of the user without being noticed. As a result, the combination of function identity and its arguments needs to be considered in security checks. This attack motivates us to provide *fine-grained access control at the level of APIs and their input parameters.*

We refer the interested reader to other types of investigated vulnerabilities in Node-RED [3], such as the impact of compromised package repository and *name squatting* [58] attack. The latter is critical since the "type" of nodes (what flows use to identify them) is simply a string, which multiple packages can possibly match. A flow defined by a third party can include the attacker's malicious node unless the user inspects each and every node to verify that there are no deviations from the expected "type" string.

The empirical study shows the implications of such attacks [3]: privacy violations may occur in 70.40% of Node-RED flows and integrity violations in 76.46%. The vast number of privacy violations in Node-RED reflects the power of malicious developers to exfiltrate private information.

2.3   Application-Level Context Vulnerabilities

Node-RED uses various levels of the shared context to exchange data across nodes and flows in an implicit manner. Figure 6b depicts the attack scenarios to exploit vulnerabilities by reading and writing to libraries and variables shared in the global and flow contexts [3]. The *Node* context shares data with the node itself; thus only the shared contexts at the levels of *Flow* and *Global* are intriguing to investigate. Malicious nodes in these scenarios can exploit other vulnerable Node-RED nodes, even if the platform is secured against attacks in Sect. 2.2.

Several Node-RED core nodes [38] make use of the shared context for their purposes, including the nodes executing any JavaScript function (`Function`), triggering a flow (`Inject`), generating text to fill out a template (`Template`), routing outgoing messages to branches of a flow by evaluating a set of rules (`Switch`), and modifying message properties and setting context properties (`Change`). It is shown that more than 228 published flows utilize flow or global context in at least one of the member nodes and more than 153 of the published Node-RED packages directly read from or modify the shared context [3].

The main purpose of using the shared context is data communication between nodes. Malicious operations on the shared data, such as tampering, adding, or erasing, may lead to integrity and availability attacks, as well as to disrupting the functionality entirely. As a real-world example, the Node-RED flow "Water Utility Complete Example" ⧉ is vulnerable considering misuse of the *Global* context. Targeting SCADA systems, this flow manages two tanks and two pumps; the first pump pumps water from a well into the first tank, and the second pump transfers water from the first to the second tank. The status of the tanks are stored in globally shared variables as follows:

```
global.set("tank1Level", tank1Level);
global.set("tank1Start", tank1Start);
global.set("tank1Stop",  tank1Stop);
```

Later, to determine whether a pump should start or stop, the flow retrieves the shared status from the *Global* context:

```
var tankLevel  = global.get("tank1Level");
var pumpMode   = global.get("pump1Mode");
var pumpStatus = global.get("pump1Status");
var tankStart  = global.get("tank1Start");
var tankStop   = global.get("tank1Stop");
if (pumpMode === true && pumpStatus === false && tankLevel
    <= tankStart){
  // message to start the pump
}
else if (pumpMode === true && pumpStatus === true &&
    tankLevel >= tankStop){
  // message to stop the pump
}
```

A malicious node installed by the user and deployed in the platform could alter the context relating to the tank's reading to either exhaust the water flow (never start) or cause physical damage through continuous pumping (never stop).

One can also use the context feature to share resources such as common libraries. In addition to integrity and availability concerns, this approach opens up possibilities for exfiltrating private data. An attacker can encapsulate a library to collect any sensitive information sent to the library. For instance, by modifying the `opencv` shared library inside a malicious node, the attacker can exfiltrate private information of video streaming for motion detection ⬀. More details and examples of such vulnerabilities are also studied [3].

These vulnerabilities motivate the need for monitoring *access control at the level of context*.

3   Formalization

Section 2 motivates the need for secure integration of untrusted code in general and restricting node-to-node and node-to-environment communications (i.e., between nodes, library functions, and contexts) for Node-RED in particular. To achieve this, we propose a runtime monitoring framework capable of enforcing allowlist policies at the granularity of modules, APIs and their input parameters, and variables used in the shared context. Our runtime framework formalizes the core of the flow-based programming model of Node-RED and was the basis when developing the JavaScript monitor SandTrap [3].

This section presents a security model for Node-RED apps and characterizes the essence of a fine-grained access control monitor for the platform. We show how to formalize and enforce security policies for nodes at the level of APIs and their values, along with the access rights to the shared context. Our main formal results are the soundness and transparency of the monitor.

3.1   Language Syntax and Semantics

Syntax. We define a core language to capture the reactive nature of nodes and flows. Nodes are reactive programs triggered by input messages to execute the code of an event handler and potentially produce an output message. Flows model connections between nodes by specifying the destination nodes for each node's output port. Given the set of member nodes with their handlers, it is sufficient to state the successor nodes on each output port to construct a flow.

A flow is syntactically defined as a set of nodes, written $F = \{N_k \mid k \in K\}$, where K is a finite subset of $\mathbb{N}$, and k indicates a unique node identifier. A Node-RED environment may execute flows simultaneously and the global environment is defined by a set of flows, written $G = \{F_l \mid l \in L\}$, where L is a finite subset of $\mathbb{N}$, and l denotes a unique flow identifier. Based on a generalization of Node-RED nodes, Fig. 7 presents the syntax of a reactive language inspired by Devriese and Piessens [17], where Val, Var, and Fun denote the set of all possible values, variables, and functions, respectively. A handler $handler\,(x)\{c\}$ is defined by an input parameter x, which is bound in a command c to perform a computation. While most commands are standard imperative constructs, we use command $send(e, i)$ to pass the value of expression e to the node's output port identified by i. For simplicity, we use functions $f(e)$ to model module imports, API calls, user-defined functions, and primitive operations such as addition and concatenation. To model the shared context, we distinguish between *node* variables Var_N, *flow* variables Var_F, and *global* variables Var_G such that $Var = Var_N \uplus Var_F \uplus Var_G$.

$v \in Val, x \in Var, f \in Fun, i \in \mathbb{N}$
$e ::= v \mid x \mid f(e)$
$c ::= skip \mid x := e \mid if\ e\ then\ c\ else\ c \mid while\ e\ do\ c \mid c\ ;\ c \mid send\ (e, i)$
$h ::= handler\ (x)\{c\}$

Fig. 7. Syntax of node handlers.

Semantics. We model the execution of Node-RED apps by defining the node semantics, flow semantics, and global semantics, respectively. Our trace-based semantics records the sequence of events produced during the execution of a flow. We use these events to define a semantic security condition that our monitor will enforce in a sound and transparent manner.

Node Semantics. A node $N = \langle config, wires, l \rangle_k$ is defined by a node configuration $config$, an array $wires$ that specifies the connected nodes in the flow associated with output ports, an identifier l that indicates the flow that the node belongs to, and a unique node identifier k. Index k refers to an element of node N_k, as in $config_k$ for the configuration of node k.

A node configuration $config = \langle c, M, I, O \rangle$ stores the state of the node during the execution, where c is a command, a handler, or a termination signal ($stop$), $M = [m_N, m_F, m_G]$ represents the memory for the three scopes of node ($m_N : Var_N \rightarrow Val$), flow ($m_F : Var_F \rightarrow Val$), and global ($m_G : Var_G \rightarrow Val$), where Var_N, Var_F, and Var_G are disjoint sets, I is the input channel, and O is the array of output channels, reflecting that a node has one input port and as many output ports as it requires . We model an input (output) channel as a sequence of values that a node receives (sends). A class of nodes, called *inject* nodes, is triggered by external events such as button click or time. Inject nodes send new messages to a flow, thus triggering the execution of the flow. The *wires* array records the nodes that can read the content of the output channel for the corresponding output port. A node receives a message if the node identifier is listed in *wires* among the recipients of the output port assigned in a send command.

Trace-Based Semantics. Figure 8 illustrates the small-step semantics of nodes. We annotate transitions with the trace of events thus generated, where $\rightarrow\ \subseteq Config \times Config$ and $\Downarrow : (Exp \times Mem) \rightarrow Val$. A trace T is a finite sequence of events $t_k \in E$ defined by variable reads $R_k(x)$, variable writes $W_k(x)$, or function calls $f_k(v)$ generated by the execution of node k in a flow.

Expression Evaluation

$$\frac{}{\langle v, M_k \rangle \Downarrow v} \text{ (VALUE)}$$

$$\frac{\langle e, M_k \rangle \Downarrow^{T_k} v}{\langle f(e), M_k \rangle \Downarrow^{T_k . f_k(v)} \overline{f}(v)} \text{ (CALL)} \qquad \frac{}{\langle x, M_k \rangle \Downarrow^{R_k(x)} M_k(x)} \text{ (READ)}$$

Command Evaluation

$$\frac{I = I'.v \qquad x \in Var_N}{\langle handler(x)\{c\}, M, I, O \rangle_k \rightarrow \langle c, M[x \mapsto v], I', O \rangle_k} \text{ (INPUT)}$$

$$\frac{}{\langle skip, M, I, O \rangle_k \rightarrow \langle stop, M, I, O \rangle_k} \text{ (SKIP)}$$

$$\frac{\langle e, M_k \rangle \Downarrow^{T_k} v \qquad M'_k = M_k[x \mapsto v]}{\langle x := e, M, I, O \rangle_k \xrightarrow{T_k . W_k(x)} \langle stop, M', I, O \rangle_k} \text{ (WRITE)}$$

$$\frac{c = \textbf{\textit{if}} \ e \ \textbf{\textit{then}} \ c_{true} \ \textbf{\textit{else}} \ c_{false} \qquad \langle e, M_k \rangle \Downarrow^{T_k} b}{\langle c, M, I, O \rangle_k \xrightarrow{T_k} \langle c_b, M, I, O \rangle_k} \text{ (IF)}$$

$$\frac{c = \textbf{\textit{while}} \ e \ \textbf{\textit{do}} \ c_{body} \qquad \langle e, M_k \rangle \Downarrow^{T_k} true}{\langle c, M, I, O \rangle_k \xrightarrow{T_k} \langle c_{body}; c, M, I, O \rangle_k} \text{ (WHILE-T)}$$

$$\frac{c = \textbf{\textit{while}} \ e \ \textbf{\textit{do}} \ c_{body} \qquad \langle e, M_k \rangle \Downarrow^{T_k} false}{\langle c, M, I, O \rangle_k \xrightarrow{T_k} \langle stop, M, I, O \rangle_k} \text{ (WHILE-F)}$$

$$\frac{\langle c_1, M, I, O \rangle_k \xrightarrow{T_k} \langle c'_1, M', I', O' \rangle_k}{\langle c_1; c_2, M, I, O \rangle_k \xrightarrow{T_k} \langle c'_1; c_2, M', I', O' \rangle_k} \text{ (SEQ-1)}$$

$$\frac{}{\langle stop; c, M, I, O \rangle_k \rightarrow \langle c, M, I, O \rangle_k} \text{ (SEQ-2)}$$

$$\frac{c = send(e, i) \qquad \langle e, M_k \rangle \Downarrow^{T_k} v \qquad O'[i] = O[i].v}{\langle c, M, I, O \rangle_k \xrightarrow{T_k} \langle stop, M, I, O' \rangle_k} \text{ (OUTPUT)}$$

Fig. 8. Node semantics.

Expression evaluation is standard and records the sequence of events produced during the evaluation, where M_k denotes the memory M in $\langle c, M, I, O \rangle_k$. Command evaluation models the execution of a node's handler. The handler executes whenever there is a message in the input channel I by consuming the message and updating the memory accordingly. Assignments operate in a similar manner and record the trace of events produced by variable reads and writes. An assignment updates the memory M_k to M'_k, subsequently triggering an update of the flow and global memories, as stated in the rule (STEP) in Fig. 9 and in the rule (GLOBAL) in Fig. 10. Send commands evaluate the expression e in the current memory, update the associated output channel, and record the trace of events. The index k distinguishes between events of different nodes. We write $\rightarrow^*$ for the reflexive and transitive closure of the $\rightarrow$ relation, and $\rightarrow^n$ for the n-step execution of $\rightarrow$.

Flow and Global Semantics. We lift node semantics to formalize the semantics of flows and the environment. A global configuration $G = \langle m_G, \{F_l \mid l \in L\} \rangle$ consists of a global shared memory m_G and a finite set of flows that are executing concurrently, where $L \subset \mathbb{N}$ is the set of flow identifiers. A flow configuration $F = \langle m_F, \{N_k \mid k \in K\}\} \rangle_l$ is a tuple consisting of a flow shared memory m_F, a finite set of nodes where $K \subset \mathbb{N}$ is the set of node identifiers, and l is the flow identifier. We use $Nodes(F_l)$ for the set of nodes in a specific flow and $Flows(G)$ for the set of flows in the environment. Nodes are distinguished by unique node identifiers in the environment and the node N_k can be present in only one flow. To unify the trigger point of the flow, we assume that a flow has only one inject node and denote it by N_l where $N_l \in Nodes(F_l)$; in practice, it can be considered as a dummy node which is the predecessor of all the inject nodes of the flow.

We model a flow by linking the output channels of a node to the input channels of the next ones based on the flow specification. Note that a node can have more than one output channel but only one input channel. The inject node of a flow, which does not appear in any of the *wires* arrays, triggers the flow execution by injecting a new message. An initial value is assigned to the input channel of the inject node to model the behavior of the external event such as a button click. We write $Exec(F_l, v_l)$ to refer to executions of a flow F_l with an initial value v_l. Also, $Exec(G, V)$ denotes executions of the environment G with the set of initial values $V = \{(N_l, v_l) \mid F_l \in Flows(G)\}$ for the member flows.

We remark that message passing in Node-RED is asynchronous and message objects traverse the graph in a non-deterministic manner, as reported in the documentation ("no assumptions should be made about ordering once a flow branches" [35] and "flows can be cyclic" [34]). Hence, we model the execution of nodes in a flow and the environment, as shown in Figs. 9 and 10, respectively. We overload the notation $\rightarrow$ for transitions between flow and global configurations. In a nutshell, the flow and global semantics implements the non-deterministic behavior of flows and the environment, and lifts the node semantics to ensure that the flow of messages follows the flow specification.

The intuition of the rules is that the inject node of a flow, i.e., the node N_l of the flow F_l, starts the execution by consuming the initial value (rule INIT), and then the execution continues according to the node semantics (rule STEP). When a node reaches a send command, it adds the output value to the input channels of the next nodes in the flow; the output value transmits out to the output channel indicated by the send command and the input channels of all nodes in the corresponding elements of the array *wires* get updated with the value (rule SEND); $wires_k$ denotes the array *wires* in $\langle config, wires, l \rangle_k$. The execution proceeds until it terminates and gets back to the initial state, ready to consume the next value in the input channel (rule TERM). Note that nodes are running concurrently; any of the ready nodes can make one execution step. The only rule in the global semantics (rule GLOBAL) shows that any of the flows with at least one ready node can make an execution step.

$$I_l = v_l \qquad \forall N_k \in (Nodes(F_l) \setminus N_l).\, I_k = \varnothing$$
$$M_l = [m_N, m_F, m_G] \qquad M_l' = [m_N', m_F, m_G]$$
$$config_l = \langle handler(x)\{c\}, M, I, O\rangle_l \qquad config_l' = \langle c, M[x \mapsto v_l], \varnothing, O\rangle_l$$
$$\frac{config_l \to config_l' \quad N_l = \langle config_l, wires, l\rangle_l \quad N_l' = \langle config_l', wires, l\rangle_l}{\langle m_F, Nodes(F_l)\rangle_l \to \langle m_F, (Nodes(F_l) \setminus \{N_l\}) \cup \{N_l'\}\rangle_l} \quad \text{(INIT)}$$

$$I_l = \varnothing \qquad M_k = [m_N, m_F, m_G] \qquad M_k' = [m_N', m_F', m_G']$$
$$config_k = \langle c, M, I, O\rangle_k \qquad config_k' = \langle c', M', I', O\rangle_k$$
$$config_k \xrightarrow{T_k} config_k'$$
$$\frac{N_k = \langle config_k, wires, l\rangle_k \quad N_k' = \langle config_k', wires, l\rangle_k}{\langle m_F, Nodes(F_l)\rangle_l \xrightarrow{T_k} \langle m_F', (Nodes(F_l) \setminus \{N_k\}) \cup \{N_k'\}\rangle_l} \quad \text{(STEP)}$$

$$config_k = \langle send(e, i); c, M, I, O\rangle_k \qquad config_k' = \langle stop; c, M, I, O'\rangle_k$$
$$O_k'[i] = O_k[i].v \qquad config_k \xrightarrow{T_k} config_k'$$
$$N_k = \langle config_k, wires, l\rangle_k \qquad N_k' = \langle config_k', wires, l\rangle_k$$
$$\omega = \{N_k\} \cup \{N_j \mid j \in wires_k[i]\}$$
$$\frac{\omega' = \{N_k'\} \cup \{N_j' \mid j \in wires_k[i],\ I_j' = v.I_j\}}{\langle m_F, Nodes(F_l)\rangle_l \xrightarrow{T_k} \langle m_F, (Nodes(F_l) \setminus \omega) \cup \omega'\rangle_l} \quad \text{(SEND)}$$

$$config_k = \langle stop, M, I, O\rangle_k \qquad config_k' = \langle handler(x)\{c\}, M, I, O\rangle_k$$
$$\frac{N_k = \langle config_k, wires, l\rangle_k \quad N_k' = \langle config_k', wires, l\rangle_k}{\langle m_F, Nodes(F_l)\rangle_l \to \langle m_F, (Nodes(F_l) \setminus \{N_k\}) \cup \{N_k'\}\rangle_l} \quad \text{(TERM)}$$

Fig. 9. Flow semantics.

$$M_k = [m_N, m_F, m_G] \qquad M_k' = [m_N', m_F', m_G']$$
$$F_l = \langle m_F, Nodes(F_l)\rangle_l \qquad F_l' = \langle m_F', Nodes(F_l')\rangle_l$$
$$\frac{F_l \xrightarrow{T_k} F_l'}{\langle m_G, Flows(G)\rangle \xrightarrow{T_k} \langle m_G', (Flows(G) \setminus \{F_l\}) \cup \{F_l'\}\rangle} \quad \text{(GLOBAL)}$$

Fig. 10. Global semantics.

Generally speaking, any node that is able to progress continues the execution for one execution step, and it might affect the flow and global contexts. An execution step of a node corresponds to one execution step of the flow it belongs to and one execution step of the environment. Considering the non-deterministic behavior of Node-RED's scheduler, any ready node can be selected for the next execution step.

3.2 Security Condition and Enforcement

We leverage our trace-based semantics to define a semantics-based security condition. The condition is parametric on node-level security policies, represented as allowlists of API calls and accesses to the shared context. Then, we present the semantics of a fine-grained node-level monitor and prove its soundness and transparency with respect to the security condition.

Security Condition. We extend the definition of nodes with allowlist policies $N = \langle config, wires, l, P, V, S \rangle_k$, where $P \subseteq APIs \subseteq Fun$ describes permitted API functions, $V : P \to 2^{Val}$ defines the allowlist of arguments for each API function, and S specifies read/write permissions on the shared global and flow variables, such that $S = \{(x, RW) \mid x \in Var_F \uplus Var_G, RW \in \{R, W\}\}$.

The security condition matches the trace of events produced by the semantics with the allowlist policies to check that any event produced by an execution is permitted by the policy.

Definition 1 (*Event Security*). *Let t_k be an event emitted from an execution of node N_k. We define a secure event with respect to $\langle P_k, V_k, S_k \rangle$, written $secure(t_k, \langle P_k, V_k, S_k \rangle)$, as follows:*

$$secure(R_k(x),\ \langle P_k, V_k, S_k \rangle) \stackrel{\Delta}{=} x \in Var_F \cup Var_G \Rightarrow (x, R) \in S_k$$
$$secure(W_k(x),\ \langle P_k, V_k, S_k \rangle) \stackrel{\Delta}{=} x \in Var_F \cup Var_G \Rightarrow (x, W) \in S_k$$
$$secure(f_k(v),\ \langle P_k, V_k, S_k \rangle) \stackrel{\Delta}{=} f \in APIs \Rightarrow f \in P_k \wedge v \in V_k(f).$$

We lift the security of events to define the security condition for node traces $secure(T_N)$, flows traces $secure(T_F)$, and global traces $secure(T_G)$ as expected. A finite sequence of events forms a trace. Hence a trace is secure if all its events are secure. We define trace security by the conjunction of security checks on the composing events.

Definition 2 (*Trace Security*). *Trace T is secure, written $secure(T)$, if*

$$T = t_k.T' \Rightarrow secure(t_k, \langle P_k, V_k, S_k \rangle) \wedge secure(T').$$

A node starts executing when it receives a value over its input channel. An execution of a node is secure if the corresponding trace is secure, according to the node policy.

Definition 3 (*Node-Level Security*). *The execution of a node $N_k = \langle config, wires, l, P, V, S \rangle_k$ with an input message $I = v$ is secure with regard to $\langle P_k, V_k, S_k \rangle$ if each step of the node execution complies with $\langle P_k, V_k, S_k \rangle$, i.e.,*

$$\forall \langle c', M', I', O' \rangle_k . \langle handler(x)\{c\}, M, v, O \rangle_k \xrightarrow{T_k}^* \langle c', M', I', O' \rangle_k \Rightarrow secure(T_k).$$

We now define the security of Node-RED app executions based on the flow and global semantics. The inject node of a flow initiates the flow execution, and it triggers other nodes by traversing the flow graph. At the global level, nodes in flows generate events while they are executing concurrently in the environment. We present flow and global execution security for the trace of events produced by their nodes at each execution step.

Expression Evaluation

$$\frac{secure(R_k(x), \langle P_k, V_k, S_k\rangle)}{\langle x, M_k\rangle \Downarrow_{\mathcal{M}}^{R_k(x)} M_k(x)} \quad \text{(READ}_{\mathcal{M}}\text{)}$$

$$\frac{\langle e, M_k\rangle \Downarrow^{T_k} v \qquad secure(f_k(v), \langle P_k, V_k, S_k\rangle)}{\langle f(e), M_k\rangle \Downarrow_{\mathcal{M}}^{T_k \cdot f_k(v)} \bar{f}(v)} \quad \text{(CALL}_{\mathcal{M}}\text{)}$$

Command Evaluation

$$\frac{secure(W_k(x), \langle P_k, V_k, S_k\rangle) \qquad \langle e, M_k\rangle \Downarrow^{T_k} v \qquad M' = M[x \mapsto v]}{\langle x := e, M, I, O\rangle_k \xrightarrow{T_k \cdot W_k(x)}_{\mathcal{M}} \langle stop, M', I, O\rangle_k} \quad \text{(WRITE}_{\mathcal{M}}\text{)}$$

Fig. 11. Excerpt of monitor semantics.

Definition 4 (*Flow-Level Security*). *Let F_l be a flow and v_l be an initial value for the inject node of the flow, i.e., $N_l = \langle\langle handler(x)\{c\}, M, v_l, O\rangle_l, wires, l\rangle_l$. We define flow executions $Exec(F_l, v_l)$ secure if*

$$N_l \in Nodes(F_l) \wedge \forall F_l'. \ F_l \xrightarrow{T_F}{}^* F_l' \Rightarrow secure(T_F).$$

The trace T_F is secure if $secure(T_F)$ holds, i.e., every event of the trace is secure according to the security policy of the corresponding node.

Definition 5 (*Global-Level Security*). *Let G be an environment and V_{init} be a set of initial values for the inject nodes of the flows in G, i.e., $\forall(N_j, v_j) \in V_{init}$. $F_j \in Flows(G) \wedge N_j \in Nodes(F_j) \wedge N_j = \langle\langle handler(x)\{c\}, M, v_j, O\rangle_j, wires, j\rangle_j$. We define global executions $Exec(G, V_{init})$ secure if*

$$\forall G'. \ G \xrightarrow{T_G}{}^* G' \Rightarrow secure(T_G).$$

Enforcement Mechanism. Figure 11 presents the core of our fine-grained monitor to enforce the above-mentioned security condition with respect to allowlist policies. We annotate evaluation relations with $\mathcal{M}$ to distinguish between the monitored behavior and the original one. We only present the rules that differ from the semantic rules given in Fig. 8; we replace $\rightarrow$ with $\rightarrow_{\mathcal{M}}$, and $\Downarrow$ with $\Downarrow_{\mathcal{M}}$. We add security constraints to the semantic rules for reading a variable from the shared context (rule READ$_{\mathcal{M}}$), calling an API function (rule CALL$_{\mathcal{M}}$), and writing to a shared variable (rule WRITE$_{\mathcal{M}}$).

For the email example ⬩ in Sect. 2, the policy requires allowlisting the API for sending the message and the list of intended recipients. The monitor intervenes whenever the API is called and ensures that the recipient is in the allowlist policy. An execution of a flow containing the malicious email node will be suppressed because the attacker's email address is not listed in the permitted values of the API call. The malicious event is detected by the rule CALL$_{\mathcal{M}}$, i.e., `sendMail` $\in P_k \wedge$ `"me@attacker.com"` $\notin V_k(\texttt{sendMail})$.

For context vulnerabilities, such as Water Utility Complete Example ⬦, the allowlist consists of access rights to shared variables for each node deployed in the environment. The monitor observes the interaction of nodes with the shared context and blocks the execution whenever the allowlist policy does not permit access to the shared variable. The attack scenario in the vulnerable water utility flow can also be prevented by specifying an allowlist policy ($\mathtt{tank1Level}, W$) only for the nodes that must write to a shared variable, which stops any attempt from other nodes to write to the global context (rule $\text{WRITE}_\mathcal{M}$).

We prove the soundness and transparency properties of our monitor. The soundness theorem shows that any global traces produced by an execution of the monitor are secure with respect to the allowlist policy.

Theorem 1 (Soundness). *The monitor enforces global-level security for any finite executions,*

$$\forall (G, V). \, \forall G'. \, G \xrightarrow{T_G}{}^{*}_{\mathcal{M}} G' \Rightarrow secure(T_G).$$

The transparency theorem shows that if a monitored execution is secure, the monitor semantics and the original semantics generate the same trace. Moreover, if both semantics run under the same scheduler, the monitor preserves the longest secure prefix of a trace.

Theorem 2 (Transparency). *The monitor preserves the longest secure prefix of a trace yielded by an execution,*

$$\forall (G_0, V). \, \forall n \in \mathbb{N}. \, G_0 \xrightarrow{T}{}^{n} G_n \Rightarrow \exists m \leq n. \, G_0 \xrightarrow{T'}{}^{m}_{\mathcal{M}} G_m \, \wedge$$
$$\left[\left(secure(T) \Rightarrow T = T' \wedge n = m \right) \vee \right.$$
$$\left(\left(\exists i < n. \, G_0 \xrightarrow{T_{pre}}{}^{i} G_i \wedge G_i \xrightarrow{T_i} G_{i+1} \wedge G_{i+1} \xrightarrow{T_{post}}{}^{n-i-1} G_n \wedge secure(T_{pre}) \wedge \right.\right.$$
$$\left.\left. \neg secure(T_i) \right) \Rightarrow T' = T_{pre} \wedge i = m \right) \Big].$$

The proofs of the theorems are reported in the online appendix [2].

4   Related Work

We discuss the most closely related work on Node-RED security and modeling, monitor implementation, and securing trigger-action platforms in general. We refer the reader to surveys on the security of IoT app platforms [7,13] for further details.

Node-RED Security and Modeling. Ancona et al. [5] investigate runtime monitoring of parametric trace expressions to check the correct usage of API functions in Node-RED. Trace expressions allow for rich policies, including temporal patterns over sequences of API calls. By contrast, our monitor supports both coarse and fine access control granularity of modules, functions, and contexts. Schreckling et al. [49] propose COMPOSE, a framework for fine-grained static and dynamic enforcement that integrates JSFlow [21], an information-flow tracker for JavaScript. COMPOSE focuses on data-level granularity, whereas our monitoring framework supports module- and API-level granularity.

Clerissi et al. [15] use UML models to generate and test Node-RED flows to provide early system validation. A preliminary set of guidelines has also been proposed to assist Node-RED flow makers in terms of user comprehension and for testing activities [16]. Focusing more on end users and less on developers, Kleinfeld et al. [27] introduce an extension of Node-RED called glue.things, enabling Node-RED easier to use by predefined trigger and action nodes. Blackstock and Lea [12] propose a distributed runtime for Node-RED apps such that flows can be hosted on various platforms. Tata et al. [53] propose a formal modeling for decomposing process-aware applications deployed in IoT environments using Petri nets; Node-RED indeed fits in this setup, thus extended as a prototype for their approach [25].

In terms of modeling, Node-RED can be intrinsically seen as a concurrent system, thus our approach shares similarities with the broad range of formal approaches such as process calculi [8,46], CSP [22], and CCS [31]. In the same spirit, our formalization is targeted to capture the execution model of Node-RED flows consisting of concurrent node executions that trigger the execution of code upon receiving messages, and modify, create, and dispatch messages to the next nodes. In contrast, our modeling is explicit and it captures the essence of the execution semantics of Node-RED. Focusing on security policies in concurrent systems, KLAIM [11,32] is a programming language providing a mechanism to customize access control policies. The mechanism, based on a hierarchical capability-based type system, enforces policies that control resource usage and authorize migration and execution of processes. While KLAIM is designed for programming distributed applications with agents and code mobility, our Node-RED model is simple and expressive enough to describe the API-based access control enforcement mechanism.

Monitor Implementation. Regarding the possible candidates for implementing our theoretical framework, it should be noted that the dynamic nature of JavaScript requires more precise analysis provided by dynamic approaches. Andreasen et al. [6] survey available methods for dynamic analysis for JavaScript, and outline three general categories: runtime instrumentation, source code instrumentation, and metacircular interpreters.

DProf [19] and NodeProf [52] are two well-known runtime instrumentation tools. DProf instruments a program at the instruction level, targeting a variety of languages, including JavaScript. NodeProf instead instruments a program at the abstract syntax tree (AST) level and is specifically made as a dynamic analysis framework for Node.js. However, some important Node.js features, such as `module.exports`, commonly used in Node-RED nodes, are not supported by NodeProf yet. In addition, to obtain the desired results, it requires the instrumentation of the entire Node-RED environment. NodeMOP [48] is a Monitoring-Oriented Programming (MOP) tool built on top of NodeProf that also looks interesting for our purposes, while the challenges in practice remain unresolved.

Ferreira et al. [18] propose a lightweight permission system to enforce the least-privilege principle at the Node.js packages level at runtime, restricting access to security-critical APIs and resources. Sharing some of our motivations, however, this work does not enforce access control policies at the context and value levels. Pyronia [29] is a fine-grained access control system for IoT applications restricting access at the function level via runtime and kernel modifications. To detect access to sensitive resources, Pyronia leverages OS-level techniques such as system call interposition and stack inspection. By contrast, our monitor needs to be implemented in language-level isolation to prevent access to sensitive resources at different levels of granularity.

Membrane-based approaches [1, 3, 20, 30, 50] seem to be the most promising compared to other techniques. Membranes are a "defensive programming pattern used to intermediate between sub-components of an application" [54]. This pattern is implemented in Node.js by recursively wrapping an object in a proxy with respect to prototype hierarchies such that the wrapped object can only be modified in protected ways. Staicu et al. [51] provide an example of this technique applied to Node.js, isolating libraries to extract taint specifications automatically.

SandTrap [3] combines the Node.jsvm module with fully structural proxy-based two-sided membranes to enforce fine-grained access control policies. Sand-Trap has been integrated with Node-RED and evaluated on a set of flows while enforcing a variety of policies yet incurring negligible runtime overhead. Our framework is a step toward providing the formal grounds for characterizing the soundness and transparency of the SandTrap instantiation to Node-RED. The formalization can be further enhanced by modeling the Node.js environment and full-featured JavaScript [28].

Securing Trigger-Action Platforms. IoTGuard [14] is a monitor for enforcing security policies written in the IoTGuard policy language. Security policies describe valid transitions in an IoT app execution. Bastys et al. [9,10] study attacks by malicious app makers in IFTTT and Zapier. They develop dynamic and static information flow control (IFC) in IoT apps and report on an empirical study to estimate to what extent IFTTT apps manipulate sensitive information of users. Wang et al. [56] develop NLP-based methods to infer information flows in trigger-action platforms and check cross-app interaction via model checking. Alpernas et al. [4] propose dynamic coarse-grained IFC for JavaScript in serverless platforms. Our presented monitor is based on access control rather than IFC. Hence, these works are complementary, focusing on information flow after access is granted. IFC supports rich dependency policies, yet arduous to track information flow in JavaScript without breaking soundness or giving up precision.

5   Conclusion

We have investigated the security of Node-RED, an open-source JavaScript-driven trigger-action platform. We have expanded on the recently-discovered critical exploitable vulnerabilities in Node-RED, where the impact ranges from massive exfiltration of data from unsuspecting users to taking over the entire platform. Motivated by the need for a security mechanism for Node-RED, we have proposed an essential model for Node-RED, suitable to reason about nodes and flows, be they benign, vulnerable, or malicious. We have formalized a principled framework to enforce fine-grained API control for untrusted Node-RED applications. Our formalization for a core language shows how to soundly and transparently enforce global security properties of Node-RED applications by local access checks, supporting module-, API-, value-, and context-level policies.

Acknowledgments. This work was partially supported by the Swedish Foundation for Strategic Research (SSF), the Swedish Research Council (VR), and Digital Futures.

References

1. Agten, P., Van Acker, S., Brondsema, Y., Phung, P.H., Desmet, L., Piessens, F.: JSand: complete client-side sandboxing of third-party JavaScript without browser modifications. In: ACSAC (2012). https://doi.org/10.1145/2420950.2420952
2. Ahmadpanah, M.M., Balliu, M., Hedin, D., Olsson, L.E., Sabelfeld, A.: Securing Node-RED Applications. Proofs. https://www.cse.chalmers.se/research/group/security/SandTrap/proofs.pdf (2021)
3. Ahmadpanah, M.M., Hedin, D., Balliu, M., Olsson, L.E., Sabelfeld, A.: SandTrap: securing JavaScript-driven trigger-action platforms. In: USENIX Security (2021). https://www.usenix.org/conference/usenixsecurity21/presentation/ahmadpanah
4. Alpernas, K., et al.: Secure serverless computing using dynamic information flow control. In: OOPSLA (2018). https://doi.org/10.1145/3276488
5. Ancona, D., Franceschini, L., Delzanno, G., Leotta, M., Ribaudo, M., Ricca, F.: Towards runtime monitoring of node.js and its application to the internet of things. In: ALP4IoT@iFM (2017). https://doi.org/10.4204/EPTCS.264.4
6. Andreasen, E., et al.: A survey of dynamic analysis and test generation for JavaScript. ACM Comput. Surv. (2017). https://doi.org/10.1145/3106739
7. Balliu, M., Bastys, I., Sabelfeld, A.: Securing IoT Apps. IEEE S&P Magazine (2019). https://doi.org/10.1109/MSEC.2019.2914190
8. Balliu, M., Merro, M., Pasqua, M., Shcherbakov, M.: Friendly fire: cross-app interactions in IoT platforms. ACM Trans. Priv. Secur. (2021). https://doi.org/10.1145/3444963
9. Bastys, I., Balliu, M., Sabelfeld, A.: If this then what? controlling flows in IoT apps. In: CCS (2018). https://doi.org/10.1145/3243734.3243841
10. Bastys, I., Piessens, F., Sabelfeld, A.: Tracking information flow via delayed output - addressing privacy in IoT and emailing apps. In: NordSec (2018). https://doi.org/10.1007/978-3-030-03638-6_2
11. Bettini, L., et al.: The klaim project: theory and practice. In: Global Computing (2003). https://doi.org/10.1007/978-3-540-40042-4_4
12. Blackstock, M., Lea, R.: Toward a distributed data flow platform for the web of things (distributed node-RED). In: WoT (2014). https://doi.org/10.1145/2684432.2684439
13. Celik, Z.B., Fernandes, E., Pauley, E., Tan, G., McDaniel, P.D.: Program analysis of commodity IoT applications for security and privacy: challenges and opportunities. ACM Comput. Surv. (2019). https://doi.org/10.1145/3333501

14. Celik, Z., Tan, G., McDaniel, P.: IoTGuard: dynamic enforcement of security and safety policy in commodity IoT. In: NDSS (2019). https://doi.org/10.14722/ndss.2019.23326
15. Clerissi, D., Leotta, M., Reggio, G., Ricca, F.: Towards an approach for developing and testing node-RED IoT systems. In: EnSEmble@ESEC/SIGSOFT FSE (2018). https://doi.org/10.1145/3281022.3281023
16. Clerissi, D., Leotta, M., Ricca, F.: A set of empirically validated development guidelines for improving node-RED flows comprehension. In: ENASE (2020). https://doi.org/10.5220/0009391101080119
17. Devriese, D., Piessens, F.: Noninterference through secure multi-execution. In: S&P (2010). https://doi.org/10.1109/SP.2010.15
18. Ferreira, G., Jia, L., Sunshine, J., Kästner, C.: Containing malicious package updates in NPM with a lightweight permission system. In: ICSE (2021). https://doi.org/10.1109/ICSE43902.2021.00121
19. Gregg, B., Mauro, J.: DTrace: Dynamic Tracing in Oracle Solaris, Mac OS X, and FreeBSD. Prentice Hall Professional (2011)
20. Groef, W.D., Massacci, F., Piessens, F.: NodeSentry: least-privilege library integration for server-side JavaScript. In: ACSAC (2014). https://doi.org/10.1145/2664243.2664276
21. Hedin, D., Birgisson, A., Bello, L., Sabelfeld, A.: JSFlow: tracking information flow in JavaScript and its APIs. In: SAC (2014). https://doi.org/10.1145/2554850.2554909
22. Hoare, C.A.R.: Communicating sequential processes. Commun. ACM (1978). https://doi.org/10.1145/359576.359585
23. IBM Cloud (2021). https://cloud.ibm.com/
24. IFTTT: If This Then That (2021). https://ifttt.com
25. Jain, R., Klai, K., Tata, S.: Formal modeling and verification of scalable process-aware distributed iot applications. In: ISPA/BDCloud/SocialCom/SustainCom (2019). https://doi.org/10.1109/ISPA-BDCloud-SustainCom-SocialCom48970.2019.00047
26. jcreedcmu: Escaping NodeJS vm (2018). https://gist.github.com/jcreedcmu/4f6e6d4a649405a9c86bb076905696af
27. Kleinfeld, R., Steglich, S., Radziwonowicz, L., Doukas, C.: glue.things: a mashup platform for wiring the internet of things with the internet of services. In: WoT (2014). https://doi.org/10.1145/2684432.2684436
28. Maffeis, S., Mitchell, J.C., Taly, A.: An operational semantics for JavaScript. In: APLAS (2008). https://doi.org/10.1007/978-3-540-89330-1_22
29. Melara, M.S., Liu, D.H., Freedman, M.J.: Pyronia: intra-process access control for IoT applications. CoRR abs/1903.01950 (2019). http://arxiv.org/abs/1903.01950
30. Miller, M.S.: Robust Composition: Towards a Unified Approach to Access Control and Concurrency Control. Ph.D. thesis, Johns Hopkins University (2006)
31. Milner, R. (ed.): A Calculus of Communicating Systems. LNCS, vol. 92. Springer, Heidelberg (1980). https://doi.org/10.1007/3-540-10235-3
32. Nicola, R.D., Ferrari, G.L., Pugliese, R.: Programming access control: the KLAIM experience. In: CONCUR (2000). https://doi.org/10.1007/3-540-44618-4_5
33. Node-RED: Community Node Module Catalogue (2021). https://github.com/node-red/catalogue.nodered.org
34. Node-RED: Cyclic Flows (2021). https://groups.google.com/g/node-red/c/C6M3HokoSTI/m/B2tqcb_cAQAJ
35. Node-RED: Making Flows Asynchronous by Default (2021). https://nodered.org/blog/2019/08/16/going-async

36. Node-RED (2021). https://nodered.org/
37. Node-RED: Securing Node-RED (2021). https://nodered.org/docs/user-guide/runtime/securing-node-red
38. Node-RED: The Core Nodes (2021). https://nodered.org/docs/user-guide/nodes
39. Node-RED: The RED Object (2021). https://github.com/node-red/node-red/blob/master/packages/node_modules/node-red/lib/red.js
40. Node-RED: Working with Context (2021). https://nodered.org/docs/user-guide/context
41. Node-RED Library (2021). https://flows.nodered.org/
42. Node.JS: VM (executing JavaScript) (2021). https://nodejs.org/api/vm.html#vm_vm_executing_javascript
43. NPM: Node Package Manager (2021). https://www.npmjs.com/
44. OWASP: NodeJS Security Cheat Sheet (2021). https://cheatsheetseries.owasp.org/cheatsheets/Nodejs_Security_Cheat_Sheet.html#do-not-use-dangerous-functions
45. Pfretzschner, B., ben Othmane, L.: Identification of Dependency-based Attacks on Node.js. In: ARES (2017). https://doi.org/10.1145/3098954.3120928
46. Roscoe, A.W.: The Theory and Practice of Concurrency. Prentice Hall PTR (1997)
47. Saltzer, J.H., Schroeder, M.D.: The protection of information in computer systems. Proc. IEEE (1975). https://doi.org/10.1109/PROC.1975.9939
48. Schiavio, F., Sun, H., Bonetta, D., Rosà, A., Binder, W.: NodeMOP: runtime verification for node.js applications. In: SAC (2019). https://doi.org/10.1145/3297280.3297456
49. Schreckling, D., Parra, J.D., Doukas, C., Posegga, J.: Data-centric security for the IoT. In: IoT 360 (2) (2015). https://doi.org/10.1007/978-3-319-47075-7_10
50. Simek, P.: Proposal for VM2: advanced vm/sandbox for Node.js (2021). https://github.com/patriksimek/vm2
51. Staicu, C., Torp, M.T., Schäfer, M., Møller, A., Pradel, M.: Extracting taint specifications for JavaScript libraries. In: ICSE (2020). https://doi.org/10.1145/3377811.3380390
52. Sun, H., Bonetta, D., Humer, C., Binder, W.: Efficient dynamic analysis for Node.js. In: CC (2018). https://doi.org/10.1145/3178372.3179527
53. Tata, S., Klai, K., Jain, R.: Formal model and method to decompose process-aware IoT applications. In: OTM (2017). https://doi.org/10.1007/978-3-319-69462-7_42
54. Van Cutsem, T.: Isolating Application Sub-components with Membranes (2018). https://tvcutsem.github.io/membranes
55. Ur, B., McManus, E., Ho, M.P.Y., Littman, M.L.: Practical trigger-action programming in the smart home. In: CHI (2014). https://doi.org/10.1145/2556288.2557420
56. Wang, Q., Datta, P., Yang, W., Liu, S., Bates, A., Gunter, C.A.: Charting the attack surface of trigger-action IoT platforms. In: CCS (2019). https://doi.org/10.1145/3319535.3345662
57. Zapier (2021). https://zapier.com
58. Zimmermann, M., Staicu, C., Tenny, C., Pradel, M.: Small world with high risks: a study of security threats in the NPM ecosystem. In: USENIX Security (2019). https://dl.acm.org/doi/10.5555/3361338.3361407

Protocol Analysis with Time and Space

Damián Aparicio-Sánchez[1], Santiago Escobar[1], Catherine Meadows[2(✉)],
José Meseguer[3], and Julia Sapiña[1]

[1] VRAIN, Universitat Politècnica de València, Valencia, Spain
{daapsnc,sescobar,jsapina}@upv.es
[2] Naval Research Laboratory, Washington DC, USA
meadows@itd.nrl.navy.mil
[3] University of Illinois at Urbana-Champaign, Champaign, USA
meseguer@illinois.edu

Abstract. We present a formal framework for the analysis of cryptographic protocols that make use of time and space in their execution. In a previous work we provided a timed process algebra syntax and a timed transition semantics. The timed process algebra only made message sending-and-reception times available to processes whereas the timed transition semantics modelled the actual time interactions between processes. In this paper we extend the previous process algebra syntax to make spatial location information also available to processes and provide a transition semantics that takes account of fundamental properties of both time and space. This time and space protocol framework can be implemented either as a simulation tool or as a symbolic analysis tool in which time and space information are not represented by specific values but by logical variables, and in which the properties of time and space are reasoned about in terms of constraints on those time and space logical variables. All these time and space constraints are carried along the symbolic execution of the protocol and their satisfiability can be evaluated as the analysis proceeds, so attacks that violate the laws of physics can be discarded as impossible. We demonstrate the feasibility of our approach by using the Maude-NPA protocol analyzer together with an SMT solver that is used to evaluate the satisfiability of timing and location constraints. We provide a sound and complete protocol transformation from our time and space process algebra to the Maude-NPA syntax and semantics, and we prove its soundness and completeness. We analyze two protocols using time and space constraints.

1 Introduction

The laws of physics are an important aspect of many cryptographic protocols, and there has been increasing interest in the formal analysis of protocols that

---

This work has been partially supported by the EU (FEDER) and the Spanish MCIU under grant RTI2018-094403-B-C32, by Generalitat Valenciana under grant PROMETEO/2019/098, by EIG-CONCERT-JAPAN under grant PCI2020-120708-2, and by NRL under contract number N00173-17-1-G002. Julia Sapiña has been supported by the Generalitat Valenciana APOSTD/2019/127 grant.

D. Dougherty et al. (Eds.): Guttman Festschrift, LNCS 13066, pp. 22–49, 2021.
https://doi.org/10.1007/978-3-030-91631-2_2

require them to function properly. Model checking of protocols that use time and space can be done using either an explicit model with time and space information, or by using an untimed model and showing it is sound and complete with respect to a time and space model. The former is more intuitive for the user, but the latter is often chosen because not all cryptographic protocol analysis tools support reasoning about either time or space.

In [1], we provided a framework for analyzing protocols involving time. We combined the advantages of both approaches: an explicit timed specification language was developed with a timed syntax and semantics, and was automatically and faithfully translated into an existing untimed language. We applied this approach to the Maude-NPA tool by taking advantage of its built-in support for constraints and analyzed Mafia fraud and distance hijacking attacks on a suite of distance-bounding protocols.

We celebrate Joshua Guttman with a paper on a tool and approach based on one of his most important contributions to security: the strand space model introduced by Thayer, Herzog, and Guttman in [21]. In this graph-based model both protocol roles and adversarial actions are represented by strands, which are lists of terms sent and received by a principal in the order that they occur. A protocol execution (or *bundle*) is constructed by matching sent terms with received terms in different strands. We have used strand spaces as the basis of Maude-NPA syntax and semantics [9], and have found that they allow us to represent them in a very natural way. We have also found [23], that this syntax and semantics can be naturally extended to a process algebra syntax and semantics. Moreover, strand spaces are very amenable to extension via adding constraints to the strand space implementation. In particular, we have found this approach useful for adding features such as state space reduction [10,11], deterministic and nondeterministic choice [23], timed protocols [1], and now, protocols that use both space and time.

In [1], we assumed a metric space with a distance function such that (i) $d(A, A) = 0$, (ii) $d(A, B) = d(B, A)$, and (iii) $d(A, B) \leq d(A, C) + d(C, B)$. In this paper, we actually compute the real distances according to a three-dimensional space: $d(A, B)^2 = (A_x - B_x)^2 + (A_y - B_y)^2 + (A_z - B_z)^2$. We extend the previous process algebra syntax to make spatial location information also available to processes and provide a transition semantics that takes account of fundamental properties of both time and location. The new time and space protocol framework clearly subsumes and extends the previous time framework.

As it already happened in [1], this time and space protocol framework can be implemented either as a simulation tool or as a symbolic analysis tool in which time and space information is not represented by specific values but by logical variables, and in which the properties of time and space are represented as constraints on those time and space logical variables. All these time and space constraints are carried along the symbolic execution of the protocol and their satisfiability can be evaluated as the analysis proceeds, so attacks that violate the laws of physics can be discarded as impossible. We realize the time and space semantics by translating it into the semantics of the Maude-NPA protocol analysis tool, in which time and space are expressed as constraints. The constraints generated during the Maude-NPA search are then checked using an embedded SMT solver.

We believe that this approach can be applied to other tools that support constraint handling as well. Many tools support constraint handling, e.g., Maude-NPA [11] and Tamarin [14]. The laws of physics can be naturally added to a process algebra. Many tools support processes, e.g., Maude-NPA [23] and AKISS [8].

The rest of this paper is organized as follows. In Sect. 2, we present our two running examples: the Brands-Chaum protocol and a secure localization protocol. In Sect. 3, we present the time and space process algebra with its intended semantics. In Sect. 4, we present a sound and complete protocol transformation from our time and space process algebra to an untimed process algebra with constraints. In Sect. 5, we present a second transformation from the untimed process algebra into Maude-NPA strand notation. We conclude in Sect. 6.

1.1 Related Work

There are a number of security protocols that make use of time. In general, there are two types: those that make use of assumptions about time, most often assuming some sort of loose synchronization, and those that guarantee these assumptions. The first kind includes protocols such as Kerberos [15], which uses timestamps to defend against replay attacks, the TESLA protocol [18], which relies on loose synchronization to amortize digital signatures, and blockchain protocols, which use timestamps to order blocks in the chain. The other kind provides guarantees based on physical properties of time: for example, distance bounding, which guarantees that a prover is within a certain distance of a verifier, and secure time synchronization, which guarantees that the clocks of two different nodes are synchronized within a certain margin of error. We refer the reader to [1] for a discussion on timed protocols.

For location-based protocols, the concepts of *physical proximity, secure localization, secure neighbor discovery* and *secure distance measurement* are used quite often. In [2,3,19], Basin et al. define formal models for reasoning about physical properties of security protocols, including timing and location, using Isabelle/HOL and a technique similar to Paulson's inductive approach [17]. The notion of *secure distance measurement* has been studied in [5–7,12]. In [12], Message Time Of Arrival Codes (MTACs) are developed, a new class of cryptographic primitives that allow receivers to verify if an adversary has manipulated the message arrival time in a similar way to how Message Authentication Codes protect message integrity.

2   Two Time and Space Protocols

Example 1. The Brands-Chaum protocol [4] specifies communication between a verifier V and a prover P. P needs to authenticate itself to V, and also needs to prove that it is within a distance "d" of it. A typical interaction between the prover and the verifier is as follows, where N_A denotes a nonce generated by A, S_A denotes a secret generated by A, $X;Y$ denotes concatenation of two messages X and Y, $commit(N, S)$ denotes commitment of secret S with a nonce N, $open(N, S, C)$ denotes opening a commitment C using the nonce N and checking whether it carries the secret S, $\oplus$ is the exclusive-or operator, and $sign(A, M)$ denotes A signing message M.

$P \rightarrow V : commit(N_P, S_P)$
//The prover sends his name and a commitment
$V \rightarrow P : N_V$
//The verifier sends a nonce and records the time when this message was sent
$P \rightarrow V : N_P \oplus N_V$
//The verifier checks the answer message arrives within two times a fixed distance

$P \rightarrow V : S_P$
//The prover sends the committed secret and the verifier opens the commitment
$P \rightarrow V : sign_P(N_V; N_P \oplus N_V)$
//The prover signs the two rapid exchange messages

In [1], we already considered this Brands-Chaum protocol. We assumed the participants were located at an arbitrary given topology (participants do not move from their assigned locations) with distance constraints, where time and distance are equivalent for simplification and are represented by a real number. We assumed a metric space with a distance function $d : \mathcal{A} \times \mathcal{A} \rightarrow Real$ from a set $\mathcal{A}$ of participants such that $d(A, B) \geq 0$, $d(A, A) = 0$, $d(A, B) = d(B, A)$, and $d(A, B) \leq d(A, C) + d(C, B)$.

In this paper, we assume coordinates P_x, P_y, P_z for each participant P and the distance function $d : \mathcal{A} \times \mathcal{A} \rightarrow Real$ calculated from the positions of the participants. From now on, we will use the following notation in order to improve readability: $\lfloor d(A, B) \rfloor$ that provides the set of constraints associated to a symbolic distance between participants A and B and $d((x, y, z), (x', y', z'))$ that calculates the actual distance between participants A and B from their given concrete coordinates:

$$\lfloor d(A, B) \rfloor := (d(A, B) \geq 0 \wedge d(A, B)^2 = (A_x - B_x)^2 + (A_y - B_y)^2 + (A_z - B_z)^2)$$

$$d((x, y, z), (x', y', z')) := \sqrt{(x - x')^2 + (y - y')^2 + (z - z')^2}$$

The previous informal Alice&Bob notation was naturally extended to include time in [1] and we further extend it here to include both time and location. First, we add the time when a message was sent or received as a subindex $P_{t_1} \rightarrow V_{t_2}$. Second, the sending and receiving times of a message differ by the distance between them just by adding the location constraints $\lfloor d(A, B) \rfloor$. Third, the distance bounding constraint of the verifier is represented as an arbitrary distance d. Time and space constraints are written using quantifier-free formulas in real arithmetic. For convenience, we allow both $2 * x = x + x$ and the monus function $x \dot{-} y = if\ y < x\ then\ x - y\ else\ 0$ as definitional extensions.

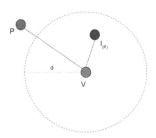

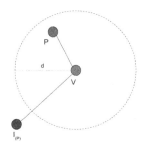

Fig. 1. Mafia attack   **Fig. 2.** Hijacking attack

In the following time and space sequence of actions, a vertical bar differentiates between the process and corresponding constraints associated to the metric space. We remove the constraint $open(N_P, S_P, commit(N_P, S_P))$ for simplification. The following action sequence differs from [1] only on the terms $\lfloor d(P,V) \rfloor$.

$$
\begin{aligned}
P_{t_1} \to V_{t_1'} &: commit(N_P, S_P) & | \ t_1' &= t_1 + d(P,V) \wedge \lfloor d(P,V) \rfloor \\
V_{t_2} \to P_{t_2'} &: N_V & | \ t_2' &= t_2 + d(P,V) \wedge t_2 \geq t_1' \wedge \lfloor d(P,V) \rfloor \\
P_{t_3} \to V_{t_3'} &: N_P \oplus N_V & | \ t_3' &= t_3 + d(P,V) \wedge t_3 \geq t_2' \wedge \lfloor d(P,V) \rfloor \\
V &: t_3' \dot{-} t_2 \leq 2 * d & & \\
P_{t_4} \to V_{t_4'} &: S_P & | \ t_4' &= t_4 + d(P,V) \wedge t_4 \geq t_3 \wedge \lfloor d(P,V) \rfloor \\
P_{t_5} \to V_{t_5'} &: sign_P(N_V; N_P \oplus N_V) & | \ t_5' &= t_5 + d(P,V) \wedge t_5 \geq t_4 \wedge \lfloor d(P,V) \rfloor
\end{aligned}
$$

The Brands-Chaum protocol is designed to defend against mafia frauds, where an honest prover is outside the neighborhood of the verifier (i.e., $d(P,V) > d$) but an intruder is inside (i.e., $d(I,V) \leq d$), pretending to be the honest prover as depicted in Fig. 1. The following is an example of an *attempted* mafia fraud, in which the intruder simply forwards messages back and forth between the prover and the verifier. We write $I(P)$ to denote an intruder pretending to be an honest prover P.

$$
\begin{aligned}
P_{t_1} \to I_{t_2} & : commit(N_P, S_P) & | \ t_2 &= t_1 + d(P,I) \wedge \lfloor d(P,I) \rfloor \\
I(P)_{t_2} \to V_{t_3} & : commit(N_P, S_P) & | \ t_3 &= t_2 + d(V,I) \wedge \lfloor d(V,I) \rfloor \\
V_{t_3} \to I(P)_{t_4} & : N_V & | \ t_4 &= t_3 + d(V,I) \wedge \lfloor d(V,I) \rfloor \\
I_{t_4} \to P_{t_5} & : N_V & | \ t_5 &= t_4 + d(P,I) \wedge \lfloor d(P,I) \rfloor \\
P_{t_5} \to I_{t_6} & : N_P \oplus N_V & | \ t_6 &= t_5 + d(P,I) \wedge \lfloor d(P,I) \rfloor \\
I(P)_{t_6} \to V_{t_7} & : N_P \oplus N_V & | \ t_7 &= t_6 + d(V,I) \wedge \lfloor d(V,I) \rfloor \\
V & : t_7 \dot{-} t_3 \leq 2 * d & & \\
P_{t_8} \to I_{t_9} & : S_P & | \ t_9 &= t_8 + d(P,I) \wedge t_8 \geq t_5 \wedge \lfloor d(P,I) \rfloor \\
I(P)_{t_{10}} \to V_{t_{11}} & : S_P & | \ t_{11} &= t_{10} + d(V,I) \wedge t_{11} \geq t_7 \wedge \lfloor d(V,I) \rfloor \\
I(P)_{t_{12}} \to V_{t_{13}} & : sign_P(N_V; N_P \oplus N_V) & | \ t_{13} &= t_{12} + d(V,I) \wedge t_{13} \geq t_{11} \wedge \lfloor d(V,I) \rfloor
\end{aligned}
$$

This attack is physically unfeasible, since it would require that $2 * d(V,I) + 2 * d(P,I) \leq 2 * d$, which is unsatisfiable by $d(V,P) > d > 0$ and the triangular inequality $d(V,P) \leq d(V,I) + d(P,I)$, satisfied in three-dimensional space. This attack was already unfeasible in [1] using only the metric space assumptions.

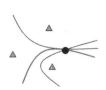
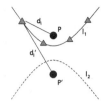

Fig. 3. Trilateration   **Fig. 4.** Insecure   **Fig. 5.** Secure

However, a distance hijacking attack is possible (i.e., the time and distance constraints are satisfiable), as depicted in Fig. 2, where an intruder located outside the neighborhood of the verifier (i.e., $d(V, I) > d$) succeeds in convincing the verifier that he is inside the neighborhood by exploiting the presence of an honest prover in the neighborhood (i.e., $d(V, P) \leq d$) to achieve his goal. The following is an example of a *successful* distance hijacking, in which the intruder listens to the exchanges messages between the prover and the verifier but builds the last message.

$$
\begin{array}{lll}
P_{t_1} \rightarrow V_{t_2} & : commit(N_P, S_P) & | \; t_2 = t_1 + d(P,V) \wedge \lfloor d(P,V) \rfloor \\
V_{t_2} \rightarrow P_{t_3}, I_{t'_3} : N_V & & | \; t_3 = t_2 + d(P,V) \wedge \lfloor d(P,V) \rfloor \\
& & | \; t'_3 = t_2 + d(I,V) \wedge \lfloor d(V,I) \rfloor \\
P_{t_3} \rightarrow V_{t_4}, I_{t'_4} : N_P \oplus N_V & & | \; t_4 = t_3 + d(P,V) \wedge \lfloor d(P,V) \rfloor \\
& & | \; t'_4 = t_3 + d(I,P) \wedge \lfloor d(I,P) \rfloor \\
V & : t_4 \dot{-} t_2 \leq 2*d & \\
P_{t_5} \rightarrow V_{t_6} & : S_P & | \; t_6 = t_5 + d(P,V) \wedge \lfloor d(P,V) \rfloor \\
& & | \; t_5 \geq t_3 \wedge t_6 \geq t_4 \\
I(P)_{t_7} \rightarrow V_{t_8} & : sign_I(N_V; N_P \oplus N_V) | \; t_8 = t_7 + d(I,V) \wedge \lfloor d(I,V) \rfloor \\
& & | \; t_7 \geq t'_4 \wedge t_8 \geq t_6
\end{array}
$$

This attack was feasible in [1] using the metric space assumptions, and it is also possible in three-dimensional space. Note that an attack may be possible in *some* metric space but it may not be possible in *all* metric spaces, let alone in Euclidean metric spaces like three-dimensional space. This inspired us to add location to our previous framework, as motivated by the following protocol.

Example 2. A secure localization protocol determines the physical location of a mobile device such as a sensor, a mobile phone, or a small computer with applications to location-based access control and security. In [20], a malicious device may lie about its location in an environment with different beacons to appear either farther away than its true location or closer than it really is.

We consider a very simple protocol in two-dimensional space. A device sends a timestamp to different beacons. All beacons are honest and receive the timestamp. Figure 3 shows how three beacons infer the position of the device by trilateration, i.e., the intersection of the hyperbolas associated to the distance travelled from the device's location. There is a base station that receives the positions inferred by the beacons and checks whether they coincide or not.

$D \rightarrow Be^i : timestamp$
      //The device broadcasts a timestamp, maybe different to its
      //actual time to appear farther or closer than its true location

$Be^i \rightarrow Ba : timediff ; \; Be^i_x ; \; Be^i_y$
      //Each beacon sends to a base station the difference between
      //the received timestamp and the actual reception time plus
      //her position.

An informal Alice-Bob presentation with time and location is as follows, where (D^i_x, D^i_y) is the inferred location of the device D according to beacon Be^i. The base calculates whether the positions of the device inferred by the beacons coincide, in symbols $D^1_x = \cdots = D^n_x$ and $D^1_y = \cdots = D^n_y$.

$$D_{t_1} \rightarrow Be^i_{t'_1} : t \qquad\qquad\qquad | \; t'_1 = t_1 + d(D, Be^i) \wedge \lfloor d(D, Be^i) \rfloor$$
$$Be^i : \bar{t} = t \dot{-} t'_1 \qquad\qquad\qquad | \; \bar{t} \geq 0$$
$$Be^i_{t_2} \rightarrow Ba_{t'_2} : \bar{t} ; \; Be^i_x ; \; Be^i_y \qquad | \; t'_2 = t_2 + d(Be^i, Ba) \wedge \lfloor d(Be^i, Ba) \rfloor$$
$$Ba : \bar{t}^2 = (D^1_x - Be^1_x)^2 + (D^1_y - Be^1_y)^2$$
$$\vdots$$
$$Ba : \bar{t}^2 = (D^n_x - Be^n_x)^2 + (D^n_y - Be^n_y)^2$$
$$Ba : D^1_x = \cdots = D^n_x \wedge D^1_y = \cdots = D^n_y$$

If the device is honest, the constraints on the real numbers computed by the base station are always satisfied. If the device is malicious, [20] shows two interesting configurations.

(i) (Insecure configuration) If the beacons are in the same lobe of a hyperbola, as shown in Fig. 4, it is possible for a malicious device at position P to choose a timestamp to pretend to be at position P'.

(ii) (Secure configuration) If there are four beacons and they form a rectangle, shown in Fig. 5, then [20] proves that the device is always caught by the base station.

Note that these two statements, (i) an attack and (ii) the absence of any attack, are verified by our time and space process algebra below without requiring exact positions. That is, (i) is verified just by showing an execution where the computed time and space constraints are satisfied and (ii) is verified by obtaining a finite search space where all the computed time and space constraints are unsatisfiable.

3   A Time and Space Process Algebra

In [1] we provided a timed process algebra syntax and a timed transition semantics. The timed process algebra only made message sending-and-reception times available to processes whereas the timed transition semantics modelled the actual time interactions between processes under metric space constraints. In this section, we extend the previous process algebra syntax to make spatial location information also available to processes and provide a transition semantics that models the actual time and space interactions between processes and Euclidean space constraints.

3.1 New Syntax for Location

In our time and space protocol process algebra, the behaviors of both honest principals and the intruders are represented by *labeled processes*. Therefore, a protocol is specified as a set of labeled processes. Each process performs a sequence of actions, namely sending $(+m)$ or receiving $(-m)$ a message m, but without knowing who actually sent it or received it. Each process may also perform deterministic or non-deterministic choices. We define a protocol $\mathcal{P}$ in the time and space protocol process algebra, written $\mathcal{P}_{TPA}$, as a pair of the form $\mathcal{P}_{TPA} = ((\Sigma_{TPA_{\mathcal{P}}}, E_{TPA_{\mathcal{P}}}), P_{TPA})$, where $(\Sigma_{TPA_{\mathcal{P}}}, E_{TPA_{\mathcal{P}}})$ is the equational theory specifying the equational properties of the cryptographic functions and the state structure, and P_{TPA} is a $\Sigma_{TPA_{\mathcal{P}}}$-term denoting a *well-formed* time and space process. The time and space protocol process algebra's syntax Σ_{TPA} is parameterized by a sort Msg of messages. Moreover, time and coordinates are represented by a new sort Real, since we allow conditional expressions on time and location to be constraints in real polynomial arithmetic.

Similar to [1,23], processes support four different kinds of choice: (i) a process expression $P\ ?\ Q$ supports *explicit non-deterministic choice* between P and Q; (ii) a choice variable $X_?$ appearing in a send message expression $+m$ supports *implicit non-deterministic choice* of its value, which can furthermore be an *unbounded* non-deterministic choice if $X_?$ ranges over an infinite set; (iii) a conditional *if C then P else Q* supports *explicit deterministic choice* between P and Q determined by the result of its condition C; and (iv) a receive message expression $-m(X_1, ..., X_n)$ supports *implicit deterministic* choice about accepting or rejecting a received message, depending on whether or not it matches the pattern $m(X_1, ..., X_n)$. This deterministic choice is implicit, but it could be made explicit by replacing $-m(X_1, ..., X_n) \cdot P$ by the semantically equivalent conditional expression $-X.\ if\ X = m(X_1, ..., X_n)\ then\ P\ else\ nilP$, where X is a variable of sort Msg, which therefore accepts any message.

The time and space process algebra has the following syntax, also similar to that of [1,23] plus the addition of the suffix @*Real* to the sending and receiving actions:

$$
\begin{aligned}
ProcConf &::= LProc \mid ProcConf\ \&\ ProcConf \mid \emptyset \\
ProcId &::= (Role, Nat) \\
LProc &::= (ProcId, Nat, Real, Real, Real)\ Proc \\
Proc &::= nilP \mid +(Msg@Real) \mid -(Msg@Real) \mid Proc \cdot Proc \mid \\
&\qquad Proc\ ?\ Proc \mid if\ Cond\ then\ Proc\ else\ Proc
\end{aligned}
$$

- *ProcConf* stands for a *process configuration*, i.e., a set of labeled processes, where the symbol & is used to denote set union for sets of labeled processes.

– *ProcId* stands for a *process identifier*, where *Role* refers to the role of the process in the protocol (e.g., prover or verifier) and *Nat* is a natural number denoting the identity of the process, which distinguishes different instances (sessions) of a process specification.
– *LProc* stands for a *labeled process*, i.e., a process *Proc* with a label $(ProcId, J)$. For convenience, we sometimes write $(Role, I, J, x, y, z)$, where J indicates that the action at stage J of the process $(Role, I)$ will be the next one to be executed, i.e., the first $J - 1$ actions of the process for role *Role* have already been executed. The three *Real* elements x, y, z represent the coordinates on three-dimensional space. Note that the I and J of a process $(Role, I, J, x, y, z)$ are omitted in a protocol specification.
– *Proc* defines the actions that can be executed within a process, where $+Msg@T$, and $-Msg@T$ respectively denote sending out a message or receiving a message *Msg*. Note that T must be a variable where the underlying Euclidean space determines the exact sending or receiving time, which can be used later in the process. Moreover, "*Proc · Proc*" denotes *sequential composition* of processes, where symbol $\_.\_$ is associative and has the empty process *nilP* as identity. Finally, "*Proc ? Proc*" denotes an explicit *nondeterministic choice*, whereas "*if Cond then Proc else Proc*" denotes an explicit *deterministic choice*, whose continuation depends on the satisfaction of the constraint *Cond*. Note that choice is explicitly represented by either a non-deterministic choice between $P_1 ? P_2$ or by the deterministic evaluation of a conditional expression *if Cond then* P_1 *else* P_2, but it is also implicitly represented by the instantiation of a variable in different runs.

In all process specifications we assume five disjoint kinds of variables, similar to the variables of [23] plus time variables as in [1] and location coordinate variables:

– **fresh variables**: each one of these variables receives a *distinct constant value* from a data type V_{fresh}, denoting unguessable values such as nonces. Throughout this paper we will denote this kind of variables as $f, f_1, f_2, \ldots$.
– **choice variables**: variables first appearing in a *sent message* $+M$, which can be substituted by any value arbitrarily chosen from a possibly infinite domain. A choice variable indicates an *implicit non-deterministic choice*. Given a protocol with choice variables, each possible substitution of these variables denotes a possible run of the protocol. We always denote choice variables by letters postfixed with the symbol "?" as a subscript, e.g., $A_?, B_?, \ldots$.
– **pattern variables**: variables first appearing in a *received message* $-M$. These variables will be instantiated when matching sent and received messages. *Implicit deterministic choices* are indicated by terms containing pattern variables, since failing to match a pattern term leads to the rejection of a message. A pattern term plays the implicit role of a guard, so that, depending on the different ways of matching it, the protocol can have different continuations. Pattern variables are written with uppercase letters, e.g., $A, B, N_A, \ldots$.
– **time variables**: a process cannot access the global clock, which implies that a time variable T of a reception or sending action $+(M@T)$ can never appear

in M but can appear in the remaining part of the process. Also, given a receiving action $-(M_1@t_1)$ and a sending action $+(M_2@t_2)$ in a process of the form $P_1 \cdot -(M_1@t_1) \cdot P_2 \cdot +(M_2@t_2) \cdot P_3$, the assumption that timed actions are performed from left to right forces the constraint $t_1 \leq t_2$. Time variables are always written with a (subscripted) t, e.g., $t_1, t_1', t_2, t_2', \ldots$.

- **coordinate variables**: a process can only access its own coordinates x, y, and z. Its coordinates can be sent and coordinate variables can be received, sent again and used in comparisons. The location of a process never changes, so coordinate variables can never be updated. Coordinate variables are always written with a (subscripted) x, y or z, e.g., $x_1, x_1', y_2, z_2', \ldots$.

These requirements about variables are formalized by the function $wf :$ $Proc \rightarrow Bool$ for *well-formed* processes given in [1]. The definition of wf uses an auxiliary function $shVar : Proc \rightarrow VarSet$ also given in [1].

Example 3. Let us specify the Brands and Chaum protocol of Example 1, where variables are distinct between processes. A nonce is represented as $n(A?, f)$, whereas a secret value is represented as $s(A?, f)$. The identifier of each process is represented by a choice variable $A?$. Recall that there is an arbitrary distance $d > 0$. Since participants in this protocol do not make use of their own coordinates, the following specification is identical to that of [1].

$$(Verifier, x, y, z) : -(Commit@t_1) \cdot$$
$$+(n(V?, f_1)@t_2) \cdot$$
$$-((n(V?, f_1) \oplus N_P)@t_3) \cdot$$
$$if \ t_3 - t_2 \leq 2 * d$$
$$then \ -(S_P@t_4) \cdot$$
$$if \ open(N_P, S_P, Commit)$$
$$then \ -(sign(P, n(V?, f_1); N_P \oplus n(V?, f_1))@t_5)$$
$$(Prover, x, y, z) : +(commit(n(P?, f_1), s(P?, f_2))@t_1) \cdot$$
$$-(N_V@t_2) \cdot$$
$$+((N_V \oplus n(P?, f_1))@t_3) \cdot$$
$$+(s(P?, f_2)@t_4) \cdot$$
$$+(sign(P?, N_V; n(P?, f_1) \oplus N_V)@t_5)$$

Example 4. Let us specify the secure localization protocol of Example 2 for four beacons. The timestamp is represented by variable t.

$$(Be^i, x, y, z) : -(t@t_1) \cdot$$
$$+(((t \dot{-} t_1) \; ; \; x \; ; \; y)@t_2) \cdot$$
$$-((ok@t_3) \cdot nilP$$
$$(Ba, x, y, z) : -((t'_1 \; ; \; x_1 \; ; \; y_1)@t_1) \cdot$$
$$-((t'_2 \; ; \; x_2 \; ; \; y_2)@t_2) \cdot$$
$$-((t'_3 \; ; \; x_3 \; ; \; y_3)@t_3) \cdot$$
$$-((t'_4 \; ; \; x_4 \; ; \; y_4)@t_4) \cdot$$
$$if \; \exists dx, dy : (t'_1)^2 = (dx - x_1)^2 + (dy - y_1)^2 \wedge$$
$$(t'_2)^2 = (dx - x_2)^2 + (dy - y_2)^2 \wedge$$
$$(t'_3)^2 = (dx - x_3)^2 + (dy - y_3)^2 \wedge$$
$$(t'_4)^2 = (dx - x_4)^2 + (dy - y_4)^2 \quad then \; +(ok@t_5) \; else \; nilP$$

3.2   Time and Space Intruder Model

The active Dolev-Yao intruder model is followed, which implies that an intruder can intercept, forward, or create messages from received messages. We assume that intruders are *located* and cannot change their location, as in [1]. In particular, they cannot change the physics of the metric space, e.g., cannot send messages from a different location or intercept a message that it is not within range.

In our time and space intruder model, we consider several located intruders, each with its own coordinates, with a family of capabilities (concatenation, deconcatenation, encryption, decryption, etc.), and each capability may have arbitrarily many instances. The combined actions of two intruders requires time, i.e., their distance; but a single intruder can perform many actions in zero time[1]. Note that, unlike in the standard Dolev-Yao model, we cannot assume just one intruder, since the time required for a principal to communicate with a given intruder is an observable characteristic of that intruder. Thus, although the Mafia fraud and distance hijacking attacks of the Brands and Chaum protocol and the insecure and secure configurations of the secure localization protocol only require one intruder, the framework itself allows general participant configurations with multiple intruders; although one intruder co-located with each honest participant is enough [16].

Example 5. In our timed process algebra, the family of capabilities associated to an intruder k are also described as processes. For instance, concatenating two received messages is represented by the process[2]

$$(k.Conc, x, y, z) : \; -(X@t_1) \; \cdot -(Y@t_2) \; \cdot +(X; Y@t_3)$$

and extracting one of them from a concatenation is described by the processes

$$(k.DeconcLeft, x, y, z) : \; -(X; Y@t_1) \; \cdot +(X@t_2)$$

---

[1] Adding time cost to single-intruder actions could be done with additional time constraints, but is outside the scope of this paper.

[2] Time variables t_1, t_2, t_3 as well as its coordinates are not actually used by the intruder but could be in the future.

$$(k.DeconcRight, x, y, z) : \ -(X; Y @ t_1) \ \cdot + (X @ t_2)$$

Roles of intruder capabilities include the identifier of the intruder, and it is possible to combine several intruder capabilities from the same or from different intruders. For example, we may say that the $+(X; Y @ t)$ of a process $I1.Conc$ associated to an intruder $I1$ may be synchronized with the $-(X; Y @ t')$ of a process $I2.DeconcLeft$ associated to an intruder $I2$. The physical space determines that $t' = t + d(I1, I2)$, where $d(I1, I2) > 0$ if $I1 \neq I2$ and $d(I1, I2) = 0$ if $I1 = I2$.

As presented in [1], a special *forwarding* intruder capability, not considered in the standard Dolev-Yao model, has to be included in order to take into account the time travelled by a message from an honest participant to the intruder and later to another participant, possibly another intruder.

$$(k.Forward, x, y, z) : \ -(X @ t_1) \ \cdot + (X @ t_2)$$

3.3 Time and Space Process Semantics

A *state* of a protocol $\mathcal{P}$ consists of a set of (possibly partially executed) *labeled processes*, a set of terms in the network $\{Net\}$, and the global clock. That is, a state is a term of the form $\{LP_1 \& \cdots \& LP_n \mid \{Net\} \mid \bar{t}\}$.

In [1], the only time information available to a process is the variable T associated to input and output messages $M @ T$; the global clock is inaccessible. However, once these messages have been sent or received, we included them in the network Net with extra information. When a message $M @ T$ is sent, we stored $M @ (A : t \to \emptyset)$ denoting that message M was sent by process A at the global time clock t, and propagated $T \mapsto t$ within the process A. When this message is received by an action $M' @ T'$ of process B (honest participant or intruder) at the global clock time t', M is matched against M' modulo the cryptographic functions, $T' \mapsto t'$ is propagated within the process B, and $B : t'$ is added to the stored message, following the general pattern $M @ (A : t \to (B_1 : t_1 \cdots B_n : t_n))$.

In our new time and space process algebra, we simply annotate stored messages with the coordinates from where the message was sent and, when the message is received by another process, we calculate actual distances between the stored coordinates and the coordinates of the current process. When a message $M @ T$ is sent by process (A, x, y, z), we store $M @ (A : x, y, z, t \to \emptyset)$ denoting that message M was sent at the global time clock t from location (x, y, z). When this message is received by an action $M' @ T'$ of process B (honest participant or intruder) at the global clock time t', M is matched against M' modulo the cryptographic functions, $T' \mapsto t'$ is propagated within the process B, and $B : t'$ is added to the stored message, following the general pattern $M @ (A : x, y, z, t \to (B_1 : t_1 \cdots B_n : t_n))$. No reception coordinates are stored, but we check that process B is reachable from process A at distance $t' - t$, i.e., $(t' - t)^2 = (B_x - A_x)^2 + (B_y - A_y)^2 + (B_z - A_z)^2$.

The rewrite theory $(\Sigma_{TPA_{\mathcal{P}}+State}, E_{TPA_{\mathcal{P}}}, R_{TPA_{\mathcal{P}}})$ characterizes the behavior of a protocol $\mathcal{P}$, where $\Sigma_{TPA_{\mathcal{P}}+State}$ extends $\Sigma_{TPA_{\mathcal{P}}}$, by adding state constructor symbols. We assume that a protocol run begins with an empty state, i.e., a state with an empty set of labeled processes, an empty network, and at time zero. Therefore, the initial empty state is always of the form $\{\emptyset \mid \{\emptyset\} \mid 0.0\}$. Note that, in a specific run, all the distances are provided a priori according to the Euclidean space and a chosen topology, whereas in a symbolic analysis, they will be represented by variables, probably occurring within space and time constraints.

State changes are defined by a set $R_{TPA_{\mathcal{P}}}$ of *rewrite rules* given below. Each transition rule in $R_{TPA_{\mathcal{P}}}$ is labeled with a tuple (ro, i, j, a, n, t), where:

- ro is the role of the labeled process being executed in the transition.
- i denotes the instance of the same role being executed in the transition.
- j denotes the process' step number since its beginning.
- a is a ground term identifying the action that is being performed in the transition. It has different possible values: "$+m$" or "$-m$" if the message m was sent (and added to the network) or received, respectively; "m" if the message m was sent but did not increase the network, "?" if the transition performs an explicit non-deterministic choice, "T" if the transition performs an explicit deterministic choice, "*Time*" when the global clock is incremented, or "*New*" when a new process is added.
- n is a number that, if the action that is being executed is an explicit choice, indicates which branch has been chosen as the process continuation. In this case n takes the value of either 1 or 2. If the transition does not perform any explicit choice, then $n = 0$.
- t is the global clock at each transition step.

Note that in the transition rules $R_{TPA_{\mathcal{P}}}$ shown below, *Net* denotes the network, represented by a set of messages of the form $M @ (A : x, y, z, t \rightarrow (B_1 : t_1 \cdots B_n : t_n))$, P denotes the rest of the process being executed and PS denotes the rest of labeled processes of the state (which can be the empty set $\emptyset$).

- *Sending a message* is represented by the two transition rules below, depending on whether the message M is stored, (TPA++), or is just discarded, (TPA+). In (TPA++), we store the sent message with its sending information, $(ro, i) : \bar{t}$, and add an empty set for those who will be receiving the message in the future $(M\sigma' @ (ro, i) : x, y, z, \bar{t} \rightarrow \emptyset)$.

$$\{(ro, i, j, x, y, z) \ (+M@t \cdot P) \ \& \ PS \mid \{Net\} \mid \bar{t}\}$$

$$\longrightarrow_{(ro,i,j,+(M\sigma'),0,\bar{t})}$$

$$\{(ro, i, j + 1, x, y, z) \ P\sigma' \ \& \ PS \mid \{(M\sigma'@(ro, i) : x, y, z, \bar{t} \to \emptyset), Net\} \mid \bar{t}\}$$
$$\textit{if} \ (M\sigma' : (ro, i) : x, y, z, \bar{t} \to \emptyset) \notin Net$$
$$\textit{where } \sigma \textit{ is a ground substitution binding choice variables in } M$$
$$\textit{and } \sigma' = \sigma \uplus \{t \mapsto \bar{t}\} \qquad\qquad\qquad\qquad\qquad\qquad \text{(TPA++)}$$

$$\{(ro, i, j, x, y, z) \ (+M@t \cdot P) \ \& \ PS \mid \{Net\} \mid \bar{t}\}$$

$$\longrightarrow_{(ro,i,j,M\sigma',0,\bar{t})}$$

$$\{(ro, i, j + 1, x, y, z) \ P\sigma' \ \& \ PS \mid \{Net\} \mid \bar{t}\}$$
$$\textit{where } \sigma \textit{ is a ground substitution binding choice variables in } M$$
$$\textit{and } \sigma' = \sigma \uplus \{t \mapsto \bar{t}\} \qquad\qquad\qquad\qquad\qquad\qquad \text{(TPA+)}$$

– *Receiving a message* is represented by the transition rule below. We add the reception information to the stored message, i.e., we replace $(M'@((ro', k) : x', y', z', t' \to AS))$ by $(M'@((ro', k) : x', y', z', t' \to (AS \uplus (ro, i) : \bar{t})))$.

$$\{(ro, i, j, x, y, z) \ (-(M@t) \cdot P) \ \& \ PS \mid$$
$$\{(M'@((ro', k) : x', y', z', t' \to AS)), Net\} \mid \bar{t}\}$$

$$\longrightarrow_{(ro,i,j,-(M\sigma'),0,\bar{t})}$$

$$\{(ro, i, j + 1, x, y, z) \ P\sigma' \ \& \ PS \mid$$
$$\{(M'@((ro', k) : x', y', z', t' \to (AS \uplus (ro, i) : \bar{t})), Net\} \mid \bar{t}\}$$
$$\text{IF } \exists \sigma : M' =_{E_{\mathcal{P}}} M\sigma, \bar{t} = t' + d((x, y, z), (x', y', z')), \sigma' = \sigma \uplus \{t \mapsto \bar{t}\} \quad \text{(TPA-)}$$

– An *explicit deterministic choice* is defined as follows. More specifically, the rule (TPAif1) describes the *then* case, i.e., if the constraint T is satisfied, then the process continues as P, whereas rule (TPAif2) describes the *else* case, that is, if the constraint C is *not* satisfied, the process continues as Q.

$$\{(ro, i, j, x, y, z) \ ((\textit{if } C \textit{ then } P \textit{ else } Q) \cdot R) \ \& \ PS \mid \{Net\} \mid \bar{t}\}$$
$$\longrightarrow_{(ro,i,j,C,1,\bar{t})} \{(ro, i, j + 1, x, y, z) \ (P \cdot R) \ \& \ PS \mid \{Net\} \mid \bar{t}\} \text{ IF } C \qquad \text{(TPAif1)}$$
$$\{(ro, i, j, x, y, z) \ ((\textit{if } C \textit{ then } P \textit{ else } Q) \cdot R) \ \& \ PS \mid \{Net\} \mid \bar{t}\}$$
$$\longrightarrow_{(ro,i,j,C,2,\bar{t})} \{(ro, i, j + 1, x, y, z) \ (Q \cdot R) \ \& \ PS \mid \{Net\} \mid \bar{t}\} \text{ IF } \neg C \qquad \text{(TPAif2)}$$

– An *explicit non-deterministic choice* is defined as follows. The process can continue either as P, denoted by rule (TPA?1), or as Q, denoted by rule (TPA?2).

$$\{(ro, i, j, x, y, z) \ ((P \ ? \ Q) \cdot R) \ \& \ PS \mid \{Net\} \mid \bar{t}\}$$
$$\longrightarrow_{(ro,i,j,?,1,\bar{t})} \{(ro, i, j + 1, x, y, z) \ (P \cdot R) \ \& \ PS \mid \{Net\} \mid \bar{t}\} \qquad \text{(TPA?1)}$$
$$\{(ro, i, j, x, y, z) \ ((P \ ? \ Q) \cdot R) \ \& \ PS \mid \{Net\} \mid \bar{t}\}$$
$$\longrightarrow_{(ro,i,j,?,2,\bar{t})} \{(ro, i, j + 1, x, y, z)(Q \cdot R) \ \& \ PS \mid \{Net\} \mid \bar{t}\} \qquad \text{(TPA?2)}$$

– *Global Time advancement* is represented by the transition rule below that increments the global clock enough to make one sent message arrive to its closest destination.

$$\{PS \mid \{Net\} \mid \bar{t}\} \longrightarrow_{(\perp,\perp,\perp,Time,0,\bar{t}+t')} \{PS \mid \{Net\} \mid \bar{t} + t'\}$$
$$\text{IF } t' = mte(PS, Net, \bar{t}) \wedge t' \neq 0 \qquad\qquad\qquad\qquad\qquad \text{(PhyTime)}$$

where the function mte is defined as follows:

$$mte(\emptyset, Net, \bar{t}) = \infty$$
$$mte(P\&PS, Net, \bar{t}) = min(mte(P, Net, \bar{t}), mte(PS, Net, \bar{t}))$$
$$mte((ro, i, j, x, y, z) \; nilP, Net, \bar{t}) = \infty$$
$$mte((ro, i, j, x, y, z) \; + (M@t) \cdot P, Net, \bar{t}) = 0$$
$$mte((ro, i, j, x, y, z) \; - (M@t) \cdot P, Net, \bar{t}) =$$
$$min\left(\left\{\begin{matrix} d((x,y,z),(x',y',z')) \mid (M'@(ro',i') : x',y',z',t' \to AS) \in Net \\ \wedge \exists \sigma : M\sigma =_B M' \end{matrix}\right\}\right)$$
$$mte((ro, i, j, x, y, z) \; (if \; T \; then \; P \; else \; Q) \cdot R, Net, \bar{t}) = 0$$
$$mte((ro, i, j, x, y, z) \; P_1?P_2, Net, \bar{t}) = 0$$

Note that the function mte evaluates to 0 if some instantaneous action by the previous rules can be performed. Otherwise, mte computes the smallest non-zero time increment required for some already sent message (existing in the network) to be received by some process (by matching with such an existing message in the network).

Further Time and Space Constraints. In [1], the timed process semantics assumed only a metric space with a distance function $d : ProcId \times ProcId \to Real$ such that (i) $d(A, A) = 0$, (ii) $d(A, B) = d(B, A)$, and (iii) $d(A, B) \le d(A, C) + d(C, B)$. For every message $M @ (A : t \to (B_1 : t_1 \cdots B_n : t_n))$ stored in the network Net, the semantics ensured that (iv) $t_i = t + d(A, B_i)$, $\forall 1 \le i \le n$. Furthermore, according to our wireless communication model, our semantics assumed (v) a *time sequence monotonicity* property, i.e., there is no other process C such that $d(A, C) \le d(A, B_i)$ for some i, $1 \le i \le n$, and C is not included in the set of recipients of the message M. Also, for each class of attacks such as the Mafia fraud or the hijacking attack analyzed in [1], (vi) some extra topology constraints were necessary (see Figs. 1 and 2). In our time and space semantics, all those assumptions except (v) are unnecessary by considering actual coordinates. This simplifies the transformation of time and space processes into untimed processes of Sect. 4 compared to the transformation presented in [1].

– New processes can be added as follows.

$$\left\{\begin{matrix} \forall \; (ro) \; P_k \in P_{PA} \\ \{PS \mid \{Net\} \mid \bar{t}\} \\ \xrightarrow{(ro,i+1,1,New,0,\bar{t})} \\ \{(ro, i+1, 1, x_?\sigma, y_?\sigma, z_?\sigma) \; P_k\sigma\rho_{ro,i+1} \; \& \; PS \mid \{Net\} \mid \bar{t}\} \\ where \; \rho_{ro,i+1} \; is \; a \; fresh \; substitution, \\ \quad \sigma \; is \; a \; ground \; substitution \; binding \; x_?, y_?, z_?, \\ \quad and \; i = id(PS, ro) \end{matrix}\right\} \quad (TPA\&)$$

The auxiliary function id counts the instances of a role

$$id(\emptyset, ro) = 0$$
$$id((ro', i, j, x, y, z)P\&PS, ro) = \begin{cases} max(id(PS, ro), i) & if \; ro = ro' \\ id(PS, ro) & if \; ro \ne ro' \end{cases}$$

where PS denotes a process configuration, P a process, and ro, ro' role names.

Therefore, the behavior of a timed protocol in the process algebra is defined by the set of transition rules $R_{TPA_P} = \{(\text{TPA} + +), (\text{TPA}+), (\text{PhyTime}), (\text{TPA}-), (\text{TPAif1}), (\text{TPAif2}), (\text{TPA?1}), (\text{TPA?2})\} \cup (\text{TPA\&})$.

Example 6. Continuing Example 3, it is possible to create a configuration of the Brands and Chaum for the mafia attack (which are impossible due to unsatisfiability of the timing and distance constraints) with a prover p, an intruder i, and a verifier v. The neighborhood distance is set to $d = 1.0$, the verifier is at coordinates $(0, 0, 0)$, the prover is at $(2, 0, 0)$, and the intruder is at $(1, 0, 0)$. That is, the distance between the prover and the verifier is $d(p, v) = 2.0$, but the distance between the prover and the intruder as well as the distance between the verifier and the intruder are $d(v, i) = d(p, i) = 1.0$, i.e., the honest prover p is outside v's neighborhood, $d(v, p) > d$, where $d(v, p) = d(v, i) + d(p, i)$.

Example 7. Continuing Example 4, it is possible to create a configuration of the beacons protocol where a malicious device is caught cheating. We consider four beacons at the following positions in two-dimensional space (we omit $z = 0$): $Be^1 : (0, 0)$, $Be^2 : (4, 0)$, $Be^3 : (0, 3)$, and $Be^4 : (4, 3)$. We assume a device at position $(4, 6)$. If the device is honest and sends the right timestamp, the distances d_1, d_2, d_3, d_4 computed by each beacon are

$$d_1 = \sqrt{(4 - 0)^2 + (6 - 0)^2} = \sqrt{16 + 36} = \sqrt{52},$$
$$d_2 = \sqrt{(4 - 4)^2 + (6 - 0)^2} = \sqrt{36} = 6,$$
$$d_3 = \sqrt{(4 - 0)^2 + (6 - 3)^2} = \sqrt{16 + 9} = \sqrt{25} = 5,$$
$$d_4 = \sqrt{(4 - 4)^2 + (6 - 4)^2} = \sqrt{9} = 3$$

the base station receives the distances and the beacons positions and computes the following set of equations

$$52 = (x - 0)^2 + (y - 0)^2$$
$$36 = (x - 4)^2 + (y - 0)^2$$
$$25 = (x - 0)^2 + (y - 3)^2$$
$$9 = (x - 3)^2 + (y - 3)^2$$

and it is not difficult to calculate x and y by Gaussian elimination:

$$x = ((36 + 16 - 36) + 16)/8 = (16 + 16)/8 = 4$$
$$y = ((52 - 25) + 9)/6 = (27 + 9)/6 = 36/6 = 6$$

If the device is malicious and sends the original timestamp plus 1 unit, the distances d_1, d_2, d_3, d_4 computed by each beacon are $d_1 = \sqrt{52} - 1$, $d_2 = 6 - 1 = 5$, $d_3 = 5 - 1 = 4$, and $d_4 = 3 - 1 = 2$. But when plugged in the previous equations, it is easy to check that the device is lying.

As it already happened in [1] with our timed protocol semantics, our new time and space protocol semantics can be implemented straightforwardly as a simulation tool. Note, however, that, since the number of different topologies is infinite, model checking a protocol for a *concrete configuration* with a simulation tool is very limited, since it cannot prove the *absence* of an attack for *all* topologies. For this reason, we follow a symbolic approach that can explore *all* relevant configurations.

In the following section we provide a sound and complete protocol transformation from our time and space process algebra to the untimed process algebra with constraints of the Maude-NPA tool, in a similar manner to the protocol transformation provided in [1]. In order to do this, we represent time and location information as well as those constraints checked by the participants as real arithmetic constraints. As a path is built, an SMT solver can be used to check that the constraints are satisfiable as we did in [1] only for time.

4   Time and Space Process Algebra into Untimed Process Algebra

In this section, we extend the general constraint satisfiability approach of [1] where all possible (not only some) runs are symbolically analyzed. This time and space semantics provides both a *trace-based insecure statement*, i.e., a run leading to an insecure secrecy or authentication property where all constraints are satisfiable is discovered given enough resources, and an *unsatisfiability-based secure statement*, i.e., there is no run leading to an insecure secrecy or authentication property due to time and space constraint unsatisfiability.

Example 8. Consider again the initial configuration for the Brands-Chaum protocol of Example 6. We can abstract away from the specific locations and just use logical variables for the coordinates of the prover (p_x, p_y), the verifier (v_x, v_y), and the intruder (i_x, i_y). Then, it is possible to obtain a symbolic trace using logical variables $\bar{t}_0, \ldots, \bar{t}_6$ where the following time constraints are accumulated:

$$t_1 = t_0 + d((p_x, p_y), (i_x, i_y))$$
$$t_2 = t_1 + d((v_x, v_y), (i_x, i_y))$$
$$t_3 = t_2 + d((v_x, v_y), (i_x, i_y))$$
$$t_4 = t_3 + d((p_x, p_y), (i_x, i_y))$$
$$t_5 = t_4 + d((p_x, p_y), (i_x, i_y))$$
$$t_6 = t_5 + d((v_x, v_y), (i_x, i_y))$$

Note that these constraints are unsatisfiable when combined with (i) the assumption $d > 0$, (ii) the verifier check $\bar{t}_6 - \bar{t}_2 \leq 2*d$, (iii) the assumption that the honest prover is outside the verifier's neighborhood, $d((p_x, p_y), (v_x, v_y)) > d$, (iv) the triangular inequality $d((p_x, p_y), (v_x, v_y)) \leq d((p_x, p_y), (i_x, i_y)) + d((v_x, v_y), (i_x, i_y))$, and (v) the assumption that there is only one intruder.

Example 9. Consider again the initial configuration for the beacons protocol of Example 7. Again, we can abstract away from the specific locations and just put logical variables for the coordinates of the four beacons $x_1, x_2, x_3, x_4, y_1, y_2, y_3, y_4$, the base station (but they are irrelevant) and the malicious device d_x, d_y. Then, it is possible to obtain a symbolic trace using logical variables $t_0, \ldots, t_4$ and the sent timestamp t where the following time and space constraints are accumulated:

$$t_1 = t_0 + d((d_x, d_y), (x_1, y_1))$$
$$t_2 = t_0 + d((d_x, d_y), (x_2, y_2))$$
$$t_3 = t_0 + d((d_x, d_y), (x_3, y_3))$$
$$t_4 = t_0 + d((d_x, d_y), (x_4, y_4))$$
$$(t - t_1)^2 = (d_x - x_1)^2 + (d_y - y_1)^2$$
$$(t - t_2)^2 = (d_x - x_2)^2 + (d_y - y_2)^2$$
$$(t - t_3)^2 = (d_x - x_3)^2 + (d_y - y_3)^2$$
$$(t - t_4)^2 = (d_x - x_4)^2 + (d_y - y_4)^2$$

It is easy to check that a malicious device will be caught if $t \neq t_0$.

As explained previously, there are some implicit conditions based on the *mte* function to calculate the time increment to the closest destination of a message. However, the *mte* function is unnecessary in the untimed process algebra, where those implicit conditions are incorporated into the symbolic run. In the following, we define a transformation of the time and space process algebra by (i) removing the global clock; (ii) adding the time data into untimed messages of a process algebra without time; (iii) adding the coordinates of each process to the untimed messages of a process algebra without space information; and (iv) adding real arithmetic conditions over the reals for the time and location constraints (those generated by the time and space semantics and those checked by the processes).

Since all the relevant time information is actually stored in messages of the form $M @ (A : x, y, z, t \rightarrow (B_1 : t_1 \cdots B_n : t_n))$ and controlled by the transition rules (TPA++), (TPA+), and (TPA-), the mapping *phy2pa* of Definition 1 below transforms each message $M @ t$ of a timed process into a message $M @ (A : x_?, y_?, z_?, t_? \rightarrow AS_?)$ of an untimed process. That is, we use a timed choice variable $t_?$ for the sending time, choice variables $x_?, y_?, z_?$ for the coordinates and a variable $AS_?$ for the reception information $(B_1 : t'_1 \cdots B_n : t'_n)$ associated to the sent message. The transformation below ensures that the choice variables for the coordinates are all the same within the messages of the untimed process. Since choice variables are replaced by specific values, $t_?, x_?, y_?, z_?$ and $AS_?$ will be replaced by the appropriate values that make the execution and all its time and space constraints possible. Note that these choice variables will be replaced by logical variables during the symbolic execution.

Definition 1 (Adding Real Variables and Time and Space Constraints).
The mapping phy2pa from time and space processes into untimed processes and its auxiliary mapping phy2pa* is defined as follows:

$phy2pa(\emptyset) = \emptyset$

$phy2pa((ro,i,j,x,y,z) P \& PS) = (ro,i,j) \, phy2pa^*(P,ro,i,x,y,z) \& phy2pa(PS)$

$phy2pa^*(nilP, ro, i, x, y, z) = nilP$

$phy2pa^*(+(M@t) . P, ro, i, x, y, z) =$
$\quad + (M@((ro,i) : x_?, y_?, z_?, t_? \rightarrow AS_?)) . phy2pa^*(P\gamma, ro, i, x, y, z)$
$\quad\quad where \; \gamma = \{t \mapsto t_?\}$

$phy2pa^*(-(M@t) . P, ro, i, x, y, z) =$
$\quad - (M@((ro',i') : x', y', z', t' \rightarrow ((ro,i) : t) \uplus AS)) .$
$\quad\quad if \, t = t' + d((x_?, y_?, z_?),(x', y', z')) \; then \; phy2pa^*(P, ro, i) \; else \; nilP$

$phy2pa^*(\; (if \, C \, then \, P \, else \, Q) . R, ro, i, x, y, z)$
$\quad = (if \, C \, then \, phy2pa^*(P,ro,i,x,y,z) \; else \; phy2pa^*(Q,ro,i,x,y)) . phy2pa^*(R,ro,i,x,y,z)$

$phy2pa^*(\; (P \, ? \, Q) . R, ro, i, x, y, z)$
$\quad = (phy2pa^*(P,ro,i,x,y,z) \, ? \, phy2pa^*(Q,ro,i,x,y,z)) . phy2pa^*(R,ro,i,x,y,z)$

where $t_?$ and $AS_?$ are choice variables different for each one of the sending actions, $x_?$, $y_?$, $z_?$ are always the same variables for all sending or receiving actions, ro', i', t', d, x', y', z', AS are pattern variables different for each one of the receiving actions, P, Q, and R are processes, M is a message, and C is a constraint.

The soundness and completeness proof of this transformation is almost identical to the soundness and completeness proof of [1], available at https://arxiv.org/abs/2010.13707, since it just replaces time constraints by the time and space constraints associated to the expression $d((x, y, z), (x', y', z'))$.

Example 10. The time and space processes of Example 3 are transformed into the following untimed processes. We remove the "else *nilP*" branches for clarity.

$(Verifier) : -(Commit @ A_1 : x_1, y_1, z_1, t'_1 \rightarrow V_? : t_1 \uplus AS_1) \cdot$
$\quad\quad if \, t_1 = t'_1 + d((x_1, y_1, z_1), (x_?, y_?, z_?)) \wedge d((x_1, y_1, z_1), (x_?, y_?, z_?)) \geq 0 \; then$
$\quad\quad +(n(V_?, f_1) @ V_? : x_?, y_?, z_?, t_{2?} \rightarrow AS_{2?}) \cdot$
$\quad\quad -((n(V_?, f_1) \oplus N_P) @ A_3 : x_3, y_3, z_3, t'_3 \rightarrow V_? : t_3 \uplus AS_3) \cdot$
$\quad\quad if \, t_3 = t'_3 + d((x_3, y_3, z_3), (x_?, y_?, z_?)) \wedge d((x_3, y_3, z_3), (x_?, y_?, z_?)) \geq 0 \; then$
$\quad\quad if \, t_3 \dot{-} t_{2?} \leq 2 * d \; then$
$\quad\quad -(S_P @ A_4 : x_4, y_4, z_4, t'_4 \rightarrow V_? : t_4 \uplus AS_4) \cdot$
$\quad\quad if \, t_4 = t'_4 + d((x_4, y_4, z_4), (x_?, y_?, z_?)) \wedge d((x_4, y_4, z_4), (x_?, y_?, z_?)) \geq 0 \; then$
$\quad\quad if \, open(N_P, S_P, Commit) \; then$
$\quad\quad -(sign(P, n(V_?, f_1)); N_P \oplus n(V_?, f_1)) @ A_5 : x_5, y_5, z_5, t'_5 \rightarrow V_? : t_5 \uplus AS_5) \cdot$
$\quad\quad if \, t_5 = t'_5 + d((x_5, y_5, z_5), (x_?, y_?, z_?)) \wedge d((x_5, y_5, z_5), (x_?, y_?, z_?)) \geq 0 \; then$
$\quad\quad nilP$
$(Prover) : +(commit(n(P_?, f_1), s(P_?, f_2))@P_? : x_?, y_?, z_?, t_{1?} \rightarrow AS_{1?}) \cdot$
$\quad\quad -(V; N_V @ A_2 : x_2, y_2, z_2, t'_2 \rightarrow V_? : t_2 \uplus AS_2) \cdot$
$\quad\quad if \, t_2 = t'_2 + d((x_2, y_2, z_2), (x_?, y_?, z_?)) \wedge d((x_2, y_2, z_2), (x_?, y_?, z_?)) \geq 0 \; then$
$\quad\quad +((N_V \oplus n(P_?, f_1))@P_? : x_?, y_?, z_?, t_{3?} \rightarrow AS_{3?}) \cdot$

$$+(s(P_?, f_2)@P_? : x_?, y_?, z_?, t_{4?} \rightarrow AS_{4?}) \cdot$$
$$+(sign(P_?, N_V; n(P_?, f_1) \oplus N_V)@P_? : x_?, y_?, z_?, t_{5?} \rightarrow AS_{5?}))$$

Example 11. The time and space processes of Example 5 for the intruder are transformed into the following untimed processes. Note that we use the intruder identifier I associated to each role instead of a choice variable $I_?$.

$(I.Conc) : -(X@ \; A_1 : x_1, y_1, z_1, t_1 \rightarrow I : t_1' \uplus AS_1) \cdot$
   $if \; t_1' = t_1 + d((x_1, y_1, z_1), (x_?, y_?, z_?)) \wedge d((x_1, y_1, z_1), (x_?, y_?, z_?)) \geq 0 \; then$
   $-(Y@ \; A_2 : x_2, y_2, z_2, t_2 \rightarrow I : t_2' \uplus AS_2) \cdot$
   $if \; t_2' = t_2 + d((x_2, y_2, z_2), (x_?, y_?, z_?)) \wedge d((x_2, y_2, z_2), (x_?, y_?, z_?)) \geq 0 \; then$
   $+(X; Y@I : x_?, y_?, z_?, t_{3?} \rightarrow AS_?)$
$(I.DeconcLeft) : -(X; Y@ \; A_1 : x_1, y_1, z_1, t_1 \rightarrow I : t_1' \uplus AS_1) \cdot$
   $if \; t_1' = t_1 + d((x_1, y_1, z_1), (x_?, y_?, z_?)) \wedge d((x_1, y_1, z_1), (x_?, y_?, z_?)) \geq 0 \; then$
   $+(X@I : x_?, y_?, z_?, t_{2?} \rightarrow AS_?)$
$(I.Forward) : -(X@ \; A_1 : x_1, y_1, z_1, t_1 \rightarrow I : t_1' \uplus AS_1) \cdot$
   $if \; t_1' = t_1 + d((x_1, y_1, z_1), (x_?, y_?, z_?)) \wedge d((x_1, y_1, z_1), (x_?, y_?, z_?)) \geq 0 \; then$
   $+(X@I : x_?, y_?, z_?, t_{2?} \rightarrow AS_?)$

Example 12. The time and space processes of Example 4 are transformed into the following untimed processes. We remove the "else *nilP*" branches for clarity.

$(Be^i, x, y, z) : -(t@x_1, y_1, z_1, t_1' \rightarrow Be_? : t_1 \uplus AS_1) \cdot$
   $if \; t_1 = t_1' + d((x_1, y_1, z_1), (x_?, y_?, z_?)) \wedge d((x_1, y_1, z_1), (x_?, y_?, z_?)) \geq 0 \; then$
   $+(((t \dot{-} t_1) \; ; \; x_? \; ; \; y_?)@x_?, y_?, z_?, t_2 \rightarrow AS_{2?}) \cdot$
   $-((ok@x_3, y_3, z_3, t_3' \rightarrow Be_? : t_3 \uplus AS_3) \cdot$
   $if \; t_3 = t_3' + d((x_3, y_3, z_3), (x_?, y_?, z_?)) \wedge d((x_3, y_3, z_3), (x_?, y_?, z_?)) \geq 0 \; then$
   $nilP$

$(Ba, x, y, z) : -((t_1' \; ; \; x_1' \; ; \; y_1')@x_1, y_1, z_1, t_1' \rightarrow Ba_? : t_1 \uplus AS_1) \cdot$
   $if \; t_1 = t_1' + d((x_1, y_1, z_1), (x_?, y_?, z_?)) \wedge d((x_1, y_1, z_1), (x_?, y_?, z_?)) \geq 0 \; then$
   $-((t_2' \; ; \; x_2' \; ; \; y_2')@x_2, y_2, z_2, t_2' \rightarrow Ba_? : t_2 \uplus AS_2) \cdot$
   $if \; t_2 = t_2' + d((x_2, y_2, z_2), (x_?, y_?, z_?)) \wedge d((x_2, y_2, z_2), (x_?, y_?, z_?)) \geq 0 \; then$
   $-((t_3' \; ; \; x_3' \; ; \; y_3')@x_3, y_3, z_3, t_3' \rightarrow Ba_? : t_3 \uplus AS_3) \cdot$
   $if \; t_3 = t_3' + d((x_3, y_3, z_3), (x_?, y_?, z_?)) \wedge d((x_3, y_3, z_3), (x_?, y_?, z_?)) \geq 0 \; then$
   $-((t_4' \; ; \; x_4' \; ; \; y_4')@x_4, y_4, z_4, t_4' \rightarrow Ba_? : t_4 \uplus AS_4) \cdot$
   $if \; t_4 = t_4' + d((x_4, y_4, z_4), (x_?, y_?, z_?)) \wedge d((x_4, y_4, z_4), (x_?, y_?, z_?)) \geq 0 \; then$
   $if \; \exists dx, dy : (t_1')^2 = (dx - x_1')^2 + (dy - y_1')^2 \wedge$
   $\qquad\qquad\quad (t_2')^2 = (dx - x_2')^2 + (dy - y_2')^2 \wedge$
   $\qquad\qquad\quad (t_3')^2 = (dx - x_3')^2 + (dy - y_3')^2 \wedge$
   $\qquad\qquad\quad (t_4')^2 = (dx - x_4')^2 + (dy - y_4')^2$
   $then \; +(ok@x_?, y_?, z_?, t_5 \rightarrow AS_{5?})$

Once a time and space process is transformed into an untimed process with time and location variables and time and locations constraints using the notation of Maude-NPA, we can easily adapt the soundness and completeness proof of [1], which relies on both a soundness and completeness proof from the Maude-NPA process notation into Maude-NPA forward rewriting semantics and on a soundness and completeness proof from Maude-NPA forward rewriting semantics into

Maude-NPA backwards symbolic semantics, see [22,23]. Since the Maude-NPA backwards symbolic semantics already considers constraints in a very general setting [11], we only need to perform the additional satisfiability check for real polynomial arithmetic.

5   Timed Process Algebra into Strands in Maude-NPA

This section is provided to help in understanding the experimental work. Although Maude-NPA accepts protocol specifications in either the process algebra notation or the strand space notation, its output is given in the stand space notation. Thus, in order to make our experiments easier to understand, we describe the translation from untimed processes with time and space constraints into untimed strands with time and location variables and time and space constraints. This translation is also sound and complete, as it replicates the transformation of [22,23].

Strands [21] are used in Maude-NPA to represent both the actions of honest principals (with a strand specified for each protocol role) and those of an intruder (with a strand for each action an intruder is able to perform on messages). In Maude-NPA strands evolve over time. The symbol | is used to divide past and future. That is, given a strand $[\ msg_1^{\pm},\ \ldots,\ msg_i^{\pm}\ |\ msg_{i+1}^{\pm},\ \ldots,\ msg_k^{\pm}\ ]$, messages $msg_1^{\pm}, \ldots, msg_i^{\pm}$ are the *past messages*, and messages $msg_{i+1}^{\pm}, \ldots, msg_k^{\pm}$ are the *future messages* ($msg_{i+1}^{\pm}$ is the immediate future message). Constraints can be also inserted into strands. A strand $[msg_1^{\pm}, \ldots, msg_k^{\pm}]$ is shorthand for $[nil\ |\ msg_1^{\pm}, \ldots, msg_k^{\pm}, nil]$. An *initial state* is a state where the bar is at the beginning for all strands in the state, and the network has no possible intruder fact of the form $m \in \mathcal{I}$. A *final state* is a state where the bar is at the end for all strands in the state and there is no negative intruder fact of the form $m \notin \mathcal{I}$.

In the following, we illustrate how the untimed process algebra can be transformed into strands specifications of Maude-NPA for our two running examples. We simply replaced · by comma, and each if-then-else by its boolean constraint.

Example 13. The untimed processes of Example 10 are transformed into the following strands.

$(Verifier) : [-(Commit @ A_1 : x_1, y_1, z_1, t_1' \rightarrow V_? : t_1 \uplus AS_1),$
$\quad (t_1 = t_1' + d((x_1, y_1, z_1), (x_?, y_?, z_?)) \wedge d((x_1, y_1, z_1), (x_?, y_?, z_?)) \geq 0),$
$\quad +(n(V_?, f_1) @ V_? : x_?, y_?, z_?, t_{2?} \rightarrow AS_{2?}),$
$\quad -((n(V_?, f_1) \oplus N_P) @ A_3 : x_3, y_3, z_3, t_3' \rightarrow V_? : t_3 \uplus AS_3),$
$\quad (t_3 = t_3' + d((x_3, y_3, z_3), (x_?, y_?, z_?)) \wedge d((x_3, y_3, z_3), (x_?, y_?, z_?)) \geq 0),$
$\quad (t_3 \dot{-} t_{2?} \leq 2 * d),$
$\quad -(S_P @ A_4 : x_4, y_4, z_4, t_4' \rightarrow V_? : t_4 \uplus AS_4),$
$\quad (t_4 = t_4' + d((x_4, y_4, z_4), (x_?, y_?, z_?)) \wedge d((x_4, y_4, z_4), (x_?, y_?, z_?)) \geq 0),$
$\quad open(N_P, S_P, Commit),$
$\quad -(sign(P, n(V_?, f_1); N_P \oplus n(V_?, f_1)) @ A_5 : x_5, y_5, z_5, t_5' \rightarrow V_? : t_5 \uplus AS_5),$
$\quad (t_5 = t_5' + d((x_5, y_5, z_5), (x_?, y_?, z_?)) \wedge d((x_5, y_5, z_5), (x_?, y_?, z_?)) \geq 0)]$

$(Prover) : [+(commit(n(P_?, f_1), s(P_?, f_2))@P_? : x_?, y_?, z_?, t_{1?} \rightarrow AS_{1?}),$

$$-(V; N_V @ A_2 : x_2, y_2, z_2, t_2' \to V_? : t_2 \uplus AS_2),$$
$$(t_2 = t_2' + d((x_2, y_2, z_2), (x_?, y_?, z_?)) \wedge d((x_2, y_2, z_2), (x_?, y_?, z_?)) \geq 0),$$
$$+((N_V \oplus n(P_?, f_1)) @ P_? : x_?, y_?, z_?, t_{3?} \to AS_{3?}),$$
$$+(s(P_?, f_2) @ P_? : x_?, y_?, z_?, t_{4?} \to AS_{4?}),$$
$$+(sign(P_?, N_V; n(P_?, f_1) \oplus N_V) @ P_? : x_?, y_?, z_?, t_{5?} \to AS_{5?}))]$$

Example 14. The untimed processes of Example 12 are transformed into the following strands.

$$(Be^i, x, y, z) : [-(t @ x_1, y_1, z_1, t_1' \to Be_? : t_1 \uplus AS_1),$$
$$(t_1 = t_1' + d((x_1, y_1, z_1), (x_?, y_?, z_?)) \wedge d((x_1, y_1, z_1), (x_?, y_?, z_?)) \geq 0),$$
$$+(((t \dot{-} t_1) \; ; \; x_? \; ; \; y_?) @ x_?, y_?, z_?, t_2 \to AS_{2?}),$$
$$-((ok @ x_3, y_3, z_3, t_3' \to Be_? : t_3 \uplus AS_3),$$
$$(t_3 = t_3' + d((x_3, y_3, z_3), (x_?, y_?, z_?)) \wedge d((x_3, y_3, z_3), (x_?, y_?, z_?)) \geq 0)]$$

$$(Ba, x, y, z) : [-((t_1' \; ; \; x_1' \; ; \; y_1') @ x_1, y_1, z_1, t_1' \to Ba_? : t_1 \uplus AS_1),$$
$$(t_1 = t_1' + d((x_1, y_1, z_1), (x_?, y_?, z_?)) \wedge d((x_1, y_1, z_1), (x_?, y_?, z_?)) \geq 0),$$
$$-((t_2' \; ; \; x_2' \; ; \; y_2') @ x_2, y_2, z_2, t_2' \to Ba_? : t_2 \uplus AS_2),$$
$$(t_2 = t_2' + d((x_2, y_2, z_2), (x_?, y_?, z_?)) \wedge d((x_2, y_2, z_2), (x_?, y_?, z_?)) \geq 0),$$
$$-((t_3' \; ; \; x_3' \; ; \; y_3') @ x_3, y_3, z_3, t_3' \to Ba_? : t_3 \uplus AS_3),$$
$$(t_3 = t_3' + d((x_3, y_3, z_3), (x_?, y_?, z_?)) \wedge d((x_3, y_3, z_3), (x_?, y_?, z_?)) \geq 0),$$
$$-((t_4' \; ; \; x_4' \; ; \; y_4') @ x_4, y_4, z_4, t_4' \to Ba_? : t_4 \uplus AS_4),$$
$$(t_4 = t_4' + d((x_4, y_4, z_4), (x_?, y_?, z_?)) \wedge d((x_4, y_4, z_4), (x_?, y_?, z_?)) \geq 0),$$
$$\begin{pmatrix} (t_1')^2 = (dx - x_1')^2 + (dy - y_1')^2 \wedge \\ (t_2')^2 = (dx - x_2')^2 + (dy - y_2')^2 \wedge \\ (t_3')^2 = (dx - x_3')^2 + (dy - y_3')^2 \wedge \\ (t_4')^2 = (dx - x_4')^2 + (dy - y_4')^2 \end{pmatrix}$$
$$+(ok @ x_?, y_?, z_?, t_5 \to AS_{5?})]$$

We specify the desired security properties in terms of *attack patterns* including logical variables, which describe the insecure states that Maude-NPA is trying to prove unreachable. The specifications, outputs, and a modified version of Maude-NPA are available at http://personales.upv.es/sanesro/guttman2021. Specifically, the tool attempts to find a *backwards narrowing sequence* path from the attack pattern to an initial state until it can no longer form any backwards narrowing steps, at which point it terminates. If it has not found an initial state, the attack pattern is judged *unreachable*.

The following examples show how a classic mafia fraud attack for the Brands-Chaum protocol can be specified in Maude-NPA's strand notation. Note that Maude-NPA uses symbol === for equality on the reals, +=+ for addition on the reals, *=* for multiplication on the reals, and -=- for subtraction on the reals. Extra time and space constraints are included in an smt section. In general, Maude-NPA requires an SMT solver that supports checking quadratic constraints over the reals, such as Yices [24], Z3 [25], or Mathematica [13].

Example 15. Following the strand specification of the Brands-Chaum protocol given in Example 13, the mafia attack of Example 1 is given as the following attack pattern. We consider one prover p, one verifier v, and one intruder i at fixed locations (px, py, pz), (vx, vy, vz) and (ix, iy, iz), respectively. Brands-Chaum is secure against the mafia fraud attack and no initial state is found in the backwards search.

```
eq ATTACK-STATE(1) --- Mafia fraud
= :: r :: ---Alice --- Verifier
[ nil,
 -(commit(n(b,r1),s(b,r2)) @ i : ix,iy,iz,t1 -> a : t2),
 ((t2 === t1 +=+ dai) and (dai > 0/1) and
 ((dai *=* dai) === (((ix -=- ax) *=* (ix -=- ax)) +=+ ((iy -=- ay) *=* (iy -=- ay)))
                                    +=+ ((iz -=- az) *=* (iz -=- az)))),
 +(n(a,r) @ a : ax,ay,az,t2 -> i : t2'''),
 -(n(a,r) * n(b,r1) @ i : ix,iy,iz,t3 -> a : t4),
 ((t4 === (t3 +=+ dai)) and (dai > 0/1) and
 (((t4 -=- t2) <= (2/1 *=* d)) and (d > 0/1)) | nil ]
&
:: r1,r2 :: ---Bob  --- Prover
[ nil,
 +(commit(n(b,r1),s(b,r2)) @ b : bx,by,bz,t1' -> i : t1''),
 -(n(a,r) @ i : ix,iy,iz,t2'' -> b : t3'),
 ((t3' === (t2'' +=+ dbi)) and (dbi > 0/1) and
 ((dbi *=* dbi) === ((((ix -=- bx) *=* (ix -=- bx)) +=+ ((iy -=- by) *=* (iy -=- by)))
                                    +=+ ((iz -=- bz) *=* (iz -=- bz))))),
 +(n(a,r) * n(b,r1) @ b : bx,by,bz,t3' -> i : t3'') | nil ]
 || smt(((dai +=+ dbi) > d) and (dbi > 0/1) and (dab > 0/1) and (dai > 0/1) and
        ((dab *=* dab) === ((((ax -=- bx) *=* (ax -=- bx)) +=+ ((ay -=- by) *=* (ay -=- by))
                                    +=+ ((az -=- bz) *=* (az -=- bz)))))
```

Example 16. Continuing Example 15, the hijacking attack of Example 1 is given as the following attack pattern. And the backwards search of Maude-NPA from this attack pattern does find an initial state.

```
eq ATTACK-STATE(2) --- Hijacking
= :: r :: --- Alice --- Verifier
[ nil,
 -(commit(n(b,r1),s(b,r2)) @ b : bx,by,bz,t1 -> a : t2),
 ((t2 === t1 +=+ dab) and (dab > 0/1) and
 ((dab *=* dab) === (((ax -=- bx) *=* (ax -=- bx)) +=+ ((ay -=- by) *=* (ay -=- by)))
                                    +=+ ((az -=- bz) *=* (az -=- bz)))),
 +(n(a,r) @ a : ax,ay,az,t2 -> b : t3 # i : t2''),
 -(n(a,r) * n(b,r1) @ b : bx,by,bz,t3 -> a : t4 # i : t4''),
 ((t4 === t3 +=+ dab)),
 ((t4 -=- t2) <= (2/1 *=* d)),
 -(s(b,r2) @ b : bx,by,bz,t5 -> a : t6),
 ((t6 === t5 +=+ dab)),
 -(sign(i,(n(a,r) * n(b,r1)) ; n(a,r)) @ i : ix,iy,iz,t7 -> a : t8),
 ((t8 === (t7 +=+ dai)) and (dai > 0/1) and
 ((dai *=* dai) === (((ax -=- ix) *=* (ax -=- ix)) +=+ ((ay -=- iy) *=* (ay -=- iy)))
                                    +=+ ((az -=- iz) *=* (az -=- iz)))) | nil ]
&
:: r1,r2 :: ---Bob  --- Prover
[ nil,
 +(commit(n(b,r1),s(b,r2)) @ b : bx,by,bz,t1 -> a : t2),
 -(n(a,r) @ a : ax,ay,az,t2 -> b : t3 # i : t3''),
 ((t3 === (t2 +=+ dab)) and (dab > 0/1) and
 ((dab *=* dab) === (((ax -=- bx) *=* (ax -=- bx)) +=+ ((ay -=- by) *=* (ay -=- by)))
                                    +=+ ((az -=- bz) *=* (az -=- bz)))),
 +(n(a,r) * n(b,r1) @ b : bx,by,bz,t3 -> a : t4 # i : t4''),
 +(s(b,r2) @ b : bx,by,bz,t5 -> a : t6) | nil]
 || smt( (dai > d) and (dab <= d))
```

Example 17. Following the strand specification of the beacons protocol given in Example 14, we can give a very general attack pattern.

```
eq ATTACK-STATE(0) =
:: r :: --- Intruder
[ nil, +(t @ i : x1,y1,z1,t0 -> Be1 : t1 # Be2 : t2 # Be3 : t3 # Be4 : t4) | nil ]
&
:: r1 :: --- Beacon 1
[ nil ,
-(t @ i : x1,y1,z1,t0 -> Be1 : t1 # Be2 : t2 # Be3 : t3 # Be4 : t4),
((t1 === t0 +=+ dbe1) and (dbe1 > 0/1) and
((dbe1 *=* dbe1) === (((be1x -=- x1) *=* (be1x -=- x1))
    +=+ ((be1y -=- y1) *=* (be1y -=- y1))) +=+ ((be1z -=- z1) *=* (be1z -=- z1)))),
+((t1 -=- t) ; be1x ; be1y @ Be1 : be1x,be1y,be1z,t1 -> Ba : t1'),
-(ok @ Ba : bax,bay,baz,t5 -> Be1 : t1'' # Be2 : t2'' # Be3 : t3'' # Be4 : t4''),
((t1'' === t5 +=+ dbabe1) and (dbabe1 > 0/1) and
((dbabe1 *=* dbabe1) === (((be1x -=- bax) *=* (be1x -=- bax))
    +=+ ((be1y -=- bay) *=* (be1y -=- bay))) +=+ ((be1z -=- baz) *=* (be1z -=- baz)))) | nil]
&
:: r2 :: --- Beacon 2
[ nil ,
-(t @ i : x1,y1,z1,t0 -> Be1 : t1 # Be2 : t2 # Be3 : t3 # Be4 : t4),
((t2 === t0 +=+ dbe2) and (dbe2 > 0/1) and
((dbe2 *=* dbe2) === (((be2x -=- x1) *=* (be2x -=- x1))
    +=+ ((be2y -=- y1) *=* (be2y -=- y1))) +=+ ((be2z -=- z1) *=* (be2z -=- z1)))),
+((t2 -=- t) ; be2x ; be2y @ Be2 : be2x,be2y,be2z,t2 -> Ba : t2'),
-(ok @ Ba : bax,bay,baz,t5 -> Be1 : t1'' # Be2 : t2'' # Be3 : t3'' # Be4 : t4''),
((t2'' === t5 +=+ dbabe2) and (dbabe2 > 0/1) and
((dbabe2 *=* dbabe2) === (((be2x -=- bax) *=* (be2x -=- bax))
    +=+ ((be2y -=- bay) *=* (be2y -=- bay))) +=+ ((be2z -=- baz) *=* (be2z -=- baz)))) | nil]
&
:: r3 :: --- Beacon 3
[ nil ,
-(t @ i : x1,y1,z1,t0 -> Be1 : t1 # Be2 : t2 # Be3 : t3 # Be4 : t4),
((t3 === t0 +=+ dbe3) and (dbe3 > 0/1) and
((dbe3 *=* dbe3) === (((be3x -=- x1) *=* (be3x -=- x1))
    +=+ ((be3y -=- y1) *=* (be3y -=- y1))) +=+ ((be3z -=- z1) *=* (be3z -=- z1)))),
+((t3 -=- t) ; be3x ; be3y @ Be3 : be3x,be3y,be3z,t3 -> Ba : t3'),
-(ok @ Ba : bax,bay,baz,t5 -> Be1 : t1'' # Be2 : t2'' # Be3 : t3'' # Be4 : t4''),
((t3'' === t5 +=+ dbabe3) and (dbabe3 > 0/1) and
((dbabe3 *=* dbabe3) === (((be3x -=- bax) *=* (be3x -=- bax))
    +=+ ((be3y -=- bay) *=* (be3y -=- bay))) +=+ ((be3z -=- baz) *=* (be3z -=- baz)))) | nil]
&
:: r4 :: --- Beacon 4
[ nil ,
-(t @ i : x1,y1,z1,t0 -> Be1 : t1 # Be2 : t2 # Be3 : t3 # Be4 : t4),
((t4 === t0 +=+ dbe4) and (dbe4 > 0/1) and
((dbe4 *=* dbe4) === (((be4x -=- x1) *=* (be4x -=- x1))
    +=+ ((be4y -=- y1) *=* (be4y -=- y1))) +=+ ((be4z -=- z1) *=* (be4z -=- z1)))),
+((t4 -=- t) ; be4x ; be4y @ Be4 : be4x,be4y,be4z,t4 -> Ba : t4'),
-(ok(r') @ Ba : bax,bay,baz,t5 -> Be1 : t1'' # Be2 : t2'' # Be3 : t3'' # Be4 : t4''),
((t4'' === t5 +=+ dbabe4) and (dbabe4 > 0/1) and
((dbabe4 *=* dbabe4) === (((be4x -=- bax) *=* (be4x -=- bax))
    +=+ ((be4y -=- bay) *=* (be4y -=- bay))) +=+ ((be4z -=- baz) *=* (be4z -=- baz)))) | nil]
&
:: r' :: --- Base Station
[ nil ,
-((t1 -=- t) ; be1x ; be1y @ Be1 : be1x,be1y,be1z,t1 -> Ba : t1'),
((t1' === t1 +=+ dbabe1) and (dbabe1 > 0/1) and
((dbabe1 *=* dbabe1) === (((be1x -=- bax) *=* (be1x -=- bax))
    +=+ ((be1y -=- bay) *=* (be1y -=- bay))) +=+ ((be1z -=- baz) *=* (be1z -=- baz)))),
-((t2 -=- t) ; be2x ; be2y @ Be2 : be2x,be2y,be2z,t2 -> Ba : t2'),
((t2' === t2 +=+ dbabe2) and (dbabe2 > 0/1) and
((dbabe2 *=* dbabe2) === (((be2x -=- bax) *=* (be2x -=- bax))
    +=+ ((be2y -=- bay) *=* (be2y -=- bay))) +=+ ((be2z -=- baz) *=* (be2z -=- baz)))),
-((t3 -=- t) ; be3x ; be3y @ Be3 : be3x,be3y,be3z,t3 -> Ba : t3'),
((t3' === t3 +=+ dbabe3) and (dbabe3 > 0/1) and
((dbabe3 *=* dbabe3) === (((be3x -=- bax) *=* (be3x -=- bax))
```

```
    +=+ ((be3y -=- bay) *=* (be3y -=- bay))) +=+ ((be3z -=- baz) *=* (be3z -=- baz)))),
-((t4 -=- t) ; be4x ; be4y @ Be4 : be4x,be4y,be4z,t4 -> Ba : t4'),
((t4' === t4 +=+ dbabe4) and (dbabe4 > 0/1) and
((dbabe4 *=* dbabe4) === (((be4x -=- bax) *=* (be4x -=- bax))
    +=+ ((be4y -=- bay) *=* (be4y -=- bay))) +=+ ((be4z -=- baz) *=* (be4z -=- baz)))),
(((t1 -=- t) *=* (t1 -=- t)) === (((dx -=- be1x) *=* (dx -=- be1x))
    +=+ ((dy -=- be1y) *=* (dy -=- be1y))) and
((t2 -=- t) *=* (t2 -=- t)) === (((dx -=- be2x) *=* (dx -=- be2x))
    +=+ ((dy -=- be2y) *=* (dy -=- be2y))) and
((t3 -=- t) *=* (t3 -=- t)) === (((dx -=- be3x) *=* (dx -=- be3x))
    +=+ ((dy -=- be3y) *=* (dy -=- be3y))) and
((t4 -=- t) *=* (t4 -=- t)) === (((dx -=- be4x) *=* (dx -=- be4x))
    +=+ ((dy -=- be4y) *=* (dy -=- be4y)))),
+(ok @ Ba : bax,bay,baz,t5 -> Be1 : t1'' # Be2 : t2'' # Be3 : t3'' # Be4 : t4''),
(t5 >= t1' and t5 >= t2' and t5 >= t3' and t5 >= t4') | nil]
|| smt((t =/== t0))
```

The insecure configuration of Fig. 4 is now obtained by just adding extra constraints to the attack pattern: (i) fixing concrete locations for the beacons in a hyperbola, (ii) adding the distances from the malicious device to the beacons, (iii) adding the distances inferred by the beacons from the malicious device, and (iv) adjusting the sent timestamp to differ from the actual sending time in the appropriate amount to fake the base station. And the backwards search of Maude-NPA from this attack pattern does find an initial state.

```
smt( --- hyperbola with a^2 = 4, b^2 = 5, c^2 = 9
(t > t0) and (t0 === 0/1) and (z1 === 0/1) and
(be1z === 0/1) and (be2z === 0/1) and (be3z === 0/1) and
(be4z === 0/1) and (baz === 0/1) and
((be1x === 3/1) and (be1y === 5/2)) and
((be2x === 3/1) and (be2y === -(5/2))) and
((be3x === 4/1) and ((be3y *=* be3y) === 60/4) and (be3y > 0/1)) and
((be4x === 4/1) and ((be4y *=* be4y) === 60/4) and (be4y < 0/1)) and
(x1 === -(3/1)) and (dx === 3/1) and (dy === y1) and (y1 === 0/1))
```

The secure configuration of Fig. 5 is now obtained by just adding extra constraints to the attack pattern: (i) fixing concrete locations for the beacons in a rectangle for a parametric height and width, and (ii) asking whether the timestamp is different from the sending time.

```
smt( (t =/== t0) and (t >= 0/1) and z1 === 0/1 and baz === 0/1 and
be1z === 0/1 and be2z === 0/1 and be3z === 0/1 and be4z === 0/1 and
(h > 0/1) and (v > 0/1) and (be1x === 0/1) and (be1y === 0/1) and
(be2x === be1x) and (be2y === be1y +=+ v) and
(be3x === be1x +=+ h) and (be3y === be1y) and
(be4x === be1x +=+ h) and (be4y === be1y +=+ v))
```

Our analysis of this protocol uncovered some interesting challenges that would need to be addressed in future research. When we gave the constraints to the SMT solvers, including Yices [24] and Z3 [25], which support non-linear real arithmetic, none of them were able to prove that they were unsatisfiable. It was not until we simplified them by hand by using Gaussian elimination on the matrix defined by the coefficients of the constraints, producing the set of constraints given below, that we were able to get one solver, Mathematica [13], to prove unsatisfiability. This suggest that more research is needed on heuristics for preprocessing the types of constraints that arise from reasoning about time and space protocols so that they can be handled by available SMT solvers.

```
In[8]:= Solve[w > 0 && h > 0 && d != 0 && d1 > 0 && d2 > 0 && d3 > 0 && d4 > 0 && (d1-d) > 0 && (d2 - d) > 0 &&
        (d3 - d) > 0 && (d4 - d) > 0 && (((d1 == d2) && (d2 == d4)) || ((d1 == d3) && d2 == d4)) &&
        x == (1 / 2) * w && y == ((((d1 ^ 2) - (d3 ^ 2)) + (w ^ 2)) / (2 * w)) && x ^ 2 + y ^ 2 == d1 ^ 2 &&
        (((2 * d * (d3 - d1)) / h) * y) ^ 2 + (d * ((d3 - d1) / h)) ^ 2 + (2 * d1 * d) - d ^ 2 == 0, {d}, Reals]

Out[8]= {}
```

6 Conclusions

We have extended our previous paper with a time model for protocols using time constraints to a time and space model for protocol analysis based on timing and space constraints. We have also extended our previous prototype of Maude-NPA handling protocols with time to handle time and space by taking advantage of Maude's support of SMT solvers, and Maude-NPA's support of constraint handling. We have used the Brands and Chaum protocol to illustrate how this extension is natural and smoothly subsumes our previous time-only framework, and a secure localization protocol with complex location and time constraints. This approach should be applicable to other tools that support constraint handling. There are several ways this work can be extended, as suggested within the paper. And there are many interesting protocols that can be tested with this time and space model, for example protocols using the Message Time Of Arrival Codes (MTACs) of [12].

References

1. Aparicio-Sánchez, D., Escobar, S., Meadows, C., Meseguer, J., Sapiña, J.: Protocol analysis with time. In: Bhargavan, K., Oswald, E., Prabhakaran, M. (eds.) INDOCRYPT 2020. LNCS, vol. 12578, pp. 128–150. Springer, Cham (2020). https://doi.org/10.1007/978-3-030-65277-7_7
2. Basin, D.A., Capkun, S., Schaller, P., Schmidt, B.: Formal reasoning about physical properties of security protocols. ACM Trans. Inf. Syst. Secur. 14(2), 16:1-16:28 (2011)
3. Basin, D., Capkun, S., Schaller, P., Schmidt, B.: Let's get physical: models and methods for real-world security protocols. In: Berghofer, S., Nipkow, T., Urban, C., Wenzel, M. (eds.) TPHOLs 2009. LNCS, vol. 5674, pp. 1–22. Springer, Heidelberg (2009). https://doi.org/10.1007/978-3-642-03359-9_1
4. Brands, S., Chaum, D.: Distance-bounding protocols (Extended abstracts). In: Helleseth, T. (ed.) EUROCRYPT 1993. LNCS, vol. 765, pp. 344–359. Springer, Heidelberg (1994). https://doi.org/10.1007/3-540-48285-7_30
5. Srdjan Capkun. Secure positioning and location-based security for IoT and beyond. In: Chang, C.-H., Rührmair, U., Holcomb, D.E., Guajardo, J., (eds.) Proceedings of the 2018 Workshop on Attacks and Solutions in Hardware Security, ASHES@CCS 2018, Toronto, ON, Canada, October 19, 2018, p. 81. ACM (2018)

6. Srdjan Capkun and Jean-Pierre Hubaux. Secure positioning of wireless devices with application to sensor networks. In INFOCOM 2005. 24th Annual Joint Conference of the IEEE Computer and Communications Societies, 13–17 March 2005, Miami, FL, USA, pages 1917–1928. IEEE, 2005

7. Capkun, S., Hubaux, J.-P.: Secure positioning in wireless networks. IEEE J. Sel. Areas Commun. **24**(2), 221–232 (2006)

8. Debant, A., Delaune, S.: Symbolic verification of distance bounding protocols. In: Nielson, F., Sands, D. (eds.) POST 2019. LNCS, vol. 11426, pp. 149–174. Springer, Cham (2019). https://doi.org/10.1007/978-3-030-17138-4_7

9. Escobar, S., Meadows, C., Meseguer, J.: A rewriting-based inference system for the NRL protocol analyzer and its meta-logical properties. Theoret. Comput. Sci. **367**(1), 162–202 (2006)

10. Escobar, S., Meadows, C., Meseguer, J., Santiago, S.: State space reduction in the maude-NRL protocol analyzer. Inf. Comput. **238**, 157–186 (2014)

11. Escobar, S., Meadows, C., Meseguer, J., Santiago, S.: Symbolic protocol analysis with disequality constraints modulo equational theories. In: Bodei, C., Ferrari, G.-L., Priami, C. (eds.) Programming Languages with Applications to Biology and Security. LNCS, vol. 9465, pp. 238–261. Springer, Cham (2015). https://doi.org/10.1007/978-3-319-25527-9_16

12. Leu, P., Singh, M., Roeschlin, M., Paterson, K.G., Capkun, S.: Message time of arrival codes: a fundamental primitive for secure distance measurement. In: 2020 IEEE Symposium on Security and Privacy (SP), pp. 500–516 (2020)

13. Mathematica (2021). https://www.wolfram.com/mathematica

14. Meier, S., Schmidt, B., Cremers, C., Basin, D.: The TAMARIN prover for the symbolic analysis of security protocols. In: Sharygina, N., Veith, H. (eds.) CAV 2013. LNCS, vol. 8044, pp. 696–701. Springer, Heidelberg (2013). https://doi.org/10.1007/978-3-642-39799-8_48

15. Neumann, C., Yu, T., Hartman, S., Raeburn, K.: The kerberos network authentication service (V5). Request Comments **4120**, 1–37 (2005)

16. Nigam, V., Talcott, C., Aires Urquiza, A.: Towards the automated verification of cyber-physical security protocols: bounding the number of timed intruders. In: Askoxylakis, I., Ioannidis, S., Katsikas, S., Meadows, C. (eds.) ESORICS 2016. LNCS, vol. 9879, pp. 450–470. Springer, Cham (2016). https://doi.org/10.1007/978-3-319-45741-3_23

17. Paulson, L.C.: The inductive approach to verifying cryptographic protocols. J. Comput. Secur. **6**(1–2), 85–128 (1998)

18. Perrig, A., Song, D., Canetti, R., Tygar, J.D., Briscoe, B.: Timed Efficient Stream Loss-Tolerant Authentication (TESLA): multicast source authentication transform introduction. Request Comments **4082**, 1–22 (2005)

19. Schaller, P., Schmidt, B., Basin, D.A., Capkun, S.: Modeling and verifying physical properties of security protocols for wireless networks. In: Proceedings of the 22nd IEEE Computer Security Foundations Symposium, CSF 2009, New York, USA, 8–10 July, pp. 109–123. IEEE Computer Society (2009)

20. Shmatikov, V., Wang, M.-H.: Secure verification of location claims with simultaneous distance modification. In: Cervesato, I. (ed.) ASIAN 2007. LNCS, vol. 4846, pp. 181–195. Springer, Heidelberg (2007). https://doi.org/10.1007/978-3-540-76929-3_17

21. Thayer, F.J., Herzog, J.C., Guttman, J.D.: Strand spaces: proving security protocols correct. J. Comput. Secur. **7**(1), 191–230 (1999)

22. Yang, F., Escobar, S., Meadows, C., Meseguer, J.: Strand spaces with choice via a process algebra semantics. Computing Research Repository (2019)

23. Yang, F., Escobar, S., Meadows, C., Meseguer, J., Santiago, S.: Strand spaces with choice via a process algebra semantics. In: Proceedings of the 18th International Symposium on Principles and Practice of Declarative Programming (PPDP 2016), pp. 76–89. ACM Press (2016)
24. The Yices SMT Solver (2021). https://yices.csl.sri.com
25. The Z3 SMT Solver (2021). https://github.com/Z3Prover/z3

Searching for Selfie in TLS 1.3 with the Cryptographic Protocol Shapes Analyzer

Prajna Bhandary[1], Edward Zieglar[2]($\boxtimes$), and Charles Nicholas[1]

[1] University of Maryland, Baltimore County (UMBC), Baltimore, MD 21250, USA
{prajnab1,nicholas}@umbc.edu
[2] National Security Agency, Fort George G. Meade, MD 20755, USA
evziegl@uwe.nsa.gov

Abstract. TLS 1.3 was developed in conjunction with several formal analyses and proofs of its security properties. However, in 2019, researchers Drucker and Gueron discovered a reflection attack, they named Selfie, against the pre-shared key (PSK) mode of authentication used by TLS 1.3 by identifying a gap in the proofs. They realized that the proofs ignored the case of external PSKs. They demonstrated that if the PSK was not associated with a particular client and server pairing, such as a single PSK between a pair of hosts which could use the key as either a client or server, implicit authentication implied by the use of the PSK would fail in a reflection attack. The proofs and tools used did not account for this, so we set out to determine if it was possible to identify this attack with the Cryptographic Protocol Shapes Analyzer (CPSA). Using CPSA, which attempts to enumerate all equivalence classes of a protocol's executions, we were able to uncover the attack and verify two proposed mitigations. We were also able to identify a previously discovered impersonation attack against the use of post handshake authentication in scenarios where a PSK is used as a network key.

Keywords: Cryptographic protocols · Cryptography · Cryptographic Protocol Shapes Analyzer (CPSA) · Cybersecurity · Formal methods · Transport Layer Security · Selfie attack · Protocol analysis

1 Introduction

Version 1.3 of the Transport Layer Security (TLS 1.3) protocol is an important protocol for the security of the Internet. The majority of the web based traffic is now encrypted using some version of TLS. In January of 2021, Google, in their Transparency Report, noted that 89% of pages loaded by Chrome were served using HTTPS. Applications such as email, instant messaging, voice over IP, VPN, and others also use TLS to provide authentication, confidentiality, and integrity. As a significant amount of traffic on the Internet relies on TLS for its security, it is important that TLS is vulnerable to few, if any forms of attack.

Earlier versions of TLS have had various security weaknesses, such as Logjam [1], Triple Handshake [6], SMACK [4], Lucky13 [3] and others. Therefore, it was

© Springer Nature Switzerland AG 2021
D. Dougherty et al. (Eds.): Guttman Festschrift, LNCS 13066, pp. 50–76, 2021.
https://doi.org/10.1007/978-3-030-91631-2_3

important to the Internet Engineering Task Force (IETF) that TLS 1.3 not be vulnerable to those and other attacks that may exploit the protocol to violate the security goals. To achieve assurance that TLS 1.3 satisfied its security goals, the IETF undertook an unprecedented effort to provide formal analysis and security proofs of the design in studies such as [5,7,8,10,13,14,17,18,20]. In spite of this effort, Drucker and Gueron [11] discovered a reflection attack, which they named the Selfie attack, against TLS 1.3's Pre Shared Key (PSK) based mutual authentication.

The existence of the Selfie attack does not take anything away from the formal analysis that was performed. The formal verification effort was successful in demonstrating that many of the weaknesses required by the known attacks were eliminated. As an example, the formal verification effort was able to demonstrate that attacks such as Logjam and Triple Handshake were not possible, even if TLS 1.3 was run in parallel with TLS 1.2. The tools that were used in the analyses, such as Tamarin, ProVerif and CryptoVerif, involve developing models of the protocols and proving theorems within the model. The reason that the Selfie attack was not discovered by the tools in the analysis was because the analyses weren't comprehensive enough to cover a case where the Client uses TLS 1.3 with an external PSK and then proceeds to talk to itself. These tools assumed that a PSK can be shared only between a Client and a Server. They also assumed that if a mutual authentication could be established between a Client and a Server or between a Client and a Client, then both are valid [5].

The Cryptographic Protocol Shapes Analyze (CPSA) [19] operates differently than other protocol verification tools. Instead of specifying the properties that one wishes to verify in the model, CPSA takes a protocol definition and a partial description of an execution, built within a particular formal model, and attempts to produce descriptions of all possible executions of the protocol that complete the partial description in the presence of a powerful network adversary. From the descriptions of the executions, referred to as shapes, it is possible to identify the properties that the protocol satisfies.

We were interested in determining whether or not the approach taken by CPSA would have identified the Selfie attack. Using CPSA, we modeled the TLS 1.3 PSK authentication protocol and analyzed the shapes that CPSA produced and were able to identify the attack. We were also able to verify that the proposed mitigations of a unique key between a client and server or the use of identifiers would prevent the Selfie attack. We describe our approach in the following sections.

2 Background

We briefly review CPSA, the TLS 1.3 Pre Shared Key authentication protocol, and the Selfie attack discovered by Drucker and Gueron.

2.1   Cryptographic Protocol Shapes Analyser

The Cryptographic Protocol Shapes Analyzer (CPSA) [15,19] is an open-source tool for automated formal analysis of cryptographic protocols. CPSA takes as input a model of a cryptographic protocol and a description of a partial execution with assumptions, and generates a set of minimal, essentially different descriptions of executions of the protocol that complete the partial execution, consistent with the assumptions. The descriptions of completed executions are referred to as shapes. When some property holds in all shapes generated, it is a property guaranteed by the protocol.

CPSA is based on strand space theory [9,12] in which events are organized into partially-ordered graphs. In strand space theory, events are transmissions or receptions of messages. Strands are sequences of events that capture a local view of a participant in the network. CPSA also has state events that consist of initializing, observing and transitioning between states. Protocols are defined as a set of legitimate participant roles that serve as a template for strands consistent with the protocol.

The underlying execution model of CPSA is the Bundle, where every reception is explained directly by a previous transmission of that exact message. A bundle of a particular protocol is a set of strands where all the strands are either (1) generic adversary behavior such as parsing or constructing complex messages, or encrypting or decrypting with the proper keys, or (2) behavior of participants in the protocol consistent with the protocol roles.

CPSA reasons about bundles indirectly by analyzing skeletons, i.e. partially-ordered sets of strands that represent only regular behavior, along with origination assumptions about the secrecy and/or freshness of particular values, such as keys unknown to the adversary or nonces, freshly chosen and therefore assumed unique. Skeletons in which all messages can be explained by some combination of legitimate or adversary behavior consistent with the secrecy and freshness assumptions are referred to as realized. A shape is the most general form of a set of realized skeletons. Non-realized skeletons may represent partial descriptions of actual executions, or may represent a set of conditions inconsistent with any actual execution [19].

The cpsagraph tool creates visualizations of skeletons as graphs in which events are shown as circles, black for transmissions and blue for receptions, in connected columns where each column represents a strand. Events within a strand are ordered from top to bottom, with the earliest event at the top. Arrows between strands indicate necessary orderings (other than orderings within strands, or those that can be inferred transitively). An arrow from event *P to* Q denotes that for *Q to take place, it is necessary that event* P take place first. A solid black arrow indicates that the message that was transmitted was exactly the same as the one received. Black dashed arrows indicate that the message was altered by some form of adversary behavior. CPSA represents states as gray circles. State is assumed to not be directly observable by the adversary. Observation of state is indicated by a blue arrow originating from a state event, represented as a gray circle. See Fig. 3 in Sect. 3.1 for an example of such a visualization.

The cpsagraph tool also outputs the skeleton information associated with the graph that has been drawn. This information is in the form of a defskeleton. A defskeleton contains all the information that is necessary to describe an execution, whether it is partial, having unrealized message receptions, or realized, a complete execution of the protocol. As such, it contains a complete list of the variables used in the skeleton, the strands which identify the protocol role, the number of messages sent and received as well as state interactions, and the variable assignments for the strand in a defstrand, the assumptions made on the variables, the action taken by CPSA to create the current skeleton, the ordering of the nodes in the skeleton, and information concerning whether or not the analysis is complete. For brevity, we have only shown the partial CPSA output of a defskeleton that includes the strands in this paper. This allows one to see whether or not the strands agree on values associated with the variables. For example, in Fig. 3, both the client and the server agree on the values of the variables, but in Fig. 8, the client and server disagree on variables a and b which represent their views of the client and server.

2.2   TLS 1.3 Pre Shared Key Authentication

TLS 1.3 [21] offers a variety of options for establishing a secure connection. Several of the options support authentication of one or more of the parties through public key certificates. Another option uses a Pre Shared Key (PSK), established externally or derived from the secret value from a previous connection. Authentication when using a PSK is predicated on the assumption that the party receiving a message authenticated with the PSK knows that the message was sent by a party that also knows the PSK. TLS 1.3 allows this use of implicit authentication to save bandwidth and latency over certificate verification and to support 0-RTT mode.

As TLS 1.3 can be used to support networks of communicating peers, where every node acts as both a client and a server, it is possible to use a single PSK for authentication as both the client and the server. It is under this scenario that Drucker and Gueron identified their attack.

2.3   Selfie Attack

The Selfie attack discovered by Drucker and Gueron [11] is a reflection attack against the use of PSK authentication in TLS. The attack relies on the assumption that if two parties share a symmetric key, the receiving party knows that the message, if it passes verification with the key, was sent by a party that knows that key. As TLS permits this implicit authentication to save bandwidth and latency in support of 0-RTT mode, it opens up the possibility of this reflection attack against a party when parties within the network can act as both client and server using the same key. In this case, the sender, when under attack, could also be the receiver of the authentic message itself.

Figure 1 taken from [11] illustrates the attack. In this case Alice, acting as the client, wishes to communicate with Bob, acting as the server. The adversary, Eve, is able to intercept and reflect the messages back to Alice. The communication takes place as follows:

- Alice sends the ClientHello message with a pre shared key extension intended for Bob.
- Eve intercepts the message and reflects it back to Alice, pretending (implicitly) to be Bob.
- Alice receives the message containing the PSK extension she uses with Bob.
- Alice, acting as server, replies (presumably to Bob) with ServerHello and ServerFinished messages which authenticate that Alice knows the PSK.
- Eve captures these messages and echoes them back to Alice.
- Alice, acting as client, authenticates the ServerHello and ServerFinish messages as being created with the PSK she shares with Bob, believing that she has authenticated Bob when she has actually opened a Selfie session with herself.
- Alice, as client, then completes the connection by authenticating herself through the ClientFinished Message.
- Eve intercepts and reflects the ClientFinished message back to Alice to complete Alice's server run of the protocol.

At the end of the run, Alice has established two sessions with herself acting as both client and server which she believes exist with Bob, in violation of the TLS claimed property of [21] [Appendix E]: "Peer authentication: The client's view of the peer identity should reflect the server's identity. If the client is authenticated, the server's view of the peer identity should match the client's identity."

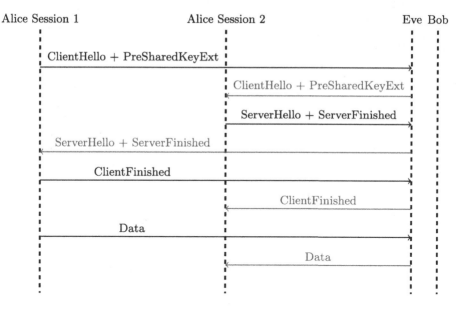

Fig. 1. The Selfie Attack [11]. Eve tricks Alice into believing she is talking to Bob while she is actually talking with herself.

3   Modeling TLS 1.3 PSK Authentication

Using CPSA, we analyze the TLS 1.3 PSK authentication when the pre-shared keys are distributed out of band in the Dolev-Yao intruder model. We develop several models of the PSK authentication and analyze them to explore the selfie attack and to verify proposed fixes in [11].

3.1   Models of the TLS 1.3 PSK Authentication

We built two models of the TLS PSK authentication. In the first model, we modeled the authentication directly as specified. In this initial model, there are no indications of who is acting as client or server. The authentication is implicit. In the second model, we made the direction of the key used explicit so that we could identify which party was acting as client and which was acting as server. We describe the models and results below.

Initial Model. The TLS 1.3 handshake, when using PSK authentication, consists of only three messages, shown in Fig. 2 taken from Sect. 2.2 of [21].

The initial message from the client is sent unencrypted. Additionally, many of the fields in the ClientHello are unlikely to change in subsequent handshakes, with the exception of the random. Our model simplifies the ClientHello to the random, n1 in our model, as that is the only component of the message that will distinguish two ClientHello messages from the same client to the same server.

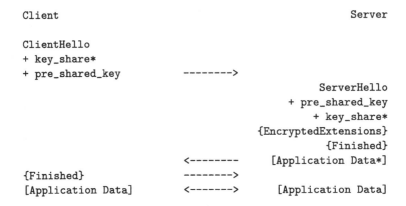

Fig. 2. Message flow for PSK handshake

The pre_shared_key is an identifier of the PSK to use for the connection. We model this simply as a unique index that is tied to the key through the use of state, observable to both the client and the server. As the key_share is an optional set of parameters that are used as a fallback to the full handshake should the PSK not be accepted, we chose not to include those additional messages.

We made similar choices for the ServerHello, pre_shared_key and key_share components of the server's response. We made a simplifying assumption that the Client did not send an extension request in the ClientHello, so we can safely ignore the EncryptedExtensions as they should only be sent if the client made a request. Finally, the Finished message is the first attempt at authenticating the server to the client. It consists of a hash of all the previous message components with the finished_key. The finished_key is created from a hash of "finished" and the base key. For this modeling, we simplified the TLS keying scheme to a single key that was produced as a hash of the PSK and the generated random nonces from each party. The key generated will be unique as long as at least one party generates a fresh nonce and the extra complication of generating additional keys is unnecessary to model the authentication.

The final message is the client's attempt to authenticate to the server by creating a finished message of its own consisting of the all the messages that it has received. The distinction between the client's finished message and the server's is that the client's message includes the server's finished message in the hash.

In addition to modeling the client and server roles in the protocol, we model an additional role that acts to distribute the key to the parties. This role, key-Placement, initializes a state with the index and the key that both the client and server can observe, representing the pre-placement of keys at both the client and the server. See Fig. 15 in the Appendix for the model.

tls 4 (realized)

client   keyPlacement   server

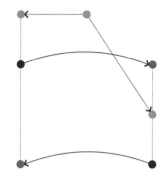

```
(defskeleton tls
  (vars (n1 n2 index text) (psk skey))
  (defstrand client 3 (index index) (n1 n1) (n2 n2) (psk psk))
  (defstrand keyPlacement 1 (index index) (psk psk))
  (defstrand server 3 (index index) (n1 n1) (n2 n2) (psk psk))
  ...
```

Fig. 3. Shape showing an execution of the protocol from the client's perspective. As identification of the parties is implicit (neither strand indicates the parties, as can be seen in the defstrand statements), the Selfie attack is included in this equivalence class represented by the shape. (Color figure online)

The Selfie attack is described as a reflection against the client. For our analysis, we defined a partial execution of the protocol consisting of a single client with the assumption that the PSK was known only to the client and server. CPSA produced a single shape for the execution, shown in Fig. 3. The shape indicates that all executions of the protocol involve only parties that share the PSK. Both the client and the server observe the same PSK, indicated by the solid blue lines. Additionally, we can see that the messages were received from the expected parties in the correct order and unaltered, as indicated by the solid black lines showing the ordering. If an adversary were able to alter the messages, a dashed line would have indicated that the message had been altered from the point of origination to the destination. As there are no indications of the parties identities in the model, the Selfie attack is also present in the shape as a single party could be acting as both client and server.

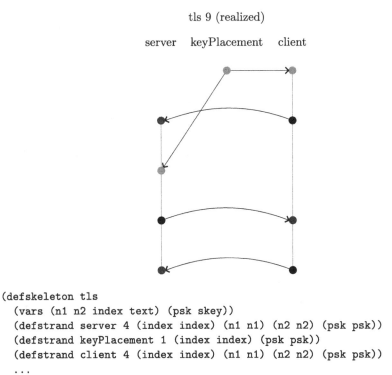

tls 9 (realized)

server   keyPlacement   client

```
(defskeleton tls
  (vars (n1 n2 index text) (psk skey))
  (defstrand server 4 (index index) (n1 n1) (n2 n2) (psk psk))
  (defstrand keyPlacement 1 (index index) (psk psk))
  (defstrand client 4 (index index) (n1 n1) (n2 n2) (psk psk))
  ...
```

Fig. 4. First shape produced by the initial model from the server's perspective. Identification is implicit. The Selfie attack is represented in the equivalence class represented by the shape.

For completeness, we also analyzed the model from the server's perspective. This analysis produced two shapes, Figs. 4 and 5, both indicating that it would only complete with a client that shared the PSK. The second shape in Fig. 5 shows an additional start of the client with the same PSK, but a different choice of nonce. It indicates that the adversary could mix messages initially from the clients, but only one can complete. As with the view from the client, the server only knows that the party acting as the client is in possession of the PSK and may in fact be the same party acting as both client and server.

Model with Identities. To better visualize which identities are communicating with each other, we modified the keyPlacement role to include the parties sharing the key, as shown in Fig. 18. Instead of a single state being initialized with the key and the index, we initialize two states, each with the same key and index, but with the identities of the parties using the key listed in the order of the client and the server. Two states were necessary, as a party could be acting as either the client or the server with the same key. With this approach, shapes representing exchanges that involve the Selfie attack would be visualized as accessing both states from the keyPlacement role, with the client accessing one state and the server accessing the other, yet communicating with each other. CPSA generated four shapes, Figs. 6, 7, 8, and 9, from the perspective of the client.

tls 12 (realized)

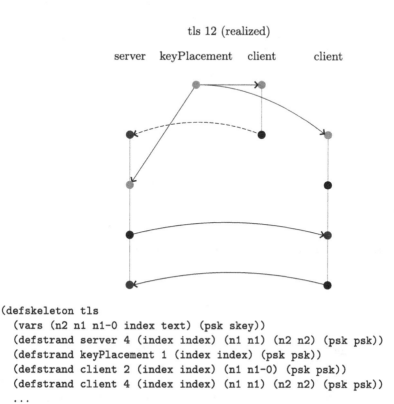

```
(defskeleton tls
  (vars (n2 n1 n1-0 index text) (psk skey))
  (defstrand server 4 (index index) (n1 n1) (n2 n2) (psk psk))
  (defstrand keyPlacement 1 (index index) (psk psk))
  (defstrand client 2 (index index) (n1 n1-0) (psk psk))
  (defstrand client 4 (index index) (n1 n1) (n2 n2) (psk psk))
  ...
```

Fig. 5. Second shape produced by the initial model from the server's perspective. This represents the possibility of additional clients that share the PSK initiating a run of the protocol. The shape indicates that the client on the left may have initiated the contact with the server before the client on the right, but the adversary changed the message from the client on the left to replace the nonce with the nonce of the client on the right. The server completes the run with the client on the right, as indicated in the variable assignments in the defstrand statements. Again, the Selfie attack is also represented in the possible executions.

tls1 20 (realized)

client   keyPlacement   server

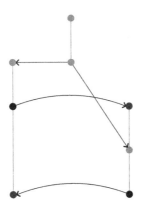

```
(defskeleton tls1
  (vars (n1 n2 index text) (a b name) (psk skey))
  (defstrand client 3 (index index) (n1 n1) (n2 n2) (a b) (b a) (psk psk))
  (defstrand keyPlacement 2 (index index) (a a) (b b) (psk psk))
  (defstrand server 3 (index index) (n1 n1) (n2 n2) (a b) (b a) (psk psk))
  . . .
```

Fig. 6. Shape illustrating a correct authentication, no Selfie Attack, where the server is assigned the name "a" and the client is assigned the name "b".

Figures 6 and 7 represent the classes of executions that are free of the Selfie attack. In each case, the client and the server accessed the same state, indicating that they agree on the assignment of values to the client, represented as variable a, and the server, represented as variable b. In Fig. 6, both parties agree that the client is "b" and the server is "a". This can be seen in the assignment of the variables, "a" representing the client and "b" representing the server, in each of the defstrand statements mapping variables of the displayed strands. Figure 7 shows the case where the key for the opposite direction is used and maps the client to "a" and the server to "b" in both the client and server strands.

tls1 23 (realized)

client   keyPlacement   server

```
(defskeleton tls1
  (vars (n1 n2 index text) (a b name) (psk skey))
  (defstrand client 3 (index index) (n1 n1) (n2 n2) (a a) (b b) (psk psk))
  (defstrand keyPlacement 1 (index index) (a a) (b b) (psk psk))
  (defstrand server 3 (index index) (n1 n1) (n2 n2) (a a) (b b) (psk psk))
  ...
```

Fig. 7. Complement to the shape in Fig. 6 illustrating a correct authentication, no Selfie Attack, where the server is assigned the name "b" and the client is assigned the name "a".

tls1 21 (realized)

client   keyPlacement   server

```
(defskeleton tls1
  (vars (n1 n2 index text) (a b name) (psk skey))
  (defstrand client 3 (index index) (n1 n1) (n2 n2) (a b) (b a) (psk psk))
  (defstrand keyPlacement 2 (index index) (a a) (b b) (psk psk))
  (defstrand server 3 (index index) (n1 n1) (n2 n2) (a a) (b b) (psk psk))
  ...
```

Fig. 8. Shape illustrating the Selfie attack where the client strand is "b" believing the server it is communicating with is "a", while the server strand it is actually communicating with is itself, "b", believing that it is communicating with client "a".

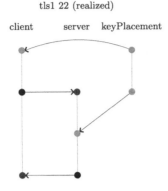

<!-- figure graphic: tls1 22 (realized) with client, server, keyPlacement -->

```
(defskeleton tls1
  (vars (n1 n2 index text) (a b name) (psk skey))
  (defstrand client 3 (index index) (n1 n1) (n2 n2) (a a) (b b) (psk psk))
  (defstrand server 3 (index index) (n1 n1) (n2 n2) (a b) (b a) (psk psk))
  (defstrand keyPlacement 2 (index index) (a a) (b b) (psk psk))
  ...
```

Fig. 9. Complement to the shape in Fig. 8 illustrating the Selfie attack where the client strand is "a" believing the server it is communicating with is "b", while the server strand it is actually communicating with is itself, "a", believing that it is communicating with client "b".

Figures 8 and 9 represent the classes of executions where the Selfie attack takes place. This is visible in the graph of the shape where the client observes one state and the server observes another. As the only difference between the states is the assignment of server and client, if two interacting strands are observing different states, it indicates that the same party is acting as both the client and the server in the communication. By making the direction a key is being used explicit, we were able to split the set of equivalent executions represented in the original model, shown in Fig. 3, into the various subsets of executions, those that show expected behavior and those that show the Selfie attack.

The models from the server's perspective also illustrate both expected executions and executions including the Selfie attack. For brevity, those shapes are not included here.

3.2   Modeling the Proposed Fixes to the Selfie Attack

The authors of [11] proposed two solutions to the Selfie attack. The first is the use of server certificates, although the authors point out that the use of certificates with the PSK defeats the purpose of using the PSK. The second approach is to require the use of a unique key between the client and the server. We validate each of the solutions in the following sections by modifying our model that supports directional use of the keys with identities. This approach allows us to visually inspect the graphs to determine if the Selfie attack has been eliminated by noting whether or not the same state is observed by both client and server, as was described in Sect. 3.

PSK with Server Identity. There are two approaches to verifying the identity of a party with a certificate. The first is to include the certificates in the handshake. The second is to request the certificate after establishing a secure connection with the PSK. To model this, we extended the protocol by adding a request for the certificate and the response.

Although the use of a certificate was proposed, we instead chose to model the addition of the server_name encrypted extension in the handshake as proposed in [16]. The analysis in the model is similar, but it has the added advantage of not requiring the additional processing necessary with the use of a certificate in an actual implementation. CPSA produced only shapes where the connected client and server were using the same state as shown in Fig. 10 and Fig. 11. As both shapes indicate, the client and server both agree on who is the client and who is the server. The mitigation of including the server's name in the response does prevent the Selfie attack.

To model the authentication request after establishing a connection, we included a certificate request message and a certificate verify message. We chose to have the server authenticate the client to continue the flow of send and receive, although we could have chosen to have the client authenticate the server. This approach creates a number of shapes that could be problematic if there were multiple parties sharing the same key. An example of one of the problematic shapes is Fig. 12. In this case, the client on the left is accessing the state for the

tls2 60 (realized)

client   keyPlacement   server

```
(defskeleton tls2
  (vars (n1 n2 index text) (b a name) (psk skey))
  (defstrand client 3 (index index) (n1 n1) (n2 n2) (a b) (b a) (psk psk))
  (defstrand keyPlacement 2 (index index) (a a) (b b) (psk psk))
  (defstrand server 3 (index index) (n1 n1) (n2 n2) (a b) (b a) (psk psk))
  ...
```

Fig. 10. Shape produced when a modified handshake is used to convey the server's name to the client. Both sides are using the same state, indicating that they agree on the values of the client and server. In this case, the client is "b" and the server is "a".

tls2 64 (realized)

client   keyPlacement   server

```
(defskeleton tls2
  (vars (n1 n2 index text) (a b name) (psk skey))
  (defstrand client 3 (index index) (n1 n1) (n2 n2) (a a) (b b) (psk psk))
  (defstrand keyplacement 1 (index index) (a a) (b b) (psk psk))
  (defstrand server 3 (index index) (n1 n1) (n2 n2) (a a) (b b) (psk psk))
  ...
```

Fig. 11. The complement to the shape in Fig. 10. In this shape, both the client and server are using the same state, therefore they agree on the values of the client and server. In this case, the client is "a" and the server is "b".

reverse key of the server, indicative of the Selfie attack. The client on the right completes the authentication as expected, but all parties share the key. There is nothing to prevent the client on the left from continuing after the authentication completes. This is an example of the Selfie attack.

Authentication outside of the handshake does not preclude a Selfie attack, but the results could be much worse. If the same keys were used for several participants, then it would be possible for any participant to impersonate another as outlined in [2]. We added an additional set of keys for a third participant to see if CPSA would identify the attack. CPSA generated a considerable number of shapes, many of which indicated that one party could impersonate another. Figure 13 is an example. In this case, the server strand is "b" and it believes that it is communicating with "b-0". The client on the left is "a" and it is communicating with the server "b" while the client on the right is "b-0" and is communicating with "a", the client on the left. The client "a" is impersonating as "b-0" to the server "b". Because all parties have access to the same key, it is possible to impersonate any party to any other with this approach. If certificates are to be used, they must be used in the handshake to prevent this attack.

Unique PSK per Client/Server Pair. The second solution proposed was the use of a unique key for any client/server pair. We were able to model this by simply creating a fresh key and index for each state initialization in the keyPlacement role, representing a unique key for each direction between a pair of parties. From the clients point of view, only one shape is possible. This is shown in Fig. 14. Both the client and server agree on all variables. It is not possible for the client to chose one key and the server to chose the other in this situation, eliminating the Selfie attack.

4   Discussion

We set out to determine if the approach used by CPSA would be effective in identifying the Selfie attack that was missed in the previous formal analysis of TLS 1.3. As the previous analysis built models of the protocol and proved theorems based upon those models, it was necessary to know what properties one hoped existed in the protocol to develop the theorems that one wished to prove. Unfortunately, there were gaps in the earlier analysis as the models either failed to consider the case of external PSKs or left the analysis of the implicit authentication properties of external PSKs for future work. The approach used by CPSA doesn't require knowledge of the properties one wishes to prove. Instead of proving particular theorems about the protocol model, CPSA attempts to enumerate all possible equivalence classes of executions of the protocol that satisfy the assumptions. From the equivalence classes, referred to as shapes, it is then possible to determine what properties hold across all executions. We were looking to see if we could identify the Selfie attack with this approach.

The shapes that CPSA generated with the initial model, Figs. 3, 4 and 5, demonstrated that only parties that share the key were able to interact. That includes the case were a party is interacting with itself. With implicit authentication, it is therefore impossible to know which parties are interacting. If a party that can interact with itself is attempting to interact with another party, then the Selfie attack is possible. The shapes produced by CPSA only show that an adversary, that does not know the PSK, cannot generate or modify the messages. The adversary can reflect the messages back to a party that can act as both client and server, confusing that party as to whom it is connecting. This is the Selfie attack.

However, since one could identify the Selfie attack in the shapes produced by CPSA in the initial model, we modified the model to include the direction a key was being used by adding the client's and the server's identities to the state. We used two states to represent a bidirectional key. The states had identical index and key, but differed in which party was the client and which was the server, with the roles swapped between the two states. This allowed CPSA to subdivide the original equivalence class into four equivalence classes from the client's perspective, shown in Figs. 6, 7, 8, and 9. By adding identities and associating direction with the keys, we were able to make the Selfie attack visually evident, as there were now shapes, Figs. 8 and 9, representing executions of the Selfie attack. This

tls4 403 (realized)

server   client   keyPlacement   client

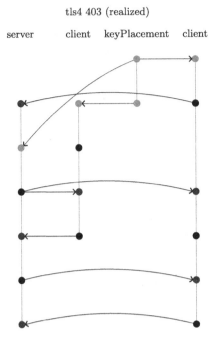

```
(defskeleton tls4
  (vars (n2 n1 index text) (ca a b name) (psk skey))
  (defstrand server 6 (index index) (n1 n1) (n2 n2) (a a) (b b) (ca ca) (psk psk))
  (defstrand client 4 (index index) (n1 n1) (n2 n2) (a b) (b a) (psk psk))
  (defstrand keyPlacement 2 (index index) (a a) (b b) (psk psk))
  (defstrand client 6 (index index) (n1 n1) (n2 n2) (a a) (b b) (ca ca) (psk psk))
  ...
```

Fig. 12. Shape produced when post handshake authentication is used. In this case the client on the left is "b" and believes that the server he has completed the handshake with is "a". The server is also "b" and believes that the handshake was completed with "a", despite completing the handshake with himself. The client on the right is "a" and completes the authentication for the client on the left, completing the Selfie attack with authentication.

also made verifying the fixes easier as it was now possible to determine if the proposed fix would eliminate those shapes.

Using our model with identities, we were able to verify the proposed fixes, and identify the attack against a post handshake authentication outlined in [2]. The introduction of the server's identity into the handshake and the use of directional keys, created by using different keys and indexes with each state, resulted in only shapes, Figs. 10 and 11 for the introduction of the server's identity and Fig. 14 for the directional keys, where both parties agreed on the identities of the client and server. None of the shapes that represented the selfie attack existed in either of those protocol modifications. The use of a post handshake authentication resulted in numerous shapes, with many containing a selfie attack with

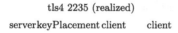

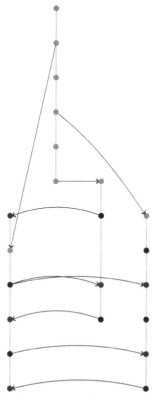

```
(defskeleton tls4
  (vars (n2 n1 index text) (ca a b b-0 name) (psk skey))
  (defstrand server 6 (index index) (n1 n1) (n2 n2) (a b-0) (b b) (ca ca) (psk psk))
  (defstrand keyPlacement 6 (index index) (a b) (b b-0) (c a) (psk psk))
  (defstrand client 4 (index index) (n1 n1) (n2 n2) (a a) (b b) (psk psk))
  (defstrand client 6 (index index) (n1 n1) (n2 n2) (a b-0) (b a) (ca ca) (psk psk))
  ...
```

Fig. 13. Shape with three parties sharing a key and using post handshake authentication to illustrate that any party could authenticate as any other party. In this case, the server is "b" and completes the handshake with the client on the left who is "a", but authenticates the client on the right who is "b-0". The client on the right believes they are authenticating to "a", the client on the left. Client "a" can now impersonate client "b-0" to the server.

authentication taking place with a different strand, as illustrated in Fig. 12. In this case, it would be possible for the server to be communicating with itself while authenticating a different client. Such a situation lends itself to anyone being able to impersonate anyone else in network keyed environments as identi-

tls3 299 (realized)

client   keyPlacement   server

```
(defskeleton tls3
  (vars (n1 n2 index0 text) (a b name) (psk0 skey))
  (defstrand client 3 (index index0) (n1 n1) (n2 n2) (a a) (b b) (psk psk0))
  (defstrand keyPlacement 1 (index0 index0) (a a) (b b) (psk0 psk0))
  (defstrand server 3 (index index0) (n1 n1) (n2 n2) (a a) (b b) (psk psk0))
  ...
```

Fig. 14. Shape produced when directional keys are used. Only one shape is produced, as only one key can be used between any pair of parties, guaranteeing agreement by the parties on who is the client and who is the server.

fied in [2]. We were able to illustrate this (see Fig. 13) by adding an additional party that was using the same key.

We have validated one of the recommendations for external PSK usage outlined in [16], that keys be used only between client/server pairs. We did not evaluate the other proposed solutions of using external PSK importers to protect against the attack, although the proposal is similar to the mitigations that have been investigated.

5   Conclusions

Using CPSA, we were able to model TLS 1.3 PSK authentication and identify the Selfie attack where other formal tools did not. We were also able to use CPSA to subdivide the shape representing the equivalence class from our original model into shapes representing classes of executions that included the Selfie attack and those that did not. This allowed us to verify that the proposed mitigations were effective. It also allowed us to demonstrate that a post handshake authentication would not be effective at preventing impersonation attacks if multiple hosts shared the PSK.

Although CPSA was able to identify an attack that was missed in the previous formal analysis, nothing is taken away from the formal analysis that was performed before. That formal verification effort was successful in verifying the elimination of a number of weaknesses that existed in previous versions of TLS. Additionally, there are properties that can be proven in the other tools that cannot be proven in CPSA. The various tools have their strengths and weaknesses, with no tool offering to verify all properties that one may wish. This effort highlights the benefits of using a variety of tools to validate the security properties of a protocol. The approach taken by CPSA may best be used when all properties of a protocol may not be well understood. We would advocate for more formal analysis using a variety of tools to provide greater coverage and assurance in the security properties of cryptographic protocols.

A   Appendix

Source code for the CPSA models used in the analysis (Figs. 16, 17, 19, 20, 21 and 22).

```
(defprotocol tls basic

  (defrole keyPlacement
    (vars (index text) (psk skey))
    (trace
     (init (cat index psk)))
    (uniq-orig index)
    (non-orig psk))

  (defrole client
    (vars (index n1 n2 text) (psk skey))
    (trace
     (obsv (cat index psk))
     (send (cat n1 index))
     (recv (cat n2 (hash (hash psk n1 n2) n1 index n2)))
     (send (hash (hash psk n1 n2) n1 index n2 (hash (hash psk n1 n2) n1 index n2)))
     )
    )

  (defrole server
    (vars (index n1 n2 text) (psk skey))
    (trace
     (recv (cat n1 index))
     (obsv (cat index psk))
     (send (cat n2 (hash (hash psk n1 n2) n1 index n2)))
     (recv (hash (hash psk n1 n2) n1 index n2 (hash (hash psk n1 n2) n1 index n2)))
     )
    )
  (comment "Protocol without identities. Shows Selfie attack.")
  )
```

Fig. 15. CPSA model of TLS 1.3 PSK authentication

```
(defskeleton tls
  (vars (n1 index text) (psk skey))
  (defstrand client 3 (n1 n1) (index index) (psk psk))
  (uniq-orig n1)
  )
```

Fig. 16. Skeleton indicating a partial run of the protocol by the client.

```
(defskeleton tls
  (vars (a b name) (n2 index text) (psk skey))
  (defstrand server 4 (n2 n2) (index index) (psk psk))
  (uniq-orig n2)
  )
```

Fig. 17. Skeleton indicating a partial run of the protocol by the server.

```
(defprotocol tls1 basic

  (defrole keyPlacement
    (vars (a b name) (index text) (psk skey))
    (trace
     (init (cat index a b psk)) ;; clientialization of key for parties a and b
     (init (cat index b a psk))) ;; added so CPSA knows the key is bidirectional
    (uniq-orig index)
    (non-orig psk))

  (defrole client
    (vars (a b name) (index n1 n2 text) (psk skey))
    (trace
     (obsv (cat index a b psk))
     (send (cat n1 index))
     (recv (cat n2 (hash (hash psk n1 n2) n1 index n2)))
     (send (hash (hash psk n1 n2) n1 index n2 (hash (hash psk n1 n2) n1 index n2)))
     )
    )

  (defrole server
    (vars (a b name) (index n1 n2 text) (psk skey))
    (trace
     (recv (cat n1 index))
     (obsv (cat index a b psk))
     (send (cat n2 (hash (hash psk n1 n2) n1 index n2)))
     (recv (hash (hash psk n1 n2) n1 index n2 (hash (hash psk n1 n2) n1 index n2)))
     )
    )
  (comment "Protocol with identities added to state. Shows Selfie attack.")
  )
```

Fig. 18. CPSA model of TLS 1.3 PSK authentication with identities associated with the key to identify direction of use.

```
(defprotocol tls2 basic

  (defrole keyPlacement
    (vars (a b name) (index text) (psk skey))
    (trace
     (init (cat index a b psk))
     (init (cat index b a psk)))
    (uniq-orig index)
    (non-orig psk)
    (neq (a b))))

  (defrole client
    (vars (a b name) (index n1 n2 text) (psk skey))
    (trace
     (obsv (cat index a b psk))
     (send (cat n1 index)) ;; client hello
     (recv (cat n2 ;; server hello
                (enc b (hash psk n1 n2)) ;;encrypted extension servername
                (hash (hash psk n1 n2) n1 index n2 (enc b (hash psk n1 n2))))) ;; server finish
     (send (hash (hash psk n1 n2) n1 index n2 (enc b (hash psk n1 n2))
                (hash (hash psk n1 n2) n1 index n2 (enc b (hash psk n1 n2))))) ;; client finish
     )
    )

  (defrole server
    (vars (a b name) (index n1 n2 text) (psk skey))
    (trace
     (recv (cat n1 index)) ;; client hello
     (obsv (cat index a b psk))
     (send (cat n2 ;; server hello
                (enc b (hash psk n1 n2)) ;; encrypted extension servername
                (hash (hash psk n1 n2) n1 index n2 (enc b (hash psk n1 n2))))) ;; server finish
     (recv (hash (hash psk n1 n2) n1 index n2 (enc b (hash psk n1 n2))
                (hash (hash psk n1 n2) n1 index n2 (enc b (hash psk n1 n2))))) ;; client finish
     )
    )
  (comment "Protocol with servername extension. No selfie attack.")
  )
```

Fig. 19. CPSA model of PSK authentication with server name included in the hand-shake.

```
(defprotocol tls3 basic

  (defrole keyPlacement
    (vars (a b name) (index0 index1 text) (psk0 psk1 skey))
    (trace
     (init (cat index0 a b psk0))
     (init (cat index1 b a psk1)) ;; clientialization of key for parties a and b
     )
    (uniq-orig index0 index1)
    (non-orig psk0 psk1)
    (neq (index0 index1) (psk0 psk1) (a b)))

  (defrole client
    (vars (a b name) (index n1 n2 text) (psk skey))
    (trace
     (obsv (cat index a b psk))
     (send (cat n1 index))
     (recv (cat n2 (hash (hash psk n1 n2) n1 index n2)))
     (send (hash (hash psk n1 n2) n1 index n2 (hash (hash psk n1 n2) n1 index n2)))
     )
    )

  (defrole server
    (vars (a b name) (index n1 n2 text) (psk skey))
    (trace
     (recv (cat n1 index))
     (obsv (cat index a b psk))
     (send (cat n2 (hash (hash psk n1 n2) n1 index n2)))
     (recv (hash (hash psk n1 n2) n1 index n2 (hash (hash psk n1 n2) n1 index n2)))
     )
    )
  (comment "Protocol with directional key, names added. Does not shows Selfie attack.")
  )
```

Fig. 20. CPSA model of PSK authentication with directional keys.

```
(defprotocol tls4 basic

  (defrole keyPlacement
    (vars (a b c name) (index text) (psk skey))
    (trace
     (init (cat index a b psk))
     (init (cat index b a psk)))
    (uniq-orig index)
    (neq (a b));; (a c) (b c))
    (non-orig psk))

  (defrole client
    (vars (a b ca name) (index n1 n2 text) (psk skey))
    (trace
     (obsv (cat index a b psk))
     (send (cat n1 index))
     (recv (cat n2 (hash (hash psk n1 n2) n1 index n2)))
     (send (hash (hash psk n1 n2) n1 index n2 (hash (hash psk n1 n2) n1 index n2)))
     (recv (enc "CertificateRequest" (hash psk n1 n2)))
     (send (enc (enc a (privk ca)) (enc (hash (hash psk n1 n2) n1 index n2
     (hash (hash psk n1 n2) n1 index n2) "CertificateRequest") (privk a)) (hash psk n1 n2)))
     )
    (non-orig (privk ca))
    )

  (defrole server
    (vars (a b ca name) (index n1 n2 text) (psk skey))
    (trace
     (recv (cat n1 index))
     (obsv (cat index a b psk))
     (send (cat n2 (hash (hash psk n1 n2) n1 index n2)))
     (recv (hash (hash psk n1 n2) n1 index n2 (hash (hash psk n1 n2) n1 index n2)))
     (send (enc "CertificateRequest" (hash psk n1 n2)))
     (recv (enc (enc a (privk ca)) (enc (hash (hash psk n1 n2) n1 index n2
     (hash (hash psk n1 n2) n1 index n2) "CertificateRequest") (privk a)) (hash psk n1 n2)))
     )
    (non-orig (privk ca))
    )
  (comment "Protocol with post authentication assuming group key, shows impact of selfie attack")
  )
```

Fig. 21. CPSA model of PSK use with post handshake authentication.

```
(defprotocol tls5 basic

  (defrole keyPlacement
    (vars (a b c name) (index text) (psk skey))
    (trace
     (init (cat index a b psk))
     (init (cat index b a psk))
     (init (cat index c b psk))
     (init (cat index b c psk))
     (init (cat index a c psk))
     (init (cat index c a psk)))
    (uniq-orig index)
    (neq (a b) (a c) (b c))
    (non-orig psk))

  (defrole client
    (vars (a b ca name) (index n1 n2 text) (psk skey))
    (trace
     (obsv (cat index a b psk))
     (send (cat n1 index))
     (recv (cat n2 (hash (hash psk n1 n2) n1 index n2)))
     (send (hash (hash psk n1 n2) n1 index n2 (hash (hash psk n1 n2) n1 index n2)))
     (recv (enc "CertificateRequest" (hash psk n1 n2)))
     (send (enc (enc a (privk ca)) (enc (hash (hash psk n1 n2) n1 index n2
     (hash (hash psk n1 n2) n1 index n2) "CertificateRequest") (privk a)) (hash psk n1 n2)))
     )
    (non-orig (privk ca))
    )

  (defrole server
    (vars (a b ca name) (index n1 n2 text) (psk skey))
    (trace
     (recv (cat n1 index))
     (obsv (cat index a b psk))
     (send (cat n2 (hash (hash psk n1 n2) n1 index n2)))
     (recv (hash (hash psk n1 n2) n1 index n2 (hash (hash psk n1 n2) n1 index n2)))
     (send (enc "CertificateRequest" (hash psk n1 n2)))
     (recv (enc (enc a (privk ca)) (enc (hash (hash psk n1 n2) n1 index n2
     (hash (hash psk n1 n2) n1 index n2) "CertificateRequest") (privk a)) (hash psk n1 n2)))
     )
    (non-orig (privk ca))
    )
  (comment "Protocol with post authentication assuming group key, shows impact of selfie attack")
  )
```

Fig. 22. CPSA model of PSK use with post handshake authentication and group keying.

References

1. Adrian, D., et al.: Imperfect forward secrecy: how Diffie-Hellman fails in practice. In: 22nd ACM Conference on Computer and Communications Security (Oct 2015)
2. Akhmetzyanova, L., Alekseev, E., Smyshlyaeva, E., Sokolov, A.: On post-handshake authentication and external psks in tls 1.3. J. Comput. Virology Hacking Tech. **16**(4), 269–274 (2020)
3. Al Fardan, N.J., Paterson, K.G.: Lucky thirteen: breaking the TLS and DTLS record protocols. In: 2013 IEEE Symposium on Security and Privacy, pp. 526–540 (2013). https://doi.org/10.1109/SP.2013.42

4. Beurdouche, B., et al.: A messy state of the union: taming the composite state machines of TLS. In: 2015 IEEE Symposium on Security and Privacy, pp. 535–552 (2015). https://doi.org/10.1109/SP.2015.39

5. Bhargavan, K., Blanchet, B., Kobeissi, N.: Verified Models and Reference Implementations for the TLS 1.3 Standard Candidate. Research Report RR-9040, Inria Paris, May 2017. https://hal.inria.fr/hal-01528752

6. Bhargavan, K., Lavaud, A.D., Fournet, C., Pironti, A., Strub, P.Y.: Triple handshakes and cookie cutters: breaking and fixing authentication over TLS. In: 2014 IEEE Symposium on Security and Privacy, pp. 98–113 (2014). https://doi.org/10.1109/SP.2014.14

7. Cremers, C., Horvat, M., Hoyland, J., Scott, S., van der Merwe, T.: A comprehensive symbolic analysis of TLS 1.3. In: Proceedings of the 2017 ACM SIGSAC Conference on Computer and Communications Security, CCS 2017, pp. 1773–1788. Association for Computing Machinery, New York (2017). https://doi.org/10.1145/3133956.3134063, https://doi.org/10.1145/3133956.3134063

8. Cremers, C., Horvat, M., Scott, S., van der Merwe, T.: Automated analysis and verification of TLS 1.3: 0-rtt, resumption and delayed authentication. In: 2016 IEEE Symposium on Security and Privacy (SP), pp. 470–485 (2016). https://doi.org/10.1109/SP.2016.35

9. Doghmi, S.F., Guttman, J.D., Thayer, F.J.: Searching for shapes in cryptographic protocols. In: Grumberg, O., Huth, M. (eds.) TACAS 2007. LNCS, vol. 4424, pp. 523–537. Springer, Heidelberg (2007). https://doi.org/10.1007/978-3-540-71209-1_41

10. Dowling, B., Fischlin, M., Günther, F., Stebila, D.: A cryptographic analysis of the TLS 1.3 draft-10 full and pre-shared key handshake protocol. Cryptology ePrint Archive, Report 2016/081 (2016). https://eprint.iacr.org/2016/081

11. Drucker, N., Gueron, S.: Selfie: reflections on TLS 1.3 with PSK. Cryptology ePrint Archive, Report 2019/347 (2019). https://eprint.iacr.org/2019/347

12. Fabrega, F.J.T., Herzog, J.C., Guttman, J.D.: Strand spaces: why is a security protocol correct? In: Proceedings of the 1998 IEEE Symposium on Security and Privacy (Cat. No.98CB36186), pp. 160–171, May 1998. https://doi.org/10.1109/SECPRI.1998.674832

13. Fischlin, M., Günther, F.: Replay attacks on zero round-trip time: the case of the TLS 1.3 handshake candidates. Cryptology ePrint Archive, Report 2017/082 (2017). https://eprint.iacr.org/2017/082

14. Fischlin, M., Günther, F., Schmidt, B., Warinschi, B.: Key confirmation in key exchange: a formal treatment and implications for TLS 1.3. In: 2016 IEEE Symposium on Security and Privacy (SP), pp. 452–469 (2016). https://doi.org/10.1109/SP.2016.34

15. Guttman, J.D., Liskov, M.D., Ramsdell, J.D., Rowe, P.D.: The Cryptographic Protocol Shapes Analyzer (CPSA). https://github.com/mitre/cpsa

16. Housley, R., Hoyland, J., Sethi, M., Wood, C.: Guidance for External PSK Usage in TLS, draft-ietf-tls-external-psk-guidance-02, August 2021

17. Krawczyk, H., Wee, H.: The optls protocol and TLS 1.3. In: 2016 IEEE European Symposium on Security and Privacy (EuroS P), pp. 81–96 (2016). https://doi.org/10.1109/EuroSP.2016.18

18. Li, X., Xu, J., Zhang, Z., Feng, D., Hu, H.: Multiple handshakes security of TLS 1.3 candidates. In: 2016 IEEE Symposium on Security and Privacy (SP), pp. 486–505 (2016). https://doi.org/10.1109/SP.2016.36

19. Liskov, M.D., Ramsdell, J.D., Guttman, J.D., Rowe, P.D.: The Cryptographic Protocol Shapes Analyser: A Manual. Manual, The MITRE Corporation, May 2020. https://github.com/mitre/cpsa
20. Paterson, K.G., van der Merwe, T.: Reactive and proactive standardisation of TLS. In: Chen, L., McGrew, D., Mitchell, C. (eds.) SSR 2016. LNCS, vol. 10074, pp. 160–186. Springer, Cham (2016). https://doi.org/10.1007/978-3-319-49100-4_7
21. Rescorla, E.: The Transport Layer Security (TLS) Protocol Version 1.3, RFC 8446, August 2018

A Tutorial-Style Introduction to DY*

Karthikeyan Bhargavan[1], Abhishek Bichhawat[2], Quoc Huy Do[3,4],
Pedram Hosseyni[3(✉)], Ralf Küsters[3], Guido Schmitz[3,5], and
Tim Würtele[3]

[1] INRIA, Paris, France
karthikeyan.bhargavan@inria.fr
[2] IIT Gandhinagar, Gandhinagar, Gujarat, India
abhishek.b@iitgn.ac.in
[3] University of Stuttgart, Stuttgart, Germany
{quoc-huy.do,pedram.hosseyni,ralf.kuesters,guido.schmitz,
tim.wuertele}@sec.uni-stuttgart.de
[4] GLIWA GmbH, Weilheim i.OB., Germany
[5] Royal Holloway University of London, Egham, Surrey, UK

Abstract. DY* is a recently proposed formal verification framework for
the symbolic security analysis of cryptographic protocol code written in
the F* programming language. Unlike automated symbolic provers, DY*
accounts for advanced protocol features like unbounded loops and mutable recursive data structures as well as low-level implementation details
like protocol state machines and message formats, which are often at the
root of real-world attacks. Protocols modeled in DY* can be executed,
and hence, tested, and they can even interoperate with real-world counterparts. DY* extends a long line of research on using dependent type
systems but takes a fundamentally new approach by explicitly modeling
the global trace-based semantics within the framework, hence bridging
the gap between trace-based and type-based protocol analyses. With this,
one can uniformly, precisely, and soundly model, for the first time using
dependent types, long-lived mutable protocol state, equational theories,
fine-grained dynamic corruption, and trace-based security properties like
forward secrecy and post-compromise security.

In this paper, we provide a tutorial-style introduction to DY*: We
illustrate how to model and prove the security of the ISO-DH protocol,
a simple key exchange protocol based on Diffie-Hellman.

Keywords: Cryptographic protocols · Protocol analysis · Mechanized
proofs · Formal methods · F*

1 Introduction

Since the proposal of the authentication protocol by Needham and
Schroeder [26], the security of such cryptographic protocols has become a continuous field of study for the research community. The first formalization for
symbolic protocol analysis has been proposed by Dolev and Yao in [13]. Still, a

© Springer Nature Switzerland AG 2021
D. Dougherty et al. (Eds.): Guttman Festschrift, LNCS 13066, pp. 77–97, 2021.
https://doi.org/10.1007/978-3-030-91631-2_4

severe protocol flaw in the public-key authentication protocol (NS-PK) proposed by Needham and Schroeder remained undiscovered for 17 years: In [23], Lowe presented an attack that breaks the security of the NS-PK protocol by mixing two concurrent protocol sessions. Lowe also proposed a fix and showed that this fix is indeed sufficient using the symbolic tool FDR [24].

Since then, the research community has developed several formal analysis techniques and (semi-)automated tools to verify cryptographic protocols (see [2,9] for detailed surveys). The approaches can be divided into two categories: i) *computational* approaches, where proofs are built on precise probabilistic assumptions of the underlying cryptographic primitives, and ii) *symbolic* approaches which build upon a simpler, abstract notion of these primitives. While computational analyses are more precise, they require significantly more effort, and even with the aid of mechanized verification tools, it becomes infeasible to cover all protocol features and attack vectors for large protocols. In contrast, symbolic analyses scale much better, but with less precision regarding cryptographic details.

The symbolic approach has also been in the research focus of Joshua Guttman for a long time: For example, in [31], Thayer, Herzog, and Guttman have proposed a framework that formalizes possible executions of a protocol together with possible actions of an adversary into so-called *strand spaces* and enables precise proofs w.r.t. different kinds of attackers. This approach is extended, exercised, and refined in several papers by Guttman (and others), e.g., (1) to prove independence of sub-protocols' security goals when combining protocols with shared cryptographic material [18]; (2) by introducing *authentication tests* [19] to prove certain authentication properties more easily and using those to not only analyze, but also to design security protocols [17]. Other contributions include work on an algebra for symbolic Diffie-Hellman protocol analysis [14] and reasoning on participant's state [27].

By now, the field has matured a lot. Many real-world protocols have been analyzed using symbolic methods, which often are based on Joshua's work. For example, important protocols like TLS [7,12], Signal [11,21], IKEv2 [1], OAuth [15], and OpenID Connect [16] have undergone symbolic analysis, often revealing severe flaws. In many cases, such protocols have been analyzed using automated provers for symbolic protocol analyses, such as AVISPA [1], ProVerif [10], and Tamarin [25], with Tamarin being based on the concept of strand spaces. These tools can quickly analyze all possible execution traces of protocols and find attacks like Lowe's and much more sophisticated ones in a matter of seconds.

Still, existing symbolic analysis tools, such as ProVerif and Tamarin, have many limitations: (1) These tools do not scale well for complex protocols, as they always perform *whole protocol analysis* and cannot break the analysis into smaller (re-usable) modules. (2) Protocols with unbounded loops, for which a proof typically needs inductive reasoning, as well as protocols that use recursive, unbounded data structures are very challenging for these tools. (3) Models for these tools are far from actual implementations that take low-level protocol details into account.

Existing symbolic analysis frameworks based on dependent-type systems (see, e.g., [3,8]) mitigate some of these limitations as they focus on implementations and modular analysis. However, they come with other restrictions: For example, these works do not model global trace-based runtime semantics and rely on external security arguments (typically proven by hand); security goals such as forward secrecy and post-compromise security are difficult to express and prove; they do not model cryptographic primitives like Diffie-Hellman or XOR that require equational theories and they only have limited support for stateful code with mutable data structures.

A recent approach, the DY* framework [5], tries to combine the best of both worlds. It allows for *modeling protocols in detail*, including implementation features, such as state management, that are usually left out in other approaches. Moreover, the models are *executable*, and hence, testable using (say) test vectors from protocol specifications. Protocols can even be implemented in DY* to a level of detail that yields implementations that *interoperate with real-world counterparts* [6]. DY* is based on the full-fledged programming language F* [29,30], which provides an advanced dependent type system and a powerful proof environment. The F* type-checker can prove that programs meet their specifications using a combination of SMT solving and interactive proofs. With F*'s type system and proof environment, DY* is also able to build and verify protocols in a *modular* way, use *induction-based proofs* and capture *unbounded and recursive protocols* with *complex data structures*.

This new approach has already been used to analyze complex protocols: In [5], we have analyzed the Signal protocol, which is used in many popular messaging systems and makes heavy use of Diffie-Hellman exponentiation, signatures, key derivation functions, symmetric encryption, and MACs. Signal employs multiple layers of recursive sub-protocols, which we have modeled/implemented and analyzed in detail in DY*. Our work on Signal is the first type-based formulation and proof of post-compromise security for any protocol. In [6], we analyzed the ACME protocol, which is used by certification authorities, such as Let's Encrypt, to verify domain ownership and issue certificates. Our model of ACME enjoys an unprecedented level of detail, sufficient to be interoperable with real-world implementations; it, among others, can interact with the Let's Encrypt server. Our model and proof of ACME totals more than 16,000 lines of F* code and is one of the largest and most in-depth analyses of a cryptographic protocol standard in the literature. Again, in the analysis we precisely handle recursive sub-protocols and implementation loops.

In this paper, we provide a tutorial-style introduction to DY* using the relatively simple ISO-DH authentication and key establishment protocol [20] as a running example. In Sect. 2, we first give an overview of DY* itself. The ISO-DH protocol is briefly described in Sect. 3. We show how to model ISO-DH in DY* in Sect. 4, with the analysis of this protocol in DY* presented in Sect. 5. The code of our analysis is available in [4]. We conclude in Sect. 6. We refer the reader to [5,6] for a detailed introduction of DY*, more complex case studies, and a more comprehensive discussion of related work. More information on the umbrella project *REPROSEC* can be found in [28].

2   The DY* Framework

The DY* framework has been proposed in [5]. In this section, we give a brief overview of this framework following the descriptions of the original publication. For full details, we refer the reader to [5].

The DY* framework is meant to model a distributed system that consists of *principals* executing protocol code and exchanging messages over an *untrusted network* which is under the control of a *Dolev-Yao adversary*.

A central component of our framework is the *global (execution) trace*. Among others, it records the history of the states of all principals at any time throughout the run of a system as well as all messages sent over the network by principals. A principal's state may contain arbitrary information. For example, it can contain long-lived keys, such as the principal's public and private keys. Also, principals may be involved in an unbounded number of sessions at the same time. Hence, a principal's state also contains the current session state for all of its sessions.

In the simplest case, at each protocol step a principal first retrieves its current state from the global trace, possibly reads a message from the network (and hence, from the trace), performs its computation, sends messages back to the network (and hence, to the trace), and at the end of the invocation saves its new state in the global trace. Being based on a fully-fledged programming language, DY*, of course, does not restrict protocol implementations to follow that pattern and it allows for arbitrary computations, including, for example, loops within protocol steps as well as iterations of subprotocols.

The trace also records the nonces generated by principals and documents whether principals or their sessions (even versions of sessions, see below) are corrupted by the adversary, who can corrupt principals dynamically in a fine-grained way.

The trace determines the attacker's knowledge at any point in a run: the attacker knows all messages that have been sent on the network thus far as well as the state of corrupted principals or corrupted sessions of principals. This knowledge in turn determines which messages the attacker can send to (sessions of) principals. An attacker can only construct and send messages it can derive from its knowledge. In particular, it cannot simply guess secrets.

For principals to interact with the trace, we provide a set of *modules* (containing APIs). These modules are *layered*: At the bottom is the *symbolic runtime layer*, which allows principals to access and manipulate the trace in a straightforward way. On top of this layer, we construct the *labeled layer*, which factors out generic security abstractions and invariants, all of which are mechanically proven sound in F* w.r.t. to the lower-level trace-based runtime semantics of the symbolic runtime layer.

We typically prove security properties in DY* with the help of the labeled layer: At the heart of our methodology is a security-oriented coding discipline for protocol code written in terms of secrecy labels and usage constraints. Labels allow us to proactively track knowledge of secrets. Whenever some secret is generated (e.g., a nonce), we annotate this secret with a label that states who is allowed to know this secret.

Usage constraints complement labeling: We annotate key material with a usage, for example: a key may only be used for signing but not for encryption (which rules out decryption oracles). Moreover, the annotation can also express that a key may only be used for cryptographic operations with certain payloads, e.g., that some key is only ever used to sign specific messages. This allows us to (by local type-checking) even reason about the behavior of other honest principals.

The labeling layer contains a generic *trace invariant* that describes a *valid* trace. For example, in a valid trace, messages sent to the network must always be publishable (according to their labeling) and principals only store terms in their states that they are allowed to know. This means that, e.g., code modeling a protocol in which principals send secrets unprotected via the public network will violate our valid trace invariant. DY* comes with generic security lemmas, proven in F* in the framework itself, which show that the labeling of messages is actually sound w.r.t. the symbolic runtime layer.

The global trace also allows us to naturally and explicitly express security properties, such as secrecy properties and authentication/integrity properties, involving features like (long-lived) mutable state, dynamic compromise, forward secrecy, and post-compromise security that require reasoning about the adversary's knowledge and the precise order of events in the global trace. As mentioned in Sect. 1, all this was lacking in previous dependent type based approaches. In order to prove such properties, we typically formulate global invariants over the global trace which the code of every principal has to preserve. The invariants must be strong enough to then imply the security properties we care about.

States and Corruption. As mentioned above, principals' states are recorded in the global trace. Every time a principal stores its state, a new (immutable) entry is appended to the trace that contains the principal's identity and the whole principal's state. This state is grouped in so-called *sessions*, each annotated with a *version* identifier. Sessions can store long-term keys, such as a principal's public and private keys, but also, as the name suggests, the principal's states of arbitrary many ongoing protocol sessions. An adversary can at any time *compromise* a specific version of a session of some principal. Such a compromise is recorded in the trace and the adversary can use all information stored in that state session. This particularly fine-grained notion of compromise allows an attacker to dynamically compromise both long-term keys and ephemeral protocol states. By this, we can model that only a subset of data stored in a principal's state leaks to the adversary, allowing us, for instance, to analyze forward secrecy and post-compromise security. The attacker, however, is not restricted by this model as it can corrupt as many versions and sessions as it likes.

Equational Theories. DY* builds upon an abstract type of byte strings called bytes and defines a series of (abstract) conversion and cryptographic functions for constructing and parsing byte strings. One can also define equational theories on bytes to capture algebraic properties. For example, for Diffie-Hellman, we have the functions dh_pk and dh, where dh_pk reflects the generation of the public key (g^y) from a private key (y), and dh reflects the computation of the shared secret (g^{xy}) from a private key (x) and public key (g^y).

We technically represent equational rules as F* lemmas. For example, the equational rule $(g^x)^y = (g^y)^x$ is expressed as follows:[1]

```
val dh_shared_secret_lemma: x:bytes → y:bytes →
   Lemma ((dh x (dh_pk y)) == (dh y (dh_pk x)))
```

DY* already provides a large set of typical equational rules, which —if needed— can easily be extended (for DH, XOR, signatures, etc.). For example, in [6] we add a property called *non-destructive exclusive ownership* for signatures.

Modeling Adversarial Behavior. We model an active network attacker, in the tradition of Dolev and Yao [13]. The attacker can intercept, modify, and block all messages sent on the network. The attacker can compromise any session state and can call any cryptographic function (using messages/principal's states it already knows), and can schedule any part of a protocol, i.e., functions that model the behavior of honest parties (see below). By using these capabilities, the attacker grows its knowledge as the global trace is extended and can try to break the protocol's security goals. Essential for an attacker's behavior is its knowledge. The *attacker's knowledge* at each index i in the global trace is logically characterized using a set of derivation rules. For example, the attacker can immediately derive literals, read any message sent on the network, read previously compromised states, and decrypt ciphertexts for which it knows the corresponding keys. To verify the correctness and expressiveness of our attacker model, we implement a (typed) API for the attacker with commonly expected operations like sending and receiving messages or corrupting principals. By typechecking this attacker API, we prove that our trace invariants do not restrict the adversary in unexpected ways, a property called *attacker typability*.

Labeled Crypto API. The core of the labeled layer is a labeled crypto API that provides labeled wrappers for all the crypto functions on the symbolic runtime layer and internally enforces labeling and usage rules. Each byte in bytes is assigned a unique label that indicates who may know it. For example, a label CanRead [P p1; P p2] indicates a secret that only the principals p1 and p2 may know, whereas the label public indicates that anyone may know it. Literals are always labeled public, nonces are assigned a label when they are generated.

---

[1] Note that we format all F* code in this paper using a pretty-printer, i.e., some syntactic constructs are displayed using well-known mathematical symbols for readability, such as →, ∀, ∃, and λ, instead of their textual representations.

Secrecy labels form a lattice, where can_flow i l1 l2 says that the label l1 is equal or less strict than the label l2 at trace index i. In particular, public flows to all other labels, and CanRead [P p] can flow to public at index i if Compromised p sid v (for some session sid and some version v) occurs in the trace at or before i.

The labeled APIs enforce a labeling discipline that ensures that secret values never flow to public channels. In particular, we require that the labels of all network messages must flow to public. If a secret value has to be sent over the network, it must first be encrypted with a key whose label is at least as strict as the message's label. We refer the reader to [4] for the full set of labeling rules.

In addition to secrecy labels, the labeled APIs also enforce usage preconditions. Each key is assigned an intended usage. For example, a signature key cannot be used as an encryption key. Furthermore, we define a global usage predicate controlling what kinds of messages a given key can encrypt/sign. Of course, these restrictions only apply to honest principals. For example, the labeled API for the signature and verification functions is as follows:[2]

```
val vk: sk:bytes → pk:bytes{is_labeled_public pk}
val sign: #p:global_usage → #i:timestamp → #l:label → #l':label →
    k:bytes{∃ s. is_signing_key p i k l s} → nonce:bytes →
    m:bytes{get_label m == l' ∧ ∀s. is_signing_key p i k l s
        ⟹ p.usage_preds.can_sign i s (vk k) m} →
    tag:bytes{can_flow i (get_label tag) l'}
val verify: pk:{is_labeled_public pk} → m:bytes → tag:bytes → bool
val verify_lemma: #p:global_usage → #i:timestamp → #l1:label → #l2:label →
    pk:bytes → m:msg p i l1 → tag:msg p i l2 →
    Lemma (if verify pk m tag then (∀ l s. is_verification_key p i pk l s
        ⟹ (can_flow i l public ∨ (∃ j . j ≤ i ∧ p.usage_preds.can_sign j s pk m)))
        else (C.verify pk m s = false))
```

Signing keys are supposed to be secrets (typically labeled with CanRead [P prin] to model that they should be known only to some principal prin) and marked to be used as signing keys (along with some string s that we can use to tag such keys in order to track them in our proofs). The corresponding verification keys (generated with vk) are always labeled public. For each protocol, we define a (global) predicate can_sign i s k m (part of the global usage data structure p) that indicates if at some timestamp i the private key corresponding to the public key k (tagged with the string s) may sign the message m. This predicate is then used as a pre-condition for sign, ensuring that protocol code does not accidentally call sign with a message that does not conform to can_sign. Conversely, if verify

---

[2] Note that the code excerpts we show in this paper are a bit simplified for presentation purposes (see [4] for the full code). Further note that we here use so-called *refinement types* provided by F* to further restrict types. For example, the result pk of the function vk is of type bytes, which is —by refinement— further required to satisfy the predicate is_labeled_public, which states that the byte string pk must be labeled as public. We also make use of so-called *implicit* arguments, which are marked by #. In many cases, these parameters can be dropped when calling the function, as F* can derive them from the context.

succeeds, then the API guarantees that the signature must be valid and the signed message must satisfy can_sign, unless the signing key can be known by the attacker (see verify_lemma above); in this lemma, l indicates the label of the *private* key of pk.

For Diffie-Hellman, each DH private key has the type dh_private_key p i l s indicating that it has a secrecy label l and that the *shared secret* generated from this private key should have the usage defined by the function dh_usage that takes as parameter the string s. The corresponding public keys have type dh_public_key p i l s. The declarations in F* are as follows:

```
val dh_usage: string → usage
val dh_pk: #p:global_usage → #i:nat → #l:label → #s:string →
    dh_private_key p i l s → dh_public_key p i l s
val dh: #p:global_usage → #i:nat → #l1:label → #l2:label → #s:string →
    dh_private_key p i l1 s → dh_public_key p i l2 s →
    b:bytes{has_label i b (join l1 l2) ∧ has_usage i b (dh_usage s)}
```

The function dh takes a private key with type dh_private_key p i l1 s and a public key with type dh_public_key p i l2 s to compute a shared secret with label join l1 l2 and usage defined by dh_usage given the string s. The label join l1 l2 means that the shared secret may be used in any session covered by l1 or l2. We define several other variants of the dh function, including for cases where the peer's public key is untrusted.

The types for the rest of the cryptographic API are similar. In each construction, the arguments must satisfy some protocol-specific usage predicate (can_aead_encrypt, can_mac, ...), and in all encryption functions, we ask that messages must flow to the labels of the decryption keys.

Specifying Protocols. A protocol is written as a set of functions, each of which defines one protocol step performed by a principal. These functions can be called by the adversary in arbitrary order. The parameters of these functions allow the adversary to specify which session of the protocol is to be invoked and which message the principal is supposed to read from the network. In particular, we have no restrictions on the number of principals or sessions in a protocol run.

When called, a function typically parses the principal's state as well as the network message to some semantically rich data type (we provide protocol-dependent parsing and serializing functions). Next, it performs the computation of the respective protocol step, serializes its results (a new state for this principal and possibly new network messages), and places these results on the trace (by storing the new state and sending the network messages). Since with F* we have a full-fledged functional programming language at our disposal, the functions can perform arbitrary computation and, in combination with global traces, easily deal with recursive, mutable, and long-lived state, unlike previous approaches.

The protocol code for each principal cannot directly read or write to the trace, but instead must use the labeled API that enforces an append-only discipline on the global trace using a custom computational and stateful (monadic) effect called LCrypto. Recall that effects (and so-called monads) are common in functional programming languages, for example, to implement stateful functions. LCrypto allows the function to use and modify the global trace, without providing the global trace as a parameter to the function. The effect also captures trace invariants (see below). Functions annotated with the LCrypto effect are total (i.e., they always terminate) but can return errors, which are automatically propagated by LCrypto.

The labeled API provides functions to generate new nonces, send and receive messages, store and retrieve states, and log security events. Using these functions, and a library of functions for cryptography and bytes manipulations, we can build stateful implementations of protocols.

The LCrypto effect enforces the global trace invariant valid_trace. Functions in the trace API and with the LCrypto effect take valid_trace as both pre- and post-condition. Hence, this generic trace invariant must hold in all global traces generated by protocol code that follows the labeling rules. The invariant consists of several components, some generic and some that have to be defined for each protocol. The following F* code specifies the generic parts with the protocol-specific invariants/predicates given in the argument pr:

```
1  let valid_trace (pr:preds) (tr:trace) =
2    (∀ (i:timestamp) (t:bytes) (s:principal) (r:principal). i < trace_len tr ⟹
3      (was_message_sent_at i s r t ⟹ (is_publishable pr.global_usage i t))) ∧
4    (∀ (i:timestamp) (p:principal) (v:version_vec) (s:state_vec). i < trace_len tr ⟹
5      (state_was_set_at i p v s ⟹ ((Seq.length v = Seq.length s) ∧
6        (∀ j. j < Seq.length v ⟹ pr.trace_preds.session_st_inv i p s[j] v[j] )))) ∧
7    (∀ (i:timestamp) (p:principal) (e:event). i < trace_len tr ⟹
8      (did_event_occur_at i p e ⟹ (pr.trace_preds.can_trigger_event i s e)))
```

The invariant states that i) (Lines 2–3) any message t that is sent on the network (at index i by the sender s to the intended receiver r) must have a label that can flow to public; ii) (Lines 4–6) any state (with sessions s and corresponding versions v)[3] that is stored by an honest principal p at index i must satisfy the protocol-specific state invariant session_st_inv i p s' v' contained in pr for each session s' (in s) and their corresponding version identifier v' (in v); iii) (Lines 7–8) any event e logged by principal p at index i must satisfy the protocol-specific event predicate can_trigger_event i p e in pr. We also prove that all functions in the attacker API preserve valid_trace (regardless of protocol-specific predicates), i.e., the attacker is not restricted by this invariant.

For a protocol model, we define the above-mentioned protocol-specific invariants pr and provide pr to the effect LCrypto as an argument. As valid_trace is parameterized by pr, the effect can then instantiate this invariant for a concrete protocol. Note that pr also contains usage predicates for cryptographic functions, such as can_sign mentioned above. Hence, these predicates are propagated in the same way as valid_trace.

---

[3] Sessions and versions are stored in two separate sequences s and v (of the same length). For each session s' that is stored at index j in s, the corresponding version identifier v' is stored at the same index j in v.

Protocol-specific invariants can be parameterized as well. This way, we can easily define re-usable modular layers, such as a generic PKI layer (which we also provide). This PKI layer, for example, provides key material to each principal stored in distinguished sessions. To enable layering, the protocol-specific invariant of this layer takes another (higher-layer) protocol-specific invariant pr as an argument and combines both to pki pr, where pki maps pr to the richer invariant.

Specifying Security Goals. The labeled layer of the DY* framework allows us to specify security goals in several ways: i) we can use labeling to specify "simple" goals such as the secrecy of certain terms; ii) we can use the state invariant and event predicate from valid_trace to specify conditions under which a certain principal may reach a certain state/record an event; iii) we can specify more complex properties independently and show that these are implied by valid_trace. In the latter case, we have to define the state invariant and event predicate such that they reflect sufficient properties of the protocol to prove the security goal.

Symbolic Execution. To enable debugging and testing protocol models, we provide a symbolic implementation of all abstract parts of the symbolic runtime layer. In particular, we provide an algebraic model for our basic data type bytes and all conversion and cryptographic functions of this layer. We emphasize that this model is mechanically proven to satisfy the equational theory, i.e., all lemmas describing this theory must hold true for the implementation.

For each protocol that we model in DY*, we can write a scheduler function which calls the protocol functions in the expected order. This scheduler essentially describes a run of the protocol and can be seen as a test case. We can then compile the scheduler along with the DY* framework and the protocol implementation to OCaml and execute this code to print out a symbolic trace of a protocol run. This way, we can inspect symbolic runs and check our model for errors, something not possible in tools like Tamarin and ProVerif. We can also implement further test cases and also implement and check known attacks for unfixed protocol code.

3   The ISO-DH Protocol

The ISO-DH protocol is a variant of the Diffie-Hellman protocol for authenticated key exchanges. More precisely, it extends the Diffie-Hellman protocol by adding an authentication mechanism as defined in [20]. The protocol is depicted in Fig. 1 with an initiator I and receiver R. For computing and verifying signatures, the protocol requires both parties to have a key pair and know the corresponding public key of the other party. We denote the private signing key of P by sk_P and the corresponding public key by pk_P.

Security Goals. The primary goal of the protocol is to provide secrecy of the generated shared key (g^{xy}) if the protocol is run between an honest initiator and an honest responder. More precisely, the protocol aims to achieve forward secrecy in the presence of an active network attacker. That is, even if the attacker corrupts the long-term secrets of the principals (the signature keys) after a shared key has been established, the attacker is not able to obtain the shared key. The protocol also aims to provide mutual authentication by means of the signatures added to the Diffie-Hellman protocol.

4 Modeling ISO-DH in DY*

We now illustrate the overall modeling process in DY* using the ISO-DH protocol as an example. This section presents the model of the first two steps of this protocol in detail (up to the point where the responder processes the first message and sends the second message) and gives a brief overview of the remaining steps. The full DY* implementation of this protocol can be found in [4]. We note that the analysis of ISO-DH has first been conducted as a case study in [5] but was only briefly sketched there. Here, we go into much more detail regarding both the formal model as well as the security analysis.

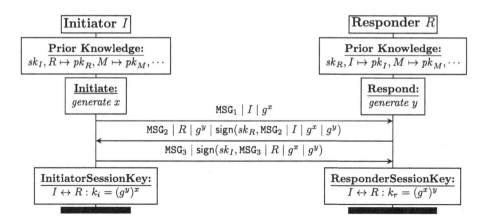

Fig. 1. Signed Diffie-Hellman Protocol (ISO-DH) [22]. We use message tags to avoid reflection and type confusion attacks. This figure is taken from [5].

Initiator: Send First Message. To model the first step of the protocol, we define a function initiator_send_msg_1 which chooses a fresh nonce x for a principal a (the initiator), sends the first protocol message to a principal b (the responder), and stores the relevant values in the principal state of a. The interface and the implementation of this function are shown in Fig. 2. As specified by the interface in Lines 2 to 6 of Fig. 2, the function has two principals a and b as input parameters. The return values are idx_msg and idx_session, where idx_msg is the trace index at which the global trace records the sent message and idx_session is the index in the trace at which the new state of the initiator is recorded. Furthermore, the function has the LCrypto effect, parametrized by pki isodh, with isodh being the protocol-specific predicates (see also Sect. 2).

Before explaining the function in detail, we note that the LCrypto effect allows us to specify pre- and post-conditions using the requires and ensures clauses. The initiator_send_msg_1 has no additional pre-conditions except those required by the effect, i.e., that the (implicit) input trace is valid (see Line 5). In Line 6, the post-condition of the function specifies a condition on the input trace t0, the return values (i, si), and the output trace t1. More precisely, the length of the output trace must be larger than the length of the input trace, and the message index i must point to the last trace entry of the output trace t1. Recall that the LCrypto effect (implicitly) also stipulates the validity of the output trace. Users do not have to state this.

```
 1 // Interface of the first protocol step
 2 val initiator_send_msg_1:
 3   a:principal → b:principal →
 4   LCrypto (idx_msg:timestamp × idx_session:nat) (pki isodh)
 5   (requires (λ _→ ⊤))
 6   (ensures (λ t0 (i,si) t1 → trace_len t1 > trace_len t0 ∧ i == trace_len t1 − 1))
 7
 8 // Implementation of the first protocol step
 9 let initiator_send_msg_1 a b =
10   let si = new_session_number a in
11   let (|t0,x|) = rand_gen (readers [V a si 0]) (dh_usage "ISODH.dh_key") in
12   let gx = dh_pk x in
13
14   let ev = initiate a b gx in
15   trigger_event a ev;
16
17   let t1 = global_timestamp () in
18   let new_ss_st = InitiatorSentMsg1 b x in
19   let new_ss = serialize_valid_session_st t1 a si 0 new_ss_st in
20   new_session a si 0 new_ss;
21
22   let t2 = global_timestamp () in
23   let msg1 = Msg1 a gx in
24   let w_msg1 = serialize_msg t2 msg1 in
25   let i = send a b w_msg1 in
26   i, si
```

Fig. 2. Interface and implementation of the first protocol step. See module ISODH.Protocol in [4].

The implementation of initiator_send_msg_1 starts with choosing a new state session index in Line 10, which is used to store information related to one protocol session. The function new_session_number is provided by DY* and returns the next available session index for the current principal state of a.

Next, the function generates a fresh nonce x using the DY* function rand_gen in Line 11. The label of this nonce is (readers [V a si 0]), indicating that only version 0 of the state session si of principal a may read the nonce. Furthermore, the usage of the nonce is specified as (dh_usage"ISODH.dh_key"). By calling the DY* function dh_pk, the DH public key g^x is calculated.

In Lines 14 and 15, an application-specific event is created and added to the trace, stating that a protocol flow is initiated with initiator a, responder b, and initiator public value gx.

The relevant information about the protocol flow is saved in the principal state of a in Lines 18 to 20. In particular, the intended responder b and the nonce x are stored in an application-specific session type InitiatorSentMsg1 and this state session is serialized (i.e., turned into a value of type bytes). In Line 20, the serialized state session is appended to the current principal state of a and the new principal state is then stored in the global trace. Recall that a principal p may only store state labeled to be readable by p. This is a time-dependent property, which is why the timestamp (Line 17) is needed.

In Lines 22 to 25, the function once more acquires a new timestamp (i.e., the current length of the trace, which is not equal to t1, as the state of principal a was updated in Line 20) and creates an application-specific message Msg1 containing the identity of the initiator and the DH public key gx. This message is serialized in Line 24 and sent in Line 25. The send function appends the message to the global trace and returns the message's trace index. (Note that the message has to be publishable, a time-dependent property.)

The function returns two indices, as already mentioned above. With these values, it is possible to write a scheduler for symbolic test cases as described in Sect. 2.

Responder: Receive Message and Send Reply. The steps performed by the receiver are shown in Fig. 3. As mentioned, DY* supports a high degree of modularity. In particular, we can split up large functions into small helper functions, as shown below: The main function modeling the second step is responder_send_msg_2 (see module ISODH.Protocol in [4]), which we split up into two helper functions, one for receiving the first protocol message and one for sending the second protocol message (for brevity, we omit the responder_send_msg_2 function, as this function simply uses the two helper functions shown in Fig. 3). The security, i.e., non-violation of the trace invariant, is proven for each (helper) function independently, modularizing proof obligations on a fine-grained level.

The function that models receiving the first message, receive_msg_1_helper, is shown in Lines 1 to 12 of Fig. 3. In Line 8, the helper function calls the receive_i function of DY*, which is given the trace index at which the message to be read is stored and the receiver's name. However, the receive function does not provide any guarantees on authenticity or confidentiality of the received message and only guarantees that a message was sent at the given trace index.

(The operation might fail and the failure is propagated by the LCrypto effect.) The received message is then parsed in Lines 9 to 12.

The second helper function send_msg_2_helper is similar to the initiator function shown above. The responder creates the values y and g^y in Lines 23 and 24, stores all relevant values in a new session in its state in Lines 26, 27, and 31, and generates an event in Line 30. The responder creates the second protocol message in Line 38, serializes it in Line 39, and sends the message in Line 40.

For computing the signature contained in the second protocol message, the responder first retrieves its private key in Line 21 using the get_private_key function. This function is provided by the PKI layer of DY* and returns the key of b of the specified key type (here, the key type is SIG, hence the function returns a signing key). The responder creates the signature in Lines 33 to 36. The function sigval_msg2 (used in Line 34) is a helper function that creates the payload for the signature, i.e., a concatenation of the identifier a, the values gx and gy, and a string "msg2" (as a tag).

The assert clause in the code states a simple property that facilitates the F* proofs (see also Sect. 5).

Remaining Protocol Steps. For details on the remaining protocol steps, we refer to the reader to [4]. The model implements the remaining steps from Fig. 1 similarly to the functions presented in this section. Upon finishing the protocol run, the initiator and responder each write events to the trace indicating that they completed a protocol run, and in these events include their names, the values gx, gy, and the shared key k. In the following, we briefly explain the verification of the signature by the initiator, as this step is crucial for the proof outlined in Sect. 5.

When the initiator receives the second message, it verifies the signature contained in the message using the helper function shown in Fig. 4. The initiator calls the function with the following arguments: the current trace length i, the session and version indices si and vi at which the initiator manages the values of the protocol flow, the principal names a and b, the public key pkb of b (for verifying the signature), the values gx and gy of the current protocol flow, and the signature sig contained in the second protocol message.

First, the initiator creates the message for which the signature should be valid in Line 2 of Fig. 4. As described previously, the sigval_msg2 function essentially concatenates the input arguments. Next, the helper function tries to verify the signature in Line 3 . If the verification is successful, the initiator calculates and returns the shared key k in Lines 5 and 7 . The remaining code is needed to prove the security properties and will be described in Sect. 5.

5   Security Analysis

In this section, we describe in detail how security properties can be proven within the DY* framework, illustrated by the ISO-DH protocol. In particular, we show how security properties can be stated as F* lemmas, encoded in trace invariants, and how these invariants are enforced on the application code layer.

5.1 Forward Secrecy

A central security property of the ISO-DH protocol is the secrecy of the resulting shared key, even if long-term secrets used by the initiator and responder become corrupted. We formalize this forward secrecy property, which was already outlined in Sect. 3, as an F* lemma as shown in Fig. 5.

```
1  val receive_msg_1_helper:
2    b:principal → idx_msg:timestamp →
3    LCrypto (now:timestamp & a:principal & gx:msg now public) (pki isodh)
4    (requires (λ _→ ⊤))
5    (ensures (λ t0 (|now, _, _|) t1 → t0 == t1 ∧ now == trace_len t0))
6
7  let receive_msg_1_helper b idx_msg =
8    let (|now,_,w_msg1|) = receive_i idx_msg b in
9    let msg1 = parse_msg w_msg1 in
10   match msg1 with
11   | Success (Msg1 a gx) → (|now,a,gx|)
12   | _→ error "responder_send_msg_2:␣not␣a␣msg1"
13
14 val send_msg_2_helper: #idx:timestamp → b:principal → a:principal →
15   gx:msg idx public → LCrypto (timestamp × nat) (pki isodh)
16   (requires (λ t0 → later_than (trace_len t0) idx))
17   (ensures (λ t0 (i,si) t1 → trace_len t1 > trace_len t0 ∧ i == trace_len t1 − 1))
18
19 let send_msg_2_helper #idx b a gx =
20   let si = new_session_number b in
21   let (|_, skb|) = get_private_key b SIG sig_key_label in
22
23   let (|t1, y|) = rand_gen (readers [V b si 0]) (dh_usage "ISODH.dh_key") in
24   let gy = dh_pk y in
25
26   let new_ss_st = (ResponderSentMsg2 a gx gy y) in
27   let new_ss = serialize_valid_session_st t1 b si 0 new_ss_st in
28
29   assert (is_eph_priv_key (t1+1) y b si 0);
30   trigger_event b (respond a b gx gy y);
31   new_session b si 0 new_ss;
32
33   let t2 = global_timestamp () in
34   let sv: msg t2 public = sigval_msg2 a gx gy in
35   let (|t3,n_sig|) = rand_gen (readers [P b]) (nonce_usage "SIG_NONCE") in
36   let sg = sign skb n_sig sv in
37
38   let msg2 = Msg2 b gy sg in
39   let w_msg2 = serialize_msg t3 msg2 in
40   let i = send b a w_msg2 in
41   i,si
```

Fig. 3. Interface and Implementation of the Second Protocol Step. See module ISODH.Protocol in [4] for full details. Note that we marked proof-related code with a gray background (see also Sect. 5).

```
1  let initiator_verify_signature i si vi a b pkb x gx gy sig =
2     let sv = sigval_msg2 a gx gy in
3     if verify pkb sv sig then (
4        can_flow_to_public_implies_corruption i (P b);
5        let k = dh x gy in
6        dh_key_label_lemma isodh_global_usage i gy;
7        k
8     ) else (error "sig␣verification␣failed")
```

Fig. 4. Helper function for verifying the signature of the second message and – if the signature is valid – calculating the shared DH key. See module `ISODH.Protocol` in [4].

```
1  val initiator_forward_secrecy_lemma: i:timestamp → a:principal → b:principal →
2        gx:bytes → gy:bytes → k:bytes → LCrypto unit (pki isodh)
3     (requires (λ t0 → i < trace_len t0 ∧ did_event_occur_at i a (finishI a b gx gy k)))
4     (ensures (λ t0 _t1 → t0 == t1 ∧ (corrupt_at i (P b) ∨ (
5        ∃si sj vi vj. is_labeled isodh_global_usage i k (join (readers [V a si vi])
6                                                              (readers [V b sj vj])) ∧
7        (corrupt_at (trace_len t0) (V a si vi) ∨ corrupt_at (trace_len t0) (V b sj vj) ∨
8           is_unknown_to_attacker_at (trace_len t0) k)
9     ))))
```

Fig. 5. Forward secrecy theorem. See module `ISODH.SecurityLemmas` in [4].

The lemma is formulated as a function of the LCrypto effect, but without a return value (i.e., the type of the return value is unit). The pre-condition of the lemma requires that the initiator a has finished the flow (modeled by a finishI event) at a trace index i. If this is the case, then the lemma ensures that either b has been corrupted at or before i, or the key has a join label (containing the specific session and version identifiers at which a and b store the key) and cannot be derived by the attacker unless it compromises one of these sessions (with the respective version). In particular, as long as the specific sessions at which a and b store their key is not corrupted, the key stays secret even if the attacker corrupts the long-term signing keys of a or b after the initiator has finished the protocol run. We formulate a similar lemma for an event type indicating that the responder has finished the protocol flow.

As explained in Sect. 2, the security properties are proven by an appropriate instantiation of the valid_trace invariant from which the security properties should follow. We show how a suitable valid_trace can be specified and how to utilize the signature and event predicates in DY* to prove that the protocol code preserves valid_trace.

Specifying valid_trace. In brief, we encode in valid_trace that, whenever a (finishI a b gx gy k) event occurs on the trace, then the key k must have the label (join (readers [V a si vi]) (readers [V b sj vj])) (for some values si, vi, sj, vj) if b is not corrupted at i. Using a generic security lemma for labels provided by DY*, we can then prove the secrecy of the key (see below). As described in Sect. 2,

DY* provides a straightforward way to define predicates on events using the parameter of the LCrypto effect. The effect parameter used in this analysis is (pki isodh), i.e., event predicates on the finishI event can be defined in the isodh invariants (at the application layer). For this purpose, we first define a predicate is_dh_shared_key as follows (see module ISODH.Sessions):

```
1  let is_dh_shared_key (i:timestamp) (key:bytes) (a:principal) (b:principal) =
2    (∃ si sj vi vj. is_aead_key isodh_global_usage i key
3      (join (readers [V a si vi]) (readers [V b sj vj])) "ISODH.aead_key")
```

By using the is_aead_key predicate as shown, we require the key to be labeled (join (readers [V a si vi]) (readers [V b sj vj])) (and to be used as an AEAD encryption key); see module Labeled.CryptoAPI in [4].

For (finishI a b gx gy k) events, we now require (using the event predicate) that (corrupt_id i (P b) ∨ is_dh_shared_key i k a b) must hold true. With such a predicate on finishI events, we can easily infer that the label of a shared key is (join (readers [V a si vi]) (readers [V b sj vj])) (for some values si, vi, sj, vj) as long as principal b is not corrupted at or before trace index i. Next, we show how we ensure that the protocol implementation fulfills this event predicate and why is_dh_shared_key is true if b is not corrupted at or before i.

Implementation Fulfills valid_trace. Recall that by using the LCrypto effect for protocol code, each function must ensure the validity of the resulting trace after the function call, e.g., whenever an initiator creates a finishI event, it must ensure that is_dh_shared_key is true if the responder is not corrupted.

Before the initiator of our model finishes the protocol run, it checks the signature contained in the second message and computes the shared key (see Fig. 4). The post-condition of the function in Fig. 4 looks as follows:

```
1  λ t0 k t1 → trace_len t0 == trace_len t1 ∧ k == CryptoLib.dh x gy ∧
2    is_msg isodh_global_usage i k (readers [V a si vi]) ∧ (
3      corrupt_id i (P b) ∨
4      (∃ y. k == CryptoLib.dh y gx ∧ is_dh_shared_key i k a b ∧
5        did_event_occur_before i b (respond a b gx gy y)))
```

Hence, when the initiator calls the helper function, it gets the shared key k and the guarantees on k needed for the validity of the trace. (The did_event_occur_before predicate is used only for authentication, see Sect. 5.2.) In the following, we show why the helper function yields this post-condition.

As described in Sect. 4, the helper function tries to verify the signature in Line 3 of Fig. 4 using a verification key belonging to b (required by the function type, not shown here). As described in Sect. 2, a successful verification guarantees that either the signature predicate can_sign holds true or the signing key is known to the attacker (see verify_lemma in Sect. 2). In the latter case, b, the principal owning the signing key, must be corrupted, which is deduced by the (generic) lemma can_flow_to_public_implies_corruption called in Line 4 of Fig. 4.

To determine which guarantees the signature predicate can_sign needs to provide, we first notice that the shared key k is calculated in Line 5 of Fig. 4 using the dh function. The label of k is the join of the label of the initiator's secret key x, i.e., (readers [V a si vi]), and the label of the responder's secret key y. The connection between gy and the label of the corresponding secret key y is established using the lemma dh_key_label_lemma called in Line 6. Therefore, to show that is_dh_shared_key i k a b holds true, the signature predicate needs to imply that the label of the private key of gy is equal to (readers [V b sj vj]), for some session sj and version vj.

The idea for connecting the successful signature verification to the label of the private key y is as follows: We formulate the signature predicate such that the successful signature verification of the second message implies that, at a previous trace index, the responder created an event, and define a predicate on this event enforcing the required label on y. Following this roadmap, we construct the application-specific signature predicate as follows:

```
1  match parse_sigval m with // parse the signature payload
2    | Success (SigMsg2 a gx gy) →
3      (∃ y. gy == (dh_pk y) ∧ did_event_occur_before i p (respond a p gx gy y))
4    ...
```

That is, the initiator code, after successful verification of the signature, can use the fact that a respond event was created for the private key y. For (respond a b gx gy y) events, we require (within the event predicate) that (∃si vi. is_eph_priv_key i y b si vi) must be true, where the is_eph_priv_key predicate enforces, amongst others, that the label of y is (readers [V b si vi]).

Overall, when the signature verification is successful, the event predicate implies that there is a private key y labeled with (readers [V b si vi]), and thus, the key k returned by initiator_verify_signature has the label join (readers [V a si vi]) (readers [V b sj vj])) (for some values si, vi, sj, vj) if b is not corrupted at i.

We highlight that every function that triggers a respond event, in particular, the responder function presented in Sect. 4, needs to ensure this property. This can be automatically done by explicitly asserting is_eph_priv_key i y b si 0 in Line 29, a statement then proven by F*.

Proving the Secrecy Lemma. The proof of the initiator_forward_secrecy_lemma (Fig. 5) essentially follows from valid_trace, in particular, from the label of the shared key shown above, i.e., whenever a finishI event occurs, the label of the shared key is (join (readers [V a si vi]) (readers [V b sj vj])) (for some values si, vi, sj, vj) unless b is corrupted. Given this label, we can use the generic security lemma secrecy_join_label_lemma provided by DY*, which states that if both ids of the join label of the key are uncorrupted, then the attacker cannot derive the key. The F* proof of initiator_forward_secrecy_lemma is now performed automatically by F*. It only needs to be hinted at secrecy_join_label_lemma:

```
1  let initiator_forward_secrecy_lemma i a b gx gy k =
2    secrecy_join_label_lemma k // generic lemma from DY*
```

5.2 Authentication Properties

Besides the key secrecy property, we formulate and prove authentication properties. Here, we give a brief overview of these properties and refer to the module ISODH.SecurityLemmas in [4] for their formal statements and proofs.

The authentication properties state that, after finishing a protocol flow, both the initiator and responder agree on all session parameters. Hence, we formulate two properties, one from the initiator's perspective and one from the responder's perspective. The property from the initiator's perspective states that, whenever the initiator a finishes the flow and creates an event indicating that it finished the run with b using the session parameters gx, gy, and the shared key k, then either the responder has previously created an event indicating that it sent the second protocol message to a with the same values gx, gy, and the private key y such that k = (dh y gx), or the responder is corrupted. The authentication property from the responder's point of view is analogous.

6 Conclusion

DY* is a recently proposed framework for formal protocol analysis and verification, a field which was shaped significantly by Joshua's work, e.g., in [14,17–19,27,31].

In this paper, we have given a tutorial-style introduction to DY* to help potential users of the framework to get started. DY* provides many more features than what we have been able to show in this paper, such as reasoning on unbounded loops, recursive data structures, low-level implementation aspects like data encoding, and interoperability. As discussed in [5,6], we plan to enrich DY* with even more features, including support for equivalence-based properties.

Acknowledgments. This work was partially supported by the *Deutsche Forschungsgemeinschaft* (DFG) through Grants KU 1434/10-2 and KU 1434/12-1, the *European Research Council (ERC)* through Grant CIRCUS-683032, and the *Office of Naval Research (ONR)* through Grant N000141812618.

References

1. Armando, A., et al.: The AVISPA tool for the automated validation of internet security protocols and applications. In: Etessami, K., Rajamani, S.K. (eds.) CAV 2005. LNCS, vol. 3576, pp. 281–285. Springer, Heidelberg (2005). https://doi.org/10.1007/11513988_27
2. Barbosa, M., et al.: SoK: computer-aided cryptography. In: IEEE S&P, pp. 777–795 (2021)
3. Bengtson, J., Bhargavan, K., Fournet, C., Gordon, A.D., Maffeis, S.: Refinement types for secure implementations. ACM TOPLAS **33**(2), 8:1-8:45 (2011)
4. Bhargavan, K., et al.: DY* Code Repository. https://github.com/REPROSEC/dolev-yao-star/tree/festschrift-guttman
5. Bhargavan, K., et al.: DY*: a modular symbolic verification framework for executable cryptographic protocol code. In: IEEE EuroS&P '21, pp. 523–542 (2021)

6. Bhargavan, K., et al.: An in-depth symbolic security analysis of the ACME standard. In: ACM CCS '21 (2021)
7. Bhargavan, K., Blanchet, B., Kobeissi, N.: Verified models and reference implementations for the TLS 1.3 standard candidate. In: IEEE S&P, pp. 483–502 (2017)
8. Bhargavan, K., Fournet, C., Gordon, A.D.: Modular verification of security protocol code by typing. In: ACM POPL, pp. 445–456 (2010)
9. Blanchet, B.: Security protocol verification: symbolic and computational models. In: POST, pp. 3–29 (2012)
10. Blanchet, B.: Modeling and verifying security protocols with the applied Pi calculus and ProVerif. Found. Trends Priv. Secur. **1**(1–2), 1–135 (2016)
11. Cohn-Gordon, K., Cremers, C.J.F., Dowling, B., Garratt, L., Stebila, D.: A formal security analysis of the signal messaging protocol. In: IEEE EuroS&P, pp. 451–466 (2017)
12. Cremers, C., Horvat, M., Hoyland, J., Scott, S., van der Merwe, T.: A comprehensive symbolic analysis of TLS 1.3. In: ACM CCS, pp. 1773–1788 (2017)
13. Dolev, D., Yao, A.C.: On the security of public key protocols. IEEE Trans. Inf. Theor. **29**(2), 198–208 (1983)
14. Dougherty, D.J., Guttman, J.D.: An algebra for symbolic diffie-hellman protocol analysis. In: Palamidessi, C., Ryan, M.D. (eds.) TGC 2012. LNCS, vol. 8191, pp. 164–181. Springer, Heidelberg (2013). https://doi.org/10.1007/978-3-642-41157-1_11
15. Fett, D., Küsters, R., Schmitz, G.: A comprehensive formal security analysis of OAuth 2.0. In: ACM CCS, pp. 1204–1215 (2016)
16. Fett, D., Küsters, R., Schmitz, G.: The web SSO standard OpenID connect: in-depth formal security analysis and security guidelines. In: IEEE CSF, pp. 189–202 (2017)
17. Guttman, J.: Security protocol design via authentication tests. In: IEEE CSFW, pp. 92–103 (2002)
18. Guttman, J., Thayer, F.: Protocol independence through disjoint encryption. In: IEEE CSFW, pp. 24–34 (2000)
19. Guttman, J.D., Thayer, F.J.: Authentication tests and the structure of bundles. Theor. Comput. Sci. **283**(2), 333–380 (2002)
20. ISO/IEC 9798–3:2019(E): IT Security techniques - Entity authentication - Part 3: Mechanisms using digital signature techniques. Technical report (2019)
21. Kobeissi, N., Bhargavan, K., Blanchet, B.: Automated verification for secure messaging protocols and their implementations: a symbolic and computational approach. In: IEEE EuroS&P, pp. 435–450 (2017)
22. Krawczyk, H.: SIGMA: the 'SIGn-and-MAc' approach to authenticated diffie-hellman and its use in the IKE protocols. In: Boneh, D. (ed.) CRYPTO 2003. LNCS, vol. 2729, pp. 400–425. Springer, Heidelberg (2003). https://doi.org/10.1007/978-3-540-45146-4_24
23. Lowe, G.: An attack on the needham-schroeder public-key authentication protocol. Inf. Process. Lett. **56**(3), 131–133 (1995)
24. Lowe, G.: Breaking and fixing the needham-schroeder public-key protocol using FDR. In: TACAS, pp. 147–166 (1996)
25. Meier, S., Schmidt, B., Cremers, C., Basin, D.: The TAMARIN prover for the symbolic analysis of security protocols. In: Sharygina, N., Veith, H. (eds.) CAV 2013. LNCS, vol. 8044, pp. 696–701. Springer, Heidelberg (2013). https://doi.org/10.1007/978-3-642-39799-8_48
26. Needham, R.M., Schroeder, M.D.: Using encryption for authentication in large networks of computers. Commun. ACM **21**(12), 993–999 (1978)

27. Ramsdell, J.D., Dougherty, D.J., Guttman, J.D., Rowe, P.D.: A hybrid analysis for security protocols with state. In: IFM, pp. 272–287 (2014)
28. REPROSEC: REPROSEC Project (2021). https://reprosec.org/
29. Swamy, N., Chen, J., Fournet, C., Strub, P., Bhargavan, K., Yang, J.: Secure distributed programming with value-dependent types. J. Funct. Program. **23**(4), 402–451 (2013)
30. Swamy, N., et al.: Dependent types and multi-monadic effects in F*. In: ACM POPL, pp. 256–270 (2016)
31. Thayer, F.J., Herzog, J.C., Guttman, J.D.: Strand spaces: proving security protocols correct. J. Comput. Secur. **7**(1), 191–230 (1999)

Security Protocols as Choreographies

Alessandro Bruni[1], Marco Carbone[1(✉)], Rosario Giustolisi[1],
Sebastian Mödersheim[2], and Carsten Schürmann[1]

[1] IT University of Copenhagen, 2300 Copenhagen S, Denmark
{brun,carbonem,rosg,carsten}@itu.dk
[2] DTU Compute, 2800 Lyngby, Denmark
samo@dtu.dk

Abstract. A choreography gives a description of how endpoints in a concurrent systems should exchange messages during its execution. In this paper, we informally introduce a choreographic language for describing security protocols and a property language for expressing non-trivial security properties of such protocols. We motivate this work using the envelope protocol [2] as an example, which ensures auditable transfers by means of a TPM, that guarantees that the issuer of a message always learns whether such message has been opened or not. We then take an implementation of the TPM formulated as an API and discuss how such implementation and the usage of the TPM in the protocol can be related. Finally, we illustrate how the protocol and property descriptions can be translated into multiset rewrite rules and metric first order logic respectively, in order to check if auditable transfer holds.

Keywords: Security protocols · Choreography · Verification

1 Introduction

Choreographic programming [13,14,34] is a programming paradigm for concurrent systems that focuses on the global flow of interactions that communicating peers are supposed to follow during execution rather than their local sequence of send and receive operations. Choreographies have been studied extensively in the context of concurrency theory and programming languages, but they have only been sporadically considered for modeling security protocols [6,11,12]. This is quite surprising, because Alice-Bob notations, which are prevalently used in security theory [3,10,27,30], are closely related to choreographies that describe the communication structure of entire systems. In fact, extensions of the Alice-Bob notation with more features such as long-term state or subprotocols [7] can be found in the literature.

In this paper, we celebrate Joshua Guttmann by proposing a choreography language extended with term algebras and equational theories for modelling various cryptographic primitives used in security protocols, for example, encryption and decryption, signatures and verifications, etc. The main idea is that security

© Springer Nature Switzerland AG 2021
D. Dougherty et al. (Eds.): Guttman Festschrift, LNCS 13066, pp. 98–111, 2021.
https://doi.org/10.1007/978-3-030-91631-2_5

protocols can be written in such language and then the minimum local behavior of each participant can be automatically generated from the choreography through an operation called *endpoint projection*. Note that a choreography *only* provides the local behavior of *honest* participants (while the intruder may not stick to the protocol and is rather defined, for instance, by a Dolev-Yao-style model). Generating the endpoint projection requires an analysis of the honest agents knowledge, and how they can compose and decompose the messages that they send and receive [3,30]. Since this problem is well-understood, here we focus on those aspects of choreographic languages that distinguish them from traditional Alice-and-Bob narrations. The (honest) local behaviour generated from a choreography specifying a protocol can then be used for two purposes. First, it can be used as a local specification for verifying that a given implementation is compliant with a given API (similarly to what is done for multiparty session types [23]), e.g., in the TPM envelope example reported in this article, where we check that the usage of the TPM in the protocol description is compatible with the TPM API. Second, it allows us to replace the local projection of API-like participants with their API implementations, and use them along with the local projections of the remaining honest agents as the input for a protocol analyser, where we can verify some security properties. A key feature of our approach is that such properties can be specified at the choreographic level and then automatically translated, in a semantic preserving way, into the language of the protocol analyser automatically, via the endpoint projection.

This paper is not a theory paper in that it does not provide a formal development of the translation of choreographies. It should be read as a position paper that elaborates the idea of choreographies applied to security protocols and their endpoint projections by the means of an example, namely the *envelope protocol*, first proposed by Ables and Ryan [2] and analyzed by Delaune et al. [17]. Joshua Guttman and colleagues [22] proposed an extension to the CPSA tool [18] to protocols with state, contributing to the first verification of the envelope protocol with unbounded reboots, while also introducing a modular approach that faithfully represents the interface offered by the trusted third party used in the protocol.

The envelope protocol uses the Trusted Platform Module (TPM) as a trusted party to guarantee a security property that we have dubbed *auditable transfer*: Alice wants to share a message with Bob such that Alice will be able to verify if Bob has opened the message or not. The TPM is used to securely store the state of this transfer.

In this paper, we give a formulation of the auditable transfer protocol as a choreography in Sect. 2, describe the result of the endpoint projection including the property in Sect. 3, and feed the result into Tamarin to verify the auditable transfer property in Sect. 4. Our main goal with this notation is to allow for a simple, clear and yet very expressive specification language. We revisit related work in Sect. 5 and assess results and outline future work in Sect. 6.

2 The Envelope Protocol and Its Choreographic Description

The envelope protocol aims at being the digital version of a sealed physical envelope. A sealed envelope allows to achieve auditable transfer: the recipient can either obtain the content inside the envelope or prove that they have not broken the seal and thus obtained the content, with no intervention required from the sender. In this paper, we use the classic example of the envelope protocol: Alice would like her parents to know where she is going out for the night only in case of necessity, so she writes this information in a letter and puts it into a sealed envelope. Alice does not necessarily trust her parents, who may behave adversarially and hence may like to know where Alice is going out without her noticing that they learned this information. The sealed envelope protects Alice in this case, as learning the information requires breaking the seal, which Alice would notice upon her comeback. Its digital counterpart cannot be implemented with cryptography alone, as revealing the content of a message usually requires obtaining the key or solving an interactive challenge.

The envelope protocol relies on a trusted third party, the TPM, which provides an interface to create a key that is concealed inside the trusted computing module, and offers functions for encryption and decryption which are bound to the internal state of the TPM. The internal state of a TPM is made of 24 Platform Configuration Registers (PCRs), which essentially implement a hash chain: the TPM allows to reset one of these registers to an initial known value (with the `Boot` command) and to extend the chain with a new value (with the `Extend, n` command). For simplicity we assume only one register, which is also what the envelope protocol requires, hence all the commands omit the first parameter. The three other commands that the TPM implements that are used by the envelope protocol are the following: the `Create, s` command that creates a new public-private key bundle and releases the public key (the corresponding private key is retained by the TPM and can only be used through the TPM interface when the `pcr` is in state `s`); the `Quote, x` command that binds the message `x` to the current value of the `pcr`, and the `Decrypt` command that takes a ciphertext and a key bundle and returns the decryption only if the state of the key bundle matches the current value of the `pcr`. In Sect. 3.2, we formalise the TPM interface and show that the envelope protocol respects this interface.

The envelope protocol uses the TPM as follows: Alice first resets the TPM to its initial `pcr` state 1 and then issues the `Extend` command with a fresh secret nonce `n`, so the TPM is now in state `hash(n,1)`. Now Alice asks the TPM to create a public key `k` for the state `hash(obtain, hash(n, 1))`, i.e., the TPM will only decrypt messages using `inv(k)`, when the TPM is in that state. The TPM can be brought into that state by performing the `Extend` command with value `obtain`, but afterwards it is impossible to bring it back to state `hash(n,1)` unless one knows the nonce `n`. Alice now encrypts her message `v` with `k` and sends it to her parent. The parent now has two options: they can either extend the PCR to the state `hash(refuse, hash(n, 1))` and obtain a proof that they refused to open

```
1  Roles: Alice, TPM[Honest], Parent
2  Knowledge: tpmk
3
4  Protocol
5    Alice → TPM: Boot
6    TPM: pcr := '1'
7    TPM → Alice: Booted
8    Alice: new n, new esk
9    Alice → TPM: Session, tpmk, aenc(esk, tpmk)
10   TPM: new sid
11   TPM → Alice: sid
12   Alice → TPM: senc((Extend, n, sid), esk)
13   TPM: pcr := hash(n, pcr)
14   TPM → Alice: Extended
15   Alice → TPM: Create, hash('obt', pcr)
16   TPM: new k
17   TPM → Alice: sign((Created, k, hash('obt', pcr)), inv(tpmk)
        )
18   Alice: new v
19   Alice → Parent: Envelope, enc(v, k)
20   Parent: new esk
21   Parent → TPM: Session, aenc(esk, tpmk)
22   TPM: new sid
23   TPM → Parent: sid
24   Parent → TPM: {
25     senc((Extend, 'ref', sid), esk):
26     TPM: pcr := hash('ref', pcr)
27     TPM → Parent: Extended
28     Parent → TPM: Quote, enc(v, k)
29     TPM → Parent: sign((Quoted, pcr, enc(v, k)), inv(tpmk))
30     event secret(v)
31   +
32     senc((Extend, 'obt', sid), esk):
33     TPM: pcr := hash('obt', pcr)
34     TPM → Parent: Extended
35     Parent → TPM: Decrypt, enc(v, k), sign((Created, k, pcr),
          inv(tpmk))
36     TPM → Parent: v
37   }
38
39 Objectives
40   Intruder learns v implies not secret(v)
```

Fig. 1. The envelope protocol as a chreography

the letter, or they can extend the PCR to the state hash(obtain, hash(n, 1))
and use the TPM to decrypt Alice's message.

We now give a precise specification of the envelope protocol as a choreography, which is depicted in Fig. 1. A choreography consist of four sections: Roles,
Knowledge, Protocol, and Objectives. The roles and initial knowledge declared

are standard. More interesting is the specification of the protocol. The TPM offers different services, such as `Boot`, `Extend`, `Create`, `Quote`, `Decrypt`, or `Envelope`, which are followed by their respective parameters. Upon completion, the TMP signals the caller that a particular service has terminated, again using messages, such as `Booted`, `Extended`, `Created`, `Quoted`, or `Decrypted`. We use M to denote messages.

Choreographies also support state. In our example the state is denoted by `pcr`, the internal state of the TPM. The expression algebra that we use, includes operations such as bit string concatenation, denoted by a comma, hashing, denoted by `hash`, and encryption, denoted by `enc`. Dereferencing `pcr` is a silient operation. Expressions are denoted by E.

The language supports two forms of command, generically denoted by C: a command to create fresh nonces written as `new`, and another command for assignment, denoted by `:=`. The scope of nonces extends to the end of the protocol specification, but a priori, only the principal who creates the nonce knows it. Let A and B be two different roles. Protocols P, Q are defined by a sequence of operations, in Alice Bob notation, message transfer of message M as $A \rightarrow B : M$, internal execution of command C as $A : C$, and choice $A \rightarrow B : \{P + Q\}$.

As part of a formal semantics in the style of [3,11,30], we rule out as *not executable* (or *not well-formed*) those specifications that require participants to produce messages that they actually cannot produce (without breaking cryptography). This, however, requires a considerable amount of formal machinery that we do not want to introduce in this more conceptual paper.

3   Projection and Refinement

In the previous section, we have shown how to use a choreographic language for specifying the envelope protocol. Besides proving the correctness of such a protocol (which we will do in the next section), we show how we can use a type-like approach for checking that an implementation of (some of) the participants is compliant with the behavioural specification given by the protocol. In order to do so, we proceed by two steps. First, we define the notion of *projection*, a well-studied concept in the theory of choreographies.

3.1   Projection

The projection of a choreography with respect to a particular endpoint is a specification of how such endpoint has to behave in the protocol. In a nutshell, given the choreography $A \rightarrow B : M_1; B \rightarrow A : M_2$ for example, the projection with respect to A is `send` M_1 ; `receive` M_2, while the projection with respect to B is `receive` M_1; `send` M_2, were `send` and `receive` are standard endpoint operations, i.e. commands. However, in general just literally taking the messages from the choreography for the endpoint actions will not be correct, e.g., if M_1 is an encrypted message that B cannot decrypt, then it must be replaced by a variable as first observed by Lowe [27]. This question is in general also related to the algebraic properties of cryptographic operators that we consider, e.g., the properties of exponentiation in Diffie-Hellman. In general such a formal semantics can be given in the style of [3]. The endpoint specification is useful, because we can use it for checking that, e.g., a given implementation of A follows the specification given by the original choreography.

In the envelope protocol, the behaviour of Alice according to the choreographic specification of the envelope protocol consists of:

```
 1  Role Alice
 2    send Boot
 3    new n
 4    send Extend(n)
 5    receive Extended
 6    send Create(hash('obt', pcr))
 7    receive Created(k, hash('obt', pcr))
 8    new v
 9    send Envelope(enc(v, k))
```

The projection of Alice corresponds to her behaviour in the choreography. Above, new n creates a fresh nonce n and works as a binder in the subsequent code. On the other hand, send Extend(n) sends a message which selects option Extend and also communicates the value n, which in this case is bound by the new n in the second line. When receiving a message, the language uses structured terms with constants and variables, implying standard pattern matching. Similarly, we can project the behaviour of the TPM:

```
 1  Role TPM
 2    receive Boot
 3    pcr := '1'
 4    receive Extend(n)
 5    send Extended
 6    receive Create(hash('obt', pcr))
 7    new k
 8    send Created(k, hash('obt', pcr))
 9    receive {
10        Extend('ref'):
11            pcr := hash('ref', pcr)
12            send Extended
13            receive Quote(enc(v, k))
14            send Quoted(pcr, enc(v, k))
15        +
16        Extend('obt'):
17            pcr := hash('obt', pcr)
18            send Extended
19            receive Decrypt(enc(v, k)), Created(k, pcr)
20            send Decrypted(v)
21  }
```

In the case of TPM, we note that the receive operation can also handle choice. Options in the choice are separated by the keyword + as in standard choreographies which corresponds to the standard external choice from the pi-calculus [29]. As mentioned in the previous sections, in order to ensure consistency of these specifications, each branch must have a unique label. In order to achieve this, while retain flexibility, we use pattern matching to distinguish branches with the same label. E.g., above, although the label Extend is identical in both branches, each branch can be identified by the constant that the branch is expecting to receive. Finally, this is the projection of the parent's expected behaviour:

```
 1  Role Parent
 2    receive Envelope(enc(v, k))
 3    send {
 4        Extend('ref'):
 5          receive Extended
 6          send Quote(enc(v, k))
 7          receive Quoted(pcr, enc(v, k)) (1)
 8    +
 9        Extend('obt'):
10          receive Extended
11          send Decrypt(enc(v, k)), Created(k, pcr)
12          receive Decrypted(v)
13    }
```

Dually to the external choice provided by the TPM, the parent's projection is making an internal choice: it either sends the ref value or the obt value.

3.2   Refinement

In the theory of choreographies, choreographic specifications are projected into endpoints behaviour. Such cut of the global behaviour can often be used by a type system to do a local type checking of code. In here, our choreographies are richer in the sense that contain information about values that the protocol being described should handle. Hence, the specification and a possible implementation are very close. In this subsection, we illustrate how a notion of refinement could be used for verifying that an implementation is compliant to the protocol specification. In order to do so, we focus on the TPM behaviour. Obviously, the projection from the choreography given above does not have to be the exact way the TPM should be implemented. In general, a TPM is a piece of hardware that can provide the TPM service to system components. Therefore, it is usually implemented as a simple API. The one below is a possible API implementation:

```
 1  TPM(pcr) = {
 2      receive Boot: {
 3          send Booted;
 4          TPM(-1)
 5      } +
```

```
 6        receive Create, s: {
 7            new k
 8            send sign((Created, k, s), inv(tpmk))
 9            TPM(pcr)
10        } +
11        receive Quote, x: {
12            send sign((Quoted, pcr, x), inv(tpmk))
13            TPM(pcr)
14        } +
15        receive Session, tpmk, aenc(esk, tpmk): {
16            new sid;
17            send sid;
18            receive senc((Extend, x, sid), tpmk);
19            send Extended, hash(x,pcr);
20            TPM(hash(x, pcr))
21        } +
22        receive Decrypt, aenc(c, pk(k)), Created(k, pcr')): {
23            if (pcr = pcr') then
24                send dec(c, k)
25            TPM(pcr)
26        }
27  }
```

Unlike the projection from the choreography, the behaviour of the TPM API is just a sum of all the possible methods that can be invoked. Note that we also enhance the local behaviour specification with recursion. We conjecture that the projection of the TPM from the choreography and the API above can be formally related. Our idea is to look at the set of possible traces that the API can perform and compare to the traces of the projection (up-to recursive behaviour). Clearly, if a trace is in the projection of the choreography then it is for sure a trace of the API. This shows that the API implementation is compliant with the envelope protocol.

4 Verification in Tamarin

Our mechanised analysis is carried out in Tamarin [28], an interactive protocol verifier that can prove reachability and equivalence-based properties in the symbolic model. It has an expressive language based on multiset rewriting rules.

In Tamarin, terms are variables and functions ranging over terms; facts are predicates that store state information and are parameterized by terms; facts may be linear (i.e. can be consumed only once) or persistent (i.e. can be consumed arbitrarily often by rules); rules are essentially defined as transitions from one multiset of facts to another. The Tamarin multiset rewriting rules define a labeled transition system. The labels are used to reason about the behaviour of a protocol. Thus, to analyse the envelope protocol in Tamarin, we need to annotate our rules with appropriate labels that will serve to the specification of our security properties. Tamarin encodes a Dolev-Yao [19] adversary that controls the network.

Conventionally, cryptographic primitives can be modelled in Tamarin by means of equational theories. An equational theory E describes the equations that hold on terms built from the signature. Terms are related by an equivalence relation $=$ induced by E. For instance, the equation $dec(enc(m, k), k) = m$ models a symmetric encryption scheme. The term m is the message, the term k is the secret key, the term enc models the encryption function, and the term dec models the decryption function, namely a deconstructor for the function enc.

Trace properties can be modelled in Tamarin via metric first-order logic. Predicates are labels and properties can be expressed using quantification over time. For example, the following lemma models a non-injective agreeement on the message x, meaning that for all got message x, there exists at least an event in which the message x has been previously sent.

$$(\text{Non-injective agreement}) \quad \forall x \ \#i. \ Get(x)@i \implies \exists \ \#j. \ Sent(x)@j \wedge j < i$$

The endpoint projection of the API of the TPM have immediate specifications into Tamarin rules: labels in a choreography can be translated to Tamarin's facts; send and receive can be mapped into the Tamarin's *Out* and *In* respectively; conditionals in choreography can be captured using pattern matching in Tamarin. For example, the rule below captures the Decrypt service.

```
1  rule Decrypt:
2     let c = enc(v,~k) in
3     [ In(c), In(Created(~k, pcr)), TPM(pcr) ]
4     --[ Decrypt(v), TPM(pcr) ]->
5     [ Out(v), TPM(pcr) ]
```

Here, the TPM outputs the value v, which is encrypted in c, if and only if the value of *pcr* in the TPM is equal to the value of *pcr* in Created.

Similarly, we can model Alice behaviour with two rules, one to capture Alice sending the commands Boot, Extend, and Create (*Alice_BEC*) and one to capture Alice sending the envelope (*Alice_Env*).

```
1  rule Alice_BEC:
2     [ Fr(~n) ]
3     --[ Alice_BEC(~n) ]->
4     [ Out(Boot()), Out(Extend(~n)), Out(Create(hash('obt',
       hash(~n, 'nil')))),
5     Alice1(~n) ]
6
7  rule Alice_Env:
8     [ Alice1(~n), Fr(~v), In(Created(~k, hash('obt', hash(~n,
       'nil')))) ]
9     --[ Alice_Env(~n, ~v, ~k) ]->
10    [ Out(enc(~v, ~k)) ]
```

We do not need to model the role the parents since they act as an adversary, thus the role is controlled by the Dolev-Yao attacker encoded in Tamarin.

The specification of auditable transfer can be modelled in Tamarin as

$$(Audic\text{ transfer}) \quad \forall n \ v \ k \ \#i \ \#j. \ Alice\_BEC(n)@i \wedge \ Alice\_Env(n,v,k)@j$$
$$\implies \neg(\exists \ \#l. \ !KU(v)@l) \vee \neg(\exists \ \#l.$$
$$!KU(Quoted(h('ref', \ h(n, \ 'nil')), \ enc(v, \ k)))@l)$$

The fact *!KU* represents the knowledge of the adversary, which in our case is the parents. Thus, the property says that whenever Alice has initialised the TPM and sent the envelope, the adversary cannot both open the envelope and learn the content *and* obtain a proof of refusal of opening the envelope.

Tamarin cannot prove automatically auditable transfer. However, we resort to the interactive proof theory feature of Tamarin to find the proof. The proof and the full Tamarin code modelling the envelope protocol are available in [1].

5   Related Work

The idea of using choreographic languages for describing security protocol is not new: in fact, Alice and Bob notations are the predominant informal notation used by protocol designers.

The first work on a formal Alice and Bob notation with automated translation to the process algebra CSP is the Casper compiler by Lowe [27]. Mödersheim [30] later proposed an Alice and Bob-like language with a formal semantics and support for algebraic properties a-la Diffie-Hellman, that is integrated into the prover OFMC [5]. Several extension to this line of work have been made, for example, to support arbitrary algebraic reasoning [3] and secure and pseudonimous channels [33] forwarding channels [10]. Alice and Bob-style languages have a level of clarity and explainability that other models lack, however they only support linear protocols, which makes it impossible to represent API-like protocols such as the one analyzed in this paper, which typically contain branching and state that persists across sessions.

Stateful protocol verification is another relevant line of work. The first tool to support stateful verification was AIF [31], which abstracts values according to their membership class. This abstraction techniques was also applied to process algebras [9] and extended to countable families of sets [32] to support unbounded principals. The TPM envelope protocol that we use here as an example motivated the work on StatVerif [4], however the first analysis of the protocol was done with a custom encoding in Horn clauses [17]. Joshua and his colleagues also took the TPM envelope protocol as inspiration to extend the CPSA tool based on strand spaces to handle stateful protocols [22]. Another tool that supports stateful protocols is the Tamarin prover [28], which uses multiset rewrite rules to describe security protocols and we employ here as our target language. Later, support to stateful protocols was also added into the protocol verifier ProVerif [15].

Carbone and Guttmann [11] proposed a simple choreographic language with boxes for writing web interactions. Their core idea is that boxes containing information that must be exchanged in a network are annotated with the sender and the receiver, respectively the creator of box and the one who can open it. Then, an endpoint projection is provided which generates local behaviour expressed in the Strand Spaces formalism. The translation introduces cryptographic enhancements to the boxes in order to ensure authentication and secrecy. Similarly, Bhargavan et al. [6] use a choreographic language inspired by multiparty session types for specifying web services. Similarly to Carbone and Guttmann, their tool adds some cryptographies to the messages specified in the choreography. Both research contributions differ from our idea in the fact that, unlike us, they abstract from the details that are necessary for achieving security properties. In particular, they do not consider expressing security properties at choreographic level.

The hallmark characteristic of auditable transfer is that it allows a party to get evidence on whether another party has learnt a secret. This seems an instantiation of the broader notion of *auditability* [21,24], which is defined as the quality of a protocol, which stores a sufficient number of pieces of evidence, to convince a third party that specific properties are satisfied. Similar properties are *verifiability*, which ensures that the failure of a protocol's goal can be detectable [16,25] and accountability [8,26], which additionally guarantees that misbehaving parties can be blamed. An interesting line of work is to study choreography for the modelling of such broader properties. For example, verifiability, accountability, and dispute resolution properties can all be defined by identifying the *tests* that decide whether a protocol's goal fails, and then check that each of the tests meets soundness, completeness, and sufficiency conditions [8,20,26]. Choreographies can be the language that enables the analyst to formulate tests and conditions, which can be then checked by a model checker of choice.

6   Conclusion

In this work we have given a formulation of the auditable transfer protocol as a choreography. We have shown how the role of the TPM can be defined with a local choreography, and that the auditable transfer protocol is shown to be a refinement of the TPM API. The choreographic constructs of branching and recursion useful language constructions to express the core properties of stateful, API-like protocols like the one we considered in this paper. It is then possible to translate to other intermediate languages for verification, like we have shown in our example for the multiset rewrite rules of Tamarin.

References

1. Tamarin   code   (2021).   https://www.dropbox.com/sh/lonxu6vmj3iilmu/AAAErB3ATSNg59MFGxBcp74Ha?dl=0
2. Ables, K., Ryan, M.D.: Escrowed data and the digital envelope. In: Acquisti, A., Smith, S.W., Sadeghi, A.-R. (eds.) Trust 2010. LNCS, vol. 6101, pp. 246–256. Springer, Heidelberg (2010). https://doi.org/10.1007/978-3-642-13869-0_16

3. Almousa, O., Mödersheim, S., Viganò, L.: Alice and bob: reconciling formal models and implementation. In: Bodei, C., Ferrari, G.-L., Priami, C. (eds.) Programming Languages with Applications to Biology and Security. LNCS, vol. 9465, pp. 66–85. Springer, Cham (2015). https://doi.org/10.1007/978-3-319-25527-9_7

4. Arapinis, M., Phillips, J., Ritter, E., Ryan, M.D.: Statverif: verification of stateful processes. J. Comput. Secur. **22**(5), 743–821 (2014). https://doi.org/10.3233/JCS-140501

5. Basin, D.A., Mödersheim, S., Viganò, L.: OFMC: a symbolic model checker for security protocols. Int. J. Inf. Sec. **4**(3), 181–208 (2005). https://doi.org/10.1007/s10207-004-0055-7

6. Bhargavan, K., Corin, R., Deniélou, P., Fournet, C., Leifer, J.J.: Cryptographic protocol synthesis and verification for multiparty sessions. In: Proceedings of the 22nd IEEE Computer Security Foundations Symposium, CSF 2009, Port Jefferson, New York, USA, 8–10 July 2009, pp. 124–140. IEEE Computer Society (2009). https://doi.org/10.1109/CSF.2009.26

7. Brøndum, C.: Languages and Translators for Stateful Protocols. Tech. rep., DTU, MSc. Thesis (2020). https://findit.dtu.dk/en/catalog/2525864377

8. Bruni, A., Giustolisi, R., Schuermann, C.: Automated analysis of accountability. In: Nguyen, P., Zhou, J. (eds.) Information Security Conference, vol. 10599, pp. 417–434. Springer, Heidelberg (2017). https://doi.org/10.1007/978-3-319-69659-1_23

9. Bruni, A., Mödersheim, S., Nielson, F., Nielson, H.R.: Set-pi: Set membership p-calculus. In: Fournet, C., Hicks, M.W., Viganò, L. (eds.) IEEE 28th Computer Security Foundations Symposium, CSF 2015, Verona, Italy, 13–17 July 2015, pp. 185–198. IEEE Computer Society (2015). https://doi.org/10.1109/CSF.2015.20

10. Bugliesi, M., Calzavara, S., Mödersheim, S., Modesti, P.: Security protocol specification and verification with anbx. J. Inf. Secur. Appl. **30**, 46–63 (2016). https://doi.org/10.1016/j.jisa.2016.05.004

11. Carbone, M., Guttman, J.D.: Choreographies with secure boxes and compromised principals. In: Bonchi, F., Grohmann, D., Spoletini, P., Tuosto, E. (eds.) Proceedings 2nd Interaction and Concurrency Experience: Structured Interactions, ICE 2009, Bologna, Italy, 31st August 2009. EPTCS, vol. 12, pp. 1–15 (2009). https://doi.org/10.4204/EPTCS.12.1

12. Carbone, M., Guttman, J.D.: Execution models for choreographies and cryptoprotocols. In: Beresford, A.R., Gay, S.J. (eds.) Proceedings Second International Workshop on Programming Language Approaches to Concurrency and Communication-cEntric Software, PLACES 2009, New York, UK, 22nd March 2009. EPTCS, vol. 17, pp. 31–41 (2009). https://doi.org/10.4204/EPTCS.17.3

13. Carbone, M., Honda, K., Yoshida, N.: Structured communication-centered programming for web services. ACM Trans. Program. Lang. Syst. **34**(2), 8:1–8:78 (2012). https://doi.org/10.1145/2220365.2220367

14. Carbone, M., Montesi, F.: Deadlock-freedom-by-design: multiparty asynchronous global programming. In: Giacobazzi, R., Cousot, R. (eds.) The 40th Annual ACM SIGPLAN-SIGACT Symposium on Principles of Programming Languages, POPL '13, Rome, Italy, 23–25 January 2013. pp. 263–274. ACM (2013). https://doi.org/10.1145/2429069.2429101

15. Cheval, V., Cortier, V., Turuani, M.: A little more conversation, a little less action, a lot more satisfaction: Global states in proverif. In: 31st IEEE Computer Security Foundations Symposium, CSF 2018, Oxford, United Kingdom, 9–12 July 2018, pp. 344–358. IEEE Computer Society (2018). https://doi.org/10.1109/CSF.2018.00032

16. Cortier, V., Galindo, D., Küsters, R., Müller, J., Truderung, T.: SoK: verifiability notions for e-voting protocols. In: IEEE Symposium on Security and Privacy, pp. 779–798 (2016)
17. Delaune, S., Kremer, S., Ryan, M.D., Steel, G.: Formal analysis of protocols based on TPM state registers. In: Proceedings of the 24th IEEE Computer Security Foundations Symposium, CSF 2011, Cernay-la-Ville, France, 27–29 June, 2011, pp. 66–80. IEEE Computer Society (2011). https://doi.org/10.1109/CSF.2011.12
18. Doghmi, S.F., Guttman, J.D., Thayer, F.J.: Searching for shapes in cryptographic protocols. In: Grumberg, O., Huth, M. (eds.) TACAS 2007. LNCS, vol. 4424, pp. 523–537. Springer, Heidelberg (2007). https://doi.org/10.1007/978-3-540-71209-1_41
19. Dolev, D., Yao, A.C.: On the security of public key protocols. IEEE Trans. Inf. Theory **29**(2), 198–208 (1983)
20. Giustolisi, R., Bruni, A., et al.: Privacy-preserving dispute resolution in the improved bingo voting. In: Krimmer, R. (ed.) E-Vote-ID 2020. LNCS, vol. 12455, pp. 67–83. Springer, Cham (2020). https://doi.org/10.1007/978-3-030-60347-2_5
21. Guts, N., Fournet, C., Zappa Nardelli, F.: Reliable evidence: auditability by typing. In: Backes, M., Ning, P. (eds.) ESORICS 2009. LNCS, vol. 5789, pp. 168–183. Springer, Heidelberg (2009). https://doi.org/10.1007/978-3-642-04444-1_11
22. Guttman, J.D., Liskov, M.D., Ramsdell, J.D., Rowe, P.D.: Formal support for standardizing protocols with state. In: Chen, L., Matsuo, S. (eds.) SSR 2015. LNCS, vol. 9497, pp. 246–265. Springer, Cham (2015). https://doi.org/10.1007/978-3-319-27152-1_13
23. Honda, K., Yoshida, N., Carbone, M.: Multiparty asynchronous session types. J. ACM **63**(1), 9:1–9:67 (2016). https://doi.org/10.1145/2827695
24. Jagadeesan, R., Jeffrey, A., Pitcher, C., Riely, J.: Towards a theory of accountability and audit. In: Backes, M., Ning, P. (eds.) ESORICS 2009. LNCS, vol. 5789, pp. 152–167. Springer, Heidelberg (2009). https://doi.org/10.1007/978-3-642-04444-1_10
25. Kremer, S., Ryan, M., Smyth, B.: Election verifiability in electronic voting protocols. In: Gritzalis, D., Preneel, B., Theoharidou, M. (eds.) ESORICS 2010. LNCS, vol. 6345, pp. 389–404. Springer, Heidelberg (2010). https://doi.org/10.1007/978-3-642-15497-3_24
26. Küsters, R., Truderung, T., Vogt, A.: Accountability: definition and relationship to verifiability. In: CCS, pp. 526–535. ACM (2010)
27. Lowe, G.: Casper: a compiler for the analysis of security protocols. J. Comput. Secur. **6**(1–2), 53–84 (1998). http://content.iospress.com/articles/journal-of-computer-security/jcs106
28. Meier, S., Schmidt, B., Cremers, C., Basin, D.: The TAMARIN prover for the symbolic analysis of security protocols. In: Sharygina, N., Veith, H. (eds.) CAV 2013. LNCS, vol. 8044, pp. 696–701. Springer, Heidelberg (2013). https://doi.org/10.1007/978-3-642-39799-8_48
29. Milner, R., Parrow, J., Walker, D.: A calculus of mobile processes I and II. Inf. Comput. **100**(1), 1–77 (1992)
30. Mödersheim, S.: Algebraic properties in alice and bob notation. In: Proceedings of the The Forth International Conference on Availability, Reliability and Security, ARES 2009, 16–19 March 2009, Fukuoka, Japan, pp. 433–440. IEEE Computer Society (2009). https://doi.org/10.1109/ARES.2009.95

31. Mödersheim, S.: Abstraction by set-membership: verifying security protocols and web services with databases. In: Al-Shaer, E., Keromytis, A.D., Shmatikov, V. (eds.) Proceedings of the 17th ACM Conference on Computer and Communications Security, CCS 2010, Chicago, Illinois, USA, 4–8 October 2010, pp. 351–360. ACM (2010). https://doi.org/10.1145/1866307.1866348

32. Mödersheim, S., Bruni, A.: AIF-ω: set-based protocol abstraction with countable families. In: Piessens, F., Viganò, L. (eds.) POST 2016. LNCS, vol. 9635, pp. 233–253. Springer, Heidelberg (2016). https://doi.org/10.1007/978-3-662-49635-0_12

33. Mödersheim, S., Viganò, L.: Secure pseudonymous channels. In: Backes, M., Ning, P. (eds.) ESORICS 2009. LNCS, vol. 5789, pp. 337–354. Springer, Heidelberg (2009). https://doi.org/10.1007/978-3-642-04444-1_21

34. W3C WS-CDL Working Group: Web services choreography description language version 1.0 (2004). http://www.w3.org/TR/ws-cdl-10/

How to Explain Security Protocols to Your Children

Véronique Cortier[1] and Itsaka Rakotonirina[2]([✉])

[1] Université de Lorraine, CNRS, Inria, LORIA, 54000 Nancy, France
[2] MPI-SP, 44799 Bochum, Germany
itsaka.rakotonirina@mpi-sp.org

Abstract. Security protocols combine two key components: a logical structure (who answers what, under which conditions?) as well as cryptography (encryption, signature, hash, ...). It is not so easy to explain their principles and weaknesses to a non expert audience. Why is something an attack or not? For which attacker? With what purpose?

In this paper, we propose an approach to introduce security protocols to a general audience, including children or even scientists from different fields. Its goal is to convey the implicit assumptions of our community, such as threat models or the participants' behaviour. This all-public introduction can be thought of as a story but, interestingly, can also be implemented physically with boxes and padlocks: manipulation helps to understand how protocols operate, even permitting non-expert participants to design their own—and thus to size the challenges of this task.

1 Introduction

How do you explain security protocols to your children? You would typically start with applications. "You see, security protocols are very useful. They are used in payment, 5G, in your messaging applications, biometric passport, and even voting." Yes, but how does it work? And here starts the complex part. You would need to explain a bit of *cryptography*, the expected behaviour of the participants, and how attackers can deviate from them. When giving examples of *attacks*— that is, the operating modes of malicious parties breaching the protection offered

This paper is dedicated to Joshua Guttman, on the occasion of his 66,66 birthday, with many thanks for his inspiring conversations.

to other users—we get recurring questions: but Bob can clearly see that he has been tricked into sending Alice's key in clear! Why doesn't he stop?

This paper describes a fictitious situation where Isabelle and Bob wish to exchange a cake while preventing the deliveryman from eating it. To this end, boxes and padlocks are used, acting as abstractions of various flavours of data encryption. The deliveryman thus represents the standard threat model in security protocols: an attacker who may see or block any package circulating on the network, who may as well create and inject messages of her own, but who cannot open encrypted messages without the corresponding keys. The objective of this story is to offer a glimpse of the subtleties of security—and of the unexpected turns of events that can arise when protecting deliveries with unbreakable padlocks. An early version has appeared on a popularisation website [19] (in French). And, of course, we have used it already in many talks and activities.

Our story progressively builds a protocol, alternating between the (playful) presentation of preliminary versions and attacks on them. It stops one step before obtaining the full Needham-Schroeder protocol [17]. Interestingly, this story can also be simulated physically, as an interactive puzzle using real boxes and padlocks. Manipulation helps understanding how protocols work, even permitting to non-expert participants to design their own protocol—often to see, to their surprise, that it can easily be breached. In our experience, this type of interaction helped general audiences to understand the pitfalls and challenges of the field, compared to a purely verbal presentation.

The images of this paper are under a creative commons licence (CC-BY-SA) so that you can reuse them on your own material. But we do not ship our boxes and padlocks.

2   Storyboard

Bob would like to buy a cake from a famous bakery run by Isabelle. The store being too far away to go in person, he orders a home delivery. Unfor-   tunately, the deliveryman is known for having a sweet tooth: he tends to compulsively eat the cakes he is supposed to deliver. It is a complex situation: Isabelle and Bob *need* the deliveryman, but they are also aware of the fact that *he cannot be trusted*. After discussing the issue over the phone, they realise that they both have *padlocks* at home: when using this unreliable postal service, they could put Isabelle's deliveries inside locked boxes to mitigate the risk of theft.

The issue is that Bob is not in possession of Isabelle's key, and thus cannot open her padlock; simply sealing the bakery's orders with it is therefore not a solution by itself. Maybe Isabelle could send the key later? But then the delivery person could get both the locked box and its key, rendering the protection ineffective.

2.1 Our First Security Protocol

A first solution is to combine the two padlocks as follows. Isabelle first places the cake in a box, locks it with her padlock, and sends the whole safe to Bob.

Of course, Bob is unable to open the box. Instead, he adds his own padlock and sends the box back to Isabelle. The safe is now locked by both padlocks.

Upon reception of the package, Isabelle removes her padlock and sends the box one final time to Bob.

Bob can finally remove his lock and get the cake. These three steps can be followed in order to send a cake while providing protection against malicious interferences; saying it differently, this is an example of a first security protocol! Let us call it V1. No keys were sent during the process and there was always at least one lock on each package given to the delivery person. Hence, he cannot eat Isabelle's cake... or can he? This statement is actually relying on implicit assumptions:

1. the deliveryman cannot open a padlocked box, and
2. he is *passive*, that is, he follows the delivery instructions he receives.

When designing a security protocol, in particular its *logical structure*, we typically assume secure building blocks such as the soundness of cryptography. In the case of encryption, it means assuming that the attacker cannot read an encrypted message unless he has the decryption key; in our story, this is the analogue of the deliveryman not being able to open locked boxes. However, what about the second assumption?

2.2 How the Postman Steals Isabelle's Cake

Actually, our first protocol is too weak against an *active* malicious deliveryman, that is, one who may deviate from the instructions Isabelle and Bob give him. Indeed, instead of delivering the box to Bob, he may add his own lock to the package and return it to Isabelle.

Isabelle does not know that the second padlock is not the one from Bob: the deliveryman's is just like any other. Therefore, Isabelle believes that everything is running as expected and proceeds with the next step of the protocol—that is, she removes her padlock.

The deliveryman may then unlock the box and eat the cake! This is a first example of an *attack*, against protocol V1: despite the locks, the deliveryman has a way to steal the cake. This did not require breaking any lock: it simply exploits a hole in the protocol's structure.

2.3 A Fix: Asymmetric Encryption

Without extra assumptions about the initial setting, it is actually impossible to design a protocol secure against an active attacker. Hence, Isabelle and her clients decide to subscribe to a large certification organisation with *public padlocks*:

- Each member of the organisation is given a personal, private key;
- Everyone can get from the organisation a padlock of a specific member.

Note that the deliveryman may also be part of the organisation like anyone: let us not prevent him from buying cakes to Isabelle without stealing them! With this organisation, there is now a simple protocol (V2): Isabelle places Bob's cake in a box and seals it with Bob's padlock, that she received from the organisation. Only Bob can open his padlock hence only Bob can get the cake.

In technical terms, this corresponds to asymmetric encryption and signature: everyone can encrypt a message with Bob's public key but only Bob can decrypt. One important issue is to be certain to use Bob's public key and not another one. Imagine for example that the deliveryman was able to make Isabelle believe that his own padlock is actually Bob's: he would again gain access to Bob's cake. This explains why public keys are typically *certified* by certification bodies and why, sometimes, your browser tells you that it cannot recognise a certificate—and hence that you should not trust the corresponding website.

2.4 Denial of Service?

In addition of having a sweet tooth, the deliveryman is also a sore loser: frustrated by such a simple but secure solution, he takes the locked box containing Bob's cake and throws it away instead of delivering it. In the Internet, a drop of one packet is not a real issue: the packet will be sent again as it is easy to keep a copy of it—at least it is much easier than re-baking a delicious cake. If an attacker tries to systematically block any packet sent by Isabelle, this forms what is called a *denial of service attack*. They are typically considered as out of scope of security protocols since they should be prevented by other means, at the network level; we therefore ignore them in our context.

3 When it Gets Really Dark

But this is not the end of the story. Bob has enemies as well as friends, and someone sends him a package with a poisoned cake and a message claiming it is a gift from Isabelle. Happy, Bob eats it, which reveals a critical weakness of the protocol: we can never be sure that the sender of a delivery is who he claims to be. When Bob returns from the hospital, he and Isabelle decide to update the delivery protocol to ensure some form of *authentication*.

3.1 Challenge and Respond

We assume that Isabelle and her client (here Bob) have obtained padlocks from the organisation. This time, the customer is the one initiating the protocol, writing on a piece of paper a (long) password that will be used to identify his order. He then sends it to Isabelle in a box sealed with her lock, and attaches a note with his own name so that Isabelle knows who to return the delivery to.

Upon receiving the box, Isabelle reads the customer's name on the note, opens the box with her key, puts the cake inside next to the paper with the password, and then seals it with the customer's padlock. She then has the package delivered.

The client checks that the cake is accompanied by the same password that he chose initially; if not, he can, say, destroys the cake. We call this new version V3. It is designed so that someone attempting to make Bob eat a poisoned cake would have to guess his password—which is considered to be impossible if it is long and unpredictable enough. This is an example of a widely-used technique, called *challenge-response*. Here, Bob challenges Isabelle to answer with his long, temporary, password. Only Isabelle can open her box, hence only Isabelle can respond with the correct password. Such a challenge-response technique is used in many protocols, such as EMV [9] or biometric passports [13].

So what do you think? Is the V3 protocol secure?

3.2   Man in the Middle Attack

Unfortunately there is yet another attack even on our reinforced version of the protocol. This is also what makes security protocols so interesting: without formal, rigorous security analyses, we often end up with such counter-intuitively broken protocols. The actual attack unfolds as follows. First of all, the protocol starts as usual: Bob places a password in a locked box and writes his name on it. On his side, the deliveryman orders a cake, then transmits Bob's order to Isabelle *but* replaces Bob's name by his own.

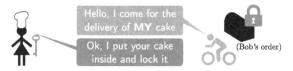

Isabelle follows the instructions of the protocol and places the cake in the safe, thinking that the password inside is from the deliveryman. She then closes the box *with the deliveryman's padlock*: this permits him to open it, poison the cake, and close it afterwards with Bob's lock.

The deliveryman then returns to Bob and gives him the poisoned delivery, pretending it is what Bob ordered from Isabelle. Bob believes it to be safe due to the presence of his password and eats the poisoned cake.

3.3   A Countermeasure

A countermeasure is to ask the customer to put his name *inside* the box, next to the password, to prevent the deliveryman from changing it. Actually, adding more information about identities inside boxes (or, inside ciphertexts in real protocols) is commonly considered as a good practice for similar reasons [1]. Calling this final version V4, it finally satisfies the expected property:

> *An active malicious delivery person can neither eat a cake sent to Bob, nor poison Bob if the latter only eats cakes he thinks are from Isabelle.*

Due to the attacks we exhibited on all successive versions of the protocol, you might be wary of that statement—as of any security statements you hear from today. The version V4 however deserves more trust than the previous ones, as its analysis has been backed up by formal, automated tools [18], thus mitigating the risk of unconsciously overlooking attack scenarios, or simply of inattention mistakes. Formal methods allow to *prove* that there is no attack, even when the deliveryman sends arbitrary packets, in any order. These techniques are applied more generally to security protocols to detect flaws and obtain enhanced guarantees. Some of them are based on strand spaces [11,12,22], Horn clauses [2], or constraint systems [20]; examples of such techniques can be found in the following survey book [8].

It is also interesting to note that protocol V4 corresponds to the first part of the Needham-Schroeder protocol [17], that has received in-depth academic scrutiny, including analyses in popular automated tools such as ProVerif [3], Tamarin [16], or Maude-NPA [10]. These tools continue to receive attention and improvements from the community up to this day [5,14], in parallel to the emergence of new techniques and analysers that with yet different approaches [4,6,7]. The attack on V3 is actually very similar to an attack found against the second part of the Needham-Schroeder protocol [15], also due to missing indications of Bob's identity. The description of many other protocols and attacks can be found in the reference book from Schneier [21].

4   A Practical Session

These stories can also be played "in real life": under the form of an interactive riddle, the protocols and their attacks are easier to understand. This also gives the opportunity for participants to design their own protocols, and thus to estimate the difficulty of the task. We explain here how we organise a practice session; we experimented with it on audiences from diverse backgrounds, ranging over children, teenagers, teachers, or adults of various ages and professional activities—and it basically works with anyone curious enough. Sessions usually last about 45 min, but can be adapted to 30 min or stretched to 1 h easily with minor adjustments. A good size for the group is about 10–15 participants, as they later need to be split into 2 or 3 smaller subgroups of 3–5 participants.

4.1   The Material

In short, a session requires the following material, discussed below:

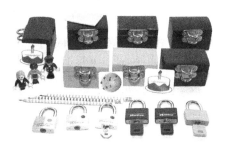

1. *boxes and padlocks*: ideally three should be available per subgroup;
2. *pens and post-its*, for the passwords of the challenge-response;
3. *small toys* to represent Isabelle, Bob, the deliveryman, the public-lock organisation, and the cakes.

Boxes can be crafted using cardboard paper; more advanced versions like the ones on the picture can be built with reasonable effort, using paintable wood chests (obtainable from hobby shops), where two metal rings are screwed (found in hardware shops, and through which padlocks can be closed to lock the boxes). It can also be fun to have various sizes of boxes to allow for "Russian dolls", that is, nested boxes that simulate several layers of encryption. As this is not necessary for solving the riddles presented here, this is simply a misleading pitfall. In our experience, providing such spurious mechanisms improves the imaginativeness of the participants, and is a good way of not guiding them too much towards the solution—making them understand that stacking all available ingredients does not necessary improve security as a result.

Regarding toys, you can just borrow them from your children or nephews. We typically use characters from a world-known brand but we did not get the permission to use them in official material or pictures. You may also use chess pieces or any wood token if you do not like gendered figurines.

4.2 A Typical Session

Part 1: Context. In a typical session, after a short introduction about the history of security and telecommunication, we follow the storyboard, using our boxes, padlocks and figurines to play the scenarios. First of all, we thus explain V1; then, before telling the attack, we ask two volunteers to come and play the protocol's roles themselves (one plays Isabelle, one Bob). This helps making sure everyone got enough time to understand the setting. Of course, *we* play the delivery person and attack the two volunteers as soon as we feel that the group is ready for it.

After explaining the notion of public locks and letting the audience find the (easy) protocol V2, we explain the new scenario: the deliveryman now wishes to poison Bob and we should find a protocol to protect him from such a disaster.

Part 2: Design. We then split the audience in 2 or 3 smaller groups and ask them to invent their own protocol for the above purpose. Each group receives material and has about 15 min for this activity. In the meantime, we regularly check on them to re-explain the goals and assumptions, or to clear misunderstandings. Recurring misconceptions are typically on the following aspects of the problem:

1. *The protocol design is not secret*: as a protocol is designed for everyone to use, we assume that everyone knows how it works—including the deliveryman. We thus deny assumptions such as "the deliveryman has no way to know Isabelle and Bob plan to do this" as soon as we overhear them.
2. *The attacker is unpredictable*: assumptions such as "if I do this, the attacker will think that, and he will therefore not do this action that would break my protocol" should also be denied by the animators.
3. *The attacker is ubiquitous*: it is not possible to keep the attacker busy somewhere else to avoid his interferences—for example by sending dummy boxes to another destination.

In our experience, younger children (10–12 years old) are more optimistic and happier with their protocol. Older ones better anticipate attacks and, as a result, may be more reluctant to propose their own design; it is usually helpful to encourage them to try anything as a starting point, to be improved step by step.

Part 3: Attacks. Then comes the time when each group explains its protocol to the rest of the participants. This leads to a friendly competition where each group tries to find attacks on the others. At this point, we consider that V3 is sufficient; more generally, we do not mention attacks that require the deliveryman to have accomplices among the clients. Interestingly, it is often the case that participants easily find attacks on other groups' protocols, while they struggle to find one against their own—even when it is deeply flawed or close to identical to another group's. It is then easy to convince them that designing TLS was not so easy.

Naturally, in case nobody finds an attack on a broken proposal, this is our task to find one (which requires to be comfortable with security analyses).

Part 4: Ending. The final part is up to you, the group, and the remaining time. One possibility is to go further into the protocol design and explain the attack on V3, present V4, and link them to real protocols that use challenge-response as a buliding block. If you feel like it, you can then continue with fancier protocols (voting, payment, passport, messaging...). Another direction is of course to talk about formal methods. At this stage, the participants are quite aware of the fact that it is difficult to design a protocol, and even more difficult to be convinced that there is no attack. They will expectedly be receptive to the message that we need rigorous techniques to *prove* that there is no flaw.

4.3   Long-Term Variants of the Design-Attack Parts (advanced)

Our experience is that even college students are receptive to this playful format. We therefore also investigated longer-term, more technical variants of the practical session, serving as a student project for introduction courses to security. One of the authors (Véronique Cortier), along with other teachers, has implemented it several years in a French engineering school, for the equivalent of third-year bachelor students. We outline in this section how this may be organised.

First of all, the Part 1 of the practical session (from the historical context to presenting the poison scenario) can be used as is to tease the overall course to the students. A couple of hours may then be spent in a more classical, academic manner to connect this game to practice: more technical definition of symmetric and asymmetric encryption, presentation of the Alice-Bob notation to specify protocols, or essentially any basic knowledge on security that the course is expected to convey. Once the students start having a minimal understanding of protocols and of a syntax to specify them, the actual project can be presented: it replaces the Parts 2 and 3 of the activity, and students will carry it out mostly out of class, in parallel to the course, under the form of an online competition.

1. Just as in Part 2 of the practical session, students form small groups and work on the design of protocol V4. A rudimentary online interface should allow each team to put their proposals in full view of all other students.
2. All along the project, as in Part 3, the goal of each team is to attack other team's protocols, in addition of proposing its owns. A scoring system is then designed to encourage playing the game; it should:

(a) reward finding attacks, all the more for attacks found quickly;
(b) reward proposing (new) protocols lasting long before an attack is found;
(c) *optional*: in case the course teaches the use of automated tools such as ProVerif or Tamarin, protocols coming with a formal analysis in one of these tools may be rewarded, just as attacks found using them;
(d) *advised*: influence the solutions to stay away from the V3/V4 protocols, which are usually found quickly, wasting the competition. We used a *cost function*: each operation (encrypting, decrypting, pairing...) has a determined cost, and the overall cost of a protocol induces a score penality, thus encouraging to avoid costly operations. It then suffices to smartly choose a cost function that spikes on V3/V4 and remains reasonably low otherwise. Our choice was to attribute a very high cost to encrypting a tuple of messages (which corresponds, in V3 for example, to putting two objects—the password and the cake—inside the same locked chest).

Of course, the competition should remain beneficial to the students to foster motivation and avoid despondency. We simply gave bonus points to the final exam to students depending on their rank in the competition. Dedicated grades could also be given, provided an honest investment secures a reasonable mark.

5 Conclusion: Have Fun!

We hope this paper and the associated activities can help explaining security protocols to a general audience and will be pursued with other ideas. At least, we had a lot of fun in all of our sessions!

Acknowledgments. We would like to thank Isabelle for her fantastic cakes at our cafeteria. It certainly fostered our motivation to work on security protocols. (and also to take a few naps.)

References

1. Abadi, M., Needham, R.: Prudent engineering practice for cryptographic protocols. IEEE Trans. Softw. Eng. **22**(1), 6–15 (1996)

2. Blanchet, B.: An efficient cryptographic protocol verifier based on prolog rules. In: Proceedings of the 14th Computer Security Foundations Workshop (CSFW'01). IEEE Computer Society Press (2001)

3. Blanchet, B.: Automatic verification of security protocols in the symbolic model: the verifier ProVerif. In: Aldini, A., Lopez, J., Martinelli, F. (eds.) FOSAD 2012-2013. LNCS, vol. 8604, pp. 54–87. Springer, Cham (2014). https://doi.org/10.1007/978-3-319-10082-1_3

4. Chadha, R., Cheval, V., Ciobâcă, Ş., Kremer, S.: Automated verification of equivalence properties of cryptographic protocols. ACM Trans. Comput. Logic (TOCL) **17**(4), 1–32 (2016).https://github.com/akiss/akiss

5. Cheval, V., Cortier, V., Turuani, M.: A little more conversation, a little less action, a lot more satisfaction: global states in proverif. In: 2018 IEEE 31st Computer Security Foundations Symposium (CSF), pp. 344–358. IEEE (2018)

6. Cheval, V., Kremer, S., Rakotonirina, I.: The deepsec prover. In: International Conference on Computer Aided Verification (CAV) (2018). https://deepsec-prover.github.io/

7. Cortier, V., Dallon, A., Delaune, S.: Sat-equiv: an efficient tool for equivalence properties. In: 2017 IEEE 30th Computer Security Foundations Symposium (CSF) (2017). https://projects.lsv.ens-paris-saclay.fr/satequiv/index.html

8. Cortier, V., Kremer, S. (eds.): Formal Models and Techniques for Analyzing Security Protocols, Cryptology and Information Security Series, vol. 5. IOS Press (2011)

9. EMVCo: Book1 - application independent ICC to terminal interface requirements. Technical report, (2011)

10. Escobar, S., Meadows, C., Meseguer, J.: A rewriting-based inference system for the NRL protocol analyzer and its meta-logical properties. Theor. Comput. Sci. **367**(1–2), 162–202 (2006)

11. Guttman, J.D.: Cryptographic protocol composition via the authentication tests. In: de Alfaro, L. (ed.) FoSSaCS 2009. LNCS, vol. 5504, pp. 303–317. Springer, Heidelberg (2009). https://doi.org/10.1007/978-3-642-00596-1_22

12. Guttman, J., Thayer, F.: Authentication tests and the structure of bundles. Theor. Comput. Sci. **283**, 333–380 (2001)

13. ICAO: Machine readable travel documents. Technical report, International Civil Aviation Organization (2006). doc 9303. Part 1

14. Jackson, D., Cremers, C., Cohn-Gordon, K., Sasse, R.: Seems legit: automated analysis of subtle attacks on protocols that use signatures. In: Proceedings of the 2019 ACM SIGSAC Conference on Computer and Communications Security (CCS), pp. 2165–2180 (2019)

15. Lowe, G.: Breaking and fixing the needham-schroeder public-key protocol using FDR. In: Margaria, T., Steffen, B. (eds.) TACAS 1996. LNCS, vol. 1055, pp. 147–166. Springer, Heidelberg (1996). https://doi.org/10.1007/3-540-61042-1_43

16. Meier, S., Schmidt, B., Cremers, C., Basin, D.: The TAMARIN prover for the symbolic analysis of security protocols. In: Sharygina, N., Veith, H. (eds.) CAV 2013. LNCS, vol. 8044, pp. 696–701. Springer, Heidelberg (2013). https://doi.org/10.1007/978-3-642-39799-8_48

17. Needham, R., Schroeder, M.: Using encryption for authentication in large networks of computers. Commun. ACM **21**(12), 993–999 (1978)

18. Rakotonirina, I.: Efficient verification of observational equivalences of cryptographic processes : theory and practice. Ph.D. thesis, Université de Lorraine (2021)

19. Rakotonirina, I.: Les livraisons dangereuses (2021). on Interstices (in French), https://interstices.info/les-livraisons-dangereuses/

20. Rusinowitch, M., Turuani, M.: Protocol insecurity with finite number of sessions is NP-complete. In: Proceedings of the 14th Computer Security Foundations Workshop (CSFW'01), pp. 174–190. IEEE Computer Society Press (2001)
21. Schneier, B.: Applied Cryptography Second Edition: Protocols, Algorithms, and Source Code in C. J. Wiley & Sons, Inc., Hoboken (1996)
22. Thayer, J., Herzog, J., Guttman, J.: Strand spaces: why is a security protocol correct? In: Proceedings of the IEEE Symposium on Security and Privacy. IEEE Computer Society Press (1998)

Verifying a Blockchain-Based Remote Debugging Protocol for Bug Bounty

Pierpaolo Degano[1,2]($\boxtimes$) , Letterio Galletta[2] , and Selene Gerali[1,2]

[1] Dipartimento di Informatica, Università di Pisa, Pisa, Italy
pierpaolo.degano@unipi.it, s.gerali@studenti.unipi.it
[2] IMT School for Advanced Studies, Lucca, Italy
letterio.galletta@imtlucca.it

Abstract. We address the problem of a mutual agreement between a bug bounty issuer and a bounty hunter in blockchain smart contracts. Our framework is VeriOSS, where a Proof of Knowledge protocol is used. Through it, the hunter communicates in clear increasingly large portions of the detected bug and gets back increasingly ample portions of the reward, provided that the issuer considers the received information plausible. The process is iterated until the entire bug is revealed and the entire reward given. We formalize this protocol using the Applied Pi-calculus and we apply ProVerif to it so as to verify its correctness, i.e., that only the relevant information and the corresponding reward are exchanged and that the integrity and the authenticity of the communications is granted.

Keywords: Bug bounty · Protocol verification · Remote debugging

1 Introduction

Most of Joshua D. Guttman's research contributions are on the field of security in particular, on cryptographic protocol modeling and verification. His contributions deeply influenced us, among which the most inspiring has been his work on *Strand Spaces* [15,16] supporting the verification tool CPSA [1]; on information flow verification on SELinux policies [11]; on firewall configuration [3]; and the column on security of the Bulletin of EATCS [10]. It has been a great pleasure and a rare privilege meeting and working with Joshua and writing this little essay in which we follow some of his scientific lines.

Recently, software developers resorted to the large community of the network for help in spotting bugs in their products. To do that, developers and also vendors offer public rewards to those who detect flaws and contribute to fix them, so launching what are called *bug bounty* programs.

This work has been partially supported by IMT PAI Project *VeriOSS*, and by the MIUR project PRIN 2017FTXR7S *IT MATTERS (Methods and Tools for Trustworthy Smart Systems)*.

D. Dougherty et al. (Eds.): Guttman Festschrift, LNCS 13066, pp. 124–138, 2021.
https://doi.org/10.1007/978-3-030-91631-2_7

In such a collective debugging, a *bounty issuer* offers a reward to any *bounty hunter* who discovers a bug. The offered reward usually depends on the type and criticality of the bug and it is paid in change of the information for reproducing it.

Bug bounty programs are subject to numerous challenges. Current programs hardly protect issuers and hunters from a dishonest party. On the one hand, hunters have to prove that they actually discovered a bug, but a dishonest issuer can take this information and yet she can deny or downgrade the reward. On the other hand, a dishonest hunter may provide a false bug to an issuer and cash the reward.

These challenges make the bounty market inefficient. Hunters are pushed to look for other opportunities to sell bugs, such as gray and black markets.[1] On their side, issuers are forced to carefully inspect the validity of the reported bugs, since it is not infrequent that forged bugs are submitted, e.g., in 2016 the majority of the security reports received by Google were considered invalid.[2]

Recently, a blockchain-based platform for bug bounties, called VeriOSS, has been proposed as a tool to increase the fairness and the efficiency of the bounty markets [6]. Reputation also plays a crucial role, and the integrity properties of the blockchain ensure that any cheating attempt is recorded and made publicly visible to all. One of the main components of the platform VeriOSS is a bug disclosure protocol, arbitrated by a smart contract.

The protocol starts from a bounty issuer publishing a smart contract on the blockchain. This contract contains a precise characterization of the eligible bugs together with the offered reward. When a bounty hunter claims the reward, she must call the smart contract and provide enough information to check the eligibility of the bug without revealing all the details for reproducing it. The blockchain arbitrates then a remote debugging protocol between the bounty issuer and the bounty hunter that, if successful, leads her to fully disclose the bug and the issuer to pay the reward. The protocol consists of a challenge-response loop, where at each step, the issuer proposes a challenge to the hunter that she can only solve if she actually knows the bug. To solve the challenge the hunter has to disclose parts of the execution trace that reproduces the bug. In exchange, the issuer pays a fraction of the total reward through the smart contract.

Note that the issuer can decide not to start or to interrupt the challenge-response loop, e.g., if the bug is already known or it is or seems of no interest. Similarly, the hunter can leave protocol because she is cheating and does not care about her reputation.

Since the security of VeriOSS strictly depends on the challenge-response protocol, it is crucial to study the behaviour of its key components for a correct functioning of the bug bounty market. To achieve that, in this paper we for-

---

[1] The activities occurring on gray and black markets are hard to document, however, some leaked emails give a glimpse on these markets. See https://tsyrklevich.net/2015/07/22/hacking-team-0day-market/.

[2] https://sites.google.com/site/bughunteruniversity/behind-the-scenes/charts/2016.

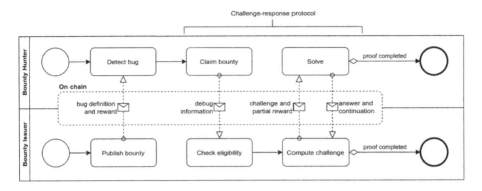

Fig. 1. The workflow of the VeriOSS protocol in the case success. The initiator is the Bounty Issuer.

malize this protocol using the Applied Pi-Calculus [2] and we study its security properties using the ProVerif analyzer [4]. More in detail, we focus here on message integrity and on authenticity of communications. This is because the bounty market as well as the execution of the protocol are to be publicly accountable by any participant. Therefore, we make sure that the issuer and the hunter are actually those who published the bounty and claimed the reward. We also verify that when the execution of the protocol reaches some predefined checkpoints, the participants have performed certain required actions in the correct order.

This paper is structured as follows. We first survey VeriOSS in Sect. 2, and then we formalize it using the Applied-Pi Calculus in Sect. 3. The verification in ProVerif is in Sect. 4. Section 5 discusses the relevant literature and draws some conclusions.

2 Background: VeriOSS

In this section we briefly recall the main components of VeriOSS and how they interact. We refer the reader to [6] for a full account of the design and description of the protocol. Briefly, VeriOSS has two goals: (*i*) support an honest bounty hunter BH in collecting a reward under the assumption of an untrusted bounty issuer BI; and (*ii*) protect BI against untrusted BHs claiming an undeserved reward. In particular, VeriOSS achieves these two goals by (*i*) requiring BI to provide a precise description of the eligible bugs; and (*ii*) driving the BH in disclosing the bug and claiming for the reward.

2.1 Workflow Overview

The general workflow of VeriOSS is in Fig. 1. Initially, the bounty issuer BI publishes a bounty on the blockchain. The bounty contains information about the type of bugs BI is interested in, and the reward offered. The bugs are classi-fied according to some standards, e.g., the Common Vulnerability Scoring System[3] and the Common Weaknesses Enumeration.[4] When the bounty hunter BH detects a bug that complies with the issued bounty, she can claim the reward. To do so, BH carries out a commitment by sending to the smart contract some initial debug information containing some meta-data about the bug and a (hash of the) faulty execution trace. The information on the trace is obfuscated in such a way that BI cannot find out where the bug is but only check the eligibility of the bug. For instance, the bug description may consist of the kind of error and of some high level information about the buggy state at the end of the exe-cution trace, e.g., a partial documentation that the program crashes because of segmentation faults. Before starting the actual protocol the issuer checks if the bug committed by the hunter is not duplicated and decides if it is worth paying for it. Note that the eligibility step is fundamental to prevent those situations where a malicious hunter tries to deceive the issuer proposing already solved bugs (replay attacks).

Once the issuer decided that the bug is eligible, an iterative challenge-response protocol starts, whose goal is to protect both participants: it prevents BI to pay for forged bugs, and at the same time ensures that BH is paid for her work. At each iteration of the protocol loop, BI synthesizes a challenge for BH to test her knowledge of the buggy trace at a specific step. If BH solves the challenge, she receives a partial reward (expressed as a fraction of the total one) and she provides information to continue the disclosure loop. Eventually, the protocol terminates when either the bug is entirely disclosed, so completing the proof, or one of the participants withdraws.

2.2   Challenge-Response Interaction

VeriOSS uses a sort of Proof of Knowledge (PoK) protocol, that is also called Σ-protocol [12]. A standard PoK consists of a prover and a verifier interact-ing through a challenge-response process, and the two parties play *both* roles. Instead, our protocol is slightly asymmetric, because BH must prove she knows the bug and BI must prove she is willing to pay the reward.

We call this protocol *Pay-per-Knowledge* (P2K) and it is an instance of a *two-party fair exchange* protocol [13]. A peculiar feature of this kind of protocols is that the two parties either achieve their individual goals *together* or they both fail. Reaching the goals simultaneously is not mandatory because, e.g., a party could receive the other's knowledge while providing an *effective commitment* to release her own knowledge within a certain time.

Typically, P2K relies on a trusted third party to mediate between the two par-ticipants, and VeriOSS implements it through a smart contract on a blockchain. The smart contract carries out a specific task when certain conditions are satis-fied, in our case when a participant knows the answer to a challenge.

---

[3] https://www.first.org/cvss/specification-document.

[4] https://cwe.mitre.org/cwss/cwss_v1.0.1.html.

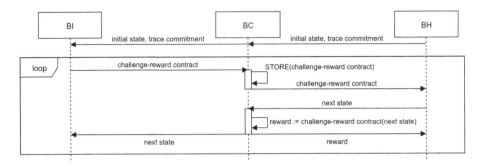

Fig. 2. The P2K protocol message sequence diagram.

The message flow in the P2K bounty claim protocol is shown in Fig. 2. The bug disclosure is a sort of remote debugging process replicating the execution of a buggy program trace. The protocol starts with BH claiming the bounty: she describes the bug without fully disclosing it, and commits the obfuscated debug trace, storing it in the blockchain BC. Actually, the commitment contains the hash of the program states appearing in the trace. Note that this hash ensures that a dishonest BH can neither craft a faked trace nor diverge from the protocol execution.

The challenge-response loop is as follows. The issuer BI stores a *challenge-reward* smart contract on the blockchain BC. The input of the smart contract is the answer to the challenge submitted by BI. In particular, the solution of the challenge is a program state from which the buggy state is reachable after a certain number of steps. Then BH submits a program state to the smart contract: if her answer correctly solves the challenge, and at the same time it is consistent with the trace committed at the beginning, then BH can collect the partial reward. Note that BI can access the submitted state since the blockchain content is public. The loop is repeated by replacing the buggy state with the state provided by BH. Eventually, the loop terminates when BH provides the initial state of the trace or one of the parties withdraws from the protocol.

2.3 Remote Debugging, and Challenge Generation and Solution

The challenge-response protocol described above implements a sort of *remote debugging* process, because the target program runs on a different location, e.g., a remote host. Under our assumptions, the hunter executes the target program and the issuer debugs it. However, P2K differs from the (standard, forward) remote debugging process because it proceeds backwards: the debugging starts from a (buggy) final state and proceeds towards an initial state, in a *reverse debugging* style.

In general, reverse debugging may disclose the whole buggy execution trace in an early stage, so failing to protect the hunter: in other words, BI might infer the initial state without interacting with BH. To address this issue, the hunter only partially reveals the current debug state.

Roughly, the challenge consists in finding a boolean assignment to a formula $\mathcal{F}$ representing the program state σ that precedes the current state σ', in the style of *weakest precondition* [8]. To solve the challenge, both σ and σ' must belong to the execution trace initially committed by the hunter BH.

It is well-known that finding the required boolean assignment to the formula $\mathcal{F}$ is NP-complete [14]. Nevertheless, this is not a problem here: a honest hunter already knows a solution to the challenge, that is the program state that she has committed. Solving the challenge is indeed feasible, and consists in evaluating $\mathcal{F}$ with the boolean assignment provided by the hunter.

Example 1. We clarify how VeriOSS works through a toy example, taken from [6]. Consider a issuer that is interested in understanding if there is a bug in the following C function:

```
float foo(unsigned char c) {
    float z = 255/(c+1);
    return 1.0/z;
}
```

The issuer publishes a bounty on the blockchain proposing a certain amount of money as reward for any bug that makes the function returns an invalid value.

An hunter can find out that in the code above there is a division by zero when c = 255. Indeed, in this case z gets assigned the result of the integer division 255/256, which is 0. Thus, the execution of the return statement makes the function to return an invalid value. More precisely, the final state reached when c = 255 is $\sigma = [\mathsf{z} \hookleftarrow 0, \mathsf{c} \hookleftarrow 255, foo_r \hookleftarrow \mathtt{inf}]$, where foo_r represents the value returned by the function. Of course, if the hunter publishes an execution trace ending in σ with no obfuscation, the input triggering the bug is trivially exposed.

We now describe how the challenge response protocol can be used to reveal the bug; two steps suffice. Since the state σ refers to the completion of the execution of the function, the hunter sends a trace ending in the state $\sigma_r = [foo_z \hookleftarrow \mathtt{inf}]$, i.e., σ projected on the returned value of the function. In this way, the issuer sees that an invalid value is actually returned, but (in principle) she does not know which input causes the mistake. However, the issuer can realize that the computation failed because the value of z is incorrect, and that this can only happen when its value is 0. Thus, she uses this information to construct a challenge for the hunter. Since the predicate z = 0 holds after the instruction `float z = 255/(c+1)`, the precondition for this last statement is a predicate P that implies $z = 0$ Also, since $z = 255/(\mathsf{c}+1)$ we have that P implies $255/(\mathsf{c}+1) = 0$. Moreover, due to the semantics of the integer division operator in C this condition is equivalent to P implies $\mathsf{c} \geq 255$. Thus, the issuer's challenge for the hunter is: Provide me with a partial trace ending in a state which satisfies the predicate c ≥ 255.

The hunter can easily solve this challenge by supplying a trace made of a single state where $[c \hookleftarrow 255]$. At the end of the interaction, the issuer has the value causing the bug and the hunter will receive her reward.

3   Protocol Encoding

We assume the reader familiar with the Applied Pi-calculus [2] that we use to formalize the P2K protocol. It consists of the parallel composition of six processes, as displayed in Fig. 5. The first three specify the blockchain, the bounty issuer and the bounty hunter, dubbed BC, BI and BH, respectively. The others are dubbed BI' and BH' and roughly act as continuations of BI and BH; as we will see in Fig. 5, they express the challenge-response loop and have a recursive definition through the replication operator "!". There is also a further auxiliary process, BC', the continuation of BC.

We assume that the communications between BC and BI (BH, respectively) take place on the channel c_{IC} (c_{HC}, respectively); the same channels are also used by their three continuations. Also, we assume to have a digital signature system that generates a pair of public and secret keys for a process X through the functions $pk(X)$ and $sk(X)$, respectively. In our case, the issuer has the pair K_{PI}, K_{SI} of public and private keys, and so have the blockchain and the hunter, referred to as K_{PC}, K_{SC} and as K_{PH}, K_{SH}, respectively.

In the Applied Pi-calculus specification we use the following notation, predicates and two abbreviations, the first for non-deterministic choice, not present in this calculus, and the second for the abridged conditional:

- the names E, T, C, N, Z, S, R, M are constants used as special messages: E for when a process abandons the protocol; T for when the protocol terminates successfully; C represents the initial contract; N signals the successful publication of a contract; Z is the notification of a claimed bug; S is a contract representing an intermediate challenge; R is an answer to a challenge S; and M is a partial reward;
- $\{msg\}_K$ indicates that the message msg has been signed by the owner of the private the key K;
- $[\{C\}_K, x]_{K^{-1}}$ besides checking if the cyphertext C equals $\{msg\}_K$, this predicate has the additional effect of substituting the plaintext msg for the variable x occurring in the process P it prefixes; otherwise, the process attempting decryption gets stuck. When the variable x is immaterial we feel free to use "$\_$".
- $valid(x)$ is a predicate that holds if and only if (i) the issuer verifies that x is a valid debug (sub-)trace or (ii) the blockchain verifies correct the answer of the hunter to a given challenge; we omit here some technical details, e.g., that the debug sub-trace is obfuscated through a hash function and that the verification step uses further data not mentioned here;
- $exit(y)$ is a predicate that holds if and only if the participant y notifies that he is going to abandon the protocol;
- $terminated(P2K)$ is a predicate that holds if and only if the protocol is successfully terminated, i.e., if the bounty issuer knows the initial state of the bugged program, because the hunter correctly answered all the challenges;
- $P + Q \triangleq (\nu a)(\bar{a}\langle m \rangle \cdot 0 \mid a(x) \cdot P \mid a(x) \cdot Q)$, where a and m are fresh names, i.e., occurring free neither in P nor in Q, the first denoting a channel and the second a dummy message.

$$BI \triangleq \overline{c_{IC}}\langle\{C\}_{K_{SI}}\rangle \cdot c_{IC}(n) \cdot [n, \_]_{K_{PC}} \cdot c_{IC}(y) \cdot [y, p]_{K_{PC}} \cdot \text{if valid}(p) \text{ then } BI'$$

$$BC \triangleq c_{IC}(c) \cdot [c, \_]_{K_{PI}} \cdot \overline{c_{IC}}\langle\{N\}_{K_{SC}}\rangle \cdot \overline{c_{HC}}\langle\{N\}_{K_{SC}}\rangle \cdot c_{HC}(z) \cdot [z, y]_{K_{PH}} \cdot \overline{c_{IC}}\langle\{y\}_{K_{SC}}\rangle \cdot BC'$$

$$BH \triangleq c_{HC}(n) \cdot [n, \_]_{K_{PC}} \cdot \overline{c_{HC}}\langle\{Z\}_{K_{SH}}\rangle \cdot BH'$$

Fig. 3. The specification of the bounty issuer BI, the blockchain BC, and the bounty hunter BH.

$$BI' \triangleq \overline{c_{IC}}\langle\{S\}_{K_{SI}}\rangle \cdot c_{IC}(n) \cdot [n, \_]_{K_{PC}} \cdot c_{IC}(t) \cdot [t, \_]_{K_{PC}} \cdot 0$$

$$BC' \triangleq c_{IC}(s) \cdot [s, \_]_{K_{PI}} \cdot \overline{c_{IC}}\langle\{N\}_{K_{SC}}\rangle \cdot \overline{c_{HC}}\langle\{N\}_{K_{SC}}\rangle \cdot c_{HC}(r) \cdot [r, t]_{K_{PH}} \cdot$$
$$\text{if valid}(t) \text{ then } \overline{c_{HC}}\langle\{M\}_{K_{SC}}\rangle \cdot \overline{c_{IC}}\langle\{t\}_{K_{SC}}\rangle \cdot 0$$

$$BH' \triangleq c_{HC}(n) \cdot [n, \_]_{K_{PC}} \cdot \overline{c_{HC}}\langle\{R\}_{K_{SH}}\rangle \cdot c_{HC}(m) \cdot [m, \_]_{K_{PC}} \cdot 0$$

Fig. 4. The continuations BI', BC' and BH' of the bounty issuer, the blockchain, and the bounty hunter.

- if *guard* then $P \triangleq$ "if *guard* then P else 0"

The processes that define the initial behaviour of the participants are in Fig. 3. Intuitively, through a send the issuer BI stores the smart contract C in the blockchain BC that in turn notifies (via the message N) both the issuer (the key used to sign is K_{SI}) and the hunter BH that the contract has been published. Note that the publication of C only succeeds if the sender is indeed BI and has correctly signed C. Upon reception of N, the hunter BH sends the piece of information about the claimed faulty trace to the issuer via the blockchain. The issuer first verifies if the message has been signed by the hunter, and then checks its validity. Then, the challenge-response loop starts by running the continuations of the three processes above.

We now comment on Fig. 4 that displays the continuations BI', BC' and BH' of the bounty issuer, the blockchain, and the bounty hunter. The first process stores in the blockchain a new challenge S, signed with his private key; it receives a notice N from BC'; it verifies the signature; later on it receives a partial trace R of the program (from BH' via the contract in BC') and stores it in t after checking its signature. The continuation BC' of the blockchain receives the new challenge in s; it verifies that the challenge has been signed by the issuer; it sends the signed acknowledge to both BI' and BH'; it receives a candidate solution to the challenge from BH' (stored in t), and it checks its signature; if t is a valid solution, BC' sends a (partial) reward to the hunter and the solution to the issuer. Finally, the hunter receives the notice from the blockchain and verifies the signature; it signs the new response R, and waits for the (partial) reward.

The process formalizing the whole P2K protocol is in Fig. 5. It consists of six components: the first three processes define the initial behaviour of the participants, namely of BI, BC and BH. The other three processes perform some non-deterministic choices, each including the continuations BI', BC' and BH'. They replicate their behaviour, so implementing the challenge-response loop of the P2K protocol. More precisely, the fourth process behaves as BI' or it

$BI \mid BC \mid BH \mid$

$\quad (!(BI' + \overline{c_{IC}}\langle\{E\}_{K_{SI}}\rangle \cdot 0 + \overline{c_{IC}}\langle\{T\}_{K_{SI}}\rangle \cdot 0 + c_{IC}(a) \cdot [a, \_]_{K_{PC}} \cdot 0) \mid$

$\quad\quad !(BC' + c_{IC}(f) \cdot [f, g]_{K_{PC}} \cdot \text{if } (\text{exit}(g) \text{ } or \text{ terminated } (g)) \text{then } \overline{c_{HC}}\langle\{g\}_{K_{SC}}\rangle \cdot 0 +$

$\quad\quad\quad c_{HC}(f) \cdot [f, g]_{K_{PH}} \cdot \text{if exit}(g) \text{ then } \overline{c_{HC}}\langle\{g\}_{K_{SC}}\rangle \cdot 0) \mid$

$\quad\quad !(BH' + \overline{c_{HC}}\langle\{E\}_{K_{SH}}\rangle \cdot 0 + c_{HC}(a) \cdot [a, \_]_{K_{PC}} \cdot 0)$

$\quad)$

Fig. 5. The specification of the protocol P2K. It consists of three processes that initiate the protocol and of three processes that replicate themselves and implement the challenge-response loop.

outputs either the constant E or T, signed with its secret key K_{SI}; through these constants this process communicates the blockchain either its intention to abandon the protocol or a successful termination. In the last alternative, the fourth is receiving from the hunter a response for the current challenge, or the signal of abandoning the protocol, both duly signed. The fifth process has three alternatives, the first of which is the continuation BC'. The second non-deterministic choice receives from the issuer a signed message that is decrypted and forwarded to the sixth process, provided that it is a notification of either abandon or termination, namely E or T. The third alternative receives from the hunter a message when it is about to abandon the protocol, and forwards the constant E to the issuer. The sixth and last process either behaves as BH', or it abandons the protocol by sending the blockchain the message E, or it receives the reward for the portion of bug revealed.

4   Verification in ProVerif

Here, we describe the security analysis of the P2Kprotocol through the tool ProVerif [4]. Since the ProVerif specification is obtained by a simple one-to-one translation of the processes described in Sect. 3, we omit it here; the interested reader can find it online.[5]

Where the Blockchain Helps. Before presenting the properties we study using ProVerif, it is worth noticing that there are some assurances that our protocol inherits from the blockchain and that we do not explicitly consider in our analysis. In particular, we can neglect some attacks that are already prevented by a typical blockchain system. For example, we do not explicitly consider a hunter-in-the-middle attack, where an attacker publishes on the blockchain a smart contract pretending to be a certain issuer, because this is already prevented by the integrity and authenticity properties of the blockchain. Since these properties rely on the fact that the private key of issuers remain secret, below we only verify that the attacker never learns it. Also, one relies on the blockchain to

---

[5] https://github.com/Selene15/P2K_ProVerif.

guarantee that messages are fresh. Finally, note that two different issuers may publish bounties that may intersect, i.e., for the same bugs and in the same software. This may happen, e.g., for an open source software that is used by different company but developed mainly by volunteers. We consider this situation legit and falls within the market mechanisms: hunters will sell bugs to the best bidder.

Expressing Corresponding Assertions. Since the execution of the protocol is required to be publicly accountable by any node of the blockchain, we do not ensure confidentiality of the communications between participants. Instead, we check authentication properties that are fundamental for a correct functioning of the bug bounty market. We need to make sure that the actual issuer is who publishes a given bounty. The same identity assurance should also hold when a hunter claims she found a bug and wants a reward. As usual, these authentication properties are expressed by using correspondence assertions [17]. Corresponding assertions are also used to verify that the participants have performed certain required actions in the correct order, when the execution of the protocol reaches some predefined checkpoints. Verifying that the execution of the protocol reaches these checkpoints in the correct state is fundamental to be confident that no misbehavior is overlooked and that the design of the protocol is correct.

To specify these properties in ProVerif we exploit the notion of *event*. Intuitively, events are emitted when the execution of the protocol reaches specific checkpoints during the verification process. Below we list the events used in our specification and their intuition:

- `startChallenge` signals the beginning of the challenge-response loop, it is therefore emitted every time the process BI' starts;
- `traceValid` marks that the issuer BI has accepted the trace submitted by BH as valid;
- `sendRewardBH` denotes that BC' paid the partial reward due for an intermediate challenge;
- `challengeResolved` occurs when BC' successfully checks the answer provided by BH' to the current challenge;
- `notifyChallengeBH` shows that the blockchain BC' has notified the other participants of the publication of a new challenge;
- `publicChallengeReward` records that the challenge and the associated reward have been published on the blockchain;
- `sendNewState` signals that BH' submits a new program state as solution of the challenge;
- `notifyChallengeReceived` indicates that BH' has been notified of a new challenge published on the blockchain;
- `notifyStateBI` occurs when BC' notifies BI' that the challenge has been correctly solved;
- `BIends` denotes a clean termination of the protocol for the issuer;
- `BIleaves` (`BHleaves`, respectively) signals that the issuer (the hunter, respectively) has abandoned the protocol;

- BCinterruptedForBH (BCinterruptedForBI, respectively) denotes that BC' received the notification of clean or not clean termination of the hunter (the issuer, respectively);
- BIterminated expresses that the issuer terminates the protocol;
- params_equal occurs when the number of the submitted solutions equals the number of the proposed challenges.

Verification of Properties. The properties that we want to verify on our protocol are expressed by using the *query* mechanism of ProVerif, which are of two kinds: reachability and correspondence assertion queries.

The reachability queries mainly concern with the knowledge of the attacker and have the following form

```
query attacker(t);
```

where t is a term. Intuitively the query verifies the secrecy of t, i.e., it holds when the attacker cannot learn it. Since we want to ensure message integrity and authenticity, we require that the messages exchanged by the participants are all signed through their private keys and that the attacker does not know them. To verify these properties, we submit to ProVerif the following queries about the attacker knowledge:

```
query attacker(ksi);   // ksi is issuer's private key
      attacker(ksh);   // ksh is hunter's private key
      attacker(ksc).   // ksc is blockchain's private key
```

All these queries get a positive answer, so proving that the messages exchanged by the P2K protocol satify the integrity and authenticity requirements. The bottom part of Fig. 7 shows the output of ProVerif.

The corresponding assertion queries verify that certain events have occurred when the execution of the protocol reaches some predefined checkpoints. These queries have the form

$$e_1 \&\& e_2 \&\& \ldots \&\& e_n \Rightarrow e$$

and intuitively they are satisfied when for each occurrence of the event e all the events e_i have previously occurred. ProVerif also supports injective events (denoted by the keyword inj-event) that express a one-to-one relationship. Below, we list the queries we have used, with an intuition about their meaning:

- event(startChallenge)⇒event(traceValid) makes sure that the challenge-response loop only starts after the reception of a valid trace;
- event(sendRewardBH)⇒event(challengeResolved) guarantees that the hunter receives the partial reward only when her solution to the challenge has been verified by the smart contract on the blockchain;
- event(notifyChallengeBH)⇒event(publicChallengeReward) requires that the blokchain has notified the hunter every time the issuer has deposited the reward on the smart contract;

```
let processT =
  in ( counter , ( i : nat , j : nat ));
  if ( i = j ) then
    event params_equal ;
    in ( counter , l : bitstring );
    let x : bitstring = l in
    if ( x = challenge ) then
      out ( counter ,( i +1 , j ));
    if ( x = response ) then
      out ( counter ,( i , j +1)).
```

Fig. 6. The counter process

- `event(sendNewState)⇒event(notifyChallengeReceived)` ensures that the hunter sends her solution to the challenge only after the issuer has deposited the reward on the smart contract;
- `event(notifyStateBI)⇒event(sendRewardBH)` guarantees that the issuer is notified of the publication of the next trace state, only after the smart contract has sent the reward to the hunter;
- `inj-event(BIends) && event(BCinterruptedForBI)⇒inj-event(BHleaves)` makes sure that if the hunter leaves the protocol then she cannot receive the reward any longer, and consequently the issuer ends the protocol;
- `event(BCinterruptedBH)⇒event(BIleaves)` checks that if the issuer leaves the protocol then she cannot receive further states of the trace (note that the hunter in turn ends the protocol);
- `event(BIterminated)⇒event(params_equal)` requires that the hunter has solved all the challenges proposed by the issuer when the protocol terminates correctly.

For technical reasons, in our specification we introduce an auxiliary process, called processT, that models and expresses the properties of the last query above. Intuitively, this additional process implements a counter that keeps the number of published challenges, dubbed i, and the number of those that have been correctly solved, dubbed j. Figure 6 shows the definition of processT that has the private channel counter. Through this channel we keep track of the number of challenges i and of the answers j, updated whenever new challenges or new states are received from the blockchain; note that the process BC' is accordingly modified to accomodate this little technical extension. When challenges and correct solutions to them match in pair, the event params_equal is fired.

The upper part of Fig. 7 shows that ProVerif successfully proved all the corresponding assertion queries proving the authentication properties of the P2K protocol.

```
--------------------------------------------------------------
Verification summary:

Query event(startChallenge) ==> event(traceValid) is true.

Query event(sendRewardBH) ==> event(challengeResolved) is true.

Query event(notifyChallengeBH) ==> event(publicChallengeReward) is true.

Query event(sendNewState) ==> event(notifyChallengeReceived) is true.

Query event(notifyStateBI) ==> event(sendRewardBH) is true.

Query event(BIends) && event(BCinterruptedForBI) ==> event(BHleaves) is true.

Query event(BCinterruptedForBH) ==> event(BIleaves) is true.

Query event(BIterminated) ==> event(params_equal) is true.

Query not attacker(ksi[]) is true.

Query not attacker(ksh[]) is true.

Query not attacker(ksc[]) is true.
--------------------------------------------------------------
```

Fig. 7. Summary of the verification task performed by ProVerif on authentication and integrity properties of P2K

5   Conclusion

We have considered the P2K protocol of VeriOSS, a recent proposal for establishing a fair bug bounty market exploiting the blockchain [6]. We have formalized the protocol using the Applied Pi-Calculus and we have verified its authenticity and integrity using the ProVerif security analyzer. This have ensured us that the issuer and the hunter are actually those who published the bounty and claimed the reward. We also have verified that the participants have performed certain required actions in the correct order.

We follow here the line of formal verification of cryptographic protocol in the symbolic model. The literature on this topic is very large and we only refer the interested reader to a couple of surveys [5,7]. The VeriOSS protocol addresses a problem similar to the one addressed by the fair exchange protocols. These are multi-parties protocol where participants want to exchange assets in a fair way, i.e., no participant gives anything away unless she gets everything she wants. There have been a great deal of work in the crytography community for defining and studying the security of these protocols, and we refer the reader to the literature for an analysis [9,13]. The main difference our setting and the setting of fair exchange is that in VeriOSS the information released by the hunter should be carefully selected. More specifically, we need to prevent the issuer from reproducing a bug before the hunter reveals the whole execution trace, so that she can obtain the expected reward.

We plan to extend our work along different directions. A first refining of our model will make it more adherent to implementations that delegate oracles to perform parts of computations that are too expensive. For example, storing the information about the obfuscated execution is quite demanding, and thus infeasible to be carried on by the blockchain. A further extension concerns studying if concurrent executions of the VeriOSS protocol will preserve its correctness. Besides ProVerif also CPSA can help in automatically verifying authentication and integrity of parallel sessions.

References

1. Cpsa: Crptographic protocol shapes analyzer. https://github.com/mitre/cpsa, Accessed May 2021
2. Abadi, M., Blanchet, B., Fournet, C.: The applied pi calculus: mobile values, new names, and secure communication. J. ACM **65**(1), 1:1–1:41 (2018)
3. Adão, P., Focardi, R., Guttman, J.D., Luccio, F.L.: Localizing firewall security policies. In: IEEE 29th Computer Security Foundations Symposium, CSF 2016, Lisbon, Portugal, 27 June–1 July 2016, pp. 194–209. IEEE Computer Society (2016). https://doi.org/10.1109/CSF.2016.21
4. Blanchet, B.: An efficient cryptographic protocol verifier based on prolog rules. In: 14th IEEE Computer Security Foundations Workshop (CSFW-14 2001), pp. 82–96. IEEE Computer Society (2001)
5. Blanchet, B.: Modeling and verifying security protocols with the applied pi calculus and proverif. Found. Trends Priv. Secur. **1**(1–2), 1–135 (2016)
6. Canidio, A., Costa, G., Galletta, L.: VeriOSS: using the blockchain to foster bug bounty programs. In: Anceaume, E., Bisière, C., Bouvard, M., Bramas, Q., Casamatta, C. (eds.) 2nd International Conference on Blockchain Economics, Security and Protocols, Tokenomics 2020. OASIcs, vol. 82, pp. 6:1–6:14. Schloss Dagstuhl - Leibniz-Zentrum für Informatik (2020)
7. Cortier, V., Kremer, S.: Formal models and techniques for analyzing security protocols: a tutorial. Found. Trends Program. Lang. **1**(3), 151–267 (2014)
8. Dijkstra, E.W.: A Discipline of Programming, vol. 613924118. Prentice-hall, Englewood Cliffs (1976)
9. Franklin, M., Tsudik, G.: Secure group barter: multi-party fair exchange with semi-trusted neutral parties. In: Hirchfeld, R. (ed.) FC 1998. LNCS, vol. 1465, pp. 90–102. Springer, Heidelberg (1998). https://doi.org/10.1007/BFb0055475
10. Guttman, J.D.: A new column: information security. Bull. EATCS **82**, 242–252 (2004)
11. Guttman, J.D., Herzog, A.L., Ramsdell, J.D., Skorupka, C.W.: Verifying information flow goals in security-enhanced linux. J. Comput. Secur. **13**(1), 115–134 (2005). http://content.iospress.com/articles/journal-of-computer-security/jcs230
12. Hazay, C., Lindell, Y.: Efficient Secure Two-Party Protocols: Techniques and Constructions, 1st edn. Springer-Verlag, Heidelberg (2010)
13. Mukhamedov, A., Kremer, S., Ritter, E.: Analysis of a multi-party fair exchange protocol and formal proof of correctness in the strand space model. In: Patrick, A.S., Yung, M. (eds.) FC 2005. LNCS, vol. 3570, pp. 255–269. Springer, Heidelberg (2005). https://doi.org/10.1007/11507840_23
14. Papadimitriou, C.: Computational Complexity, 1st edn. Pearson, Boston (1993)

15. Thayer, F.J., Herzog, J.C., Guttman, J.D.: Strand spaces: why is a security protocol correct? In: Security and Privacy - 1998 IEEE Symposium on Security and Privacy, Oakland, CA, USA, 3–6 May 1998, Proceedings, pp. 160–171. IEEE Computer Society (1998). https://doi.org/10.1109/SECPRI.1998.674832

16. Thayer, F.J., Herzog, J.C., Guttman, J.D.: Strand spaces: Proving security protocols correct. J. Comput. Secur. **7**(1), 191–230 (1999). http://content.iospress.com/articles/journal-of-computer-security/jcs117

17. Woo, T.Y., Lam, S.S.: A semantic model for authentication protocols. In: Proceedings 1993 IEEE Computer Society Symposium on Research in Security and Privacy, pp. 178–194. IEEE (1993)

Quantum Machine Learning and Fraud Detection

Alessandra Di Pierro$^{(\boxtimes)}$ (iD) and Massimiliano Incudini

Dipartimento di Informatica, Università di Verona,
Strada le Grazie 15, 34137 Verona, Italy
{alessandra.dipierro,massimiliano.incudini}@univr.it

Abstract. One of the most common problems in cybersecurity is related to the fraudulent activities that are performed in various settings and predominantly through the Internet. Securing online card transactions is a tough nut to crack for the banking sector, for which fraud detection is an essential measure. Fraud detection problems involve huge datasets and require fast and efficient algorithms. In this paper, we report on the use of a quantum machine learning algorithm for dealing with this problem and present the results of experimenting on a case study. By enhancing statistical models with the computational power of quantum computing, quantum machine learning promises great advantages for cybersecurity.

Keywords: Quantum computing · Support vector machine · Cybersecurity and fraud

1 Introduction

As technology keeps advancing at a very rapid pace, we can rely on computational resources increasingly bigger beyond any prediction that could have been made by Moore's law (at least by the strictest definition of doubling chip densities every two years). Importantly, the idea of using quantum physics for building computers that are in principle exponentially more powerful than any classical super computer is now becoming a reality although in the form of limited and error-prone computers, aka Noisy Intermediate-Scale Quantum computers [21]. This is already having a significant impact on some areas of cybersecurity, such as cryptography (where quantum devices generating truly random numbers can be used), secure communication (cf. quantum key exchange protocols), and machine learning algorithms for identifying and defeating cyberattack methods.

In this paper we will address some of the aspects related to the impacts of this general trend and its consequences on the analysis of security, a theme dear to Joshua.

When the first author first met Joshua, her main objective in research was the analysis of security properties by means of a formal tool that we called probabilistic abstract interpretation, where abstraction, probability and program semantics play a crucial role. Contrary to the main trend in probabilistic

© Springer Nature Switzerland AG 2021
D. Dougherty et al. (Eds.): Guttman Festschrift, LNCS 13066, pp. 139–155, 2021.
https://doi.org/10.1007/978-3-030-91631-2_8

static analysis we realized that considering linear algebra and functional analysis, instead of set-based structures of probability or measure functions, was an 'easy' way to achieve practically more useful approximations and analyses which are closer in nature to average case rather than to the worst case analysis of complexity theory. This translates in real applications to the possibility of reducing the number of false positives at the expense of correctness, and vice versa, thus leaving to the user the choice of the appropriate trade-offs.

Another aspect of probabilistic abstract interpretation that is somehow a byproduct of its mathematical definition is closer to the current investigations that we are carrying out and that we are going to discuss in this paper. This is related to a dual nature of the probabilistic abstract interpretation framework, namely as a tool for both *probabilistic* and *statistic* analysis. It is well known that while probability deals with predicting the likelihood of future events by deducing it from some known distribution, statistics involves the analysis of the frequency of past events for inferring such likelihoods. We have shown the use of probabilistic abstract interpretation in both its functionalities, namely for probabilistic static analysis [11] and for regression analysis [14]. This also implies that machine learning and static analysis should be used as complementary and not alternative tools for the successful identification and prevention of cyberattacks.

In this paper we go a step further by showing the relation between probabilistic abstract interpretation and a quantum machine learning method for classification. Quantum machine learning is a relatively new research field, where investigations are made on the use of quantum computing for speeding up machine learning algorithms and the analysis of big data. We will present a quantum classifier defined in [22] in analogy with the support vector machine method of classical machine learning, and demonstrate this method for a very topical problem in cybersecurity, namely fraud detection. The enormous amount of data and their statistical nature make the problem a good example of the advantages coming from the combined use of quantum computing and machine learning.

In the next section we will introduce the problem and a classical machine learning approach to solve it, i.e. the Support Vector Machine. In Sect. 3 we will briefly introduce quantum machine learning, and in Sect. 4 we will illustrate the application of quantum support vector machine to fraud detection, showing its analogy with probabilistic abstract interpretation.

2   Detecting Fraudulent Transactions

Today, fraudulent activities are predominantly performed through the Internet. Malware and phishing methods are engineered for this purpose. Some of the most common types of fraud are customer information altering, ATM fraud, credit card application fraud, account theft, fake credit cards and card duplication [5,7].

Due to today's global superhighways of communication and the refinement of technological tools, fraud is increasing dramatically causing major disruptions especially in the financial sector and resulting in the loss of billions of dollars worldwide each year. In fact, the increase of online transactions is forcing banks to deal with an unforeseen number of fraudulent activities. For obvious reasons, the literature on fraud detection is very limited and mainly related to general methodological approaches rather than specialized methods of fraud detection on a specific dataset (companies are often loath to release fraud figures as this could frighten customers but also because the figures change over time).

Since anomaly detection methods are very context dependent, much of the published literature in the area concentrates on supervised classification methods.

Supervised methods, using samples from the fraudulent/non-fraudulent classes as the basis to construct classification rules to detect future cases of fraud, suffer from the problem of unbalanced class sizes, as the legitimate transactions generally far outnumber the fraudulent ones. When the probability of fraud is very low, as it is often the case, simple mis-classification rate such as *accuracy* cannot be used as a performance measure. This is because the formula

$$\text{accuracy} = \frac{true\_non\_fraud + true\_fraud}{total\_examples}$$

would assign a very high accuracy to a classifier answering 'no' all the times. Other metrics could give a more meaningful evaluation of a classifier performance, e.g. *precision* which answers the question: When the model predicts fraud, how often is it correct? Or, how many predicted frauds are truly frauds? In fact, by calculating the formula

$$\text{precision} = \frac{true\_fraud}{true\_fraud + false\_fraud},$$

we can get an estimate of how many times we get wrong by using a given classifier (the closer to 1 the precision, the less false positives). Note that precision is the most commonly used metric of measuring the quality of static analyses; in the case of the quantitative static analyses that are performed using probabilistic abstract interpretation, this precision can also be numerically estimated, thus providing a basis for possible trade-offs [12].

Many fraud detection problems involve huge datasets that are constantly evolving. Processing these datasets in a search for fraudulent transactions needs fast and efficient algorithms. Clearly this is one of those cases where the potential of Quantum Computing [20] promises huge advantages. We will show this by focusing on a specific machine learning algorithm that can be used for fraud detection, i.e. support vector machine, which we will first introduce in its original classical version in the next section.

2.1   Support Vector Machines

A natural way of classifying a given dataset in two classes (e.g. fraud and non-fraud) is to draw a separating boundary between the two classes. The standard Support Vector Machine (SVM) [8] is a method that tries to maximize the margin, i.e. the distance of the decision hyperplane to the nearest data points; this induces a labeling on the dataset assigning each object to a class depending on which part of the hyperplane they are positioned.

SVM is the best known member of a class of algorithms for pattern analysis called *kernel methods* [8]. Kernel methods employ a so-called kernel function in order to map data points, living in a input space V, to a higher dimensional feature space V', where separability between classes of data becomes easier due to the reduction of a possibly non-linear separation boundary into a linear one. Kernel methods allow us to avoid the explicit calculation of the embedding map into the new space V' and yet exploit its structure by representing the inner product function in this new feature space (see Fig. 1).

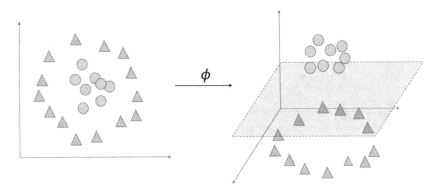

Fig. 1. Visual explanation of the kernel trick. After the application of the map ϕ, a previously non linearly separable dataset becomes such in a higher feature space.

In fact, if ϕ is the embedding map, $\phi : V \rightarrow V'$, the kernel $K : V \times V \rightarrow \mathbb{R}$ is the function defined by

$$K(\vec{x}_i, \vec{x}_j) \equiv \langle \phi(\vec{x}_i), \phi(\vec{x}_j) \rangle,$$

(where $\langle \, , \, \rangle$ is the inner product in V'), satisfying the Mercer condition of positive semi-definiteness, i.e. for all possible choices of n real numbers $(c_1, \ldots, c_n)$, the following relation must hold

$$\sum_{i=1}^{M} \sum_{j=1}^{M} K(\vec{x}_i, \vec{x}_j) c_i c_j \geq 0.$$

Hence calculating the kernel $K(\vec{x}_i, \vec{x}_j)$ is computationally cheaper than computing each new coordinate of $\phi(\vec{x})$. On the other hand, a classifier defined via a kernel never involves or requires the computation of $\phi(\vec{x}_i)$; thus we only need the guarantee provided by the Mercer theorem stating that a mapping ϕ does exist whenever the kernel function $K(\vec{x}_i, \vec{x}_j)$ gives rise to a kernel matrix obeying the positive semi-definiteness condition, or positive semi-definite (PSD) matrix. Common examples of kernels defined on a Euclidean space $\mathbb{R}^d$ include:

- Linear kernel: $K(x, y) = x^T y, \quad x, y \in \mathbb{R}^d$.
- Polynomial kernel: $K(x, y) = (x^T y + r)^n, \quad x, y \in \mathbb{R}^d, r \geq 0$.
- Gaussian kernel (RBF Kernel): $K(x, y) = e^{-\frac{\|x - y\|^2}{2\sigma^2}}, \quad x, y \in \mathbb{R}^d, \sigma > 0$

However, some kernel might be harder to compute than others like those that are defined in terms of some distance which is inherently hard to compute. An example could be the graph edit distance based kernels. The graph edit distance (GED) is a measure of similarity (or dissimilarity) between two graphs whose mathematical definition depends on the characteristics of the graphs under study, i.e. whether they are labeled, directed, planar etc. In general, given a set of graph edit operations $\{e_1, \ldots . e_n\}$, the GED between two graphs is defined as

$$GED(g_1, g_2) = \min_{(e_1, \ldots, e_k) \in \mathcal{P}(g_1, g_2)} \sum_{i=1}^{k} c(e_i),$$

where $\mathcal{P}(g_1, g_2)$ denotes the set of edit paths transforming g_1 into (a graph isomorphic to) g_2 and $c(e) \geq 0$ is the cost of an edit operation e. The problem of computing GED is in general NP-hard, which means that also obtaining the GED based kernel belongs at least to the same class.

As already mentioned, SVM is the best known example of kernel methods. It is a supervised binary classifier that learns the optimal discriminative hyperplane based on a set of M labeled vectors $\{(\vec{x}, y) \mid \vec{x} \in \mathbb{R}^N, \ y \in \{-1, +1\}\}$. A SVM maximizes the distance, i.e. the margin, between the decision hyperplane and the closest points, called support vectors [8].

The SVM optimization problem with hard-margin is defined by the objective function

$$\arg \min_{(\vec{w}, b)} \left\{ \frac{1}{2} \|\vec{w}\|^2 \right\}$$

subject to the constraint

$$\forall_i \ y_i (\vec{w} \cdot \vec{x}_i - b) \geq 1,$$

where $(\vec{x}_i, y_i)$, with $i = 1 \ldots M$ and $y_i \in \{-1, +1\}$ is the pair of training vector and label, $\vec{w}$ is the vector normal to the discriminative hyperplane, and b is the offset of the hyperplane.

An important extension of SVM is the so called soft margin SVM, where the best hyperplane is the one that reaches the optimal trade-off between two factors: the minimization of the margin and the error introduced by points on the 'wrong' side of the hyperplane, expressed using slack variables ξ_i tuned by the hyper-parameter C. The soft margin SVM optimization problem is of the form:

$$\arg \min_{(\vec{w}, b)} \left\{ \frac{1}{2} \|\vec{w}\|^2 + C \sum_{i=1}^{M} \xi_i \right\}$$

subject to the constraint

$$\forall_i \ y_i (\vec{w} \cdot \vec{x}_i - b) \geq 1 - \xi_i, \quad \xi_i \geq 0. \tag{1}$$

Usually it is convenient to switch to the dual form where we introduce Lagrange multipliers α_i in order to include the constraint in the objective function:

$$\arg\max_{(\alpha_i)} \sum_{i=1}^{M} \alpha_i - \frac{1}{2} \sum_{i,j} \alpha_i \alpha_j y_i y_j (\vec{x}_i^T \vec{x}_j) \tag{2}$$

subject to

$$\sum_i \alpha_i y_i = 0 , \ \forall_i \, \alpha_i \geq 0$$

where the relation $\vec{w} = \sum_i \alpha_i y_i \vec{x}_i$ has been used to obtain Eq. 2. Note that only a sparse subset of the α_is are non-zero and the corresponding $\vec{x}_i$ are the support vectors which lie on the margin and determine the discriminant hyperplane.

In this context, a non-linear classification boundary for the SVM is obtained by replacing the term $(\vec{x}_i^T \vec{x}_j)$ in Eq. 2 with a kernel function $K(\vec{x}_i, \vec{x}_j) \equiv \phi(\vec{x}_i)^T(\phi(\vec{x}_j))$ satisfying the Mercer condition of positive semi-definiteness. The Lagrangian optimization problem for the soft margin SVM now becomes

$$\arg\max_{(\alpha_i)} \sum_{i=1}^{M} \alpha_i - \frac{1}{2} \sum_{i,j} \alpha_i \alpha_j y_i y_j K(\vec{x}_i, \vec{x}_j) \tag{3}$$

subject to

$$\sum_i \alpha_i y_i = 0 \ \text{ with } \forall_i \, \alpha_i \geq 0.$$

The dual form of the SVM optimization problem is quadratic in the parameter α_i and can be efficiently solved with quadratic programming algorithms.

This is the principal (but by no means the only) use of kernel methods in machine learning, one which vastly extends the utility of the SVM by enabling the mapping of the input decision space into a large variety of alternative higher-dimensional spaces (thus guaranteeing linear separability). The decision boundary in the input space may thus undergo significant morphology variation while crucially retaining the low parametric support vector characterization of the decision boundary in the embedding space, i.e. the space defined by $\phi(\vec{x})$, where $K(\vec{x}_i, \vec{x}_j) \equiv \phi(\vec{x}_i)^T(\phi(\vec{x}_j))$. Critically, at no stage are we required to compute $\phi(\vec{x}_i)$. The Mercer condition guarantees the existence of ϕ, but the kernel itself may be calculated based on any similarity function that gives rise to a legitimate (i.e. PSD) kernel matrix.

An alternative version of SVM that has a central role in the quantum setting is the least squares support vector machine of [28], and will be discussed in Sect. 3.1.

2.2   Quantum Matrix Inversion and Probabilistic Abstract Interpretation

The least squares version of SVM's for classification problems with two classes as formulated in [28] represents the classical counterpart of the Quantum Support

Vector Machine (QSVM) that we will introduce in Sect. 3.1. This is based on a matrix inversion subroutine that shares strong similarities with the key notions of probabilistic abstract interpretation (PAI).

One basic common aspect is the reference to a system of linear equations and their *least* solution. Linear equations play an important role in virtually all fields of science and engineering. Where their use in PAI is to guarantee a form of correctness of the analysis, in quantum machine learning they are essential in dealing with the rapidly growing size of the datasets that is easily reaching the order of terabytes and even petabytes in most ML applications. Like in the PAI setting the general idea is to find a best approximation rather than trying to find the full solution of N linear equations (which would scale at least as N). The QSVM defined in [22] and described in Sect. 3.1 shows how to use a quantum computer for finding such an approximation in time which scales logarithmically in N and polynomially in the desired precision. We now briefly introduce the basic notions of PAI and describe the quantum matrix inversion algorithms in order to highlight their relation.

Probabilistic Abstract Interpretation [12,14] is based on a correspondence between Hilbert spaces, which is defined by a bounded linear operator[1] (representing an abstraction or property) and its Moore-Penrose pseudo-inverse (representing a concretization operator). If $\mathcal{C}$ and $\mathcal{D}$ are two Hilbert spaces, and $\mathbf{A} : \mathcal{C} \to \mathcal{D}$ and $\mathbf{G} : \mathcal{D} \to \mathcal{C}$ are bounded linear operators between (the concrete domain) $\mathcal{C}$ and (the abstract domain) $\mathcal{D}$, such that $\mathbf{G}$ is the Moore-Penrose pseudo-inverse of $\mathbf{A}$, then we say that $(\mathcal{C}, \mathbf{A}, \mathcal{D}, \mathbf{G})$ forms a *probabilistic abstract interpretation*.

Definition 1. *Let $\mathcal{H}_1$ and $\mathcal{H}_2$ be two Hilbert spaces and $\mathbf{A} : \mathcal{H}_1 \mapsto \mathcal{H}_2$ a bounded linear map between them. A bounded linear map $\mathbf{A}^\dagger = \mathbf{G} : \mathcal{H}_2 \mapsto \mathcal{H}_1$ is the Moore-Penrose pseudo-inverse of $\mathbf{A}$ iff*

$$\mathbf{A} \circ \mathbf{G} = \mathbf{P_A} \ and \ \mathbf{G} \circ \mathbf{A} = \mathbf{P_G},$$

where $\mathbf{P_A}$ and $\mathbf{P_G}$ are orthogonal projections onto the ranges of $\mathbf{A}$ and $\mathbf{G}$, respectively.

The operation 'o' indicates function composition and corresponds to matrix multiplication in reverse order, so that $\mathbf{A} \circ \mathbf{G} = \mathbf{GA}$ and $\mathbf{G} \circ \mathbf{A} = \mathbf{AG}$.

The properties of the Moore-Penrose pseudo-inverse [4,6,10] guarantee a form of optimality of the abstractions (abstract semantics) that we can construct via PAI: they are the *closest* to the concrete semantics one can construct, where closeness is defined via the distance induced by the norm on the Hilbert space (thus often referred to as *least squares approximation*). This follows from the following theorem [4].

---

[1] For the purposes of this paper, it is sufficient to restrict ourselves to the finite-dimensional case where bounded linear operators can always be represented as matrices.

Definition 2. *A least squares solution to a system of linear equations* $A\vec{x} = \vec{b}$ *is a vector* $\vec{x_0}$ *such that*

$$\|A\vec{x_0} - \vec{b}\| \leq \|A\vec{x} - \vec{b}\|.$$

Theorem 1. *If* $A^\dagger$ *is the Moore-Penrose pseudo-inverse of* A, *then* $\vec{x_0} = A^\dagger\vec{b}$ *is the best approximate solution of* $A\vec{x} = \vec{b}$, *and is unique.*

We can restrict w.l.o.g. to abstraction operators that are surjective, i.e. $\mathbf{A}(\mathcal{C}) = \mathcal{D}$. In fact, given a PAI $(\mathcal{C}, \mathbf{A}, \mathcal{D}, \mathbf{G})$, we can always partition the abstract domain $\mathcal{D}$ by identifying those elements with the same concrete meaning. In this way we can ensure that any abstract object in $\mathcal{D}$ is the image of a concrete object in $\mathcal{C}$, i.e. we reduce the abstract domain to one which does not contain redundant objects, or equivalently, we turn the abstraction operator $\mathbf{A}$ into a surjective one. In this case the closed subspace of $\mathcal{C}$ corresponding to the projection $\mathbf{G} \circ \mathbf{A} = \mathbf{P_G}$ is isomorphic to $\mathbf{A}(\mathcal{C})$. This allows us to identify orthogonal projections on a Hilbert space $\mathcal{H}$ (or equivalently its closed subspaces) with all probabilistic abstract interpretations for the given concrete domain $\mathcal{H}$ [13]. In particular, we can show that the quantum matrix inversion performed by the HHL algorithm (that will describe below) on a kernel matrix corresponds to one such projection and therefore to a PAI.

The HHL Algorithm [17] was introduced by Aram Harrow, Avinatan Hassidim, and Seth Lloyd (thus its name) in 2009. This is a 'big data' quantum algorithm that outclasses any classical algorithm for inverting huge matrices, achieving an exponential speed-up in the size of the system. The problem is still (as previously) to find a solution to $A\vec{x} = \vec{b}$, but this time the matrix A must be a square matrix, $A \in \mathbb{C}^{N \times N}$, and Hermitian. The exponential advantage is achieved by reformulating the problem in a quantum setting and essentially reducing it to a Quantum Phase Estimation (QPE) problem, for which a solution can be found very efficiently on a quantum computer [20].

There are two important aspects of this algorithm that must be taken into consideration. One is that, contrary to the classical algorithm, HHL does not return the full solution, but only approximate functions of the solution vector. The other point is that it makes the assumption that the encoding of the classical data into a quantum state can be performed efficiently [1]. This is a strong assumption as the data loading phase in a quantum ML circuit often jeopardizes the overall efficiency. One way around would be the use of a Quantum Random Access Memory (QRAM) [16], which is however very hard to realize with the currently available technologies.

The quantum matrix inversion performed by the HHL algorithm plays an essential role in the quantum support vector machine method that we are going to describe in Sect. 3.1. It is also strongly related to PAI as we will show in Sect. 3.2.

3   Quantum Machine Learning

The recent developments in the study of the application of quantum computing to machine learning tasks have shown that the synergy of the two fields, known as Quantum Machine Learning (QML) [26,31], can be leveraged to improve existing cybersecurity strategies.

The potential risks that quantum computing implies for existing widespread cryptographic and key exchange protocols for secure communication[2], is balanced by the benefits that a quantum computer can provide in the improvement of all those security tasks where ML is already used, such as behavior anomaly detection, classification of data, users, threat actors or malware, and prevention.

A unifying framework for various quantum ML approaches that have been introduced in the literature up to now is based on the notion of *quantum model* [24]. A quantum model is a quantum algorithm replacing a classical ML model, such as a classifier or a generator, and consisting of a data encoding phase followed by a measurement. The data encoding effectively corresponds to the embedding of the input data into the Hilbert space of quantum states, while the measurement corresponds to the output of the model.

3.1   Quantum Support Vector Machines

A classification via kernel methods has been defined within the context of quantum computing by Rebentrost, Mohseni and Lloyd [23].

The quantum SVM they propose uses the least squares re-implementation of the classic kernelized SVM [29] so as to implicate the efficient quantum matrix inversion of Harrow, Hassidim & Lloyd [17].

In this reformulation, the constraint defined in Eq. (1) is replaced with the equality constraint

$$\forall_i \; y_i(\vec{w} \cdot \phi(\vec{x}_i) - b) = 1 - e_i, \tag{4}$$

where e_i are error terms. In this way, optimal parameters $\vec{\alpha}$ and b that identify the decision hyperplane are found by solving a set of linear equations, instead of using quadratic programming. Thus the problem can be formulated as follows:

$$F\begin{pmatrix} b \\ \vec{\alpha} \end{pmatrix} = \begin{pmatrix} 0 & \vec{1}^T \\ \vec{1} & K + \gamma^{-1}I \end{pmatrix} \begin{pmatrix} b \\ \vec{\alpha} \end{pmatrix} = \begin{pmatrix} 0 \\ \vec{y} \end{pmatrix} \tag{5}$$

where F is a $(M+1) \times (M+1)$ matrix, $\vec{1}^T \equiv (1,1,1\ldots)^T$, K is the kernel matrix and γ^{-1} is the trade-off parameter that plays a similar role as C in soft margin SVM. Training object classifications are denoted by the vector $\vec{y} \in ([-1,1]^M)^T$, for the M training objects order-correlated with the kernel matrix K (training object vectors $\vec{x}_k$ are represented in their own basis). Finally, $\vec{\alpha}$ and b (the object of the optimization) are respectively the weight and bias offset parameters of the

---

[2] The security of RSA and Diffie-Hellman cannot be demonstrated anymore with the prospective use of a quantum computer, since efficient quantum algorithms exist for factorization and for computing the discrete logarithm.

decision hyperplane within the Mercer embedding space induced by the kernel. These SVM parameters are determined schematically by

$$\begin{pmatrix} b \\ \vec{\alpha} \end{pmatrix} = F^{-1} \begin{pmatrix} 0 \\ \vec{y} \end{pmatrix}.$$

For the quantum support vector machine (QSVM) the task is to generate a quantum state $|\vec{\alpha}, b\rangle$ describing the hyperplane with quantum matrix inversion of F. This produces the solution state:

$$|\vec{\alpha}, b\rangle = \frac{1}{b^2 + \sum_{k=1}^{M} \alpha_k^2} \left(b\,|0\rangle + \sum_{k=1}^{M} \alpha_k\,|k\rangle \right) \tag{6}$$

Note that the alpha are non-sparse and represent distances from the margin; we do not thus obtain support vectors as in the dual Lagrangian formulation.

Utilization of these parameters for classification of novel data requires the implementation of a *query oracle* implicating all of the labeled data:

$$|\tilde{u}\rangle = \frac{1}{\left(b^2 + \sum_{k=1}^{M} \alpha_k^2 |\vec{x}_k|^2 \right)^{\frac{1}{2}}} \left(b\,|0\rangle\,|0\rangle + \sum_{k=1}^{M} |\vec{x}_k|\,\alpha_k\,|k\rangle\,|\vec{x}_k\rangle \right) \tag{7}$$

and also the query state:

$$|\tilde{x}\rangle = \frac{1}{M|\vec{x}|^2 + 1} \left(|0\rangle\,|0\rangle + \sum_{k=1}^{M} |\vec{x}_k|\,|k\rangle\,|\vec{x}_k\rangle \right) \tag{8}$$

($|k\rangle$ is thus an index state over training vectors).

The classification is then carried out as the inner product of the two states, i.e. by performing a swap test [30] and allocating class labels on the basis of the inner product probability being greater or less than $\frac{1}{2}$. Note that the swap test is performed via the use of an ancilla to construct the state $\frac{1}{\sqrt{2}}(|0\rangle\,|\tilde{u}\rangle + |1\rangle\,|\tilde{x}\rangle)$ which is then measured in the basis $\frac{1}{\sqrt{2}}(|0\rangle - |1\rangle)$.

Quantum kernelization can be achieved by directly acting on the training vector basis, an approach that lends itself most readily to polynomial kernels (radial basis functions are possible, but less straightforward within this approach).

Thus, it is possible to construct in quantum terms the kernel:

$$K(\vec{x}_j, \vec{x}_k) = (\vec{x}_j \cdot \vec{x}_k)^D \equiv \phi(\vec{x}_j) \cdot \phi(\vec{x}_k) \tag{9}$$

where ϕ is a non-linear feature map into the linear Hilbert embedding space (that is not explicitly calculated in the SVM calculation). (The D parameter can be used to control the relative likelihood of over-fitting/under-fitting the training data by varying the polynomial degree).

The QVM methods we have just described is illustrative of the *raison d'être* of QML, namely the ability of performing computations that are hard to perform classically. However, we can achieve computational advantages in classical

ML too, e.g. via the kernel trick (cf. Sect. 2.1). Recently it has been advocated that a more systematic approach than merely replacing quantum for classical procedures is needed to understand when we can expect speed-ups, which may assume a general-purpose quantum computer rather than the currently available NISQ devices [18].

3.2 Quantum Support Vector Machines as PAI

The quantum matrix inversion performs an approximation of the kernel matrix F that essentially corresponds to a PAI. This can be realized by observing that the application of the HHL algorithm to the $M \times M$ kernel matrix K forces a filtering of the eigenvalues by discarding all those eigenvalues whose value is below a certain threshold in order to keep the efficiency of the procedure [22]. More precisely, given a $N \times M$ data matrix $X = (\vec{x_1}, \ldots, \vec{x_M})$, we can construct the kernel matrix as $K = X^\dagger X$, which in terms of probabilistic abstraction corresponds to the projection onto the abstract domain of the training dataset $\{\vec{x_1}, \ldots, \vec{x_M}\}$. As projections are not invertible (the identity apart), the quantum matrix inversion necessarily produces an approximation of K^{-1} consisting in the filtering mentioned above. This approximation is effectively the PAI generated by the $N \times N$ covariance matrix $\Sigma = XX^\dagger = \sum_{m=1}^{M} \vec{x_m}\vec{x_m}^T$, which can be seen as determining an orthogonal projection on (or a closed subspace of) the original dataset, as explained in Sect. 2.2. As the matrices $X^\dagger X$ and $XX^\dagger$ have the same non-zero eigenvalues, keeping the largest eigenvalues and corresponding eigenvectors of the kernel matrix retains the *principal components* of the covariance matrix, i.e. the most important features of the data.

4 Implementation of Quantum Fraud Detection

From a computational viewpoint, solving the quadratic programming problem or the least-squares SVM has complexity $O(M^3)$ in the number M of the training data. A bottleneck to the speed of computation is determined by the kernel: computing a polynomial kernel $K(\vec{x_i}, \vec{x_j}) = (\vec{x_i}^T \vec{x_j} + c)^d$ takes $O(M^2 d)$, but in other cases the complexity could be much higher, e.g. for those kernels depending on a distance whose calculation is itself a NP problem. An important part of the research in QML is devoted to the study of methods and techniques using quantum computation for the evaluation of kernel functions as part of a hybrid classification model. In this model, the classical data are embedded in a Hilbert space via a quantum circuit translating them into quantum states. This transformation essentially corresponds to a feature map that is computed explicitly in order to produce a kernel matrix as the matrix of the inner products of all pairs of states in the new higher dimensional space. We refer to [19] for a survey of various quantum approaches to kernel-based machine learning.

In order to investigate possible advantages in terms of efficiency that could be obtained by using a quantum computer, we have analyzed the performance of the QSVM classification method for the fraud detection problem. We have used the implementation described in [9] (see also the IBM documentation page https://qiskit.org/documentation/stubs/qiskit.aqua.algorithms.QSVM.html).

Instead of running our quantum circuits on the IBM real quantum computer,[3] we have used the IBM simulator, which is available on the Qiskit platform [2]. Clearly, simulation relies on classical resources, which means that we have to deal with the exponential growth of the quantum spaces to be simulated. More precisely, by encoding each feature in one qubit, we are easily confronted with matrices of one terabyte and more (20 features lead to $2^{20} \times 2^{20}$ matrices). This forces us to 'simplify' the dataset of the case study presented in Sect. 4.1 in order to reduce the number of the original features.

4.1 Experiments on the IBM Quantum Platform

We report here on the results obtained by running the QSVM on the IBM quantum platform. We have also run some experiments by using other methods such as the quantum variational circuit or QNN [25], which we did not address in this paper.

The payment fraud dataset we considered for our experiments has more than 150000 payments, most of which are non-fraud. We extracted some features corresponding to the most important fields of the payment:

- id_operation;
- amount;
- country;
- merchant_category (which type of product was buyed);
- channel (ATM, Internet, ...);
- card_type;
- circuit (none, Visa, Mastercard, ...);
- target (fraud or legit).

We considered two different subsets of this dataset:

- FRAUD_SHORT: the training set has 1092 legit payments and 212 fraud payments; the testing set has 70 payments per class. All the payments has country set to *Italy*, category set to *Business Services*, channel set to *Internet*;
- FRAUD_MEDIUM: the training set has 2056 legit payments and 327 fraud payments; the testing set has 109 payments per class. All the payments has country set to *Italy* and category set to *Business Services*.

Because the testing set is balanced (same number of items for both fraud and non-fraud) we can choose the *accuracy* metric to evaluate the classifier. As already mentioned in Sect. 2, in the case of a non-balanced dataset (with much more non-frauds than frauds), the classifier would learn that most payments are

---

[3] The quantum computer currently available to the public is a very limited 16-qubit device, which is much too primitive (in terms of both stability and error tolerance) for practical problems.

non-fraud and led to classify everything as non-fraud, and yet get a high accuracy. Alternatively, we could have chosen a more sophisticated metric such as *precision*, which would be a more reasonable choice in the unbalanced case.

Then we pre-processed some fields. As an example, `amount` is log scaled and then normalized (log scaling is applied when some payments are very high and the normalization technique sets most of the other small payments to values close to zero). The continuous variables are always encoded in a real number between zero and one. The categorical variables can be encoded as either a real value between zero and one, as a binary integer or as one-hot encoding binary string.

The quantum circuit acts itself as the kernel function $K(\vec{x}_j, \vec{x}_k) \equiv \phi(\vec{x}_j) \cdot \phi(\vec{x}_k)$. The part of the circuit implementing ϕ is called *feature map* and, although the size of $\phi(\vec{x})$ is exponential in the number of qubits of the circuit, the dot product $\phi(\vec{x}_j) \cdot \phi(\vec{x}_k)$ can be performed efficiently on a quantum computer.

The way we encode the input data affects the number of qubits that we need to use for the circuit. The continuous variables and the categorical ones encoded with real values only use a single qubit, and the encoding is performed by a single rotation gate. The categorical variable having m possible values can be encoded as one-hot binary string and needs m qubits; each bit corresponds to a qubit and exactly one X gate is needed to flip the only bit set to one. In this case, it might be useful to introduce the QRAC encoding [3] of binary variables that can slightly reduce the number of qubits needed to encode a binary string.

Table 1 schematizes the results of our experiments in terms of the accuracy of the quantum classifier. Quantum circuits implementing some of the feature maps considered in our experiments are shown in Fig. 2. These results promise some benefits from the use of a quantum computer for detecting fraudulent transactions, although the limited computing resources available still do not allow us to elaborate massive data.

Table 1. Accuracy of the many configurations tested.

Configuration	SVM	QSVM							
	%	R	Z	ZZ	Z+ZZ	P1	P2	P3	QR
		%	%	%	%	%	%	%	%
Dataset FRAUD_SHORT									
Continuous encoding (CE)	55.3	54.6	57.4	**66.6**	55.3		64.5	58.8	60.2
Discrete encoding (DE)	56.0	57.4	60.9	58.1	**64.6**	63.8	56.7	60.2	58.9
Dataset FRAUD_MEDIUM									
Continuous encoding (CE)	57.3	57.3	56.4	56.8	**59.2**		58.2	58.2	52.7

Legend: CE: all the fields are encoded with real numbers; DE: continuous fields are encoded with real numbers while categorical ones are encoded with one-hot bit strings; R: the feature map is Qiskit's `RawFeatureVector`; Z: the feature map is Qiskit's `ZFeatureMap` repeated once; ZZ: the feature map is Qiskit's `ZZFeatureMap` repeated once with full entanglement; P1: the feature map is Qiskit's `PauliFeatureMap` using gates Z and ZZ; P2: the feature map is Qiskit's `PauliFeatureMap` using only gates ZZ; P3: the feature map is Qiskit's `PauliFeatureMap` using gates Z and XX; P4: the feature map is Qiskit's `PauliFeatureMap` using only gates ZY; P5: the feature map is Qiskit's `PauliFeatureMap` using gates Z, YY and ZXZ; QR: the feature map is Qiskit's `ZZFeatureMap` with categorical data encoded with QRAC.

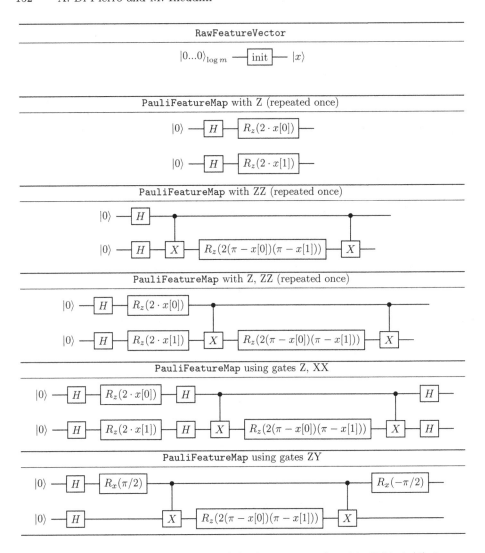

Fig. 2. Circuits corresponding to some of the feature maps listed in Table 1. $|0\rangle$ denotes the initial state 'ket-zero' corresponding to the column vector $\binom{1}{0}$; $|0...0\rangle_k$ is the tensor product of k ket-zeros; $|x\rangle$ is the normalized vector x. Each single qubit gate corresponds to a 2×2 unitary matrix, each two-qubits gate corresponds to a 4×4 unitary matrix. A n-qubits circuit corresponds to a $2^n \times 2^n$ unitary matrix obtained by applying tensor product and matrix multiplication to the unitary matrices associated with each gate. The **RawFeatureVector** implements Shende's algorithm ([27]) which encodes 2^n features with $O(n)$ qubits and $O(2^n)$ gates. The other feature maps all creates a complex state which depends from the input data by means of circuits whose length is proportional to the number of features.

An important question that we are currently investigating is the effect that the choice of a particular feature map can make on the resulting classification. The different feature maps are related to different boundaries in the Hilbert feature space, but identifying them is not immediate not least because we do not have any analytical expression as often is the case in the classical setting. Investigations on this question may nevertheless also affect classical ML, where heuristics are also used to define the implicit feature mapping in the context of kernel methods, thus giving no guarantee that the pre-defined kernel can lead to a more favorable feature space where data has better distribution towards the application.

5   Conclusion

Static analysis and machine learning are two methods that can be used for the identification and the prevention of cyberattacks: they are both necessary in constructing an integrated layered platform of defense. We have shown an analogy between probabilistic static analysis as formulated in [14,15] and the quantum machine learning technique for classification introduced in [22]. We have applied this technique to the problem of fraud detection and shown the results of some experiments that we have performed on a small dataset by using the IBM quantum platform Qiskit.

These results are promising for a future more extensive use of quantum computing in cybersecurity, but there are still substantial challenges to address.

The most immediate challenge is to achieve sufficient numbers of fault-tolerant qubits to allow the use of the full power of quantum computing.

Recently there has been a substantial investment in solving the core problems hindering the scaling of qubit count and designing error correction codes and new algorithms. From a cybersecurity perspective, while quantum computing may render some existing encryption protocols obsolete, it has the promise to enable a substantially enhanced level of communication security and privacy, and (as we have partially shown in this paper) facilitate the analysis and detection of cyberattacks.

References

1. Aaronson, S.: Read the fine print. Nat. Phys. **11**(4), 291–293 (2015). https://doi.org/10.1038/nphys3272
2. Aleksandrowicz, G., et al.: Qiskit: an open-source framework for quantum computing (2019). https://doi.org/10.5281/zenodo.2562110
3. Ambainis, A., Leung, D., Mancinska, L., Ozols, M.: Quantum random access codes with shared randomness (2008). arXiv preprint arXiv:0810.2937
4. Ben-Israel, A., Greville, T.N.E.: Gereralized Inverses - Theory and Applications. CMS Books in Mathematics, 2nd edn. Springer, Heidelberg (2003). https://doi.org/10.1007/b97366
5. Bolton, R.J., Hand, D.J.: Statistical fraud detection: a review. Stat. Sci. **17**(3), 235–255 (2002)

6. Campbell, S.L., Meyer, C.D.: Generalized Inverses of Linear Transformations. Dover, Pitman, London (1979)
7. Can, B., Yavuz, A.G., Karsligil, E.M., Guvensan, M.A.: A closer look into the characteristics of fraudulent card transactions. IEEE Access **8**, 166095–166109 (2020). https://doi.org/10.1109/ACCESS.2020.3022315
8. Cortes, C., Vapnik, V.: Support-vector networks. Mach. Learn. **20**(3), 273–297 (1995)
9. Córcoles, A.D., Temme, K., Harrow, A.W., Kandala, A., Chow, J.M., Gambetta, J.M.: Supervised learning with quantum-enhanced feature spaces. Nature **567**, 209–212 (2019)
10. Deutsch, F.: Best Approximation in Inner-Product Spaces. Springer, Heidelberg (2001). https://doi.org/10.1007/978-1-4684-9298-9
11. Di Pierro, A., Hankin, C., Wiklicky, H.: Approximate non-interference. J. Comput. Secur. **12**(1), 37–81 (2004)
12. Di Pierro, A., Wiklicky, H.: Measuring the precision of abstract interpretations. In: LOPSTR 2000. LNCS, vol. 2042, pp. 147–164. Springer, Heidelberg (2001). https://doi.org/10.1007/3-540-45142-0_9
13. Di Pierro, A., Wiklicky, H.: Semantic abstraction and quantum computation. In: 4th International Workshop on Quantum Programming Languages. Electronic Notes in Computer Science, vol. 210, pp. 49–63. Elsevier (2008)
14. Di Pierro, A., Wiklicky, H.: Probabilistic abstract interpretation: from trace semantics to DTMC's and linear regression. In: Probst, C.W., Hankin, C., Hansen, R.R. (eds.) Semantics, Logics, and Calculi. LNCS, vol. 9560, pp. 111–139. Springer, Cham (2016). https://doi.org/10.1007/978-3-319-27810-0_6
15. Di Pierro, A., Wiklicky, H.: Probabilistic analysis of programs: a weak limit approach. In: Dal Lago, U., Peña, R. (eds.) FOPARA 2013. LNCS, vol. 8552, pp. 58–76. Springer, Cham (2014). https://doi.org/10.1007/978-3-319-12466-7_4
16. Giovannetti, V., Lloyd, S., Maccone, L.: Quantum random access memory. Phys. Rev. Lett. **100**, 160501 (2008)
17. Harrow, A.W., Hassidim, A., Lloyd, S.: Quantum algorithm for linear systems of equations. Phys. Rev. Lett. **103**(15) (2009). https://doi.org/10.1103/physrevlett.103.150502
18. Kübler, J.M., Buchholz, S., Schölkopf, B.: The inductive bias of quantum kernels (2021). arXiv preprint arXiv:2106.03747
19. Mengoni, R., Di Pierro, A.: Kernel methods in quantum machine learning. Quant. Mach. Intell **1**(3), 65–71 (2019)
20. Nielsen, M.A., Chuang, I.L.: Quantum Computation and Quantum Information. Cambridge University Press, New York (2011)
21. Preskill, J.: Quantum computing in the nisq era and beyond. Quantum **2**, 79 (2018). https://doi.org/10.22331/q-2018-08-06-79
22. Rebentrost, P., Mohseni, M., Lloyd, S.: Quantum support vector machine for big data classification. Phys. Rev. Lett. **113**, 130503 (2014)
23. Rebentrost, P., Mohseni, M., Lloyd, S.: Quantum support vector machine for big data classification. Phys. Rev. Lett. **113**, 130501 (2014)
24. Schuld, M.: Quantum machine learning models are kernels methods (2021). arXiv preprint arXiv:2101.11020v1
25. Schuld, M., Bocharov, A., Svore, K.M., Wiebe, N.: Circuit-centric quantum classifiers. Phys. Rev. A **101**, 032308 (2020)
26. Schuld, M., Petruccione, F.: Prospects for near-term quantum machine learning. In: Supervised Learning with Quantum Computers. QST, pp. 273–279. Springer, Cham (2018). https://doi.org/10.1007/978-3-319-96424-9_9

27. Shende, V.V., Bullock, S.S., Markov, I.L.: Synthesis of quantum-logic circuits. IEEE Trans. Comput.-Aided Des. Integr. Circ. Syst **25**(6), 1000–1010 (2006). https://doi.org/10.1109/TCAD.2005.855930
28. Suykens, J., Vandewalle, J.: Least squares support vector machine classifiers. Neural Process. Lett. **9**(3), 293–300 (1999)
29. Suykens, J., Vandewalle, J.: Least squares support vector machine classifiers. Neural Process. Lett. **9**(3), 293–300 (1999). https://doi.org/10.1023/A:1018628609742
30. Wiebe, N., Braun, D., Lloyd, S.: Quantum algorithm for data fitting. Phys. Rev. Lett. **109**(5), 050505 (2012)
31. Wittek, P. (ed.): Quantum Machine Learning. Academic Press, Boston (2014). https://doi.org/10.1016/B978-0-12-800953-6.00015-3, http://www.sciencedirect.com/science/article/pii/B9780128009536000153

Model Finding for Exploration

Daniel J. Dougherty(⊠)

Worcester Polytechnic Institute, Worcester, USA
dd@wpi.edu

Abstract. We survey recent results in model finding, focusing on the notion of a model finding assistant to help users, even users not trained in logic, understand their software artifacts. The technical results discussed have all been previously published; the presentation here highlights two themes: (i) geometric logic and homomorphism orders as natural foundations for model finding, and (ii) an implemetation dichotomy between direct model finding and model finding with the aid of SAT- and SMT-solvers. We give generic high-level algorithms for the central problems of programming against such solvers; lower-level details are determined based on the category of homomorphisms being used.

1 Introduction

We are interested in the following situation. A user (a software developer, a protocol designer, a system administrator ...) would like to gain confidence in a certain artifact (a data structure or algorithm design, a protocol, a data center configuration ...). Our user has at hand a specification of their artifact in a logical language, but is not a trained logician. Nor do they have formal assertions to be verified. Our user may even have to work with a specification they didn't compose: many applications compile artifacts such as security policies or UML class diagrams into logic [47,48,55].

What kind of tool might help them?

One possibility is to treat their specification as a logical theory T and use *model finding* (we sometimes use the phrase *scenario finding*) to explore the possibilities inherent in their specification.

Model finding—the process of constructing finite models for first-order theories—is already a well-studied problem. Often model finding is a secondary component of another primary activity; it plays a role in *saturation-based theorem proving* [8–10,33, 42,60], *SMT solving* [60], and *property-based testing,* [6,11,12,14,26,40,49,52,56, 66], to name a few areas.

But the game is subtler when we want our tool to help our user *understand* their theory T. The model-finding approach we have in mind consists in generating and displaying concrete examples of the abstract specification at hand with an eye towards either reassuring the user when the scenarios match what is expected, or—more interestingly—uncovering surprising scenarios that elicit reactions of the form "whoops, I didn't mean to allow that!"

This work was partially supported by the U.S. National Science Foundation
Dedicated to Joshua Guttman, with appreciation for his insights and with gratitude for his friendship.

D. Dougherty et al. (Eds.): Guttman Festschrift, LNCS 13066, pp. 156–174, 2021.
https://doi.org/10.1007/978-3-030-91631-2_9

Indeed, we have in mind an *interaction* between the tool and the human, in the spirit of proof assistants, but for the purpose of building models rather than proofs. Thus the phrase, implicitly representing a slogan: *model finding assistant.*

The notions above of "reassuring" or "surprising" the user are, as stated, a bit squishy[1]. Can we find *principled* approaches to answering questions like the following?

1. How do we choose a collection of models to show to give a good picture of the space of *all* models?
2. Given the fact that our theory, if consistent, probably has lots of models, what counts as "reassurance" to our user?
3. If we do have a surprise to show the user, what models do the best job of showing them what went wrong?
4. If we decide to present a certain model, can we provide some tools to understand how it works: which parts of the model are necessary for it to satisfy the theory, which parts conspire to satisfy or fail to satisfy certain queries?

After the introductory material of Sects. 2 and 3, Sect. 4 offers some principles to guide our answers. The rest of the paper reports some technical progress on realizing these answers, along two conceptually different lines. The first is to build models "directly:" this is mathematically satisfying but—in the current state of the art—can have performance problems in some domains. The other broad approach is to leverage the amazing recent advances of SAT-solvers and SMT-solvers: here we typically face a tradeoff of expresssive power for efficiency. We shed light on some existing tools in this category by showing that they can be seen as instantiations of some simple abstract building blocks.

Proofs Have Been Omitted Here. Our goal is to create a sense of how the results fit together, and proofs are all available in the originally published papers.

This is a good place to point out that Joshua Guttman has embraced a spirit of "scenarios over deductions" throughout his career. The CPSA project, which he helped found and has guided for years, is an exemplar of domain-specific model-finding, and indeed one that already does quite a good job of addressing our motivating questions (especially the 1st and 3rd questions). This will become clearer as we detail more about CPSA below.

The Human Factor. An important dimension for any user-facing tool for formal methods is the human factor. Tools should provide mathematically sound help, but they are valuable only to the extent that people will use and understand them. Every one of our motivating questions above has a psychological component as well as a logical one.

Formal methods tools must therefore thread a needle between mathematical rigor and accessibility. So the truly "principled" approaches to our informal questions should reflect both mathematical and psychological considerations. Much more user-focused

---

[1] A technical philosophical term Joshua has been known to employ ....

formal methods research is called for. User studies [17] are one aspect; for a wider discussion see the abstract of Krishnamurthi and Nelson's recent invited talk [43] and the references therein.

In this paper we focus on the mathematical aspects of model finding, while trying to keep in mind the users who are actually using the tools.

2   Foundations

We work in a first-order signature Σ with relations and functions, and we take for granted the standard notions of model for Σ, satisfaction of a formula in a model, and model of a theory. We mostly focus on finite models.

If α is a formula and $a_1, \ldots, a_n$ are elements of a model $\mathbb{A}$ we will sometimes write $\mathbb{A} \models \alpha[a_1, \ldots, a_n]$ as shorthand to mean that $\mathbb{A} \models \alpha(x_1, \ldots, x_n)$ under the environment sending each x_i to a_i.

Definition 1 (Homomorphism). *Let $\mathbb{A}$ and $\mathbb{B}$ be Σ-models. A function $h : |\mathbb{A}| \to |\mathbb{B}|$ is a* homomorphism *if, for functions f and relations R from Σ,*

- $\mathbb{A} \models f[a_1, \ldots, a_n] = a$ *implies* $\mathbb{B} \models f[h(a_1), \ldots, h(a_n)] = h(a)$ *and*
- $\mathbb{A} \models R[a_1, \ldots, a_n]$ *implies* $\mathbb{B} \models R[h(a_1), \ldots, h(a_n)]$

Model $\mathbb{A}$ is a *submodel* of $\mathbb{B}$ if $|\mathbb{A}| \subseteq |\mathbb{B}|$ and the inclusion function is a homomorphism.

Categories of Models. We will consider various *categories* of models: a family of structures with a certain class of homomorphisms between them. For a theory T, the models of T form the objects of a category $\mathcal{T}$ whose arrows are the homomorphisms. We identify three subcategories of interest:

- the subcategory of $\mathcal{T}$ with injective homomorphisms;
- the full subcategory of $\mathcal{T}$ with finite models;
- the subcategory of $\mathcal{T}$ with finite models and injective homomorphisms.

2.1   Homomorphism Orderings

- Fix a category $\mathcal{C}$.
    - write $\mathbb{A} \precsim \mathbb{B}$ if there is a $\mathcal{C}$ map $h : \mathbb{A} \to \mathbb{B}$.
    - write $\mathbb{A} \approx \mathbb{B}$ if $\mathbb{A} \precsim \mathbb{B}$ and $\mathbb{B} \precsim \mathbb{A}$.
    - write $\mathbb{A} \precnsim \mathbb{B}$ if $\mathbb{A} \precsim \mathbb{B}$ and not $\mathbb{B} \precsim \mathbb{A}$.
- A model $\mathbb{A}$ is *a-minimal* for T if it is a minimal element in the homomorphism preorder on models of T.

    A model $\mathbb{A}$ is *i-minimal* for T if it is a minimal element in the injective-homomorphism preorder on models of T.

Well-Foundedness of Homomorphism Orderings. In a category of finite models, the ordering determined by injective homomorphisms is well-founded, by cardinality considerations. But the ordering determined by homomorphisms is not well-founded in general. For example, in the signature with one unary function symbol, define the model $\mathbb{C}_n$ consisting of a chain of n elements $a, f(a), \ldots f^{(n)}(a)$ with f mapping $f^{(n)}(a)$ to itself. Then each $\mathbb{C}_{i+1} \precsim \mathbb{C}_i$.

But if there happen to be only finitely many $\mathbb{M}_i$ for a theory T (as for example when we uniformly bound the size of models of T), it is easy to see that we cannot have an infinite strictly descending chain of homomorphisms.

Lemma 2. *For any theory T, the injective-homomorphism preorder on models of T is well-founded.*

If T has only finitely many models up to isomorphism, the $\precsim$ order on models of T is well-founded.

We will often add axioms to a theory to ensure that there is an upper bound on the size of its models. In such a case Lemma 2 will apply, even in the arbitrary-homomorphism situation.

Set of Support The following notion will be crucial for us, as it will supply our primary notion of completeness for model finders.

Definition 3 (Set of Support). *If $\mathcal{C}$ is a category of models and $\mathcal{M}$ is a collection of models in $\mathcal{C}$ we say that $\mathcal{M}_0$ is a set of support for $\mathcal{M}$ if for all $\mathbb{M} \in \mathcal{M}$, there exists $\mathbb{M}_0 \in \mathcal{M}_0$ with $\mathbb{M}_0 \precsim_{\mathcal{C}} \mathbb{M}$.*

3   Approaches to Model Finding

In its simplest form, model finding is the following problem. Given a theory T presented as input, either determine that T is unsatisfiable or construct one or more models satisfying T. Typically T is a first-order theory, and typically we ask for finite models; indeed sometimes the input includes a bound on the size of models searched for.

There are many tools that might be termed "standalone" model finders. It is traditional to see them as falling into two categories: *MACE style* and *SEM style*, after McCune's tool MACE [51] and the SEM tool of Zhang and Zhang [73]. These designations correspond to differences in the underlying techniques used to construct models, reduction to propositional logic (MACE-style) *vs.* more-or-less direct searching for a model (SEM-style). There are too many tools to catalog here, but the introductions to either of Claessen et al. [13] or Baumgartner et al. [4] will provide a good list of examples of each kind of tool and a good entry point into the literature.

We should make special mention of Kodkod [69], though. Kodkod is the backend for Alloy [41], is available as a stand-alone Java library and is used in many projects, including several of the tools discussed below: Margrave [55], Aluminum [54], Amalgam [53], and CompSAT [58].

Many model finders resist a simple MACE-vs-SEM taxonomy, especially if we recognize that SMT solving is a blend of propositional and first-order reasoning. For example Fortress [70] is a tool that reduces problems to the theory EUF of equality with uninterpreted functions, and uses an SMT solver. The method of Reynolds et al. [60] might best be described as SEM-style over SMT. By contrast, Elghazi and Taghdiri [27] translate Alloy theories to (non-propositional) SMT-LIB in order to do search with unbounded scopes.

For our purposes here, surveying model-finding *assistants* it is more useful to distinguish tools based on whether they work directly with first-order theories or incorporate the use of SAT- or SMT-solving: this will guide our organization in the rest of the paper.

4   Three Principles for Model Finding Assistants

The case for building a model finder that can be viewed as a *model finding assistant* was made implicitly in [54] and explicitly in [63]. We offer the following pre-theoretic intuitions about such a tool.

1. It should specify and respect a notion of "fitness" for the models it returns
2. It should provide for exploration of individual models
3. Most important: it should satisfy reasonable soundness and completeness properties

4.1   Fitness

"Fitness" is intentionally less-than-specific. One would like to see a commitment to fitness *for a given purpose.* In this general discussion we don't want to argue for a notion of fitness applying to all model-finding activities.

If one wants to check a safety property of a specification, one may hope that no counterexample models will be found, and if such models exist it is probably best to show the user models that have no extraneous information: minimal models. This principle is manifest in the universal injunction to "provide a minimal bug report."

On the other hand if our user is truly exploring a system in the early stages of a design, they may be interested in a robust selection of *consistent* phenomena: lots of things that *could* happen, even if they don't always happen. If a model finder only produces minimal models it will not be of any help in detecting *underconstraint* in a specification.

The main force of this principle is simply that the output of a model finder should not be determined by accidents of the underlying SAT- or SMT-technology.

By the way, as we will see, there are purely technical benefits of having a tool produce minimal models automatically, see the discussions of *provenance*, *augmentation*, and *set of support* below, each of which is easier to implement when we start with minimal models.

We have elsewhere [21] discussed the relative pros and cons of minimality in the respective categories of arbitrary and injective homomorphisms.

4.2   Exploration of Individual Models

Provenance. Suppose $\mathbb{A}$ is a model of a theory T (think of T as comprising a background theory perhaps together with some conjecture). If a certain fact F holds in $\mathbb{A}$ the user might very well wonder, "does that F have to be there in order that $\mathbb{A}$ satisfies T? Or is it an accident?" If F is not an accident, the user will be interested to know *why* F is there: what is it in T that makes F hold? The analogous questions can be asked about a given *element a* of the model: is a present in order to satisfy some existence requirement imposed by T, or is a superfluous?.

We call these questions of *provenance*. Several recent tools ([53,58,63,64]) afford the user the capability of asking provenance questions.

Augmentation. A model finder with augmentation will allow the user to (attempt to) add a fact F to a given scenario. If the model finder reports that F is inconsistent with the model under consideration, this may call attention to an *overconstraint* in the specification. More subtly, it might happen that a commitment to adding F means that another, surprising, ancillary fact F' must necessarily hold. Augmentation is typically a straightforward functionality to add to a model finder ([54,63,64].)

4.3 Completeness

We propose the following (ambitious) criterion for completeness: for each input theory T, every finite model of T should be reachable in principle.

A natural strategy to achieve this in a category $\mathcal{C}$ of models is the following:

1. ensure that the tool automatically produces a stream of models (perhaps on-demand by the user) comprising a **set of support** (Definition 3).
2. ensure that whenever $\mathbb{A} \precsim \mathbb{B}$ then user-directed **augmentation** of $\mathbb{A}$ can reach $\mathbb{B}$.

As will be explained below, this strategy relies on a commitment to having the tool produce *minimal* models by default.

5 Geometric Logic

Geometric logic is a variant of first-order logic that makes a rich specification language and supports a view of model finding that is congenial to the analysis goals introduced earlier. In this section we describe the sense in which model finding for a geometric theory is in a sense "syntax directed,"

Positive-Existential Formulas. A formula is *positive-existential* if it is built from atomic formulas (including $\top$ and $\bot$) using finitary $\wedge$, infinitary $\vee$ and $\exists$; with the requirement that each subformula has only finitely many free variables. (Positive existential formulas are referred to in the database community as *unions of conjunctive queries*.)

Suppose α is a positive-existential formula. Let $\mathbb{M}$ be a model and η an environment such that $\mathbb{M} \models_\eta \alpha$. Then there is a *finite* submodel $\mathbb{M}_0$ of $\mathbb{M}$ such that $\mathbb{M}_0 \models_\eta \alpha$ (in particular $\mathbb{M}_0$ encompasses the range of η). For this reason, properties defined by positive-existential formulas are sometimes called *observable* properties [1]. It is important to note that infinite disjunctions—but not conjunctions—are accommodated easily here.

It is also worth noting that if we come to learn (or come to ensure) that a positive-existential fact $\alpha[\vec{a}]$ is true in a model $\mathbb{A}$, perhaps based on the fact that $\mathbb{A}$ has not been fully constructed, then further information added to $\mathbb{A}$ cannot make $\alpha[\vec{a}]$ false. So we might also call positive-existential formulas "imperturbable".

It is a classical result that positive-existential formulas are precisely those preserved under homomorphisms; Rossman [61] has shown that this holds even if we restrict attention to finite models only.

Theorem 4. *The following are equivalent, for a formula $\alpha(\vec{x})$:*

1. α *is preserved by homomorphism: if $h : \mathbb{A} \to \mathbb{B}$ is a homomorphism, and $\vec{a}$ is a vector of elements from $\mathbb{A}$ such that $\mathbb{A} \models \alpha[\vec{a}]$, then $\mathbb{B} \models \alpha[\vec{ha}]$.*
2. α *is logically equivalent to a positive-existential formula.*
3. α *is equivalent to a positive-existential formula in the category of finite models.*

Thus the homomorphism preorder captures the observable properties of models: this is the sense in which we view this preorder as an "information-preserving" one.

Geometric Theories. A theory T is a *geometric theory* if has an axiomatization by sentences of the form

$$\forall \vec{x}. \quad \alpha(\vec{x}) \to \beta(\vec{x}) \tag{1}$$

where α and β are positive-existential. [2] A geometric formula is *coherent* if all of its disjunctions are finite.

To gain intuition for why geometric logic is well-adapted to model finding, consider that a geometric formula $\alpha(\vec{x}) \to \beta(\vec{x})$ is true of a tuple $\vec{a}$ in a model $\mathbb{A}$ whenever $\mathbb{A}$ passes the test: "whenever $\alpha[\vec{a}]$ is observed, $\beta[\vec{a}]$ must also be observed."

The case for geometric logic as a logic of observable properties was made clearly by Abramsky [1]. Geometric logic plays a role in categorical logic [46] and topos theory [44]; and geometric logic is a natural formalism for specification [22,65,71,72]. Independently, Guttman observed [36,38] that a robust class of security goals for protocols are naturally expressed in the form (1).

There have been several investigations into deductive calculi for coherent logic [5,15,16,18,31,68]. Geometric sentences make a *Glivenko class*. That is to say, if a geometric formula is classically derivable from a geometric theory then it is in fact derivable intuitionistically.

Expressivity of Geometric Logic. Many theories are naturally geometric: any algebraic theory, any Horn theory, the theories that arise in disjunctive logic programming, etc. The fact that infinite disjunctions are permitted means that common inductive notions are geometric: transitive closure, an abelian group having torsion, the notion of a model of successor being standard, etc.

More interestingly, *any* first-order theory has a conservative geometric extension. There are a variety of approaches to this result; Dyckhoff and Negri [25] have given a particularly illuminating treatment of the issues.

---

[2] Confusingly, some authors use "geometric" to refer to what is more broadly called "positive existential". For them a "geometric theory" is a collection of quantified implications between "geometric formulas" (thus the axioms themselves are not "geometric formulas").

Set of Support and Completeness. A set of support for a class of models provides a complete "testbed" for entailment of geometric sentences.

Theorem 5. *Suppose T is a geometric theory and $\forall \vec{x} . \alpha(\vec{x}) \rightarrow \beta(\vec{x})$ is a geometric sentence. Let $\vec{a}$ be a sequence of fresh constants appropriate for $\vec{x}$ and suppose $\{\mathbb{A}_1, \mathbb{A}_2 \dots\}$ is an arbitrary-homomorphisms set of support for $T \cup \{\alpha[\vec{a}]\}$. Then*

$$T \models \forall \vec{x} . \alpha(\vec{x}) \rightarrow \beta(\vec{x})$$

if and only if, each $\mathbb{A}_i \models \beta[\vec{a}]$.

Notice that when we can compute a *finite* set of support of finite models $\{\mathbb{A}_1, \mathbb{A}_2 \dots \mathbb{A}_k\}$ for $T \cup \{\alpha[\vec{a}]\}$, Theorem 5 yields a decision procedure. Indeed it suffices that the $\{\mathbb{A}_1, \mathbb{A}_2 \dots \mathbb{A}_k\}$ be, even if infinite, presented in such a way that $T \cup \{\alpha[\vec{a}]\}$ is decidable. This is the key to the decidability result in [23].

6 Direct Model Finding Methods

6.1 Chase-Based Approaches

The Chase is a method for building a model of a geometric theory T, or detecting that T is unsatisfiable. In fact the Chase as we present it here is a natural adaptation of the well-studied [19,29,30,34,34,45] Chase algorithm in the database community, used for checking implications between constraints and computing solutions to data exchange problems.

So let T be a geometric theory. We need to assume that T is written without function symbols other than constants. This is no real constraint, though, since the axioms required when replacing function symbols by relation symbols are themselves geometric.

By standard manipulations we can bring any geometric formula into the form

$$\forall \vec{x} . P(\vec{x}) \rightarrow \bigvee \{\exists \vec{y}_j . Q_j(\vec{x}, \vec{y}_j) \mid j \in J\} \tag{2}$$

where P and each Q_j are conjunctions of atomic formulas. As usual, we view an empty disjunction as representing Falsehood, so that a formula as above with $J = \emptyset$ encodes $\forall \vec{x} . \neg P(\vec{x})$.

Assume now that each axiom of T is in this standard form.

Let C be an infinite set of fresh constants, to be used to name elements of the model we construct. Say that a *fact* over C is a closed atomic sentence over C. We build our model by starting with the empty set of facts, and gradually adding to it until it represents a model of T. Our set of facts is enlarged by doing *Chase steps* in a fair manner.

A Chase Step. Suppose F is a set of facts over C. Let σ be a formula in the form (2).

Suppose $\theta \equiv \{x_1 \mapsto c_1, \dots, x_k \mapsto c_k\}$ is a substitution making P false in F, i.e., $P(\theta \vec{x})$ holds in F yet for no j do we have $Q_j(\theta \vec{x})$ true in F. A Chase-step on F, σ, and θ is the result of

1. choosing some disjunct $E_j \equiv \exists y_{j1} \dots y_{jk} . Q_j(\vec{x}, y_{j1} \dots y_{jk})$

2. adding new elements $d_1, \ldots, d_k$ to C ;
3. adding each of the facts in $\theta' Q_j$ to F, where θ' is the substitution obtained by adding to θ each of the bindings $y_{ji} \mapsto d_i$.

The *Chase* consists of starting with the empty set of facts and iterating the above process.

We halt with success if we reach a finite set F of facts where we cannot apply a step, *i.e.*, when F is a model of T. We halt with failure if we reach a set F of facts where a formula with empty right-hand-side fails in F (which is to say, its left-hand-side is true): we cannot "repair" F to make such a formula true. It is possible that the Chase may not halt: conditions under which termination is guaranteed are an active area of study.

When the Chase is done in a "fair" manner and does not terminate, the resulting infinite set of facts will be a model of T: this is the essential content of the claim that The Chase is a complete deduction method for geometric logic.

Theorem 6 (Deductive Completeness). *Let T be geometric. Then T is satisfiable if and only if there is a fair run of the Chase which does not fail.*

A crucial thing about Chase calculations is that they make no commitments to facts that are not required by the theory. This leads to the following key theorem for model finding.

Theorem 7 (Set of Support). *Let T be geometric. For any model $\mathbb{M}$ of T there is an $\mathbb{M}_i$ obtained by some execution of the Chase and a homomorphism from $\mathbb{M}_i$ to $\mathbb{M}$.*

Provenance in Chase Models. Another aspect of the fact noted above that models built by the Chase are built "by need" is that provenance is easy to compute.

Referring to the general form of axioms (2) above, the only elements in a Chase model are those added to instantiate existential quantifiers $\exists \vec{y}$, and the only atomic facts in the model are those added to make the $Q_j(\vec{x}, \vec{y})$ true. It is easy enough to keep track of these justifications by introducing Skolem functions in the implementation to name elements, so that any fact in the model (Skolemized under the hood) can be traced back through the line of Chase steps that led to its addition. In this way we can answer provenance queries from the user.

The Chase in Practice. The Chase algorithm is described above as a nondeterministic procedure. The choice of rule to fire is one source of nondeterminism, but the important source is the disjunctions on the right-hand sides. Different choices of disjuncts to satisfy will (usually) lead to different output models. An implementation must negotiate this tree of models-in-progress. The original version of Razor managed this structure directly, but this was seen to be too slow for *general* use. (Specifically, performance on the TPTP suite of problems [67] was unacceptable).

Subsequent versions of Razor [63] take a hybrid approach. Roughly speaking, an SMT solver is used to manage the disjunctions, while Chase steps are used to construct elements and facts.

The Chase is used by Rowe, Ramsdell, and Kretz [62] to discover adversary behaviors that thwart layered attestation specifications. This implementation has good performance [59] in its domain without resorting to mechanisms external to the Chase.

6.2 CPSA

The CPSA protocol analyzer [20] is an example of a direct model finder. Actually CPSA is—superficially—of a different character from the other model finders discussed in this paper, since it is does not explicitly take a first-order theory as input. But the theory of strand spaces can be axiomatized, as a geometric theory [22] and the skeletons it returns are readily seen as first-order structures. And CPSA has always been founded on a notion of homomorphism as organizing principle [36]. The theory of strand spaces is not first-order, since a well-foundedness assumption about causality is imposed. But this well-foundedness can be enforced using the infinite disjunctions available in geometric logic.

The CPSA algorithm is not Chase-based, rather it relies instead on the Authentication Test mechanism [39]. (There is however, at least one project, an undergraduate thesis, implementing the strand space approach using the Chase [57].)

CPSA satisfies [37] the set of support criterion expressed by Theorem 5. As such it represents a sound and complete method for establishing security goals (for an unbounded number of sessions) that are represented as geometric sentences. As a technical remark, the category of models that CPSA works with has homomorphisms that are injective on nodes representing message events and arbitrary otherwise.

7   Programming Against a Solver: Theory

We present generic algorithms for model finding that rely on the primitive operation of asking a SAT or SMT solver, or an algorithm like the Chase, for a single finite model of a given theory.

To see that there is some work to do beyond simply invoking a solver, note the following.

1. Once the solver has determined that a theory T is satisfiable, and computed— internally—a model for T, the application must extract the model from the solver. But the API for doing this—in the solvers we are familiar with—is quite restricted. In any event, SMT-Lib compliant solvers are not *required* to make this process particularly convenient. Quoting from the SMT-Lib Standard (v.2.6) [2]:

   The internal representation of the model A is not exposed by the solver. Similarly to an abstract data type, the model can be inspected only through ... [certain commands] ... As a consequence, it can even be partial internally and extended as needed in response to successive invocations of some of these commands.

2. A typical solver makes no promises about the models it returns other that they satisfy the input theory. So *fitness* requires some attention.

3. Repeated requests to a solver for the same theory will often return the same model. So *completeness* must be explicitly managed. (The Alloy tool does priority of excluding—in a best-effort way—models isomorphic to those previously seen.)

The generic algorithms in this section assume that they are working in categories of finite models that have a well-founded homomorphism ordering. In practice for us this means that our categories have finite models as objects and either (i) there is a uniform bound on the domain size of models, or (ii) homomorphisms are injective or inclusions.

Space doesn't permit a review of solver-based augmentation or provenance here, even though tools such as Aluminum, Amalgam, and CompoSAT pursue ambitious goals and solve interesting problems along the way.

7.1 Building Blocks

There are two key sentences we can construct about a model that serve as the essential API with the solver. We'll show how to construct our models using these two building blocks, then make some remarks about how to compose these sentences. In each case there is no mystery about writing *some* sentence that works—the interesting task is to write sentences that behave well in practice.

Fix a theory T and a category of models of T.

1. $homTo_\mathbb{A}$: a sentence defining the models $\mathbb{P} \models T$ such that there is a homomorphism $h : \mathbb{P} \to \mathbb{A}$.
2. $homFrom_\mathbb{A}$: a sentence defining the models $\mathbb{P} \models T$ such that there is a homomorphism $h : \mathbb{A} \to \mathbb{P}$.

So

$$\neg homFrom_\mathbb{A}$$

defines the models $\mathbb{P} \models T$ that are not in the homomorphism cone of $\mathbb{A}$. Thus

$$below_\mathbb{A} := (homTo_\mathbb{A} \wedge \neg homFrom_\mathbb{A})$$

defines the models $\mathbb{P} \models T$ strictly below $\mathbb{A}$ in the homomorphism order.

Note that the above notions make sense whether we consider arbitrary homomorphisms or restrict to injective homomorphisms.

7.2 Minimization

If we bound the size of the domain(s) of our models then a-minimal models exist for any satisfiable theory: the $\precsim$ preorder is well-founded, so the set of minimal elements with respect to this order is non-empty. The question is, how do we compute a-minimal models?

The idea is that, given a model $\mathbb{A}$, we can use the sentences $homTo_\mathbb{A}$ and $homFrom_\mathbb{A}$ to iterate the process of constructing a model that is strictly below $\mathbb{A}$ in the $\precsim$ ordering.

Algorithm 8 (Minimize)

    // A relevant category $\mathcal{C}$ of models of T is part of the context
    input: theory T and model $\mathbb{A} \models T$
    output: model $\mathbb{M} \models T$ such that $\mathbb{M}$ is minimal for $\mathcal{C}$ and $\mathbb{M} \precsim \mathbb{A}$
    initialize: set $\mathbb{M}$ to be $\mathbb{A}$
    while $T' \stackrel{def}{=} T \cup \{below_\mathbb{M}\}$ is satisfiable, set $\mathbb{M}$ to be a model of T'
    return $\mathbb{M}$

Lemma 9. *Algorithm 8 is correct: if the category $\mathcal{C}$ has a well-founded homomorphism ordering and $\mathbb{A}$ is a finite model of T then Algorithm 8 terminates on $\mathbb{A}$, and the output $\mathbb{M}$ is an a-minimal model of T with $\mathbb{M} \precsim \mathbb{A}$*

7.3   Set of Support

We take the ability to generate a set-of-support for the class of all models of a theory T to be a natural notion of "completeness" in model-finding. Theorem 5 makes a precise claim of completness with respect to reasoning about geometric consequences of T.

Computing sets-of-support is another application of $homFrom_A$, or more to the point, $\neg homFrom_A$. Given theory T and model A, if we construct the theory $T' \overset{\text{def}}{=} T \cup \{\neg homFrom_A\}$ then calls to the SMT solver on theory T' are guaranteed to return models of T outside the hom-cone of A if any exist. So a set-of-support for T can be generated by iterating this process.

Recall that we can instrument any theory with a set of extra sentences uniformly bounding the size of the models of the enriched theory.

Algorithm 10 (SetOfSupport)

> // A relevant category $\mathcal{C}$ of models of T is part of the context
> *input: theory T with a uniformly bounded model size.*
> *output: a stream $M_1, M_2, \ldots$ of minimal models of T such that for any $\mathbb{P} \models T$, there is some i such that $M_i \precsim \mathbb{P}$.*
> *initialize: set theory T^* to be T*
> **while** T^* *is satisfiable*
> > *let M be a (minimal)[3] model of T^**
> > *output M*
> > *set T^* to be $T^* \cup \{\neg homFrom_M\}$*

If desired, of course, we can generate a potentially infinite set of support for a theory with unbounded domain sizes by "iterative deepening," letting the bounds increase indefinitely.

8   Programming Against a Solver: Practice

The generic model-finding algorithms above rely on two crucial building blocks: the sentences $homFrom_A$ and $homTo_A$, characterizing $\{\mathbb{P} \mid A \precsim \mathbb{P}\}$ and $\{\mathbb{P} \mid \mathbb{P} \precsim A\}$ respectively. It turns out that writing versions of these sentences to behave efficiently depends on the category of models we work in.

8.1   Constructing HomTo and HomFrom for Arbitrary Homomorphisms

The "Homomorphism Problem," deciding whether $M \precsim N$ for arbitrary homomorphisms, is NP-complete [32]. The more general problems of characterizing, for fixed A, the sets $\{\mathbb{P} \mid A \precsim \mathbb{P}\}$ and $\{\mathbb{P} \mid \mathbb{P} \precsim A\}$ are deep and well-studied [3,7,35,50]. Here we focus, not on the computational complexity of the problem but the practical problem of asking SAT- and SMT-solvers to produce appropriate models, using *homFrom* and *homTo* sentences.

---

[3] Completeness of this algorithm does not require that the models M we work with are minimal. But if we do work with minimal models there will be fewer iterations.

homTo. Constructing a *homTo*$_\mathbb{A}$ sentence is straightforward ([21]) and even a naive such sentence seems to not cause our tools any trouble. We simply add a function symbol to the signature and write axioms saying that it is a homomorphism.

Algorithm 11 (Constructing homTo)

> *input:* model $\mathbb{A}$ over signature Σ.
> *output:* sentence homTo$_\mathbb{A}$ in an expanded signature Σ^+, such that for any model $\mathbb{P} \models \Sigma$, $\mathbb{P} \precsim \mathbb{A}$ iff there is an expansion $\mathbb{P}^+$ of $\mathbb{P}$ to Σ^+ with $\mathbb{P}^+ \models$ homTo$_\mathbb{A}$.
>
> *define* Σ^+ to be the extension of Σ obtained by
> - adding a set of fresh constants naming elements of the domain of $\mathbb{A}$
> - adding a function symbol $h_S : S \to S$ at each sort S
>
> *return* homTo$_\mathbb{A}$ as the conjunction of the following sentences, one for each function symbol f and predicate R in Σ. Here $\vec{e}$ and e' range over the names for elements of $\mathbb{A}$.

$$\forall \vec{x}, y \, . \, f\vec{x} = y \; \to \; \bigvee \{ (\vec{hx} = \vec{e} \wedge y = e') \mid \mathbb{A} \models f\vec{e} = e' \}$$

$$\forall \vec{x} \, . \, R\vec{x} = true \; \to \; \bigvee \{ (\vec{hx} = \vec{e}) \mid \mathbb{A} \models R\vec{e} = true \}$$

If we are working in a category of injective maps, simply add a sentence to say that h is injective.

Lemma 12. *There is a homomorphism from $\mathbb{B}$ to $\mathbb{A}$ iff there is a model $\mathbb{B}^+ \models$ homTo$_\mathbb{A}$ such that $\mathbb{B}$ is the reduction to Σ of $\mathbb{B}^+$.*

Constructing HomFrom. Let $\mathbb{A}$ be a finite model over signature Σ. Define an expanded signature Σ^+ by adding, for each element e of the domain of $\mathbb{A}$, a constant c_e, and let $\mathbb{A}^+$ be the corresponding expansion of $\mathbb{A}$. The *diagram* $\Delta_\mathbb{A}$ of $\mathbb{A}$ is the set of atomic sentences and negations of atomic sentences true in $\mathbb{A}^+$. If we take only the atomic sentences, the result is the *positive diagram* $\Delta_\mathbb{A}^+$ of $\mathbb{A}$.

The sentence—in the original signature Σ—obtained by converting the new constants in the positive diagram to variables and existentially quantifying them is called the *characteristic sentence ch*$_\mathbb{A}$ of $\mathbb{A}$.

It is easy to see that the models of *ch*$_\mathbb{A}$ are precisely those models $\mathbb{B}$ with $\mathbb{A} \precsim \mathbb{B}$.

But observe that for our purposes we are interested in characterizing (by a first-order sentence) the *complement* of the set of $\mathbb{B}$ such that $\mathbb{A} \precsim \mathbb{B}$. Certainly the negation $\neg ch_\mathbb{A}$ suffices. But simply negating *ch*$_\mathbb{A}$ leads to computationally unwieldy formulas, since universal quantifiers are bottlenecks for SMT-solvers.

The ideal outcome would be to construct an existential sentence capturing the complement of the hom cone of $\mathbb{A}$. Equivalently we might look for a structure $\mathbb{D}$ such that for any $\mathbb{X}$, $\mathbb{X} \precsim \mathbb{D}$ iff $\mathbb{A} \not\precsim \mathbb{X}$. This is called "homomorphism duality" in the literature. Such a structure doesn't always exist, and even if it does, it can be exponentially large in the size of $\mathbb{A}$ [28]. So we must turn to heuristic methods.

The model finders Razor and LPA work with arbitrary homomorphisms. The former tool uses, essentially, *homTo*$_\mathbb{A}$ as defined in Algorithm 11, and uses the straightforward *ch*$_\mathbb{A}$ in building *homFrom*$_\mathbb{A}$. LPA inherits this approach from Razor. Elsewhere we have written [21,24] about some best-effort techniques for constructing *homFrom*$_\mathbb{A}$ sentences.

8.2   Constructing HomTo and HomFrom for Submodel Morphisms

"Bounded model finding" as represented by (for example) Alloy imposes a uniform bound on the sizes of models for the duration of each analysis session. Indeed it introduces a set of *names* for model elements[3]. Let us choose to respect distinctness of names in our homomorphisms. We arrive at the notion of a "submodel" category $\mathcal{B}$ of models, with the following properties.

- There is a fixed finite set C of constants, and every element of a model in $\mathcal{B}$ is named by a constant in C (we do not assume unique names per element).
- The ordering $\mathbb{A} \sqsubseteq \mathbb{B}$ on models is the submodel ordering

It is not obvious that ordering by submodel, which requires that relationships between models respect names, is the best choice for model exploration. The next section takes up this question.

In these submodel categories it turns out that $homTo_{\mathbb{A}}$ and $homFrom_{\mathbb{A}}$ can be expressed compactly, with propositional formulas.

Constructing homTo.   Given model $\mathbb{A}$ we take $homTo_{\mathbb{A}}$ to be the propositional sentence

$$\bigwedge \{\neg\alpha \mid \alpha \text{ is atomic}, \mathbb{A} \models \neg\alpha\}$$

Note in particular that if c and c' are constants naming distinct elements of $\mathbb{A}$, then $c \neq c'$ is one of the conjuncts of $homTo_{\mathbb{A}}$. This sentence works: if $\mathbb{B}$ satisfies this then the identity map on names is a homomorphism, since there are no facts of $\mathbb{B}$ that make an obstacle.

Constructing homFrom.   Given model $\mathbb{A}$ we take $homFrom_{\mathbb{A}}$ to be the propositional sentence

$$\bigwedge \{\beta \mid \beta \text{ is atomic}, \mathbb{A} \models \beta\}$$

so that $\neg homFrom_{\mathbb{A}}$, used to avoid the homomorphism-cone of $\mathbb{A}$, is

$$\bigvee \{\neg\beta \mid \beta \text{ is atomic}, \mathbb{A} \models \beta\}$$

This sentence works: it is just a version of the naive $ch_{\mathbb{A}}$ but we do not have to introduce existential quantifiers since our homomorphisms are so constrained.

Minimization and Set of Support are now easily computed. One might wonder whether the SAT-solving iteration required, in Algorithm 8, to reduce a model to a minimal one might be expensive. But experimental evaluation [54] has shown that in fact minimal models are returned quite quickly.

Examples.   The model finders Aluminum, and Amalgam work with the inclusion ordering on models. (They inherit this aspect from Kodkod, their core model-finding engine.) They use the versions of $homTo_{\mathbb{A}}$ and $homFrom_{\mathbb{A}}$ developed in this section.

---

[3] somewhat confusingly, names are called "bounds" in the Alloy community.

8.3   Constructing homTo and homFrom for Injective Morphisms

As a final note, we observe the somewhat surprising fact that if we relax the notion of homomorphism in bounded categories to require only injectivity, as opposed to preservation of names, then analysis is almost as easy as working with submodels.

For minimization: to say that there is an injective homomorphism from $\mathbb{A}$ to $\mathbb{B}$ is to say that $\mathbb{A}$ is isomorphic to a submodel of $\mathbb{B}$. Since we only care about models up to isomorphism, the problem of minimization with respect to injective maps is the same problem as minimization with respect to the submodel ordering.

For set of support: this is not quite "the same problem" in the two orderings. We require one more idea. The key fact is this: if $\mathbb{B}$ is a *minimal* model of a theory and there is an injective homomorphism from $\mathbb{A}$ to $\mathbb{B}$ then in fact $\mathbb{A}$ and $\mathbb{B}$ are isomorphic. Since: our assumption implies that $\mathbb{A}$ is isomorphic to a submodel of $\mathbb{B}$. If this submodel is not $\mathbb{B}$ itself, it would provide a counterexample to the minimality of $\mathbb{B}$.

The upshot of this is that the only obstacle to the correctness of the Set of Support algorithm for injective homomorphism when we use the submodel-based *homTo* and *homFrom* constructions is that we might construct isomorphic copies of previously-derived models. So all we have to do is add an isomorphism check at the end of the next-model algorithm. Such a check is not known to be asymptotically efficient, but is a standard operation and behaves well in practice.

9   Conclusion

Motivated by the idea of using model finding to explore theories as opposed to simply checking satisfiability, we have argued for development of *model-finding assistants* to aid users in understanding software artifacts. We have (i) suggested some core design principles for a model finding tool, (ii) argued for geometric logic as a convenient formalism for a specifications supporting a computational interpretation, and (iii) outlined some fundamental building blocks that supply core functionality in generating a set of support for the finite models of a theory.

Note and Acknowledgements. This paper surveys some recent work—foundational and applied—by a variety of authors in model finding. All of it has been previously published. My purpose in gathering this material into one place is to point out the shared foundations for a number of different model finders and to identify some differences in their aspirations and in their functionalities.

As the technical content of this paper draws so heavily on previous work with coauthors, my feeling of gratitude to my colleagues is stronger than usual. I want to particularly thank *Natasha Danas, Joshua Guttman, Kathi Fisler, Shriram Krishnamurthi, Timothy Nelson, John Ramsdell, and Salman Saghafi* for their insights and contributions.

References

1. Abramsky, S.: Domain theory in logical form. Ann. Pure Appl. Logic **51**(1–2), 1–77 (1991)
2. Barrett, C., Fontaine, P., Tinelli, C.: The Satisfiability Modulo Theories Library (SMT-LIB) (2016). www.SMT-LIB.org

3. Barto, L., DeMeo, W.J., Mottet, A.: The complexity of the homomorphism problem for boolean structures (2020). CoRR **abs/2010.04958**, https://arxiv.org/abs/2010.04958

4. Baumgartner, P., Fuchs, A., Nivelle, H.D., Tinelli, C.: Computing finite models by reduction to function-free clause logic. J. Appl. Logic **7**(1), 58–74 (2009)

5. Bezem, M., Coquand, T.: Automating coherent logic. In: Sutcliffe, G., Voronkov, A. (eds.) LPAR 2005. LNCS (LNAI), vol. 3835, pp. 246–260. Springer, Heidelberg (2005). https://doi.org/10.1007/11591191_18

6. Blanchette, J.C., Nipkow, T.: Nitpick: a counterexample generator for higher-order logic based on a relational model finder. In: Kaufmann, M., Paulson, L.C. (eds.) ITP 2010. LNCS, vol. 6172, pp. 131–146. Springer, Heidelberg (2010). https://doi.org/10.1007/978-3-642-14052-5_11

7. Bodirsky, M., Feller, T., Knäuer, S., Rudolph, S.: On logics and homomorphism closure (2021). CoRR abs/2104.11955, https://arxiv.org/abs/2104.11955

8. Bouajjani, A., Fernandez, J.-C., Halbwachs, N.: Minimal model generation. In: Clarke, E.M., Kurshan, R.P. (eds.) CAV 1990. LNCS, vol. 531, pp. 197–203. Springer, Heidelberg (1991). https://doi.org/10.1007/BFb0023733

9. Bry, F., Yahya, A.: Minimal model generation with positive unit hyper-resolution tableaux. In: Miglioli, P., Moscato, U., Mundici, D., Ornaghi, M. (eds.) TABLEAUX 1996. LNCS, vol. 1071, pp. 143–159. Springer, Heidelberg (1996). https://doi.org/10.1007/3-540-61208-4_10

10. Bry, F., Yahya, A.: Positive unit hyperresolution tableaux and their application to minimal model generation. J. Autom. Reas **25**, 35–82 (2000)

11. Bulwahn, L.: The new quickcheck for isabelle. In: Hawblitzel, C., Miller, D. (eds.) CPP 2012. LNCS, vol. 7679, pp. 92–108. Springer, Heidelberg (2012). https://doi.org/10.1007/978-3-642-35308-6_10

12. Chamarthi, H.R., Dillinger, P.C., Kaufmann, M., Manolios, P.: Integrating testing and interactive theorem proving. In: Hardin, D., Schmaltz, J. (eds.) Proceedings 10th International Workshop on the ACL2 Theorem Prover and its Applications, ACL2 2011, Austin, Texas, USA, 3–4 November 2011. EPTCS, vol. 70, pp. 4–19 (2011)

13. Claessen, K., Sorensson, N.: New techniques that improve MACE-style finite model finding. In: Proceedings of the CADE-19 Workshop: Model Computation-Principles, Algorithms, Applications. Citeseer (2003)

14. Claessen, K., Hughes, J.: QuickCheck. In: Proceedings of the Fifth ACM SIGPLAN International Conference on Functional Programming - ICFP '00. ACM Press (2000)

15. Coquand, T.: A completeness proof for geometric logic. In: Logic, Methodology and Philosophy of Science. Proceedings of the Twelfth International Congress, pp. 79–90 (2010)

16. Coste, M., Lombardi, H., Roy, M.F.: Dynamical method in algebra: effective nullstellensätze. Ann. Pure Appl. Logic **111**(3), 203–256 (2001)

17. Danas, N., Nelson, T., Harrison, L., Krishnamurthi, S., Dougherty, D.J.: User studies of principled model finder output. In: Cimatti, A., Sirjani, M. (eds.) SEFM 2017. LNCS, vol. 10469, pp. 168–184. Springer, Cham (2017). https://doi.org/10.1007/978-3-319-66197-1_11

18. de Nivelle, H., Meng, J.: Geometric resolution: a proof procedure based on finite model search. In: Furbach, U., Shankar, N. (eds.) IJCAR 2006. LNCS (LNAI), vol. 4130, pp. 303–317. Springer, Heidelberg (2006). https://doi.org/10.1007/11814771_28

19. Deutsch, A., Nash, A., Remmel, J.: The chase revisited. In: ACM SIGMOD-SIGACT-SIGART Symposium on Principles of Database Systems, pp. 149–158 (2008)

20. Doghmi, S.F., Guttman, J.D., Thayer, F.J.: Searching for shapes in cryptographic protocols. In: Grumberg, O., Huth, M. (eds.) TACAS 2007. LNCS, vol. 4424, pp. 523–537. Springer, Heidelberg (2007). https://doi.org/10.1007/978-3-540-71209-1_41

21. Dougherty, D.J., Guttman, J.D., Ramsdell, J.D.: Homomorphisms and Minimality for Enrich-by-Need Security Analysis. ArXiv e-prints (2018)

22. Dougherty, D.J., Guttman, J.: Geometric logic and strand spaces. In: 5th International Workshop on Security and Rewriting Techniques (2010)
23. Dougherty, D.J., Guttman, J.D.: Decidability for lightweight Diffie-Hellman protocols. In: IEEE 27th Computer Security Foundations Symposium, CSF 2014, Vienna, Austria, 19–22 July 2014, pp. 217–231 (2014)
24. Dougherty, D.J., Guttman, J.D., Ramsdell, J.D.: Security protocol analysis in context: computing minimal executions using SMT and CPSA. In: Furia, C.A., Winter, K. (eds.) IFM 2018. LNCS, vol. 11023, pp. 130–150. Springer, Cham (2018). https://doi.org/10.1007/978-3-319-98938-9_8
25. Dyckhoff, R., Negri, S.: Geometrisation of first-order logic. Bull. Symb. Logic **21**, 123–163 (2015)
26. Eastlund, C.: Doublecheck your theorems. In: Proceedings of the Eighth International Workshop on the ACL2 Theorem Prover and its Applications, pp. 42–46 (2009)
27. El Ghazi, A.A., Taghdiri, M.: Analyzing alloy constraints using an SMT solver: a case study. In: 5th International Workshop on Automated Formal Methods (AFM) (2010)
28. Erdős, P.L., Pálvölgyi, D., Tardif, C., Tardos, G.: Regular families of forests, antichains and duality pairs of relational structures. Combinatorica **37**(4), 651–672 (2017). https://doi.org/10.1007/s00493-015-3003-4
29. Fagin, R., Kolaitis, P.G., Popa, L.: Data exchange: getting to the core. ACM Trans. Database Syst. (TODS) **30**(1), 174–210 (2005)
30. Fagin, R., Kolaitis, P.G., Miller, R.J., Popa, L.: Data exchange: semantics and query answering. Theor. Comput. Sci. **336**(1), 89–124 (2005)
31. Fisher, J., Bezem, M.: Skolem machines. Fundamenta Informaticae **91**(1), 79–103 (2009)
32. Garey, M.R., Johnson, D.S.: Computers and intractability. w. h (1979)
33. Geisler, T., Panne, S., Schütz, H.: Satchmo - the compiling and functional variants. J. Autom. Reas. **18**(2), 227–236 (1997)
34. Gottlob, G.: Computing cores for data exchange: new algorithms and practical solutions. In: ACM SIGMOD-SIGACT-SIGART Symposium on Principles of Database Systems, pp. 148–159 (2005)
35. Grohe, M.: The complexity of homomorphism and constraint satisfaction problems seen from the other side. J. ACM (JACM) **54**(1), 1–24 (2007)
36. Guttman, J.D.: Security theorems via model theory. EXPRESS Express. Conc. (EPTCS) **8**, 51 (2009). https://doi.org/10.4204/EPTCS.8.5
37. Guttman, J.D.: Shapes: surveying crypto protocol runs. In: Cortier, V., Kremer, S. (eds.) Formal Models and Techniques for Analyzing Security Protocols. IOS Press, Cryptology and Information Security Series (2011)
38. Guttman, J.D.: Establishing and preserving protocol security goals. J. Comput. Secur. **22**(2), 203–267 (2014)
39. Guttman, J.D., Thayer, F.J.: Authentication tests and the structure of bundles. Theor. Comput. Sci. **283**(2), 333–380 (2002)
40. Hughes, J.: QuickCheck testing for fun and profit. In: Hanus, M. (ed.) PADL 2007. LNCS, vol. 4354, pp. 1–32. Springer, Heidelberg (2006). https://doi.org/10.1007/978-3-540-69611-7_1
41. Jackson, D.: Alloy: a language and tool for exploring software designs. Commun. ACM **62**(9), 66–76 (2019)
42. Koshimura, M., Nabeshima, H., Fujita, H., Hasegawa, R.: Minimal model generation with respect to an atom set. In: International Workshop on First-Order Theorem Proving (2009)
43. Krishnamurthi, S., Nelson, T.: The human in formal methods. In: ter Beek, M.H., McIver, A., Oliveira, J.N. (eds.) FM 2019. LNCS, vol. 11800, pp. 3–10. Springer, Cham (2019). https://doi.org/10.1007/978-3-030-30942-8_1

44. Mac Lane, S., Moerdijk, I.: Sheaves in Geometry and Logic: A First Introduction to Topos Theory. Universitext, Springer, New York (1992). https://doi.org/10.1007/978-1-4612-0927-0

45. Maier, D., Mendelzon, A.O., Sagiv, Y.: Testing implications of data dependencies. ACM Trans. Database Syst. (TODS) **4**(4), 455–469 (1979)

46. Makkai, M., Reyes, G.E.: First Order Categorical Logic. LNM, vol. 611. Springer, Heidelberg (1977). https://doi.org/10.1007/BFb0066201

47. Maldonado-Lopez, F.A., Chavarriaga, J., Donoso, Y.: Detecting network policy conflicts using Alloy. In: Ameur, Y.A., Schewe, K. (eds.) Abstract State Machines, Alloy, B, TLA, VDM, and Z - 4th International Conference, ABZ 2014, Toulouse, France, 2–6 June 2014. Proceedings. Lecture Notes in Computer Science, vol. 8477, pp. 314–317. Springer, Heidelberg (2014). https://doi.org/10.1007/978-3-662-43652-3_31

48. Maoz, S., Ringert, J.O., Rumpe, B.: CD2Alloy: class diagrams analysis using alloy revisited. In: Whittle, J., Clark, T., Kühne, T. (eds.) MODELS 2011. LNCS, vol. 6981, pp. 592–607. Springer, Heidelberg (2011). https://doi.org/10.1007/978-3-642-24485-8_44

49. Marinov, D., Khurshid, S.: Testera: a novel framework for automated testing of java programs. In: Proceedings 16th Annual International Conference on Automated Software Engineering (ASE 2001), pp. 22–31. IEEE (2001)

50. Marx, D.: Tractable hypergraph properties for constraint satisfaction and conjunctive queries. J. ACM (JACM) **60**(6), 1–51 (2013)

51. McCune, W.: Mace4 reference manual and guide (2003). arXiv preprint cs/0310055

52. Milicevic, A., Misailovic, S., Marinov, D., Khurshid, S.: Korat: a tool for generating structurally complex test inputs. In: 29th International Conference on Software Engineering (ICSE'07), pp. 771–774. IEEE (2007)

53. Nelson, T., Danas, N., Dougherty, D.J., Krishnamurthi, S.: The power of Why and Why Not: enriching scenario exploration with provenance. In: Proceedings of the 2017 11th Joint Meeting on Foundations of Software Engineering, ESEC/FSE 2017, Paderborn, Germany, 4–8 September 2017, pp. 106–116 (2017)

54. Nelson, T., Saghafi, S., Dougherty, D.J., Fisler, K., Krishnamurthi, S.: Aluminum: Principled scenario exploration through minimality. In: 35th International Conference on Software Engineering (ICSE), pp. 232–241 (2013)

55. Nelson, T., Barratt, C., Dougherty, D.J., Fisler, K., Krishnamurthi, S.: The Margrave tool for firewall analysis. In: Proceedings of the 24th USENIX Large Installation System Administration Conference (LISA 2010) (2010)

56. Paraskevopoulou, Z., Hriţcu, C., Dénès, M., Lampropoulos, L., Pierce, B.C.: Foundational property-based testing. In: Urban, C., Zhang, X. (eds.) ITP 2015. LNCS, vol. 9236, pp. 325–343. Springer, Cham (2015). https://doi.org/10.1007/978-3-319-22102-1_22

57. Pombrio, J.L.: Protocol analysis via the chase. Technical report, Worcester Polytechnic Institute (2011)

58. Porncharoenwase, S., Nelson, T., Krishnamurthi, S.: CompoSAT: specification-guided coverage for model finding. In: Havelund, K., Peleska, J., Roscoe, B., de Vink, E. (eds.) FM 2018. LNCS, vol. 10951, pp. 568–587. Springer, Cham (2018). https://doi.org/10.1007/978-3-319-95582-7_34

59. Ramsdell, J.: Personal communication (2021)

60. Reynolds, A., Tinelli, C., Goel, A., Krstić, S.: Finite model finding in SMT. In: Sharygina, N., Veith, H. (eds.) CAV 2013. LNCS, vol. 8044, pp. 640–655. Springer, Heidelberg (2013). https://doi.org/10.1007/978-3-642-39799-8_42

61. Rossman, B.: Homomorphism preservation theorems. J. ACM (JACM) **55**(3), 15 (2008)

62. Rowe, P.D., Ramsdell, J.D., Kretz, I.D.: Automated trust analysis for layered attestations. Submitted for publication (2021)

63. Saghafi, S., Danas, R., Dougherty, D.J.: Exploring theories with a model-finding assistant. In: Felty, A.P., Middeldorp, A. (eds.) CADE 2015. LNCS (LNAI), vol. 9195, pp. 434–449. Springer, Cham (2015). https://doi.org/10.1007/978-3-319-21401-6_30

64. Saghafi, S., Dougherty, D.J.: Razor: provenance and exploration in model-finding. In: 4th Workshop on Practical Aspects of Automated Reasoning (PAAR) (2014)

65. Saghafi, S., Nelson, T., Dougherty, D.J.: Geometric logic for policy analysis. In: International Workshop on Automated Reasoning in Security and Software Verification (ARSEC 2013), pp. 12–20 (2013)

66. Shao, D., Khurshid, S., Perry, D.E.: Whispec: white-box testing of libraries using declarative specifications. In: Proceedings of the 2007 Symposium on Library-Centric Software Design, pp. 11–20 (2007)

67. Sutcliffe, G.: The TPTP problem library and associated infrastructure. From CNF to TH0, TPTP v6.4.0. J. Autom. Reas. **59**(4), 483–502 (2017)

68. Thorstensen, E.: Instance-Based Hyper-Tableaux for Coherent Logic. Master's thesis, University of Oslo (2009)

69. Torlak, E., Jackson, D.: Kodkod: a relational model finder. In: Conference on Tools and Algorithms for the Construction and Analysis of Systems (2007)

70. Vakili, A., Day, N.A.: Finite model finding using the logic of equality with uninterpreted functions. In: Fitzgerald, J., Heitmeyer, C., Gnesi, S., Philippou, A. (eds.) FM 2016. LNCS, vol. 9995, pp. 677–693. Springer, Cham (2016). https://doi.org/10.1007/978-3-319-48989-6_41

71. Vickers, S.: Geometric logic in computer science. In: Burn, G.L., Gay, S.J., Ryan, M. (eds.) Theory and Formal Methods 1993, Proceedings of the First Imperial College Department of Computing Workshop on Theory and Formal Methods, Isle of Thorns Conference Centre, Chelwood Gate, Sussex, UK, 29–31 March 1993, pp. 37–54. Workshops in Computing, Springer, Heideleberg (1993). https://doi.org/10.1007/978-1-4471-3503-6_4

72. Vickers, S.: Geometric logic as a specification language. In: Hankin, C., Mackie, I., Hankin, R.N., Mackie, I., Nagarajan, R. (eds.) Proceedings for the Second Imperial College Department of Computing Workshop on Theory and Formal Methods, pp. 321–340 (1995)

73. Zhang, J., Zhang, H.: SEM: a system for enumerating models. In: IJCAI, vol. 95, pp. 298–303 (1995)

Secure Key Management Policies
in Strand Spaces

Riccardo Focardi$^{(\boxtimes)}$ and Flaminia L. Luccio

DAIS, Ca' Foscari University, Venice, Italy
{focardi,luccio}@unive.it

Abstract. Key management is the Achilles heel of cryptography. In recent years, several attacks have been identified due to poor key management or too liberal APIs, which do not provide a policy that precisely determines the intended use of cryptographic keys. In this paper, we have taken advantage of the expressiveness and simplicity of strand spaces, first introduced in 1998 by Joshua Guttman et al., to specify a significant subset of key management APIs. We used the automatic CPSA tool to rediscover, in an extremely clear and effective way, some known attacks. We have therefore defined a generic key management policy model and proved a key secrecy theorem for a typed version of the API. The proof highlighted the necessary requirements of the policy that we formalized through a closure property that, in fact, computes which types a key can take at runtime.

Keywords: Crypto API · Key management · Strand spaces · Automated verification

1   Introduction

This paper is dedicated to Joshua Guttman, on the occasion of his 66th and 2/3 birthday. Joshua's work has been a source of inspiration for ours. His work is always foundational and insightful. He always explores different perspectives and finds elegant and meaningful solutions to challenging problems. Strand spaces are a great example of Joshua's contribution. They allow us to prove properties of security protocols and, at the same time, deeply understand the actual requirements for security. In this work we celebrate Joshua's research work by applying the strand space formalism to the simple but delicate problem of key management in security devices. The proof of security was challenging and insightful, even more than expected! So thanks Joshua . . . and happy birthday!

Cryptography is becoming more and more pervasive. The expansion of IoT, home automation and industry 4.0 has dramatically increased the attack surface, making it necessary to use cryptographic protocols to protect communications and data. However, encryption is complex as not all cryptographic mechanisms offer the same level of protection. Protocols and implementations, may present

© Springer Nature Switzerland AG 2021
D. Dougherty et al. (Eds.): Guttman Festschrift, LNCS 13066, pp. 175–197, 2021.
https://doi.org/10.1007/978-3-030-91631-2_10

bugs that weaken or, in some cases, cancel the security guarantees offered by the adopted mechanisms.

Key management is often the Achilles heel of cryptographic systems. Cryptographic keys must be stored securely, using tamper-resistant hardware, such as Hardware Security Modules (HSMs), or through appropriate keystores protected by passwords or other cryptographic keys. Keys, to be useful, must be shared using secure channels. A typical example is the export of cryptographic keys from an HSM using the so-called *wrap* operation, in which a sensitive key is encrypted with another key before being exported, so that its value is never exposed in the clear. This simple operation has caused several problems and attacks on real devices. In some cases they were simply due to erroneous key management, in other cases to overly liberal APIs, which do not allow to provide a policy that precisely determines the intended use of a certain class of keys. See, for example, the numerous papers on PKCS#11 standard API vulnerabilities [4,7,9,11,23,31].

Joshua Guttman is very well known for the introduction of the notion of strand spaces, in a joint work with F. Fabrega and J. Herzog [15]. In this paper we have exploited the expressiveness and simplicity of strand spaces to study the security of the key management APIs. We have specified a significant subset of key management APIs that include symmetric key encryption, decryption, wrap, and unwrap operations. To demonstrate that the specified set is already expressive enough to exhibit interesting attacks, we have used the automatic CPSA tool, proposed by Joshua Guttman et al. [1,25] to rediscover, in an extremely clear and effective way, some known attacks. We have therefore defined a generic key management policy model based on dynamic types for keys. When a key is created, it is assigned to a particular type, then, the policy determines which cryptographic operations can be performed by a certain type, towards other types of keys and data.

The operations modeled are simply encryption and decryption, as key wraps and unwraps are in fact nothing more than encryption and decryption performed between cryptographic keys. We then used strand spaces to prove a key secrecy theorem for a typed version of the API. The proof highlighted the necessary requirements of the key management policy and some assumptions that, inductively, allow us to first demonstrate the secrecy of keys starting from those that do not depend on others (intuitively the master keys). In some cases, the policy is too permissive and it is not possible to apply the theorem. In the examples, we illustrate that these cases usually correspond to attacks that allow to discover the value of a cryptographic key in the clear. In order to analyze the policies, we have formalized a *closure* operation which over-approximates which types a key can take at runtime. By inspecting this closure it is possible to immediately see the critical cases that correspond to attacks.

Paper Structure. In Sect. 2 we give some technical background and discuss related work; in Sect. 3 we define a generic model for key management policies, giving some examples; in Sect. 4 we formalize a key management API in strand spaces showing that an untyped version is subject to known attacks (using CPSA), and then proving a security theorem for a typed version.

2   Background and Related Work

In this section we first introduce the strand space model (Sect. 2.1), and the CPSA tool (Sect. 2.2). We then present the PKCS#11 standard (Sect. 2.3), illustrating some known attacks. We finally discuss the related work (Sect. 2.4).

2.1   The Strand Space Model

The strand space formalism was introduced in [15] to analyze protocol executions. Events are defined using a partially-ordered graph, and this graph is generated by causal interaction. The model analyzes the interaction among the participants in the network from a viewpoint of a single participant. The events consist of a message M being transmitted ($+M$) or received ($-M$). The set of all possible events is denoted ($\pm M$), and a finite sequence of such events is called a *strand*, denoted s, and is an element of $(\pm M)^*$. Also the attacker, called a *penetrator*, can be viewed as a strand, and his strands are sequences of sending and receiving of messages. Activities the penetrator may perform are, e.g., sending concatenated messages, sending out guessable data, etc. A collection of strands is called a *strand space* and it includes strands of the legitimate participants and strands of the penetrator.

Bundles define the underlying execution model. In a bundle, every reception is related to a previous transmission of that message. More precisely, the relation $a \rightarrow b$ on the nodes specifies that a and b respectively send and receive a message. A bundle is always acyclic and represents the causal dependencies of the nodes in terms of both communication and natural ordering of events in the strands. A bundle of a correct protocol is a bundle in which there is one strand for each party, and each of them agree on different issues such are participants, keys, nonces, etc. In the bundle there are also penetrator strands that however, do not prevent the legitimate participant operations. Moreover, the adversary is able to guess only those values that could have been received. Finally, protocol correctness depends on the freshness of nonces and session keys.

We recall the definition of terms and subterm relation from [15] [Sect. 2.3]. We assume a set $\mathbf{T}$ of atomic messages (texts) and a set $\mathbf{K}$ of cryptographic keys, disjoint from $\mathbf{T}$. We then write$\{g\}_k$ to denote term g encrypted under symmetric key k and $g\ h$ to denote the concatenation of terms g and h. The concatenation of z terms will be noted as $g_1\ g_2\ \dots\ g_n$. We let $\mathbf{A}$ denote the set of all terms constructed by applying encryption and concatenation starting from $\mathbf{T}$ and $\mathbf{K}$.

Definition 1 (Subterm relation). *The subterm relation $\sqsubset$ is defined inductively, so that:*

- *$a \sqsubset t$ for $t \in \mathbf{T}$ iff $a = t$;*
- *$a \sqsubset k$ for $k \in \mathbf{K}$ iff $a = k$;*

$- \ a \sqsubset \{g\}_k \ \textit{iff} \ a \sqsubset g \ \textit{or} \ a = \{g\}_k;$
$- \ a \sqsubset g \ h \ \textit{iff} \ a \sqsubset g \ \textit{or} \ a \sqsubset h \ \textit{or} \ a = g \ h;$

Notice that the subterm relation does not inspect cryptographic keys as their are never deducible from a ciphertext.

We recall the definition of penetrator traces from [15] [Definition 3.1] that we will need next, and provide a very intuitive example of how strands are defined:

Definition 2 (Penetrator). *Let* **T** *be a set of atomic messages (texts) and let* $\mathbf{K}_\mathcal{P} \subseteq \mathbf{K}$ *be a set of keys initially known by the attacker. A penetrator trace* $s \in \mathcal{P}$ *is one of the following:*

M. *Text message:* $\langle +t \rangle$ *with* $t \in \mathbf{T}$
F. *Flushing:* $\langle -g \rangle$
T. *Tee:* $\langle -g, \ +g, \ +g \rangle$
C. *Concatenation:* $\langle -g, \ -h, \ +g \ h \rangle$
S. *Separation:* $\langle -g \ h, \ +g, \ +h \rangle$
K. *Key:* $\langle +k \rangle$ *with* $k \in \mathbf{K}_\mathcal{P}$
E. *Encryption:* $\langle -k, \ -m, \ +\{m\}_k \rangle$
D. *Decryption:* $\langle -k, \ -\{m\}_k, \ +m \rangle$

Notice that, since we will only consider symmetric key cryptography we do not consider inverse keys in the definition above.

2.2   The CPSA Tool

The Cryptographic Protocol Shapes Analyzer (CPSA) is a tool developed at The MITRE Corporation. Several people work on the tool Joshua D. Guttman, John D. Ramsdell, Jon C. Herzog, Shaddin F. Doghmi, F. Javier Thayer, Paul D. Rowe, and Moses D. Liskov on the theory and John D. Ramsdell and Moses D. Liskov on the implementation [1,25].

CPSA can be used to design and analyze security protocols and is grounded on the strand space theory. The output of the analysis can be visualized using a standard browser (Chrome, Firefox, Safari, etc.). It is one of the many tools that are available to formally analyze secure protocol executions (see, e.g., Maude-NPA [14], Tamarin, [26], and ProVerif [3]).

In CPSA cryptographic protocols are defined as patterns of interaction between parties. CSPA is able to give a complete characterization of possible protocol executions, that are called *shapes*, starting from an initial behavior of one participant and analyzing, from his point of view, the behavior of the other participants, and what shapes are compatible with the description (typically few of them). This can be done even in the presence of a penetrator that can execute different operations as, e.g., manipulate, alter, drop messages, even breaking secrecy or authentication of the protocol (cf. Sect. 2.1).

The search of the shapes is done with a high-level algorithm that enumerates all the shapes, and that can be considered complete relative to natural role semantics, [1,2]. The analysis is done within a pure Dolev-Yao model [13].

$$\textbf{Wrap}(h_1, h_2) \rightarrow c$$
$$\textbf{Decrypt}(c, h_2) \rightarrow k_1$$

Fig. 1. *wrap-then-decrypt* attack.

2.3   Attacks on the PKCS#11 API

The Public Key Cryptography Standard #11 (PKCS#11), was first proposed by RSA in 1995, its latest version is 3.0 and belongs to OASIS [27]. It contains an API called 'Cryptoki' that can be used by HSMs, cryptographic tokens and smart cards for cryptographic and key management functions. All operations are performed inside the device, thus cryptographic keys are protected and never exposed in the clear to external applications.

Once a session has been established, the application may access *objects* using some *handles*. Objects are keys or certificates, and have *attributes* that are used to specify properties or roles. Attributes can be boolean values and can be set and unset. Handles are only pointers to the objects, and do not disclose any information about them. As all the cryptographic functions use key handles to refer to keys their value is never exposed outside the device. New objects may be created either using a key generation command or by specific operations that will be later defined, i.e., unwrapping an encrypted blob. A fresh handle will then point at them.

As an example, to encrypt and decrypt data we should use keys respectively with the attributes `encrypt` and `decrypt` set. To export and import keys in the device under so called *wrapping* keys, we have to use the `wrap` and `unwrap` attributes. The `wrap` attribute is used to encrypt and then to export as a cipher-text a key. To import keys we use the `unwrap` attribute that takes an encrypted key, decrypts it, imports it in the device as a new object, and returns a fresh handle.

Sequences of different operations may occur in API level attacks. The first attack dates back to 2003 and was presented in [10] by Clulow. The idea of the attack is to execute two operations on a `sensitive` key, first a wrap, and then a decrypt. For this reason it is called the *wrap-then-decrypt* attack. More precisely, the attacker has two keys, a target sensitive key k_1 and a key k_2 with attributes `wrap` and `decrypt` set. It also has two handles: handle h_1 associated to key k_1, and handle h_2 associated to a key k_2.

The attacker executes two operations: First wraps key k_1 under key k_2 obtaining ciphertext c (using the two handles), then decrypts the ciphertext c using key k_2 (through its handle h_2), thus leaking the sensitive key k_1 in the clear (cf. Fig. 1). The attack is possible since the device is not able to distinguish between keys and plaintexts, and given that the operations wrap and decrypt are allowed by the `wrap`and `decrypt` attributes set on h_2.

There are similar versions of the attack, an example is the *encrypt-then-unwrap* attack in which the attacker encrypts a known key k under h_2 and then unwraps it, since h_2 has attributes `unwrap` and `encrypt` set. Then, it imports it in the device with a fresh handle h_3 and attribute `wrap` set, and this is possible since once a key is unwrapped, attributes might be changed. Then h_1 (that refers to the sensitive key k_1) can be wrapped using the fresh handle h_3 obtaining the encryption of k_1 under the known key k, thus allowing the attacker to perform decryption.

These attacks could be in principle prevented by forbidding the use of conflicting roles, e.g., `wrap`, `decrypt` or `unwrap`, `encrypt`. However, in practice this solution does not work as attributes can be set and unset liberally. An extended analysis of different attacks can be found in [12,17]. The only mechanism that was added to prevent API-level attacks is the `wrap_with_trusted` attribute. This was introduced only in Version 2.20 of the standard and allows keys to be wrapped only under keys with attribute `trusted` set. While this is suggested, it is however not imposed by the standard. Note that, this `wrap_with_trusted` attribute cannot be unset anymore. The only user that can set a key as `trusted` is the Security Officer. While this mechanism could, in theory, prevent some attacks, it does not offer any flexibility and does not scale to more sophisticated key hierarchies.

2.4   Related Work

The strand space model has been widely used in different contexts. Some examples are the following. In [22] the authors use the strand spaces formalism to model and analyze layered security protocols, in a setting where there is an application layer protocol on top of a secure transport protocol. In [33] the authors extend the standard strand space model by proposing a way of representing choices in cryptographic protocols in order to compose strand spaces. To achieve this, they use a process algebra for cryptographic protocols that supports choice primitives. Another line of research is towards connecting strand spaces to other formal models. E.g., in [21] the authors study the relationship between strand spaces and multi-agent systems, and they prove that the main difference between the two models is how agents are handled. They are unspecified in strand spaces and explicit in multi-agent systems. They show there is some lack of expressiveness in strand spaces as some multi agent systems cannot be directly mapped into them and they also propose extensions to the strand model. In [5] the authors study the relationship between strand spaces and distributed temporal logic. It turns out that they are compatible, but provide different views of protocol executions. Finally, [8] compares strand spaces with multiset rewriting with existential quantification. In order to prove the relation, the authors extend strand spaces to incrementally construct bundles so to emulate an execution with parametric strands.

CPSA has been used widely used to perform the analysis of cryptographic protocols. Examples are, e.g., the proof of the CAVES Attestation protocol by describing the protocol using logical formulas and the rely-guarantee method, and proving the protocol correctness using CPSA [28]. Some other works concentrate on state changes. Joshua Guttman in [20] proposes a model to connect protocol execution with state and" state change, and uses this model to provide a proof of a known fair exchange protocol. Some of the proofs are done using CPSA. In [29] the authors present a way of modeling stateful protocols. They achieve this by extending CPSA to systems with a state component, and by using Prototype Verification System to reason about computations over state. In [24] the authors analyze the forced-latency defense against the chess grandmaster attack using CPSA, validate the security properties of the protocol and first find, and then fix, a small message-space attack. Recently, in [30] the authors have analyzed the Secure Remote Password (SRP) protocol, used, e.g., by iCloud Keychain and iPassword, with CPSA, and proved a new attack based on the fact that a malicious server can fake an authentication session with a client that does not participate.

Regarding PKCS#11 we want to focus on possible API level attacks and on different analysis of Security APIs (see, e.g., [4,6,10–12,16–18]). As we have mentioned in Sect. 2.3 there are different known attacks based specific operations over keys with contrasting attributes. Example are the *wrap-then-decrypt* attack [10] and its extensions. Starting from these attacks, different analysis of Security APIs have been proposed. In [12] the authors propose the first automated analysis of PKCS#11. The model either finds attacks or derives security properties on the device. In [4] the authors propose an extension and refinement of the model based on a reverse-engineering tool. This tool was able to find attacks based on the leaking of sensitive keys on real devices. A mechanism to prevent some attacks was proposed in [11] but was never included in the standard, even when formally proposed to Oasis [32]. The idea is to run *authenticated wrapping*, i.e., attributes should be wrapped together with the key thus remaining unchanged once imported and exported. Different works focused on the proof of correctness of some specific key configurations, e.g., one based on the use of the wrap_with_trusted attribute in a controlled way (see [18]), or other configurations proposed in [6,23] and [4]. A limit of all the mentioned works is that they assume that the attributes of keys are immutable, which is not true in practice. A configuration for cloud HSMs that does require any change in the API has been proposed in a recent work by the present authors [16]. There are few works that propose an analysis of PKCS#11 and are closer to the present one. In [19] the authors propose an analysis of the PKCS#11 in Maude-NPA and consider the attacks indicated by Delaune et al. in [12]. Another work that analyses PKCS#11 in the Tamarin tool is [23].

3   Key Management Policies

We define a very general model for key management policies that regulates what can be encrypted/decrypted by a given key. We consider N key types $K_1, K_2, \ldots, K_N$, and a separate type D, representing data. Input to cryptographic functions will always be associated to at least one of these types.

Definition 3 (Key management policy). *A key management policy is a relation $P \subseteq \mathcal{K} \times \mathcal{L} \times \mathcal{KD}$ where :*

Fig. 2. Plain hierarchical policy.

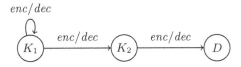

Fig. 3. An insecure self-wrapping policy.

- $\mathcal{K} = \{K_1, K_2, \ldots, K_N\}$;
- $\mathcal{L} = \{enc, dec\}$;
- $\mathcal{KD} = \{K_1, K_2, \ldots, K_N, D\}$.

When $(K, l, J) \in P$ we equivalently write $K \xrightarrow{l}_P J$. We will also write $K \xrightarrow{enc/dec}_P J$ if we have both $K \xrightarrow{enc}_P J$ and $K \xrightarrow{dec}_P J$. When there is no ambiguity about what policy P we are referring to (which will be the usual situation), we will simply write $K \xrightarrow{l} J$.

Intuitively, we write $K \xrightarrow{l} J$ when K can perform operation l over J. Possible operations are encryption and decryption, respectively denoted by enc and dec. For example $K_1 \xrightarrow{enc} K_2$ means that keys of type K_1 can encrypt (i.e., wrap) keys of type K_2, while $K_3 \xrightarrow{dec} D$ means that keys of type K_3 can decrypt data. Notice that, $D \xrightarrow{l} J$ is not a valid policy entry, as $D \notin \mathcal{K}$. In fact, data should not be used as cryptographic keys.

A policy should be interpreted as a specification of the intended usage of keys. The way a policy is enforced depends on the actual API implementation as we will discuss in Sect. 4.

Example 1 (Simple hierarchy). A simple way to organize key types is through a total strict ordering $K_1 < K_2 < \ldots < K_N < D$, depicted in Fig. 2. Intuitively, any key type can encrypt/decrypt the next type in the ordering, while K_N can only encrypt/decrypt data. This appears to be a rather safe approach as there is no confusion or non-determinism about key roles: any time a decryption/unwrapping happens there is a unique possible type for the obtained plaintext.

Example 2 (Self wrapping keys). Consider now the example of Fig. 3. We have two key types: K_2 that only encrypts and decrypts data, and K_1 that can wrap/unwrap keys of types K_1 and K_2. This policy is non-deterministic: when we perform an unwrap operation with keys of type K_1 we might import the decrypt key either as K_1 or as K_2. This non-deterministic behavior is tricky and allows for changing the type of a key through a wrap-then-unwrap pattern. For example, a key k_1 of type K_1 could wrap itself and then unwrap with type

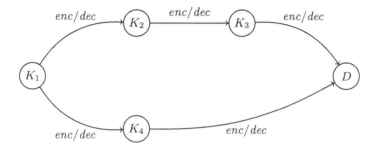

Fig. 4. Flawed tree-like hierarchical policy.

K_2, producing a copy of itself in a different type. This pattern is allowed by the policy but it clearly enables a wrap-then-decrypt attack: once k_1 is unwrapped with type K_2 it can be used to decrypt itself as data, leaking the value in the clear. More precisely, the problematic sequence of API calls would be:

API call	Output	Types
$\mathtt{wrap}(k_1, k_1)$	$\{k_1\}_{k_1}$	$k_1 : K_1$
$\mathtt{unwrap}(\{k_1\}_{k_1}, k_1, K_2)$		$k_1 : K_1, K_2$
$\mathtt{decrypt}(\{k_1\}_{k_1}, k_1)$	k_1	$k_1 : K_1, K_2$

Example 3 (Tree hierarchy). One might expect that the plain hierarchical policy of Example 1 can be generalized to a tree-like hierarchy. Surprisingly, this is not the case in general. Consider the example of Fig. 4. It might happen that a key k_2 of type K_2 is wrapped by a key k_1 of type K_1 and then unwrapped as a key of type K_4. Then, k_2 can be used to carry out a wrap-then-decrypt attack over keys of type K_3 since it has both type K_2 and type K_4.

More precisely the problematic sequence of API calls would be:

API call	Output	Types
$\mathtt{wrap}(k_2, k_1)$	$\{k_2\}_{k_1}$	$k_1 : K_1, k_2 : K_2, k_3 : K_3$
$\mathtt{unwrap}(\{k_2\}_{k_1}, k_1, K_4)$		$k_1 : K_1, k_2 : K_2, K_4, k_3 : K_3$
$\mathtt{wrap}(k_3, k_2)$	$\{k_3\}_{k_2}$	$k_1 : K_1, k_2 : K_2, K_4, k_3 : K_3$
$\mathtt{decrypt}(\{k_3\}_{k_2}, k_2)$	k_3	$k_1 : K_1, k_2 : K_2, K_4, k_3 : K_3$

Example 4 (Secure templates). In [4], a secure policy is proposed, named *secure templates*, that have a unique type for unwrapped keys that prevent conflicting roles. Keys can be generated either as wrap/unwrap keys or as encrypt/decrypt keys. When unwrap happens, the imported key is only allowed to unwrap and encrypt. The rationale is that unwrap and encrypt operations do not conflict with the initial key roles. There are two cases: (*i*) if a wrap/unwrap key is unwrapped, it acquires an encryption capability (unwrap is already possible) that might enable an encrypt-then-unwrap attack which imports a known key in the device. However, since unwrapping a key never enables a wrap operation

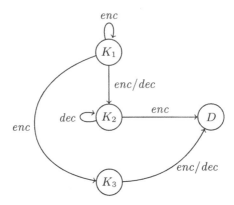

Fig. 5. Secure templates of [4].

the imported key would never be allowed to wrap and leak other keys; (*ii*) if an encrypt/decrypt key is unwrapped, it acquires an unwrap capability (encrypt is already possible) which, again, could be used in a encrypt-then-unwrap attack with no success.

The secure templates policy can be easily encoded in our formalism using three key types, as illustrated in Fig. 5. K_1 keys can encrypt (wrap) any other keys K_3 keys can encrypt/decrypt data. When a key is unwrapped by K_1 the only possible type is K_2 that can encrypt data or unwrap other keys, as required by the policy. The fact that this policy is correct cannot be trivially deduced by the specification but we will prove its correctness in Sect. 4.3.

4   Key Management APIs

We now define a core model of a key management API in the strand space formalism [15]. The model supports key creation, wrap, unwrap, encrypt and decrypt functionalities for symmetric key cryptography.

We start with an untyped model, where any key can be used to perform any of the above functionalities. As we discussed in Sect. 2.3, this excessive flexibility allows for a number of critical attacks that extract cryptographic keys in the clear. Interestingly, we leverage the CPSA tool [1,25] to automatically search for these attacks (cf. Sect. 4.1).

Then, we enrich the model with key types that are assigned when a key is created. Since keys are stored in a device, assigning a type is plausible and useful. We modify the API so to make all the functionalities consistent with the assigned types and a key management policy defined along Definition 3. However, notice that, when a key is wrapped and exported the typing information is lost and an unwrap operation will allow any of the types consistent with the given policy. As we will see, this approach requires a minimal modification to the API and does not require any modification of the actual cryptographic operations. As a matter of fact, we will not include any typing information about the wrapped key in the ciphertext, differently, e.g., from the *wrapped attribute* approach proposed for PKCS#11 (e.g., [11,32]).

Our proof of the security of the typed API is carried out in the strand space formalism and is parametric with respect to a given key management policy. A very interesting feature of strand spaces is that they allow one to distill the minimal requirements for security. In our case, this will translate into the minimal requirements for a secure key management policy. Thus, we will define a static check to determine when a key management policy is secure, while types will be used at execution time to guarantee that the API treat keys consistently with the given policy (cf. Sect. 4.2).

As a side note, despite the apparent simplicity of the core model that we will treat, we could not perform any automated proof using CPSA, even for fixed simple policies such as the one of Example 1 with $N = 2$. When generating all the possible executions compatible with a given strand, the tool was looping around inverse functionalities, such as wrap and unwrap. We had similar experiences with other state-of-the-art automated tools. We leave as a future work the study of possible automation of the analysis presented in this paper.

4.1   An Untyped, Vulnerable API

We model a key k stored in a device as if it were wrapped under a device's master key mk, i.e., $\{k\}_{mk}$. We will assume many such keys corresponding to an unbounded set of devices, moreover master keys could be pre-shared among devices allowing key sharing of freshly generated keys. In fact, the presence of one of more devices is immaterial for the analysis.

Notice that, this model is realistic, as it is often the case that devices store keys outside their memory in an encrypted form. This modeling strategy makes it possible to model key management APIs purely as a stateless protocol, since stored keys will be just sent as output and retrieved when necessary. This seems to contradict the usual approach in the literature for, e.g., PKCS#11 models, where a mutable state is considered (e.g., [4,12,23]). However, in these works the state is necessary in order to model the key attributes that we do not consider here.

Definition 4 (Untyped key management API). *An infiltrated strand space Σ, $\mathcal{P}$ is a Untyped Key Management (UKM) space if Σ is the union of the following kinds of strands:*

```
1 (herald "APIs"
2   (comment "Untyped API: finds all attacks"
3     "Note: it diverges, so we stop it and check the attacks")
      )
4
5 (defprotocol api basic
6   (defrole create
7     (vars (k text) (mk skey))
8     (trace
9     (send (enc k mk))
10    )
11   (uniq-orig k) ; k is fresh
12   (non-orig mk) ; mk is uncompromised
13   )
14  (defrole encrypt
15    (vars (m k text) (mk skey))
16    (trace
17    (recv (cat m (enc k mk)))
18    (send (enc m k)))
19    (non-orig mk) ; mk is uncompromised
20    )
21  (defrole decrypt
22    (vars (m k text) (mk skey))
23    (trace
24    (recv (cat (enc m k) (enc k mk)))
25    (send m))
26    (non-orig mk) ; mk is uncompromised
27    )
28  (defrole wrap
29    (vars (k1 k2 text) (mk skey))
30    (trace
31    (recv (cat (enc k1 mk) (enc k2 mk)))
32    (send (enc k1 k2)))
33    (non-orig mk) ; mk is uncompromised
34    )
35  (defrole unwrap
36    (vars (k1 k2 text) (mk skey))
37    (trace
38    (recv (cat (enc k1 k2) (enc k2 mk)))
39    (send (enc k1 mk)))
40    (non-orig mk) ; mk is uncompromised
41    )
42
43 (defskeleton api
44   (vars (k text) (mk skey))
45   (defstrand create 1 (k k) (mk mk))
46   (deflistener k) ; check secrecy of created keys!
47   (comment "Analyze from the create's perspective"))
```

Fig. 6. Flawed APIs in CPSA.

create   wrap   decrypt

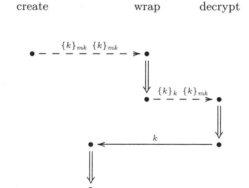

Fig. 7. Wrap-then-decrypt with a single key k.

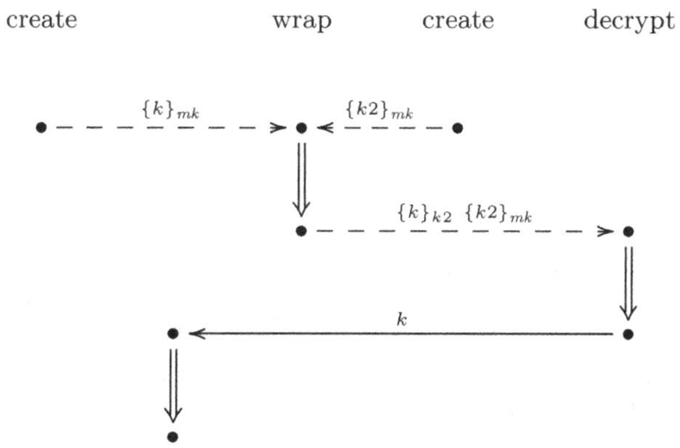

create   wrap   create   decrypt

$$\bullet\ \text{---} \ \underset{\{k\}_{mk}}{\text{------}} \ \text{-->} \ \bullet \ \text{<--} \ \underset{\{k2\}_{mk}}{\text{-----}} \ \bullet$$

Fig. 8. Wrap-then-decrypt with two keys: k and $k2$.

1. *Penetrator strands: $s \in \mathcal{P}$ (cf. Definition 2)*
2. *Create: $\langle +\{k\}_{mk}\rangle$*
3. *Encrypt: $\langle -m\ \{k\}_{mk},\ +\{m\}_k\rangle$*
4. *Decrypt: $\langle -\{m\}_k\ \{k\}_{mk},\ +m\rangle$*
5. *Wrap: $\langle -\{k_1\}_{mk}\ \{k_2\}_{mk},\ +\{k_1\}_{k_2}\rangle$*
6. *Unwrap: $\langle -\{k_1\}_{k_2}\ \{k_2\}_{mk},\ +\{k_1\}_{mk}\rangle$*

We know that this liberal API is subject to all the known attacks in the literature. Interestingly, we have modeled it in the CPSA tool so to re-discover all the attacks, very efficiently. The CPSA specification is reported in Fig. 6. Intuitively, **defrole** specifications correspond to the five API functionalities that we model: create, encrypt, decrypt, wrap and unwrap. We declare the master key mk of sort **skey**, for symmetric keys, and any other variable as **text**. We will also assume that mk is never exposed to the attacker. This reflects our interest in

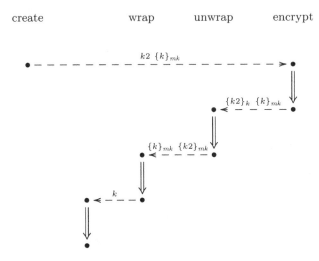

Fig. 9. Encrypt-then-unwrap with a single key k and an attacker key $k2$.

analyzing key management under the assumption that keys are stored securely in the device, so we will not model any attack over the master key(s) mk.

Strands are specified using the `trace` keyword and are just a syntactic renaming of the honest strands of Definition 4. For example, $\{k1\}_{k2}$ is written as (`enc k1 k2`) while the concatenation of terms m and $\{k\}_{mk}$ is written as (`cat m (enc k mk)`). Strand symbols − and + for input and output are translated into `recv` and `send`. The skeleton at the end of the specification specifies an instance of a create strand adding a listener for `k`. This will force the tool to look for executions where `k` is learned by the attacker. If no such execution exists, the secrecy of generated keys is guaranteed, which is not the case for this API.

The tool does not converge on this analysis, but if we stop it after just 1 s we find 6 traces corresponding to known attacks. Conveniently, CPSA has an option to produce output directly in LATEX. For more readability, we have only added on the arcs the terms that the strand gets as input. Notice that, dashed arrows represent interactions where the attacker, in the middle, performs some operation. In Fig. 7 we have the simplest attack found: a *self* wrap-then-decrypt sequence, where a single key k is used to wrap and then decrypt itself. Notice that, the create strand produces term $\{k\}_{mk}$, but the attacker can duplicate it as $\{k\}_{mk}$ $\{k\}_{mk}$ to provide a correct input to the wrap strand (we decorate arrows with input terms). Wrap produces a self wrapping $\{k\}_k$ and the attacker adds again $\{k\}_{mk}$ to provide input for the decrypt strand. These two arrows are dashed to represent some attacker's activity in between: in fact the output of the originating strand does not match the input of the receiving one. Finally, decrypt produces k that is sent to the implicit listener strand that has the only purpose of pointing out a successful leak.

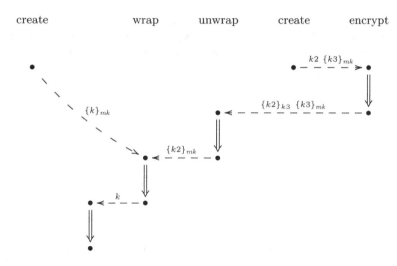

Fig. 10. Encrypt-then-unwrap with two keys k, $k3$ and an attacker key $k2$.

Figure 8 reports the second attack found by CPSA, which is the same as Fig. 7 based on two keys k and $k2$. In Fig. 9 we found another classic attack: encrypt-then-unwrap. Here, the attacker provides her own key $k2$ and asks to encrypt and unwrap it under k, in order to import it in the device as $\{k2\}_{mk}$. At this point, it is enough to wrap k under $k2$ to obtain k in the clear. In fact, notice that, the attacker can decrypt the ciphertext $\{k\}_{k2}$ generated by the wrap operation (this Dolev-Yao decryption is hidden in the final dashed arrow). Figure 10 is the same attack carried out with two keys k and $k3$ and an attacker key $k2$. Even if we cannot be guaranteed that there are no more interesting attacks, by inspecting subsequent attacks found by CPSA we noticed that they seem to add only useless steps, such as importing an attacker key to unwrap another attacker key that is finally used to wrap k, or attacking a key $k3$ and then wrapping the target key k under $k3$.

As we mentioned, the tool loops over these attack variants and never terminates. However, since this untyped API is insecure, we still find the tool very insightful as it automatically and very efficiently spots attacks. We focus on proving security of a fixed API in the next section.

4.2   A Secure, Typed API

Our typed API is based on the following idea: when a key is created a type is assigned and is encrypted together with the key in order to enforce the policy at execution time. For example, key k_1 of type K_1 is modeled as $\{k_1, K_1\}_{mk}$. When a key is unwrapped any type admitted by the policy is assigned to the unwrapped key, making it possible to have multiple types for the same key. This is modeled by creating another ciphertext with the new assigned type, e.g., $\{k_1, K_2\}_{mk}$.

Definition 5 (Typed key management API). *Let P be a key management policy and let K, K_1, K_2 range over $\mathcal{K}$. Let $\mathbf{K}_d, \mathbf{K}_m \subseteq \mathbf{K}$, such that $\mathbf{K}_d \cap \mathbf{K}_m = \emptyset$, respectively be a set of fresh device keys and of master keys which we assume to be unknown to the penetrator, i.e., $(\mathbf{K}_d \cup \mathbf{K}_m) \cap \mathbf{K}_\mathcal{P} = \emptyset$ (cf. Defintion 2). We let mk range over $\mathbf{K}_m$. An infiltrated strand space $\Sigma, \mathcal{P}$ is a P-Typed Key Management (TKM$_P$) space if Σ is the union of the following kinds of strands:*

1. *Penetrator strands: $s \in \mathcal{P}$;*
2. *Create: $\langle +\{k, K\}_{mk} \rangle$ with $k \in \mathbf{K}_d$ uniquely originating*
3. *Encrypt: $\langle -m, -\{k, K\}_{mk}, +\{m\}_k \rangle$ if $K \xrightarrow{enc} D$*
4. *Decrypt: $\langle -\{m\}_k, -\{k, K\}_{mk}, +m \rangle$ if $K \xrightarrow{dec} D$*
5. *Wrap: $\langle -\{k_1, K_1\}_{mk}, -\{k_2, K_2\}_{mk}, +\{k_1\}_{k_2} \rangle$ if $K_2 \xrightarrow{enc} K_1$*
6. *Unwrap: $\langle -\{k_1\}_{k_2}, -\{k_2, K_2\}_{mk}, +\{k_1, K_1\}_{mk} \rangle$ if $K_2 \xrightarrow{dec} K_1$*

The security of this API depends on the security of the policy P. We have noticed how keys of certain types can acquire new types when they are wrapped and then unwrapped under certain keys (cf. Examples 2 and 3). In order to capture this runtime behavior, we define a new relation $\hat{P}$, starting from a policy P, that represents all the cryptographic capabilities that can be acquired, at runtime, by a key of initial type K. We also compute the set of types that are *reachable* from an initial type K, noted R_K.

Definition 6 (Closure $\hat{P}, \mathcal{R}$ of P). *Given a key management policy, $P \subseteq \mathcal{K} \times \mathcal{L} \times \mathcal{KD}$, noted $K \xrightarrow{l} J$, we define its closure $\hat{P}, \mathcal{R}$, where $\hat{P} \subseteq \mathcal{KD} \times \mathcal{L} \times \mathcal{KD}$ and $\mathcal{R} = \{R_{K_1}, \ldots, R_{K_N}, R_D\}$ with $R_i \subseteq 2^{\mathcal{KD}}$, noted $K \xRightarrow{l} J$, as the smallest sets/relation such that:*

1. *$K \xrightarrow{l} J$ implies $K \xRightarrow{l} J$;*
2. *$K \in R_K$;*
3. *$D \xRightarrow{l} D$;*
4. *$K \xRightarrow{enc} J$ and $K \xRightarrow{dec} Z$ implies $Z \in R_J$;*
5. *$K \xrightarrow{dec} J$ and $K \in R_Z$ implies $Z \xRightarrow{dec} J$*
6. *$K \xRightarrow{enc} J$ and ($K \in R_Z$ or $Z \in R_K$) implies $Z \xRightarrow{enc} J$*
7. *$J \xRightarrow{enc} K$ and ($K \in R_Z$ or $Z \in R_K$) implies $J \xRightarrow{enc} Z$*

The first four items are quite intuitive: whatever is allowed by P is also allowed by $\hat{P}$ (item 1); a type K is always reachable by itself (item 2); D can perform any operation over D, in order to account for penetrator's behaviour (item 3); if a type K can acquire the capability of wrapping J and then decrypt it as Z, then Z should belong to the types R_J that are reachable from J (item 4).

The next four items are necessary to prove the subsequent lemmas and theorem on the security of the typed API. Item 5 backward propagates decryption capability over a given type J, i.e., if K can decrypt J and K is reachable from Z then also Z can decrypt J. Notice that, 5 uses P in the hypothesis. Finally, items 6 and 7 propagate encryption capabilities bidirectionally: if K can encrypt

J and K can reach/can be reached by Z then Z can also encrypt J (item 6); if J can encrypt K and K can reach/can be reached by Z then J can also encrypt Z (item 7).

Notice that, keys $k \in \mathbf{K}_d$ uniquely originate in the Create strand (cf. Definition 4). In the following we let K_k denote the initial (unique) type of key k in a bundle, i.e., the type assigned when the key was originated. For terms $m \notin \mathbf{K}_d$, including the penetrator keys $\mathbf{K}_{\mathcal{P}}$, we let $K_m = D$. We also let $\sqsubset_{\mathbf{K}_m}$ be a variant of $\sqsubset$ (cf. Definition 1) which does enter ciphtertext encrypted under master keys $\mathbf{K}_m$. It is enough to split the $a \sqsubset \{g\}_k$ case as follows:

- $a \sqsubset \{g\}_k$ with $k \notin \mathbf{K}_m$ iff $a \sqsubset g$ or $a = \{g\}_k$;
- $a \sqsubset \{g\}_{mk}$ with $mk \in \mathbf{K}_m$ iff $a = \{g\}_k$.

The next theorem proves that the closure $\hat{P}, \mathcal{R}$ over-approximates the set of types that are assigned at run-time. Intuitively, for each node n, if $\{k, K\}_{mk}$ occurs in n then K is reachable from the initial type K_k of k, written $K \in R_{K_k}$; if $\{k\}_{k'}$ occurs in n then there exit two types K, K' that are reachable from the initial types of k and k' and such that K' can encrypt K, written $K' \overset{enc}{\Longrightarrow} K$; finally, if tuple $m_1 \ldots m_z$ occurs in n then D is reachable from all initial types of $m_1 \ldots m_z$, written $D \in R_{K_{m_i}}$ for $i \in 1, \ldots, z$. In fact, tuples are only generated by the penetrator, except for the terms encrypted under master keys that are excluded by $\sqsubset_{\mathbf{K}_m}$. For this reason, tuple members are all required to reach D, the type that represents public data which is under the control of the penetrator.

Theorem 1 (Type soundness). *Let Σ be a TKM_P space, and $\mathcal{C}$ be a bundle. Then $\forall k, k' \in \mathbf{A} \setminus \mathbf{K}_m, n \in \mathcal{C}$:*

1. $\{k, K\}_{mk} \sqsubset n$ *implies* $K \in R_{K_k}$;
2. $\{k\}_{k'} \sqsubset n$ *implies* $\exists K, K' \in \mathcal{KD}, n' \in \mathcal{C}$ *such that* $K' \overset{enc}{\Longrightarrow} K, K \in R_{K_k}$, $K' \in R_{K_{k'}}$;
3. $m_1 \ldots m_z \sqsubset_{\mathbf{K}_m} term(n)$ *implies* $D \in R_{K_{m_i}}$ *for* $i \in 1, \ldots, z$.

Proof. Let S be the set of nodes that violate the theorem thesis:

$$S = \{ \, n \in \mathcal{C} : \exists k \in \mathbf{A} \setminus \mathbf{K}_m \, . \, \{k, K\}_{mk} = term(n) \, \wedge \, K \notin R_{K_k} \}$$
$$\cup$$
$$\{ \, n \in \mathcal{C} : \exists k, k' \in \mathbf{A} \setminus \mathbf{K}_m \, . \, \{k\}_{k'} = term(n) \, \wedge$$
$$\forall K, K' \in \mathcal{KD}, n' \in \mathcal{C} \text{ with } K' \overset{enc}{\Longrightarrow} K \text{ we have } K \notin R_{K_k} \vee K' \notin R_{K_{k'}} \}$$
$$\cup$$
$$\{ \, n \in \mathcal{C} : m_1 \ldots m_z \sqsubset_{\mathbf{K}_m} term(n) \, \wedge \, \exists i \in 1 \ldots z \text{ such that } D \notin R_{K_{m_i}} \}$$

We prove that S is empty by proving that it does not have a minimal element (cf [15] [Lemma 2.6]).

We first prove that no minimal element of S is a regular node. Suppose, by contradiction, that $n \in S$ is minimal and it is a regular node. The sign must be positive by [15] [Lemma 2.7]. We consider all the possibilities:

Create: The trace has the form $\langle +\{k, K\}_{mk}\rangle$ with $mk \in \mathbf{K}_m$ with $k \in \mathbf{K}_d$ uniquely originating in Σ with type $K = K_k$. For n to belong to S we must have $K \notin R_{K_k}$ which is false as $K = K_k \in R_{K_k}$ (cf. Definition 6, item 2), leading to a contradiction.

Encrypt: the trace has the form $\langle -m, \ -\{k', K'\}_{mk'}, \ +\{m\}_{k'}\rangle$ with $K' \xrightarrow{enc} D$, which implies $K' \stackrel{enc}{\Longrightarrow} D$ (cf. Definition 6, item 1). Minimal node n must be positive so the third node is the only candidate. Notice that, if $+\{m\}_{k'}$ is in S because of a subterm of m then $-m$ would also be in S, giving a contradiction. Thus, we have the following cases:

- $\{m\}_{k'} = \{k, K''\}_{mk''}$ which implies $k' = mk''$ but mk'' never originates in Σ so it cannot be that term $\{mk'', K'\}_{mk'}$ in the second node occurs in $\mathcal{C}$.
- $\{m\}_{k'} = \{k\}_{k'}$. Since first and second nodes cannot be in S, and $m = k$, we respectively have that $D \in R_{K_k}$ and $K' \in R_{K_{k'}}$. Moreover, $K_{term(n)} = D$ for all compound terms and $D \in R_{K_D}$ by (cf. Definition 6, item 2) which implies $D \in R_{K_{term(n)}}$. In summary, we have $K = D \in R_{K_{k'}}$, $K' \in R_{K_{k'}}$, $K' \stackrel{enc}{\Longrightarrow} D$, $\{k', K'\}_{mk'}$ and $D \in R_{K_{term(n)}}$, which prove that node $+\{m\}_{k'}$ does not belong to S, leading to a contradiction.
- $D \notin R_{K_{term(n)}}$. This case does not apply, as we discussed in the previous item.

Decrypt: the trace has the form $\langle -\{m\}_{k'}, \ -\{k', K'\}_{mk'}, \ +m\rangle$ with $K' \xrightarrow{dec} D$, which implies $K' \stackrel{dec}{\Longrightarrow} D$ (cf. Definition 6, item 1). n must be the last node. Notice that, if $+m$ is in S because of a subterm of m then $-\{m\}_{k'}$ would also be in S, giving a contradiction. Thus, we have the following cases:

- $\{m\}_{k'} = \{k, K''\}_{mk''}$ which implies $k' = mk''$ but mk'' never originates in Σ so it cannot be that term $\{mk'', K'\}_{mk'}$ in the second node occurs in $\mathcal{C}$;
- $\{m\}_{k'} = \{k\}_{k'}$. Since the first node cannot be in S we have that $\exists K, K'' \in \mathcal{KD}, K'' \stackrel{enc}{\Longrightarrow} K$ such that $K \in R_{K_k}, K'' \in R_{K_{k'}}$. Moreover, since the second node cannot be in S we additionally have that $K' \in R_{K_{k'}}$. By Definition 6, item 6 we have that $K'' \stackrel{enc}{\Longrightarrow} K$ implies $K_{k'} \stackrel{enc}{\Longrightarrow} K$ and then $K' \stackrel{enc}{\Longrightarrow} K$. By Definition 6, item 7 we also have that $K' \stackrel{enc}{\Longrightarrow} K_k$ Thus, by Definition 6, item 4 we have that $D \in R_{K_k}$ and so n belongs to S, giving a contradiction.
- $D \notin R_{K_{term(n)}}$. The only interesting case in when $K_{term(n)} \neq D$ which only happens when $m = k \in \mathbf{K}_d$ and we already covered in the previous item, getting a contradiction.

Wrap: the trace has the form $\langle -\{k_1, K_1\}_{mk'}, \ -\{k_2, K_2\}_{mk'}, \ +\{k_1\}_{k_2}\rangle$ with $K_2 \xrightarrow{enc} K_1$, which implies $K_2 \stackrel{enc}{\Longrightarrow} K_1$ (cf. Definition 6, item 1). n can only be the third node. Notice that, if $+\{k_1\}_{k_2}$ is in S because of a subterm of k_1 then $-\{k_1, K_1\}_{mk'}$ would also be in S, giving a contradiction. Thus, we have the following cases:

- $k_1, k_2 \in \mathbf{A} \setminus \mathbf{K}_m$. Since the first and second nodes cannot be in S we have that $K_1 \in R_{K_{k_1}}$ and $K_2 \in R_{K_{k_2}}$. Moreover, $K_{term(n)} = D$ for all compound terms and $D \in R_{K_D}$ by (cf. Definition 6, item 2) which implies $D \in R_{K_{term(n)}}$. So node $+\{k_1\}_{k_2}$ is in S, giving a contradiction.

- $\{k_1\}_{k_2} = \{k, K''\}_{mk''}$ which implies $k_2 = mk''$ but mk'' never originates in Σ so it cannot be that term $\{mk'', K_2\}_{mk'}$ in the second node occurs in $\mathcal{C}$.
- $D \notin R_{K_{term(n)}}$. This case does not apply, as we discussed in the first item.

Unwrap: the trace has the form $\langle -\{k_1\}_{k_2}, \ -\{k_2, K_2\}_{mk'}, \ +\{k_1, K_1\}_{mk'} \rangle$ with $K_2 \xrightarrow{dec} K_1$, which implies $K_2 \xRightarrow{dec} K_1$ (cf. Definition 6, item 1). n can only be the third node. Notice that, if $+\{k_1, K_1\}_{mk'}$ is in S because of a subterm of k_1 then $-\{k_1\}_{k_2}$ would also be in S, giving a contradiction. Notice also that, $K_{term(n)} = D$ for all compound terms and $D \in R_{K_D}$ by (cf. Definition 6, item 2) which implies $D \in R_{K_{term(n)}}$. Since the first node cannot be in S we have that $\exists K, K' \in \mathcal{KD}, K' \xRightarrow{enc} K$ such that $K \in R_{K_{k_1}}, K' \in R_{K_{k_2}}$. Moreover, since the second node cannot be in S we additionally have that $K_2 \in R_{K_{k_2}}$. By Definition 6, item 6 we have that $K \xRightarrow{enc} K$ implies $K_{k_2} \xRightarrow{enc} K$ and then $K_2 \xRightarrow{enc} K$. By Definition 6, item 7 we also have that $K_2 \xRightarrow{enc} K_{k_1}$ Thus, by Definition 6, item 4 we have that $K_1 \in R_{K_{k_1}}$ and so n belongs to S, giving a contradiction.

We now prove that no minimal element of S is a penetrator node. Suppose, by contradiction, that $n \in S$ is minimal and it is a penetrator node. As for the previous case, the sign must be positive by [15] [Lemma 2.7]. We consider all the possibilities:

F. Flushing: $\langle -g \rangle$. There is no positive node so this case does not apply.
T. Tee: $\langle -g, +g, +g \rangle$. If $+g \in S$ also $-g \in S$ so positive nodes cannot be minimal in S, giving a contradiction.
C. Concatenation: $\langle -g, -h, +g\,h \rangle$. If n is in S because of a subterm of g or h then, of course, $-g\,h \in S$. Thus, the only interesting case is $D \notin R_{K_{g_i}}$, with $g = g_1 \ldots g_z$ or $D \notin R_{K_{h_j}}$, with $h = h_1 \ldots h_w$, but this would also imply that $-g\,h \in S$ since g_i or h_j clearly appear in $-g\,h$, giving a contradiction.
S. Separation: $\langle -g\,h, +g, +h \rangle$. W.l.o.g., assume that $n = +g$. If n is in S because of a subterm then, of course, $-g\,h \in S$. Thus, the only interesting case is $D \notin R_{K_{g_i}}$, with $g = g_1 \ldots g_z$, but this would also imply that $-g\,h \in S$ since g_i clearly appears in $-g\,h$, giving a contradiction.
K. Key: $\langle +k' \rangle$ with $k' \in \mathbf{K}_\mathcal{P}$. The only interesting case is $D \notin R_{K_k}$ but this is not possible since $K_{k'} = D$ for $k' \in \mathbf{K}_\mathcal{P}$.
E. Encryption: $\langle -k', -m, +\{m\}_{k'} \rangle$. Minimal node n must be positive so the third node is the only candidate. Notice that, if $+\{m\}_{k'}$ is in S because of a subterm of m then $-m$ would also be in S, giving a contradiction. Thus, we have the following cases:

- $\{m\}_{k'} = \{k, K''\}_{mk''}$ which implies $k' = mk''$ but mk'' never originates in Σ so it cannot be that term mk' in the first node occurs in $\mathcal{C}$.
- $\{m\}_{k'} = \{k\}_{k'}$. Since first and second nodes cannot be in S, and $m = k$, we respectively have that $D \in R_{K_k}$ and $D \in R_{K_{k'}}$. Moreover, $K_{term(n)} = D$ for all compound terms and $D \in R_{K_D}$ by (cf. Definition 6, item 2) which

implies $D \in R_{K_{term(n)}}$. In summary, we have $K = D \in R_{K_{k'}}, D \in R_{K_{k'}}$, $D \overset{enc}{\Longrightarrow} D, \{k', K'\}_{mk'}$ and $D \in R_{K_{term(n)}}$, which prove that node $+\{m\}_{k'}$ does not belong to S, leading to a contradiction.

- $D \notin R_{K_{term(n)}}$. This case does not apply, as we discussed in the previous item.

D. Decryption: $\langle -k', -\{m\}_{k'}, +m \rangle$. n must be the last node. Notice that, if $+m$ is in S because of a subterm of m then $-\{m\}_{k'}$ would also be in S, giving a contradiction. Thus, we have the following cases:

- $\{m\}_{k'} = \{k, K''\}_{mk''}$ which implies $k' = mk''$ but mk'' never originates in Σ so it cannot be that term $\{mk'', K'\}_{mk'}$ in the second node occurs in $\mathcal{C}$;
- $\{m\}_{k'} = \{k\}_{k'}$. Since the first node cannot be in S we have that $D \in R_{K_{k'}}$ Since the second node cannot be in S we additionally have that $\exists K, K'' \in \mathcal{KD}, K'' \overset{enc}{\Longrightarrow} K$ such that $K \in R_{K_k}, K'' \in R_{K_{k'}}$. By Definition 6, item 6 we have that $K'' \overset{enc}{\Longrightarrow} K$ implies $K_{k'} \overset{enc}{\Longrightarrow} K$ and then $D \overset{enc}{\Longrightarrow} K$. By Definition 6, item 7 we also have that $D \overset{enc}{\Longrightarrow} K_k$. Since $D \overset{dec}{\Longrightarrow} D$, by Definition 6, item 4 we have that $D \in R_{K_k}$ and so n belongs to S, giving a contradiction.
- $D \notin R_{K_{term(n)}}$. The only interesting case in when $K_{term(n)} \neq D$ which only happens when $m = k \in \mathbf{K}_d$ and we already covered in the previous item, getting a contradiction.

We can now state our security theorem: any key such that D is not reachable from its initial type is never leaked in the clear.

Theorem 2 (Security). *Let Σ be a TKM$_P$ space, $\mathcal{C}$ be a bundle and $k \in \mathbf{K}_d$ be (uniquely originating) key such that $D \notin R_{K_k}$. Then, for all nodes $n \in \mathcal{C}$ we have $k \neq term(n)$.*

Proof. By Theorem 1 we have that $k = term(n)$ implies $D \in R_{K_k}$, from which the thesis.

4.3 Examples

We reconsider the examples of policies of Sect. 3 and we apply Theorem 2 to analyze their security.

In Example 1 the closure $\hat{P}$ is identical to the initial policy P. In fact, keys can only be unwrapped to their initial type (cf. Fig. 2). Sets in $\mathcal{R}$ only contain the singleton initial type, i.e., $R_{K_i} = \{K_i\}$, for $i = 1, \ldots, N$, and $R_D = \{D\}$. By Theorem 2 we obtain that all keys are secure as $D \notin R_{K_i}$, for $i = 1, \ldots, N$.

In Example 2 we have an insecure policy (cf. Fig. 3). In fact, when we compute its closure we obtain that any key can encrypt/decrypt any other key and data. In particular, we obtain that $R_{K_1} = R_{K_2} = R_D = \{K_1, K_2, D\}$ and Theorem 2 cannot be applied as D belongs to all the sets.

Interestingly, in Example 3 we obtain the following reachable types: $R_{K_1} = \{K_1\}$, $R_{K_2} = R_{K_4} = \{K_2, K_4\}$, $R_{K_3} = R_D = \{K_3, D\}$. We can apply Theorem 2 to prove the secrecy of K_1, K_2, K_4. In fact, keys of type K_3 can be leaked through the previously described wrap-then-decrypt attack using a key which assumes both type K_2 and type K_4.

Finally, Example 4 shows that types over-approximate the behavior as we obtain the following reachable types: $R_{K_1} = \{K_1, K_2, D\}$, $R_{K_2} = R_D = \{K_2, D\}$ and $R_{K_3} = \{K_3, K_2, D\}$. Unfortunately, we cannot apply the theorem even if the policy is intuitively secure. The bidirectional propagation of the encryption capabilities along the reachable types, in this case, approximates too much the analysis. We leave as a future work the investigation of improvements that might prove also this example secure.

5   Conclusion

In this paper we have used strand spaces to analyze key management APIs. We have shown how to rediscover known attacks using the CPSA tool and have defined a typed version of the API that is based on a key management policy expressed in a generic model. A theorem allows one to prove the correctness of the security policy by computing a closure and inspecting a few simple critical cases. The use of strand spaces has proved very useful for extracting the minimum requirements that a key management policy must meet. As a future work we intend to analyze other key management policies proposed in the literature and compare them using our generic model. We will also investigate techniques to improve the precision of the analysis.

Acknowledgments. We would like to thank the anonymous reviewers for their very interesting and insightful comments. This work has been partially supported by the European Regional Development Fund project *SAFE PLACE: Sistemi IoT per ambienti di vita salubri e sicuri* (POR FESR 2014–2020 AZIONE 1.1.4 DGR 822/2020—ID 10288513).

References

1. CPSA: A cryptographicprotocol shapes analyzer. In: Hackage. The MITRE Corporation (2009). http://hackage.haskell.org/package/cpsa
2. Completeness of CPSA: The MITRE Corporation (2011). https://www.mitre.org/sites/default/files/pdf/12_0038.pdf
3. Blanchet, B., Smyth, B., Cheval, V., Sylvestre, M.: ProVerif 2.02pl1: Automatic Cryptographic Protocol Verifier, User Manual and Tutorial (2020). https://prosecco.gforge.inria.fr/personal/bblanche/proverif/manual.pdf
4. Bortolozzo, M., Centenaro, M., Focardi, R., Steel, G.: Attacking and fixing PKCS#11 security tokens. In: Proceedings of the 17th ACM Conference on Computer and Communications Security (CCS 2010), pp. 260–269. ACM Press, October 2010. https://doi.org/10.1145/1866307.1866337
5. Caleiro, C., Viganó, L., Basin, D.: Relating strand spaces and distributed temporal logic for security protocol analysis. Logic J. IGPL **13**, 637–663 (2005)
6. Centenaro, M., Focardi, R., Luccio, F.: Type-based analysis of key management in PKCS#11 cryptographic devices. J. Comput. Secur. **21**(6), 971–1007 (2013)

7. Centenaro, M., Focardi, R., Luccio, F., Steel, G.: Type-based analysis of PIN processing APIs. In: Springer (ed.) Proceedings of the 14th European Symposium on Research in Computer Security (ESORICS 09), vol. 5789, pp. 53–68 (2009). https://doi.org/10.1007/978-3-642-04444-1_4

8. Cervesato, I., Durgin, N., Lincoln, P., Mitchell, J., Scedrov, A.: A comparison between strand spaces and multiset rewriting for security protocol analysis. In: Okada, M., Pierce, B.C., Scedrov, A., Tokuda, H., Yonezawa, A. (eds.) ISSS 2002. LNCS, vol. 2609, pp. 356–383. Springer, Heidelberg (2003). https://doi.org/10.1007/3-540-36532-X_22

9. Clulow, J.: The Design and Analysis of Cryptographic APIs for Security Devices. Master's thesis, University of Natal, Durban (2003)

10. Clulow, J.: On the security of PKCS#11. In: Proceedings of the 5th Int. Workshop on Cryptographic Hardware and Embedded Systems (CHES 2003). LNCS, vol. 2779, pp. 411–425. Springer (2003). https://doi.org/10.1007/978-3-540-45238-6_32

11. Dax, A., Künnemann, R., Tangermann, S., Backes, M.: How to wrap it up - a formally verified proposal for the use of authenticated wrapping in PKCS#11. In: 2019 IEEE 32nd Computer Security Foundations Symposium (CSF 2019), pp. 62–6215 (2019). https://doi.org/10.1109/CSF.2019.00012

12. Delaune, S., Kremer, S., Steel, G.: Formal analysis of PKCS#11 and proprietary extensions. J. Comput. Secur. 18(6), 1211–1245 (2010). https://doi.org/10.3233/JCS-2009-0394

13. Dolev, D., Yao, A.: On the security of public-key protocols. IEEE Trans. Inf. Theory 29, 198–208 (1983)

14. Escobar, S., Meadows, C., Meseguer, J.: Maude-NPA: Cryptographic Protocol Analysis Modulo Equational Properties, pp. 1–50. Springer, Berlin, Heidelberg (2009). https://doi.org/10.1007/978-3-642-03829-7_1

15. Fabrega, F., Herzog, J., Guttman, J.: Strand spaces: why is a security protocol correct? In: Proceedings. 1998 IEEE Symposium on Security and Privacy, pp. 160–171 (1998). https://doi.org/10.1109/SECPRI.1998.674832

16. Focardi, R., Luccio, F.L.: A formally verified configuration for hardware security modules in the cloud. In: Vigna, G., Shi, E. (eds.) The ACM Conference on Computer and Communications Security (CCS), 2021. ACM (2021). (to appear)

17. Focardi, R., Luccio, F.L., Steel, G.: An introduction to security API analysis. In: Foundations of Security Analysis and Design VI - FOSAD Tutorial Lectures, pp. 35–65 (2011)

18. Fröschle, S., Sommer, N.: Concepts and proofs for configuring PKCS#11. In: Formal Aspects of Security and Trust - 8th International Workshop, (FAST 2011), Revised Selected Papers. LNCS, vol. 7140, pp. 131–147. Springer (2011). https://doi.org/10.1007/978-3-642-29420-4_9

19. González-Burgueño, A., Santiago, S., Escobar, S., Meadows, C., Meseguer, J.: Analysis of the PKCS#11 API using the Maude-NPA tool. In: Chen, L., Matsuo, S. (eds.) SSR 2015. LNCS, vol. 9497, pp. 86–106. Springer, Cham (2015). https://doi.org/10.1007/978-3-319-27152-1_5

20. Guttman, J.: State and progress in strand spaces: proving fair exchange. J. Autom. Reasoning 48, 159–195 (2012)

21. Halpern, Y., Pucella, J.R.: On the relationship between strand spaces and multi-agent systems. ACM Trans. Inf. Syst. Secur. 61, 43–70 (2003)

22. Kamil, A., Lowe, G.: Understanding abstractions of secure channels. In: Degano, P., Etalle, S., Guttman, J.D. (eds.) Formal Aspects of Security and Trust - 7th International Workshop, FAST 2010. Revised Selected Papers. Lecture Notes in Computer Science, vol. 6561, pp. 50–64. Springer (2010). https://doi.org/10.1007/978-3-642-19751-2_4

23. Künnemann, R.: Automated backward analysis of PKCS#11 v2.20. In: Principles of Security and Trust - 4th International Conference (POST 2015). LNCS, vol. 9036, pp. 219–238. Springer (2015). https://doi.org/10.1007/978-3-662-46666-7_12

24. Lanus, E., Zieglar, E.: Analysis of a forced-latency defense against man-in-the-middle attacks. J. Inf. Warfare **16**(2), 66–78 (2017)

25. Liskov, M., Ramsdell, J., Guttman, J., Rowe, P.: The Cryptographic Protocol Shapes Analyzer: A Manual. The MITRE Corporation. CPSA Version 3. Available at https://hackage.haskell.org/package/cpsa-3.3.2/src/doc/cpsamanual.pdf (2016)

26. Meier, S., Schmidt, B., Cremers, C., Basin, D.: The TAMARIN prover for the symbolic analysis of security protocols. In: Sharygina, N., Veith, H. (eds.) CAV 2013. LNCS, vol. 8044, pp. 696–701. Springer, Heidelberg (2013). https://doi.org/10.1007/978-3-642-39799-8_48

27. OASIS: PKCS #11 Cryptographic Token Interface Base Specification Version 3.0, June 2020. Accessed May 2021. https://docs.oasis-open.org/pkcs11/pkcs11-base/v3.0/pkcs11-base-v3.0.html

28. Ramsdell, J., Guttman, J.D., Millen, J.K., O'Hanlon, B.: An Analysis of the CAVES Attestation Protocol using CPSA. eprint arXiv:1207.0418 (2012). https://arxiv.org/abs/1207.0418

29. Ramsdell, J.D., Dougherty, D.J., Guttman, J.D., Rowe, P.D.: A hybrid analysis for security protocols with state. In: Albert, E., Sekerinski, E. (eds.) IFM 2014. LNCS, vol. 8739, pp. 272–287. Springer, Cham (2014). https://doi.org/10.1007/978-3-319-10181-1_17

30. Sherman, A., et al.: Formal methods analysis of the secure remote password protocol. In: Logic, Language, and Security, vol. 12300. Springer (2020). https://doi.org/10.1007/978-3-030-62077-6_9

31. Stanley-Oakes, R.: A provably secure PKCS#11 configuration without authenticated attributes. In: Financial Cryptography and Data Security, pp. 145–162. Springer International Publishing (2017). https://doi.org/10.1007/978-3-319-70972-7_8

32. Steel, G.: Proposal: Authenticated Attributes for Key Wrap in PKCS#11 (2014). https://lists.oasis-open.org/archives/pkcs11/201408/msg00006/pkcs11-authenticated-encryption-key-transport.pdf

33. Yang, F., Escobar, S., Meadows, C., Meseguer, J., Santiago, S.: Strand spaces with choice via a process algebra semantics. In: Proceedings of the 18th International Symposium on Principles and Practice of Declarative Programming, PPDP 2016, pp. 76–89. ACM (2016). https://doi.org/10.1145/2967973.2968609

A Declaration of Software Independence

Wojciech Jamroga[1], Peter Y. A. Ryan[1(✉)], Steve Schneider[2],
Carsten Schürmann[3], and Philip B. Stark[4]

[1] University of Luxembourg, Esch-sur-Alzette, Luxembourg
`peter.ryan@uni.lu`
[2] University of Surrey, Guildford, England
[3] IT University of Copenhagen, Copenhagen, Denmark
[4] University of California, Berkeley, USA

Abstract. A voting system should not merely report the outcome: it should also provide sufficient evidence to convince reasonable observers that the reported outcome is correct. Many deployed systems, notably paperless DRE machines still in use in US elections, fail certainly the second, and quite possibly the first of these requirements. Rivest and Wack proposed the principle of *software independence* (SI) as a guiding principle and requirement for voting systems. In essence, a voting system is SI if its reliance on software is "tamper-evident", that is, if there is a way to detect that material changes were made to the software without inspecting that software. This important notion has so far been formulated only informally.

Here, we provide more formal mathematical definitions of SI. This exposes some subtleties and gaps in the original definition, among them: what elements of a system must be trusted for an election or system to be SI, how to formalize "detection" of a change to an election outcome, the fact that SI is with respect to a set of detection mechanisms (which must be legal and practical), the need to limit false alarms, and how SI applies when the social choice function is not deterministic.

1 Introduction

Using digital technologies in elections opens up possibilities of enriching democratic processes, but it also brings a raft of new and often poorly understood threats to election accuracy, security, integrity, and trust. This is particularly clear with the so-called *DRE*, Direct-Recording Electronic voting machines, deployed widely in the U.S. after the Help America Vote Act (HAVA) of 2002, which passed in the aftermath of the controversial 2000 presidential election. The original DREs recorded, reported, and tallied cast votes using just software, with no paper record. Thus, an error in or change to that software could alter the outcome without leaving a trace.

It might be argued that the software could be analysed and proven to always deliver a correct result given the input votes. In practice, such analysis and testing is immensely difficult and prohibitively expensive. Moreover, access to

D. Dougherty et al. (Eds.): Guttman Festschrift, LNCS 13066, pp. 198–217, 2021.
https://doi.org/10.1007/978-3-030-91631-2_11

the code is often restricted due to commercial or legal constraints. And even if the software could be analysed completely and proven correct, there is still the challenge of guaranteeing that the software actually running on all the machines throughout the voting period is the "correct", verified version.

Consequently, for paperless DRE machines, BMDs, and existing Internet voting systems, voters, election officials et al. are required to place total blind confidence in the correctness of the code running on the devices.

Such concerns prompted calls to add a Voter-Verifiable Paper Audit Trial (VVPAT) to DREs, essentially a printer attached to the DRE that prints the voter's choice, in sight of the voter. In principle, each voter can check whether the paper accurately recorded her preferences, and correct the record if not.[1]

An alternative response—piloted but not yet widely adopted for political elections—is cryptographic end-to-end verifiable voting (E2E-V), which provides voters a means to verify that their vote reaches the tally unaltered and is correctly included in the tally. An accessible introduction to such systems can be found at [4], and a more extensive description at [9].

To capture the essential goal of being able to detect whether faulty software altered the outcome while remaining agnostic with respect to the technology employed to achieve that goal (e.g., a paper record or cryptographic methods), [12,13] proposed the principle of *software independence*, which seeks to exclude systems for which the trust in the correctness of the outcome requires trusting the software. The original definition is given as follows:

A voting system is *software-independent* if an (undetected) change or error in its software cannot cause an undetectable change or error in an election outcome.

[12,13] also define a stronger requirement, a system that does not require trusting software, and that is resilient to software-caused errors:

A voting system is *strongly software-independent* if it is software independent *and moreover, a detected change or error in an election outcome (due to change or error in the software) can be corrected without re-running the election.*

Version 2.0 of the U.S. Voluntary Voting System Guidelines [7], adopted 10 February 2021, incorporates the principle of Software Independence:

9.1 - An error or fault in the voting system software or hardware cannot cause an undetectable change in election results.

The principle seems very natural and compelling. It clearly rules out paperless DRE machines and—subject to certain assumptions about voter eligibility and the curation of paper ballots—it clearly admits systems based on hand-marked paper ballots supporting manual recounts, risk-limiting audits [14], and other

---

[1] There is considerable evidence that voters rarely check machine-generated printout and are unlikely to notice that votes were altered. See, e.g., [5,6,8,10].

forms of audits. However, as soon as we start to consider applying it to other systems, such as end-to-end cryptographically verifiable systems, things are less clear. In particular, many of the terms used in the definition require careful interpretation:

- What exactly do we mean by *the system*? Does it include pollworkers? Auditors? Where do we draw the boundaries?
- What exactly is the *software*? Does it include software involved in determining voter eligibility? Auditing software?
- What exactly does it mean to *detect* an error? Is it enough simply to flag a problem, or must evidence be provided that there really is a problem? What kind of evidence? To whom is the evidence available [1]? What rules out systems that always cry "foul", even when the election outcome is correct?
- What do we mean by *outcome*, in particular, where the social choice function is non-deterministic?

All of this motivates a more formal statement of the principle, which is the aim of this paper. This reveals a number of subtleties, notably that the original definition, read literally, does not exclude systems that reject every declared outcome: there is no penalty for false alarms. We argue that while software independence is a necessary property for a system to be able to deliver a verifiable outcome, it is not sufficient. We also stress the distinction between a *system* being *verifiable* and an *election* being *verified*.

We do not here address vote anonymity, receipt-freeness, coercion resistance, and related concerns. We focus just on the issues of detecting and correcting wrong outcomes while controlling false alarms. In practice, of course, great care needs to be taken in designing a system to provide sufficient transparency and generate sufficient evidence without violating privacy requirements.

We should also remark that, while software independence means that we should not have to place blind faith in the correct behaviour of the code, this does not imply that we should do away with all verification and testing of code. The latter is still important to help ensure the smooth running of any election run using the system, but the assurance of the outcome should not depend on the rigor etc. of such measures.

SI is a desirable property, but the use of an SI system does not by itself give the public adequate reason to trust election outcomes. The fact that it is possible to detect malfunctions of the software does not mean that checks will be performed nor that appropriate action will be taken if problems are detected. And errors or corruption may occur outside the software, e.g. breaches of chain of custody, faulty procedures, incorrect electoral roles, etc.

The notion of software independence is related to notions of end-to-end verifiability (E2E-V); we discuss the relationship in Sect. 3.2.

2 Formalizing Software Independence

In this section we set the ground for a definition that seeks to capture more formally the spirit of the original natural-language definition. We believe it is faithful to the spirit of the original, but as we shall see, the definition reveals some subtleties, and motivates the game-theoretic definition of the notion of *evidence-based elections* [2,15], presented below.[2]

2.1   Software Independence... of What?

To merit public confidence, a voting system should generate evidence that can be used to check whether it behaved correctly; typically, that involves a tamper-evident record of voters' expressed preferences, to which the social choice function can be applied to check the reported result. That record might be in the form of a well curated paper audit trail, or, as in many E2E-V systems, data (some of which is encrypted) posted to a public bulletin board (ledger). Furthermore, the system should provide for various checks to be performed on this evidence by the stakeholders: voters, observers, candidates etc. Such checks might be performed before the election starts (e.g. verifying that a transparent ballot box is initially empty), during (e.g. Benaloh challenges), or after (e.g. risk limiting-audits, risk-limiting tallies, verification of zero-knowledge proofs, digital signatures etc.). We refer to such checks generically as "audits".

We consider *software independence as a property of a voting system* $\mathcal{P}$ *with respect to a set of audits* $\mathcal{A}$. The voting system $\mathcal{P}$ represents all the components and aspects relevant for how the election is run, starting with the voting protocol, including its implementation (software) and deployment (hardware, physical infrastructure), specification of the environment, assumptions about human users, threat models, etc. The set of audits $\mathcal{A}$ captures the notion of "detectability" by providing an abstract representation of the methods available for detecting something is amiss.

We emphasize that it only makes sense to talk about software independence with a particular view of detection methods. For example, a voting system might be SI if a very powerful (and expensive) kind of instrument or audit can be used, but not if the requisite tools and methods are unaffordable, too time-consuming, or not mandated in law or regulation. On the other hand, another voting system might not be SI with respect to any known audit method, yet may become SI if a new forensic method is invented.[3] We elaborate on both aspects of this characterisation below.

2.2   Voting System and Its Software

Let $\mathcal{P}$ be a specification of how the voting protocol should work. This refers to the overall election system, including hardware, software, procedural, and human components. More precisely, $\mathcal{P}$ denotes the system running "correct" software, i.e., software that correctly computes the chosen social choice function over the

---

[2] The idea of evidence-based elections is that election officials should not only find the correct winner(s), but should also produce convincing public evidence that they found the correct winner(s)—or else admit that they cannot.

[3] E.g., think of what happened to criminal forensics when DNA tests were introduced.

voted preferences of eligible voters. The software, denoted $\mathcal{S}$, is considered a part of the system. However, in an actual execution of the system, $\mathcal{S}$ may be under the control of the adversary. Thus, $\mathcal{S}$ denotes a part of the system on whose correct behaviour we do not want to rely for evidence that the result is correct. In practise, that might comprise more than software. The spirit of the original definition corresponds to taking $\mathcal{S}$ to be the software that records and interprets votes, applies the social choice function to them, and reports an outcome. It does not include software that may form part of the surrounding system, such as software involved in giving each voter the correct ballot, software used to verify voter eligibility (e.g. voter registration systems and electronic pollbooks), or software involved in auditing the results. Nor does it include the behavior of voters, pollworkers, or election officials.

When we want to make the software $\mathcal{S}$ explicit in the voting system $\mathcal{P}$, then we write $\mathcal{P}[\mathcal{S}]$. Note that it is straightforward to generalise our approach to quantify over other parts of the system, e.g., hardware, people, procedures, etc.

The relevant aspects of system $\mathcal{P}[\mathcal{S}]$ are characterized, on an abstract level, by the following sets and functions:

- $m(\mathcal{P})$: a function that returns all the relevant mutations $\mathcal{P}[\mathcal{S}']$ of the voting system $\mathcal{P}$. We consider $\mathcal{P}[\mathcal{S}']$ as a relevant mutation of $\mathcal{P}[\mathcal{S}]$ if $\mathcal{P}[\mathcal{S}']$ can be obtained from $\mathcal{P}[\mathcal{S}]$ through changing only the software of $\mathcal{P}[\mathcal{S}]$, i.e., $\mathcal{S}$. Hardware and processes and protocols must be the same for $\mathcal{P}[\mathcal{S}]$ and $\mathcal{P}[\mathcal{S}']$. The software that can be changed is restricted to the software involved in collecting voter selections (votes), applying the social choice function to the votes, and reporting the results.

- In: the set of possible input sequences. Typically, an input sequence will comprise all the votes expressed[4] by the voters. Depending on the level of granularity in our modelling, it may also include other election-related activity, such as voter registration steps, eligibility verification, coercion attempts, generation of cryptographic keys, where and how each vote was cast, etc. It may also include the full expressed preferences of all the voters. In general, $v \in In$ contains much more information than is needed to determine who won.

- Ω: the set of possible election outcomes. Typically, an outcome is either the tally, or the winner(s) of the election. Depending on the level of granularity, it may also include any other publicly available output of the voting system, such as the content of the web bulletin board. We assume that Ω is finite. For example, in a plurality contest with two contestants, A and B, the possible outcomes in Ω might be "A wins," "B wins," and "A and B are tied." If the social choice function breaks ties, then there would be only two possible outcomes: "A wins" and "B wins."

---

[4] By *expressed*, we mean what the voter did: the marks the voters make on the paper or the cell they press on a touchscreen. Of course, a confusing user interface—including poor ballot layout—can cause voters' expressed preferences to differ from their intended preferences. See, e.g. [1].

– $exec(\mathcal{P}[\mathcal{S}], v)$: a function that returns the set of all the possible executions (runs) of system $\mathcal{P}[\mathcal{S}]$ on the sequence of inputs $v \in In$. Any particular election system with a particular input sequence might have a number of possible executions arising from the different choices that can be made at various points of the voting protocol. For example if a voter is required to provide inputs other than just selections (e.g., to decide whether to challenge an encryption, as allowed in some E2E-V protocols), then different possible executions can arise. In practice, there will usually be just one possible execution given $(\mathcal{P}[\mathcal{S}], v)$, but there may be boundary conditions (e.g. tie-breaking, or randomness in transferring votes) where more than one result is possible. Naturally, $exec(\mathcal{P}[\mathcal{S}'], v)$ is the set of all possible executions of the mutated system $\mathcal{P}[\mathcal{S}']$ on the input sequence v.

– $result(E)$: the outcome of the election for execution E. We lift the function to sets of executions X by fixing $result(X) = \{result(E) \mid E \in X\}$. In the case of the correct system $\mathcal{P}[\mathcal{S}]$, we would expect any outcome in $result(exec(\mathcal{P}[\mathcal{S}], v))$ to be a valid result of the election.

Note that the composition $result(exec(\mathcal{P}[\mathcal{S}], v))$ can be seen as a generalisation of a *social choice function*.

2.3   Available Audits

In the process of running the election, including recording, tallying, and broadcasting the election results, the overall voting system $\mathcal{P}[\mathcal{S}]$ generates evidence that can be used to audit the election. The auditing of an election may overlap with, or be completely separate from the voting procedure. The evidence is provided as input to a decision-making process, represented by a function a, which then provides a judgement. The software in a is assumed to be trustworthy. Such an assumption of trustworthiness needs of course to be justified, and this will usually be by arguing that, if its inputs and intended function are public, anyone who wishes to check the correctness of its outputs could write it again from scratch, or a reputable authority such as the Electronic Frontier Foundation (EFF) could provide a reference implementation.

Evidence produced in the election might include voter registration databases, poll books, physical ballots, encrypted choices, cryptographic receipts, public bulletin boards, zero-knowledge proofs (ZKPs), security videos, the condition of physical seals on ballot boxes, chain-of-custody logs, logs from telephone complaint lines or websites that record "anomalies" voters witnessed during the election, etc. The evidence might not include the "plaintext" voter preferences and generally will not include a voter's actual interaction with a DRE or BMD.

Some evidence generated during the election will be unreliable or unavailable. For instance, paper ballots do not provide reliable evidence of the outcome if they might have been tampered with, replaced, augmented, or lost; or if voter eligibility checks were not sufficiently accurate. In some E2E-V systems, plaintext votes are not available to check the correctness of the outcome; a system designed to allow voters to check that their intent was recorded correctly (e.g., using

a VVPAT or through a Benaloh challenge) does not provide public evidence
that voter intent was correctly recorded unless there is both evidence about the
number of voters who checked, how effectively they checked, and a mechanism
by which it would become known that they found errors, if they find errors. It
must be also noted that, by the time a preliminary outcome is available, evidence
could be lost, altered, or counterfeited; the election officials might have reacted
to some detected problems during the election; and that in turn might generate
new possibilities for things to go wrong.

Formally, the capability of the voting authorities (possibly together with
independent auditors, public observers, or with voters, e.g., in case of mechanisms for voter verification) to detect malfunctioning of the voting system is
characterised by the set $\mathcal{A} = \{a_1, a_2, \dots\}$ of available audit procedures. Let T
and F denote the truth values of *true* and *false*, respectively. Each element a_i of
$\mathcal{A}$ is a function that takes an execution E of the voting system, and returns an
audit judgement $a_i(E) \in \{T, F\}$ such that $a_i(E) = F$ only if there is a change or
error in the election outcome. (Below we also consider audits that have a random
component, and thus have some probability of returning T or F for any given
the voting system execution E.) It is required that a_i must be compatible with
the voting system, in the sense that the judgment $a_i(E)$ is based entirely on the
evidence available in the execution E of the voting system.

For instance, $\mathcal{A}$ might include verifying poll book signatures, comparing the
number of pollbook signatures to the number of votes cast in each precinct, a
manual audit of results against a paper trail, checking ZKPs, checking whether
digital signatures on cryptographic receipts are authentic, reviewing chain-of-
custody records, inspecting equipment log files and security videos, etc.

An exemplar a_i might specify, among its branches, "before opening each box
of ballots for central counting, check the seal on the box against a photograph
of the seal taken in the polling place. If the seal has been disturbed, interview
everyone who has had custody of the box since it was sealed, examine every
ballot by hand for signs of tampering or forgery, and compare the number of
ballots in the box with the number of pollbook signatures."

3   Possibilistic Formulation of Software Independence

The original definition of SI talks about whether a change to the result is always
detectable. This is expressed in terms of possibilities rather than probabilities.
Here we see how far we can get with expressing SI possibilistically without involving probabilities. We will also show that it is natural to introduce probabilities
into the audit process.

3.1   Basic Formulation

Using the notation introduced in Sect. 2, the property of Software Independence
with respect to a particular election input v and audit method a can be expressed
as follows:

$$SI_1(\mathcal{P}[\mathcal{S}], v, a) \iff \tag{1}$$
$$\forall \mathcal{P}[\mathcal{S}'] \in m(\mathcal{P}[\mathcal{S}]) \,.$$
$$\big(\forall E' \in exec(\mathcal{P}[\mathcal{S}'], v) \,.\, \exists E \in exec(\mathcal{P}[\mathcal{S}], v) \,.\, (result(E) = result(E'))\big)$$
$$\lor \big(\exists E' \in exec(\mathcal{P}[\mathcal{S}'], v) \,.\, a(E') = F\big).$$

The formula states that every execution of any mutation of $\mathcal{P}[\mathcal{S}]$ gives a correct result, or else the malfunction is detectable. More precisely, either every execution of a mutation of $\mathcal{P}[\mathcal{S}]$ gives a result that could have been produced by the correct software, or there is some execution that will fail the audit.

Then, Software Independence holds with respect to a set of possible election inputs $v \in In$ and allowable audit procedures $\mathcal{A}$ if there is some audit procedure $a \in \mathcal{A}$ such that SI holds for all possible inputs:

$$SI_1(\mathcal{P}[\mathcal{S}], \mathcal{A}) \iff \exists a \in \mathcal{A} \,.\, \forall v \in In \,.\, SI_1(\mathcal{P}[\mathcal{S}], v, a). \tag{2}$$

Arguably, Formula (1) captures software independence of particular *election*, given the set of votes and actual audit strategy used in the election. In contrast, Formula (2) expresses software independence of the *voting system* defined by the voting infrastructure and the available audit strategies.

Remark. Formulas (1)–(2) capture a rather weak notion of Software Independence. First, they only say that $\mathcal{P}[\mathcal{S}']$ cannot undetectably add incorrect outcomes to the set of possible results of the election. However, a software mutation *removing* some of the correct results may as well satisfy the conditions. We address this issue in Sect. 3.5.

Secondly, the formalisation is based on a weak notion of detectability. The conditions require that significant software mutations *might* be detected (i.e., they are detected on some possible executions), but there is no guarantee that they can be detected for every execution that produces incorrect outcomes.

A stronger definition of SI is obtained by replacing the right hand side of the disjunction (1) as follows:

$$\forall E' \in exec(\mathcal{P}[\mathcal{S}'], v) \,.\, \big((\exists E \in exec(\mathcal{P}[\mathcal{S}], v) \,.\, result(E) = result(E')) \lor (a(E') = F)\big).$$

This removes the existential quantification over executions and brings E' under the universal quantification. The first formalisation allows for some executions of a mutation not to be caught by an audit even if they give the wrong result. This stronger formalisation states that any execution of a mutation that does not give the correct result should be caught by an audit.

Note also that our formalisation is focused on the potential irregularities due to software mutations. Thus, disturbances of the election outcome due to failures of hardware, dishonest voter behaviour, etc., must only be handled in $\mathcal{P}[\mathcal{S}']$ if they would be caught and dealt with in the ideal system $\mathcal{P}[\mathcal{S}]$.

Audit Strategies. We recall that the characterisation of $\mathcal{A}$ encapsulates the audit methods that are allowable. Considerations as to what should be allowable can include what is possible, affordable (in terms of cost or time), legal (to fit with local election law, preserve the anonymity of votes, etc.), and other considerations as appropriate to the situation. Identifying the limits of what is allowable is itself part of the consideration as to whether a system is software independent. From a technical point of view, the definition of $\mathcal{A}$ will also need to depend on the evidence provided explicitly by the voting system. Thus the formalisation of possible executions E also constrains the audits that are possible, because a is a function on executions: two runs giving rise to the same execution record E must give the same result on audit. For example, if the only evidence collected for audit is the set of paper ballots, then forensic analysis of the hard disks of the voting machines is outside the scope of audit. Conversely if the audit includes the possibility of such analysis, then the evidence provided by an election run should include the relevant state of the hard disks to enable the audit function to be defined.

The sanity condition (or soundness) on an auditing mechanism a for system $\mathcal{P}[\mathcal{S}]$ is that any correct execution of the ideal system will verify positively:

$$\mathbf{sound}(a, \mathcal{P}[\mathcal{S}]) \iff \forall v \in In \ . \ \forall E \in exec(\mathcal{P}[\mathcal{S}], v) \ . \ a(E) = T.$$

Although this is not stated explicitly within the original definition of Software Independence, correct election outcomes should not be flagged by the audit as incorrect, so we will require that every a function in $\mathcal{A}$ be *sound*.

3.2   Relationship to End-to-End Verifiability

The definitions above enable us to highlight an important distinction between Software Independence and End-to-end Verifiability (E2E-V), cf. [3] for an introduction and [11] for a well-known formalisation. In particular, in a description of a system $\mathcal{P}[\mathcal{S}]$ the component $\mathcal{S}$ explicitly represents only the software, and the context $\mathcal{P}$ remains unchanged. This amounts to requiring that the context $\mathcal{P}$ is trusted in the characterisation of SI. However, when we consider whether the system $\mathcal{P}[\mathcal{S}]$ is end-to-end verifiable, we consider this question with respect to the entire system.

We should note that not all formulations of E2E-V in the literature actually imply correctness of the outcome. Early formulations focused on the ability to detect the corruption of any vote between casting and input to the tally function. To achieve guarantees of correctness we also need measures to prevent ballot stuffing and ballot collisions. Taken together, these imply a bijection between the set of cast votes and the set of votes input to the tally. Here we assume a definition that does encompass these requirements, as does [11]. Here they refer to such a strengthened notion, that does imply correctness if all verification steps give true, as *global verifiability*.

To illustrate the difference, consider the following toy example, which shows that SI does not imply E2E-V: A voting system consists of a ballot box for paper ballots, a scanner, and a software component $\mathcal{S}$ that controls the scanner, interprets the scans, applies the social choice function to the votes, and reports the result. There is a trusted individual $\mathcal{I}$ (appointed by the Election Authority, say) who will also play a key part. A description of the system formulated as $\mathcal{P}[\mathcal{S}]$ would include $\mathcal{I}$ within the definition of $\mathcal{P}$.

Voting: To vote, voters fill out their ballot form, run it through the scanner, then drop it in the ballot box.

Tallying: At the end of the election, $\mathcal{I}$ privately counts the votes from the ballot box and calculates the result r_1. The electronic component $\mathcal{S}$ computes the result r_2 from the scans, and provides this result to $\mathcal{I}$, who privately checks whether $r_1 = r_2$. If so, then $\mathcal{I}$ reports the result. Otherwise an alarm is raised and an audit occurs, consisting of comparing r_1 and r_2. if they are distinct then the audit returns the value F.

The system $\mathcal{P}[\mathcal{S}]$ is SI, because an undetected change in $\mathcal{S}$ cannot undetectably change the result, and the system meets the definition in Line 1. Given a change to the software, either the resulting software still gives the same result, or the audit will return the value F. Note that this relies on the honesty and correct behaviour of $\mathcal{I}$; this is assumed for the characterisation of SI.

The system $\mathcal{P}[\mathcal{S}]$ is not E2E-V. Voters are not able to check that their vote is included in the tally, and there is no check for independent observers that the tally is computed correctly. In particular, $\mathcal{I}$ can simply report a different result and not raise the alarm.

One key difference is that for SI, any part of the system that is not the software is presumed to be acting as it should. Hence, the question is whether a change to $\mathcal{S}$ can change the result when $\mathcal{P}$ behaves correctly.

On the other hand for E2E-V we also consider that $\mathcal{P}$ can behave dishonestly. So $\mathcal{P}[\mathcal{S}]$ is not E2E-V: it is possible for the wrong result to be reported without any verification checks showing incorrect behaviour.

A further distinction is that SI makes no mention of who does the "detecting," whereas E2E-V is quite explicit: each voter can perform the individual check and anyone can perform the universal check. The example above illustrates this point, too.

E2E-V $\Rightarrow$ SI: Conversely, we can reason informally that E2E-V implies SI, via a contrapositive argument as follows. If a system with verification mechanisms is not SI, then by Definition 2 for some input v there is a change to the software $\mathcal{S}'$ that can result in an execution E' with an incorrect result $result(E')$ that passes every audit $audit \in \mathcal{A}$, i.e. it produces an undetectable change to the result. But if the incorrectness of the result is undetectable, then the verification mechanisms cannot detect this, and hence will verify an incorrect result. But this means the system is not E2E-V, since E2E-V requires that if all potential verification steps pass[5] then the result is correct. Note that here we are assuming a strong notion of verifiability, such as global verifiability.

Observe that both audits and verifications can raise an alarm even when the result is correct. We are not concerned with this case in this section, but rather

---

[5] I.e., every voter checks what individual voters can check (individual verifiability), someone checks the aggregation of votes (universal verifiability), and someone checks that every vote has come from a different eligible voter (eligibility verifiability).

the converse case where the audits and verifications do not raise the alarm even though the result is incorrect.

3.3 SI with Adaptive Audits

The formalization of SI by Formulas (1)–(2) assumes that there exists a single audit strategy in $\mathcal{A}$ that can detect malfunction and/or tampering with the voting software. Another option is to swap the quantifiers, and assume that different audit procedures may be applicable on different runs of the voting system (e.g., against different kinds of threats). Now, SI with respect to a set of available audits becomes:

$$
\begin{aligned}
SI_2(\mathcal{P}[\mathcal{S}], \mathcal{A}) &\iff \forall v \in In \;.\; SI_2(\mathcal{P}[\mathcal{S}], v, \mathcal{A}); \\
SI_2(\mathcal{P}[\mathcal{S}], v, \mathcal{A}) &\iff \\
&\forall \mathcal{P}[\mathcal{S}'] \in m(\mathcal{P}[\mathcal{S}]) \;. \\
&\big(\forall E' \in exec(\mathcal{P}[\mathcal{S}'], v) \;.\; \exists E \in exec(\mathcal{P}[\mathcal{S}], v) \;.\; (result(E) = result(E'))\big) \\
&\vee \big(\exists E' \in exec(\mathcal{P}[\mathcal{S}'], v) \;.\; \exists a \in \mathcal{A} \;.\; a(E') = F\big).
\end{aligned}
\tag{3}
$$

That is, either every execution of any mutation of $\mathcal{P}[\mathcal{S}]$ gives a result that could have been produced by the correct software, or there is some execution that will fail at least one audit procedure in the available audit set. Again, Formula (3) captures software independence of an election, and (2) expresses SI of the voting system. Note that these notions of detection are still somewhat weak in that they do not ensure that anyone can tell *which* $a \in \mathcal{A}$ suffices for any particular execution E.

3.4 A Refinement

Audit procedures are often nondeterministic by design (e.g., audits that inspect a random sample of ballots, including risk-limiting audits). In our definition of SI, it can be beneficial to separate the randomness of the audit from randomness in the rest of the system. This view can be incorporated by treating audit procedures as functions on system executions E that return a probability distribution on $\{T, F\}$.

For example, for statistical audit of the paper trail, different audit runs result from inspecting different random samples of ballots, each of which has some probability; for some runs, the audit might return T and for others F.

The soundness sanity condition on the auditing mechanism a stays as before.

Having separated the audit non-determinism from the system non-determinism, we can now redefine "undetectable change" to apply to those *system runs* for which the probability that the audit returns F is zero. Let Pr denote probability computed with respect to the audit, treating. Now, software independence of system $\mathcal{P}[\mathcal{S}]$ with respect to the audit set $\mathcal{A}$ becomes:

$$SI_3(\mathcal{P}[\mathcal{S}], \mathcal{A}) \iff \exists a \in \mathcal{A} . \forall v \in In . SI_3(\mathcal{P}[\mathcal{S}], v, a); \qquad (4)$$

$$SI_3(\mathcal{P}[\mathcal{S}], v, a) \iff \qquad\qquad\qquad\qquad\qquad (5)$$
$$\forall \mathcal{P}[\mathcal{S}'] \in m(\mathcal{P}[\mathcal{S}]) . \forall E' \in exec(\mathcal{P}[\mathcal{S}'], v) .$$
$$(\exists E \in exec(\mathcal{P}[\mathcal{S}], v) . result(E) = result(E')) \vee$$
$$Pr(a(E') = F) > 0.$$

The definition can be equivalently phrased as follows. Let

$$AccResults(\mathcal{P}[\mathcal{S}'], a, v) = \{\omega \mid \exists E' \in exec(\mathcal{P}[\mathcal{S}'], v) .$$
$$(\omega = result(E') \wedge Pr(a(E') = T) = 1)\}$$

be the set of *surely accepted results* for $\mathcal{P}[\mathcal{S}']$ on v. That is, these are the possible outcomes of running $\mathcal{P}[\mathcal{S}']$ on input v for which the audit has zero probability of reporting that the outcome is wrong. Note that, for the ideal system $\mathcal{P}[\mathcal{S}]$, if the audit meets the soundness condition this is just the set of possible (correct) outcomes, i.e., $AccResults(\mathcal{P}[\mathcal{S}], a, v) = \{result(E) \mid E \in exec(\mathcal{P}[\mathcal{S}], v)\}$. Since in that case the set does not depend on the audit strategy, we will often write $AccResults(\mathcal{P}[\mathcal{S}], v)$ instead of $AccResults(\mathcal{P}[\mathcal{S}], a, v)$. Then, Formula (5) can be rephrased as:

$$SI_3(\mathcal{P}[\mathcal{S}], v, a) \iff$$
$$\forall \mathcal{P}[\mathcal{S}'] \in m(\mathcal{P}[\mathcal{S}]) . AccResults(\mathcal{P}[\mathcal{S}'], a, v) \subseteq AccResults(\mathcal{P}[\mathcal{S}], v).$$

3.5   Software Resilience

The above definition says that every execution of $\mathcal{P}[\mathcal{S}']$ either simulates a legitimate execution of $\mathcal{P}[\mathcal{S}]$ or has a strictly positive chance of being "detected" by the audit. This kind of property is arguably closest to the spirit of the proposal by Rivest and Wack. Also, it corresponds to the intuition that, usually, the only evidence that one has to determine a property of an election system comes from the actual run of the system during the actual election. However, as a system property, it is rather weak. Ideally, one would also like to guarantee the "vice versa" condition, saying that every outcome of the ideal software can be produced by the mutation $\mathcal{P}[\mathcal{S}']$. That is, $\mathcal{P}[\mathcal{S}']$ not only does not introduce any illegal winners, but also does not remove any legally possible ones. Then, every mutation $\mathcal{P}[\mathcal{S}']$ must produce exactly the same set of acceptable election outcomes as the ideal system $\mathcal{P}[\mathcal{S}]$. We call the new property *software resilience (SR)*, and define it formally as follows:

$$SR(\mathcal{P}[\mathcal{S}], \mathcal{A}) \iff \exists a \in \mathcal{A} . \forall v \in In . SR(\mathcal{P}[\mathcal{S}], v, a);$$
$$SR(\mathcal{P}[\mathcal{S}], v, a) \iff$$
$$\forall \mathcal{P}[\mathcal{S}'] \in m(\mathcal{P}[\mathcal{S}]) . AccResults(\mathcal{P}[\mathcal{S}'], a, v) = AccResults(\mathcal{P}[\mathcal{S}], v).$$

In other words, $SR(\mathcal{P}[\mathcal{S}], v, a)$ requires that every mutation $\mathcal{P}[\mathcal{S}']$ is trace-equivalent to $\mathcal{P}[\mathcal{S}]$ with respect to the surely accepted election outcomes that they can produce.

In practice of course, what the electorate needs is a way to determine, as the end of a given election, whether the reported outcome was not only one of the possible correct outcomes, but also fair in some sense. Where the outcome is uniquely defined this is fine: it is enough that we can determine that it was correct. Where the outcome is not uniquely defined, for example in the event of a tie in a simple plurality vote resolved by the system's software (rather than, for instance, by a public coin toss), this is more delicate: we would like to be able to establish that no possible outcomes were excluded by that particular software running at the time. If the tie is resolved by the software, there is no way to establish one the basis of observation of a single run.

In order to resolve such situations it seems necessary to externalise the mechanism that makes the choice amongst possible outcomes, for example based on a publicly observable coin toss or equivalent. How to provide a truly random source that cannot be predicted or influenced by any way is a topic in its own right, outside the scope of this paper.

Another approach is to regard the outcome as the raw tally, and the resolution of any ties etc. to be outside the scope of the definition. However, the outcome can be correct even when the tally is not—indeed, this is why risk-limiting audits can be efficient. Machine tallies of hand-marked paper ballots are rarely if ever perfectly accurate.

Moreover, non-determinism may be buried in the tabulation algorithm itself, and so not neatly separable. This is for instance the case in the STV variant used in New South Wales, Australia , as well as the D'Hondt method of allocating seats in the parliament in many European countries.

3.6   Thought Experiment

A simple voting system with rather a weak audit highlights some aspects of the definitions.

Consider a voting system $\mathcal{P}_{weak}$ defined as follows:

Voting

1. Votes are cast on paper (filling in a bubble by hand), scanned, and then deposited into a ballot box. The scans are linked to the corresponding paper ballots in a way that allows the scan corresponding to a particular ballot to be retrieved, and vice versa.
2. All of the scans are then published, and the result declared.

Here the software $\mathcal{S}$ controls the scanning, tabulation, and reporting. We assume that there is good physical security of the ballots, and that the total number of ballots is known.

Audit

1. Auditors check whether the number of scans matches the number of ballots. If not, the audit returns F.

2. Auditors inspect every scan and tabulate the resulting interpretation of the votes to obtain an electoral outcome. If that outcome differs from the reported outcome, the audit returns F.
3. A paper ballot is selected at random. Its corresponding scan is retrieved and checked to see whether the human interpretation of that scan matches the human interpretation of the ballot. If not, the audit returns F.

According to the Rivest/Wack definition of SI this system is SI, because any change in the result (caused by a change in the software) can be in principle detected. Thus, it meets the formal characterisation in Line 1. However, this audit may have a low probability of detecting an attack that alters or substitutes scans. If the fraction of the altered scans is δ, then δ is also the chance of detecting the attack. (Moreover, this audit may produce false alarms: the reported outcome could be correct even if some scans were altered.)

3.7   Software Independence for Probabilistic Audits

The thought experiment illustrates that audits can be (and usually are) probabilistic. Although the Rivest/Wack definition of software independence is expressed in possibilistic terms, a comment (almost in passing) in [12] indicates that in practice there should be a high probability of detecting software misbehaviour:

> The detection of any software misbehavior does not need to be perfect; it only needs to happen with sufficiently high probability, in an assumed ideal environment with alert voters, pollworkers, etc.

This is a rather stronger requirement, and introduces probability into the characterisation. Where should this probability be introduced?

The idea should be that whatever mutation of $\mathcal{P}$ is considered, and for any execution of that mutation, if the result has been changed then this should be detectable with high probability. The 'detectable' element of this definition is the responsibility of the audit function.

Then we can adjust the definition of Software Independence of Sect. 3.4 to incorporate the additional requirement that when the result has been changed, the audit has a probability $p_0 > 0$ to notice that:

$$SI_4(\mathcal{P}[\mathcal{S}], \mathcal{A}, p_0) \iff \exists a \in \mathcal{A} . \forall v \in In . SI_4(\mathcal{P}[\mathcal{S}], v, a, p_0);$$
$$SI_4(\mathcal{P}[\mathcal{S}], v, a, p_0) \iff$$
$$\forall \mathcal{P}[\mathcal{S}'] \in m(\mathcal{P}[\mathcal{S}]) . \forall E' \in exec(\mathcal{P}[\mathcal{S}'], v) .$$
$$(\exists E \in exec(\mathcal{P}[\mathcal{S}], v) . result(E) = result(E'))$$
$$\vee Pr(a(E') = F) \geq p_0.$$

This is clearly stronger than the previous definition in Eqs. (4)–(5).

4 Probabilistic/Game-Theoretic Definition

In the previous section, we proposed a possibilistic definition of software independence. It was based on the assumption that we can quantify over possibilities (possible mutations of the software, executions of the system, etc.) but cannot formulate constraints with respect to quantitative measures over the possibilities (e.g., probability of executions or computational complexity of a mutation strategy). The first step towards a more quantitative approach was discussed in Sect. 3.7 where we considered audits with a random component. Here, we present a full-blown quantitative definition of SI. We assume the following:

1. The execution of $\mathcal{P}[\mathcal{S}]$ on an input v defines a probability distribution over all the possible runs in $exec(\mathcal{P}[\mathcal{S}], v)$;
2. The execution of audit method a given a system execution E defines a probability distribution on $\{T, F\}$;
3. The choice of a software mutation belongs to a potentially malicious "attacker," whereas the auditing method is selected by the "defender." The input sequence $v \in In$ is chosen by Nature;
4. The defender must select the audit without knowing the mutation the attacker selected. (However, the audit procedure can be adaptive.) The attacker knows the defender's audit strategy in advance, but not any random elements involved in that strategy. E.g., the attacker might know that the auditor will examine a random sample of ballots, but does not know which particular ballots will be examined.

4.1 Terminology and Notation

As before, Pr denotes probability. Moreover, we will use $\mathsf{Exec}(\mathcal{P}[\mathcal{S}], v)$, $\mathsf{Res}(E)$, and $\mathsf{Aud}(E)$ for the random variables ranging over possible runs $E \in exec(\mathcal{P}[\mathcal{S}], v)$, possible election outcomes $\omega \in result(E)$, and audit judgments in $\{T, F\}$, respectively.

Election Environment. Given the input $v \in In$ (in particular, the voters' expressed preferences), the voting system $\mathcal{P}[\mathcal{S}]$ defines a probability distribution $Pr(\mathsf{Exec}(\mathcal{P}[\mathcal{S}], v) = E)$ over the possible runs $E \in exec(\mathcal{P}[\mathcal{S}], v)$. Similarly, given a run E of the voting system, $Pr(\mathsf{Res}(E) = \omega)$ denotes the probability that the election outcome is $\omega \in \Omega$. Note that the social choice function can be now represented by the probability distribution

$$Pr(\mathsf{Res}(\mathcal{P}[\mathcal{S}], v) = \omega) = \sum_{E \in exec(\mathcal{P}[\mathcal{S}], v)} Pr(\mathsf{Exec}(\mathcal{P}[\mathcal{S}], v) = E) \cdot Pr(\mathsf{Res}(E) = \omega).$$

Deterministic social choice functions amount to randomized functions that put all their mass on a single $\omega \in \Omega$.

For instance, in a two-candidate plurality contest with ties broken at random, the set of outcomes can be defined as $\Omega = \{a, b\}$ with a standing for "Alice wins" and b for "Bob wins." If the election input $v \in In$ contains more votes for Alice than for Bob, then $Pr(\mathsf{Res}(\mathcal{P}[\mathcal{S}], \mathsf{v}) = a) = 1$ and $Pr(\mathsf{Res}(\mathcal{P}[\mathcal{S}], \mathsf{v}) = b) = 0$. If v contains more votes for Bob than for Alice, then $Pr(\mathsf{Res}(\mathcal{P}[\mathcal{S}], \mathsf{v}) = a) = 0$ and $Pr(\mathsf{Res}(\mathcal{P}[\mathcal{S}], \mathsf{v}) = b) = 1$. If v has the same number of votes for Alice and Bob, then $Pr(\mathsf{Res}(\mathcal{P}[\mathcal{S}], \mathsf{v}) = a) = Pr(\mathsf{Res}(\mathcal{P}[\mathcal{S}], \mathsf{v}) = b) = \frac{1}{2}$.

If an election produces outcome ω that has probability zero, that is, if $Pr(\mathsf{Res}(\mathcal{P}[\mathcal{S}], \mathsf{v}) = \omega) = 0$, then the outcome is presumptively incorrect.[6] For a single election, if $Pr(\mathsf{Res}(\mathcal{P}[\mathcal{S}], \mathsf{v}) = \omega) > 0$, we cannot tell whether $\mathcal{P}[\mathcal{S}]$ assigns the *correct* probability to ω: that would require replicating the execution. Hence, we consider an outcome ω to be *admissible* for $\mathcal{P}[\mathcal{S}]$ and v if the probability of that outcome is strictly positive, that is, if $Pr(\mathsf{Res}(\mathcal{P}[\mathcal{S}], \mathsf{v}) = \omega) > 0$ (the outcome is expected to occur sometimes for that vote profile and that social choice function). We denote the set of such outcomes by $\mathcal{W}_{\mathcal{P}[\mathcal{S}], v}$.

Attack and Defense Strategies. We model the interplay between threats (regardless of their cause) and mitigations as the election unfolds by means of two *strategies* that play against each other: an *attack strategy* and a *defense strategy*.

An *attack strategy* f interferes with the ideal operation of the election by changing the "software" of the election system. (Recall that we use the term "software" abstractly, to denote those things under consideration that might behave incorrectly, which might include more than computer code, depending on context.) Each f amounts to a (possibly randomized) plan that specifies the action that the attacker will take if a given circumstance occurs. It involves the vulnerabilities and failure modes of the overall election, and represents how outcomes and evidence might be altered by failures or adversarial attacks. The involved software mutations are drawn from $m(\mathcal{P}[\mathcal{S}])$. The input v is the set of "true" votes of the eligible voters.

We denote the set of *feasible attack strategies* by $\mathcal{F}_{m(\mathcal{P}[\mathcal{S}])}$. Note that such strategies may have to satisfy some constraints. For instance, it might not be computationally feasible to fake a ZKP. Or it might not be possible to alter marks on paper ballots undetectably, to steal a ballot box and its contents undetectably, or to corrupt a multipartisan group of auditors into faking audit results.

A *defense strategy* g conducts tests and countermeasures to judge whether the announced outcome of the election is correct. Each g amounts to a (possibly randomized) conditional plan that specifies the actions the defender will take in a given set of circumstances. Defense strategies consist of actions that the "checkers" (elections officials, auditors, public, etc.) can take before, during, and after the election to try to ensure that the outcome is correct, and to assess whether the outcome is correct, despite the fact that things might have gone wrong—that is, despite f. Clearly, they can have random elements, such as statistical audits. Given an election run E, $Pr(\mathsf{Aud}(\mathsf{g}, \mathsf{E}) = AJ)$ is the probability that the defense strategy g returns audit judgment $AJ \in \{T, F\}$ on E. The set of possible defense strategies based on audit methods $\mathcal{A}$ is denoted by $\mathcal{G}_{\mathcal{A}}$ The set $\mathcal{G}_{\mathcal{A}}$ is fixed after $\mathcal{F}_{m(\mathcal{P}[\mathcal{S}])}$ is known, but before the apparent outcome ω is known, and without knowledge of f. That is, methods for assessing the outcome may

---

[6] Recall that the set of outcomes is assumed to be finite.

depend on the kind of evidence the system generates, the ways the ideal evidence might be corrupted, and the execution trace E, including reported tallies and outcomes. The strategies in $\mathcal{G}_A$ must satisfy legal and practical constraints, as discussed above.

Both f and g are "interactive," in the sense that the actions taken under a particular g can depend on circumstances generated by the actions under f, and *vice versa*, as well as on random elements. The defense strategy is restricted to the "audits"; the attacker has no influence on audits other than through $\mathcal{S}$.

Execution Semantics for Strategies. The choice of attack (f) and defense (g) strategies determine how probable different election runs are, which in turn affects the chance that the audit identifies incorrect outcomes. We model this through the probability distribution $Pr(\mathsf{Exec}(\mathcal{P}[\mathcal{S},f],v) = E)$ on the set of system executions, for system software $\mathcal{S}$, attack strategy f, and input votes v. For any given g, this induces a probability distribution on the audit decisions $\mathsf{Aud}(g,E)$. Now,

$$Pr(\mathsf{Aud}(f,g,v) = AJ \mid \mathcal{W}) =$$
$$\sum_{w \in \mathcal{W}} \sum_{E \in exec(\mathcal{P}[\mathcal{S},f],v)} Pr(\mathsf{Exec}(\mathcal{P}[\mathcal{S},f],v) = E) \cdot Pr(\mathsf{Res}(E) = w) \cdot Pr(\mathsf{Aud}(g,E) = AJ)$$

denotes the probability that the announced outcome will be accepted (for $AJ = T$) or rejected (for $AJ = F$), given that the announced outcome is in $\mathcal{W}$.

As in Sect. 3, we take v to be fixed when defining software independence of a particular *election*. Moreover, we are interested in $\mathcal{W} = \{w\}$, where w is the outcome that has been announced. In defining software independence of an *election system*, we quantify over the possible election inputs $v \in In$, and do not condition on $\mathcal{W} = \{w\}$.

4.2   Game-Theoretic Definition of SI

We will cast software independence in terms of a game, in a manner analogous to how semantic security of cryptographic algorithms is captured, or to how estimation problems are formalized in statistical decision theory. An election is seen as a strictly competitive game between the adversary choosing an attack strategy $f \in \mathcal{F}_{m(\mathcal{P}[\mathcal{S}])}$ and the checker choosing a defense strategy $g \in \mathcal{G}_A$. The payoffs of the checker are multicriterial (and thus only partially ordered), and given by the respective probabilities of false positive and false negative output of the audit procedure. The solution concept is based on *minimax*, i.e., the checker minimizes the loss assuming the worst case (most damaging) of the adversary. (Since the payoff is multicriterial, there is no minimax strategy *sensu stricto*, but the analysis is worst-case.) Moreover, the adversary is assumed to adapt the attack strategy f to the defense strategy g selected by the checker. On the other hand, the checker must choose the defense strategy without knowing the attack strategy.

Formally, given a defense strategy $g \in \mathcal{G}_A$, an election input $v \in In$, and a set of admissible election outcomes $\mathcal{W}_{\mathcal{P}[\mathcal{S}],v}$, we define two kinds of costs that the checker wants to minimize:

$$\epsilon(g, v) = \sup_{f \in \mathcal{F}_{m(\mathcal{P}[\mathcal{S}])}} Pr(\mathsf{Aud}(f, g, v) = F \mid \mathcal{W}_{\mathcal{P}[\mathcal{S}], v}),$$

$$\delta(g, v) = \sup_{f \in \mathcal{F}_{m(\mathcal{P}[\mathcal{S}])}} Pr(\mathsf{Aud}(f, g, v) = T \mid \overline{\mathcal{W}}_{\mathcal{P}[\mathcal{S}], v})$$

$$= 1 - \inf_{f \in \mathcal{F}_{m(\mathcal{P}[\mathcal{S}])}} Pr(\mathsf{Aud}(f, g, v) = F \mid \overline{\mathcal{W}}_{\mathcal{P}[\mathcal{S}], v}).$$

That is, ϵ is the largest chance that the checker rejects an admissible outcome (*false negative*), and δ is the largest chance that he fails to reject an inadmissible outcome (*false positive*).

Definition 1 ((ϵ, δ)-SI). *Consider an election where v was the actual input and g the used defense strategy. The election is (ϵ_0, δ_0)-software independent if $\epsilon(g, v) \leq \epsilon_0$ and $\delta(g, v) \leq \delta_0$, i.e., the probability of false negative is bounded by ϵ_0, and the probability of false positive is bounded by δ_0.*

Moreover, the voting system is (ϵ_0, δ_0)-software independent if there exists $g \in \mathcal{G}_A$ such that for all $v \in In$, the resulting election is (ϵ_0, δ_0)-SI.

Ideally, elections should be fully reliable. This motivates the following definition.

Definition 2 (Strict SI). *An election (respectively, voting system) is strictly software independent if it is (0, 0)-software independent.*

Unfortunately, strict SI might be hard to achieve in realistic scenarios. In that case, we should at least require that the defense strategy is more effective than random guessing. Suppose that the checker tosses a biased coin (independently of all other election processes) that has probability p of landing heads, and then rejects the announced outcome if the coin lands heads and accepts the outcome if the coin lands tails. That rule g_p attains $\epsilon(g_p, v) = p$ and $\delta(g, v) = 1 - p$, so $\epsilon(g_p, v) + \delta(g_p, v) = 1$. By using the available evidence one should be able to do better. This leads to the following definition:

Definition 3 (loose SI). *An election (respectively, voting system) is loosely software independent if it is (ϵ, δ)-software independent with $\epsilon + \delta < 1$.*

For example, consider a voting system based on hand-marked paper ballots kept secure and trustworthy, with trustworthy eligibility determinations, subject to a risk-limiting audit with risk limit $\alpha < 1$. Such a voting system is $(0, \alpha)$-SI and loosely SI. If there were an automatic recount instead of a risk-limiting audit, the system would be strictly SI.

5   Conclusions

We have presented several formalisations of the notion of software independence. In doing so we have shown that, like many security properties, this seemingly simple and intuitive notion actually harbours many subtleties. For example we observe that it is important to exclude trivial systems that simply reject all runs of an election. The original definition clearly intended this but did not explicitly require it. Many of the terms used in the definition require precise definition. For example, "detection" should not just mean claiming to have observed a departure from correct behaviour but also to be able to provide evidence that such a departure did indeed occur. This is related the notion of dispute resolution: the ability of a third party to be able to determine whether alarm is genuine or false.

We have enriched our definitions to allow for non-determinism or randomisation in the execution of the protocols, and in particular in the social choice function. Further, we have argued that purely possibilistic definition is not necessarily that useful, rather one should extend that definition to account for the probabilities of detecting erroneous behaviour.

Another insight from our formalisation is the need to precisely define when is meant by the "system" and the "software". By the latter we mean those parts of the system on whose behaviour we do not want the correctness of the outcome to depend. However, for many systems this will not include all the software of the system, for example, the auditing components and procedures may require software and we typically assume that such software is correct with respect to its specification. Such assumptions can typically be justified by arguing that auditing algorithms can typically be rerun on independent implementations, so corruption of an instance of this software is itself detectable.

In future work we plan to apply our definitions to a representative sample of verifiable voting systems. We also plan to generalise the notion of software independence to include other components of the system: hardware, people, procedures etc. This brings us back to the question of defining the boundaries of the sub-system that we require the correctness of the outcome to be independent.

Acknowledgements. Peter Y.A. Ryan would like to thank the FNR (Fond Nationale de Research Luxembourg) and the Velux Foundation for support during his sabbatical and to ITU Copenhagen for hosting him when this work was initiated. Steve Schneider is grateful to EPSRC for funding through the VOLT project EP/P031811/1. Wojciech Jamroga acknowledges the support of the National Centre for Research and Development, Poland (NCBR), and the FNR Luxembourg under the PolLux/FNR-CORE projects VoteVerif (POLLUX-IV/1/2016) and STV (POLLUX-VII/1/2019).

References

1. Appel, A., DeMillo, R., Stark, P.: Ballot-marking devices cannot assure the will of the voters. Election Law J. Rules Polit. Policy **19**(3) (2020). https://doi.org/10.1089/elj.2019.0619
2. Appel, A., Stark, P.: Evidence-based elections: create a meaningful paper trail, then audit. Georgetown Law Technol. Rev. **4**(2), 523–541 (2020). https://georgetownlawtechreview.org/wp-content/uploads/2020/07/4.2-p523-541-Appel-Stark.pdf
3. Benaloh, J., Rivest, R., Ryan, P.Y., Stark, P., Teague, V., Vora, P.: End-to-end verifiability (2015). arXiv:1504.03778

4. Bernhard, M., et al.: Public evidence from secret ballots. In: Krimmer, R., Volkamer, M., Braun Binder, N., Kersting, N., Pereira, O., Schürmann, C. (eds.) E-Vote-ID 2017. LNCS, vol. 10615, pp. 84–109. Springer, Cham (2017). https://doi.org/10.1007/978-3-319-68687-5_6

5. Bernhard, M., et al.: Can voters detect malicious manipulation of ballot marking devices? In: 2020 IEEE Symposium on Security and Privacy (SP), pp. 679–694 (2020). https://doi.org/10.1109/SP40000.2020.00118

6. DeMillo, R., Kadel, R., Marks, M.: What voters are asked to verify affects ballot verification: a quantitative analysis of voters' memories of their ballots. Technical report (2018)

7. Election Assistance Commission: Voluntary voting system guidelines VVSG 2.0 (2021). https://www.eac.gov/sites/default/files/TestingCertification/Voluntary_Voting_System_Guidelines_Version_2_0.pdf

8. Everett, S.: The Usability of Electronic Voting Machines and How Votes Can Be Changed Without Detection. Ph.D. thesis, Rice University (2007)

9. Hao, F., Ryan, P.Y.A.: Real-World Electronic Voting: Design, 1st edn. Analysis and Deployment. Auerbach Publications, USA (2016)

10. Haynes, A., III, M.H.: Georgia voter verification study. Technical report (2021)

11. Küsters, R., Truderung, T., Vogt, A.: Verifiability, privacy, and coercion-resistance: new insights from a case study. In: 32nd IEEE Symposium on Security and Privacy, pp. 538–553 (2011)

12. Rivest, R.: On the notion of "software independence" in voting systems. Philos. Trans. Royal Soc. A: Math. Phys. Eng. Sci. **366**(1881), 3759–3767 (2008)

13. Rivest, R., Wack, J.: On the notion of "software independence" in voting systems (draft version of July 28, 2006). Technical report, Information Technology Laboratory, National Institute of Standards and Technology (2006)

14. Stark, P.: Conservative statistical post-election audits. Ann. Appl. Stat. **2**, 550–581 (2008)

15. Stark, P., Wagner, D.: Evidence-based elections. IEEE Secur. Priv. **10**, 33–41 (2012)

Formal Methods and Mathematical Intuition

Dale M. Johnson$^{(\boxtimes)}$

The MITRE Corporation, McLean, VA 22102, USA
`dalejohnson3@verizon.net`

*Dedicated to Joshua Guttman, Colleague
and Friend.*

Abstract. The paper offers a retrospective on earlier developments and
work in formal methods at The MITRE Corporation, emphasizing the
leading work of Joshua Guttman and some of his colleagues. It then
provides a short introduction to dimension theory and its history as
a methodologically contrasting development in mathematics in which
counterintuitive examples and counterexamples play a role in motivating
mathematical growth by means of conjectures and refutations or proofs
and refutations. The paper ends with a broad methodological comparison
between developments in formal methods and developments in domains
of mathematics like dimension theory in which mathematical intuition
and proofs and refutations play a significant role.

Keywords: Conjectures and refutations · Counterexamples ·
Cybersecurity · Dimension theory · Formal methods · Heuristics ·
Invariance · Macetes · Mathematical intuition · Proofs and refutations

1 Introduction

Upon joining The MITRE Corporation in 1985 I became associated with a small
group of logicians, mathematicians, and computer scientists at the organization
actively engaged in research into formal methods and formal verification techniques, primarily directed at framing and solving problems in computer security,
or as it is now called cybersecurity. Joshua Guttman was a prominent member
of the group. His ideas became and still are highly influential at MITRE and in
the larger formal methods research community. Joshua became a close colleague
and good friend. Others were also involved in the research—to mention a few,

© Springer Nature Switzerland AG 2021
D. Dougherty et al. (Eds.): Guttman Festschrift, LNCS 13066, pp. 218–231, 2021.
https://doi.org/10.1007/978-3-030-91631-2_12

Leonard Monk, Jonathan Millen, Javier Thayer Fábrega, William (Bill) Farmer, John Ramsdell, Ron Watro, and Vipin Swarup.

The work at MITRE was exciting, especially with the press of the rapidly developing field of security for computers and computer networks. Joshua offered many ideas and insights for us to consider on the formal side, drawing on his background in mathematical logic aa well as computer science. In the broader research community those taking a formal approach to cybersecurity adopted and adapted formal methods, mathematical logical techniques, formal specification and verification, formal protocol descriptions and modeling, as well as more formalized procedural methods for securing computing and network systems in efforts to defend against potential attackers and make these systems safe and secure to use. Somewhat later the tremendous growth of the Internet and World Wide Web spurred even more development in cybersecurity, including further work in formal methods.

The aim of this paper is to provide a brief retrospective on some of the earlier work in formal methods at MITRE. Then I want to make some comparisons with certain other kinds of mathematical thinking and 'mathematical intuition' in an area in which I have a strong background: dimension theory and its history. Formal methods as an approach to cybersecurity seeks to model and specify formally selected computing systems, security protocols, hardware, and software as completely as possible and state their intended functional and security properties, and then demonstrate assertions stating that the specified entities satisfy these properties by using mathematical logic and related methods. In other areas of mathematics like dimension theory the aim is to model broader mathematical objects and situations and develop corresponding geometrical and topological intuitions, heuristics, and conjectures, with a view to laying out carefully defined theories and articulating theorems to be proved. Examples and counterexamples, and conjectures and refutations are often a part of this development, especially in the unusual situations found in the geometry and topology. Mathematical intuition is sharpened in the process. Overall, there are reasonable comparisons to be made between formal methods for cybersecurity and dimension theory, both positive and negative, as we shall see.

The retrospective on formal methods at MITRE is not intended to be complete. This paper is dedicated to my colleague and friend Joshua.

2   Formal Methods and Research at MITRE

Given the nature of computers and associated communications networks, their detailed computations and processes, their underlying hardware, firmware, and software, their hierarchical nature, and their need to run by using formal computer languages with well-defined syntax and semantics, the necessity of having formal definitions of computer languages and formal theoretical explorations of their processes becomes clear. To examine cybersecurity issues using formal methods then becomes quite natural.

Formalizing mathematical and logical theories forms a large part of later nineteenth century and twentieth century developments in mathematical logic.

One can point back to Gottlob Frege (1848–1925), who studied the strict logical basis of arithmetic [14,15], and Bertrand Russell (1872–1970) and Alfred North Whitehead (1861–1947), who formalized large chunks of mathematics in the massive three-volume *Principia Mathematica*, in an effort to demonstrate the logicist thesis that mathematics is reducible to logic [33,34]. Note, though, that in the history of modern mathematical logic, efforts have not been directed merely toward formalization of mathematical theories per se, but mainly toward the demonstration of metalogical or metamathematical results. Some of the most celebrated results in this domain are Kurt Gödel's (1906–1978) completeness theorem for first-order predicate calculus and his limitative incompleteness and consistency theorems for formal theories containing arithmetic and also Alfred Tarski's (1901–1983) results on truth in formalized languages.

One of the first tasks I was assigned at MITRE was to join with Javier Thayer Fábrega and Bill Farmer in an analysis of the formal design verification of a special device called the Restricted Access Processor (RAP) [32]. Offered by another organization, the formal verification aimed to show that RAP functionally satisfied its formal security specification, or to use other terms, that RAP's top-level specification as a system satisfied it formal security model. It used an early verification language and tool, which yielded a rather messy and hard-to-understand verification of RAP. The verification details seemed to us as readers to overwhelm the main thrust of the argument. Admittedly, the early verification language and tool used may not have been fully up to the job. Moreover, the verification lacked the clarity one would expect from a good exposition of a mathematical theory.

Our assessment of the verification motivated the three of us to write a paper [13] proposing that the formal verification of a computer system be regarded as an endeavor in applied mathematics. As applied mathematics it should involve three separate processes, a modeling process, a theorem proving process, and a review and acceptance process. This meant establishing formal mathematical models of the system being analyzed and the directly related natural-language requirements and specifications. Then on the basis of the modeling, it should be possible to use mathematical techniques to reason about the formal models obtained, essentially building a formal theory of the system and its requirements to derive the formal verification result. Finally, it is important that the formal theory be understandable by a larger group to help determine its validity as a verification. Thus, there should be a reviewing and acceptance process available for a larger interested community. Just as in mathematics and its research community, there should be a social acceptance process validating the argument of the verification.

The critique of the RAP design verification was the first time I became involved with formal verification. Efforts in formal specification and formal verification, the building of tools related to support such efforts became a significant part of the work at MITRE, with interactions with many other organizations. The need for highly secure computing and networked systems led to work with so-called 'A1' systems according to the *Trusted Computer Security Evaluation Criteria (The Orange Book)* [6]. Many of us at MITRE became involved with a number of those applied efforts.

In the nineties Bill Farmer, Joshua Guttman, and Javier Thayer Fábrega set out to build an Interactive Mathematical Proof System offering computational support for traditional techniques of mathematics [9,10,12] (full IMPS bibliography, https://imps.mcmaster.ca/doc/imps-bibliography.html). The resulting IMPS is based on simple type theory and uses the axiomatic method to build interconnected 'little theories' of coherent pieces of mathematics [11]. I want to point to a particular facet of the IMPS work that will be related to the theme of this paper. As an efficient device to apply theorems or collections of theorems directly in deductive proof sequences IMPS includes 'macetes' [12, pp. 227, 234–235]. Somewhat formally, a macete is used to apply a theorem or a collection of theorems to a deductive sequent in a formal deduction graph, thereby simplifying the graph. In colloquial Brazilian Portuguese, a 'macete' is a clever trick, a term Javier Thayer Fábrega introduced into IMPS. These tricks are analogous to a mathematician simplifying a chain of reasoning in the argumentation by applying previously proven theorems. They are a kind of heuristic to abbreviate some of the excessive details in the elaborated formal mathematical deductions. In informal mathematics mathematicians do this all the time. This technique appears as a formalization of heuristics used in informal mathematics with the advantage that the formal mechanism can check the mathematics to avoid errors.

In a short paper published in 1994, Joshua Guttman and I summarized three applications of formal methods, which formed part of our work at MITRE [18]. These applications were: an effort devoted to specifying TCP using Communication Sequential Processes (CSP) and state machine methods, with partial proofs that it would meet its reliable delivery requirement; a formalization of a simple virtual memory scheme, carried out using IMPS; and a verified implementation of the programming language Scheme, which was named VLISP. I was doing some of the protocol work with colleagues, and through it I became acquainted with larger international efforts using formal methods and specialized formal languages and tools to understand protocol behaviors formally.

About this time Joshua Guttman together with colleagues, Javier Thayer Fáabre-ga and Jonathan Herzog, began studying security protocols, such as authentication protocols or cryptographic protocols, using a modeling approach called 'strand spaces' [7,8,16,17]. Informally, a security protocol is a sequence of messages among two or more communicating parties in which encryption is used to provide authentication or to distribute cryptographic keys for new conversations. Determining that such protocols are secure and resistant to attacks can be tricky. Strand spaces provide a way to capture these kinds of protocol conversations as interwoven strands of the conversations. The security is rigorously analyzed by examining possible attackers trying to defeat the security by joining in the conversations. The strand space approach has been very successful. Unfortunately, I do not have the space in this paper to go further into the approach and the results.

Formal methods applied to solving problems of cybersecurity has come a long way in the last few decades. While by no means the only approach, the application of formal methods to problems of cybersecurity has yielded very valuable results and real successes. A strong indication of progress is the report of the National Science Foundation-sponsored Workshop on Formal Methods for Security [5]. The workshop was held in November 2015. The workshop highlighted four main areas: (i) hardware architecture, (ii) operating systems, (iii) distributed systems, and (iv) privacy. Each of these ares requires careful scrutiny of their underlying foundations, their elaborated details, and their explicit requirements for proofs of correctness and security. Progress has been made on a variety of fronts with the aid of special formal languages and tools, yielding results of significant value. Moreover, challenge problems have been identified that can drive further progress.

MITRE has added much to developments in formal methods for cybersecurity. I have mentioned just a few contributions in my summary. Joshua Guttman has played leading roles in a majority of these. His list of publications, many with other MITRE authors, is extensive—well over a hundred—with numerous citations.

3   Mathematical Intuition and Heuristics

I shall now turn to considering a different style of mathematics in which mathematical 'intuition' and heuristics play a greater role in the solution of mathematical problems. Problems have always been crucial to developing new mathematics over its long history. Formal details of exposition and proof do matter, but key insights to solving significant or long-standing problems often have enormous value. These insights are the 'ah-ha!' experiences so gratifying to mathematicians. They touch on the realm of heuristics in mathematics, highlighted through many examples by George Polya [28–30], and the area of conjectures and refutations or proofs and refutations, characterized philosophically by my teachers Sir Karl Popper [31] and Imre Lakatos [23]. In the course of solving problems creative mathematicians often move from a problem to a conjectured solution to a correction to the tentative solution to an enhanced problem and better solution.

I shall take examples from the history of dimension theories[1] to illustrate points about mathematical intuition and heuristics. Of course, many other areas of mathematics would offer examples equally well.

4   Example: Development of Dimension Concepts and Dimension Theories

Problems concerning dimension go back to the ancients, particularly the ancient Greeks. Two fundamental problems motivated the ancients to consider notions of dimension. First, they asked the question: What is the nature of dimension? Attempts to solve this problem resulted in definitions and simple descriptive theories of dimension. Second, they posed the question: Why does our space

---

[1] See my papers [19–21]. I am writing a book on dimension theories and their history deriving from these papers and including much new material.

have three dimensions? Trying to solve this problem resulted in explanations of the observed fact about our space. Evidence of theories of dimension can be found in writings of the Pythagoreans, Aristotle (384–322 BCE), and Euclid (fl. 300 BCE). The mathematician and astronomer Claudius Ptolemy (c. 100–170 CE) wrote an entire book *On Dimension*, in which he put forward an argument for the 3-dimensionality of physical bodies and the universe. Unfortunately, the book is not extant.

Moving to the modern era of mathematics a new problem of dimension arose from ground-breaking developments of set theory and point-set topology that Georg Cantor (1845–1918) and Richard Dedekind (1831–1916) initiated toward the end of the nineteenth century. Cantor arrived at early important results in set theory, showing that while the set of all real algebraic numbers is countable, the set of all real numbers (the linear continuum) is not countable. This led him to pose the following research problem, which he stated in a letter of 5 January 1874 to his mathematical colleague, Dedekind [4, page 20]:

> Can a surface (perhaps a square including its boundary) be put into one-one correspondence with a line (perhaps a straight line segment including its endpoints), so that to each point of the surface there corresponds a point of the line and inversely to each point of the line there corresponds a point of the surface?[2]

There is no record of Dedekind's initial response to Cantor's question. Others with whom Cantor discussed the question at meetings and conferences around the time thought it was obvious that the answer would be negative. However, Cantor persisted in seeking an answer to the research question. Even by posing his research question he introduced something quite new and important into thinking about dimension. *He related mappings and correspondences to considering the dimensions of figures and spaces.* For Cantor this new way of thinking was natural, because he was already interested in the cardinality of infinite sets. Cantor effectively moved the notion of dimension to a different mathematical problem situation.

Cantor continued his quest, but *he switched his line of attack*. In a letter to Dedekind of 20 June 1877 he asserts a positive generalization [4, page 25]:

> ... that surfaces, solids, even continuous figures of ρ dimensions can be put into one-one correspondence with continuous lines, thus figures of only *one* dimension; therefore, that surfaces, solids, even figures of ρ dimensions have the same *power* as curves ... .[3]

---

[2] In German: Lässt sich eine Fläche (etwa ein Quadrat mit Einschluss der Begrenzung) eindeutig auf eine Linie (etwa eine gerade Strecke mit Einschluss der Endpunkte) eindeutig beziehen, so dass zu jedem Puncte der Fläche ein Punct der Linie und umgekehrt zu jedem Puncte der Linie ein Punct der Fläche gehört?

[3] In German: ... dass Flächen, Körper, ja selbst stetige Gebilde von ρ Dimensionen sich eindeutig zuordnen lassen stetigen Linien, also Gebilden von nur *einer* Dimension, dass also Flächen, Körper, ja sogar Gebilde von ρ Dimensionen, dieselbe *Mächtigkeit* haben, wie Curven ... .

and offers an initial proof that the points of a unit ρ-dimensional cube, denoted as a system of real values $(x_1, x_2, ..., x_p)$, where $0 \leq x_i \leq 1$, can be put in one-one correspondence with the points of the unit line segment, denoted as values of a variable y, $0 \leq y \leq 1$. The proof uses *infinite* decimal expansions of the coordinates of the points. Essentially the digits of the array of ρ numbers,

$$x_1 = 0.\alpha_{11}\alpha_{12} \ldots \alpha_{1\nu} \ldots,$$
$$x_2 = 0.\alpha_{21}\alpha_{22} \ldots \alpha_{2\nu} \ldots,$$
$$\ldots\ldots\ldots\ldots\ldots\ldots\ldots\ldots$$
$$x_\rho = 0.\alpha_{\rho 1}\alpha_{\rho 2} \ldots \alpha_{\rho\nu} \ldots,$$

can be counted off in order, ρ of them at a time (first place digits, then second place digits, and so forth) as the successive digits of a single decimal number for each value of y:

$$y = 0.\beta_1\beta_2\beta_\nu \ldots,$$

such that

$$\beta_1 = \alpha_{11}, \beta_2 = \alpha_{21}, \ldots \beta_\rho = \alpha_{\rho 1}, \beta_{\rho+1} = \alpha_{12} \ldots.$$

Inversely, from each value of y one can count off successive sets of ρ digits to yield the digits for each ρ-tuple, $(x_1, x_2, \ldots, x_p)$.

Dedekind almost immediately pointed out an error in Cantor's proof. The correspondence between Cantor and Dedekind is fascinating in showing the back and forth of attempted proof and critical counterexample [4]. I shall not go into the details. Cantor did come up with a correct proof that satisfied Dedekind, which he then published. It used continued fractions rather than decimal expansions. Even Cantor was surprised by his paradoxical discovery. In a letter to Dedekind of 29 June 1877 he exclaimed [4, page 34]:

...I see it, but I don't believe it.[4]

Cantor and Dedekind in the course of their exchange realized that Cantor's one-one correspondence between line segment and either the square or the ρ-dimensional cube is very discontinuous. That observation might be a way to save the dimension concept, but a theorem needed to be formulated and proved.

Soon, another surprising and 'complementary' discovery was made. The Italian mathematician Giuseppe Peano (1858–1932) in 1890 defined a continuous mapping from a line segment to a square—a space-filling curve—whereby the entire square was covered as the range of the mapping (and so the mapping is surjective). This time the mapping was not one-one (injective). Many points of the square were covered multiple times.

In his short paper, 'Sur une courbe, qui remplit toute une aire plane' ('Concerning a curve that covers an entire plane area'), Peano defines the continuous mapping of the unit line segment to the unit square analytically with no geometrical explanations or diagrams [25] (English translation with commentary [22, pp. 143–149]). Other mathematicians, such as David Hilbert (1862–1943),

---

[4] In French: ...je le vois, mais je ne le crois pas.

soon provided these. Much later Peano gave a geometrical explanation of the construction of his curve [27, pp. 239–240]. One way to picture the successive steps of construction of the mapping geometrically is through the diagrams in Fig. 1. Consider the left diagram as the first step of an iterative construction, dividing the square into 9 subsquares and drawing a continuous line from the bottom left to the top right as given. Then consider the right diagram in Fig. 1 as the second step, dividing each subsquare into 9 subsubsquares and drawing a continuous line through the newly divided square in similar ways through each of the 81 subsquares, moving from bottom left to top right. Continue the construction by dividing squares in steps ad infinitum, and the result is Peano's curve at the limit covering all the points of the original square. Peano's curve is continuous, though certainly not one-one (injective), with many points covered multiple times. It should be said that Peano was quite proud of his counterintuitive curve.[5]

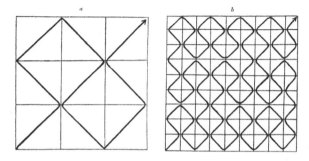

Fig. 1. Digrams for initial two steps in construction of Peano curve

As a mathematician Peano had a longstanding passionate interest in advancing formal methods, in presenting mathematics in a symbolic logical way, and in furthering the use of the axiomatic method. He is well known for his axiomatization of the theory of the natural numbers, the so-called Peano postulates, and its rigorous logical development, presented in his *Arithmetices principia, Nova methodo exposita* (*Principles of Arithmetic, Presented by a New Method*) [24]. (Dedekind independently developed a very similar axiomatization of the theory.) In an effort covering many years of his mathematical career, he set out to present large chunks of mathematics in symbolic logical form. His work went through five editions: *Formulaire de mathématiques* (*Formulation of mathematics*) [26] to *Formulario mathematico* (*Mathematical Formulation*) [27]. Though Peano's mathematical logic does not fully conform to modern standards, his work is impressive, and his chosen symbolic form is largely still readable today.

---

[5] See Kennedy's statement [22, page 7]: 'Peano was so proud of this discovery that he had one of the curves in the sequence put on the terrace of his home, in black tiles on white.'.

An assessment of Peano's mathematical corpus suggests that his work with formal methods is only loosely related to his discovery of a space-filling curve and his important contributions to analysis. His work in formal methods and the formalization of mathematical results seems to constitute a precise, systematic way to capture them.[6]

By the end of the nineteenth century, given Cantor's highly discontinuous mapping of the line segment to the ρ-cube and Peano's surjective but certainly not injective mapping from the line segment to the square, the space-filling curve, the need to save the dimension concept emerged as the need to prove a dimensional-invariance theorem. Several mathematicians proved partial results, but none in full generality.

5   L. E. J. Brouwer's Breakthrough to Invariance of Dimension

At this point we consider L.E.J. Brouwer (1881–1966) and his breakthrough to showing dimensional invariance. Among philosophers of mathematics and logicians Brouwer is known for his philosophy of intuitionism and his intuitionist logic and mathematics. Among topologists he is known for his fixed-point theorem, his characterization and elaboration of the concept of mapping degree, his theory of dimension, and his invariance theorems. We are concerned with his key topological result demonstrating invariance of dimension, presented in a paper of a mere five pages, which Brouwer submitted in June 1910 and which was published in 1911 [3]. This paper effectively swept away all previous attempts to prove the invariance of dimension.

Brouwer's approach to the problem of demonstrating that an m-dimensional manifold (or Euclidean space) and an $(m + h)$-dimensional manifold ($h > 0$) cannot be put into one-one continuous correspondence, i.e., that the manifolds are not homeomorphic, is through the proof of an important lemma [3, page 164]:

> In a q-dimensional manifold if for a single-valued continuous mapping of a q-dimensional cube the maximum of the displacements [of the points] is less than half the side length, then there exists a concentric and homothetic cube which is contained entirely in the image set.[7]

The intuitive appeal of the lemma is immediate. It is a weak form of domain invariance: the mapping satisfying the given conditions on displacements yields an image set that must contain a (smaller) q-dimensional cube. In their classic

---

[6] Compare [22] for English translations of some of Peano's works and notes on and appraisals of his mathematics.

[7] In German: Wenn in einer q-dimensionalen Mannigfaltigkeit bei einer eindeutigen und stetigen Abbildung eines q-dimensionalen Kubus das Maximum der Verrückungen kleiner ist als die halbe Kantenlänge, so existiert ein konzentrischer und homothetischer Kubus, der ganz in der Bildmenge enthalten ist.

book on topology, Alexandroff and Hopf call it Brouwer's invariance principle [1, pp. 364–365]. It is a key to dimensional invariance.

In the Brouwer *Nachlass* there is an interesting manuscript in Brouwer's hand that is clearly related to the published proof of dimensional invariance, a manuscript entitled 'De invariantie van het aantal dimensies eener ruimte' ('The invariance of the number of dimensions of a space'). It is almost certainly a draft of a lecture that he gave to the Wiskundig Genootschap, the Dutch Mathematical Society, in October 1910. The five-page draft of the lecture contains essentially the same proof as the published paper, but, as the lecture was delivered four months after the paper was submitted, it includes improvements and is more informal. For example, it contains diagrams that nicely capture Brouwer's geometrical thoughts in two dimensions. Figure 2 is a copy of a diagram from the notebook with the draft lecture, illustrating the situation with the concentric, homothetic squares K and K' in two dimensions. Square K has side length $2a$ and the mapping displaces points in it by at most $b < a$, whereby the larger square is potentially squeezed by the mapping down to an image set that must still contain the smaller square K' with side length $2(a - b)$. The condition $< 2(a - b)$ at the top of the smaller square.refers to all the points inside the smaller square, which must satisfy that condition.

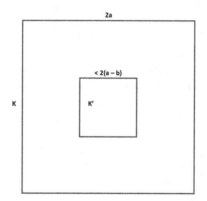

Fig. 2. Digram from Brouwer's Notebook

It is not possible to analyze the proof in the short space of this paper, but I think the diagram provides a good illustration of Brouwer's mathematical intuition in a broad sense of the term. The proof is broadly 'constructive,' providing the reader a way to work through the mental construction of the geometrical situation. It relies on simplicial mappings, simplicial approximations, and the concept of mapping degree. The proof proceeds by contradiction; it is *not* intuitionistically acceptable.

There is much more to dimension theory. However, I must stop now to consider my theme of formal methods and mathematical intuition and make some comparisons.

6   Conclusion: Formal Methods, Mathematical Intuition, and Rigorous Mathematical Exposition

Recent experiences have shown the value of applying formal methods to cybersecurity in several domains. The NSF Report provides a good indicator of important successes [5]. Modeling and specifying formally computing systems, protocols, or other situations involving security and then rigorously proving that they satisfy their intended functional and/or security properties have provided insightful results. Other, longer experiences with the development of fields of mathematics have yielded differing kinds of successes. Topology is a field in which increasingly well-honed mathematical intuitions, heuristics, and conjectural thinking have guided developments that have been successful, but often hard won. Conjectures and refutations or proofs and refutations have led to refined definitions and fundamental theorems with rigorous proofs. Topology is a field in which very careful distinctions are required. A small change in the basis can be the difference between a theorem and a refuting counterexample. Hence, a point of striking similarity between the development of formal methods for cybersecurity and that of topology and dimension theory is the need to pay extremely close attention to the details of rigorous specification/definition and proof.

There is a key ontological difference between the objects to which formal methods have been applied and the mathematical objects of dimension theory and domains of pure mathematics. Formal methods are applied to real-world artifacts, computers, hardware, firmware, and software, and also related networks. It should be possible ideally to check the specific modeling derived using formal methods with the corresponding artifacts to determine if the modeling is correct. In the case of dimension theory and more generally pure mathematics the objects of study are abstract entities. Such entities do gain a kind of 'quasi-real' existence known at least to those developing the mathematics for them, no matter whether the practicing mathematician believes in a Platonic universe of mathematical objects or in some lesser form of abstract existence. In dealing with models for either domain, one can apply logical reasoning to develop useful results and also check the models against the underlying 'reality,' whether an abstract reality or a computing artifact. The geometrical objects or point sets of dimension theory or topology have an abstract existence beheld by the practicing mathematician similar to the concrete existence of computers and computer programs beheld by the practitioners of formal methods.

In the domain of formal methods for cybersecurity, developing accurate applied models, laying out precise formal specifications, and carefully crafting assertions to be proven are crucial to success. Part of this development rests on having expressive formal languages and versatile tools. The end result depends on the art of the modeler to capture the essence of the situation to derive a result useful to developing the implementation. One critical issue, which others have raised before, is the inevitable gap between a formal model and the related, eventual implementation. The formal elaboration should yield sufficiently useful results to make a difference in the practical development. In the end, there is still likely to be a need for thorough practical testing of the implementation beyond the formal methods, using systematic functional and security testing methods, including red-team testing, This last point suggests an area of comparison between the broader functional correctness and cybersecurity of a computing system and the kind of mathematics represented by topological dimension theory. The back and forth between a developing or even delivered implementation and the potentially destructive attacks against the implementation, whether by a red team working on the implementation in development or by real attackers going after the delivered implementation, is analogous to conjectures and refutations in certain domains of mathematics. However, for the mathematical domain there is no exact equivalent to the attacker against the implementation. In mathematics correctness depends on mathematicians exercising their critical powers through exacting criticism and counterexample.

In the short space of this paper I have only provided a few highlights of the different kind of development of dimension theory; the full story is much richer and more intricate. My hope is that the reader may get the idea that examples, many counterintuitive, and counterexamples have been important drivers in building theories of dimension. The development of several theories of dimension over a longer period of time has been less formal than with formal theory construction à la formal methods. Nonetheless, the critical social process occurring over time among mathematicians and others has led to exacting, rigorous results. There have also been shifts to new methods and foundations, for example, by applying results in point set and/or algebraic topology. Careful distinctions concerning dimension as a concept, including 0-dimensionality, as well as connectedness, disconnectedness, and compactness have helped build rigorous theories of dimension.[8]

Reasonably exacting formalization and semi-formal methods have been critical at certain junctures in the growth of topology and dimension theory. The layout of formal definitions of dimension, including comparisons among those definitions for a variety of spaces, and the accompanying axiomatization of point set topology and related mathematical theories have had their place in modern developments. Simplifying computational shortcuts in set theory, algebraic topology, and homological algebra have had their place too. These are analogous to the 'tricks' or 'macetes' of IMPS.[9]

Both formal methods for cybersecurity and dimension theory falling under topology drive for greater precision and rigor. Ultimately, their results must be judged by the critical social process of comment, critique, and revision.

---

[8] For an additional case of the drive for improved results through counterexamples, one may look to the celebrated case of Brouwer's work of his 1910 paper, 'Zur Analysis Situs' ('On Analysis Situs') [2], in which, through a set of counterintuitive examples, he demolished the previous topological work of Arthur Schoenflies (1853–1928).

[9] However, it must be pointed out that to build full mathematical theories of topology and dimension at the level of IMPS formalization would take considerable effort in formal theory construction. Algebraic simplification rules could be a part of that construction.

References

1. Alexandroff, P., Hopf, H.: Topologie I: Erster Band. Grundbegriffe der Mengentheoretischen Topologie Topologie der Komplexe Topologische Invarianzsatze und Anschliessende Begriffsbildungen Verschlingungen im n-Dimensionalen Euklidischen Raum Stetige Abbildungen von Polyedern. Julius Springer-Verlag (1935). https://doi.org/10.1007/978-3-662-02021-0

2. Brouwer, L.E.J.: Zur Analysis Situs. Mathematische Annalen **68**(3), 422–434 (1910)

3. Brouwer, L.E.J.: Beweis der Invarianz der Dimensionenzahl. Mathematische Annalen **70**(2), 161–165 (1911)

4. Cantor, G., Dedekind, R.: Briefwechsel Cantor-Dedekind. Hermann (1937)

5. Chong, S., et al.: Report on the NSF workshop on formal methods for security. arXiv preprint arXiv:1608.00678 (2016)

6. Department of Defense: Department of Defense Trusted Computer System Evaluation Criteria. Department of Defense (1985), doD 5200.28-STD

7. Fábrega, F.J.T., Herzog, J.C., Guttman, J.D.: Strand spaces: Why is a security protocol correct? In: Proceedings. 1998 IEEE Symposium on Security and Privacy (Cat. No. 98CB36186), pp. 160–171. IEEE (1998)

8. Fábrega, F.J.T., Herzog, J.C., Guttman, J.D.: Strand spaces: Proving security protocols correct. J. Comput. Secur. **7**(2/3), 191–230 (1999)

9. Farmer, W.M., Guttman, J.D., Fábrega, F.J.T.: IMPS: an updated system description. In: International Conference on Automated Deduction, pp. 298–302. Springer (1996)

10. Farmer, W.M., Guttman, J.D., Thayer, F.J.: IMPS: System description. In: International Conference on Automated Deduction, pp. 701–705. Springer (1992). https://doi.org/10.1007/3-540-55602-8_207

11. Farmer, W.M., Guttman, J.D., Thayer, F.J.: Little theories. In: International Conference on Automated Deduction. pp. 567–581. Springer (1992). https://doi.org/10.1007/3-540-55602-8_192

12. Farmer, W.M., Guttman, J.D., Thayer, F.J.: IMPS: an interactive mathematical proof system. J. Autom. Reason. **11**(2), 213–248 (1993)

13. Farmer, W.M., Johnson, D.M., Thayer, F.J.: Towards a discipline for developing verified software. In: 9th National Computer Security Conference, pp. 91–98. Citeseer (1986)

14. Frege, G.: Begriffsschrift. Eine der arithmetischen nachgebildete Formalsprache der reinen Denkens, Louis Nebert (1879)

15. Frege, G.: Die Grundlagen der Arithmetik: Eine logisch mathematische Untersuchung über den Begriff der Zahl. W. Koebner (1884)

16. Guttman, J.D.: Security goals: Packet trajectories and strand spaces. In: International School on Foundations of Security Analysis and Design. pp. 197–261. Springer (2000). https://doi.org/10.1007/3-540-45608-2_4

17. Guttman, J.D.: State and progress in strand spaces: proving fair exchange. J. Autom. Reason. **48**(2), 159–195 (2012)

18. Guttman, J.D., Johnson, D.M.: Three applications of formal methods at MITRE. In: International Symposium of Formal Methods Europe. pp. 55–65. Springer (1994). https://doi.org/10.1007/3-540-58555-9_87

19. Johnson, D.M.: Prelude to dimension theory: the geometrical investigations of Bernard Bolzano. Archive History Exact Sci. **17**(3), 261–295 (1977)

20. Johnson, D.M.: The Problem of the Invariance of Dimension in the Growth of Modern Topology, part I. Archive History Exact Sci. **20**(2), 97–188 (1979)
21. Johnson, D.M.: The problem of the invariance of dimension in the growth of modern topology, part II. Arch. History Exact Sci. **25**(2–3), 85–266 (1981)
22. Kennedy, H.: Selected Works of Giuseppe Peano. University of Toronto Press, Toronto (1973)
23. Lakatos, I.: Proofs and Refutations: The Logic of Mathematical Discovery. Cambridge University Press, Cambridge (2015)
24. Peano, G.: Arithmetices principia: Nova methodo exposita. Fratres Bocca (1889)
25. Peano, G.: Sur une courbe, qui remplit toute une aire plane. Mathematische Annalen **36**(1), 157–160 (1890)
26. Peano, G.: Formulaire de mathématiques. Bocca frères, Ch. Clausen, 1 edn. (1895)
27. Peano, G.: Formulario Mathematico. Fratres Bocca, Ch. Clausen, 5 edn. (1908)
28. Pólya, G.: Mathematics and Plausible Reasoning: Induction and Analogy in Mathematics, vol. 1. Princeton University Press, Princeton (1954)
29. Pólya, G.: Mathematics and Plausible Reasoning: Patterns of Plausible Inference, vol. 2. Princeton University Press, Princeton (1968)
30. Pólya, G.: How to Solve It: A New Aspect of Mathematical Method. Princeton University Press, Princeton (2004)
31. Popper, K.: Conjectures and Refutations: The Growth of Scientific Knowledge. Routledge, Milton Park (2002)
32. Proctor, N.: The restricted access processor: an example of formal verification. ACM SIGSOFT Softw. Eng. Notes **10**(4), 116–118 (1985)
33. Whitehead, A.N., Russell, B.: Principia Mathematica. Cambridge University Press, Cambridge (1910–1913)
34. Whitehead, A.N., Russell, B.: Principia Mathematica. Cambridge University Press, Cambridge. Second edn. (1925–1927)

Establishing the Price of Privacy
in Federated Data Trading

Kangsoo Jung$^{(\boxtimes)}$, Sayan Biswas$^{(\boxtimes)}$, and Catuscia Palamidessi$^{(\boxtimes)}$

Inria and Ecole Polytechnique, Palaiseau, France
{gangsoo.zeong,sayan.biswas}@inria.fr, catuscia@lix.polytechnique.fr

Abstract. Personal data is becoming one of the most essential resources in today's information-based society. Accordingly, there is a growing interest in data markets, which operate data trading services between data providers and data consumers. One issue the data markets have to address is that of the potential threats to privacy. Usually some kind of protection must be provided, which generally comes to the detriment of utility. A correct pricing mechanism for private data should therefore depend on the level of privacy. In this paper, we propose a model of data federation in which data providers, who are, generally, less influential on the market than data consumers, form a coalition for trading their data, simultaneously shielding against privacy threats by means of differential privacy. Additionally, we propose a technique to price private data, and an revenue-distribution mechanism to distribute the revenue fairly in such federation data trading environments. Our model also motivates the data providers to cooperate with their respective federations, facilitating a fair and swift private data trading process. We validate our result through various experiments, showing that the proposed methods provide benefits to both data providers and consumers.

Keywords: Data trading · Federated data market · Differential privacy · Revenue splitting mechanism · Game theory

1 Introduction

The use of data analytics is growing, as it plays a crucial role in making decisions and identifying social and economical strategies. Not all data, however, are equally useful, and the availability of accurate data is crucial for obtaining high-quality analytics. In line with this trend, data are considered an asset and commercialized, and data markets, such as Datacoup [1] and Liveen [15], are on the rise.

Unlike traditional data brokers, data markets provide a direct data trading service between data providers and data consumers. Through data markets, data providers can be informed of the value of their private data, and data consumers can collect and process personal data directly at reduced costs, as intermediate entities are not needed in this model.

© Springer Nature Switzerland AG 2021
D. Dougherty et al. (Eds.): Guttman Festschrift, LNCS 13066, pp. 232–250, 2021.
https://doi.org/10.1007/978-3-030-91631-2_13

Two important issues that need to be addressed for the success of such data markets are (a) the prevention of privacy violation, and (b) an appropriate pricing mechanism for personal data. Data owners are increasingly aware of the privacy risks, and are less and less inclined to expose their sensitive data without proper guarantees. If the data market cannot be trusted concerning the protection of the sensitive information, the data providers will not be willing to trade their data. For example, Cambridge Analytica collected millions of Facebook users' profiles under the pretext of using them for academic purposes, while in reality they used this information to influence the 2016 US presidential election [8]. When media outlets broke news of Cambridge Analytica's business practices, many Facebook users felt upset about the misuse of their data and left Facebook.

Differential privacy [3] can prevent exposure of personal information while preserving statistical utility, hence it is a good candidate to protect privacy in the data market. Another benefit of differential privacy is that it provides a metric, i.e., the parameter ϵ, which represents the amount of obfuscation, and therefore the level of privacy and utility of the sanitized data. Hence ϵ can be used directly to establish the price of personal data as a function of the level of privacy protection desired by an individual.

We envision a data trading framework in which groups of data providers ally to form federations in order to increase their bargaining power, following the traditional model of trade unions. At the same time, federations guarantee that the members respect their engagement concerning the trade. Another important aspect of the federation is that the value of the collection of all data is usually different from the sum of the values of all members' data. It could be larger, for instance because the accuracy of the statistical analyses increases with the size of the dataset, or could be smaller, for instance because of some discount offered by the federation. Data consumers are supposed to make a collective deal with a federation rather than with the individual data providers, and, from their perspective, this approach can be more reliable and efficient than dealing with individuals. Thus, data trading through federations can benefit both parties.

Given such a scenario, two questions are in order:

1. How is the price of data determined in a federation environment?
2. How does the federation fairly distribute the earnings to its members?

In this paper, we consider these issues, and we provide the following contributions:

1. We propose a method to determine the price of collective data based on the differential privacy metric.
2. We propose a distribution model based on game theory. More precisely, we borrow the notion of Shapley value [18,20] from the theory of cooperative games. This is a method to determine the contribution of each participant to the payoff, and we will use it to ensure that each member of the federation receives a compensation according to his contribution.

The paper is organized as follows: Sects. 2 recalls some basic notions about differential privacy and Shapley values. Section 3 summarizes related works.

Section 4 describes the federation-based data trading and our proposal for the distribution of the earnings. Section 5 validates the proposed technique through experiments. Section 6 concludes and discusses potential directions for future work.

2   Preliminaries

In this section, we recall the basics about differential privacy and Shapley values.

2.1   Differential Privacy

Differential privacy (DP) is a method to ensure privacy on datasets based on obfuscating the answers to queries. It is parametrized by $\epsilon \in \mathbb{R}^+$, that represents the level of privacy. We recall that two datasets D_1 and D_2 are neighboring if they differ by only one record.

Definition 1 (Differential privacy [3]). *A randomized function $\mathcal{R}$ provides ϵ-differential privacy if for all neighboring datasets D_1 and D_2 and all $S \subseteq Range(\mathcal{R})$, we have*

$$\mathbb{P}[\mathcal{R}(D_1) \in S] \leq e^\epsilon \times \mathbb{P}[\mathcal{R}(D_2) \in S]$$

For example, if we have $\mathbb{D}$ as the space of all datasets, and some $m \in \mathbb{N}$, then the randomized function $\mathcal{R} : \mathbb{D} \mapsto \mathbb{R}^m$ could be such that $\mathcal{R}(D) = \mathcal{Q}(D) + X$, where $\mathcal{Q}$ is a statistical query function executed on D, such as the counting or histogram query, and X is some added noise to the true query response. For $\Delta_{\mathcal{Q}} = \max_{D,D' \in \mathbb{D}} |\mathcal{Q}(D) - \mathcal{Q}(D')|$, if $X \sim \text{Lap}(0, \frac{\Delta_{\mathcal{Q}}}{\epsilon})$, $\mathcal{R}$ will guarantee ϵ-DP.

DP is typically implemented by adding controlled random noise to the true answer to the query before reporting the result. ϵ is a positive real number parameter, and the value of ϵ affects the amount of privacy, which decreases as ϵ increases. For simplicity of discussion, we focus on the non-interactive and pure ϵ-differential privacy.

Recently, a local variant of differential privacy (LDP), in which the data owner directly obfuscate their data, has been proposed [5]. This variant considers the individual data points (or records), rather than queries on datasets. Its definition is as follows:

Definition 2 (Local differential privacy [5]). *A randomized function $\mathcal{R}$ satisfies ϵ-local differential privacy if, for all pairs of individual data x and x', and for any subset $S \subseteq Range(\mathcal{R})$, we have*

$$\mathbb{P}[\mathcal{R}(x) \in S] \leq e^\epsilon \cdot \mathbb{P}[\mathcal{R}(x')] \in S,$$

When the domain of data points is finite, one of the simplest and most used mechanisms for LDP is kRR [12]. In this paper, we assume that all data providers use this mechanism to obfuscate their data.

Definition 3 (kRR Mechanism [12]). *Let $\mathcal{X}$ be an alphabet of size $k < \infty$. For a given privacy parameter ϵ, and given an input $x \in \mathcal{X}$, the kRR mechanism returns $y \in \mathcal{X}$ with probability:*

$$\mathbb{P}(y|x) \quad = \quad \frac{1}{k - 1 + e^{\epsilon}} \begin{cases} e^{\epsilon}, & \text{if } y = x \\ 1, & \text{if } y \neq x \end{cases}$$

2.2   Shapley Value

When participating in data trading through a federation, *Pareto efficiency* and *symmetry* are the important properties for the intra-federation earning distribution. Pareto efficiency means that at the end of the distribution process, no change can be made without making participants worse off. Symmetry means that all players who make the same contribution must receive the same share. Obviously, the share should vary according to the member's contribution to the collective data.

The Shapley value [18,20] is a concept from game theory named in honor of Lloyd Shapley, who introduced it. Thanks to this achievement, Shapley won the Nobel Prize in Economics in 2012. The Shapley value applies to cooperative games, and it is a method to distribute the total gain that satisfy Pareto efficiency, symmetry, and differential distribution according to a player's contribution. Thus, all participants have the advantage of being fairly incentivized. The solution based on the Shapley value is unique. Due to these properties, the Shapley value is regarded as an excellent approach to design a distribution method.

Let $N = \{1, \ldots, n\}$ be a set of players involved in a cooperative game and $M \in \mathbb{R}^{+}$ be a financial revenue from the data consumer. Let $v : 2^{N} \mapsto \mathbb{R}^{+}$ be the characteristic function, mapping each subset $S \subseteq N$ to the total expected sum of payoffs the members of S can obtain by cooperation. (i.e., $v(S)$ is the total collective payoff of the players in S). According to the Shapley value, the benefit received by player i in the cooperative game is given follows:

$$\psi_i(v, M) \quad = \quad \sum_{S \subseteq N \setminus \{i\}} \frac{|S|! \times (n - |S| - 1)!}{n!} (v(S \cup \{i\}) - v(S))$$

We observe that $v(A) > v(B)$ for any subsets $B \subset A \subseteq N$, and hence, $v(S \cup \{i\}) - v(S)$ is positive. We call this quantity the *marginal contribution* of player i in a given subset S. Note that $\psi_i(v, M)$ is the expected marginal contribution of player i over all subsets $S \subseteq N$.

In this paper, we use the Shapley value to distribute the earnings according to the contributions of the data providers in the federations.

3   Related Works

Data markets, such as Datacoup [1] and Liveen [15], need to provide privacy protection in order to encourage the data owners to participate. One of the key questions is how to appropriately price data obfuscated by a privacy-protection mechanism. When we use differential privacy, the accuracy of data depends on the value of the noise parameter ϵ, which determines the privacy-utility trade-off. Thus, this question is linked to the problem of how to establish the value of ϵ. Researchers have debated how to choose this value since the introduction of differential privacy, and there have been several proposals [2,9,13,19]. In particular, [13] showed that the privacy protection level by an arbitrary ϵ can be infringed by inference attacks, and it proposed a method for setting ϵ based on the posterior belief. [2] considered the relation between differential privacy and t-closeness, a notion of group privacy which prescribes that the earth movers distance between the distribution in any group E and the distribution in the whole dataset does not exceed the threshold t, and showed that both ϵ-differential privacy and t-closeness are satisfied when the $t = \max_E \frac{|E|}{N}\left(1 + \frac{N-|E|-1}{|E|})e^\epsilon\right)$ where N is the number of records of the database.

Several other works have studied how to price the data according to the value of ϵ [6,7,10,11,14,16,17,21]. The purpose of these studies is to determine the price and value of the ϵ according to the data consumer's budget, accuracy requirement of information, the privacy preference of the data provider, and the relevance of the data. In particular, the study in [21] assumed a dynamic data market and proposed an incentive mechanism for data owners to truthfully report their privacy preferences. In [16], the authors proposed a framework to find the balance between financial incentive and privacy in personal data markets where data owners sell their own data, and suggested the main principles to achieve reasonable data trading. Ghosh and Roth [7] proposed a pricing mechanism based on auctions that maximizes the data accuracy under the budget constraint or minimizes the budget for the fixed data accuracy requirement, where data is privatized with differential privacy.

Our study differs from previous work in that, unlike the existing approaches assuming a one-to-one data trading between data consumers and providers, we consider trades between a data consumer and a federation of data providers. In such a federated environment, the questions are (a) how to determine the price of the collective data according to the privacy preferences of each member, and (b) how to determine the individuals' contribution to the overall data value, in order to receive a share of the earnings accordingly.

In this paper, we estimate the value of ϵ for the kRR mechanism [12], and we fairly distribute the earnings to the members of the federations using the Shapley value. We propose a valuation function that fits the characteristics of differential privacy. For example, increasing value of ϵ does not infinitely increase the price (we will elaborate on this in Sect. 4). Furthermore, we characterize the conditions required for setting up the earning distribution schemes.

4   Differentially Private Data Trading Mechanism

4.1   Mechanism Outline

Overview: We focus on an environment with multiple federations of data providers and one data consumer who interacts with the federations in order to obtain information (data obfuscated using kRR mechanism with varying values of ϵ) in exchange of financial revenues. We assume that federations and consumer are aware that the data providers use kRR mechanism, independently and with their desired privacy level (which can differ from provider to provider). Our method provides a sensible way of splitting the earnings using the Shapley value. In addition, it also motivates an individual to cooperate with the federation she is a part of, and penalises intentional and recurring non-cooperation.

Notations and Set-up: Let $\mathcal{F} = \{F_1, \dots, F_k\}$ be a set of k federations of data providers, where each federation F_i has n_{F_i} members for each $i \in \{1, \dots, k\}$. For a federation $F \in \mathcal{F}$, let its members be denoted by $F = \{p_1^F, \dots, p_{n_F}^F\}$. And finally, for every federation F, let $p_*^F \in F$ be an elected representative of F interacting with the data consumer. This approach to communication benefits both the data consumer and the data providers because (a) the data consumer minimizes her communication cost by interacting with just one representative of the federation, and (b) the reduced communication induces an additional layer of privacy.

We assume that each member p of a federation F has a maximum privacy threshold ϵ_p^T with which she, independently, obfuscates her data using the kRR mechanism. We also assume that p has d_p data points to potentially report.

We know from [4] that if there are m data providers reporting $d_1, \dots, d_m$ data points, independently privatizing them using the kRR mechanism with the privacy parameters $\epsilon_1, \dots, \epsilon_m$, the federated data of all the m providers also follow a kRR mechanism with the privacy parameter defined as:

$$e^\epsilon = \frac{1}{\sum_{i=1}^m d_i} \sum_{i=1}^m d_i \frac{e_i^\epsilon}{k - 1 + e_i^\epsilon}.$$

We call the quantity $d_p \epsilon_p^T$ the *information limit* of data provider $p \in F$, and

$$\eta_F^T = \sum_{p \in F} d_p \frac{e^{\epsilon_p^T}}{k - 1 + e^{\epsilon_p^T}}$$

the *maximum information threshold of the federation F.*

We now introduce the concept of *valuation function* $f(.)$, that maps financial revenues to information, representing the amount of information to be obtained for a given price. It is reasonable to require that $f(.)$ is strictly monotonically increasing and continuous. In this work we focus on the effect on the privacy parameter, hence we regard the collection of data points as a constant, and assume that only ϵ can vary. We will call $f(.)$ the *privacy valuation function.*

Definition 4 (Privacy valuation function). *A function* $f : \mathbb{R}^+ \mapsto \mathbb{R}^+$ *is a* privacy valuation function *if* $f(.)$ *is strictly monotonically increasing and continuous.*

As $f(.)$ is strictly monotonically increasing and continuous, it is also invertible. We denote the inverse of $f(.)$ as $f^{-1}(.)$, where $f^{-1} : \mathbb{R}^+ \mapsto \mathbb{R}^+$, maps a certain privacy parameter ϵ to the financial revenue evaluated with selling data privatized using kRR mechanism with ϵ as the privacy parameter.

As $f(.)$ is essentially determining the privacy parameter of a differentially private mechanism (kRR, in this case), it is reasonable to assume that $f(.)$ should be not only increasing, but also increasing exponentially for a linear increase of money. In fact, when ϵ is high, it hardly makes any difference to further increase its value. For example, when ϵ increases from 200 to 250, it practically makes no difference to the data as they were already practically no private. On the other hand, if we increase ϵ from 0 to 50, it creates a huge difference, conveying much more information. Therefore, it makes sense to set $f(.)$ to increase exponentially with a linear increase of the financial revenue.

An example of a privacy valuation function that we consider in this paper is $f(M) = K_1(e^{K_2 M} - 1)$, taking the financial revenue $M \in \mathbb{R}^+$ as its argument, satisfying the reasonable assumptions of evaluating the differential privacy parameter that should be used to privatize the data in exchange of the financial revenue of M. Here the parameters $K_1 \in \mathbb{R}^+$ and $K_2 \in \mathbb{R}^+$ are decided by the data consumer according to her requirements (Fig. 1).

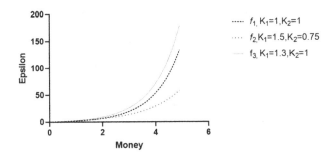

Fig. 1. Some examples of the privacy valuation function $f(.)$ illustrated with different values of K_1 and K_2. The data consumer decides the values of the parameters K_1 and K_2 according to her requirement, and broadcasts the determined function to the federations.

Finalizing and Achieving the Deal: Before the private-data trading commences, the data consumer, D, truthfully broadcasts her financial budget, $\$B$, and a privacy-valuation function, $f(.)$, chosen by her to all the federations. At this stage, each federation computes their maximum privacy threshold. In particular, for a federation F with members $F = \{p_1, \ldots, p_n\}$, and a representative p_*, p_i

reports d_{p_i} and $\epsilon_{p_i}^T$ to p_* for all $i \in \{1, \ldots, n\}$. p_* computes the maximum information threshold,

$$\eta_F^T = \sum_{i=1}^{n} d_{p_i} \frac{e^{\epsilon_{p_i}^T}}{k - 1 + e^{\epsilon_{p_i}^T}},$$

of federation F.

At this point, p_* places a bid to D to obtain \$M, which maximises the earning for F under the constraint of their maximum privacy threshold and the maximum budget available from D, i.e., p_* wishes to maximize M within the limits $M \leq B$ and $f(M) \leq \epsilon_F^T$. Thus, p_* bids for sending data privatized using the kRR mechanism with ϵ_F^T in exchange of $f^{-1}(\epsilon_F^T)$.

At the end of this bidding process by all the federations, D ends up with $\epsilon = \{\epsilon_{F_1}^T, \ldots, \epsilon_{F_k}^T\}$, the maximum privacy thresholds of all the federations. At this stage D must ensure that $\sum_{i=1}^{k} f^{-1}(\epsilon_{F_i}^T) \leq B$, adhering to her financial budget. In all probability, $\sum_{i=1}^{k} f^{-1}(\epsilon_{F_i}^T)$ is likely to exceed B in a realistic setup. Here, D needs a way to "seal the deal" with the federations staying within her financial budget, maximizing her information gain, i.e., maximizing $\sum_{i=1}^{k} d_{F_i} \epsilon_{F_i}$, where d_{F_i} is the total number of data points obtained from the ith federation F_i, and ϵ_{F_i} is the overall privacy parameter of the kRR differential privacy with the combined data of all the members of F_i.

A way D could finalize the deal with the federations is by proposing to receive information obfuscated with $w^* \epsilon_{F_i}^T$ using kRR mechanism to $F_i \, \forall i \in \{1, \ldots, k\}$, where

$$w^* = \max \left\{ w : \sum_{i \in \{1, \ldots, k\}} f^{-1}(w \epsilon_{F_i}^T) \leq B, w \in [0, 1] \right\},$$

i.e., proportional to every federation's maximum privacy threshold ensuring that the price to be paid to the federations is within D's budget. Note that $w \in [0, 1]$ guarantees that $w \epsilon_F^T \leq \epsilon_F^T$ for every federation F, making the proposed privacy parameter possible to achieve by every federation, as it's within their respective maximum privacy thresholds. Let the combined privacy parameter for federation F_i, proposed by D to successfully complete the deal, be $\epsilon_{F_i}^P = w^* \epsilon_{F_i}^T$ $\forall i \in \{1, \ldots, k\}$.

The above method to scale down the maximum privacy parameters to propose a deal, maximizing D's information gain, is just one of the possible approaches. In theory, any method that ensures the total price to be paid to all the federations, in exchange of their data, is within D's budget, and the privacy parameters proposed are within the corresponding privacy budgets of the federations, could be implemented to propose a revised set of privacy parameters and, in turn, the price associated with them.

Definition 5 (Seal the deal). *When all the federations are informed about the revised privacy parameters desired of them, and they agree to proceed with the private-data trading with the data consumer by achieving the revised privacy* *parameter by combining the data of their members, we say* the deal has been sealed *between the federations and the data consumer.*

Once the deal is sealed between the federations and the data consumer, F_i is expected to provide data gathered from its members with an overall obfuscation with the privacy parameter $\epsilon_{F_i}^P$ using the kRR mechanism, in exchange of a price $M^i = f^{-1}(\epsilon_{F_i}^P)$ for every $i \in \{1, \ldots, k\}$. Failing to achieve this parameter of privacy for any federation results in a failure to uphold the conditions of the "deal" and makes the deal void for that federation, with no price received.

A rational assumption made here is that if a certain federation F fails to gather data from its members such that the overall kRR privacy parameter of F is less than ϵ_F^P, then F doesn't receive any partial compensation for its contribution, as it would incur an increase in communication cost and time for the data consumer in proceeding to this stage and "seal a new deal" with F, instead of investing the revenue to a more responsible federation.

The rest of the process consists in collecting the data and it takes place within every federation F which has sealed the deal. At the tth round, for $t \in \{1, 2, \ldots\}$, any member p of F has the freedom of contributing $d_p^t \leq d_p - \sum_{i=1}^{t-1} d_p^i$ data points privatized using kRR mechanism with any parameter ϵ_p^t. The process continues until the overall information collected until then achieves an information of at least η_F^T. Let T denote the number of rounds needed by F to achieve the required privacy level. As per the deal sealed between F and D, F needs to submit $D_F = \sum_{p \in F} \sum_{i=1}^T d_p^i$ data points to D such that the overall kRR privacy level of the collated data,

$$\eta_F = \sum_{p \in F} \sum_{t=1}^{T} d_p^t \frac{e^{\epsilon_p^t}}{k - 1 + e^{\epsilon_p^t}}$$

is at least η_F^T, and in return F receives a financial revenue of \$$M$ from D.

4.2 Earning Splitting

We use the Shapley value to estimate the contribution of each data provider of the federation, in order to split the whole earning M, which F would receive from D at the end of the trade. Let $\psi : \mathbb{R}^+ \times \mathbb{R}^+ \mapsto \mathbb{R}^+$ be the valuation function used for evaluating the Shapley values of the members after each contribution. If a certain member, p, of F reports d differentially private data points with privacy parameter ϵ, $\psi_i(v)$ should give the share of "contribution" made by p over the total budget, M, of F, to be split across all its members. It is assumed that each member, p, of F computes her Shapley value, knows what share of revenue she would receive by contributing her data privatized with a chosen privacy parameter, and uses this knowledge to decide on ϵ_p^t at every round t, depending on her financial desire. In our model, characteristic function $v(S)$ is as follows:

$$v(S) = \begin{cases} M, & \text{if } \epsilon_F \geq \epsilon_F^P \\ 0, & \text{if } \epsilon_F < \epsilon_F^P \end{cases}$$

where n is the number of data provider in subset S .

Example 1. As an example, let us assume that there are p_1, p_2, p_3, and each provider's contribution $\sum_{t=1}^{T} d_p^t \frac{e^{\epsilon_p^t}}{k-1+e^{\epsilon_p^t}}$ are 1.0, 0.5 and 0.3. And we assume that ϵ_F^P is 1.4 and financial revenue of M is 60. In this case, the calculation of each provider's revenue using Shapley value is as follows:

Case 1) Only one data provider participates:

$$p_1 : v(p_1) = 0$$
$$p_2 : v(p_2) = 0$$
$$p_3 : v(p_3) = 0$$

Case 2) Two providers participate: $v(p_1+) = 0, v(p_2) = 0$,

$$p_1 : v(p_1 + p_2) - v(p_2) = M, v(p_1 + p_3) - v(p_3) = M$$
$$p_2 : v(p_1 + p_2) - v(p_1) = M, v(p_2 + p_3) - v(p_3) = 0$$
$$p_3 : v(p_1 + p_3) - v(p_1) = 0, v(p_2 + p_3) - v(p_2) = 0$$

Case 3) All providers participate:

$$p_1 : v(p_1 + p_2 + p_3) - v(p_2 + p_3) = M$$
$$p_2 : v(p_1 + p_2 + p_3) - v(p_1 + p_3) = M$$
$$p_3 : v(p_1 + p_2 + p_3) - v(p_1 + p_2) = 0$$

According to the above results, the share of each user, according to their Shapley values, is as follows:

$$\psi_1(v) = \frac{0!2!}{3!}0 + \frac{1!1!}{3!}M + \frac{1!1!}{3!}M + \frac{2!0!}{3!}M = \frac{4M}{6} = 40$$
$$\psi_2(v) = \frac{0!2!}{3!}0 + \frac{1!1!}{3!}M + \frac{1!1!}{3!}0 + \frac{2!0!}{3!}M = \frac{2M}{6} = 20$$
$$\psi_3(v) = \frac{0!2!}{3!}0 + \frac{1!1!}{3!}0 + \frac{1!1!}{3!}0 + \frac{2!0!}{3!}0 = \frac{0M}{6} = 0$$

In this example, p_3 has no effect on achieving the η_F^T . Thus, p_3 is excluded from the revenue distribution. If the revenue were distributed proportionally, without considering the Shapley values, the revenue of p_1 would be 33, p_2 is 17, and p_3 is 10. It would mean p_1 and p_2 would receive lower revenues even though their contribution are sufficient to achieve the η_F^T, irrespective of the participation of p_3. The Shapley value enables the distribution of revenues only for those who have contributed to achieving the goal.

One of the problems of computing the Shapley values is the high computational complexity involved. If there is a large number of players, i.e., the size of a federation is large, the total number of subsets to be considered becomes considerably large, engendering a limitation to real-world applications. To overcome this, we use a *pruning technique* to reduce the computational complexity of the mechanism. A given federation F receives revenue M only when $\eta_F \geq \eta_F^T$, as per the deal sealed with the data consumer. Therefore, it is not necessary to calculate for Shapley values for the cases where $\eta_F < \eta_F^P$, since such cases do not contribute towards the overall Shapley value evaluated for the members of F.

It is reasonable to assume this differentially private data trading between the data consumer and the federations would continue periodically for a length of time. For example, Acxiom, a data broker company, periodically collects and manages personal data related to daily life, such as consumption patterns and occupations. Periodic data collection has higher value than one-time data collection because it can track temporal trends. For simplicity of explanation, let's assume that the trading occurs ever year. Hence, we consider a yearly period to illustrate the final two steps of our proposed mechanism - "swift data collection" and the "penalty scheme". This would ensure that the data collection process is as quick as possible for every federation in every year. Additionally, this would motivate the members to cooperate and act in the best interests of their respective federations by not, unnecessarily, withholding their privacy contributions to hinder achieving the privacy goals of their group, as per the deal finalized with D.

Let $R \in \mathbb{N}$ be the "tolerance period". For a member $p \in F$, we denote $d(m)_p^i$ to be the number of data points reported by p in the ith round of data collection of year m and we denote $\epsilon(m)_p^i$ to be the privacy parameter used by p to obfuscate the data points in the ith round of data collection of year m. Let T_m be the number of rounds of data collection needed in year m by federation F to achieve their privacy goal. We denote the total number of data points reported by p in the year m by $d(m)_p$, and observe that $d(m)_p = \sum_{i=1}^{T_m} d(m)_p^i$. Let $\epsilon(m)^P$ denote the value of the privacy parameter of the combined kRR mechanism of the collated data that F needs, in order to successfully uphold the condition of the deal sealed with D.

Definition 6 (Contributed privacy level). *For a given member $p \in F$, we define the* contributed privacy level *of p in year m as*

$$\epsilon(m)_p = \sum \epsilon(m)_p^i$$

.

Definition 7 (Privacy saving). *For a given member $p \in F$, we define the* privacy saving *of p over a tolerance period R (given by a set of some previous years), decided by the federation F, as*

$$\Delta_p = \sum_{m \in R} \left(d(m)_p \epsilon_p^T - d(m)_p \epsilon(m)_p \right)$$

Swift Data Collection: It is in the best interest of F, and all its members, to reduce the communication cost, time, and resources over the data collection rounds, and achieve the goal of ϵ^P as soon as possible, to catalyze the trade with D, and receive the financial revenue. We aim to capture this through our mechanism, and enable the members not to "hold back" their data well below their capacity.

To do this, in our model we design the Shapley valuation function, $\psi(.)$, such that for $p \in F$, in year m, $\psi(N_p \epsilon(m)_p^{t+1}, d(m)_p, M) = \psi(\epsilon(m)_p^t, d(m)_p, M)$, where $N_p \in \mathbb{Z}^+$ is the *catalyzing parameter* of the data collection, decided by the federation, directly proportional to Δ_p. In particular, for $p \in F$, and a tolerance period R decided, in prior, by F, it is a reasonable approach to make $N_p \propto \Delta_p$, as this would mean that any member $p \in F$, reporting $d(m)_p$ data points, would need to use N_p times higher value of ϵ in the $(t+1)^{st}$ round of data collection in the year m, as compared to that in the tth round for the same number of data points reported to get the same share of the benefit of the federation's overall revenue, where N_p is decided by how much privacy savings p has had over a fixed period of R.

This is made to ensure that if a member of a federation has been holding back her information by using high values of privacy parameters over a period of time, she should need to compensate in the following year by helping to quicken up the process of data collection of her federation. This should motivate the members of F to report their data with a high value of the privacy parameter in earlier rounds than later, staying within their privacy budgets, so that the number of rounds needed to achieve $\epsilon(m)^P$ is reduced.

Penalty Scheme: It is also desirable to have every member of any given federation to cooperate with the other members of the same federation, and facilitate the trading process in the best interest of the federation, to the best of their ability. That is why, in our mechanism, we incorporate an idea of a "penalty scheme" for the members of a federation who are being selfish by keeping a substantial gap between their maximum privacy threshold and their contributed privacy level, wishing to enjoy benefits of the revenue at an unfair cost of other members providing information privatized with almost their maximum privacy threshold. To prevent such non-cooperation and attempted "free ride", we design a "penalty scheme" in the mechanism.

Definition 8 (Free rider). *We call a certain member $p \in F$ to be a* free rider *if $\Delta_p \geq \delta_F$, for some $\delta_F \in \mathbb{R}^+$. Here, δ_F is a threshold decided by the federation F beforehand and informed to all the members of F.*

Thus, in the ideal case, every member of F would have their privacy savings to be 0 if everyone contributed information to the best of their abilities, i.e., provided data obfuscated with their maximum privacy parameter. But as a federation, a threshold amount of privacy savings is tolerated for every member. Under the "penalty scheme", if a certain member $p \in F$ qualifies as a free rider, she is excluded from the federation, and is given a demerit point by the federation, that can be recorded by a central system keeping a track of every member of every federation, preventing p from getting admission to any other federation for her tendency to free ride. This would mean p and has the responsibility of trading with the data consumer by herself. We could define the

Shapley valuation function used to determine the share of p's contribution such that $f^{-1}(\epsilon_p^T) < \psi(v, M)$, implying that the revenue to be received by p dealing directly with D, providing one data point obfuscated with her maximum privacy threshold with respect to the privacy valuation function $f(.)$, would be giving a much lower revenue than what p would receive being a member of federation F.[1]

Theorem 1. *If the privacy valuation function used by the data consumer, D, is $f(m) = K_1(e^{K_2 m} - 1)$, in order to impose the penalty scheme to any member $p \in F$ of a federation F, the Shapley valuation function, $\psi(.)$, chosen by F, must*

$$\text{satisfy } \frac{\ln(\frac{\epsilon_p^T}{K_1}+1)}{K_2} < \psi\left(\epsilon_p^T, \frac{\ln(\frac{w^* \epsilon_p^T}{K_1}+K)}{K_2}\right), \text{ where } K = \frac{\sum_{p' \neq p \in F} d_{p'} \epsilon_{p'}^T}{K_1} + 1, \, d_\pi \text{ is the}$$

number of data points reported by any $\pi \in F$, and w^* is the suggested scaling parameter computed by D to propose a realistic deal, as described in Sect. 4.1.

Proof. See Appendix A   □

Imposing the "penalty scheme" is expected to drive every member of a given federation to be cooperating with the interests of the federation and all the other fellow members to the best of their abilities, preventing potential free riders.

We show the pseudocode for the entire process in Algorithm 1 and describe the swift data collection and penalty scheme in Algorithm 2 and 3.

Algorithm 1: Federation based data trading algorithm

Input: Federation F, Data consumer D;
Output: ϵ_F^P and M;
D broadcasts total budget B and $f(.)$;
Federation F computes the $\epsilon_F^T = \sum_{i=1}^{n} d_{p_i} \epsilon_{p_i}^T$;
p_* places a bid to D to obtain revenue M;
F and D "seal the deal" to determine the ϵ_F^P and M;
while $\epsilon_F \leq \epsilon_F^P$ *and* $t \leq T$ **do**
 | SWIFTDATACOLLECTION(F, ϵ_F^P);
 | p_* computes the overall privacy ϵ_F
if $\epsilon_F \geq \epsilon_{F_i}^P$ **then**
 | F receives the revenue M;
 | p_* computes the Shapley value $\psi_i(v, M)$;
 | p_i get their share of the revenue M
else
 | deal fails

---

[1] Here, $v(.)$ is the characteristic function of $\psi(.)$, depending on ϵ_p^T.

Algorithm 2: Swift data collection algorithm

Input: $F = \{p_1, \ldots, p_{n_F}\}, \epsilon_F^P$;
Output: $\epsilon(m)_p^t$;
Function SwiftDataCollection(F, ϵ_F^P):

>   **while** $i \leq n_F$ **do**
> >   Compute Δ_{p_i};
> >   Compute the catalyzing parameter N_{p_i};
> >   Determine the $\epsilon(m)_{p_i}^t = N_{p_i} \epsilon(m)_{p_i}^{t-1}$

Algorithm 3: Penalty scheme

Input: $F = \{p_1, \ldots, p_{n_F}\}, \Delta_F = \{\Delta_{p_1}, \ldots, \Delta_{p_{n_F}}\}, \delta_F$;
Output: Updated F;
while $i \leq n_F$ **do**

>   **if** $\Delta_{p_i} \geq \delta_F$ **then**
> > $F \setminus \{i\}$

---

5 Experimental Results

5.1 Experimental Environments

In this section, we show some experiments that support the claim that proposed method succeeds to obtain the promised ϵ and reduce the computation time for Shapley value evaluation. The number of data providers constituting the federation is set to 25, 50, 75, and 100, respectively. The value of ϵ_p^T is selected from the normal distribution between 1 and 10 with mean 5 and standard deviation 1 independently for all participants p in the federation. The experimental environment is a Intel(R) i5-9400H CPU and 16 GB of memory.

5.2 Number of Rounds Needed for Data Collection

Achieving the η_F^T is the key for the participation of F in the data trading. If η_F^T is not achieved as the collated information level for the federation, there is no revenue from the data consumer. Thus, it is important to encourage the data providers to report sufficient data in order to reach the goal of the deal sealed with the data consumer. The swift data collection is a way to catalyze the process of obtaining data from the members of every federation F, minimising the number of rounds of data-collection, to achieve η_F^T. Furthermore, we set $N_p = \frac{\Delta_p}{d(m)_p \epsilon_p^T}$ for a certain member p in federation F, to motivate the data providers who have larger privacy savings to provide more information per round.

In the experiment, η_F^T is set to be 125, 250, 375 and 500, respectively. Data provider p determines $\epsilon(m)_p^t$ randomly in first round, and then computes $\epsilon(m)_p^t$ according to N_p, for every p in the federation. We compare two cases, the catalyzing method and the non-catalyzing method.

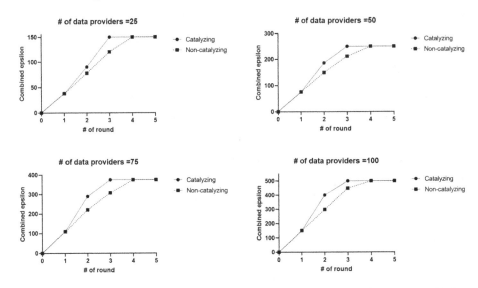

Fig. 2. Experimental results for combined ϵ. Combined ϵ refers to the amount of information provided by the data providers.

As illustrated in Fig. 2, the experimental results show that both catalyzing data collection and its non-catalyzing counterpart achieve the promised epsilon values within 5 rounds, but it can be seen that the catalyzing method achieves ϵ_F^P in an earlier round because data providers decide the privacy level used to obfuscate their data with, considering their privacy savings, resulting in a *swift data collection*.

5.3   Number of Free Riders by Penalty Scheme

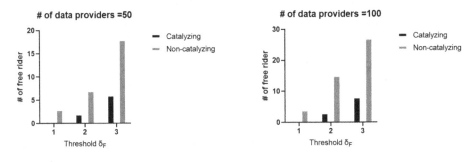

Fig. 3. Experimental results for number of free riders. We compared the number of free riders incurred by the penalty scheme in catalyzing and non-catalyzing methods for cases where the number of data providers is 50 and 100.

The penalty scheme that prevents free riders is based on the premise that trading data by participating in a federation is more beneficial than trading data directly with data consumers (Theorem 1). We evaluated the number of free riders in the catalyzing and non-catalyzing methods according to the increase of the threshold δ_F in the experiment.

As shown in the Fig. 3, we can see that the number of free riders increases in both techniques as the threshold value δ_F is increased to 1,2,3. However, the non-catalyzing method makes more free riders than the catalyzing method that changes the amount of provided information according to privacy saving Δ_P. In other words, the catalyzing method and penalty scheme help to keep members in the federation by inducing them to reach the target epsilon in an earlier time.

5.4 Reduced Shapley Value Computation Time

As mentioned in Sect. 4.2, one of the limitations of Shapley value evaluation is to compute it for all combinations of subsets. Through this experiment, we demonstrate that the proposed pruning technique reduces the computation time for calculating the Shapley values. We compared the computation times of the proposed method with brute force method that calculates all the cases by increasing the number of data providers in the federation, by 3, from 15 to 27 (Table 1).

Table 1. Computation time of brute force and proposed pruning method

# of data providers	Brute force (Sec)	Pruning method (Sec)
15	0.003	0.0007
18	0.02	0.001
21	0.257	0.0049
24	2.313	0.009
27	19.706	0.019

As shown in the table, the computation time of Shapley value evaluation increases exponentially because the total number of subsets to be considered does the same. The proposed method can calculate the Shapley values in less time by removing unnecessary computations.

6   Conclusion

With the spreading of data-driven decision making practices, the interest in personal data is increasing. The data market gives a new opportunity to trade personal data, but a lot of research is still needed to solve privacy and pricing issues. In this paper, we have considered a data market environment in which data providers form federations and protect their data with the locally differentially private kRR mechanism, and we have proposed a pricing and earnings-distribution method. Our method integrates different data providers' values of the privacy parameter ϵ and combines them to obtain the privacy parameter of the federation. The received earning is distributed using the Shapley values of the members, which guarantees the *Pareto efficiency* and *symmetry*. In addition, we have proposed a swift data collection mechanism and a penalty scheme to catalyze the process of achieving the target amount of information quickly, by penalizing the free riders who do not cooperate with their federation's best interest.

Our study has also disclosed new problems that need further investigation. Firstly, we are assuming that the data providers keep the promise for the "seal the deal", but, in reality, the data providers can always add more noise than what they promised. We plan to study how to ensure that data providers uphold their data trading contracts. Another direction for future work is considering more differential privacy mechanisms, other than kRR.

Appendix A   Proofs

Theorem 1. *If the privacy valuation function used by the data consumer, D, is $f(m) = K_1(e^{K_2 m} - 1)$, in order to impose the* penalty scheme *to any member $p \in F$ of a federation F, the Shapley valuation function, $\psi(.)$, chosen by F, must satisfy $\frac{\ln(\frac{\epsilon_p^T}{K_1}+1)}{K_2} < \psi\left(\epsilon_p^T, \frac{\ln(\frac{w^* \epsilon_p^T}{K_1}+K)}{K_2}\right)$, where $K = \frac{\sum_{p' \neq p \in F} d_{p'} \epsilon_{p'}^T}{K_1} + 1$, d_π is the number of data points reported by any $\pi \in F$, and w^* is the suggested scaling parameter computed by D to propose a realistic deal, as described in Sect. 4.1.*

Proof. Using the privacy valuation function $f(m) = K_1(e^{K_2 m} - 1)$, we have $f^{-1}(\epsilon) = \frac{\ln(\frac{\epsilon}{K_1}+1)}{K_2}$. Let p be an arbitrary member of F with a maximum privacy threshold ϵ_p^T. Therefore, in order to impose a penalty scheme on p, it needs to be ensured that

$$\frac{\ln(\frac{\epsilon_p^T}{K_1} + 1)}{K_2} < \psi(v, M)$$

$$\implies \frac{\ln(\frac{\epsilon_p^T}{K_1} + 1)}{K_2} < \psi(v, f^{-1}(\epsilon_F^P))$$

$[w^* \in [0,1]$ is the scaling parameter chosen by D and $\epsilon_F^P = w^* \epsilon_F^T]$

$$\implies \frac{\ln(\frac{\epsilon_p^T}{K_1} + 1)}{K_2} < \psi\left(v, \frac{\ln(\frac{\epsilon_F^P}{K_1} + 1)}{K_2}\right)$$

$$\implies \frac{\ln(\frac{\epsilon_p^T}{K_1} + 1)}{K_2} < \psi \left(v, \frac{\ln(\frac{C_0 + w^* \epsilon_p^T}{K_1} + 1)}{K_2} \right)$$

$$[\text{ where } C_0 = \sum_{p' \neq p \in F} d'_p \epsilon_{p'}^T \text{ is a constant}]$$

$$\implies \frac{\ln(\frac{\epsilon_p^T}{K_1} + 1)}{K_2} < \psi \left(v, \frac{\ln(\frac{C_0 + w^* \epsilon_p^T}{K_1} + 1)}{K_2} \right)$$

$$\frac{\ln(\frac{\epsilon_p^T}{K_1} + 1)}{K_2} < \psi \left(v, \frac{\ln(\frac{w^* \epsilon_p^T}{K_1} + K)}{K_2} \right)$$

$$\tag{1}$$

$$[\text{for the constant } K = \frac{C_0}{K_1} + 1.]$$

$\square$

References

1. Datacoup - reclaim your personal data. https://datacoup.com/, Accessed 26 May 2021
2. Domingo-Ferrer, J., Soria-Comas, J.: From t-closeness to differential privacy and vice versa in data anonymization. Knowl.-Based Syst. **74**, 151–158 (2015)
3. Dwork, C., Roth, A., et al.: The algorithmic foundations of differential privacy. Found. Trends Theor. Comput. Sci. **9**(3–4), 211–407 (2014)
4. Elsalamouny, E., Palamidessi, C.: reconstruction of sensitive distributions under free-will privacy, draft paper
5. Erlingsson, Ú., Pihur, V., Korolova, A.: Rappor: randomized aggregatable privacy-preserving ordinal response. In: Proceedings of the 2014 ACM SIGSAC Conference on Computer and Communications Security, pp. 1054–1067 (2014)
6. Fleischer, L.K., Lyu, Y.H.: Approximately optimal auctions for selling privacy when costs are correlated with data. In: Proceedings of the 13th ACM Conference on Electronic Commerce, pp. 568–585 (2012)
7. Ghosh, A., Roth, A.: Selling privacy at auction. In: Proceedings of the 12th ACM Conference on Electronic Commerce, pp. 199–208 (2011)
8. Hinds, J., Williams, E.J., Joinson, A.N.: "it wouldn't happen to me": privacy concerns and perspectives following the Cambridge analytica scandal. Int. J. Hum.-Comput. Stud. **143**, 102498 (2020)
9. Holohan, N., Antonatos, S., Braghin, S., Mac Aonghusa, P.: (k, ϵ)-anonymity: k-anonymity with ϵ-differential privacy (2017). arXiv preprint arXiv:1710.01615
10. Hsu, J., et al.: Differential privacy: an economic method for choosing epsilon. In: 2014 IEEE 27th Computer Security Foundations Symposium, pp. 398–410. IEEE (2014)

11. Jung, K., Park, S.: Privacy bargaining with fairness: privacy-price negotiation system for applying differential privacy in data market environments. In: 2019 IEEE International Conference on Big Data (Big Data), pp. 1389–1394. IEEE (2019)

12. Kairouz, P., Bonawitz, K., Ramage, D.: Discrete distribution estimation under local privacy. In: International Conference on Machine Learning, pp. 2436–2444. PMLR (2016)

13. Lee, J., Clifton, C.: How much is enough? choosing ε for differential privacy. In: Lai, X., Zhou, J., Li, H. (eds.) ISC 2011. LNCS, vol. 7001, pp. 325–340. Springer, Heidelberg (2011). https://doi.org/10.1007/978-3-642-24861-0_22

14. Li, C., Li, D.Y., Miklau, G., Suciu, D.: A theory of pricing private data. ACM Trans. Database Syst. (TODS) **39**(4), 1–28 (2014)

15. Liveen - blockchain-based social network platform that provides fair rewards for the users' contents. https://www.liveen.com/, Accessed 26 May 2021

16. Nget, R., Cao, Y., Yoshikawa, M.: How to balance privacy and money through pricing mechanism in personal data market (2017). arXiv preprint arXiv:1705.02982

17. Roth, A.: Buying private data at auction: the sensitive surveyor's problem. ACM SIGecom Exchang. **11**(1), 1–8 (2012)

18. Roth, A.E.: The Shapley Value: Essays in Honor of Lloyd S. Cambridge University Press, Shapley (1988)

19. Tang, J., Korolova, A., Bai, X., Wang, X., Wang, X.: Privacy loss in Apple's implementation of differential privacy on MacOS 10.12 (2017). arXiv preprint arXiv:1709.02753

20. Winter, E.: The shapley value. Handb. Game Theory Econ. Appl **3**, 2025–2054 (2002)

21. Zhang, T., Zhu, Q.: On the differential private data market: endogenous evolution, dynamic pricing, and incentive compatibility (2021). arXiv preprint arXiv:2101.04357

On the Complexity of Verification of Time-Sensitive Distributed Systems

Max Kanovich[1,6], Tajana Ban Kirigin[2($\boxtimes$)], Vivek Nigam[3,4], Andre Scedrov[5], and Carolyn Talcott[7]

[1] University College, London, UK
m.kanovich@ucl.ac.uk
[2] Department of Mathematics, University of Rijeka, Rijeka, Croatia
bank@uniri.hr
[3] Federal University of Paraíba, João Pessoa, Brazil
vivek@ci.ufpb.br
[4] Munich Research Center, Huawei, Munich, Germany
[5] University of Pennsylvania, Philadelphia, USA
scedrov@math.upenn.edu
[6] Computer Science Department, HSE University, Moscow, Russia
[7] SRI International, Menlo Park, USA
clt@csl.sri.com

Abstract. This paper develops a Multiset Rewriting language with explicit time for the specification and analysis of Time-Sensitive Distributed Systems (TSDS). Goals are often specified using explicit time constraints. A good trace is an infinite trace in which the goals are satisfied perpetually despite possible interference from the environment. In our previous work [14], we discussed two desirable properties of TSDSes, *realizability* (there exists a good trace) and *survivability* (where, in addition, all admissible traces are good). Here we consider two additional properties, *recoverability* (all compliant traces do not reach points-of-no-return) and *reliability* (the system can always continue functioning using a good trace). Following [14], we focus on a class of systems called *Progressing Timed Systems* (PTS), where intuitively only a finite number of actions can be carried out in a bounded time period. We prove that for this class of systems the properties of recoverability and reliability coincide and are PSPACE-complete. Moreover, if we impose a bound on time (as in bounded model-checking), we show that for PTS the reliability property is in the Π_2^p class of the polynomial hierarchy, a subclass of PSPACE. We also show that the bounded survivability is both NP-hard and coNP-hard.

Keywords: Multiset rewriting · Time-sensitive distributed systems · Complexity

Dedicated to Joshua Guttman with gratitude for his inspiration and friendly and insightful discussions.

D. Dougherty et al. (Eds.): Guttman Festschrift, LNCS 13066, pp. 251–275, 2021.
https://doi.org/10.1007/978-3-030-91631-2_14

1   Introduction

In our previous work [14], we considered the verification of Time-Sensitive Distributed Systems (TSDS) motivated by applications with autonomous drones performing surveillance of an area. The drones must always collectively have recent pictures, *i.e.*, at most M time units old, of certain strategic locations. In attempting to achieve this goal, the drones consume energy and must return to the base station to recharge their batteries. In addition, the environment may interfere as there may be winds that move the drone in a certain direction, or other flying objects may block a drone's path.

In [14] we considered two verification properties, realizability and survivability. Here we introduce two more properties, reliability and recoverability. Let us explain all four properties in a little more detail. The *realizability* problem consists of checking, whether under the given time constraints, the specified system can achieve the assigned goal, *e.g.*, always collect recent pictures of the sensitive locations. In many settings, the drones themselves or the environment may behave non-deterministically. For example, if a drone wants to reach a point in the northeast, it may initially move either north or east, both being equally likely. Similarly, there could be wind at a particular location, causing any drone under the influence of the wind to move in the direction of the wind. A stronger property, *survivability*, accounts for such nondeterminism and tests whether the specified system can achieve the assigned goal for all possible outcomes (of drone actions and environmental influences). The properties of realizability and survivability represent the two extremes w.r.t. requirements placed on a system. A system that is realizable can achieve the designed goal in some way. A system that satisfies survivability will always achieve the goal, under all circumstances. In some cases, realizability may not be satisfactory, while in others, survivability may be too costly or unattainable. For such systems, intermediate solutions are of interest.

To model such intermediate requirements in system design, in this paper we introduce additional properties, namely *reliability* and *recoverability*. In order to ensure system goals, drones should always be able to function. In particular, drones should always be able to come back to recharge, both in terms of distance and energy. In other words, drones should never go too far and reach so-called *points-of-no-return* where it may no longer be possible to safely return to home base. Engineers should strive to program drones to avoid reaching points-of-no-return. This property is referred to as *recoverability*. A system satisfies *reliability* if the system is always able to successfully continue its expected performance, *i.e.*, the system never gets stuck. For example, drones should always be able to ensure the system goals, regardless of the disturbances they have experienced in the environment. At any point in time, after the drones have successfully monitored sensitive locations for a certain period of time, they should be able to find a way to continue with their good performance. For example, considering possible technical failures and maintenance of the drones, it may be necessary for engineers to call in additional drones to collectively provide up-to-date images of the entire area of interest.

Following [14], we focus on a class of systems called *Progressing Timed Systems* (PTS), which are specified as timed multiset rewriting theories. In a PTS, only a finite number of actions can be carried out in a bounded time interval. In addition to formalizing the properties, we show that the following relations hold for PTS:

$$S_{urvivability} \implies R_{eliability} \iff R_{ecoverability} \implies R_{ealizability} .$$

In their spirit, these properties seem similar to safety and liveness properties [1] or a combination of these properties. However, it is not straightforward to classify them in these terms. Namely, the properties we consider, formally defined in Sect. 3.3, contain an alternation of quantifiers, which makes it more challenging to formally represent them as a combination of safety and liveness properties [1].

In our previous work [13, 17–19], we proposed a timed Multiset Rewriting (MSR) framework for specifying compliance properties similar to quantitative safety properties [1, 6] and investigated the complexity of a number of decision problems. These properties were defined over sets of finite traces, *i.e.*, executions of a finite number of actions. The above properties, on the other hand, are defined over *infinite traces*. The transition to properties over infinite traces leads to many challenges, as one can easily fall into undecidable fragments of verification problems. The main challenge is to identify the syntactic conditions on specifications so that the verification problems fall into a decidable fragment and, at the same time, that interesting examples can be specified.

The remainder of the paper is organized as follows:

- Following [14], in Sect. 2 we discuss *Progressing Timed Systems*.
- In Sect. 3 we define concepts for specifying the relevant quantitative temporal properties of timed systems used to define the properties of *realizability, reliability, recoverability* and *survivability*.
- In Sect. 4 we then formally compare the expressiveness of these properties.
- Sect. 5 investigates the complexity of verification problems that involve the above properties. While these problems are undecidable in general [19], we show that they are PSPACE-complete for PTSes. We also show that, when we bound time (as in bounded-model checking), realizability of PTSes is NP-complete, survivability is in the Δ_2^p class of the polynomial hierarchy [27] and the reliability is in the Π_2^p class of the polynomial hierarchy. We also obtain the NP and co-NP lower bound for the n-time bounded survivability problem.
- Sect. 6 provides a discussion on related and future work.

Relation to Our Previous Work. This paper considerably extends the conference paper [14]. All the material involving properties of reliability and recoverability is new, including the investigation of the relations among all four properties from Sect. 4, the complexity results relating to reliability from Sect. 5, and the lower bound complexity results for n-time bounded survivability are new. Due to space constraints, many proofs and detailed considerations are placed in the technical report [16].

2 Multiset Rewriting Systems

We briefly review timed multiset rewriting with discrete time of [19].

Assume a finite first-order typed alphabet, Σ, with variables, constants, function and predicate symbols. Terms and formulas are constructed as usual (see [10]) by applying symbols of correct type (or sort). We assume that the alphabet contains the constant $z : Nat$ denoting zero and the function $s : Nat \rightarrow Nat$ denoting the successor function. Whenever it is clear from the context, we write n for $s^n(z)$ and $(n + m)$ for $s^n(s^m(z))$. In addition, we allow an unbounded number of fresh values [5,9] to be involved.

If P is a predicate of type $\tau_1 \times \tau_2 \times \cdots \times \tau_n \rightarrow o$, where o is the type for propositions, and $u_1, \ldots, u_n$ are terms of types $\tau_1, \ldots, \tau_n$, respectively, then $P(u_1, \ldots, u_n)$ is a *fact*. A fact is *ground* if it contains no variables.

In order to specify timed systems, we attach a timestamp to each fact. *Timestamped facts* are of the form $F@t$, where F is a fact and $t \in \mathbb{N}$ is a natural number called *timestamp*. For simplicity, we often just say facts instead of timestamped facts. Also, when we want to emphasize the difference between a fact F and a timestamped fact $F@t$, we say that F is an *untimed fact*.

Note that timestamps are *not* constructed using the successor function. Rather, timestamps can take any natural number value. To obtain the complexity results, we use a symbolic representation of the problems and abstractions that can handle unbounded time values. For more insight see discussion after Definition 2.

There is a special predicate symbol $Time$ with arity zero that is used to represent global time. A *configuration* is a finite multiset of ground timestamped facts, $\mathcal{S} = \{\ Time@t,\ F_1@t_1, \ldots, F_n@t_n\ \}$ with a single occurrence of a $Time$ fact.

Given a configuration $\mathcal{S}$ containing $Time@t$, a fact $F@t_F$ in $\mathcal{S}$ is a *future fact* if its timestamp is greater than the global time t, *i.e.*, if $t_F > t$. Similarly, a fact $F@t_F$ in $\mathcal{S}$ is a *past fact* if $t_F < t$, and a fact $F@t_F$ in $\mathcal{S}$ is a *present fact* if $t_F = t$.

Configurations are to be interpreted as states of the system, *e.g.*, configuration

$$\mathcal{S}_1 = \{\ Time@4,\ Dr(d1, 1, 2, 10)@4,\ Dr(d2, 5, 5, 8)@4,\ P(p1, 1, 1)@3,\ P(p2, 4, 6)@1\ \}$$

denotes a scenario with two drones located at positions $(1, 2)$ and $(5, 5)$, with 10 and 8 energy units, and with two points to be monitored at positions $(1, 1)$ and $(4, 6)$. The former was last photographed at time 3 and the latter at time 1. The global time is 4.

Using variables, including time variables, we are able to represent configurations of particular form. For example, configuration

$$Time@(T + D),\ Dr(X, 5, 6, Y)@(T + D),\ P(p2, 4, 6)@T$$

specifies that some drone X with Y energy units is currently at the position $(5, 6)$ and that the point of interest at position $(4, 6)$ was last photographed D

time units ago. This holds for any configuration containing the above facts for some instantiation of the variables T, D, X and Y.

Configurations are modified by rewrite rules which can be interpreted as actions of the system. There is only one rule, $Tick$, which represents how global time advances:

$$Time@T \longrightarrow Time@(T+1), \tag{1}$$

where T is a time variable denoting the global time. With an application of a $Tick$ rule, a configuration, $\{\ Time@t, F_1@t_1, \ldots, F_n@t_n\ \}$, representing the state of a system at time t, is replaced with the configuration $\{\ Time@(t+1), F_1@t_1, \ldots, F_n@t_n\ \}$ representing the system at time $t+1$.

The remaining rules are *instantaneous*, since they do not modify global time, but may modify the remaining facts of configurations (those different from $Time$). Instantaneous rules have the form:

$$\begin{aligned}
Time@T, W_1@T_1, \ldots, W_p@T_p, F_1@T_1', \ldots, F_n@T_n' \mid \mathcal{C} \longrightarrow \\
\exists \vec{X}.[\ Time@T, W_1@T_1, \ldots, W_p@T_p, Q_1@(T+d_1), \ldots, Q_m@(T+d_m)\ ]
\end{aligned} \tag{2}$$

where $d_1, \ldots, d_m$ are natural numbers, $W_1@T_1, \ldots, W_p@T_p, F_1@T_1', \ldots, F_n@T_n'$ are timestamped facts, possibly containing variables, and $\mathcal{C}$ is the guard of the rule which is a set of constraints involving the time variables that appear as timestamps of facts in the pre-condition of the rule, *i.e.*, the variables $T, T_1, \ldots, T_p, T_1', \ldots, T_n'$. The facts W_i, F_j and Q_k are all different from the fact $Time$ and $\vec{X}$ are variables that do not appear in $W_1, \ldots, W_p, F_1, \ldots, F_n$.

Constraints may be of the form $T > T' \pm d$ or $T = T' \pm d$, where T and T' are time variables, and $d \in \mathbb{N}$ is a natural number. Here and throughout the rest of the paper, the symbol $\pm$ stands for either $+$ or $-$, *i.e.*, constraints may involve addition or subtraction. We use $T' \geq T' \pm d$ to denote the disjunction of $T > T' \pm d$ and $T = T' \pm d$. All variables in the guard of a rule are assumed to appear in the rule's pre-condition.

Finally, the variables $\vec{X}$ that are existentially quantified in a rule (Eq. 2) are to be replaced by fresh values, also called *nonces* in the protocol security literature [5,9]. As in our previous work [12], we use nonces whenever unique identification is required, for example for drone identification.

A rule $\mathcal{W} \mid \mathcal{C} \longrightarrow \exists \vec{X}.\mathcal{W}'$ can be applied to a configuration $\mathcal{S}$ if there is a ground substitution σ such that $\mathcal{W}\sigma \subseteq \mathcal{S}$ and that $\mathcal{C}\sigma$ is true. The resulting configuration is $((\mathcal{S} \setminus \mathcal{W}) \cup \mathcal{W}')\sigma$, where variables $\vec{X}$ are fresh. More precisely, given a rule r, an instance of a rule is obtained by substituting constants for all variables appearing in the pre- and post-condition of the rule. This substitution applies to variables appearing in terms inside facts, to variables representing fresh values, and to time variables used to specify timestamps of facts. An instance of an instantaneous rule can only be applied if all the constraints in its guard are satisfied.

Following [9] we say that a timestamped fact $F@T$ is *consumed* by a rule r if this fact occurs more times on the left side than on the right side of the rule r. A timestamped fact $F@T$ is *created* by some rule r if that fact occurs more times on the right side than on the left side of the rule r. Hence, facts $F_1@T_1', \ldots, F_n@T_n'$ are consumed by rule (Eq. 2) while facts $Q_1@(T + d_1), \ldots, Q_m@(T + d_m)$ are created by this rule. Note that a fact F can appear in a rule with different timestamps, but for the above notions we count instances of the same timestamped fact $F@T$. In a rule, we usually color red the consumed facts and blue the created facts.

Remark 1. Using constraints we are able to formalize time-sensitive properties and problems that involve explicit time requirements. The set of constraints may, however, be empty, *i.e.*, rules may have no constraints attached.

We write $S \longrightarrow_r S'$ for the one-step relation where the configuration S is rewritten into S' using an instance of rule r. For a set of rules $\mathcal{R}$, we define $S \longrightarrow_{\mathcal{R}}^* S'$ to be the transitive reflexive closure of the one-step relation on all rules in $\mathcal{R}$. We omit the subscript $\mathcal{R}$, when it is clear from the context, and simply write $S \longrightarrow^* S'$.

Note that due to the nature of multiset rewriting, there are various aspects of non-determinism in the model. For example, different actions and even different instantiations of the same rule may apply to the same configuration S, leading to different resulting configurations S'.

Definition 1 (Timed MSR System). *A timed MSR system $\mathcal{T}$ is a set of rules containing only instantaneous rules (Eq. 2) and the Tick rule (Eq. 1).*

A trace of a timed MSR system is constructed by a sequence of its rules. In this paper, we consider both finite and infinite traces. A *finite trace* of a timed MSR system $\mathcal{T}$ starting from an initial configuration S_0 is a sequence
$$S_0 \longrightarrow S_1 \longrightarrow S_2 \longrightarrow \cdots \longrightarrow S_n$$
and an *infinite trace* of $\mathcal{T}$ starting from an initial configuration S_0 is a sequence
$$S_0 \longrightarrow S_1 \longrightarrow S_2 \longrightarrow \cdots \longrightarrow S_n \longrightarrow S_{n+1} \longrightarrow \cdots$$
where for all $i \geq 0$, $S_i \longrightarrow_{r_i} S_{i+1}$ for some $r_i \in \mathcal{T}$. When a configuration S apperas in a trace P we write $S \in P$.

We will pay particular attention to periods of time represented by traces. Since time advances by one unit of time per *Tick* rule, a finite (infinite) number of *Tick* rules in a trace represents a finite (infinite) time period. One can easily imagine traces containing a finite number of *Tick* rules and an infinite number of instantaneous rules. Such traces would represent an infinite number of actions performed in a finite time interval. In this paper we are not interested in such traces and focus on so called *infinite time traces*.

Definition 2 (Infinite Time Trace). *A trace P of a timed MSR $\mathcal{T}$ is an infinite time trace if the time tends to infinity in P, i.e., $(\forall n \in \mathbb{N}) \, (\exists \, S \in P)$ such that $Time@T \in S$ and $T > n$.*

Since in any trace, the global time ticks in single time units, any infinite time trace is an infinite trace, and it contains an infinite number of *Tick* rules.

We have shown in our previous work [12,13,17,19,20] that reachability problems for MSR are undecidable if no further restrictions are imposed, already when considering only finite traces. In order to obtain decidability, among other restrictions, we assume a bound on the size of facts. The size of a timestamped fact $P@T$, written $|P@T|$, is the total number of symbols appearing in P, not considering the timestamp. For instance, $|P(s(z), f(a, X), a)@12| = 7$. Without this bound, interesting decision problems can be shown undecidable by encoding the Post correspondence problem [9]. For our complexity results, it is also important to assume that the system is *balanced* [19,20]. A timed MSR system $\mathcal{T}$ is *balanced* if for all instantaneous rules $r \in \mathcal{T}$, r creates the same number of facts as it consumes, *i.e.*, the instantaneous rules are of the form:

$$Time@T, \mathcal{W}, F_1@T_1', \ldots, F_n@T_n' \mid \mathcal{C} \longrightarrow$$
$$\exists \vec{X}. [\, Time@T, \mathcal{W}, Q_1@(T + d_1), \ldots, Q_n@(T + d_n)\,].$$

By consuming and creating facts, rewrite rules can increase and decrease the number of facts in configurations throughout a trace. However, in balanced MSR systems, the number of facts in configurations is constant throughout a trace.

2.1 Progressing Timed Systems

Following [14], we discuss a particular class of timed MSR systems, called *progressing timed MSR systems* (PTSes), in which only a finite number of actions can be carried out in a bounded time interval. This is a natural condition for many systems, similar to the *finite-variability assumption* used in the temporal logic and timed automata literature.

Definition 3 (Progressing Timed System). *A timed MSR system $\mathcal{T}$ is a progressing timed MSR system (PTS) if $\mathcal{T}$ is balanced and for all instantaneous rules $r \in \mathcal{T}$:*

i) Rule r creates at least one fact with timestamp greater than the global time, i.e., in (Eq. 2), $d_i \geq 1$ for at least one $i \in \{1, \ldots, n\}$;
ii) Rule r consumes only facts with timestamps in the past or at the current time, i.e., in (Eq. 2), the set of constraints $\mathcal{C}$ contains the set $\mathcal{C}_r = \{\, T \geq T_i' \mid F_i@T_i', 1 \leq i \leq n \,\}$.

For the sake of readability, from this point on we assume that for all rules r the set of their constraints implicitly contains the set $\mathcal{C}_r$, as shown in Definition 3, and do not always write $\mathcal{C}_r$ explicitly in our specifications.

The following rule, which denotes the action of a drone taking a photo of a point of interest, is an example of a rule in a PTS:

$$Time@T, P(I, X, Y)@T', Dr(Id, X, Y, E + 1)@T \mid \{\, T' < T \,\} \longrightarrow$$
$$Time@T, P(I, X, Y)@T, Dr(Id, X, Y, E)@(T + 1)$$

The constraint $T' < T$ is used to prevent drones from repeatedly photographing the same point of interest at the same time to save energy.

The following result [14] establishes a bound on the number of instances of instantaneous rules appearing between two consecutive instances of $Tick$ rules in a trace of a PTS. This bound is then used to formalize the intuition that PTSes always move things forward.

Proposition 1. *Let T be a PTS, S_0 an initial configuration and m the number of facts in S_0. For all traces P of T starting from S_0, let*

$$S_i \longrightarrow_{Tick} S_{i+1} \longrightarrow \cdots \longrightarrow S_j \longrightarrow_{Tick} S_{j+1}$$

be any subtrace of P with exactly two instances of the $Tick$ rule, one at the beginning and the other at the end. Then $j - i < m$. [14]

Proof. Let P be an arbitrary trace in T and

$$S_i \longrightarrow_{Tick} S_{i+1} \longrightarrow \cdots \longrightarrow S_j \longrightarrow_{Tick} S_{j+1}$$

an arbitrary subtrace of P with exactly two instances of the $Tick$ rule. All the rules between $Tick$ rules in the above subtrace are instantaneous.

Since T is a PTS, the application of any instantaneous rule creates at least one future fact and consumes at least one present or past fact. In other words, an application of an instantaneous rule reduces the total number of past and present facts in the configuration.

Since the system T is balanced, all the above configurations $S_i, \ldots, S_j$ have the same number of facts, m. Recall also that the fact $Time$ does not change when the instantaneous rules are applied. Thus, since there are at most $m - 1$ present or past facts different from $Time$ in any S_k, $i < k \leq .j$, a series of at most $m - 1$ instantaneous rules can be applied between two $Tick$ rules.   □

As per the above statement, in a PTS an unbounded number of instantaneous rules cannot be applied in a bounded interval of time. Hence, infinite traces in PTSes represent infinite time periods. In particular, there are no Zeno-type phenomena in traces of PTSes.

Proposition 2. *Let T be a PTS. All infinite traces of T are infinite time traces, i.e., traces where time tends to infinity. [14]*

Proof. Assume that in some infinite trace P of a PTS T the current time does not exceed some value M. Then, as time advances by a single time unit, there are at most M time ticks in P. According to Proposition 1, there are at most $m - 1$ instantaneous rules between any $Tick$ rule and the next $Tick$ rule in P. Consequently, in total, there are at most $(M+1) \cdot (m-1) + M$ rules in P, i.e., P is a finite trace. Contradiction.   □

Finally, notice that the PTS model has many carefully developed syntactic conditions, e.g., balanced condition, the form of time constraints, the form of instantaneous rules (Eq. 2). As we have previously shown [19], relaxing any of these conditions leads to undecidability of important verification problems over finite traces. Clearly, these conditions are also needed for infinite traces. The additional challenge in allowing infinite traces is to represent arbitrarily large time periods. Our definition of PTS is a simple and elegant way to enforce this.

Moreover, as we show in [14] and the technical report [15], it is still possible to specify many interesting examples with our PTS model and still prove the decidability of our verification problems involving infinite traces.

3 Quantitative Temporal Properties

Following [14], we begin the Sect. 3.1 by discussing critical configurations, a language used to define desirable properties of systems. This is a key concept in our framework, used to describe explicit timing constraints that a system should satisfy. In Sect. 3.2 we discuss lazy time sampling, which is a condition on traces that intuitively enforces that systems react at the expected time. Then in Sect. 3.3, we discuss a number of verification problems.

3.1 Critical Configurations and Compliant Traces

Critical configurations represent bad configurations that should be avoided by a system. *Critical configuration specification* is a set of pairs $CS = \{\langle S_1, C_1 \rangle, \ldots, \langle S_n, C_n \rangle\}$. Each pair $\langle S_j, C_j \rangle$ in CS is of the form $\langle \{F_1 @ T_1, \ldots, F_{p_j} @ T_{p_j}\}, C_j \rangle$, where $T_1, \ldots, T_{p_j}$ are time variables, $F_1, \ldots, F_{p_j}$ are facts (possibly containing variables) and C_j is a set of time constraints involving only the variables $T_1, \ldots, T_{p_j}$.

Given a critical configuration specification CS, we classify a configuration S as *critical* w.r.t. CS if for some $1 \leq i \leq n$, there is a grounding substitution σ, such that $S_i \sigma \subseteq S$ and all constraints in $C_i \sigma$ are satisfied. The substitution application ($S\sigma$) is defined as usual [10], *i.e.*, by mapping time variables in S to natural numbers, nonce names to nonce names (renaming of nonces), and non-time variables to terms. Notice that nonce renaming is assumed, since the particular nonce name should not matter for classifying a configuration as critical. Nonce names cannot be specified in advance, since they are freshly generated in a trace, *i.e.*, during the execution of the process being modelled. Several examples illustrating these concepts are discussed in [14] and [15], along with proofs showing how the explicit time conditions are handled symbolically.

Definition 4 (Compliant Trace). *A trace $\mathcal{P}$ of a timed MSR system is compliant w.r.t. a given critical configuration specification CS if $\mathcal{P}$ does not contain any configuration that is critical w.r.t. CS.*

Note that if the critical configuration specification is empty, no configuration is critical, *i.e.*, all traces are compliant.

3.2 Time Sampling

To define sensible quantitative verification properties, we need to assume some conditions on when the Tick rule is applicable. Otherwise, any MSR system allows traces containing only instances of *Tick* rules:

$$\mathcal{S}_1 \longrightarrow_{Tick} \mathcal{S}_2 \longrightarrow_{Tick} \mathcal{S}_3 \longrightarrow_{Tick} \mathcal{S}_4 \longrightarrow_{Tick} \cdots$$

In such a trace, the system never acts to avoid critical configurations and would easily contain a critical configuration $\mathcal{S}_j$, related to some constraint $T > T' + d$, involving global time T and sufficiently large j.

Imposing a *time sampling* is one way to avoid such traces. Time sampling is used, for example, in the semantics of verification tools such as Real-Time Maude [25]. In particular, time sampling dictates when the $Tick$ rule must be applied and when it cannot be applied. Such a treatment of time is used for both dense and discrete times in searching and model checking timed systems.

Definition 5 (Lazy Time Sampling (l.t.s.)). *A (possibly infinite) trace $\mathcal{P}$ of a timed MSR system $\mathcal{T}$ uses* lazy time sampling *if for any occurrence of the Tick rule $\mathcal{S}_i \longrightarrow_{Tick} \mathcal{S}_{i+1}$ in $\mathcal{P}$, no instance of any instantaneous rule in $\mathcal{T}$ can be applied to the configuration $\mathcal{S}_i$.*

In the lazy time sampling instantaneous rules are given a higher priority than the $Tick$ rule. In the remainder of this paper, we focus on the lazy time sampling. We leave it to future work to investigate whether similar results hold for other time sampling schemes.

3.3 Verification Problems

Four properties are discussed in this section: realizability and survivability from [14] and the new properties of reliability and recoverability. Figure 1 illustrates these properties, which we define below. Since the names of the properties sound similar in English, we also introduce one-letter names for the properties for better readability and differentiation.

The first property we discuss is realizability. It guarantees that the given system can achieve the assigned goal under the given time constraints and design specifications, *e.g.*, that drones can repeatedly collect up-to-date images of the sensitive locations.

Realizability is useful for increasing confidence in a specified system, since a system that is not realizable cannot accomplish the given tasks (specified by a critical specification) and the designer would therefore have to reformulate it.

However, if a system is shown to be realizable, the trace, $\mathcal{P}$, that proves realizability could also provide insights into the sequence of actions that lead to accomplishment of the specified tasks. This can be used to refine the specification and reduce possible non-determinism.

Open distributed systems are inherently non-deterministic due to, *e.g.*, the influence of the environment. Therefore, it is important to know whether the system can avoid critical configurations despite non-determinism. We call this property *survivability*.

Definition 6 (Realizability/Z property). *A timed MSR system $\mathcal{T}$ satisfies* realizability *w.r.t. an initial configuration $\mathcal{S}_0$, a critical configuration* *specification $\mathcal{CS}$ and the l.t.s. if there exists a compliant infinite time trace from $\mathcal{S}_0$ that uses the l.t.s.[1] [14]*

The Z property of a timed MSR $\mathcal{T}$ w.r.t. $\mathcal{S}_0, \mathcal{CS}$ and l.t.s. can be expressed using the formula:

$$F_Z\left(\mathcal{T}, \mathcal{S}_0\right) := \exists t \in \mathsf{T}^{\mathcal{T}, \mathcal{S}_0}.[t \in \mathsf{T}_{time}^{\mathcal{T}} \cap \mathsf{T}_{lts}^{\mathcal{T}} \cap \mathsf{T}_c^{\mathcal{T}}],$$

where $\mathsf{T}^{\mathcal{T}, \mathcal{S}_0}$ is the set of all traces of $\mathcal{T}$ starting from $\mathcal{S}_0$, $\mathsf{T}_{time}^{\mathcal{T}}$ is the set of all infinite time traces of $\mathcal{T}$, $\mathsf{T}_{lts}^{\mathcal{T}}$ is the set of all traces of $\mathcal{T}$ that use the l.t.s. and $\mathsf{T}_c^{\mathcal{T}}$ is the set of all traces of $\mathcal{T}$ compliant w.r.t. $\mathcal{CS}$.

Definition 7 (Survivability/S property). *A timed MSR $\mathcal{T}$ satisfies survivability w.r.t. an initial configuration $\mathcal{S}_0$, a critical configuration specification $\mathcal{CS}$ and the l.t.s. if it satisfies realizability with respect to $\mathcal{S}_0$, $\mathcal{CS}$, and the l.t.s. and if all infinite time traces from $\mathcal{S}_0$ that use the l.t.s. are compliant. [14]*

Using the above notation, the S property of a timed MSR $\mathcal{T}$ can be expressed with:

$$F_S\left(\mathcal{T}, \mathcal{S}_0\right) := F_Z\left(\mathcal{T}, \mathcal{S}_0\right) \wedge \forall t \in \mathsf{T}^{\mathcal{T}, \mathcal{S}_0}.[t \in \mathsf{T}_{time}^{\mathcal{T}} \cap \mathsf{T}_{lts}^{\mathcal{T}} \Rightarrow t \in \mathsf{T}_c^{\mathcal{T}}].$$

Although survivability is a desirable property, much more so than realizability, it can sometimes be a rather severe requirement for a system, or even unachievable. Hence, when designing a system, one may want to compromise and consider less demanding properties. For example, one may want to avoid configurations that appear as "dead-ends", *i.e.*, configurations that necessarily lead to critical configurations. We call such configurations *points-of-no-return*. For example, drones should not fly so far that it is no longer possible to reach a recharging station due to energy consumption.

Definition 8 (Point-of-No-Return) *Given a timed MSR system $\mathcal{T}$, a configuration $\mathcal{S}$ is called a* point-of-no-return *with respect to a critical configuration specification $\mathcal{CS}$, and the l.t.s. if $\mathcal{S}$ is not critical w.r.t. $\mathcal{CS}$, and if all infinite traces of $\mathcal{T}$ starting with $\mathcal{S}$ and using the l.t.s. are not compliant w.r.t. $\mathcal{CS}$.*

The set of all configurations that are points-of-no-return of a timed MSR $\mathcal{T}$, $\mathsf{C}_{pon}^{\mathcal{T}}$, can be described as $\mathsf{C}_{pon}^{\mathcal{T}} := \{\mathcal{S} \mid \mathcal{S} \notin \mathsf{C}_{cr}^{\mathcal{T}} \wedge \forall t.[t \in \mathsf{T}^{\mathcal{T}, \mathcal{S}} \cap \mathsf{T}_{\infty}^{\mathcal{T}} \cap \mathsf{T}_{lts}^{\mathcal{T}} \Rightarrow t \notin \mathsf{T}_c^{\mathcal{T}}]\}$, where $\mathsf{C}_{cr}^{\mathcal{T}}$ is the set of all critical configurations of $\mathcal{T}$ and $\mathsf{T}_{\infty}^{\mathcal{T}}$ is the set of all infinite traces of $\mathcal{T}$.

---

[1] For simplicity, in the rest of the paper, for properties of systems and configurations, we will not always explicitly state the critical configuration specification, initial configuration, and/or time samplingwith respect to which the property is considered. For example, when it is clear from the context, we simply say that a system satisfies Z property or that it is *realizable*.
Also, when for a property of an MSR $\mathcal{T}$ we only consider traces that use the l.t.s., we also say that $\mathcal{T}$ *uses the lazy time sampling*.

There exists no compliant infinite trace from a point-of-no-return that uses the l.t.s. A point-of-no-return itself is not critical, but must eventually lead to a critical configuration on every infinite trace that uses the l.t.s. Therefore, points-of-no-return should be avoided when searching for (infinite) compliant traces.

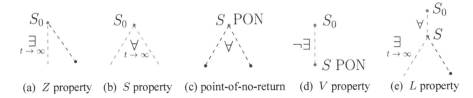

(a) *Z* property   (b) *S* property   (c) point-of-no-return   (d) *V* property   (e) *L* property

Fig. 1. Illustration of properties of (a) realizability, (b) survivability, (d) recoverability, and (e) reliability, as well as configurations that are a point-of-no-return (c). Green lines represent compliant traces that use the l.t.s., while red lines represent traces that use the l.t.s. but are not compliant. Red circles represent critical configurations, while green circles are not critical. Quantification marked with $t \to \infty$ denotes quantification over infinite time traces. (Color figure online)

Remark 2. A point-of-no-return represents the system that still satisfies the required conditions, but it will inevitably fall into a bad state where this is no longer the case. Therefore, to better distinguish between points-of-no-return and critical configurations, the condition that a point-of-no-return is not critical is included in the definition.

We use the notion of points-of-no-return, to introduce new properties of our systems. Configurations that are points-of-no-return should be avoided. For example, a drone may enter an area where it may end up with empty batteries due to frequent high winds. Such points should be avoided.

Definition 9 (Recoverability/V property). *A timed MSR system $\mathcal{T}$ satisfies recoverability with respect to an initial configuration $\mathcal{S}_0$, a critical configuration specification $\mathcal{CS}$, and the l.t.s. if it satisfies realizability with respect to $\mathcal{S}_0$, $\mathcal{CS}$, and the l.t.s. and if no point-of-no-return is reachable from $\mathcal{S}_0$ on a compliant trace that uses the l.t.s. That is, if a configuration $\mathcal{S}$ is reachable from $\mathcal{S}_0$ on a compliant trace that uses the l.t.s., then $\mathcal{S}$ is not a point-of-no-return.*

The *V* property of a timed MSR $\mathcal{T}$ can be expressed with the following formula:

$$F_V\left(\mathcal{T}, \mathcal{S}_0\right) := F_Z\left(\mathcal{T}, \mathcal{S}_0\right) \wedge [\forall t \in \mathsf{T}^{\mathcal{T}, \mathcal{S}_0} \cap \mathsf{T}_c^{\mathcal{T}} \cap \mathsf{T}_{lts}^{\mathcal{T}}. \forall \mathcal{S} \in t.\mathcal{S} \notin \mathsf{C}_{pon}^{\mathcal{T}}].$$

In fact, with the *V* property we want to ensure that all finite compliant traces from the initial configuration that use the l.t.s. can be extended to infinite compliant traces that use the l.t.s.

Next, with the reliability property we want to ensure that as long as one follows a compliant trace, there is a way to extend the trace to a compliant infinite time trace. In our drone scenario, a reliable system should be designed so that as long as the drones follow instructions, including rules for flying in high winds, there is always a way for the drones to avoid critical configurations.

Definition 10 (Reliability/L property). *A timed MSR system T satisfies reliability w.r.t. an initial configuration S_0, a critical configuration specification CS and the l.t.s. if it satisfies realizability with respect to S_0, CS, and the l.t.s. and if for any configuration S reachable from S_0 on a compliant trace that uses the l.t.s., there exists a compliant infinite time trace from S that uses the l.t.s.*

The L property of a timed MSR T can be expressed with the following formula:

$$F_L\left(T, S_0\right) := F_Z\left(T, S_0\right) \wedge$$
$$[\forall t \in \mathsf{T}^{T, S_0} \cap \mathsf{T}_c^T \cap \mathsf{T}_{lts}^T. \forall S \in t. \exists t' \in \mathsf{T}^{T, S}. t' \in \mathsf{T}_c^T \cap \mathsf{T}_{lts}^T \cup \mathsf{T}_{time}^T].$$

A timed MSR system that satisfies the L property represents a system that is always able to avoid points-of-no-return. Such a system satisfies the Z property, but it may not satisfy the S property. Indeed, the class of systems satisfying the Z property is a proper superclass of the class of systems satisfying the L property. Systems satisfying the L property also satisfy the V property, while the class of systems satisfying the V property is a proper superclass of the class of systems satisfying the S property. We present these results in Sect. 4, for general MSR systems and PTSes.

Some of these relations clearly follow since the Z property is included in the definitions of the other properties. Although this is an intuitive approach where for the more demanding properties we only consider systems that can accomplish their tasks, *i.e.*, satisfy the Z property, given a non-critical initial configuration, the Z property would follow from the V property and from the L property anyway. Similarly, by including the Z property, we avoid the vacuously survivable systems with no infinite time traces that use the l.t.s. For details see [15, Remark 3].

Time-Bounded Versions of Verification Problems

Motivated by bounded model checking, we also investigate the time-bounded versions of the above problems. Instead of infinite traces, in time-bounded versions of verification problems we consider traces with a fixed number of occurrences of Tick rules.

Definition 11 (n-Time Realizability/n-Z property). *A timed MSR system T satisfies n-time realizability w.r.t. the l.t.s., a critical configuration specification CS, and an initial configuration S_0 if there exists a compliant trace, P, from S_0 that uses the l.t.s. such that global time advances by exactly n time units in P. [14]*

Definition 12 (n-Time Survivability/n-S property). *A timed MSR system $\mathcal{T}$ satisfies n-time survivability property w.r.t. the l.t.s., a critical configuration specification $\mathcal{CS}$ and an initial configuration $\mathcal{S}_0$ if it satisfies n-Z property and if all traces with exactly n instances of the Tick rule starting with $\mathcal{S}_0$ and using the l.t.s. are compliant. [14]*

Analogously, we define the n-time bounded version of the reliability problem. We consider all compliant traces covering *at most* n time units, and extend them to compliant traces over *exactly* n time units.

Definition 13 (n-Time *Reliability/n-L* property). *A timed MSR system $\mathcal{T}$ satisfies n-time reliability w.r.t. an initial configuration $\mathcal{S}_0$, a critical configuration specification $\mathcal{CS}$, and the l.t.s. if it satisfies n-time realizability with respect to $\mathcal{S}_0$, $\mathcal{CS}$, and the l.t.s. and if for any configuration $\mathcal{S}$, reachable from $\mathcal{S}_0$ on a compliant trace $\mathcal{P}$ that uses the l.t.s. and has at most n instances of the Tick rule, there exists a trace $\mathcal{P}'$ that uses the l.t.s. such that $\mathcal{P}'$ extends $\mathcal{P}$, $\mathcal{P}'$ is compliant, and $\mathcal{P}'$ has exactly n instances of the Tick rule.*

Since the notion of a point-of-no-return is defined to be inseparable from infinite traces, the time-bounded version of the recoverability system problem makes little sense. Hence, we do not consider this problem separately.

4   Relations Among Properties of Timed MSR

In this section we formally relate all the different properties discussed in Sect. 3.3. To compare these properties, we review in the accompanying technical report [15] the machinery introduced in our previous work [19] called δ-representations. This machinery is also used in Sect. 5 to obtain complexity results for the verification problems.

In the accompanying technical report [15] we show that the Z property implies the n-Z property, as expected, but also that for a sufficiently large n, the converse implication also holds. Namely, in a trace with a sufficiently large number of $Tick$ rules, the same δ-representation is repeated, forming a loop that can be repeated to obtain an infinite time trace showing the Z property. The same implications hold for the other properties.

4.1   Relations Among Different Properties of Timed MSR and PTS

We now relate different properties defined over infinite traces. We can distinguish all these properties for general timed MSR, but only some for PTSes, as stated below.

Proposition 3. *Let $\mathcal{T}$ be a timed MSR system that uses the l.t.s., $\mathcal{S}_0$ an initial configuration and $\mathcal{CS}$ a critical configuration specification.*

If $\mathcal{T}$ satisfies the L property, then $\mathcal{T}$ satisfies the V property.

If $\mathcal{T}$ satisfies the V property, then $\mathcal{T}$ does not necessarily satisfy the L property.

Proof. Let $\mathcal{T}$ be a timed MSR system that satisfies the L property.
Assume $\mathcal{T}$ does not satisfy the V property. Then, since $\mathcal{T}$ satisfies the Z property, there is a compliant trace from $\mathcal{S}_0$ to some point-of-no-return $\mathcal{S}_P$ that uses the l.t.s. Since $\mathcal{T}$ satisfies the L property, there is a compliant infinite time trace from $\mathcal{S}_P$ that uses the l.t.s. As $\mathcal{S}_P$ is a point-of-no-return, this contradicts the notion of point-of-no-return.

We give an example of a timed MSR system, $\mathcal{T}$, that satisfies the V property, but does not that satisfy the L property.

Let $\mathcal{S}'_0 = \{Time@0, C@1\}$, $\mathcal{CS}' = \emptyset$, and let $\mathcal{T}'$ contain only the following instantaneous rules:

$$Time@T, C@T' \mid T' \leq T \; \longrightarrow \; Time@T, D@T \tag{3a}$$

$$Time@T, C@T' \mid T' \leq T \; \longrightarrow \; Time@T, A@T \tag{3b}$$

$$Time@T, A@T' \; \longrightarrow \; Time@T, B@T \tag{3c}$$

$$Time@T, B@T' \; \longrightarrow \; Time@T, A@T \tag{3d}$$

The system $\mathcal{T}'$ satisfies the Z property since there is a compliant infinite time trace from $\mathcal{S}'_0$ that uses l.t.s.:

$$Time@0, C@1 \; \longrightarrow_{Tick} \; Time@1, C@1 \; \longrightarrow_{(3a)} \; Time@1, D@1 \; \longrightarrow_{Tick}$$
$$Time@2, D@1 \; \longrightarrow_{Tick} \; Time@3, D@1 \; \longrightarrow_{Tick} \; Time@4, D@2 \; \longrightarrow_{Tick} \; \dots$$
$$\tag{4}$$

There is only one other infinite trace form $\mathcal{S}_0$ that uses the l.t.s.:

$$Time@0, C@1 \; \longrightarrow_{Tick} \; Time@1, C@1 \; \longrightarrow_{(3b)} \; Time@1, A@1 \; \longrightarrow_{(3c)}$$
$$Time@1, B@1 \; \longrightarrow_{(3d)} \; Time@1, A@1 \; \longrightarrow_{(3c)} \; Time@1, B@2 \; \longrightarrow_{(3d)} \; \dots \tag{5}$$

Its subtrace obtained from $\mathcal{S}_0$ by applying the $Tick$ rule followed by the rule (3b) reaches the configuration $Time@1, A@1$. This subtrace is compliant but it cannot be extended to a compliant infinite time trace that uses the l.t.s. Hence, $\mathcal{T}'$ does not satisfy the L property.

However, $\mathcal{T}'$ trivially satisfies the V property since there are no critical configurations and, hence, no points-of-no-return. $\qquad\square$

The properties of timed MSR defined in Sect. 3.3 involve infinite time traces that use the l.t.s. Recall that for any given PTS $\mathcal{T}$ and any configuration $\mathcal{S}$, there exists an infinite time trace of $\mathcal{T}$ that starts with $\mathcal{S}$ and uses the l.t.s.

Although V and L are different properties of timed MSR systems in general, it turns out that for the class of PTSes these properties coincide.

Proposition 4. *Let $\mathcal{T}$ be a PTS that uses the l.t.s., $\mathcal{S}_0$ an initial configuration, and $\mathcal{CS}$ a critical configuration specification.*
System $\mathcal{T}$ satisfies the L property iff $\mathcal{T}$ satisfies the V property.

Proof. Since a PTS is a timed MSR system, it follows from Proposition 3 that a PTS, which satisfies the L property, also satisfies the V property.

Assume that a PTS $\mathcal{T}$ does not satisfy the L property. If $\mathcal{S}_0$ is critical, then $\mathcal{T}$ does not satisfy the Z property and consequently, does not satisfy the V property. If $\mathcal{S}_0$ is not critical, there is a compliant trace from $\mathcal{S}_0$ to some configuration $\mathcal{S}_1$ that uses the l.t.s. which cannot be extended to a compliant infinite time trace that uses the l.t.s.

Then, $\mathcal{S}_1$ is a point-of-no-return. Namely, if P is an infinite trace from $\mathcal{S}_1$ that uses the l.t.s., by Proposition 2, P is an infinite time trace that uses the l.t.s. Then, P is not compliant. Since the point-of-no-return $\mathcal{S}_1$ is reachable from $\mathcal{S}_0$ on a compliant trace using the l.t.s., $\mathcal{T}$ does not satisfy the V property.   □

We show that the remaining properties are different even for PTSes. Furthermore, we provide the relations among the properties for PTSes and for timed MSR systems in general. We first show that L and S are different properties of PTSes, and, consequently, different properties of timed MSR systems.

Proposition 5. *Let $\mathcal{T}$ be a PTS that uses the l.t.s., $\mathcal{S}_0$ an initial configuration and $\mathcal{CS}$ a critical configuration specification.*

If $\mathcal{T}$ satisfies the S property, then $\mathcal{T}$ satisfies the L property.

If $\mathcal{T}$ satisfies the L property, it may not satisfy the S property.

Proof. Assume that $\mathcal{T}$ satisfies the S property, but does not satisfy the L property. Then, since $\mathcal{T}$ satisfies the Z property, there exists a compliant trace, $\mathcal{P}$, from $\mathcal{S}_0$ to some configuration $\mathcal{S}_1$ that cannot be extended to a compliant infinite time trace that uses the l.t.s. Let $\mathcal{P}'$ be an infinite time trace which is an extension of $\mathcal{P}$ that uses the l.t.s. Such a trace $\mathcal{P}'$ exists due to Proposition 2, but it is not compliant.

Since $\mathcal{T}$ satisfies the S property, all infinite time traces from $\mathcal{S}_0$ that use the l.t.s. are compliant, including $\mathcal{P}'$. Contradiction.

The following example of a PTS satisfies the L property, but does not satisfy the S property.

Let $\mathcal{S}_0 = \{Time@0, A@0, B@0\}$, $\mathcal{CS} = \{\langle \{B@T, D@T'\}, \emptyset \rangle\}$ and let PTS $\mathcal{T}$ contain only the following instantaneous rules:

$$Time@T, A@T', B@T'' \mid \{T' \leq T, T'' \leq T\} \longrightarrow Time@T, B@T'', C@(T+1) \quad (6a)$$

$$Time@T, A@T', B@T'' \mid \{T' \leq T\} \longrightarrow Time@T, B@T'', D@(T+1) \quad (6b)$$

$$Time@T, B@T', C@T'' \mid \{T' \leq T, T'' \leq T\} \longrightarrow Time@T, A@T, B@(T+1) \quad (6c)$$

The following trace from $\mathcal{S}_0$ uses the l.t.s. and is not compliant:

$$Time@0, A@0, B@0 \longrightarrow_{(6b)} Time@0, B@0, D@1 .$$

Hence, $\mathcal{T}$ does not satisfy the S property.

To show that $\mathcal{T}$ satisfies the L property, we first show that $\mathcal{T}$ satisfies the Z property. The following trace from $\mathcal{S}_0$ is a compliant infinite time trace that uses the l.t.s.:

$$Time@0, A@0, B@0 \longrightarrow_{(6a)} Time@0, B@0, C@1 \longrightarrow_{Tick}$$
$$\longrightarrow_{Tick} Time@1, B@0, C@1 \longrightarrow_{(6c)} Time@1, A@1, B@2 \longrightarrow_{Tick}$$
$$\longrightarrow_{Tick} Time@2, A@1, B@2 \longrightarrow_{(6a)} Time@2, B@2, C@3 \longrightarrow_{Tick} \cdots$$

Next, assume $\mathcal{P}$ is a compliant trace from $\mathcal{S}_0$ to some $\mathcal{S}_1$ that uses the l.t.s. Then $\mathcal{P}$ does not contain rule (6b), which always results in a critical configuration. Hence, only rules (6a), (6c) and $Tick$ are used in $\mathcal{P}$, so $\mathcal{S}_1$ is either $\{\,Time@t,\ A@t',\ B@t''\,\}$ or $\{\,Time@t,\ B@t',\ C@t''\,\}$. Using only the rules (6a), (6c) and $Tick$, the trace $\mathcal{P}$ can be extended to a compliant infinite time trace that uses the l.t.s. Hence, $\mathcal{T}$ satisfies the L property. $\square$

However, the above does not hold for general MSR systems, $i.e.$, MSR systems that satisfy the S property do not necessarily satisfy the L property.

Proposition 6. *Let $\mathcal{T}$ be a timed MSR that uses the l.t.s., $\mathcal{S}_0$ an initial configuration and $\mathcal{CS}$ a critical configuration specification.*
   If $\mathcal{T}$ satisfies the S property, it may not satisfy the L property.
   If $\mathcal{T}$ satisfies the L property, it may not satisfy the S property.

Proof. Let $\mathcal{T}'$, $\mathcal{S}_0'$ and $\mathcal{CS}'$ be as specified in the proof of Proposition 3. Recall that $\mathcal{T}'$ does not satisfy the L property.
   The system $\mathcal{T}'$ satisfies the S property. Namely, there are only two infinite traces from $\mathcal{S}_0'$ that use the l.t.s., traces (4) and (5) specified in the proof of Proposition 3. However, trace (5) is not an infinite time trace, so there is only one infinite time trace from $\mathcal{S}_0'$ that uses the l.t.s., trace (4). Therefore, since trace (4) is compliant, $\mathcal{T}'$ satisfies the S property.
   By Proposition 5 there is a PTS, and therefore an MSR, that satisfies the L property but does not satisfy the S property. $\square$

Next, we show how the V property relates to the Z property.

Proposition 7. *Let $\mathcal{T}$ be a timed MSR that uses the l.t.s., $\mathcal{S}_0$ an initial configuration, and $\mathcal{CS}$ a critical configuration specification.*
   If $\mathcal{T}$ satisfies the V property, then $\mathcal{T}$ satisfies the Z property.
   A system $\mathcal{T}$ that satisfies the Z property may not satisfy the V property.

Proof. Assume $\mathcal{T}$ satisfies the V property. Then, $\mathcal{T}$ satisfies the Z property by definition.
   We prove the other statement by providing an example of a PTS that satisfies the Z property, but does not satisfy the V property. Let $\mathcal{S}_0'' = \{Time@0, A@0\}$, $\mathcal{CS}'' = \{\,\langle\{D@T\}, \emptyset\,\rangle\}$ and let PTS $\mathcal{T}''$ contain only the following instantaneous rules:

$$Time@T,\ A@T' \mid \{T' \leq T\} \ \longrightarrow \ Time@T,\ B@(T+1) \tag{7a}$$

$$Time@T,\ A@T' \mid \{T' \leq T\} \ \longrightarrow \ Time@T,\ C@(T+1) \tag{7b}$$

$$Time@T,\ B@T' \mid \{T' \leq T\} \ \longrightarrow \ Time@T,\ A@(T+1) \tag{7c}$$

$$Time@T,\ C@T' \mid \{T' \leq T\} \ \longrightarrow \ Time@T,\ D@(T+1) \tag{7d}$$

The following trace, which uses the l.t.s., shows the Z property of $\mathcal{T}''$:

$$Time@0,\ A@0 \ \longrightarrow_{(7a)} \ Time@0,\ B@1 \ \longrightarrow_{Tick} \ Time@1,\ B@1 \ \longrightarrow_{(7c)}$$
$$Time@1,\ A@2 \ \longrightarrow_{Tick} \ Time@2,\ A@2 \ \longrightarrow_{(7a)} \ Time@2,\ B@3 \ \longrightarrow_{Tick} \ \cdots$$

The configuration $\widetilde{S} = \{Time@0, C@1\}$ is reachable from S_0'' by a compliant trace that uses the l.t.s.: $Time@0, A@0 \longrightarrow_{(7b)} Time@0, C@1$. $\widetilde{S}$ is a point-of-no-return as rule (7d) is the only instantaneous rule that can be applied after a $Tick$, so all infinite traces from $\widetilde{S}$ that use the l.t.s. contain the critical configuration $\{Time@1, D@2\}$.

Since $\widetilde{S}$ is a point-of-no-return, $\mathcal{T}''$ does not satisfy the V property.   □

Using transitivity of the subset relation, we can infer relations among all our properties for both PTSes and timed MSR systems in general. We summarize our results in the following corollaries.

Corollary 1. *Let* $_{reali}Z_{ability}^{MSR}$, $_{re}L_{iability}^{MSR}$, $_{reco}V_{erability}^{MSR}$ *and* $S_{urvivability}^{MSR}$ *be the classes of timed MSR systems satisfying the* Z, L, V *and* S *properties, respectively, w.r.t. the l.t.s. Then, the following relations hold:*

$$S_{urvivability}^{MSR} \neq {}_{re}L_{iability}^{MSR} \subset {}_{reco}V_{erability}^{MSR} \subset {}_{reali}Z_{ability}^{MSR}$$

Proof. The statement follows directly from the Propositions 6, 3, and 7.   □

Corollary 2. *Let* $_{reali}Z_{ability}^{PTS}$, $_{re}L_{iability}^{PTS}$, $_{reco}V_{erability}^{PTS}$ *and* $S_{urvivability}^{PTS}$ *be the classes of PTSes satisfying the* Z, L, V *and* S *properties, respectively, w.r.t. the l.t.s. Then the following proper subset relations hold:*

$$S_{urvivability}^{PTS} \subset {}_{re}L_{iability}^{PTS} = {}_{reco}V_{erability}^{PTS} \subset {}_{reali}Z_{ability}^{PTS}$$

Proof. The statement follows directly from the Propositions 5 and 4, and the proof of proposition 7.   □

Corollary 3. *Let* $_{reali}nZ_{ability}^{PTS}$, $_{re}nL_{iability}^{PTS}$ *and* $nS_{urvivability}^{PTS}$ *be the classes of PTSes satisfying the* n-Z, n-L *and* n-S *properties, respectively, w.r.t. the l.t.s. Then, the following proper subset relations hold:*

$$nS_{urvivability}^{PTS} \subset {}_{re}nL_{iability}^{PTS} \subset {}_{reali}nZ_{ability}^{PTS}.$$

Proof. Let a PTS $\mathcal{T}$ satisfy the n-S property. We check that $\mathcal{T}$ satisfies the n-L property. Let $\mathcal{S}$ be a configuration that is reachable from $\mathcal{S}_0$ on a compliant trace $\mathcal{P}$ that uses the l.t.s. and has at most n instances of the $Tick$ rule. Since $\mathcal{T}$ is a PTS, only a bounded number of instantaneous rules can be applied before a $Tick$ rule appears in a trace that uses the l.t.s. (Proposition 1). Hence, the trace $\mathcal{P}$ can be extended to a compliant trace $\mathcal{P}'$ that contains exactly n instances of the $Tick$ rule and uses the l.t.s. Since $\mathcal{T}$ satisfies the n-S property, $\mathcal{P}'$ is compliant. Consequently, $\mathcal{T}$ satisfies the n-L property.

Now, let $\mathcal{T}$ satisfy the n-L property. Then, the trivial trace of length 1 from $\mathcal{S}_0$ (containing only $\mathcal{S}_0$) can be extended to a compliant trace $\mathcal{P}'$ that contains exactly n instances of the $Tick$ rule and uses the l.t.s. Hence, $\mathcal{T}$ satisfies the n-Z property.

To show that the inclusions are proper, we give examples of PTSes that satisfy one, but not the other property. The PTS given in the proof of Proposition 7 is an example of a system that satisfies the n-Z property, $\forall n > 0$, which does not satisfy even the 1-S property. Similarly, the PTS given in the proof of Proposition 5 satisfies the n-L property, $\forall n > 0$, but it does not even satisfy the 1-S property. □

5 Complexity Results for PTSes

In this section we investigate the complexity of the verification problems defined in Sect. 3.3 for PTSes. Recall that the L and V properties for PTSes coincide.

5.1 PSPACE-Completeness of Verification Problems for PTSes

For the Z problem and the S problem, PSPACE-completeness for PTSes was proved in [14,16]. Here we show PSPACE-completeness of the L problem for PTSes, that is for the problem of deciding whether a given PTS satisfies the L property.

Let Σ be a finite alphabet, $\mathcal{T}$ a PTS, $\mathcal{S}_0$ an initial configuration, m the number of facts in $\mathcal{S}_0$, $\mathcal{CS}$ a critical configuration specification, k an upper-bound on the size of the facts, and D_{max} an upper-bound on the numerical values in $\mathcal{S}_0, \mathcal{T}$, and $\mathcal{CS}$. Let the functions $\mathcal{N}, \mathcal{X}$, and $\mathcal{L}$ run in Turing space bounded by a polynomial in $m, k, \log_2(D_{max})$ and return 1, respectively, when a rule in $\mathcal{T}$ is applicable to a given δ-representation, when a δ-representation is critical w.r.t. $\mathcal{CS}$, and when a $Tick$ rule should be applied to the given δ-representation using the l.t.s.

Proposition 8 (L problem for PTSes is PSPACE hard).
The L problem for PTSes that use the l.t.s. is PSPACE-hard.

Proof. The Z problem is an instance of the problem of checking whether a configuration is not a point-of-no-return. Recall that a system satisfies the Z property if there exists a compliant infinite time trace $\mathcal{P}$ from the initial configuration in which global time tends to infinity. Since $\mathcal{T}$ is progressing, we obtain the condition on time (time tends to infinity) from Proposition 2. Indeed, a system satisfies the Z property if and only if the initial configuration is not a point-of-no-return. Since PSPACE and co-PSPACE are the same complexity class and the Z property is PSPACE-hard, the problem of determining whether a configuration is a point-of-no-return is PSPACE-hard.

Since the L property problem comprises checking whether a configuration is a point-of-no-return, it is PSPACE-hard. □

Proposition 9 (L problem for PTSes is in PSPACE).
For a PTS $\mathcal{T}$ assume $\Sigma, \mathcal{S}_0, m, \mathcal{CS}, k, D_{max}, \mathcal{N}, \mathcal{X}$, and $\mathcal{L}$ as described above.
There is an algorithm that, given an initial configuration $\mathcal{S}_0$, decides whether $\mathcal{T}$ satisfies the L property with respect to the l.t.s., $\mathcal{CS}$, and $\mathcal{S}_0$ and the algorithm runs in a space bounded by a polynomial in m, k and $\log_2(D_{max})$.

Proof. We first propose an algorithm that, for a fixed system $\mathcal{T}$ and a fixed critical configuration specification $\mathcal{CS}$, checks whether some δ-representation corresponds to a configuration that is a point-of-no-return w.r.t. $\mathcal{T}$ and $\mathcal{CS}$.

Let $REAL$ denote the Z problem PSPACE algorithm over δ-representations (see proof of [16, Theorem 1] for details). When given δ-representation $\mathcal{W}$, as input, the algorithm $REAL(\mathcal{W})$ returns ACCEPT if and only if there is an infinite time trace of $\mathcal{T}$ that starts with $\mathcal{W}$, uses the l.t.s., and is compliant w.r.t. $\mathcal{CS}$, and it runs in polynomial space w.r.t. the given parameters, m, k and $log_2(D_{max})$. Since PSPACE and co-PSPACE are the same complexity class, we switch the ACCEPT and FAIL and obtain a deterministic algorithm $NOTREAL$ that runs in polynomial space w.r.t. m, k and $log_2(D_{max})$. $NOTREAL(\mathcal{W})$ accepts if and only if there is no compliant infinite time trace from $\mathcal{W}$ that uses the l.t.s. Then, using $NOTREAL$ we construct the algorithm PON that checks whether the given δ-representation $\mathcal{W}$ corresponds to a point-of-no-return. Let PON be the following algorithm, which takes a δ-representation $\mathcal{W}$ as input:

1. If $\mathcal{X}(W) = 1$, *i.e.*, if W represents a critical configuration, then return FAIL, otherwise continue;
2. If $NOTREAL(W) = 1$, *i.e.*, if W represents a point-of-no-return, then return ACCEPT, otherwise return FAIL.

When given δ-representation $\mathcal{W}$, as input, the algorithm $PON(\mathcal{W})$ accepts if and only if $\mathcal{W}$ is a δ-representation of a point-of-no-return w.r.t. $\mathcal{T}$ and $\mathcal{CS}$. Since $\mathcal{X}$, and $NOTREAL$ run in the polynomial space w.r.t. m, k and $log_2(D_{max})$, PON is a deterministic algorithm that also runs in such a polynomial space.

Next, we check that for any configuration $\mathcal{S}$ reachable from $\mathcal{S}_0$ using the l.t.s., there is a compliant infinite time trace from $\mathcal{S}$, *i.e.*, that $\mathcal{S}$ is not a point-of-no-return. The following algorithm accepts when no point-of-no-return is reachable from $\mathcal{S}_0$ in $\mathcal{T}$ on a compliant trace that uses the l.t.s., and fails otherwise. It begins with $i = 0$ and W_0 set to be the δ-representation of $\mathcal{S}_0$, and iterates the following sequence of operations:

1. If W_i represents a critical configuration, *i.e.*, if $\mathcal{X}(W_i) = 1$, then return FAIL, otherwise continue;
2. If W_i represents a point-of-no-return, *i.e.*, if $PON(W_i) = 1$, then return FAIL, otherwise continue;
3. If $i > L_\Sigma(m, k, D_{max})$, then ACCEPT; else continue;
4. If $\mathcal{L}(W_i) = 1$, then replace W_i by W_{i+1} obtained from W_i by applying the *Tick* rule; Otherwise non-deterministically guess an instantaneous rule, r, from $\mathcal{T}$ applicable to W_i, *i.e.*, such a rule r that $\mathcal{N}(r, W_i) = 1$. If so, replace W_i with the δ-representation W_{i+1} resulting from applying the rule r to the δ-representation W_i. Otherwise, continue;
5. Set $i = i + 1$.

Since PON, $\mathcal{N}, \mathcal{X}$, and $\mathcal{L}$ run in Turing space bounded by a polynomial in m, k and $log_2(D_{max})$, the above algorithm runs in deterministic polynomial space. □

The following result follows directly from Propositions 8 and 9.

Theorem 1. *For a PTS $\mathcal{T}$ assume $\Sigma, \mathcal{S}_0, m, \mathcal{CS}, k, D_{max}, \mathcal{N}, \mathcal{X},$ and $\mathcal{L}$ as described at the beginning of Sect. 5.1. The L problem for PTSes that use the l.t.s. is PSPACE-complete.*

Remark 3. When considering the time bounded versions of the Z , L and S problems we use auxiliary functions with configurations as their arguments. For simplicity, we still use the same notation, $\mathcal{N}, \mathcal{X},$ and $\mathcal{L}$, as types of arguments are clear from the context. We will assume that $\mathcal{N}$, $\mathcal{X}$, and $\mathcal{L}$ run in time bounded by a polynomial in m and k, and return 1, respectively, when a rule in $\mathcal{T}$ is applicable to a given configuration, when a configuration is critical with respect to $\mathcal{CS}$, and when a $Tick$ rule should be applied to the given configuration using the l.t.s. Note that for the examples we considered, one can construct such functions.

Complexity results for the time bounded versions of the Z and S problems were also obtained in [14]. It was shown that the n-Z problem is NP-complete and that the n-S problem is in the Δ_2^p class of the polynomial hierarchy, a subclass of PSPACE. The technical report accompanying this paper [15] also discusses the complexity result for the time bounded version of the L problem.

Theorem 2. *For a PTS $\mathcal{T}$ assume $\Sigma, \mathcal{S}_0, m, \mathcal{CS}, k, D_{max}, \mathcal{N}, \mathcal{X},$ and $\mathcal{L}$ as described at the beginning of Sect. 5.1.*

The n-Z problem for $\mathcal{T}$ w.r.t. the l.t.s., $\mathcal{CS}$, and $\mathcal{S}_0$ is NP-complete with input $\mathcal{S}_0$. [14]

The n-S problem for $\mathcal{T}$ w.r.t. the l.t.s., $\mathcal{CS}$, and $\mathcal{S}_0$ is both NP-hard and coNP-hard with input $\mathcal{S}_0$. Furthermore, the n-S problem for $\mathcal{T}$ w.r.t. the l.t.s., $\mathcal{CS}$, and $\mathcal{S}_0$ is in the class Δ_2^p of the polynomial hierarchy (P^{NP}) with input $\mathcal{S}_0$. [14]

The n-L problem for $\mathcal{T}$ w.r.t. the l.t.s., $\mathcal{CS}$ and $\mathcal{S}_0$ is in the class Π_2^p of the polynomial hierarchy with input the $\mathcal{S}_0$.

The proof of Theorem 2 can be found in [15]. The upper bound results rely on Proposition 1, which provides bounds on the length of traces with a bounded number of instances of $Tick$ rules for PTSes. The complexity lower bounds are obtained by encoding the 3-SAT problem. For details see [15, Section 6.2].

6   Related and Future Work

In this paper, we study a subclass of timed MSR systems called progressing timed systems introduced in [14], which is defined by imposing syntactic restrictions on MSR rules.

We discuss two verification problems, namely realizability and survivability, introduced in [14], and also consider two new properties, reliability and recoverability, defined over infinite traces. We show that these problems are PSPACE-complete for progressing timed systems, and when we additionally impose a bound on time, the realizability becomes NP-complete, the survivability is in the class Δ_2^p of the polynomial hierarchy, the reliability is in the class Π_2^p of the polynomial hierarchy, and the survivability is both NP-hard and coNP-hard. The lower bound for the n-time reliability is left for future work.

These problems involve quantitative temporal properties of timed systems and explicit time constraints, and to the best of our knowledge have not been studied in the rewriting literature. We review some of the formalisms for specifying quantitative temporal properties of timed systems such as timed automata, temporal logic, and rewriting.

Our progressing condition is related to the finite-variability assumption used in the temporal logic and timed automata literature [2,3,11,22,23], requiring that in any bounded interval of time, there can be only finitely many observable events or state changes. Similarly, progressing systems have the property that only a finite number of instantaneous rules can be applied in any bounded interval of time (Proposition 1). Such a property seems to be necessary for the decidability of many temporal verification problems.

The work [1,6] classifies (sets of) traces as safety, liveness, or properties that can be reduced to subproblems of safety and liveness. Following this terminology, properties that relate to our verification problems over infinite traces contain alternation of quantifiers, *i.e.*, involve both elements of safety and elements of liveness. We do not see how this can be expressed precisely in terms of [1,6]. We leave this investigation to future work.

As discussed in detail in the Related Work section of our previous work [19], there are some important differences between our timed MSR model and timed automata [2,3], both in terms of expressive power and decidability proofs. For example, a description of a timed MSR system uses first order formulas with variables, whereas timed automata can only refer to transitions on ground states. That is, timed MSR is essentially a first-order language, while timed automata are propositional. Replacing a first order description of timed MSR by all its instantiations, would lead to an exponential explosion. Furthermore, in contrast with the timed automata paradigm, in timed MSR we can naturally manipulate facts both in the past, in the future, as well as in the present.

The temporal logic literature has proposed many languages for the specification and verification of timed systems. Many temporal logics contain quantitative temporal operators, *e.g.*, [22,23], including time-constrained temporal operators. Metric Temporal Logic (MTL) [21] involves (bounded or unbounded) timing constraints on temporal operators similar to our time constraints. The growing literature on MTL explores the expressivity and decidability of fragments of such temporal logics [26]. However, the temporal logic literature does not discuss notions similar to *e.g.*, realizability or survivability. In addition to that, an important feature of our model is that the specifications are executable. As we have shown through experiments in [14], it is feasible to analyze fairly large progressing systems using the rewriting logic tool Maude [7].

Real-Time Maude [25] is a tool for simulation and analysis of real-time systems. Rewrite rules are partitioned into instantaneous rules and rules that advance time, with instantaneous rules taking priority. Our the lazy time sampling is inspired by such management of time in traces. Time advance rules in

Real-Time Maude may place a bound on the amount of time to advance, but do not determine a specific amount, thus, allowing the system to be continuously observed. Time sampling strategies are used to implement search and model-checking analysis. Ölveczky and Messeguer [24] investigate conditions under which the maximal time sampling strategy used in Real-Time Maude is complete. One of the required conditions is tick-stabilizing, which is similar to progressing and finite variability assumption in that one assumes a bound on the number of actions that can be applied in a finite time.

Cardenas *et al.* [4] discuss possible verification problems of cyber-physical systems in the presence of malicious intruders. They discuss surviving attacks, such as denial of service attacks on control mechanisms of devices. We believe that our progressing timed systems can be used to define meaningful intruder models and formalize the corresponding survivability notions. This may lead to automated analysis of such systems similar to the successful use of the Dolev-Yao intruder model [8] for protocol security verification. Given the results of this paper, the decidability of any security problem would most likely involve a progressing timed intruder model. We intend to investigate the security aspects of this work in the future. For example, the introduction of timed intruder models [12], and resource-bounded intruder models [28] may enable verification of whether intruders can cause PTSes to reach hazardous situations, *e.g.*, harm to people or crashes.

We believe that some of our properties, in particular survivability, can be interpreted using game theory. We find that our model has some features that are better suited for applications relating to TSDSes, in particular explicit time, quantitative time conditions and nonces. It would be interesting to investigate connections and differences between our rewriting approach to these problems and the game theory approach.

Finally, we have already done some preliminary research into ways to extend this work to dense time domains. We expect our results to hold for dense time domains as well, given our previous work [17,28,29]. There, instead of the $Tick$ rule (Eq. 1), we assume a $Tick$ rule of the form $Time@T \longrightarrow Time@(T + \varepsilon)$, where ε can be instantiated by any positive real number. The assumption of dense time is a challenge that considerably increases the machinery needed to prove our results, but we are confident of finding ways to combine the results of [17] with those presented in this paper. Similarly, for our future work, we intend to investigate extensions of our models with probabilities.

Acknowledgments. We thank the anonymous reviewers for their valuable comments and careful remarks, which have significantly improved the presentation of the paper. Ban Kirigin is supported in part by the Croatian Science Foundation under the project UIP-05-2017-9219. The work of Max Kanovich was partially supported by EPSRC Programme Grant EP/R006865/1: "Interface Reasoning for Interacting Systems (IRIS)." Nigam is partially supported by NRL grant N0017317-1-G002, and CNPq grant 303909/2018-8. Scedrov was partially supported by the U. S. Office of Naval Research under award numbers N00014-20-1-2635 and N00014-18-1-2618. Talcott was partially supported by the U. S. Office of Naval Research under award numbers N00014-15-1-2202 and N00014-20-1-2644, and NRL grant N0017317-1-G002.

References

1. Alpern, B., Schneider, F.B.: Recognizing safety and liveness. Distrib. Comput. **2**(3), 117–126 (1987)
2. Alur, R., Henzinger, T.A.: Logics and models of real time: a survey. In: Real-Time: Theory in Practice, REX Workshop, pp. 74–106 (1991)
3. Alur, R., Madhusudan, P.: Decision problems for timed automata: a survey. In: SFM, pp. 1–24 (2004)
4. Cárdenas, A.A., Amin, S., Sastry, S.: Secure control: Towards survivable cyber-physical systems. In: ICDCS, pp. 495–500 (2008)
5. Cervesato, I., Durgin, N.A., Lincoln, P., Mitchell, J.C., Scedrov, A.: A meta-notation for protocol analysis. In: CSFW, pp. 55–69 (1999)
6. Clarkson, M.R., Schneider, F.B.: Hyperproperties. J. Comput. Secur. **18**(6), 1157–1210 (2010)
7. Clavel, M., et al.: All About Maude - A High-Performance Logical Framework. LNCS, vol. 4350. Springer, Heidelberg (2007). https://doi.org/10.1007/978-3-540-71999-1
8. Dolev, D., Yao, A.: On the security of public key protocols. IEEE Trans. Inf. Theor. **29**(2), 198–208 (1983)
9. Durgin, N.A., Lincoln, P., Mitchell, J.C., Scedrov, A.: Multiset rewriting and the complexity of bounded security protocols. J. Comput. Secur. **12**(2), 247–311 (2004)
10. Enderton, H.B.: A Mathematical Introduction to Logic. Academic Press, Cambridge (1972)
11. Faella, M., Legay, A., Stoelinga, M.: Model checking quantitative linear time logic. Electr. Notes Theor. Comput. Sci. **220**(3), 61–77 (2008)
12. Kanovich, M., Ban Kirigin, T., Nigam, V., Scedrov, A.: Bounded memory Dolev-Yao adversaries in collaborative systems. Inf. Comput. **238**, 233–261 (2014)
13. Kanovich, M., Ban Kirigin, T., Nigam, V., Scedrov, A., Talcott, C.: Discrete vs. dense times in the analysis of cyber-physical security protocols. In: Principles of Security and Trust - 4th International Conference, POST, pp. 259–279 (2015)
14. Kanovich, M., Ban Kirigin, T., Nigam, V., Scedrov, A., Talcott, C.: Timed multiset rewriting and the verification of time-sensitive distributed systems. In: 14th International Conference on Formal Modeling and Analysis of Timed Systems (FORMATS) (2016)
15. Kanovich, M., Ban Kirigin, T., Nigam, V., Scedrov, A., Talcott, C.: On the complexity of verification of time-sensitive distributed systems: Technical report (2021). http://arxiv.org/abs/2105.03531
16. Kanovich, M., Ban Kirigin, T., Nigam, V., Scedrov, A., Talcott, C.L.: Timed multiset rewriting and the verification of time-sensitive distributed systems: Technical report (2016). http://arxiv.org/abs/1606.07886
17. Kanovich, M., Ban Kirigin, T., Nigam, V., Scedrov, A., Talcott, C.L.: Time, computational complexity, and probability in the analysis of distance-bounding protocols. J. Comput. Secur. **25**(6), 585–630 (2017)
18. Kanovich, M., Ban Kirigin, T., Nigam, V., Scedrov, A., Talcott, C., Perovic, R.: A rewriting framework for activities subject to regulations. In: RTA, pp. 305–322 (2012)
19. Kanovich, M., Kirigin, T.B., Nigam, V., Scedrov, A., Talcott, C., Perovic, R.: A rewriting framework and logic for activities subject to regulations. Math. Struct. Comput. Sci. **27**(3), 332–375 (2017)

20. Kanovich, M., Rowe, P., Scedrov, A.: Collaborative planning with confidentiality. J. Autom. Reasoning **46**(3–4), 389–421 (2011)
21. Koymans, R.: Specifying real-time properties with metric temporal logic. Real-time Syst. **2**(4), 255–299 (1990)
22. Laroussinie, F., Schnoebelen, P., Turuani, M.: On the expressivity and complexity of quantitative branching-time temporal logics. Theor. Comput. Sci. **297**(1–3), 297–315 (2003)
23. Lutz, C., Walther, D., Wolter, F.: Quantitative temporal logics: PSPACE and below. In: TIME, pp. 138–146 (2005)
24. Ölveczky, P.C., Meseguer, J.: Abstraction and completeness for real-time maude. Electr. Notes Theor. Comput. Sci. **176**(4), 5–27 (2007)
25. Ölveczky, P.C., Meseguer, J.: The real-time maude tool. In: Ramakrishnan, C.R., Rehof, J. (eds.) TACAS 2008. LNCS, vol. 4963, pp. 332–336. Springer, Heidelberg (2008). https://doi.org/10.1007/978-3-540-78800-3_23
26. Ouaknine, J., Worrell, J.: Safety metric temporal logic is fully decidable. In: Hermanns, H., Palsberg, J. (eds.) TACAS 2006. LNCS, vol. 3920, pp. 411–425. Springer, Heidelberg (2006). https://doi.org/10.1007/11691372_27
27. Papadimitriou, C.H.: Computational Complexity. Academic Internet Publishers, Cambridge (2007)
28. Urquiza, A., et al.: Resource and timing aspects of security protocols. J. Comput. Secur. **29**(3), 299–340 (2021)
29. Urquiza, A., et al.: Resource-bounded intruders in denial of service attacks. In: 2019 IEEE 32nd Computer Security Foundations Symposium (CSF), pp. 382–396. IEEE (2019)

Adapting Constraint Solving to Automatically Analyze UPI Protocols

Sreekanth Malladi[1] and Jonathan Millen[2(✉)] (iD)

[1] CMR Institute of Technology, Bengaluru, India
sreekanth.m@cmrit.ac.in
[2] Newburyport, MA, USA
j.millen@computer.org

Abstract. UPI (Unified Payment Interface) is a system in India for electronic payment using mobile phones. Here, a group of UPI servers act as intermediaries between customers, merchants and banks. Customers can register themselves to UPI servers using registration protocols and send the details of payments using payment protocols. Recently, these registration protocols were shown to have exploitable flaws using manual analysis [24]. However, automatic analysis is very much desirable, since manual inspection may not reveal all flaws in protocols, as often observed. With this motivation, we have developed and implemented a technique using the Constraint Solver tool for cryptographic protocol analysis [22] (which is based on Guttman-Thayer-Herzog's strand space framework [29]) to automatically analyze UPI protocols. In this paper, we explain the technique and illustrate our implementation.

Keywords: Cryptographic protocols · Formal methods · Constraint solving · Mobile computing · UPI · Financial security

1 Introduction

Electronic transactions in India between customers having bank accounts started with direct communication with their banks. The payer would send the details of the payee's bank account along with the payment amount to the payer's bank, which in turn communicates with the payee's bank using protocols such as RTFS, IMPS and NEFT to send the payment to be made into the payee's bank account. This is illustrated in Fig. 1.

However, in 2015, the National Payments Consortium of India (NPCI), with support from the government of India, has developed the Unified Payments Interface (UPI), which is an approach that optimizes the process of transactions by employing intermediaries between banks, customers and merchants [11,23]. Typically, both customers and merchants register themselves with UPI servers that are placed all over the country. When a customer wishes to pay a merchant, the customer sends the payment information to the nearby UPI server, which in turn forwards it to the recipient's bank. This is illustrated in Fig. 2.

© Springer Nature Switzerland AG 2021
D. Dougherty et al. (Eds.): Guttman Festschrift, LNCS 13066, pp. 276–292, 2021.
https://doi.org/10.1007/978-3-030-91631-2_15

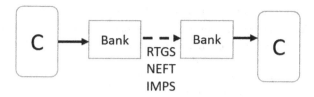

Fig. 1. Electronic transactions before UPI

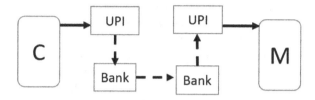

Fig. 2. Electronic transactions with UPI

This process obviates the need for the customer to enter all the details of the bank account corresponding to the merchant each time a fresh transaction is initiated. Instead, it is only necessary to include a unique UPI ID of the merchant or the recipient. Customers use a UPI-compliant app that implements the registration and payment protocols. NPCI provides a reference implementation called BHIM, but third-party implementations are also available, including Google Pay.

UPI has released two versions so far. The first version had three registration protocols. The first protocol is used under normal circumstances when the user's phone is able to send SMS (Short Message Service, text) to the server, so that the server may retrieve the user's phone number from it. The second one is used when the first protocol doesn't work because the SMS either fails to reach the server or could not be decoded properly. In that case, the user enters the phone number manually and sends it to the server. The third protocol is used when the user wishes to change the mobile device but retaining the phone number with which the UPI account has already been registered.

With the proliferation of mobile devices, such protocols are being developed ubiquitously with features that include messages sent on mobile networks via SMS and that use OTPs (One-Time Passwords). There are certain assumptions about these messages and authentication inferences that are drawn about them that weren't present in older, conventional cryptographic protocols. These have to be accounted for, in order to perform accurate analyses of modern-day protocols. The threat model also has to be modified, since the attacker now has new capabilities in these environments, such as installing malware on devices to read secrets, something not assumed in previous protocol analysis approaches over the last few decades.

We started our research with the above issues in mind and focused on formal analysis of UPI protocols. We found only one significant work reported by

Kumar et al. who analyzed UPI protocols and found an attack in the second protocol [24]. However, their analysis was informal and manual which does not give a guarantee of security even in finite models such as a limited number of simultaneously executing principals.

We could not find any published papers that discussed the application of formal and automated approaches to analyze protocols like UPI. The closest in spirit we found is by Cortier et al. in [7] who designed and formally verified a mobile payment protocol. Their protocol differs from UPI in many ways including the operational model, devices used, network assumptions etc. But most importantly, it does not involve the use of two separate channels of communication like UPI does (the cellular and data channels).

To address these issues, we have extended the constraint solving procedure for cryptographic protocol analysis by Millen and Shmatikov [22] to formally and automatically analyze UPI protocols, augmenting an approach that was previously outlined by one of us in [19]. Millen-Shmatikov's procedure uses Guttman-Thayer-Herzog's strand spaces [29] as the underlying framework to model protocols. Constraint solving can be used to analyze protocols in bounded-process scenarios, where the number of instances of each role in the protocol is specified. The **Csolver** tool, which implements the constraint-solving procedure, was used to test UPI protocols in several scenarios. We describe our approach, implementation and testing in this paper.

Our efforts are not only useful toward the security of UPI protocols, but also as a set of general guidelines to apply constraint solving to analyze any protocols used anywhere in the world on mobile networks and a general approach in which the technique may be extended for the myriad protocol variations that may be designed for secure communication in an ever-changing computing landscape.

Organization. In Sect. 2, we explain UPI protocols in detail. In Sect. 3, we describe the technique of constraint solving for cryptographic protocol analysis. In Sect. 5 we explain our modeling of UPI registration protocols with Csolver. In Sect. 6, we describe the handling of SMS messages in Csolver. In Sect. 7, we illustrate our implementation and testing of the protocols in various scenarios. We conclude with a discussion of future work.

2   Background

UPI 1.0 works by placing servers all over the country that act as intermediaries between customers, merchants and banks. Customers and merchants can register themselves with UPI using the following protocols.

The first is the default protocol, given informally in Fig. 3. A is the user, or, more accurately, the user's smartphone with a payment app installed, and B is the UPI server.

In this protocol, the customer sends her device details in the first message such as make, model etc. of the phone or device that she would be using to make transactions. She receives a registration token (a hash of the device details and

1. $A \rightarrow B$: *Device Details*
2. $B \rightarrow A$: *Registration Token (R_A)*
3. $A \rightarrow B$: R_A as SMS
4. $B \rightarrow A$: Confirmation Msg 3 Received
5. $A \rightarrow B$: Is my device registered?, R_A
6. $B \rightarrow A$: Yes your device verified
7. $A \rightarrow B$: sha(*passcode*, PhoneNumber)
8. $B \rightarrow A$: Login Token (confirms profile is set up)
9. $A \rightarrow B$: Selected Bank ID
10. $B \rightarrow A$: Bank account details

Fig. 3. UPI default protocol

a nonce) in the second message from the server, which she sends back in the third message as an SMS. The server tries to extract the phone number from the SMS and sends a confirmation in the fourth message if it was successful. In the fifth message the customer checks with the server if the device was successfully verified, to which the server responds in the sixth message. The customer then selects a passcode and sends a hash of it along with the phone number in the seventh message, which the server stores, and it responds in the eighth message with a login token to confirm that the profile has been set up in the server. The final steps 9 and 10 are where the customer selects a bank to make payments from, chosen from a list of bank accounts held by the customer in various banks (found using her phone number) and the server sends back partially masked account details of the chosen bank account. Those details are obtained from an interaction between UPI and the bank that is not explicit in the protocol.

If message 3 in the default protocol does not reach the server properly or is corrupted, then the alternate protocol I is executed, in Fig. 4, wherein a user may manually key-in the phone number.

As can be seen from the figure, the alternate protocol is similar to the default protocol until message 3. But if message 3 was not received properly, the server sends message 4 to indicate that message 3 could not be decoded. Then the user manually enters the phone number which is sent in message 5 along with the device hard binding request and the registration token. This phone number is verified by the server to be associated to the device by sending a one-time passcode OTP in message 6, which is to be returned in message 7 by the user. A careful examination of the protocol should expose the weakness in the protocol—the OTP used in message 6 is the only piece of authentication from the user to the server. If that is somehow managed to be obtained and sent back in message 7 by the attacker, the protocol's security is violated.

If a user wants to transfer to a new device, having the same phone number, then the alternate protocol II in Fig. 5 is executed.

1. $A \rightarrow B$: *Device Details*
2. $B \rightarrow A$: *Registration Token*, R_A
3. $A \rightarrow B$: R_A as SMS(*failed*)
4. $B \rightarrow A$: SendTokenandPhoneNumber
5. $A \rightarrow B$: Device hard binding request, PhNo, R_A
6. $B \rightarrow A$: Verification Status, OTP, CustID, R_A
7. $A \rightarrow B$: OTP, sha(*passcode*, PhNo)
8. $B \rightarrow A$: LoginToken
9. $A \rightarrow B$: Selected BankID
10. $B \rightarrow A$: Bank account details

Fig. 4. UPI alternate protocol I

1. $A \rightarrow B$: *Device Details*
2. $B \rightarrow A$: *Registration Token*, R_A
3. $A \rightarrow B$: R_A as SMS
4. $B \rightarrow A$: Conf Msg 3 Recd
5. $A \rightarrow B$: Device hard binding request, R_A
6. $B \rightarrow A$: Account already exists
7. $A \rightarrow B$: sha(*passcode*, PhNo)
8. $B \rightarrow A$: Existing Bank acct details

Fig. 5. UPI alternate protocol II

This protocol is the same as the default protocol until step 6, wherein the server sends a message that the account already exists if it is registered in the server. The server sends back the user's bank account information to restore the app.

There are certain features in these protocols that are unconventional. In particular, protocol messages are sent both on the Internet (using mobile data) and as SMS messages. Further, the phone number is not sent as plaintext, but is supposed to be derived from the SMS sent by the phone. A DolevYao (DY) attacker is not powerful enough to capture all the possible actions by an attacker in this environment. For instance, an OTP sent as an SMS cannot be sniffed from the data connection. These features make it hard to apply existing protocol analysis techniques directly on these protocols. In the next section, we will examine the way that we have modeled the protocols in order to analyze them with Csolver.

3 Constraint Solving

Thayer, Herzog, and Guttman pioneered the strand spaces framework [29,30]. Their formulation was the wellspring for a wealth of subsequent work on protocol security analysis. It gave rise to theoretical results [3,12–15,28] and it has also been applied and elaborated to support automated tools [9,20,22,26,27].

Constraint solving, as introduced by Millen and Shmatikov in [22], applies the strand space model to specify protocols. It is a technique for analyzing protocols in scenarios where there is a bound to the number of sessions interacting in the protocol runs. With this limitation, constraint solving was shown to be sound, complete, and terminating.

The original strand spaces framework had penetrator strands to model attacker actions on messages obtained by sniffing the network. The main innovation of the constraint solving approach was to separate the analysis into two phases: first, an enumeration of message sequences consistent with the protocol specification of legitimate parties, and the generation of a set of algebraic constraints per sequence that are solved by term reduction rules to test their realizability. The constraint solver also improved on prior approaches by allowing symmetric keys to be modeled with expressions rather just constants.

Several improvements or extensions of constraint solving have been published for use in a variety of contexts and for a variety of applications. For example:

- a more efficient solver by Corin & Etalle [5];
- to find guessing attacks on password protocols by Corin & Malladi et al. [4];
- an improved variation called "constraint differentiation" by Basin et al. [1]; and
- to analyze distance-bounding protocols in wireless networks by Malladi et al. [20].

In constraint solving, a protocol is specified as a set of roles, each of which is a *parametric strand* listing the sequence of message transmissions and receptions performed by a principal in the protocol[1]. A parametric strand can also be called a "strand schema" or a "strand template", that is, an expression which is instantiated to a *strand* once the variables representing the principal and other message data fields have been substituted.

A protocol run is a sequence of messages that can be viewed as an interleaving of protocol role instances. In particular, each message received in one role instance must have been sent in accordance with some other role instance, or by an attacker subject to general realizability constraints. The strand space model characterizes the attacker behavior with additional penetrator strands. The constraint solving model, on the other hand, characterizes attacker behavior as term replacement actions that construct new messages from previously sent messages. The rules for attacker behavior are specified as a set of reduction rules.

In a realizable protocol run, each role may be instantiated multiple times or not at all, and by the same or different principals. Boundedness means that the total number of role instances is fixed for a given realizability analysis.

---

[1] A former MITRE employee, James Williams, once commented that a protocol is like the script of a play in which the lines have been sorted by character.

4   CSolver

Csolver is a Prolog program that implements constraint solving for protocol security analysis. Its principles of operation are covered by the published constraint solving paper [22], but the details of encoding protocols, setting up scenarios, and understanding the program's output are documented only on the author's website, namely http://jonmillen.com/csolver/csolve.html. We will not attempt to explain the program usage in full here, but rather just highlight a few details to help the reader follow the modeling and testing discussion in the subsequent sections.

A protocol is a sequence of roles; a role is an expression of the form
strand($rolename, A_1, A_2, ..., $[send($M_1$), recv($M_2$),...]).

The A_i are variables that appear in the event list at the end. The identifiers send and recv correspond to + and − in strand space notation. A message M_i has the format $[S, R, C]$ where S and R are variables or constants representing the sender and receiver, and C is a term representing the content of the message. This format is not required by the strand space model or constraint solving generally, but it is needed by Csolver to generate protocol run diagrams after the analysis.

Testing the protocol requires a scenario specification indicating how many instances of each role are to be included in a protocol run. This is necessary because of the boundedness limitation of constraint solving. A test specification has the form $testname($[$S_1, S_2,...$]) :- $role1, role2$, etc. The roles on the right are specified as above, except for three differences: first, the event list is shown only as one of the variables S_i; second, roles may be partially instantiated; and third, the same role may appear more than once, with different partial instantiations and variable names. In strand space terms, a scenario specification might be described as a partial bundle schema.

A test is invoked through the Prolog command line. After the protocol and some scenario specifications are loaded, a scenario and the search function are invoked. The goal of the search is expressed by choosing symbolic parameter values in the scenario that exhibit a security violation. The search function enumerates possible strand interleavings to find a realizable protocol run satisfying the goal scenario. As explained in [22], there is a partial order search optimization that reduces the number of interleavings to be enumerated, and realizability is tested by the term reduction procedure applied to the constraint set generated from each interleaving.

Csolver output for a successful search shows the sequence of events in the protocol run, both as a simple list and also as a diagram. The appearance and interpretation of the diagram will be discussed below for the UPI test output.

5   Modeling in the Constraint Solver

In order to use the constraint solver to analyze UPI protocols, we have to abstract the protocols so that they fit the solver's vocabulary and support the expected threat environment. The effort illuminated the way existing Csolver features could be brought into play, and suggested a minor syntactic extension as well.

Two immediate problems for the encoding of UPI protocols were (1) how to abstract the benefits of the HTTPS envelope and (2) how to model SMS. In addition, in order to reproduce one of the attacks in Kumar et al. [24], the operation of a partially privileged Trojan horse, hypothesized in that paper, had to be modeled.

HTTPS commonly provides certificate-based authentication of a server and end-to-end symmetric encryption of a session. For our analysis, secure session key distribution is simply assumed, since that is handled outside of the UPI registration protocol. Authentication of a UPI server is abstracted away by treating the UPI address and phone number as well-known constants. A counterfeit UPI server might very well fool a client payment app, but it is much less likely to fool a UPI-approved bank, so it was not taken as an urgent threat to be modeled. So the HTTPS effect is modeled as a session key chosen by the client that initiates the session.

Although Malladi [19] suggested using a signature to handle the security properties of SMS, the present encoding goes further. A more complex model seemed necessary to encode the effect of the Trojan horse "Mally" in Kumar et al. [24]. Our SMS encoding is discussed in the next section.

It seems worth mentioning, in passing, that while we were considering ways in which the signature operator could be used, it was observed that it is sometimes inconvenient because it only represents an encrypted checksum, represented in Csolver by a term of the form M/pk(A). Given this checksum, the public key of A can be applied to obtain the unencrypted checksum, which should match the checksum of the original message. However, an attacker cannot analyze a checksum to recover the message M. It is useful to a legitimate receiver only if a claimed value for M is already known or received separately. The full message might be written [M,M/pk(A)], but the duplication of a long expression for M is wordy. So there is now a new concise operator $//$ such that M//A is invertible; the attacker, as well as a legitimate user, can read M from it, but only principal A can create this type of signature. For the UPI example, we did not need the new feature.

Finally, in order to focus on the most serious attacks, we condensed the protocols by eliminating inessential details in some of the messages and left out other messages entirely. We had informal arguments that nothing important was left out, but it is quite possible that some interesting attacks might rest on those details.

6   Representation of SMS

The security-relevant properties of SMS are these:

- Messages are addressed by phone number;
- The correct source phone number of a message is available to the receiver;
- Messages cannot be read or modified in transit;
- Message and service access privileges for apps at endpoints are user options.

The SMS service is modeled as a single principal **sms** in the network that forwards messages. The message-forwarding protocol role looks like this:

$$1. \quad A \rightarrow \text{sms} \; : \; |A, \textit{B-phone}, M|$$
$$2. \quad \text{sms} \rightarrow B \quad : \; |\textit{A-phone}, B, M|$$

The vertical bars around the message contents are intended to indicate that the SMS message content is protected from external access, while the actual source and destination of the messages are not. That is, the attacker can intercept SMS messages and replay them through SMS from a different phone number. However, the SMS service modifies the message content to ensure that the source phone number and the intended destination principal are included in the content of the delivered message. The actual SMS encoding includes the principal-to-phone-number pairing.

In the Csolver encoding, it was not necessary to add new syntax for message protection. Instead, we just took advantage of the fact that new function symbols can be used to construct messages within protocols. So the content of the first message above will be written as `sp(A,Bphone,M)`. Because the constraint solver has no reduction rules for new function symbols like `sp`, the attacker will be unable to analyze or construct terms with that function symbol; that is exactly the kind of protection we want.

The constraint solver allows messages to and from SMS to be redirected. Such actions correspond to interference by Trojan horse apps that have excessive SMS access privileges. Kumar et al. [24] have determined that this is possible.

The full SMS encoding is included in Appendix 8.

7   Implementation and Testing

The default registration protocol and the Alternate I version were encoded as shown in the Appendices. We did not find any new attacks, but we confirmed that the SMS model and the attack hypothesized in Kumar et al. could be exercised as expected.

The protocol defines the roles of a user A, a UPI server, and the SMS service using a variation of the strand space model originated by Thayer-Herzog-Guttman [30]. As usual for Prolog programs, identifiers beginning with capital letters are variables. A role strand is a sequence of send and receive actions, as seen by each type of principal. A test bundle is a set of role instances. Csolver, invoked by the search predicate, is supposed to merge the roles and instantiate the remaining variables into a trace that respects causality constraints. Csolver also allows an attacker to intercept messages and modify them with data available to the attacker, to implement man-in-the-middle attacks.

The default protocol in Appendix 8 has constants that abbreviate standard messages used in the UPI protocols. For example, **drr** is the device registration request, and **rc** is the registration confirmation. Messages have the form [*sender, receiver, content*]. As remarked earlier, some messages were not represented because they were not relevant to the class of attacks we were studying. The last message in the UPI role is an artificial test message reporting the final values of each variable of interest. The test was instantiated with no trouble and showed the expected registration sequence.

Symmetric encryption of a message M with the session key K is represented as $M + K$. Explicit encryption acts as a modeling abstraction here, because the applications that send and receive messages are not aware of the session key. In reality, unencrypted messages are passed to-and-from an internal API that takes care of TLS or SSL encryption. Because the legitimate protocol principals "know" K, the message content M is available to them, and the encryption serves indirectly to preserve its secrecy and session association.

The Alternate I Protocol in Appendix 8 uses the same SMS role and adds a "Mally" role to reproduce the Kumar et al. Attack 1, in which the attacker, Eve, registers herself with the legal protocol, but gives UPI the phone number of the victim, Alice. The security problem is that bank accounts are identified by the associated phone number, giving Eve access to Alice's accounts. The SMS message confirming the phone number is compromised using a Trojan horse Mally on Alice's phone. Subsequent payment activities are conducted over the Internet.

Using potentially available SMS privileges, Mally can intercept communication between Alice's payment app and the SMS service on Alice's phone. In this way Mally intercepts the SMS confirmation to Alice and sends it to Eve. The two Mally actions are these, when the OTP is sent:

```
recv([sms,A,sp(upiPh,A,OTP)]),
send([A,sms,sp(A,eph,OTP)])
```

Mally cannot prevent the SMS service from including Alice's actual source phone in the SMS message arriving at Eve's payment app. That app should expect the OTP message to come from the UPI phone, so an additional intervention is required to cause Eve's otherwise normal payment app to ignore the incorrect source phone. Kumar et al. describe how an app might claim RECEIVE_SMS and other permissions to achieve this. In our encoding of the Alternate I protocol, the action that receives the OTP has a blank in the place of the source phone to indicate the missing source phone check.

Test runs are set up by defining a Prolog predicate that accepts a bundle schema as a list of role strands. Nonces and other originated data must be symbolically instantiated for the strands that introduce them. The bounded-process restriction for Csolver means that all and only the strands listed will be realized. However, multiple strands may be included for any role. In the future, Csolver might automatically discard strands that are not needed, but presently, each listed strand must be instantiated completely in a given test.

The test run for the attack includes a user role, roleA, instantiated with e, the Eve principal. It also includes a UPI role, two SMS strands, and a Mally role. Several variables are left for Csolver to discover. The resulting trace output by Csolver is below, arranged with some comments added to clarify what happened:

```
send/recv([e,upi,dd+ke])
send([upi,e,[e,ra]+ke])
send([upi,e,rr+ke])                  % registration rejected
recv([upi,e,[e,ra]+ke])
recv([upi,e,rr+ke])
send/recv([e,upi,[ra,aph]+ke])   % e sends A's phone no.
send/recv([upi,sms,sp(upi,aph,otp)])
send/recv([sms,a,sp(upiPh,a,otp)])
send/recv([a,sms,sp(a,eph,otp)]) % Mally intercepted OTP SMS
send/recv([sms,e,sp(aph,e,otp)]) % and sent it to e's app,
send/recv([e,upi,otp+ke])        % which accepted it
send([upi,e,roleUPI(e,upi,dd,ra,aph,otp,ke)]) % report
```

Csolver allowed the registration rejection notice to be sent early as part of a search optimization that determined that it made no difference, given the Alternate I protocol.

The final test message from upi shows that the UPI server thinks that Alice's phone number aph belongs to Eve. Other test runs that omitted the Mally role, or that did not ignore the OTP source, did not yield a realizable trace, as expected.

We tried other tests on the registration protocols, including some on the Alternate II protocol, with no interesting results. The Alternate II encoding is not included here because no new techniques were needed and no attacks were found.

The Csolver diagram output for the trace is shown in Fig. 6. The arrows and vertical spacing have been edited to make the diagram fit better on the page. The central vertical line separates sent messages from received messages. Since we do not have "penetrator strands", it is necessary to show that some sent messages might not be received, and some received messages might appear out of order or might be modified or constructed by an attacker. Alterations of this kind happened not to be needed for this attack.

Csolver output diagrams always have three columns. The two outside columns indicate which legitimate principal sent or received a message. Thus, principals do not get their own exclusive columns, so labels are needed to tell which principal is using a column for a series of messages. The advantages of this are that no horizontal message line ever has to cross over a column, and the diagram never gets too wide to fit on an ordinary printed page.

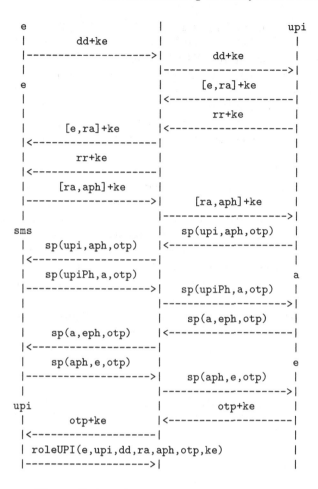

Fig. 6. Csolver diagram for alternate I attack

8 Conclusion

In this paper, we have implemented a method with which we may automatically analyze UPI registration protocols in the protocol analysis tool, the Constraint Solver (Csolver). We have analyzed the protocols in several scenarios wherein multiple participants run the protocols simultaneously (as many as four per role) and found only one known attack on the alternate protocol I of UPI 1.0. The other protocols are also vulnerable to similar attacks if SMS messages can be forged and if passcodes are learnt by attacker. We can easily demonstrate this by simply removing the sp(...) encapsulation which turns off SMS protection and adding *passcode* to the initial attacker knowledge. However, though passcodes can be learnt by attackers through overlays or malware [24], SMS messages are unforgeable using current technologies to the best of our knowledge.

As future work, our implementation could be used to analyze other similar protocols used world-wide such as UPI 2.0 protocols. Note that UPI 2.0 protocols do not actually differ much from UPI 1.0 except that the alternate protocol I of UPI 1.0 was removed from UPI 2.0 and the device details in the first message of the protocols now includes the unique IMEI number of the mobile device as well, so that at the time of the payment, the server accepts payments only received from a device that was configured with that IMEI number. Hence, future analyses should include the payment protocol steps as well, in addition to the registration protocols.

Another direction for future work is to analyze or verify the protocols amidst an unbounded number of participants playing roles of the protocol. While unbounded analysis can be performed using tools such as CPSA [8] and MaudeNPA [10], unbounded verification can be performed using tools such as ProVerif [2] and Tamarin [21]. Another approach for verification is to use completeness or decidability results such as [6,18,25], possibly modifying the protocols slightly to suit the assumptions in those results and conclude the security of the protocols. Yet another approach is to use techniques such as rank functions [16,17] which (to our knowledge) have not been provided with an automated search tool. All these approaches most likely require changes to their frameworks, techniques and implementations (if any).

Appendix 1

UPI Default Protocol for Csolver

```
% UPI Default Protocol

strand(roleA,A,UPI,DD,Ra,K,
[
   send([A,UPI,DD+K]),
   recv([UPI,A,[A,Ra]+K]),
   send([A,sms,sp(A,upiPh,Ra)]),
   recv([UPI,A,recd+K]),
   send([A,UPI,[drr,Ra]+K]),
   recv([UPI,A,[rc,Ra]+K])
   % further messages omitted
]).

strand(roleUPI,A,UPI,DD,Ra,Aph,K,
[
   recv([A,UPI,DD+K]),
   send([UPI,A,[A,Ra]+K]),
   recv([sms,UPI,sp(Aph,UPI,Ra)]),
   send([UPI,A,recd+K]),
   recv([A,UPI,[drr,Ra]+K]),
```

```
    send([UPI,A,[rc,Ra]+K]),
    send([UPI,UPI,roleUPI(A,DD,Aph)])  % report
]).
```

% SMS role as central service

```
strand(roleSMS,A,B,M,
[
  recv([A,sms,sp(A,Bph,M)]),  % sp for SMS encapsulation
  send([sms,B,sp(Aph,B,M)])   % SMS ensures phone number
]) :- phone(A,Aph),phone(B,Bph).
```

```
% correct phone numbers known to SMS locally
phone(a,aph).
phone(upi,upiPh).
phone(e,eph).
```

% To test this bundle use upi0(B),search(B).

```
upi0([Sa,Sm,Sb]) :-
    strand(roleA,a,upi,dd,Ra,k,Sa),
    strand(roleSMS,A,B,M,Sm),
    strand(roleUPI,A,UPI,DD,ra,Aph,K,Sb).
```

Appendix 2

Alternate I Protocol Attack

% Eve's repackaged BHIM role

```
strand(roleA,A,UPI,DD,Ra,Aph,OTP,K,
[
  send([A,UPI,DD+K]),
  recv([UPI,A,[A,Ra]+K]),
%  send([A,sms,sp(A,upiPh,Ra)]),  % Ra SMS not sent
  recv([UPI,A,rr+K]),             % registration rejection
  send([A,UPI,[Ra,Aph]+K]),
  recv([sms,A,sp(_,A,OTP)]),  % ignore source phone
  send([A,UPI,OTP+K])
  % further messages omitted
]).
```

% UPI role for Alternate I Protocol

```
strand(roleUPI,A,UPI,DD,Ra,Aph,OTP,K,
```

```
[
  recv([A,UPI,DD+K]),
  send([UPI,A,[A,Ra]+K]),
% recv([A,UPI,sp(Aph,upi,junk)]), % bad Ra not received
  send([UPI,A,rr+K]),
  recv([A,UPI,[Ra,Aph]+K]),
  send([UPI,sms,sp(UPI,Aph,OTP)]), % SMS
  recv([A,UPI,OTP+K]),
  send([UPI,A,roleUPI(A,UPI,DD,Ra,Aph,OTP,K)]) % report
 % further messages omitted
]).

% SMS role as central service
% Same as in default protocol

% Mally can redirect SMS messages from UPI at A

strand(roleMal,A,M,
[
  recv([sms,A,sp(upiPh,A,M)]),
  send([A,sms,sp(A,eph,M)]) % (can't fake source phone)
]).

% normal Alt 1 bundle instance

upialt10([Sa,Sm2,Sb]) :-
  strand(roleA,a,upi,dd,ra,aph,otp,ka,Sa),
  strand(roleSMS,upi,a,otp,Sm2),
  strand(roleUPI,a,upi,dd,ra,aph,otp,ka,Sb).

% Kumar et al attack test bundle

upialtK([Sa,Sm2,Sb,Sx,Sm3]) :-
  strand(roleA,e,upi,dd,Ra,Aph,OTP,ke,Sa),
% (unreceived SMS strand not included)
  strand(roleSMS,U,B,M1,Sm2), member(B,[a,e]),
  strand(roleMal,a,M,Sx),
  strand(roleSMS,a,e,M2,Sm3),
  strand(roleUPI,A,UPI,DD,ra,Aph,otp,K,Sb).
```

References

1. Basin, D., Mödersheim, S., Viganò, L.: Constraint differentiation: a new reduction technique for constraint-based analysis of security protocols. In: CCS 2003, pp. 335–344. ACM Press, New York (2003)

2. Blanchet, B.: Modeling and verifying security protocols with the applied pi calculus and proverif. In: Foundations and Trends in Privacy and Security, pp. 1 (1–2):1–135 (October 2016)
3. Cervesato, I., Durgin, N.A., Mitchell, J.C., Lincoln, P., Scedrov, A.: Relating strands and multiset rewriting for security protocol analysis. In: Proceedings of the 13th IEEE Computer Security Foundations Workshop, CSFW 2000, Cambridge, England, UK, July 3–5, 2000. pp. 35–51. IEEE Computer Society (2000). https://doi.org/10.1109/CSFW.2000.856924
4. Corin, R., Malladi, S., Alves-Foss, J., Etalle, S.: Guess what? Here is a new tool that finds some new guessing attacks. In: Workshop in the Issues of Theory of Security (WITS03), Poland, Warsaw (April 2003)
5. Corin, R., Etalle, S.: An improved constraint-based system for the verification of security protocols. In: Hermenegildo, M.V., Puebla, G. (eds.) SAS 2002. LNCS, vol. 2477, pp. 326–341. Springer, Heidelberg (2002). https://doi.org/10.1007/3-540-45789-5_24
6. Cortier, V., Delaune, S., Sundararajan, V.: A decidable class of security protocols for both reachability and equivalence properties. J. Autom. Reasoning **65**, 479–520 (2021)
7. Cortier, V., Filipiak, A., Florent, J., Gharout, S., Traoré, J.: Designing and proving an emv-compliant payment protocol for mobile devices. In: 2nd IEEE European Symposium on Security and Privacy (EuroSP 2017), pp. 467–480 (2017)
8. Doghmi, S., Guttman, J.D., Thayer, F.J.: Searching for shapes in cryptographic protocols. In: TACAS, pp. 523–537 (2007)
9. Doghmi, S., Guttman, J.D., Thayer, F.J.: Skeletons, homomorphisms, and shapes: characterizing protocol executions. Electron. Notes Theor. Comput. Sci. **173**, 85–102 (2007)
10. Escobar, S., Meadows, C., Meseguer, J.: Equational cryptographic reasoning in the Maude-NRL protocol analyzer. Electr. Notes Theor. Comput. Sci. **171**(4), 23–36 (2007)
11. Gochhwal, R.: Unified payment interface—an advancement in payment systems. Am. J. Ind. Bus. Manage. **7**, 1174–1191 (2017). https://doi.org/10.4236/ajibm.2017.710084
12. Guttman, J.D.: Cryptographic protocol composition via the authentication tests. In: de Alfaro, L. (ed.) FoSSaCS 2009. LNCS, vol. 5504, pp. 303–317. Springer, Heidelberg (2009). https://doi.org/10.1007/978-3-642-00596-1_22
13. Guttman, J.D., Thayer, F.J.: Protocol Independence through Disjoint Encryption. In: 13th IEEE Computer Security Foundations Workshop, pp. 24–34 (July 2000)
14. Heather, J.: Strand spaces and rank functions: More than distant cousins. In: Computer Security Foundations Workshop (CSFW), p. 104. IEEE Computer Society Press (2002)
15. Heather, J., Lowe, G., Schneider, S.: How to prevent type flaw attacks on security protocols. J. Comput. Secur. **11**(2), 217–244 (2003)
16. Heather, J., Schneider, S.: Towards automatic verification of security protocols on an unbounded network. In: Proceedings of 13th Computer Security Foundations Workshop, pp. 132–143. IEEE Computer Society Press (2000)
17. Heather, J., Schneider, S.: A decision procedure for the existence of a rank function. J. Comput. Secur. **13**(2), 317–344 (2005)
18. Lowe, G.: Towards a completeness result for model checking of security protocols. J. Comput. Secur. **7**(2–3), 89–146 (1999)

19. Malladi, S.: Towards automatic analysis of UPI protocols. In: (To Appear) Proceedings of the 3rd International Conference on Intelligent Communication Technologies and Virtual Mobile Networks (ICICV 2021), IEEE Computer Society (2021)
20. Malladi, S., Bruhadeshwar, B., Kothapalli, K.: Automatic analysis of distance bounding protocols. In: Proceedings of Workshop on Foundations of Computer Security. Affiliated to LICS Symposium (2009)
21. Meier, S., Schmidt, B., Cremers, C., Basin, D.: The TAMARIN Prover for the Symbolic Analysis of Security Protocols. In: Sharygina, N., Veith, H. (eds.) CAV 2013. LNCS, vol. 8044, pp. 696–701. Springer, Heidelberg (2013). https://doi.org/10.1007/978-3-642-39799-8_48
22. Millen, J., Shmatikov, V.: Constraint solving for bounded-process cryptographic protocol analysis. In: Proceedings of ACM Conference on Computer and Communication Security, pp. 166–175. ACM press (2001), Prolog implementation available online at http://jonmillen.com/csolver/csolve.html
23. NPCI: Unified Payment Interface API and Technology Specifications Version 1.0 (DRAFT). Technical Report, National Payment Corporation of India (2015). http://www.mygov.in/digidhan/pages/pdf/sbi/NPCIUnifiedPaymentInterface.pdf
24. R. Kumar, S. Kishore, H.L., Prakash, A.: Security analysis of unified payments interface and payment apps in India. In: USENIX Security Symposium (2020)
25. Ramanujam, R., Suresh, S.P.: A decidable subclass of unbounded security protocols. In: Workshop in the Issues of Theory of Security (WITS03) (2003)
26. Rowe, P.D., Guttman, J.D., Ramsdell, J.D., et al.: Assumption-based analysis of distance-bounding protocols with CPSA. In: Nigam, V. (ed.) Logic, Language, and Security. LNCS, vol. 12300, pp. 146–166. Springer, Cham (2020). https://doi.org/10.1007/978-3-030-62077-6_11
27. Song, D.X.: Athena: a new efficient automatic checker for security protocol analysis. In: Proceedings of 12th IEEE Computer Security Foundations Workshop, pp. 192–22. IEEE Computer Society Press (1999)
28. Stoller, S.D.: Brief announcement: Lower and upper bounds for attacks on authentication protocols. In: Proceedings of Eighteenth ACM Symposium on Principles of Distributed Computing (PODC) (May 1999)
29. Thayer, F.J., Herzog, J.C., Guttman, J.D.: Strand spaces: why is a security protocol correct? In: Proceedings of IEEE Symposium on Research in Security and Privacy, pp. 160–171. IEEE Computer Society Press (1998)
30. Thayer, F.J., Herzog, J.C., Guttman, J.D.: Strand spaces: proving security protocols correct. J. Comput. Secur. **7**(2,3), 191–230 (1999)

Three Branches of Accountability

Sebastian Mödersheim[1]($^{(\boxtimes)}$) and Jorge Cuellar[2]

[1] Technical University of Denmark, Lyngby, Denmark
samo@dtu.dk
[2] University of Passau, Passau, Germany
jc@sec.uni-passau.de

Abstract. Security protocols usually describe how *honest* agents behave, and one proves some security goals to hold even in the presence of an intruder who just does whatever he is capable of where cryptography alone does not provide sufficient protection, accountability can help as a deterrent for the intruder, because his actions may be detected and he could be punished. The novelty of this work is to model actually all three branches of government that are relevant here. First, instead of protocols we have a legal system that defines which actions are *legal*. Second, we have the police that may detect some crimes and collect evidence. Third, we have a justice system that evaluates evidence, can subpoena participants, and finally may convict players. The broad definition of a legal system allows us to avoid defining all protocols that honest participants may engage in. Rather we describe *players* (no matter if honest or dishonest) who *may* do anything that is legal and who *can* do anything except breaking the cryptography.

Keywords: Accountability · Formal methods · Security protocols

1 Introduction

The work of Joshua Guttman has deeply influenced the way we think about security and protocols. It is a great pleasure and inspiration to meet, discuss and work with Joshua, and we would like to thank him with this little article!

In security protocols, we often need to rely on trusted third parties, i.e., parties that will behave exactly according to protocol. An example is a keyserver who can issue public-key certificates: if this keyserver is dishonest and issues certificates to hackers for a bribe, the entire security argument of a system can break down. While for many applications we can ensure that operations are performed correctly (e.g., by some zero-knowledge proofs), there is no general *cryptographic* way to ensure honesty of a participant (even though one may see distributed ledgers as a paradigm to replace trusted third parties). Accountability we can regard as a measure to deter people from misbehaving, because this may be detected and punished.

This is especially interesting in situations where participants collaborate across organizations with a variety of protocols and distributed applications, and who have different and conflicting interests and cannot fully trust each other.

© Springer Nature Switzerland AG 2021
D. Dougherty et al. (Eds.): Guttman Festschrift, LNCS 13066, pp. 293–311, 2021.
https://doi.org/10.1007/978-3-030-91631-2_16

Accountability aims to ensure that, if a problem becomes apparent that was caused by a policy violation, then one can identify at least one participant who misbehaved and caused the given problem. Of course we must ensure fairness, i.e., that no innocent participant is punished, and that problems cannot arise when everybody behaves correctly.

Küsters, Truderung and Vogt [13] give a general framework for accountability that was in fact our starting point. They define protocols for honest and dishonest participants, i.e., one is dishonest when performing at least one of the dishonest protocols. For the open scenario described above it however gives us a *frame* problem: we do not want to have to describe all protocols that may occur in the environment, i.e., that honest participants legally can participate in. Actually, we often do not want to really describe a protocol in a classical sense at all, but rather talk about certain messages (like credentials) that have a certain meaning and can be used in various contexts.

This paper presents a novel model for formalizing and analyzing accountability with tree types of rules or processes, similar to the three branches of government. We neither formalize protocols as a set of processes nor do we have a notion of honest agents. Rather, agents are modeled basically as intruders: they may do whatever they are capable of. We model a legal system that formalizes what is legal and what is not. This legal system is actually formalizing something *similar to* a security protocol. For instance, the system may consider some keys as legally bound to particular agents and the signatures they make with them to have legal relevance. Thus a signed claim may be considered to be a *crime* (an illegal action) if it violates certain legal requirements. In this way, the legal system can indirectly define something like protocols, but without preventing agents in engaging in other activities (e.g., with keys that have no legal relevance) in their "private lives".

While the legislative branch defines which actions are legal and which are not, also the other two branches of government, executive and judicial, play a role in our approach. We model that the "police" may detect *some* crimes (collecting partial evidence) and hand it to a judge. We do not want to model here police investigations, but this is a way to model all kinds of detections of illegal behavior that is considered realistic in a given system. Note that all detections are just a possibility, i.e., crimes may go unnoticed.

One of the key ideas in the judicial system is that the judge may employ a subpoena, i.e., require an agent to present details about an action they performed. This can be for instance a server who issued a credential and who should reveal on which basis this was, because the produced credential may hide the identity of the legal owner. Both the subpoena and the conviction have to be based on the legal system however, so that no innocent agent can ever be convicted or forced to answer a subpoena that they cannot answer.

The keystone of our approach is the *perfect crime assumption* that we define precisely after introducing the three branches of government. Roughly speaking, the perfect crime assumption is the assumption that agents will engage in illegal actions only if it is risk-free for them, i.e., if they are sure that they can never be convicted for this action. Thus, we will try to design a system so that every crime bears at least a small risk of getting caught and convicted. If that is achieved, then from the perfect crime assumption follows that no agent is going to commit any crimes, and this fact we can use in security proofs of the system. We will in fact show that we can further relax this: for the security goals of a protocol some crimes may be irrelevant, and thus we do not need to ensure that there is a risk of detection for those crimes. Instead, we let us guide by what we need for the proof of the system's security.

Of course we cannot model the complexity of real-world legal systems in this article and thus restrict ourselves to the essential items that are needed to complete formal proofs. Nonetheless we believe that the formal connection between legal and technical systems that we sketch here can indeed be used in national legislation or even international treaties, or within larger organizations and consortia, where partners may not blindly trust each other, but where some basic agreements about the legal meaning of signatures can be made.

2   The Agent Model

We start off with an important difference to many standard models of protocols and accountability. It is standard to define by a *protocol* the behavior of *honest* agents, and all other behavior is summarized under the concept of the intruder who controls the network and represents all *dishonest* agents. In contrast, our model does directly describe a protocol, but rather a legal system that tells us what is *allowed* and what is not. This legal system indirectly also defines a few protocols, namely by messages that have a formal meaning in the legal system, and have to meet certain requirements, while it allows agents to engage in other communication that is not governed by the legal system. Thus, it is perfectly legal for agents to engage in all kinds of communications with each other that are not regulated by the legal system.

As a consequence, we do not need the classical distinction between honest and dishonest agents—and in fact we thus rather like to call them *players* in the following. Our model does not need to talk about honesty, because the players are simply formalized by the set of all behaviors they are cryptographically capable of, e.g. in a Dolev-Yao style model they can encrypt and decrypt any messages they know with any keys they know. Some of these behaviors may be perfectly legal even though they do not correspond to any protocol formalized in the legal system. Of course, we will later consider whether players have behaved in a legal way or not, but in the definition of the players it does not matter—with the exception of trusted third parties, i.e., where the security and accountability relies on the legal behavior of a party like a judge.

In fact, our framework allows the modeler to freely chose a particular message model (the operators, their properties, and the derivability) as well as the details of the communication infrastructure. For instance one may want to simply model a standard open network where all players can send messages and see all sent messages, or instead particular communication channels with restricted access like a channel monitored by a trusted third party or a special log-file channel where one can only append.

Definition 1. *A three-branches system consists of the following items:*

- *A set of* players Player,
  - *among them are two distinguished players p and j, representing the executive and judicial branches, respectively.*
- *A set S of* states*; the contents of such states may be freely chosen by the modeler but states must include at least the following:*
  - *For every P ∈* Player *the current* knowledge $M(P)$ *as a set of messages (or as a frame); linked to this we also assume a (state-independent) notion of derivability.*
  - *A set of players who have been convicted (found guilty).*
- *An initial state containing the initial knowledge $M_0(P)$ of every player P and where nobody is guilty.*
- *A set of* transactions $\mathcal{T}$ *that give rise to a transition relation on S; moreover, each transition is associated with a player performing the transaction.*
  - *The player j is the only one who can make a guilty verdict, i.e., no other player can modify this field.*
  - *There are several requirements on the transactions for p and j that we will introduce later.*
- *There is a legal system characterizing what actions are illegal, which messages have legal relevance in the system, and what obligations the players have; this is discussed in the next section.*

Example 1 (Running example heavy løg log (HLL)). As a running example throughout the paper we consider a credential system called HLL (the name will actually be explained in Sect. 7). It is a toy credential system with a feature that could be called "poor man's privacy": to make the usage of credentials privacy friendly, especially to hide unnecessary information from the relying party and to make several uses unlinkable, players can turn to so-called brokers who can issue a new credential based on an existing one—under the condition that the new one must only attest features that the old one does. Players may also use several brokers sequentially in credential creation if they do not trust a particular broker in terms of privacy.

We write in the following $A, B, \ldots$ for variables of type player, i.e., from set Player. Every player A has a fixed property $\phi(A)$; this can contain attributes like pre- and surname, date of birth, memberships in several groups or employment in a company. This property $\phi(A)$ contains enough information to identify A, e.g., a unique CPR number as in Scandinavian countries. To keep the example simple, A has a credential on this property signed by a universally trusted *rootCA*:

$$\mathsf{sign}(\mathsf{inv}(\mathsf{pk}(rootCA)), f_1(\mathsf{pk}(A), \phi(A), 0))$$

The message model used here is a standard Dolev-Yao style model. First, for every player A, let $\mathsf{pk}(A)$ denote the fixed long-term key of A, and for a public key PK (not necessarily a fixed long-term key), $\mathsf{inv}(PK)$ is the corresponding private key of PK. Every player A initially knows its key-pair $(\mathsf{pk}(A), \mathsf{inv}(\mathsf{pk}(A)))$ and a number of public keys of servers such as pk($rootCA$). As part of the derivation relation, it is also possible for players to create a new key pair $(PK, \text{inv}(PK))$.

The functions sign and f_1 (as well as the later introduced f_2, f_3 and h) are *public* functions: every player can apply them to known messages. The function sign represents digital signatures, and knowing sign($\text{inv}(PK), m$) one also knows m (i.e., signatures include the clear text of the signed message), and further knowing PK one can verify the signature (i.e., that it was indeed signed by the private key corresponding to PK). The function f_1 is a *format* i.e., some way to structure messages; here the f_1-message consists of three components, a public key, an attested property, and a hash value that is 0 for the initial credentials. As it is standard, formats are transparent functions: knowing $f_1(x_1, x_2, x_3)$ one can obtain the components x_1, x_2, x_3.

Let LRB be a subset of Player called the *legally recognized brokers* (who will be allowed to issue f_1-credentials, thus $rootCA \in$ LRB).

The initial knowledge of every $A \in Player$ is thus

$$M_0(A) = \{\text{pk}(X) \mid \text{pk}(X) \in \text{LRB}\} \cup \{\text{pk}(A), \text{inv}(\text{pk}(A)), \text{pk}(rootCA),$$
$$\text{sign}(\text{inv}(\text{pk}(rootCA)), f_1(\text{pk}(A), \phi(A), 0))\}$$

The states of HLL (the elements of $\mathcal{S}$), we define as consisting of the following components:

- for every player A a set $M(A)$ of messages known by A, initially $M_0(A)$,
- for every player A and a set LBK(A) of public keys that are legally bound to A (as explained in Sect. 3), initially containing only pk(A),
- and a set N of messages that have been sent on the open network and have not yet been received.

For every player A except the trusted third parties $rootCA$, p and j we define the following transaction: A can update N and $M(A)$ to be any set of messages N' and $M'(A)$ such that all messages in N' and $M'(A)$ can be derived from knowing N and $M(A)$. This allows players to receive or intercept messages, store them in their own knowledge, compute new messages from them, send messages out on the network, and actually, even "forget" messages (i.e., remove them from their knowledge).

In the following, we say that a message m is *accessible to player A*, if A can derive m from its knowledge $M(A)$ and the messages N on the network. We say a player A has *produced a signature message* $m = \text{sign}(\text{inv}(k), m_0)$, if $k \in$ LBK(A) and m is accessible to at least one other agent besides A. This complicated formulation is necessary, since A is always able to *derive* all kinds of signatures, but legally relevant is only which signatures A actually performs and makes available to others. We define transactions for p and j when we continue this example.   □

3   The Legislative Branch

In contrast to many other models, we so far have a model where players are free to do whatever they want, but the first important element is that we consider a definition of *legality*: several actions are deemed to have a special legal status, and depending on this status, some actions are deemed illegal and thus punishable. Note that it is a completely different question whether an illegal action can actually be *discovered* (and punished)—which is considered in the next sections.

This is different from the approach in [13] where everything that is not part of the protocol rules of the *honest* agents is considered dishonest, but may be tolerated. We in contrast say: everything that is not explicitly forbidden, is considered legal ("nulla poena sine lege"). Thus we allow agents a broad range of actions (e.g., using the credentials we define in HLL in all kinds of protocols) without getting into a "gray area"—as long as they do not violate any laws.

Definition 2. *The legal system is defined by a function crimes that maps from states to sets of* records, *where a record is an attribute-value type that can store all relevant information about a particular crime, especially who is the culprit and which actions are relevant to the case. Let us say A is a culprit in S if crimes(S) contains a record with A as the culprit.*

Finally, we also require that the legal system must be reasonable *in the sense that a player can only become criminal through its own actions or by not answering a subpoena.*

Note that some illegal actions may never be detected by anybody and the culprit may never be convicted for them—the goal of this approach is not to prevent all possible crimes. The legal system gives only a clear definition of what is allowed and what is not, and the justice system will be ensuring that only guilty players (who committed a crime) can be convicted.

One may wonder about the requirement of "reasonability", as this seems self-evident and maybe also irrelevant. To that end, observe that $crimes(S)$ is defined with respect to a state S and not to particular actions. A modeler may by accident specify an unreasonable *crimes* function, where the action of a player leads to a state S in which another player is the culprit. In fact we need later in our argumentation that players cannot become a culprit without having committed some illegal *action* themselves.

The legal system may specify other functions on states that define certain legal terms, e.g., that certain keys are legally bound to a particular player; these may have relevance in the definition of *crimes*. Also the definition of states may be chosen by the modeler in such a way that these definitions are made explicit for each given state: in the HHL example, we have already included in the state the set LBK of legally bound keys for each player.

The legal system may also define that an agent who performs a particular transaction is (a) forced to delete certain data after the transaction or (b) is forced to retain certain data after a transaction. In the latter case, the agent may later be subpoenaed by the judicial branch to reveal the data they were obliged to store.

Example 2 (HLL cont.). Let us actually formulate the legal system for HLL first as a set of laws, and then turn them into the function *crimes* in a second step. Our laws are:

§1 The key pair $(\mathsf{pk}(A), \mathsf{inv}(A))$ is *legally bound* to A.

§2 If a private key that is legally bound to A is known to another player B, then A is punishable.

§3 The legally recognized brokers (LBR) are given explicitly by a list of players fixed in the law.

§4 There are three legally recognized formats:

 f_1 for issuing certificates; this format has three fields, and in $f_1(PK, \phi, n)$, PK is a public key, ϕ is a property attested by the certificate, and n is a hash-value.

 f_2 for certificate requests; this format has two fields, and in $f_2(PK, \phi)$ again PK is a public key and ϕ is a property.

 f_3 for signing any other matters. (This is to allow players to use their keys for signing of messages that have nothing to do with the certificates here. For instance, one can thus use one's certificate for all kinds of private business, and f_3 distinguishes the purpose from f_1 and f_2.)

§5 If a private key is bound to player A and has been used for signing a message that is not one of the formats in §4, then A is punishable.

§6 If a private key is bound to player B and has been used for signing a message that is of format $f_1(PK, \phi, m)$, then B is punishable if any of the following conditions is violated:

 1. B is a legally recognized broker according to §3
 2. B has received and stored a certificate of the form

 $$\mathsf{sign}(\mathsf{inv}(\mathsf{pk}(C)), f_1(PK', \phi', n))$$

 where C is a legally recognized broker according to §3 and ϕ' implies ϕ.[1]
 3. B has received and stored a certificate request of the form

 $$\mathsf{sign}(\mathsf{inv}(PK'), f_2(PK, \phi))$$

 4. m is the hash of the inputs, i.e.,

 $$m = h(\ \mathsf{sign}(\mathsf{inv}(\mathsf{pk}(C)), f_1(PK', \phi', n)),\ \mathsf{sign}(\mathsf{inv}(PK'), f_2(PK, \phi))\ )\ .$$

 (The purpose of this hash value will be explained below.)
 5. Whenever a judge issues a subpoena to B concerning such a certificate, B supplies the received and stored signatures.

---

[1] In fact, for properties ϕ one must choose a language with a formal semantics, in particular formalizing implication from ϕ' to ϕ, and this implication must be efficiently decidable. An simple example could be attribute value pairs with selective disclosure and comparison of attributes, e.g. "at least 66.6 years of age".

§7 If PK is bound to player A and $\mathsf{inv}(PK)$ has been used for signing a message $f_2(PK', \phi')$, then PK' becomes legally bound to A.[2]

A few comments on the law are in order. The distribution of private keys and signatures is already a tricky notion. It is actually not forbidden that a player backs up their data (including their private key) on a remote server—provided that this data is encrypted in some way that prevents any other player from accessing it. However, in this case it is illegal to distribute the corresponding decryption key, because this enables others to obtain the private key. Our law avoids here the complications of defining precisely how one has to handle private keys and simply defines the *effect* as punishable that the private key ends up in another agent's knowledge.

This actually neglects the fact that honest players may in fact get hacked and thereby lose their private key to a hacker without any intention, and the law in this example does not require intent for the player to be guilty. Note however that HLL has no "hacking transitions" where one player gets access to another players knowledge. Our approach does not preclude a more complicated system (with hacking transitions and users being able to revoke keys) but that requires correspondingly a more complicated legal system in order to be reasonable.

As a third comment, the issuer of certificates is obliged to store the incoming messages and reveal them upon request from the judicial branch as explained below. Failure to produce the incoming messages will also be punishable.

We now define the function *crimes* based on these laws, but we have to make one adaptation of the transition system first to reflect §7. In a transition where player A produces an f_2-signature (recall that this is the case as soon as the signature is accessible), the corresponding public key in the f_2-part is added to the legally bound keys $\mathsf{LBK}(A)$.

Now $crimes(S)$ returns all of the following records, where each record is just an attribute value list containing the violated law, the culprit and any relevant other information:

- $(Law = \S2, Perp = A, Key = PK, Wit = B)$:
  if $PK \in \mathsf{LBK}(A)$ and $\mathsf{inv}(PK)$ is accessible to player $B \neq A$.
- $(Law = \S5, Perp = A, Key = PK, Wit = B)$:
  if $PK \in \mathsf{LBK}(A)$ and $\mathsf{sign}(\mathsf{inv}(PK), m)$ is accessible to player $B \neq A$ where m is not of the formats f_1, f_2, f_3.
- $(Law = \S6, Perp = A, Sig = m_0, Wit = B)$:
  if $PK_A \in \mathsf{LBK}(A)$, $m_0 = \mathsf{sign}(\mathsf{inv}(PK_A), f_1(PK, \phi, m))$ is accessible to player $B \neq A$ and either

---

[2] One could make additional clauses that define it to be illegal, if A does not know $\mathsf{inv}(PK')$, but it would put a legal requirement on A never to lose old keys (and if A is using here a key that is already legally bound to somebody else, then A is already punishable according to §2). Further one could define it as illegal if A here asks for a ϕ that is not implied by ϕ'. However, since every broker is obliged by §6 to check that, this is not necessary. In fact, one may argue that it could be counter-productive if it were illegal to ask for attestation of properties one does not have; a server could rely on the fact they are "off the hook" once a user asks for a wrong property.

- $A \notin \mathsf{LRB}$
- or A cannot derive (from $M(A)$ and N) messages of the form $m_c = \mathsf{sign}(\mathsf{inv}(\mathsf{pk}(C)), f_1(PK', \phi', n))$ and $m_r = \mathsf{sign}(\mathsf{inv}(PK'), f_2(PK, \phi))$ such that $C \in \mathsf{LRB}$, ϕ' implies ϕ, and $m = h(m_c, m_r)$

Note there is no violation for laws §1, §3, §4 and §7 as they are merely providing legal definitions for other laws. Also note that these records are just part of our model definition—what can actually be observed by any party is considered in the next section.

Finally, we show that the legal system is reasonable. Observe that for A to be guilty of a crime or be subpoenaed, another player B has to have obtained a particular message, namely a private key of which the public key is legally bound to A or a signature with such a private key. Let S be a state and A is not the culprit of any $crimes(S)$, then A cannot have leaked any of her legally bound keys. Thus, all signatures with a key legally bound to A must have indeed been produced by A. Therefore A cannot become culprit of any crime through the actions of other players. If there is a subpoena for an f_1 credential that A has issued, then by the fact that A is currently not a culprit it follows that A knows suitable input messages (see violation record for §6) and can thus answer the subpoena. Besides subpoenas, A is not obliged to send any particular messages, and can thus always send a message without any legal implications.   □

4   The Executive Branch

So far, we only have a definition of what is legal, i.e., what players *may* do, and the definition of the transition system formalizes what they *can* do. They can be discouraged from doing anything illegal, if there is a risk of being detected and punished. If the punishment is of monetary nature, aspiring criminals may compute the expected value from punishment and the risk of being caught, and weigh it against the profit they can make from their illegal actions, and thus commit only crimes that are *profitable*, i.e., where the expected value is positive for them. In order to avoid here a quantitative model, we propose a simple assumption: that the expected value is negative and thus crimes are not profitable. This means that we assume that neither the risk to get caught nor the punishment are insignificant.

To this end, the modeler shall specify one or more transactions that represent the *discovery* (or *detection*, we use as a synonym) of particular criminal offenses. This may model in an abstract way whatever can "go wrong" from the perspective of a criminal. For instance, after issuing an illegal credential in our running example, the recipient of this credential may get caught using it. This may be described rather abstractly, i.e., without modeling the details of police investigations. Also note that this is just a *possibility*: there is no guarantee that every crime is detected. However, as said before, the chance of getting caught must be non-negligible as we would otherwise would have to make a more detailed quantitative model.

The modeler has ample liberty in the design of such discovery transactions, in fact, one may even model that players can give false testimony to the police to start an investigation, but in most cases it is recommendable to focus on detecting messages that are suitable as evidence of a crime (e.g., signed messages with legally binding keys), and also only when it is realistic that this may be detected. This models that certain crimes may go undetected (even if they satisfy the specified situation), but they come with the risk of being detected. Thus being detected is simply a *reachable* state in our model.

Definition 3. *A discovery transaction is a transaction whose player is the police p, and that augments the knowledge of the judge j with a police report, i.e., a record that specifies the observations of p.*

We may also say that this *triggers* (enables) a judicial proceeding, because judge j may now be able to perform transactions that further investigate the crime, as explained in the next section. Note that one may model a dishonest police that could lie about evidence, but this has then to be appropriately reflected in the judicial process.

Example 3 (HLL cont.). Before we define the police for HLL, let us first define a *security goal* that we strive to achieve. An *attack state for HLL* is a state where a player A can derive both a credential $\mathsf{sign}(\mathsf{inv}(\mathsf{pk}(B)), f_1(PK, \phi, n))$ and the private key $\mathsf{inv}(PK)$ such that $B \in \mathsf{LRB}$ and $\phi(A)$ does not imply ϕ. This means that A knows a credential for a property she does not have and she can use this credential as she knows the private key of PK to which the credential is bound. The goal of HLL is that such a state is not reachable, but actually so far it is, because a dishonest B can just illegally issue such a credential.

However, to reach an attack state, at least one player must commit a crime: this situation cannot happen if all players perform only legal actions. (The proof of this statement will actually later follow from the final accountability proof of HLL: if the situation arises, then necessarily somebody has committed a crime they can be convicted for.)

Let us simply define the discovery transaction for this situation: it can fire in an attack state, i.e., when a player A can derive both a private key $\mathsf{inv}(PK)$ a credential $\mathsf{sign}(\mathsf{inv}(\mathsf{pk}(B)), f_1(PK, \phi, n))$ with $B \in LRB$ and $\phi(A)$ does not imply ϕ. The transition simply adds the following record to j's knowledge: $(Evid = \{\mathsf{inv}(PK), \mathsf{sign}(\mathsf{inv}(\mathsf{pk}(B)), f_1(PK, \phi, n))\}, Loc = A)$. In fact, the police may not even know the identity A and have $Loc =?$ instead; this can model the situation that an obviously fraudulent use of a credential is detected, but one could not determine the identity of A.

One may wonder if this discover rule models that the police can "examine the knowledge" of a participant, but rather it is a simple and abstract way to model the following: if B illegally gives a credential to A, then B has the risk that A might get caught using them (e.g., parents observe that their children access an gambling site for adults using a credential they obtained illegally on the Internet), or that A is a police informant. The discovery rule thus just models the risk attached to handing a usable credential illegally to another party. □

We model here an executive branch that always produces just accurate evidence of crimes. There may be situations where the evidence is potentially inaccurate (e.g., false witness testimony), not conclusive (e.g., we cannot be sure it represents a crime), or manipulated (if the police is dishonest). For the first two, the judicial process that follows must evaluate that the evidences are sufficient to convict any suspect, but the latter in general cannot be solved unless we can rely solely on unforgeable evidences.

5   The Judicial Branch

A key element of our approach is defining a process for the judicial branch, namely for the case that they get invoked by the executive branch after detecting illegal activity. This is a process that consists of various transactions that may lead to discovering more evidence and finally comes to a decision such as declaring one or more of the players guilty. It is necessary that this process obeys *in dubio pro reo* or *fairness*, i.e., we need to ensure by design that the judicial process cannot lead to the conviction of any innocent player.

Apropos *dubio*: one may wonder about the term *reasonable doubt* that we have in traditional legal courts. For instance, we have already discussed that a player may be victim of a hacker attack, so illegal signatures could exist that the player is held responsible for, without actually having done anything wrong. Vice-versa, a player who did perform illegal actions may try to avoid prosecution by claiming their private keys must have been stolen, or that somebody could have broken the cryptographic primitives. Are these reasonable doubts that should lead to acquittal of the suspect?

For this paper, the simple answer is: we define a transition system that includes everything that we expect can reasonably happen. In the HLL example, we do not have deduction rules for breaking cryptography or performing hacking attacks on other players. However, one can of course model systems with special transitions representing particular hacker attacks and the judicial branch must take this properly into account. Thus, in general a *reasonable doubt* means that the transition system can reach a state that is consistent with all the evidence gathered in the trial and where the accused player did not perform any illegal action.

The next key element of our approach is that the process of the judicial branch can include *subpoenas*: we can specify that particular players have the obligation to provide further evidence during an investigation, e.g., open log files or decrypt messages they have the key to. Failure to answer the subpoena means that the player in question is convicted as guilty. Thus fairness requires that we ensure by design that all subpoena transactions can always be answered by honest players. Said conversely, a subpoena must not require from a law-abiding player to produce documents that they actually cannot produce.

Definition 4. *The modeler can define two kinds of transactions for the judge j. First, j can convict a player A, i.e., make a transition from a state S to S'* *where A is added to the set of convicted players in S'; this requires however that there is a record R ∈ crimes(S) such that A is the culprit in R, i.e., the judge never convicts an innocent player. This requirement is called* fairness.

Second, the modeler can define special subpoena double-transitions for j and a player A chosen by j. Formally, a subpoena *is defined by a relation subp(M, m) where the query M is a set of messages and a valid answer m is a message. The* subpoena transaction *is a double-transition where*

- *the first part, performed by j, is that the judge sends M to a player A*
- *the second part, performed by A, is that A answers with an arbitrary message m that can be derived from M(A) and the network N. This answer m is just added to j's knowledge and if it does not satisfy subp(M, m) then A is directly added to the guilty set.*

We require that any such subpoena double-transition must be specified in the legal system, i.e., under which circumstances it can be raised by the judge j, what the relation subp is, and that the player A is punishable for not answering the subpoena according to subp. From the requirement that the legal system must be reasonable follows that an agent who did not commit any crime can only be subpoenaed for a message m that they indeed can produce.   □

Note that we allow A to choose any message from their knowledge, even if it does not fulfill $subp(M, m)$. This represents that A may not answer or answer in a non-meaningful way, but this would lead to A's immediate conviction. Note also that in general A may be able to lie at this point, i.e., give an answer that is not the truth but satisfies $subp(M, m)$. By simply allowing all messages (not specifying a strategy) we can leave this to a game-type definition below.

Example 4 (HLL Cont.). In the HLL example, the judicial process is started when the police has provided a report of the form

$$(Evid = \{\text{inv}(PK), \text{sign}(\text{inv}(\text{pk}(B)), f_1(PK, \phi, n))\}, Loc = A)$$

where $B \in \mathsf{LRB}$ and the entity A on which the credential and private key was found does not satisfy the property ϕ.

The case that $B = rootCA$ is handled below. For the case $B \neq rootCA$, we define now a subpoena transaction: for the credential $\text{sign}(\text{inv}(\text{pk}(B)), f_1(PK, \phi, n))$ the judge can ask the broker B to reveal the input message for issuing this credential according to §6.5. This subpoena satisfies fairness since nobody but B could have produced the credential (unless B has illegally leaked $\text{inv}(\text{pk}(B))$) and §6 obliges B to store the input credentials; thus if B has followed the law, it can produce these inputs now.

If B does not comply with the subpoena, B is considered guilty and the judicial process stops. This might be the case when B originally did not issue the credential lawfully (maybe for its own use or for selling to somebody else), or when B did so far nothing wrong, but now protects another player by not answering the subpoena. In that case, we cannot find out who that other player is, but in B we have a culprit who provably violated the law.

If B however complies with the subpoena then the investigation obtains the corresponding input credentials, i.e., a credential $\mathsf{sign}(\mathsf{inv}(\mathsf{pk}(C)), f_1(PK', \phi', n))$ and a certificate request $\mathsf{sign}(\mathsf{inv}(PK'), f_2(PK, \phi))$ where C is a legally recognized broker, ϕ' implies ϕ, and the hash m in the credential issued by B must be the hash of these two messages.

We can then just "climb up the ladder" by continuing with the subpoena of C in the same way until we either reach a broker who does not comply with the subpoena and is thus convicted, or we reach a credential from the $rootCA$. This regression with subpoenas cannot run into an infinite loop (i.e., never reaching the $rootCA$ or a non-compliant broker). This is because every credential, except the base credentials from the $rootCA$, must include a hash of a previous credential that acted as input; this gives a well-ordering on the credentials.

It is thus a necessity that this process of subpoenas in HLL will eventually terminate at an f_1 credential signed by $rootCA$, and containing the real name A_0 of its rightful owner. We then have a chain of credentials from the original credential to the one discovered by the police. From that follows that all public keys in that chain are legally bound to A_0 (§1 and §7) in particular the key PK in the discovered credential. Moreover, the property ϕ in the discovered credential is implied by $\phi(A_0)$ due to the requirement along the chain. However $\phi(A)$ does not imply ϕ (this actually triggered the investigation). Thus $A \neq A_0$ and therefore A_0 has violated §2. Thus j now convicts A_0.

Example 5. Let us consider a variant of our setup where we replace the hash-value in the f_1 format with just 0 (like in the base credentials from $rootCA$). Suppose a criminal broker $B \in \mathsf{LRB}$ generates fresh key pairs $(PK, \mathsf{inv}(PK))$ and $(PK', \mathsf{inv}(PK'))$ and the following signatures for some arbitrary property ϕ:

1. $\mathsf{sign}(\mathsf{inv}(\mathsf{pk}(B)), f_1(PK, \phi, 0))$
2. $\mathsf{sign}(\mathsf{inv}(PK), f_2(PK', \phi))$
3. $\mathsf{sign}(\mathsf{inv}(PK'), f_2(PK, \phi))$

and sends the first two of them to an honest broker C who issues

$$\mathsf{sign}(\mathsf{inv}(\mathsf{pk}(C)), f_1(PK', \phi, 0))$$

At this point, B can without danger use the "illegal" credentials or sell them: if it gets ever detected, B can point to C's credential in a subpoena. It is then clear that either B or C must have broken the law, but neither can be proved guilty due to the symmetry of the situation.

But is this truly a *perfect crime*? B can possibly make money with illegal credentials without a risk of getting caught—with one exception. At the moment when B sends the two signatures to C, a crime has happened for which the discovery transaction can fire, because B has a credential and the corresponding private key, attesting a property B actually does not have. At this moment, B has no way to answer the subpoenas and is convicted, so apparently, this crime is actually not perfect.

However, suppose ϕ is a property that B actually has. Then it is still illegal for B to issue the said credential, however our detection rule does not trigger (since B is in possession of only a credential certifying a property that B indeed has). Then, if C issues the corresponding other credential, it is risk free for B to sell the credentials and private keys on the black market to somebody who does not have property ϕ.

This attack is the reason for including the hashes in the f_1-credentials.   □

6   Security Based on Perfect Crimes

The keystone in our construction is now that we perform verification of the goals of a system under the assumption that no player performs an action that bears the risk of being punished. To define this precisely, we need to see this as a game: focusing on a particular player A we distinguish transitions that the player is performing and that others are performing.[3] Recall that in a subpoena double-transaction, the first part consists of a request from j followed by an answer from the challenged player A.

Definition 5. *For every player A we perform the following least fixedpoint computation on the state space. We label every state S red where at least one of the following holds:*

- *A is convicted in S,*
- *from S exists a non-A transition to a red state, or*
- *in a subpoena double-transition on A all answers from A in the second part lead to red states.*

We say that an A-transition that involves illegal behavior is a perfect crime *for A, if the resulting state is not labeled red. Said another way: a player A can get away with an illegal action if there is no path to a conviction given that A "plays perfectly" in subpoenas. We define the* perfect crime assumption *as the assumption that a player performs an illegal action only if it is a perfect crime.*

The important consequence of the perfect crime assumption is that no player will ever be convicted, provided that the legal system is reasonable (Definition 2) and the justice is fair (Definition 4). In an unreasonable legal system or in an unfair justice system, this does not hold in general, because a player may become a culprit (and get convicted) without having done anything, or get convicted without even being a culprit.

Example 6 (HLL example (Cont.)). As said before, the security goal of HLL is that we cannot reach an attack state which was defined as a player A knowing a credential and corresponding private key for a property they do not have, i.e., a player A knows $\mathsf{sign}(\mathsf{inv}(\mathsf{pk}(B)), f_1(PK, \phi, m))$ and $\mathsf{inv}(PK)$ while $\phi(A) \not\models \phi$ and B is an LRB.

---

[3] In general, one could model transactions that represent the behavior of more than one player performed collaboratively. This then needs to be decoupled according to the choices each player makes.

It is now easy to see that no attack state is reachable under the perfect crime assumption. Suppose an attack state S were reachable. Then from S also a discovery transition of the police is possible, triggering a judicial investigation. We have already seen that this investigation will necessarily lead to the conviction of some player A. The state S must be labeled red for A because there is a path from S to the conviction of A, and on this path A has not made A-transitions except possibly answering subpoenas. The perfect crime assumption dictates that A will answer these subpoenas to the best of her abilities: if A can answer a subpoena, she will, because everything else would be an imperfect crime. Thus the state S itself is the result of an imperfect crime of A, contradicting the perfect crime assumption.

7 Løglog

Recall that the HLL uses in all f_1-credentials the third field as a hash of the inputs to achieve well-foundedness. Actually, a slight modification can allow for a substantial improvement: we can avoid the brokers obligation to remember the input to all credentials they have issued by a self-encryption scheme as follows. Let us replace the value $h(m_1, m_2)$ (where m_1 and m_2 are the two input messages) by $\mathsf{crypt}(\mathsf{pk}(B), f_4(m_1, m_2))$ for a distinguished new format f_4 and where B is the broker issuing and crypt denotes asymmetric encryption. The full credentials would thus take the form

$$\mathsf{sign}(\mathsf{inv}(\mathsf{pk}(B)), f_1(PK, \phi, \mathsf{crypt}(\mathsf{pk}(B), f_4(m_1, m_2))))$$

This means that now every credential contains a field that represents the inputs upon which B has issued the credentials. Only B can read them (unless B has illegally given out its public key). After this modification, B does not have to remember the input messages m_1 and m_2 anymore: if B gets subpoenaed for this credential, B can simply decrypt this field and reveal m_1 and m_2 (unless B is dishonest and did not follow the encryption requirements, but that is equivalent to B simply refusing to follow the subpoena).

Since credentials now essentially ship with a small encrypted log-file that contains the parent credential, the entire ancestry of credential is present in an onion shaped log. Since the Danish word for onion is "løg" (pronounced like "loy"), we call the system Løglog.

This comes at the cost that the credentials get longer as compared to HLL, i.e., outsourcing the storage problem to the owner of the credentials. However note that this in practice reduces the risk and thus possibly the price of offering a broker service: it is costly to keep data not only secret but available for indefinite times; we reduce the amount of data from all credentials ever issued by a given server to just one private key, which is not only a much lower volume but also something static (i.e., no live connection from the data processing to the backup facility). For the user, in contrast, there is no risk attached to it: in the worst case they cannot use their credentials anymore if they lose them, but they cannot become liable. Also the size should not be excessive unless one builds long chains of credentials. The proof of security can be slightly adapted: an honest server can just decrypt its logs to reveal the input, thus preserving fairness.

Finally, we could now even require that brokers *must not* store input and output messages of credential actions: we can define it as a crime if any credentials or credential requests are derivable from the knowledge of a broker, and define an additional discovery transaction to that effect. However, this is tricky to do without making the legal system unreasonable. For instance, a broker may receive and store a message from another player that contains a certificate that the broker is not allowed to store without the broker being aware of that. One can however define brokers to be dedicated entirely to the credential issuing; such a broker can then, in an atomic transaction, fetch the input credentials from the network, perform all necessary checks and send the reply back to the network without ever storing any of these messages in its knowledge.

8   Related Work and Conclusion

The term accountability is used in a variety of fields, ranging from protocol-based approaches, over works in the field of trust and access control policies, to rather abstract and high-level concepts in usage control. Obviously, our approach belongs to the protocol area, but borrowing many ideas from the other areas.

Protocol-Based. The starting point of our work was a paper by Küsters, Truderung and Vogt [13]. It defines explicitly protocols for a given number of participants, and a subset of these protocols are for honest participants. Thus, the behavior of the dishonest participants must also be specified by sufficiently broad protocols, and an agent is called honest when they only execute an honest protocol. In contrast, our notion of legality follows a different design philosophy: players can arbitrarily interact with each other and the legal system gives only some legal boundaries. This indirectly specifies something like a protocol, but allows that players engage also in other protocols. In the running example, for instance, the players may use the credentials for instance for privacy-friendly authentication in other web service protocols (they have to just use the f_3 format when signing messages that are meant for purposes other than legal issue or request of credentials, or use keys that are not legally bound).[4] This allows us to verify security goals using accountability arguments in a very general way, i.e., independent of a fixed environment of protocols.

Further, the approaches have in common that not all illegal activities are necessarily detectable. [13] requires that illegal activities that lead to violations of the security goals must be detectable and allow for a judge to identify either one or all culprits. In contrast, our executive branch is a decoupling of that from security goals, modeling that "by chance" some crimes may be detected no matter if this is relevant for security goals or not. We also have no requirement

---

[4] Note that our legal system does not even regulate how the exchange between a player and a broker to obtain a credential is organized: this may be transmitted over a TLS channel or even clear text, either way can be done in a legal way.

that this must necessarily lead to a conviction. This is side-stepping the question whether we really need to get *all* criminals, because we use the possibility of detection as a deterrent: if the criminals are deterred enough so that violations of our security goals cannot occur, then this is sufficient.

In the judicial system we have the common similarity that systems must be fair, i.e., must not convict the innocent. The most significant differences however may be in the concept of subpoenas and the perfect crime assumption, because here we get aspects of games into the picture, namely that agents will not engage in actions that could lead to their conviction. For this reason we have also required the (to our knowledge) novel property of the legal system being reasonable, i.e., that players can only become guilty by their own actions, not by of actions of others or through a discriminatory legal system. This is necessary because our broad definition would otherwise allow for legal systems in which agents cannot by rational behavior avoid punishment and thus the perfect crime assumption no longer helps in security proofs.

Automation. Another interesting question is the automation of a verification procedure for accountability, such as in [4]. In fact, here a major difference is that for us accountability is not a goal in itself, but a means to achieve the actual security goals, namely by deterring illegal behavior. The main verification task is thus in showing that any violation of the security goals that can occur would lead to a conviction of a suspect, and perfect crime assumption, fairness and reasonability then imply that that cannot happen. The classical protocol verification tasks of analyzing a state-space are thus less prominent in our work and at the center is thus more an inductive argument like the process of obtaining a culprit. Note for instance the main difficulty in the proof here was the well-foundedness (cf. examples 4 and 5) which may not be a suitable question for automation.

Another related research area is Runtime Verification; see for instance [8] for a taxonomy of tools. The purpose is to model and specify policies that describe what actions are allowed and to use a log of actions to check whether a given run of a system satisfies the specification, see e.g., [2,16]. Sometimes the actors want to reach a common goal and the question is to automatically construct a *plan* (in the sense of Operations Research and AI) to implement a compliant solution, compare [11].

Other approaches in the protocol realm are as follows: Bella and Paulson [3] take an approach in which parties obtain lasting evidence, typically digitally signed, about actions performed by their peers. Künnemann and Backes [12] take a *causality* point of view: a party misbehaves if the fact that it deviates *causes* a violation of some given security property. Formalizing causality is challenging, and in fact, legality should be evaluated independently of the question whether it causes a problem or not. Thus, in our work the perfect crime assumption does not prevent agents from causing damage, but from getting caught.

Beyond Protocols. Also in other fields, accountability as a security goal has been studied at least since the work of [14]. Recently, the concept and methods have obtained wide recognition as a practical, real-life set of security mechanisms for ensuring compliance to policies based on deterrence, rather than on the more traditional approaches of cryptography-based or policy-based access control. Central to this deterrence idea is the creation of a system that detects and punishes participants that behave dishonestly. For instance [9] defines that a participant is accountable if there is a non-zero probability for being punished whenever the they violate the policy. They use traces of events with a utility function on maximal traces. The idea is that agents will obtain lower utility from traces that include their own security-policy violations than they do from those in which all of their actions are policy-compliant. Our notion of detection is similar, though we do not include any quantitative aspects, and use in the perfect crime assumption that the deterrence works, allowing to directly use it in security proofs.

In fact, accountability can also be regarded as particular incarnations of *Trust Management*, including policy-based and reputation-based systems. In [17], [6,7], and others the different parties in a decentralized system have the responsibility of recording information events that will be used as "proof obligations" before executing a sensitive action. Those proofs will be relevant to future assessment of accountability to some set of policies. Those works also discuss further aspects like *regret* or *dynamic* (time-dependent) trust. In our approach this is similar to the notion of subpoenas, although it has in the protocol-area a new flavor since when looking at concrete messages exchanged, this includes the question whether players may be able to forge evidence and thus lie in a subpoena without that maybe being provable.

In the domain of *Data Protection* accountability is gaining importance. In this context the term *accountability* is used in a very broad sense that is difficult to formalize, namely as an obligation of "an organization to be answerable for its actions" [5]. See [1] for the history of the term in a legal-technical context.

We believe accountability is an exciting field that will see further developments. One of the questions is for instance accountability in distributed ledgers [10]. We are currently investigating to practical use of accountability ideas in workflow processes where players may at each point have snippets (signed pieces of a workflow) and where investigation of detected misbehavior can lead to a chain of discoveries as in our running example [15].

Acknowledgements. This paper was inspired by discussions with Omar Almousa, Bud Brügger, and Max Tuengerthal. This work has been supported by the EU H2020-SU-ICT-03-2018 Project No. 830929 CyberSec4Europe (https://www.cybersec4europe.eu).

References

1. Alhadeff, J., Van Alsenoy, B., Dumortier, J.: The accountability principle in data protection regulation: origin, development and future directions. In: Guagnin, D., Hempel, L., Ilten, C., Kroener, I., Neyland, D., Postigo, H. (eds.) Managing Privacy through Accountability, pp. 49–82. Palgrave Macmillan UK, London (2012). https://doi.org/10.1057/9781137032225_4

2. Basin, D., Caronni, G., Ereth, S., Harvan, M., Klaedtke, F., Mantel, H.: Scalable offline monitoring. In: Bonakdarpour, B., Smolka, S.A. (eds.) RV 2014. LNCS, vol. 8734, pp. 31–47. Springer, Cham (2014). https://doi.org/10.1007/978-3-319-11164-3_4

3. Bella, G., Paulson, L.C.: Accountability protocols: formalized and verified. ACM Trans. Inf. Syst. Secur. (TISSEC) 9(2), 138–161 (2006)

4. Bruni, A., Giustolisi, R., Schürmann, C.: Automated analysis of accountability. In: Nguyen, P.Q., Zhou, J. (eds.) ISC 2017. vol. 10599, pp. 417–434. Springer, Cham (2017). https://doi.org/10.1007/978-3-319-69659-1_23

5. Cavoukian, A., Taylor, S., Abrams, M.E.: Privacy by design: essential for organizational accountability and strong business practices. Identity Inf. Soc. 3(2), 405–413 (2010)

6. Cederquist, J., Conn, R., Dekker, M., Etalle, S., Den Hartog, J.: An audit logic for accountability. In: Sixth IEEE International Workshop on Policies for Distributed Systems and Networks (POLICY 2005), pp. 34–43. IEEE (2005)

7. Corin, R., Etalle, S., den Hartog, J., Lenzini, G., Staicu, I.: A logic for auditing accountability in decentralized systems. In: Dimitrakos, T., Martinelli, F. (eds.) Formal Aspects in Security and Trust. IIFIP, vol. 173, pp. 187–201. Springer, Boston (2005). https://doi.org/10.1007/0-387-24098-5_14

8. Falcone, Y., Krstić, S., Reger, G., Traytel, D.: A taxonomy for classifying runtime verification tools. Int. J. Softw. Tools Technol. Transfer 23(2), 255–284 (2021). https://doi.org/10.1007/s10009-021-00609-z

9. Feigenbaum, J., Jaggard, A.D., Wright, R.N.: Towards a formal model of accountability. In: Proceedings of the 2011 New security paradigms workshop, pp. 45–56 (2011)

10. Graf, M., Küsters, R., Rausch, D.: Accountability in a permissioned blockchain: Formal analysis of hyperledger fabric. In: EuroS&P, IEEE (2020)

11. Kanovich, M., Kirigin, T.B., Nigam, V., Scedrov, A., Talcott, C., Perovic, R.: A rewriting framework and logic for activities subject to regulations. Math. Struct. Comput. Sci. 27(3), 332–375 (2017)

12. Künnemann, R., Garg, D., Backes, M.: Accountability in the decentralised-adversary setting. In: 2021 IEEE 34th Computer Security Foundations Symposium (CSF), pp. 95–110. IEEE Computer Society (2021)

13. Küsters, R., Truderung, T., Vogt, A.: Accountability: definition and relationship to verifiability. In: Proceedings of the 17th ACM conference on Computer and Communications Security, pp. 526–535 (2010)

14. Lampson, B.: Privacy and security usable security: how to get it. Commun. ACM 52(11), 25–27 (2009)

15. Popp, W.: Workflow-aware access control and accountability in IoT workflows, master Thesis, Uni Passau (2020)

16. Schneider, J., Basin, D., Brix, F., Krstić, S., Traytel, D.: Scalable online first-order monitoring. Int. J. Softw. Tools Technol. Transfer 23(2), 185–208 (2021). https://doi.org/10.1007/s10009-021-00607-1

17. Weitzner, D.J., Abelson, H., Berners-Lee, T., Feigenbaum, J., Hendler, J., Sussman, G.J.: Information accountability. Commun. ACM 51(6), 82–87 (2008)

Benign Interaction of Security Domains

Flemming Nielson[1(✉)], René Rydhof Hansen[2], and Hanne Riis Nielson[1,2]

[1] Department of Mathematics and Computer Science,
Technical University of Denmark, Kgs. Lyngby, Denmark
fnie@dtu.dk
[2] Department of Computer Science, Aalborg University, Aalborg, Denmark
rrh@cs.aau.dk

Abstract. Whenever data is communicated outside a security domain there is the risk that it may influence data coming back in a way that is not permitted by the security domain. This may arise when different security domains relate to different parallel processes that exchange information through communication. We provide general definitions of the demands on the communication and sanitisation primitives so as to mitigate the risk. For interesting instantiations of these definitions we provide algorithms for checking that the demands have been met. The development is illustrated by a worked example dealing with the outsourcing of data management to the cloud.

1 Introduction

In an ideal world one might be able to devise a security policy (perhaps expressed in XACML [16]) and impose it upon all participants, but in real life there is likely to be cooperation between groups of entities that already have their security policies in place and are reluctant to make major changes in order to merely cooperate a little bit.

This paper builds on [5] and [13] in exploring ways that such preexisting security policies may interact in a benign manner when the various groups of entities are equipped with the possibility of communicating with one another. This development is supplemented by a worked example suggesting ways that medical organisations may exchange information between them while keeping to their own security policies.

A key consideration is to determine the security implications of admitting communication between groups of entities that already have their security policies in place. Motivated by considerations of *non-interference* we take the view that this should be acceptable as long as groups of entities are *unable to observe* that information flows throughout the system in a manner that violates their own security policies. While this might be less than what could ideally be hoped for, we believe that it reflects the established rules of society in that no individual is likely to succeed in making complaints about the information gathering activities of intelligence agencies or service providers (like Google or Facebook) unless the individual can demonstrate that a violoation has taken place.

D. Dougherty et al. (Eds.): Guttman Festschrift, LNCS 13066, pp. 312–331, 2021.
https://doi.org/10.1007/978-3-030-91631-2_17

This paper develops the syntax (Sect. 2) and semantics (Appendix A) for a programming language supporting this development. Based on local security considerations (Sect. 3) it then studies the implications of global communication (Sect. 4). It then goes deeper into studying what extra information flow might be permitted due to communication (Sect. 5) before concluding (Sect. 6),

2   Syntax

In this section we extend Dijkstra's Guarded Commands language [6] with parallelism, communication and security domains. The development is an adaptation of the one in [15] by removing the considerations of symmetric cryptography and instead using explicit security domains. Unlike the development in [13] we do not add constructs for relocation of processes as this is not essential for our worked example.

The main syntactic category of *Secure Guarded Commands with Security Domains* (GCwSD) is that of programs (denoted P). A program

$$E \text{ par } L_1 \, S_1 \, D_1 \, C_1 \; \square \; \cdots \; \square \; L_n \, S_n \, D_n \, C_n \text{ rap}$$

consists of an environment (E) defining the communication channels used in the program and a number of parallel processes, each having a local list of sanitisation constructs (S_i), a local declaration (D_i) of variables, and a command (C_i). We shall assume that each command has its own security lattice L_i and that data changes security domain when communicated between them. The syntax is summarised in Fig. 1 and explained below.

The commands include those of Dijkstra's Guarded Commands so we have the basic command of assignment ($x := e$) in addition to sequencing ($C_1 \, ; C_2$) and constructs for conditionals (if $e_1 \to C_1 \; \square \; ... \; \square \; e_n \to C_n$ fi) and iteration (do $e_1 \to C_1 \; \square \; ... \; \square \; e_n \to C_n$ od). On top of this we introduce basic commands for output ($c \, ! \, e$) and input ($c \, ? \, x$) over a channel (c) and a command performing an 'external' non-deterministic choice among commands (sum $C_1 \; \square \; ... \; \square \; C_n$ mus); it will typically be the case that each C_i in sum $C_1 \; \square \; ... \; \square \; C_n$ mus takes the form $c \, ! \, e \, ; C$ or $c \, ? \, x \, ; C$ but we do not need to impose this.

We shall not fully specify the expressions but surely they must include numbers (n), strings (s), variables (x), arithmetic operations (e.g. $e_1 + e_2$), truth values (e.g. true), relational operations (e.g. $e_1 = e_2$), and logical operations (e.g. $e_1 \wedge e_2$). An expression may also be a sanitisation construct ($d \downarrow e_1$) for bypassing the security policy expressed by the security domain; assuming that the security modifier of d is $\ell' \mapsto^{\phi} \ell''$ the intention is that the security label of e_1 is changed from ℓ' to ℓ'' because of the intended security violations given by ϕ.

We shall not fully specify the data types and merely use a generic type data encompassings integers (int), booleans (bool), and strings (string). We shall leave the syntax of channels (c), sanitisers (d) (used for declassification and endorsement), and security violations (ϕ) to the concrete examples; when the security violations are of no interest they may be omitted (as we shall do in the worked example below).

programs: $P ::= E$ par $L_1 S_1 D_1 C_1$ $\square$ $\cdots$ $\square$ $L_n S_n D_n C_n$ rap $(n > 0)$

environment: $E ::=$ chan$[\ c_1 : t_1 \ell_1' \mapsto^{\phi_1} \ell_1''; \cdots ; c_n : t_n \ell_n' \mapsto^{\phi_n} \ell_n''\ ]$ $(n \geq 0)$

sanitisations: $S ::=$ san$[\ d_1 : t_1 \ell_1' \mapsto^{\phi_1} \ell_1''; \cdots ; d_n : t_n \ell_n' \mapsto^{\phi_n} \ell_n''\ ]$ $(n \geq 0)$

declarations: $D ::=$ var$[\ x_1 : t_1 \ell_1; \cdots ; x_n : t_n \ell_n\ ]$ $(n \geq 0)$

commands: $C ::= x := e \mid c!e \mid c?x \mid C_1 ; C_2$
$\qquad\qquad\quad\ \mid$ if $e_1 \to C_1$ $\square$ ... $\square$ $e_n \to C_n$ fi $(n > 0)$
$\qquad\qquad\quad\ \mid$ do $e_1 \to C_1$ $\square$ ... $\square$ $e_n \to C_n$ od $(n > 0)$
$\qquad\qquad\quad\ \mid$ sum C_1 $\square$ ... $\square$ C_n mus $(n > 0)$

expressions: $e ::= n \mid s \mid x \mid e_1 + e_2 \mid \cdots \mid$
$\qquad\qquad\quad$ true $\mid e_1 = e_2 \mid \cdots \mid e_1 \wedge e_2 \mid \cdots$
$\qquad\qquad\quad d \downarrow e_1$

data types: $t ::=$ data $\mid \cdots$

security labels: $\ell \in L_1 \cup \cdots \cup L_n$

security violations: $\phi \quad \cdots$

Fig. 1. Syntax of secure guarded commands with security domains.

Security labels (ℓ) range over $L_1 \cup \cdots \cup L_n$ and we shall leave their syntax to the concrete example; we shall assume that the sets L_i are pairwise disjoint. The fundamental idea is that the partial order $\sqsubseteq$ indicates the direction in which the security classification of data may freely change; in approaches based on the Decentralised Label Model [12] this is called 'restriction'.

National Health Service: A Worked Example

Imagine the British National Health Service (NHS) having data involving both medical and financial aspects of the care and treatment of their patients. In order to ensure the confidentiality of this data, the NHS classifies data using a simple security lattice allowing financial data to be managed mostly seperately from medical data:

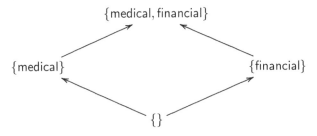

Because of pressure from the US in getting a trade agreement between the US and the UK, the NHS is forced to open up to outside data management. With respect to the medical data it engages with a New York based company (NY) that offers two security levels LoNY and HiNY, ordered as you would imagine:

Interaction between NHS and NY is restricted to channels with security modifiers {medical} ↦ LoNY, LoNY ↦ {medical}, {medical, financial} ↦ HiNY, HiNY ↦ {medical, financial}. In particular, financial data can only be communicated at the highest security levels:

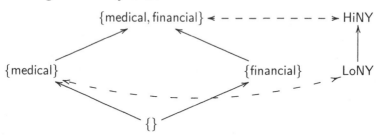

The above channels can be declared in GCwSD as follows:

```
chan [ #putLoNY : data {medical}           ↦ LoNY,
       #getLoNY : data LoNY                ↦ {medical},
       #putHiNY : data {medical, financial} ↦ HiNY,
       #getHiNY : data HiNY                ↦ {medical, financial} ]
```

Conversely, to handle the financial data the NHS engages with a New Hampshire based company (NH) that also classifies data into two security levels: LoNH and HiNH also ordered as one would imagine. Interaction between NHS and NH takes place through channels having security modifiers {financial} ↦ LoNH, LoNH ↦ {financial}, {medical, financial} ↦ HiNH, and HiNH ↦ {medical, financial}:

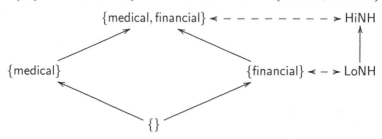

Again it is straightforward to declare the corresponding channels directly in GCwSD:

```
chan [ #putLoNH : data {financial}          ↦ LoNH,
       #getLoNH : data LoNH                ↦ {financial},
       #putHiNH : data {financial}          ↦ HiNH,
       #getHiNH : data HiNH                ↦ {medical, financial} ]
```

The following GCwSD snippet illustrates some of the above communication patterns, where the NHS forwards medical data to the NY data manager and financial data to the NH data manager:

```
 1  nhs = // The NHS
 2      var [ financial : data {financial}, medical : data {medical} ]
 3      // ...
 4      #putLoNY ! medical;
 5      // ...
 6      #putLoNH ! financial;
 7
 8  ny = // NY (handler of medical data)
 9      var [ nhsdata : data LoNY, result : data LoNY ]
10      // ...
11      #putLoNY ? nhsdata;
12      // ...
13      #getLoNY ! result;
14
15  nh = // NH (handler of financial data)
16      var [ nhsdata : data LoNH, result : data LoNH ]
17      // ...
18      #putLoNH ? nhsdata;
19      // ...
20      #getLoNH ! result;
```

The problem tackled next is to ensure that this program adheres to the intended security policies.

3 Local Security: Information Flow Type System

In this section we develop an information flow type system for ensuring that each of the parallel processes adheres to the declarations and the overall information flow policy that we impose.gene

The information flow type system presented here is responsible for ensuring that data types match, that security levels match subject to the free use of 'restriction' (i.e. $\sqsubseteq$), and that we deal correctly with the security modifiers associated with channels and sanitisers.

Within a parallel command we may bypass the security policy by means of sanitisation [7]; in approaches based on the Decentralised Label Model [12] this is called 'declassification' in case of confidentiality and 'endorsement' in case of integrity. In GCwSD it is the $d \downarrow e_1$ construct that is responsible for this. As already stated, the assumption here is that for d to have security modifier $\ell' \mapsto^\phi \ell''$ such that ℓ' and ℓ'' belong to the same security domain, and it is natural to assume that $\ell' \not\sqsubseteq \ell''$.

Between two parallel commands we need to change the security label of the data communicated. We have decided to integrate that with the actual communication and to this effect also channels have security modifiers that indicate the change of security level: $\ell' \mapsto^\phi \ell''$. The assumption here is that ℓ' and ℓ'' belong

$$\rho \vdash n : \text{data} \perp \qquad \rho \vdash s : \text{data} \perp \qquad \rho \vdash \text{true} : \text{data} \perp$$

$$\frac{}{\rho \vdash x : t\,\ell} \text{ if } \rho(x) = (t, \ell) \qquad \frac{\rho \vdash e_1 : \text{data}\,\ell_1 \quad \rho \vdash e_2 : \text{data}\,\ell_2}{\rho \vdash e_1 + e_2 : \text{data}\,(\ell_1 \sqcup \ell_2)}$$

$$\frac{\rho \vdash e_1 : t\,\ell_1 \quad \rho \vdash e_2 : t\,\ell_2}{\rho \vdash e_1 = e_2 : \text{data}\,(\ell_1 \sqcup \ell_2)} \qquad \frac{\rho \vdash e_1 : \text{data}\,\ell_1 \quad \rho \vdash e_2 : \text{data}\,\ell_2}{\rho \vdash e_1 \wedge e_2 : \text{data}\,(\ell_1 \sqcup \ell_2)}$$

$$\frac{\rho \vdash e_1 : t\,\ell'}{\rho \vdash d \downarrow e_1 : t\,\ell''} \text{ if } \rho(d) = (t, \ell' \mapsto^\phi \ell'')$$

Fig. 2. Types and security levels for expressions.

to different security domains and this is the novel construct of GCwSD. The formal development borrows from that of [15] in the way it deals with communication and parallelism but handles security domains in a different manner due to the security modifiers given to channels and sanitisers. It will make use of well-typing judgements for expressions, commands and processes. They are inspired by traditional approaches such as those of [17,18] but need to be extended to deal with parallelism and non-determinism. In doing so, we are exploiting that the semantics prescribes a lack of shared variables.

General Assumptions. Syntactic well-formedness of a program P as above also needs to impose the following conditions:

- Each channel used for output in any C_i is declared in E and its security modifier $\ell' \mapsto^\phi \ell''$ satisfies $\ell' \in L_i$.
- Each channel used for input in any C_i is declared in E and its security modifier $\ell' \mapsto^\phi \ell''$ satisfies $\ell'' \in L_i$.
- Each sanitiser used in any C_i is declared in S_i and its security modifier $\ell' \mapsto^\phi \ell''$ satisfies $\ell', \ell'' \in L_i$.
- Each variable used in any C_i is declared in D_i, hence no global variables.

This ensures that each command C_i only needs to be aware of the security labels relating to its own security lattice L_i. For the sake of readability of the type system developed below we shall not incorporate the above demands into the type system but shall feel free to rely on them when needed.

Well-typed Expressions. For expressions the judgement takes the form

$$\rho \vdash e : t\,\ell$$

It is defined by the axiom schemes and rules of Fig. 2 and will be explained below. The judgement makes use of a type environment ρ that assigns types and security levels to all variables, and types and security modifiers to all channels

$$\frac{\rho \vdash e_1 : t\,\ell_1}{\rho \vdash x := e_1 : [\ell,\ell]} \ \text{if} \ \begin{cases} \rho(x) = (t,\ell) \\ \ell_1 \sqsubseteq \ell \end{cases} \qquad\qquad \frac{\rho \vdash C_1 : L_1 \quad \rho \vdash C_2 : L_2}{\rho \vdash C_1 \,;C_2 : L_1 \sqcap L_2}$$

$$\frac{\bigwedge_i \rho \vdash e_i : \textbf{data}\,\ell_i \quad \bigwedge_i \rho \vdash C_i : L_i}{\rho \vdash \textbf{if}\ e_1 \to C_1 \ \square \ \cdots \ \square \ e_n \to C_n \ \textbf{fi} : L_1 \sqcap \cdots \sqcap L_n} \ \text{if} \ \begin{cases} \bigwedge_i \ell_i \sqsubseteq L_i \\ \bigwedge_{(i,j)\in\text{cosat}} \ell_j \sqsubseteq L_i \\ \bigwedge_{(i,j)\in\text{cosat}} \textbf{uniq}(L_i) \end{cases}$$

$$\frac{\bigwedge_i \rho \vdash e_i : \textbf{data}\,\ell_i \quad \bigwedge_i \rho \vdash C_i : L_i}{\rho \vdash \textbf{do}\ e_1 \to C_1 \ \square \ \cdots \ \square \ e_n \to C_n \ \textbf{od} : L_1 \sqcap \cdots \sqcap L_n} \ \text{if} \ \begin{cases} \bigwedge_i \ell_i \sqsubseteq L_i \\ \bigwedge_{(i,j)\in\text{cosat}} \ell_j \sqsubseteq L_i \\ \bigwedge_{(i,j)\in\text{cosat}} \textbf{uniq}(L_i) \end{cases}$$

$$\frac{\bigwedge_i \rho \vdash C_i : L_i}{\rho \vdash \textbf{sum}\ C_1 \ \square \ \cdots \ \square \ C_n \ \textbf{mus} : L_1 \sqcap \cdots \sqcap L_n} \ \text{if} \ \bigwedge_i \textbf{uniq}(L_i)$$

$$\frac{\rho \vdash e_0 : t\,\ell_0}{\rho \vdash c\,!\,e_0 : [\ell',\ell']} \ \text{if} \ \begin{cases} \rho(c) = (t,\ell' \mapsto^\phi \ell'') \\ \ell_0 \sqsubseteq \ell' \end{cases} \qquad \frac{}{\rho \vdash c\,?\,x : [\ell,\ell]} \ \text{if} \ \begin{cases} \rho(c) = (t,\ell' \mapsto^\phi \ell'') \\ \rho(x) = (t,\ell) \\ \ell'' \sqsubseteq \ell \end{cases}$$

Fig. 3. Types and pairs of security levels for commands.

and sanitisers. For simplicity of presentation we have amalgameted all occurrences of types for integers (int), booleans (bool), and strings (string) into a generic type (data).

The overall idea is that $\rho \vdash e : t\,\ell$ should ensure that the type of the expression e is t and that the security level is $\ell = \bigsqcup_i \rho(x_i)_2$ where x_i ranges over all free variables of e and $\rho(x)_2 = \ell$ whenever $\rho(x) = (t,\ell)$. This is in line with the development in [17,18] and takes care of explaining the axiom schemes and rules of Fig. 2 except for sanitisation. For sanitisation $d \downarrow e_1$ we merely change the type as indicated by the security modifier associated to d.

Well-typed Commands. For commands the typing judgement takes the form

$$\rho \vdash C : L$$

It is defined by the axiom schemes and rules of Fig. 3 and further explained below. The judgement makes use of a security label L being a *pair* of security levels, written as $[\ell_1,\ell_2]$ with $\ell_1 \sqsubseteq \ell_2$. We shall allow to write $\ell \sqsubseteq [\ell_1,\ell_2]$ for $\ell \sqsubseteq \ell_1$ and define

$$[\ell_1,\ell_2] \sqcap [\ell_1',\ell_2'] = [\ell_1 \sqcap \ell_1', \ell_2 \sqcup \ell_2']$$

(which is the greatest lower bound operation with respect to a partial order $\sqsubseteq'$ defined by $[\ell_1,\ell_2] \sqsubseteq' [\ell_1',\ell_2']$ whenever $\ell_1 \sqsubseteq \ell_1'$ and $\ell_2 \sqsupseteq \ell_2'$). We shall write $\textbf{uniq}([\ell_1,\ell_2])$ for the condition that $\ell_1 = \ell_2$.

The overall idea is that $\rho \vdash C : [\ell_1,\ell_2]$ should ensure that $\ell_1 = \bigsqcap_i \rho(x_i)_2$ where x_i ranges over all modified variables of C, and this is in line with the development in [17,18]. However, we shall see that we need a bit more to deal

$$\frac{\bigwedge_i \rho_i \vdash C_i : L_i}{\vdash E \text{ par } L_1\, S_1\, D_1\, C_1 \; \square \; \cdots \; \square \; L_n\, S_n\, D_n\, C_n \text{ rap} : \checkmark} \quad \text{where } \rho_i = \text{env}(E)\text{env}(S_i)\text{env}(D_i)$$

Fig. 4. Types for processes.

with non-determinism and so we will additionally ensure that $\ell_2 = \bigsqcup_i \rho(x_i)_2$ so as to record the variety of variables modified in the command.

The rule for assignment records the security level of the variable modified and checks that the explicit information flow is admissible. The rule for sequencing is straightforward given our explanation of $\rho \vdash C : L$ and the operation $L_1 \sqcap L_2$.

The rule for 'external' non-deterministic choice takes care of correlation flows [14,15]. It makes use of $\text{uniq}(L_i)$, i.e. $L_i = [\ell', \ell']$ for some ℓ', to ensure that all modified variables have the same security level.

The rules for conditional and iteration are essentially identical and make use of guards of the form $e_1 \to C_1 \; \square \; \cdots \; \square \; e_n \to C_n$. They take care of implicit flows by checking that $\ell_i \sqsubseteq L_i$ whenever $\bigwedge_i \rho \vdash e_i : \text{data}\, \ell_i$ and $\bigwedge_i \rho \vdash C_i : L_i$. They take care of bypassing flows [14,15] whenever some $e_i \wedge e_j$ is satisfiable for $i \neq j$. This is expressed using the set cosat that contains those *distinct* pairs (i, j) of indices such that $e_i \wedge e_j$ is satisfiable; it may be computed using a Satisfaction Modulo Theories (SMT) solver such as Z3 [10] or it may be approximated using the DAG-based heuristics described in [14]. Whenever this is the case, the condition $\ell_j \sqsubseteq L_i$ checks that the bypassing flows are admissible, and the condition $\text{uniq}(L_i)$ checks the correlation flows are admissible.

The rule for output and the axiom scheme for input are somewhat similar to the one for assignment, essentially treating output $c\,!\,e$ as an assignment $c := e$, and input $c\,?\,x$ as an assignment $x := c$. However, we are careful about which security level to use from the security modifier.

Well-typed Processes. For processes the typing judgement takes the form $\vdash P : \checkmark$. It is defined by the rule in Fig. 4 and makes use of $\text{env}(\cdots)$ to construct the appropriate environments for the commands. For $\text{env}(\text{chan}[\; \cdots \;])$ it is given by

$$\text{env}(\text{chan}[\; c_1 : t_1\, \ell_1' \mapsto^{\phi_1} \ell_1''; \cdots ; c_n : t_n\, \ell_n' \mapsto^{\phi_n} \ell_n'' \;]) = \begin{bmatrix} c_1 \mapsto (t_1, \ell_1' \mapsto^{\varphi_1} \ell_1'') \\ \cdots \\ c_n \mapsto (t_n, \ell_n' \mapsto^{\varphi_n} \ell_n'') \end{bmatrix}$$

and similarly for $\text{env}(\text{san}[\; \cdots \;])$ and $\text{env}(\text{var}[\; \cdots \;])$. We shall only allow to use the semantics on well-typed programs P (i.e. satisfying $\vdash P : \checkmark$).

National Health Service: A Worked Example

We have admittedly been very sketchy in providing the actual code for the NHS, NY and NH processes and so it should come as no surprise that the GCwSD snippets do adhere to the type system as formulated above. In particular, the code snippet

```
  var [ nhsdata : data LoNH, result : data LoNH ]
  // ...
  #putLoNH ? nhsdata;
  // ...
  #getLoNH ! result;
```

passes the type system whereas an erroneous code snippet

```
  var [ nhsdata : data LoNH, result : data HiNH ]
  // ...
  #putLoNH ? nhsdata;
  // ...
  #getLoNH ! result;
```

would be captured by the type system. The challenge however is to ensure the benign interaction between the three different security domains and this will be addressed next.

So imagine that after a while NY and NH are acquired by Amazon that over time use them simply as frontends to their own systems offering security levels Low and High ordered straightforwardly. Interaction between NY and AMZ takes place through channels having security modifiers, LoNY ↦ Low, Low ↦ LoNY, HiNY ↦ High, High ↦ HiNY. Similarly, interaction between NH and AMZ are through channels having security modifiers LoNH ↦ Low, Low ↦ LoNH, HiNH ↦ High, High ↦ HiNH:

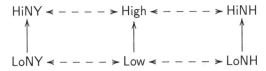

Declaring these channels is straightforward in GCwSD:

```
chan [ #takeLoNY : data LoNY ↦ Low,
       #takeHiNY : data HiNY ↦ High,
       #giveLoNY : data Low ↦ LoNY,
       #giveHiNY : data High ↦ HiNY,
       #takeLoNH : data LoNH ↦ Low,
       #takeHiNH : data HiNH ↦ High,
       #giveLoNH : data Low ↦ LoNH,
       #giveHiNH : data High ↦ HiNH ]
```

Redefining the NY process to a simple forwarding agent is also straightforward:

```
ny = // NY (handler of medical data)
  var [ lony : data LoNY, hiny : data HiNY ]
  do true →
    sum
      #putLoNY ? lony; #takeLoNY ! lony
    []
      #giveLoNY ? lony; #getLoNY ! lony
    []
      #putHiNY ? hiny; #takeHiNY ! hiny
    []
```

$$\frac{\ell' \sqsubseteq \ell'' \text{ is in } \boldsymbol{L}_i}{P \vdash_i \ell' \mapsto^\varepsilon \ell''} \qquad \frac{\ell' \mapsto^\phi \ell'' \text{ is in } S_i}{P \vdash_i \ell' \mapsto^\phi \ell''} \qquad \frac{P \vdash_i \ell' \mapsto^{\pi'} \ell \quad P \vdash_i \ell \mapsto^{\pi''} \ell''}{P \vdash_i \ell' \mapsto^{\pi'\pi''} \ell''}$$

Fig. 5. Local paths.

```
11      #giveHiNY ? hiny;  #getHiNY ! hiny
12    mus
13  od
```

And similarly for the NH process.

However, inspection of the channels now suggests a potential problem. Not knowing the code running on AMZ there is no way we can be ensured that it does not (by mistake or as a result of being hacked) contain a piece of code like

```
1   var [ low  : data Low, high  : data High ]
2   // ...
3   #takeLoNY ? low ;
4   // ...
5   #giveLoNH ! low ;
6   // ...
```

which might give rise to data of security label {medical} ending up as data of security label {financial}. This is not captured by the type system presented in this section.

4   Global Security: Change of Security Domain

Our current setup creates the risk that the communications between a process and its environment (i.e. the other processes) gives rise to information flow that would not be admitted within the process itself unless it resorts to additional sanitisations. (So far our working example has been conceived without the need to use any sanitisation.) Hence there is the risk that communication leads to local information flow not captured by the type system of the previous section. To guard against this we need to establish a bit of terminology for the i'th component of the program P of interest.

We shall be interested in recording when the declarations $\boldsymbol{L}_i S_i D_i$ might give rise to an information flow from some $\ell' \in \boldsymbol{L}_i$ to some $\ell'' \in \boldsymbol{L}_i$ and we shall write this as

$$P \vdash_i \ell' \mapsto^\pi \ell''$$

where π explains the way the information flow takes place. We say that there is an *i-local path* labelled π from $\ell' \in \boldsymbol{L}_i$ to $\ell'' \in \boldsymbol{L}_i$. This relation is defined by a number of cases summarised in Fig. 5 and explained below. There is an i-local path labelled ε from $\ell' \in \boldsymbol{L}_i$ to $\ell'' \in \boldsymbol{L}_i$ whenever $\ell' \sqsubseteq \ell''$ Furthermore, there is an i-local path labelled ϕ from $\ell' \in \boldsymbol{L}_i$ to $\ell'' \in \boldsymbol{L}_i$ whenever S_i declares some sanitiser with security modifier $\ell' \mapsto^\phi \ell''$ and $\ell', \ell'' \in \boldsymbol{L}_i$. Paths can be combined by concatenation where $\pi\varepsilon = \varepsilon\pi = \pi$.

$$\frac{\ell' \sqsubseteq \ell'' \text{ in some } L_j \text{ for } i \neq j}{P \vdash^{[i]} \ell' \mapsto^\varepsilon \ell''} \qquad \frac{\ell' \mapsto^\phi \ell'' \text{ in some } S_j \text{ for } i \neq j}{P \vdash^{[i]} \ell' \mapsto^\phi \ell''}$$

$$\frac{P \vdash^{[i]} \ell' \mapsto^{\pi'} \ell \quad P \vdash^{[i]} \ell \mapsto^{\pi''} \ell'' \quad \ell \notin L_i}{P \vdash^{[i]} \ell' \mapsto^{\pi'\pi''} \ell''} \qquad \frac{\ell' \mapsto^\phi \ell'' \text{ in } E}{P \vdash^{[i]} \ell' \mapsto^\phi \ell''}$$

Fig. 6. Remote paths.

We shall also be interested in recording when communication with the other components might give rise to an information flow from some $\ell' \in \bigcup_i L_i$ to some $\ell'' \in \bigcup_i L_i$ without exploiting the internals of the i'th component. We shall write this as

$$P \vdash^{[i]} \ell' \mapsto^\pi \ell''$$

and the definition is summarised in Fig. 6. It differs from that of Fig. 5 in recording a flow from $\ell' \in L_j$ to $\ell'' \in L_k$ whenever the environment E for the entire program P declares a channel c of security modifier $\ell' \mapsto^\phi \ell''$ and in restricting the other flows to happen outside of the i'th component. (This includes not concatenating paths that connect via the i'th component.) The definition specialises to the case where $\ell' \in L_i$ and $\ell'' \in L_i$ and motivates defining

$$P \vdash^i \ell' \mapsto^\pi \ell'' \text{ iff } P \vdash^{[i]} \ell' \mapsto^\pi \ell'' \wedge \ell' \in L_i \wedge \ell'' \in L_i$$

and we say that there is an i-*remote path* labelled π from $\ell' \in L_i$ to $\ell'' \in L_i$. We are now ready to define our first notion of when a program P is secure.

Definition 1. *A program P is* naively i-secure *whenever for every i-remote path (with some label) from some $\ell' \in L_i$ to some $\ell'' \in L_i$ there also is an i-local path (with some possibly different label) from $\ell' \in L_i$ to $\ell'' \in L_i$:*

$$\forall \ell', \ell'' \in L_i : \forall \pi_r : P \vdash^i \ell' \mapsto^{\pi_r} \ell'' \Rightarrow \exists \pi_l : P \vdash_i \ell' \mapsto^{\pi_l} \ell''$$

A program P is naively secure *whenever it is naively i-secure for all values of $i \in \{1, \cdots, n\}$.*

It is possible to check for naive security in cubic time with respect to the size of the program P. To see this, first note that the number of security labels, security violations and security modifiers considered is linear in the size of the program P. Next note that using Figs. 5 and 6 to compute $\exists \pi : P \vdash_i \ell' \mapsto^\pi \ell''$ and $\exists \pi : P \vdash^i \ell' \mapsto^\pi \ell''$ amounts to computing the transitive closure of binary relations and that this can be done in cubic time. (To avoid confusion, note that $\{\pi \mid P \vdash_i \ell' \mapsto^\pi \ell''\}$ and $\{\pi \mid P \vdash^i \ell' \mapsto^\pi \ell''\}$ may be infinite and hence cannot necessarily be computed.)

National Health Service: A Worked Example

Let us now consider the two variations of our worked example as presented in Sects. 2 and 3. In each variation we shall focus our attention on the NHS.

The Original System. The system as presented in Sect. 2 admits only the NHS-local paths directly given by the security lattice for the NHS as there are no sanitisers declared for NHS:

$$P \vdash_{NHS} \{\} \mapsto^{\varepsilon} \{\}$$
$$P \vdash_{NHS} \{\} \mapsto^{\varepsilon} \{medical\}$$
$$P \vdash_{NHS} \{\} \mapsto^{\varepsilon} \{financial\}$$
$$P \vdash_{NHS} \{\} \mapsto^{\varepsilon} \{medical, financial\}$$
$$P \vdash_{NHS} \{medical\} \mapsto^{\varepsilon} \{medical\}$$
$$P \vdash_{NHS} \{medical\} \mapsto^{\varepsilon} \{medical, financial\}$$
$$P \vdash_{NHS} \{financial\} \mapsto^{\varepsilon} \{financial\}$$
$$P \vdash_{NHS} \{financial\} \mapsto^{\varepsilon} \{medical, financial\}$$
$$P \vdash_{NHS} \{medical, financial\} \mapsto^{\varepsilon} \{medical, financial\}$$

Turning to the NHS-remote paths there are no sanitisers outside of NHS either, and the channels between NHS and NY and between NHS and NH give rise to the following:

$$P \vdash^{NHS} \{medical\} \mapsto^{\varepsilon} \{medical\}$$
$$P \vdash^{NHS} \{medical\} \mapsto^{\varepsilon} \{medical, financial\}$$
$$P \vdash^{NHS} \{financial\} \mapsto^{\varepsilon} \{financial\}$$
$$P \vdash^{NHS} \{financial\} \mapsto^{\varepsilon} \{medical, financial\}$$
$$P \vdash^{NHS} \{medical, financial\} \mapsto^{\varepsilon} \{medical, financial\}$$

The second and fourth contributions arise because of the security lattices in NY and NH.

It is now immediate to check that the worked example of Sect. 2 is naively NHS-secure and by extending the reasoning one can show that the entire system is naively secure.

The System Involving Amazon. Turning to the system as presented Sect. 3 there is no change to the NHS-local paths but we get additional NHS-remote paths due to the channels between NY and Amazon and between NH and Amazon. In particular we get the following NHS-remote paths in addition to those displayed above:

$$P \vdash^{NHS} \{medical\} \mapsto^{\varepsilon} \{financial\}$$
$$P \vdash^{NHS} \{financial\} \mapsto^{\varepsilon} \{medical\}$$

as was already hinted at in Sect. 3.

Since there are no NHS-local paths corresponding to these NHS-remote paths it follows that the modified system is not naively secure. In other words, our notion of naive security would seem to be able to ensure that the interaction between security domains is benign.

5   Taking Security Violations into Account

So far we ignored the labels of paths indicating the security violations being performed along the way. To rectify this we shall imagine a partially ordered structure over which paths can be interpreted. We denote it by $(\mathcal{C}, \preccurlyeq)$ and let $\beta(\pi)$ denote the interpretation of π in $\mathcal{C}$; we shall provide examples shortly.

Definition 2. *A program P is i-*secure wrt. β whenever for every i-remote path (with label π_r) from some $\ell' \in \mathbf{L}_i$ to some $\ell'' \in \mathbf{L}_i$ there also is an i-local path (with some potentially different label π_l) from $\ell' \in \mathbf{L}_i$ to $\ell'' \in \mathbf{L}_i$ such that $\beta(\pi_l) \preccurlyeq \beta(\pi_r)$:*

$$\forall \ell', \ell'' \in \mathbf{L}_i : \forall \pi_r : P \vdash^i \ell' \mapsto^{\pi_r} \ell'' \Rightarrow \exists \pi_l : P \vdash_i \ell' \mapsto^{\pi_l} \ell'' \wedge \beta(\pi_l) \preccurlyeq \beta(\pi_r)$$

A program P is secure wrt. β *whenever it is i-secure wrt. β for all values of $i \in \{1, \cdots, n\}$.*

The notion of *naively secure* is the same as that of *secure with respect to a constant function* (e.g. $\beta(\pi) = *$, $\mathcal{C} = \{*\}$ and $\preceq$ being equality) and we already indicated that this would be checkable in cubic time.

A very demanding notion of *secure with respect to the identify function* may be obtained by setting $\mathcal{C}$ to be all strings over the security violations, setting the partial order $\preccurlyeq$ to be equality, and setting $\beta(\pi) = \pi$. This merely states that every i-remote path must also be a i-local path. To effectively check this condition we might construct regular expressions for $\{\pi \mid P \vdash^i \ell' \mapsto^\pi \ell''\}$ and $\{\pi \mid P \vdash_i \ell' \mapsto^\pi \ell''\}$ for all pairs (ℓ', ℓ'') and subsequently to use appropriate algorithms from automata theory to check $\{\pi \mid P \vdash^i \ell' \mapsto^\pi \ell''\} \subseteq \{\pi \mid P \vdash_i \ell' \mapsto^\pi \ell''\}$ for all pairs (ℓ', ℓ''). This can be done in at most exponential time (involving the conversion from regular expressions to deterministic finite automata).

It will useful to rephrase the security condition of Definition 2 using the *Smyth*-ordering $\preccurlyeq_S$ defined by

$$X \preccurlyeq_S Y \text{ if and only if } \forall y \in Y : \exists x \in X : x \preccurlyeq y$$

Then $\forall \ell', \ell'' \in \mathbf{L}_i : \forall \pi_r : P \vdash^i \ell' \mapsto^{\pi_r} \ell'' \Rightarrow \exists \pi_l : P \vdash_i \ell' \mapsto^{\pi_l} \ell'' \wedge \beta(\pi_l) \preccurlyeq \beta(\pi_r)$ is equivalent to

$$\forall \ell', \ell'' \in \mathbf{L}_i : \{\beta(\pi) \mid P \vdash_i \ell' \mapsto^\pi \ell''\} \preccurlyeq_S \{\beta(\pi) \mid P \vdash^i \ell' \mapsto^\pi \ell''\}$$

It will usually not be the case that $\{\beta(\pi) \mid P \vdash^i \ell' \mapsto^\pi \ell''\}$ contains a least element. Also, even if $(\mathcal{C}, \preccurlyeq)$ is a complete lattice, it will not usually be the case that $\forall \ell', \ell'' \in \mathbf{L}_i : \exists \pi : P \vdash_i \ell' \mapsto^\pi \ell'' \wedge \beta(\pi) \preccurlyeq \bigsqcap \{\beta(\pi) \mid P \vdash^i \ell' \mapsto^\pi \ell''\}$ is equivalent to the above condition. This means that checking information flow in a global setting will be somewhat different from checking information flow in a local setting (as was done in Sect. 3).

Given a subset $C \subseteq \mathcal{C}$ we shall say that C' is a *frontier* of C whenever $C' \subseteq C \wedge C' \preccurlyeq_S C$. Furthermore, a *minimal frontier* of C is a frontier C' such that no proper subset of C' is also a frontier. The minimal frontier of the empty set is the empty set, and the minimal frontier of a singleton set is the singleton set.

Proposition 1. *Minimal frontiers are unique if they exist, in the sense that if C' and C'' are both minimal frontiers of C we have $C' = C''$.*

If $(\mathcal{C}, \preccurlyeq)$ is well-founded, a subset $C \subseteq \mathcal{C}$ always has a minimal frontier given by $C^* = \{c \in C \mid \neg \exists c' \in C : c' \prec c\}$ where $\prec$ is the irreflexive part of $\preccurlyeq$.

Proof. For the first claim we first show that $C' \subseteq C''$. So let $c_1 \in C'$, so that there exists $c_2 \in C''$ with $c_2 \preccurlyeq c_1$, and then there exists $c_3 \in C'$ with $c_3 \preccurlyeq c_2$. We must be able to take $c_3 = c_1$ as otherwise C' would not be minimal. Since $\preccurlyeq$ is a partial order this shows $c_1 = c_2$ and hence $C' \subseteq C''$. That $C'' \subseteq C'$ is shown similarly.

For the second claim suppose that $(\mathcal{C}, \preccurlyeq)$ is well-founded; i.e. there is no infinite sequence $\cdots c_n \prec c_{n-1} \prec \cdots \prec c_0$. Clearly $C^* \subseteq C$ and we show $C^* \preccurlyeq_{\mathsf{S}} C$ by contradiction. So suppose there is some $c_0 \in C$ such that $\neg \exists c' \in C^* : c' \preccurlyeq c_0$. Then $c_0 \notin C^*$ and there must be some $c_1 \in C$ with $c_1 \prec c_0$ for which $\neg \exists c' \in C^* : c' \preccurlyeq c_1$. Continuing like this we construct the sequence $\cdots c_n \prec c_{n-1} \prec \cdots \prec c_0$ assumed not to exist.

This allows us in many cases to restate Definition 2 in the following way that may make it easier to test the condition.

Proposition 2. *If $(\mathcal{C}, \preccurlyeq)$ is well-founded then a program P is i-secure wrt. β whenever*

$$\forall \ell', \ell'' \in \mathbf{L}_i : \{\beta(\pi) \mid P \vdash_i \ell' \mapsto^\pi \ell''\}^* \preccurlyeq_{\mathsf{S}} \{\beta(\pi) \mid P \vdash^i \ell' \mapsto^\pi \ell''\}^*$$

A program P is secure wrt. β whenever it is i-secure wrt. β for all values of $i \in \{1, \cdots, n\}$.

Proof. Under the assumptions stated we have $X \preccurlyeq_{\mathsf{S}} Y$ if and only if $X^* \preccurlyeq_{\mathsf{S}} Y^*$.

In the context of Proposition 2 the minimal frontiers $\{\beta(\pi) \mid P \vdash_i \ell' \mapsto^\pi \ell''\}^*$ and $\{\beta(\pi) \mid P \vdash^i \ell' \mapsto^\pi \ell''\}^*$ can be seen as the *Pareto*-optimal [4] ways of creating a local or remote information flow from $\ell' \in \mathbf{L}_i$ to $\ell'' \in \mathbf{L}_i$.

National Health Service: A Worked Example

We now reconsider our worked example as presented in Sects. 2, 3 and 4.

The idea is that a security violation is a set of *regulations/laws* used to legitimise bypassing the normal security considerations after a certain *duration*:

$$\phi :: = (\{r_1, \cdots, r_n\}, m) \tag{1}$$

where ϕ is the security violation that allows access after the period of m years using (some of) the regulations or laws r_i for $i \in \{1, \cdots, n\}$.

As an example, some data may be released under a *Freedom of Information Act* (FOIA) request after at least 30 years. This could be represented as $(\{FOIA\}, 30)$ while simlar legislation in other jurisdictions may require a moratorium of at least 60 years: $(\{FOIA\}, 60)$.

Similarly some countries/jurisdictions have legislation in place that allows researchers access to highly private data (in the interest of public health) with almost no delay, represented as $(\{RES\}, 0)$. This suggests imposing a partial order on regulations because clearly if information becomes generally available under a FOIA request it is automatically available also to researchers. So we impose a partial ordering $\sqsubseteq$ on regulations such that $FOIA \sqsubseteq RES$.

We now introduce a cost structure to summarise the effect of a sequence of security violations:

$$\mathcal{C} = \mathsf{DownClosure}(Reg) \times \mathbb{N}_0 \tag{2}$$

Here Reg is a *finite* set of regulations containing the r_i mentioned above. Furthermore, $\mathsf{DownClosure}(Reg)$ restricts $\mathsf{PowerSet}(Reg)$ to contain only those sets of regulations that are downwards closed under the partial ordering on regulations; let us write

$$\mathsf{close}(r_1, \cdots, r_n) = \{r \in Reg \mid \exists i \in \{1, \cdots, n\} : r \sqsubseteq r_i\} \tag{3}$$

and note that this ensures that

$$\{r_1, \cdots, r_n\} \subseteq \mathsf{close}(\{r_1, \cdots, r_n\}) = \mathsf{close}(\mathsf{close}(\{r_1, \cdots, r_n\}))$$

We have $\mathsf{close}(\{FOIA\}) = \{FOIA\}$ and $\mathsf{close}(\{RES\}) = \{RES, FOIA\}$.

The definition of the partial order on the cost structure is straightforward (where we use R to range over sets of regulations, including those that are downward closed):

$$(R_1, m_1) \preccurlyeq (R_2, m_2) \quad \text{iff} \quad \mathsf{close}(R_1) \subseteq \mathsf{close}(R_2) \wedge m_1 \leq m_2 \tag{4}$$

We can now define the cost function:

$$\beta(\pi) = \begin{cases} (\{\}, 0) & \text{if } \pi = \epsilon \\ (R' \cup \mathsf{close}(R), \max(m, m')) & \text{if } \pi = \pi'(R, m) \text{ and } \beta(\pi') = (R', m') \end{cases} \tag{5}$$

This ensures that the cost function constructs the downwards closure of the union of *all* sets of regulations used together with the *maximum* delay imposed.

We introduce two *sanitisers* modelling FOIA requests with two different time limits (30 and 60 years respectively): one for the NY and one for LHS:

$$\begin{aligned} &\texttt{foia30: LoNY} \mapsto^{(FOIA, 30)} \texttt{PubNY} \\ &\texttt{foia60: \{medical\}} \mapsto^{(FOIA, 60)} \{\} \end{aligned} \tag{6}$$

By using the sanitisers we can introduce additional local NHS paths, representing that medical data can be released to the public after 60 years:

$$P \vdash_{NHS} \{\text{medical}\} \mapsto^{\texttt{foia60}} \{\} \tag{7}$$

Similarly, the data handled by NY can be released to the public, but already after 30 years:

$$P \vdash_{NY} \texttt{LoNY} \mapsto^{\texttt{foia30}} \texttt{PubNY} \tag{8}$$

The gives rise, among others, to the following remote NHS path

$$P \cdot \vdash^{NHS} \{\text{medical}\} \mapsto^{\texttt{foia30}} \{\} \tag{9}$$

which does *not* have a corerponding local path and hence is *insecure*.

Algorithmic Considerations of Worked Example

The cost structure $(\mathsf{DownClosure}(Reg) \times \mathbb{N}_0, \preccurlyeq)$ satisfies the conditions of Proposition 2 (because Reg is finite) so that we should aim at computing the minimal frontiers $\{\beta(\pi) \mid P \vdash_i \ell' \mapsto^\pi \ell''\}^*$ and $\{\beta(\pi) \mid P \vdash^i \ell' \mapsto^\pi \ell''\}^*$ for all choices of $\ell', \ell'' \in \mathbf{L}_i$.

Minimal Frontiers for Local Paths. To develop an efficient approach for computing $\{\beta(\pi) \mid P \vdash_i \ell' \mapsto^\pi \ell''\}^*$ we need a bit of notation. For $C_1, C_2 \subseteq \mathcal{C}$ write

$$C_1 \otimes C_2 = \{(R_1 \cup R_2, \max(m_1, m_2)) \mid (R_1, m_1) \in C_1, (R_2, m_2) \in C_2\}^*$$

and note that $\{\beta(\pi_1 \pi_2)\} = \{\beta(\pi_1)\} \otimes \{\beta(\pi_2)\}$. Similarly write

$$C_1 \oplus C_2 = (C_1 \cup C_2)^*$$

and in case C_1 and C_2 are already minimal frontiers (i.e. $C_1 = C_1^*$ and $C_2 = C_2^*$) we have

$$
\begin{aligned}
C_1 \oplus C_2 = \ & \{(R, m) \in C_1 \mid R \notin \mathsf{dom}(C_2)\} \ \cup \\
& \{(R, m) \in C_2 \mid R \notin \mathsf{dom}(C_1)\} \ \cup \\
& \{(R, \min(m_1, m_2)) \mid (R, m_1) \in C_1, (R, m_2) \in C_2\}
\end{aligned}
$$

where $\mathsf{dom}(C) = \{R \mid \exists m : (R, m) \in C\}$.

We next aim at constructing $\{\beta(\pi) \mid P \vdash_i \ell' \mapsto^\pi \ell''\}^*$ using dynamic programming. For $\ell', \ell'' \in \mathbf{L}_i$ define

$$\mathcal{P}_i[0](\ell' \rightsquigarrow \ell'') = \big(\{(\emptyset, 0) \mid \ell' \sqsubseteq \ell''\} \cup \{(R, m) \mid S_i \text{ contains } \ell' \mapsto^{(R,m)} \ell''\}\big)^*$$

$$\mathcal{P}_i[n+1](\ell' \rightsquigarrow \ell'') = \mathcal{P}_i[n](\ell' \rightsquigarrow \ell'') \oplus \bigoplus_{\ell \in \mathbf{L}_i} (\mathcal{P}_i[n](\ell' \rightsquigarrow \ell) \otimes \mathcal{P}_i[n](\ell \rightsquigarrow \ell''))$$

where the idea is that $\mathcal{P}_i[n](\ell' \rightsquigarrow \ell'')$ summarises the costs over "paths" of length at most 2^n.

Proposition 3. $\{\beta(\pi) \mid P \vdash_i \ell' \mapsto^\pi \ell''\}^* = \mathcal{P}_i[\lceil \log_2(\mathsf{size}(\mathbf{L}_i)) \rceil](\ell' \rightsquigarrow \ell'')$

Proof. The key observation is that $\beta(\pi_1 \pi_3) \preccurlyeq \beta(\pi_1 \pi_2 \pi_2)$ whenever π_2 arises from a "loop" $P \vdash_i \ell \mapsto^{\pi_2} \ell$ so that in the construction of the minimal frontier for $\{\beta(\pi) \mid P \vdash_i \ell' \mapsto^\pi \ell''\}$ it suffices to consider "paths" that do not involve any repeated occurrences of any security levels in $\mathbf{L}_i$.

Minimal Frontiers for Remote Paths. To develop an efficient approach for computing $\{\beta(\pi) \mid P \vdash^i \ell' \mapsto^\pi \ell''\}^*$ we adapt the above development. For $\ell', \ell'' \in \bigcup_i \mathbf{L}_i$ define

$$\mathcal{P}^{[i]}[0](\ell' \rightsquigarrow \ell'') = \left(\begin{array}{l} \{(\emptyset, 0) \mid \ell' \sqsubseteq \ell'' \text{ in some } \mathbf{L}_j \text{ for } i \neq j\} \ \cup \\ \{(R, m) \mid S_j \text{ contains } \ell' \mapsto^{(R,m)} \ell'' \text{ for } i \neq j\} \ \cup \\ \{(R, m) \mid E \text{ contains } \ell' \mapsto^{(R,m)} \ell''\} \end{array} \right)^*$$

$$\mathcal{P}^{[i]}[n+1](\ell' \rightsquigarrow \ell'') = \mathcal{P}^{[i]}[n](\ell' \rightsquigarrow \ell'') \oplus \bigoplus_{\ell \notin \mathbf{L}_i} (\mathcal{P}^{[i]}[n](\ell' \rightsquigarrow \ell) \otimes \mathcal{P}^{[i]}[n](\ell \rightsquigarrow \ell''))$$

where as before the idea is that $\mathcal{P}^{[i]}[n](\ell' \rightsquigarrow \ell'')$ summarises the costs over "paths" of length at most 2^n.

Proposition 4. *For $\ell', \ell'' \in L_i$ we have*

$$\{\beta(\pi) \mid P \vdash^i \ell' \mapsto^\pi \ell''\}^* = \mathcal{P}^{[i]}[\lceil \log_2(\text{size}(L_1 \cup \cdots \cup L_n)) \rceil]](\ell' \rightsquigarrow \ell'')$$

A better bound could be obtained by omitting L_i in the above set union.

6 Conclusion

We have illustrated a way in which it may be ensured that local security policies are not violated when communication between lecal systems are admitted. One might see this as a light-weight attempt at adapting notions of non-interference to distributed systems in a way that is compatiable with how our society operates, in particular what is required in order to document a security violation.

Existing work on enforcing security in a distributed system with data sharing includes the *myKlaim* calculus [8] that proposes as a way to model and reason about *open* systems in which external, third-party code may be allowed inside a system to then be executed in a 'sandbox' environment to maintain security. The *Fabric* framework [1,9] aims at developing a programming language and underlying system for designing and implementing distributed systems in a safe and secure manner. The security policies are based on an extended version of the *decentralised label model* [11,12]. This allows *principals*, essentially programs, to specify degrees of trust in other (remote) programs and thereby bound the potential security impact if that node should be compromised. The main problems, insights, and solutions concerning the relationship between secure information flow and trust are distilled and further explored in the *Flow-Limited Authorization Model* [2] and the *Flow-Limited Authorization Calculus* [3] for reasoning about dynamic authorisation decisions.

Our approach was motivated by the development of [5] that studies the notion of *Lagois connection* (a modification of Galois connections) to avoid information flow breaches when connnecting security domains. As argued in [13] (that deals with mobility of agents) we find our graph based approach to be more flexible and this is the basis for our ability to develop the concept of *secure wrt. β*.

Acknowledgement. The first author was supported in part by the EU H2020-SU-ICT-03-2018 Project No. 830929 *CyberSec4Europe* (cybersec4europe.eu). The first and second authors were supported in part by the Danish project *Security by Design* granted by The Danish Industry Foundation. The third author is retired from the Department of Mathematics and Computer Science, Technical University of Denmark, Kgs. Lyngby, Denmark.

A Semantics

As in [15] and [13] we use operational semantics to define the semantics of Secure Guarded Commands with Security Domains.

Expressions are evaluated with respect to a memory σ that assigns values to all variables of interest and the semantic judgement defined in Fig. 7 takes the

$$\frac{}{\sigma \vdash n \rhd n} \qquad \frac{}{\sigma \vdash s \rhd s} \qquad \frac{}{\sigma \vdash \mathbf{true} \rhd \mathbf{tt}}$$

$$\frac{\sigma \vdash e_1 \rhd v_1 \quad \sigma \vdash e_2 \rhd v_2}{\sigma \vdash e_1 + e_2 \rhd v_1 + v_2} \qquad \frac{\sigma \vdash e_1 \rhd v_1 \quad \sigma \vdash e_2 \rhd v_2}{\sigma \vdash e_1 = e_2 \rhd v_1 = v_2} \qquad \frac{\sigma \vdash e_1 \rhd v_1 \quad \sigma \vdash e_2 \rhd v_2}{\sigma \vdash e_1 \wedge e_2 \rhd v_1 \wedge v_2}$$

$$\frac{}{\sigma \vdash x \rhd \sigma(x)} \text{ if } \sigma(x) \text{ defined} \qquad \frac{\sigma \vdash e_1 \rhd v_1}{\sigma \vdash d {\downarrow} e_1 \rhd v_1}$$

Fig. 7. Semantics of expressions.

$$\frac{\sigma \vdash e \rhd v}{(x := e, \sigma) \to^\tau (\sqrt{}, \sigma[x \mapsto v])} \text{ if } \sigma(x) \text{ is defined}$$

$$\frac{(C_1, \sigma) \to^\varphi (C_1', \sigma')}{(C_1 ; C_2, \sigma) \to^\varphi (C_1' ; C_2, \sigma')} \text{ if } C_1' \neq \sqrt{} \qquad \frac{(C_1, \sigma) \to^\varphi (\sqrt{}, \sigma')}{(C_1 ; C_2, \sigma) \to^\varphi (C_2, \sigma')}$$

$$\frac{\sigma \vdash e_i \rhd \mathbf{tt}}{(\mathbf{if} \ e_1 \to C_1 \ \Box \ \cdots \ \Box \ e_n \to C_n \ \mathbf{fi}, \sigma) \to^\tau (C_i, \sigma)}$$

$$\frac{\sigma \vdash e_i \rhd \mathbf{tt}}{(\mathbf{do} \ \cdots \ \Box \ e_i \to C_i \ \Box \ \cdots \ \mathbf{od}, \sigma) \to^\tau (C_i ; \mathbf{do} \ \cdots \ \Box \ e_i \to C_i \ \Box \ \cdots \ \mathbf{od}, \sigma)}$$

$$\frac{\sigma \vdash e_1 \rhd \mathbf{ff} \quad \cdots \quad \sigma \vdash e_n \rhd \mathbf{ff}}{(\mathbf{do} \ e_1 \to C_1 \ \Box \ \cdots \ \Box \ e_n \to C_n \ \mathbf{od}, \sigma) \to^\tau (\sqrt{}, \sigma)}$$

$$\frac{(C_i, \sigma) \to^\varphi (C_i', \sigma')}{(\mathbf{sum} \ C_1 \ \Box \ \cdots \ \Box \ C_n \ \mathbf{mus}, \sigma) \to^\varphi (C_i', \sigma')}$$

$$\frac{\sigma \vdash e \rhd v}{(c!e, \sigma) \to^{c!v} (\sqrt{}, \sigma)} \qquad \frac{}{(c?x, \sigma) \to^{c?v} (\sqrt{}, \sigma[x \mapsto v])} \text{ if } \sigma(x) \text{ is defined}$$

Fig. 8. Semantics of commands.

form $\sigma \vdash e \rhd v$. Evaluation is undefined if the expression accesses a variable for which the memory does not assign a value. Note that the value of $d {\downarrow} e_1$ is the same as the value of e_1.

Commands are executed with respect to a memory and produce a new memory. The semantic judgement defined in Fig. 8 takes the form $(C, \sigma) \to^\varphi (C', \sigma')$. the superscript φ indicates whether the action is silent (τ), an input ($c?v$) or an output ($c!v$). We allow C and C' to range both over commands and the special symbol $\sqrt{}$ indicating a terminated configuration.

Processes have disjoint memories so they can only exchange values by communicating over the channels. More precisely this means that for each process we will have a local memory assigning values to the variables of interest and we shall be based on synchronous communication. For processes the semantic judgement defined in Fig. 9 takes the form

$$(E \ \mathbf{par} \ L_1 \ S_1 \ D_1 \ C_1 \cdots L_n \ S_n \ D_n \ C_n \ \mathbf{rap}, \sigma_1 \cdots \sigma_n)$$
$$\to (E \ \mathbf{par} \ L_1 \ S_1 \ D_1 \ C_1' \cdots L_n \ S_n \ D_n \ C_n' \ \mathbf{rap}, \sigma_1' \cdots \sigma_n')$$

where once more we allow C and C' to range both over commands and the special symbol $\sqrt{}$ indicating a terminated configuration. The first rule says that we can let one of the constituent processes perform a silent step adn the second

$$\frac{(C_i, \sigma_i) \to^\tau (C'_i, \sigma'_i)}{\begin{array}{l}(E \text{ par } \cdots L_i \, S_i \, D_i \, C_i \cdots \text{rap}, \cdots \sigma_i \cdots) \\ \to (E \text{ par } \cdots L_i \, S_i \, D_i \, C'_i \cdots \text{rap}, \cdots \sigma'_i \cdots)\end{array}} \quad \text{if } \mathsf{dom}(\sigma_i) \supseteq \mathsf{dom}(\mathsf{env}(D_i))$$

$$\frac{(C_i, \sigma_i) \to^{c \,!\, v} (C'_i, \sigma'_i) \qquad (C_j, \sigma_j) \to^{c \,?\, v} (C'_j, \sigma'_j)}{\begin{array}{l}(E \text{ par } \cdots L_i \, S_i \, D_i \, C_i \,\llbracket\, L_j \, S_j \, D_j \, C_j \cdots \text{rap}, \cdots \sigma_i \sigma_j \cdots) \\ \to (E \text{ par } \cdots L_i \, S_i \, D_i \, C'_i \,\llbracket\, L_j \, S_j \, D_j \, C'_j \cdots \text{rap}, \cdots \sigma'_i \sigma'_j \cdots)\end{array}} \quad \text{if } \begin{cases} \mathsf{dom}(\sigma_i) \supseteq \\ \quad \mathsf{dom}(\mathsf{env}(D_i)) \\ \mathsf{dom}(\sigma_j) \supseteq \\ \quad \mathsf{dom}(\mathsf{env}(D_j)) \\ c \in \mathsf{dom}(\mathsf{env}(E)) \end{cases}$$

Fig. 9. Semantics of systems.

rule says (omitting the details needed to deal with input and output being placed in another order) that we can let two constituent processes produce matching input and output actions. The side conditions of the rules insist that the domain of local memories (written $\mathsf{dom}(\sigma_i)$) includes the local variables declared in the program (written $\mathsf{dom}(\mathsf{env}(D_i))$) and that the channel used for communication is indeed declared in the program (written $\mathsf{dom}(\mathsf{env}(E))$) where the environments and declarations are constructed using $\mathsf{env}(\cdots)$ as defined previously. Note that if one of the processes terminates then the corresponding component in the configuration will contain $\sqrt{}$ and it will not be able to evolve further.

References

1. Arden, O., George, M.D., Liu, J., Vikram, K., Askarov, A., Myers, A.C.: Sharing mobile code securely with information flow control. In: Proceedings of the Symposium on Security and Privacy (SP 2012), pp. 191–205 (2012). https://doi.org/10.1109/SP.2012.22
2. Arden, O., Liu, J., Myers, A.C.: Flow-limited authorization. In: Proceedings of the 28th Computer Security Foundations Symposium (CSF 2015), pp. 569–583 (2015). https://doi.org/10.1109/CSF.2015.42
3. Arden, O., Myers, A.C.: A calculus for flow-limited authorization. In: Proceedings of the 29th Computer Security Foundations Symposium (CSF 2016), pp. 135–149 (2016). https://doi.org/10.1109/CSF.2016.17
4. Aslanyan, Z., Nielson, F.: Pareto efficient solutions of attack-defence trees. In: Focardi, R., Myers, A. (eds.) POST 2015. LNCS, vol. 9036, pp. 95–114. Springer, Heidelberg (2015). https://doi.org/10.1007/978-3-662-46666-7_6
5. Bhardwaj, C., Prasad, S.: Only connect, securely. In: Pérez, J.A., Yoshida, N. (eds.) FORTE 2019. LNCS, vol. 11535, pp. 75–92. Springer, Cham (2019). https://doi.org/10.1007/978-3-030-21759-4_5
6. Dijkstra, E.W.: Guarded commands, nondeterminacy and formal derivation of programs. Commun. ACM **18**(8), 453–457 (1975)
7. Gollmann, D.: Computer Security, 3rd edn. Wiley, Hoboken (2011)
8. Hansen, R.R., Probst, C.W., Nielson, F.: Sandboxing in myKlaim. In: Proceedings of the International Conference on Availability, Reliability and Security (ARES 2006), pp. 174–181 (2006). https://doi.org/10.1109/ARES.2006.115

9. Liu, J., Arden, O., George, M.D., Myers, A.C.: Fabric: building open distributed systems securely by construction. J. Comput. Secur. **25**(4–5), 367–426 (2017). https://doi.org/10.3233/JCS-15805

10. de Moura, L., Bjørner, N.: Z3: an efficient SMT solver. In: Ramakrishnan, C.R., Rehof, J. (eds.) TACAS 2008. LNCS, vol. 4963, pp. 337–340. Springer, Heidelberg (2008). https://doi.org/10.1007/978-3-540-78800-3_24

11. Myers, A.C., Liskov, B.: A decentralized model for information flow control. In: Proceedings of the 16th ACM Symposium on Operating Systems Principles (SOSP 1997) (1997)

12. Myers, A.C., Liskov, B.: Protecting privacy using the decentralized label model. ACM Trans. Softw. Eng. Methodol. **9**(4), 410–442 (2000)

13. Nielson, F., Hansen, R.R., Nielson, H.R.: Adaptive security policies. In: Margaria, T., Steffen, B. (eds.) ISoLA 2020. LNCS, vol. 12477, pp. 280–294. Springer, Cham (2020). https://doi.org/10.1007/978-3-030-61470-6_17

14. Nielson, F., Nielson, H.R.: Lightweight information flow. In: Boreale, M., Corradini, F., Loreti, M., Pugliese, R. (eds.) Models, Languages, and Tools for Concurrent and Distributed Programming. LNCS, vol. 11665, pp. 455–470. Springer, Cham (2019). https://doi.org/10.1007/978-3-030-21485-2_25

15. Nielson, F., Nielson, H.R.: Secure guarded commands. In: Di Pierro, A., Malacaria, P., Nagarajan, R. (eds.) From Lambda Calculus to Cybersecurity Through Program Analysis. LNCS, vol. 12065, pp. 201–215. Springer, Cham (2020). https://doi.org/10.1007/978-3-030-41103-9_7

16. Ramli, C.D.P.K., Nielson, H.R., Nielson, F.: The logic of XACML. Sci. Comput. Program. **83**, 80–105 (2014)

17. Volpano, D.M., Irvine, C.E.: Secure flow typing. Comput. Secur. **16**(2), 137–144 (1997)

18. Volpano, D.M., Irvine, C.E., Smith, G.: A sound type system for secure flow analysis. J. Comput. Secur. **4**(2/3), 167–188 (1996)

Probabilistic Annotations
for Protocol Models

Dedicated to Joshua Guttman

Dusko Pavlovic[⊠]

University of Hawaii, Honolulu, HI, USA
dusko@hawaii.edu

Abstract. We describe how a probabilistic Hoare logic with localities can be used for reasoning about security. As a proof-of-concept, we analyze Vernam and El-Gamal cryptosystems, prove the security properties that they do satisfy, and disprove those that they do not. We also consider a version of the Muddy Children puzzle, where children's trust and noise are taken into account.

1 Introduction

When it was first suggested that I should study security protocols, it was with a remark that the problem was largely solved and that I should simply look for a way to apply the solution to a particular protocol of interest, which happened to be one of the proposals for the IPSec suite. I found a paper that was circulating under the title *'How to solve any protocol problem'* [8], and spent some time studying the methods of multi-party computation described in it. When I realized that I was not making any progress towards analyzing the IPSec protocol at hand, I went back and found out that the suggested solution of all protocol problems was not the multi-party computation, but strand spaces [10,11,15–17]. I drew the strand space bundles corresponding to the IPSec proposal the same afternoon.

Trying to save the science of security protocol design and analysis from its foretold demise, I spent a good part of the next 10 years looking for problems that could not be solved using the strand space model. Each time, I would then meet Joshua Guttman over dinner, usually at one of the Protocol eXchange meetings, and told him that there was this conceptual mismatch between his model and the reality, and he would then suggest how the problem of reality could be adjusted to match the strand spaces, and transformed towards a solution. On one or two occasions when I was too far down the road towards different solutions, I avoided asking about the details.

D. Pavlovic—Partially supported by NSF and AFOSR.

D. Dougherty et al. (Eds.): Guttman Festschrift, LNCS 13066, pp. 332–347, 2021.
https://doi.org/10.1007/978-3-030-91631-2_18

But here is a record of something that definitely cannot be done by strand spaces. It has been clear from the outset that the strand space bundles can be annotated by Floyd-Hoare-style logical annotations [4, 6, 7], and that the various forms of dynamic and epistemic logics, worked out for reasoning about the preconditions, postconditions, and invariants of computations, can be elevated and generalized for reasoning about protocol security [2, 12] and about the higher-order properties of distributed systems and network interactions [13]. But what if we need to reason about the guessing chances, and have to go beyond the Dolev-Yao type of models [5][1]?

2   Crypto-Logical Systems

Towards a definition of a *crypto-logical system*, we begin from two basic data types: *states* S and *predicates* $\mathcal{P}$. It is assumed that they are generated by a stratified set of algebraic operations, which allow us to write programs that lead to the states in S, and to specify the resulting properties in $\mathcal{P}$. In particular, both S and $\mathcal{P}$ are built over the same algebra $\mathcal{T}$ of terms, usually multisorted, assumed to contain enough variables, constants, and function symbols to specify keys, nonces, encryptions, decryptions, hashes, etc. These terms are computed, sent, and received by some actions that may be recorded in $q, s \ldots \in S$, while they may be compared, tested, and reasoned about in $\varphi, \psi \ldots \in \mathcal{P}$.

2.1   Crude and Overly General Definition

Given a state space S, an algebra of predicates $\mathcal{P}$, a set of agents $\mathcal{A}$, and a lattice of observations $\mathcal{O}$, a *crypto-logical system* is defined by the following data:

– a family of *semantic* maps

$$\mathcal{P} \times S \times \mathcal{P} \xrightarrow{\ -\{-\}_A-\ } \mathcal{O}$$

indexed over the agents $A \in \mathcal{A}$,
– a measure

$$S \xrightarrow{\ \mu\ } \mathbb{R}_+$$

given with a decomposition of S into a disjoint union $S = \coprod_{i \in I} S_i$ of unit sets S_i, i.e. such that $\Pr(S_i) = 1$ holds for each $i \in I$. (Each restriction $\Pr_i$ of $\Pr$ to S_i is thus a probability measure.)

---

[1] There are, of course, many ways to go beyond the Dolev-Yao models and formalize probabilistic and computational reasoning in cryptography. One of the reviewers suggests that Easycrypt [1] should be mentioned. The point here is, however, to try to extend by probabilities the usual Floyd-Hoare annotations, which naturally fit with strand spaces.

Remarks. The above definition is more general than will be needed in this paper. But it conveys the big picture and the general path.

First of all, we do not need an abstract lattice of observations $\mathcal{O}$, but will always take $\mathcal{O} = \{0, 1\}$, and work with the usual Hoare triples $\varphi\{q\}_A\psi$, which are simply the elements of a ternary relation over $\mathcal{P} \times \mathcal{S} \times \mathcal{P}$. The reason for the above formulation is that the probabilistic analysis below will suggest that the *probabilistic* Hoare triples, evaluated in $\mathcal{O} = [0, 1]$, are also of interest, and in fact simplify some aspects of the reasoning. This option should be kept in mind for future work.

The decomposition of the state space $\mathcal{S} = \coprod_{i \in I} \mathcal{S}_i$ allowing the decomposition of the measure μ into the probability measures μ_i will also not play a significant role. It is in principle needed in the examples in Sects. 3 and 4, where the state spaces will be certain powers of the monoid $\Sigma = \{0, 1\}^*$ of bitstrings, decomposed into $\Sigma = \coprod_{n=0}^{\infty} \{0, 1\}^n$, with the uniform probability distribution over each finite component $\{0, 1\}^n$. But this is spelled out in many textbooks, and the decomposition would flood the notations by information that is inessential for this paper, and hide the aspects that are essential. So we reduce the measure $\mu : \mathcal{S} \longrightarrow \mathbb{R}_+$ to the component probabilities $\Pr : \mathcal{S} \longrightarrow [0, 1]$, omitting the indices as they are easily reconstructed in all cases.

Furthermore, a state q in the space $\mathcal{S}$ may or may not contain a record of a particular computation, run, or process that led to it. Short of a better word, we stretch the word "state" to mean "a result of a computation"—whatever part of it we may choose to record. Sometimes it may be the whole history, even including the intermediary results; sometimes just the outcome. A consequence is that $\mathcal{S}$ may be closed under the usual programming and process operations, or it may be structured by the recorded data alone. In the former case, the usual rules of the Hoare logic will apply. In the latter case, when the concrete computations are not reflected by modal operators in $\mathcal{S}$, the Hoare notation boils down to

$$q \underset{A}{\models} \psi \iff \top \{q\}_A \psi$$

On the other hand, when the preconditions do play an essential role, relying upon the Hoare logic tradition and intuition seems appropriate, and useful.

In any case, we always require that the semantic maps $\mathcal{P} \times \mathcal{S} \times \mathcal{P} \longrightarrow \mathcal{O}$ preserve the lattice structure of $\mathcal{P}$, contravariantly in the first, precondition argument, and covariantly in the postcondition.

2.2 Information Sets and Preorders of States

We say that, for an agent A, a process q' *refines* a process q, or that it *contains more information than* q, and we write $q \underset{A}{\sqsubseteq} q'$, whenever q' satisfies, as far as A can tell, all the requirements that q satisfies:

$$q \underset{A}{\sqsubseteq} q' \iff \forall \varphi \psi. \, \varphi\{q\}_A\psi \leq \varphi\{q'\}_A\psi$$

Two processes are indistinguishable for the agent A if they satisfy the same requirements

$$q \underset{A}{\sim} q' \iff q \underset{A}{\sqsubseteq} q' \wedge q \underset{A}{\sqsupseteq} q'$$
$$\iff \forall \varphi \psi. \; \varphi \{q\}_A \psi = \varphi \{q'\}_A \psi$$

The $\underset{A}{\sim}$-equivalence classes are A's *information sets*. The quotient $\mathcal{S}_A = \mathcal{S}/\underset{A}{\sim}$ is A's information view. A's information set at q is written $q_A \in \mathcal{S}_A$.

2.3   Refining the Definition of Crypto-Logical Systems

The data type $\mathcal{P}$ of predicates is assumed to support the usual logical connectives, which make it into a lattice. Moreover, it is also closed under a family of modalities W_ι, indexed over some *subjective evaluations* $\iota \in \mathcal{J}[0,1]$, which will be just numbers between 0 and 1 in the simple examples below, but need to be generalized for some more involved cryptographic constructions. Semantics of these logical operations is defined by the following conditions

$$(\varphi_1 \vee \varphi_2) \{q\}_A \; \psi \iff (\varphi_1\{q\}_A\psi) \wedge (\varphi_2\{q\}_A\psi) \tag{1}$$

$$\varphi \{q\}_A (\psi_1 \wedge \psi_2) \iff (\varphi\{q\}_A\psi_1) \wedge (\varphi\{q\}_A\psi_2) \tag{2}$$

$$\varphi \{q\}_A (W_\iota\psi) \iff \Pr\left(\varphi \{s\}_A \; \psi \; \middle| \; s \underset{A}{\sim} q\right) \in \iota \tag{3}$$

The Hoare triples here are the standard ones, evaluated in $\mathcal{O} = \{0,1\}$, as explained in Sect. 2.1. Clause (3) extends the standard Hoare logic for probabilistic reasoning. The idea is that

- A's subjective probability that ψ holds after φ at q is equal to
- the objective probability that ψ holds after φ at a randomly chosen state $s \underset{A}{\sim} q$.

By definition, the conditional probability in the last clause unfolds to

$$\Pr\left(\varphi \{s\}_A \; \psi \; \middle| \; s \underset{A}{\sim} q\right) = \frac{\Pr\left\{s \in \mathcal{S} \mid s \underset{A}{\sim} q \wedge \varphi \{s\}_A \; \psi\right\}}{\Pr\left\{s \in \mathcal{S} \mid s \underset{A}{\sim} q\right\}}$$

The subjective vs objective probability conundrum goes back to the earliest days of probability theory [3] and persists as a useful distinction even in cryptographic reasoning. The objective probability is a number, which can be obtained, e.g., by counting frequencies. An observer of a random process, however, may only be able to estimate that a probability falls within a certain interval, or just in a set, measurable modulo computational indistinguishability. There are thus various generality levels at which the family $\mathcal{J}[0,1]$ of subjective evaluations may need to be modeled. To capture the standard cryptographic definitions in Sect. 3, the subjective evaluations from $\mathcal{J}[0,1]$ will need to be feasibly computable subintervals of $[0,1]$. For the simple examples presented in Sect. 4, on the other hand, rational numbers will suffice.

2.4   Probability vs. Knowledge

Note that the statement $W_1\psi$, saying that ψ is satisfied with probability 1,

$$\varphi \{q\}_A (W_1\psi) \iff \Pr\left(\varphi \{s\}_A \psi \mid s \underset{A}{\sim} q\right) = 1$$

can be viewed as a generalization of the knowledge modality $K\psi$ for A defined by

$$\varphi \{q\}_A(K\psi) \iff \forall s \in \mathcal{S}.\; s \underset{A}{\sim} q \Rightarrow \varphi\{s\}\psi$$

where the logical implication $s \underset{A}{\sim} q \Rightarrow \varphi\{s\}\psi$ is replaced by the stochastic implication

$$\left[s \underset{A}{\sim} q \Rightarrow \varphi\{s\}\psi\right] \iff \Pr\left(\varphi \{s\}_A \psi \mid s \underset{A}{\sim} q\right) = 1$$

Intuitively, this stochastic implication says that the implication is valid almost everywhere, i.e. everywhere except at a set of measure 0. While the usual semantics of knowledge tells that $K\psi$ is satisfied for A after φ at q if ψ is satisfied after φ at every $s \underset{A}{\sim} q$, the probabilistic knowledge $W_1\psi$ is satisfied after φ for almost all $s \underset{A}{\sim} q$, i.e. with a possible exception of a set of measure 0. For each A, the statements $K\psi$ and $W_1\psi$ are *almost everywhere* equivalent, i.e. they only differ at a set of states of measure 0. Since cryptographic proofs are not just up to sets of measure 0, but usually identify even the ensembles that are computationally indistinguishable[2] the knowledge modality should, for all cryptographic purposes, be identified with W_1.

2.5   Global Semantics

We say that a requirement is satisfied globally if some agent observes that it is satisfied

$$\varphi \{q\} \psi \iff \exists X.\; \varphi \{q\}_X \psi \tag{4}$$

In practice, crypto-logical systems are often given by

- a *global semantics*

$$\mathcal{P} \times \mathcal{S} \times \mathcal{P} \xrightarrow{\;-\{-\}-\;} \mathcal{O}$$

---

[2] Two ensembles are computationally indistinguishable when their differences cannot be detected by polynomially bounded computations, e.g. because they occur only superpolynomially far down the strings of digits of their probabilities.

– a family of *views*

$$\mathcal{S} \xrightarrow{(-)_A} \mathcal{S}$$

indexed by $A \in \mathcal{A}$ such that

$$(\forall X.\ q_X = q'_X) \iff q = q' \text{ and} \tag{5}$$
$$\varphi \{q\}\ \psi \iff \exists X.\ \varphi \{q_X\}\ \psi \tag{6}$$

Local semantics can then be defined by

$$\varphi \{q\}_A\ \psi \iff \varphi \{q_A\}\ \psi$$

Condition (6) implies that (4) recovers the global semantics. Condition (5) implies that $q \sim_A q' \iff q_A = q'_A$. In other words, since all $q' \sim_A q$ satisfy the same requirements $\varphi\{q'\}_A\psi$ if and only if q_A satisfies them, then q_A can be taken as the canonical representative of the information set $[q]_A \in \mathcal{S}_A$.

2.6 Knowledge of Probability vs Probability of Knowledge

The *logical* interpretation of the probabilistic modality W_ι, proposed in (3), was stated over the observations in $\mathcal{O} = \{0,1\}$. Allowing the observations to be evaluated in $\mathcal{O} = [0,1]$, and replacing the logical equivalence in (1) and (2) by the equality or indistinguishability of probabilities, leads to the probabilistic interpretation of the knowledge modality

$$\varphi \{q\}_A(\mathsf{K}\psi) = \Pr\left(\varphi \{s\}\ \psi\ \middle|\ s \underset{A}{\sim} q\right)$$

and promotes W_ι into a *confidence* modality

$$\varphi \{q\}_A(\mathsf{W}_\iota\psi) = \Pr\left(\Pr\left(\varphi \{s\}\ \psi\ \middle|\ s \underset{A}{\sim} q\right) \in \iota\right)$$

But this refined view has to be left for future work, as it requires first spelling out the standard view of familiar concepts, which barely fit in the rest of this paper.

3 Cryptographic Definitions in Crypto-Logic

A *cryptosystem* consists of three agents, each executing a single probabilistic algorithm:

– key generation $\mathsf{Gen} : \mathcal{R} \longrightarrow \mathcal{K} \times \mathcal{K}$,
– encryption $\mathsf{Enc} : \mathcal{K} \times \mathcal{R} \times \mathcal{M} \longrightarrow \mathcal{C}$, and
– decryption $\mathsf{Dec} : \mathcal{K} \times \mathcal{C} \longrightarrow \mathcal{M}$,

such that

$$\mathsf{Dec}(\overline{k}, \mathsf{Enc}(k, x, m)) = m$$

where $\langle k, \overline{k} \rangle = \mathsf{Gen}(y)$ for some $y \in \mathcal{R}$. Here $\mathcal{R}$ represents the data type of random seeds, $\mathcal{K}$ is the datatype of keys, $\mathcal{M}$ the datatype of plaintext messages, and $\mathcal{C}$ the ciphertexts. All datatypes are assumed to be finite, although unfeasibly large, so that it is sometimes convenient to assume that they are countably infinite. Each of them is given with a frequency measure

$$\Pr : \mathcal{X} \longrightarrow [0, 1]$$

When no confusion seems likely, we shall denote a random variable sampling from $\mathcal{X}$ also by $\mathcal{X}$, and write $\Pr(x \in \mathcal{X})$ where most probability theory textbooks would write $\Pr(\mathcal{X} = x)$.

Besides the principals of the cryptosystem, a definition of a security property that it may satisfy involves an attacker Att, which may operate any number of algorithms.

Remark. The notion of an *algorithm* is used here in the broadest sense, accomodating the various notions of computation. While the *computational* notions of security are defined assuming Probabilistic Polynomial-time Turing (PPT) machine as the standard model of computation, the *information-theoretic* security is defined over a notion of computation which boils down to mere *guessing* (of a message, a key, etc.), according to given frequency distributions. We begin with an information-theoretic definition.

Definition 1. *A cryptosystem is* perfectly secure *if Attacker's chance to guess a message m at a state C, when he is given a ciphertext $c = E(k, x, m)$ is the same as his chance to guess that message at a state O, where he is not given any data, and can just randomly sample the space $\mathcal{M}$ of messages:*

$$C \models \mathsf{W}_\iota(m \in \mathcal{M}) \qquad \Longleftrightarrow \qquad O \models \mathsf{W}_\iota(m \in \mathcal{M}) \qquad \text{(IT-SEC)}$$

Definition 2. *Semantic (or chosen plaintext) security of a cryptosystem is tested by the following protocol:*

- *the Attacker computes (or randomly selects) two messages, m_0 and m_1, and sends them to the Encryption oracle;*
- *the Encryption oracle tosses a coin, i.e. randomly selects a bit b, and a seed $x \in \mathcal{R}$, computes the ciphertext $c = E(k, x, m_b)$, and sends it to the Attacker.*

The cryptosystem is semantically secure *if Attacker's chance to compute (or to guess) the bit b at the final state C, when c is known to him, is not greater than his chance to guess b at the initial state O, without any data, i.e.*

$$C \models \mathsf{W}_\iota(b = 1) \qquad \Longleftrightarrow \qquad O \models \mathsf{W}_\iota(b = 1) \qquad \text{(IND-CPA)}$$

Definition 3. Adaptive *(or* chosen ciphertext*) security of a cryptosystem is tested by the following protocol:*

- *the Attacker computes (or randomly selects) two messages, m_0 and m_1, and sends them to the Encryption oracle;*
- *the Encryption oracle tosses a coin, i.e. randomly selects a bit b, and a seed $x \in \mathcal{R}$, computes the ciphertext $c = E(k, x, m_b)$, and sends it to the Attacker,*
- *the Attacker is then allowed to consult the Decryption oracle, to obtain the decryption $d = D(\overline{k}, c')$, of a chosen piece if ciphertext c' is feasibly constructed from m_0, m_1 and c, but differs from c, i.e. $c' \neq c$.*

The cryptosystem is adaptive secure if Attacker's chance to compute (or to guess) the bit b at the final state C, when the ciphertext c and the decryption d are known to him, is not greater than his chance to guess b at the initial state O, without any data, i.e.

$$C \models \mathsf{W}_\iota\, (b = 1) \qquad \Longleftrightarrow \qquad O \models \mathsf{W}_\iota\, (b = 1) \qquad \text{(IND-CCA)}$$

Remark. Varying the notion of computation in the above definition results in different notions of security. If the notion of computation is reduced to guessing, i.e. if the Attacker can only randomly choose m_0 and m_1, and only randomly guess b, but possibly following a probability distribution skewed by the knowledge of c, then we get a weaker notion of security than the one where the Attacker can perform more structured computation, e.g. of a Probabilistic Polynomial-Time Turing Machine (PPT).

4   Examples of Reasoning in Crypto-Logic

4.1   Security of the Vernam Cryptosystem

In the Vernam cryptosystem, we take

$$\mathcal{K} = \{0, 1\}^\ell$$
$$\mathcal{M} = \mathcal{K}^j$$
$$\mathcal{C} = \mathcal{M}$$
$$\mathcal{R} = 1$$

and then define

$$E(k, m) \;=\; D(k, m) = k^j \oplus m$$

where $\oplus$ is the *exclusive or* operation, and k^j is the j-tuple concatenation of a key k. We assume that the messages have a fixed number of blocks j just to avoid inessential notational details. The probability distributions over $\mathcal{K}$ and over $\mathcal{M}$ are given, and they determine

$$\Pr(c \in \mathcal{C}) = \sum_{k^j \oplus m = c} \Pr(m \in \mathcal{M}) \cdot \Pr(k \in \mathcal{K})$$

The Vernam cryptosystem is called *one-time pad* when $j = 1$, i.e. when a key is used to encrypt just one block.

Proposition 1. *One-time pad is perfectly secure. The Vernam cryptosystem is not perfectly secure for $j \geq 2$.*

Proof. To model the (IT-SEC) testing of the Vernam cryptosystem, we use as the states in $\mathcal{S}$ the substrings of the triples $\langle k, m, c \rangle \in \mathcal{K} \times \mathcal{M} \times \mathcal{C}$, subject to the constraint that $c = k^j \oplus m$. Each state can be construed as the record of an encryption session, where the key k is first generated and sent from Gen to Enc, then the message m is chosen and encrypted by Enc into $c = k \oplus m$, and finally, the ciphertext c is sent to Dec and Att.

For each agent $X \in \{\mathsf{Gen}, \mathsf{Enc}, \mathsf{Dec}, \mathsf{Att}\}$ we define the view function $\mathcal{S} \xrightarrow{(-)_X} \mathcal{S}$ to be

$$\langle k, m, c \rangle_{\mathsf{Gen}} = \langle k \rangle$$
$$\langle k, m, c \rangle_{\mathsf{Enc}} = \langle k, m, c \rangle$$
$$\langle k, m, c \rangle_{\mathsf{Dec}} = \langle k, c \rangle$$
$$\langle k, m, c \rangle_{\mathsf{Att}} = \langle c \rangle$$

The data type $\mathcal{P}$ of predicates is generated from the formulas of binary arithmetic, extended with the probabilistic modalities W_ι.

We define semantics by stipulating that $\varphi \{q\}_X \psi$ is satisfied whenever the implication $\varphi(q_X) \Rightarrow \psi(q_X)$ is provable in binary arithmetic and elementary probability theory, starting from the given distributions $\Pr_{\mathcal{M}}$, and $\Pr_{\mathcal{K}}$.

Towards a proof of (IT-SEC) property for $j = 1$, first note that

$$\langle \rangle \models \mathsf{W}_a(m \in \mathcal{M}) \qquad \Longleftrightarrow \qquad \Pr(m \in \mathcal{M}) = a$$
$$\langle c \rangle \models \mathsf{W}_b(m \in \mathcal{M}) \qquad \Longleftrightarrow \qquad \Pr(m \in \mathcal{M} \mid c \in \mathcal{C}) = b$$

On the other hand,

$$\Pr(m \in \mathcal{M} \mid c \in \mathcal{C}) = \frac{\Pr(c \in \mathcal{C} \mid m \in \mathcal{M}) \cdot \Pr(m \in \mathcal{M})}{\Pr(c \in \mathcal{C})}$$
$$= \Pr(m \in \mathcal{M})$$

holds because

$$\Pr(c \in \mathcal{C} \mid m \in \mathcal{M}) = \Pr(c = k \oplus m \in \mathcal{C} \mid m \in \mathcal{M})$$
$$= \Pr(k = c \oplus m \in \mathcal{K} \mid m \in \mathcal{M})$$
$$= \Pr(k \in \mathcal{K})$$

and

$$\Pr(c \in \mathcal{C}) = \sum_{m \in \mathcal{M}} \Pr(c \in \mathcal{C} \mid m \in \mathcal{M}) \cdot \Pr(m \in \mathcal{M})$$
$$= \Pr(k \in \mathcal{K}) \sum_{m \in \mathcal{M}} \Pr(m \in \mathcal{M})$$
$$= \Pr(k \in \mathcal{K})$$

It follows that $\langle\rangle \models W_a(m \in \mathcal{M})$ and $\langle c \rangle \models W_b(m \in \mathcal{M})$ are satisfied if and only if $a = b$.

For the Vernam cipher with $j \geq 2$, the probability $\Pr(c \in \mathcal{C} \mid m \in \mathcal{M})$ does not boil down to $\Pr(k \in \mathcal{K})$. Given $m = m_1 :: m_2 :: \cdot\, m_j$, then c must be in the form $c = c_1 :: c_2 :: \cdot\, c_j$ where $c_1 \oplus m_1 = c_2 \oplus m_2 = \cdots = c_j \oplus m_j$ equals the key k. For $c \in \mathcal{C}$ which are not in that form, $\Pr(c \in \mathcal{C} \mid m \in \mathcal{M}) = 0$. For those that are, $\Pr(c \in \mathcal{C} \mid m \in \mathcal{M}) = \Pr(k \in \mathcal{K})$ remains valid. By a similar reasoning,

$$\Pr(m \in \mathcal{M} \mid c \in \mathcal{C}) = \begin{cases} \Pr(k \in \mathcal{K}) & \text{for } m_1 \oplus c_1 = \cdots = m_j \oplus c_j \\ 0 & \text{otherwise} \end{cases}$$

This shows that the Vernam cryptosystem does not satisfy (IT-SEC) for $j \geq 2$. □

Proposition 2. *If a Vernam cryptosystem is used to encrypt even one bit more than one block, then it is not semantically (IND-CPA) secure, i.e. it can be broken by a chosen-plaintext attack.*

Remark. Note that Attacker's capability to choose a plaintext is computational, and not just stochastic: they can determine the structure of the messages m_0 and m_1 in the CPA-test, and not just rather than just randomly sample from some source.

Proof of Proposition 2. To model the Vernam cryptosystem where one bit more than one block is encrypted, we take

$$\mathcal{M} = \mathcal{C} = \mathcal{K} \times \{0, 1\}$$

To model the (IND-CPA) testing of this cryptosystem, we use as the states in $\mathcal{S}$ the substrings of the triples $\langle k, m_0, m_1, b, c \rangle \in \mathcal{K} \times \mathcal{M}^2 \times \{0, 1\} \times \mathcal{C}$, subject to the constraint that $c = k' \oplus m$, where $k' = k :: k_0$ is the key k with the first bit repeated at the end. Each state can be construed as the record of an encryption session, where the key k is first generated by Gen, and securely conveyed to Enc and Dec, while on the other side the messages m_0, m_1 are generated by Att and sent to Enc, who then chooses the bit b, computes the ciphertext $c = k^j \oplus m_b$ and sends it c to Dec and Att.

For each agent $X \in \{\mathsf{Gen}, \mathsf{Enc}, \mathsf{Dec}, \mathsf{Att}\}$ we define the view function $\mathcal{S} \xrightarrow{(-)x} \mathcal{S}$ to be

$$\begin{aligned} \langle k, m_0, m_1, b, c \rangle_{\mathsf{Gen}} &= \langle k \rangle \\ \langle k, m_0, m_1, b, c \rangle_{\mathsf{Enc}} &= \langle k, m_0, m_1, b, c \rangle \\ \langle k, m_0, m_1, b, c \rangle_{\mathsf{Dec}} &= \langle k, c \rangle \\ \langle k, m_0, m_1, b, c \rangle_{\mathsf{Att}} &= \langle m_0, m_1, c \rangle \end{aligned}$$

The data type of predicates $\mathcal{P}$ and the semantics of $\varphi \ \{q\}_X \ \psi$ are just like in the proof of the preceding proposition.

Towards a proof that (IND-CPA) not satisfied, we note that $\langle\rangle \models W_{\frac{1}{2}}(b = 1)$ holds, because[3] $\Pr(b = 1) = \frac{1}{2}$.

On the other hand, we show that the attacker can construct the messages m_0 and m_1 in such a way that $\langle c \rangle \models W_1(b = 1)$ holds if and only if $c = k' \oplus m_1$, and otherwise $\langle c \rangle \models W_0(b = 1)$ holds. Either way, $\langle c \rangle \models W_{\frac{1}{2}}(b = 1)$ does not hold, which implies that

$$\left(\langle c \rangle \models W_{\frac{1}{2}}(b = 1) \right) \quad \not\Longleftrightarrow \quad \left(\langle\rangle \models W_{\frac{1}{2}}(b = 1) \right)$$

Towards the counterexample for (IND-CPA), let

$$m_0 = 0^\ell :: 0$$
$$m_1 = 0^\ell :: 1$$

which gives

$$c_0 = k_0 :: k_1 :: \cdots :: k_0$$
$$c_1 = k_0 :: k_1 :: \cdots :: \neg k_0$$

and

$$\langle c_0 \rangle \models W_0(b = 1)$$
$$\langle c_1 \rangle \models W_1(b = 1)$$

$\square$

4.2 El-Gamal

Let $\mathbb{G}$ be a cyclic group[4] of order n with a generator g. In other words, the elements of $\mathbb{G}$ can be listed in the form $g, g^2, g^3, \ldots, g^{n-1}, 1$. The types of the El-Gamal cryptosystem are taken to be

$$\mathcal{K} = \mathbb{G} \times \mathbb{Z}_n$$
$$\mathcal{R} = \mathbb{Z}_n$$
$$\mathcal{M} = \mathbb{G}$$
$$\mathcal{C} = \mathbb{G} \times \mathbb{G}$$

The keys $\langle k, \overline{k} \rangle = \mathsf{Gen}(a)$ are set to be

$$k = g^a$$
$$\overline{k} = a$$

---

[3] We assume that the coin is fair. If it is biased, the argument goes through for any probability p instead of $\frac{1}{2}$, provided that $p \neq 0$ and $p \neq 1$.

[4] Here we hide away some details. $\mathbb{G}$ is usually taken to be a cyclic subgroup of the multiplicative group of a field $\mathbb{Z}_p$. But while the reader familiar with the system, or a student of any cryptography textbook, will have no trouble recovering the details swept under the carpet, carrying them around here would distract from the main idea.

and the encryption and decryption functions are

$$E(k, r, m) = \langle g^r, k^r \cdot m \rangle$$
$$D(\overline{k}, c) = \frac{c_2}{c_1^{\overline{k}}}$$

where $c = \langle c_1, c_2 \rangle$. This defines a cryptosystem because

$$D\left(\overline{k}, E(k, r, m)\right) = \frac{k^r \cdot m}{(g^r)^{\overline{k}}} = \frac{g^{a \cdot r} \cdot m}{g^{r \cdot a}} = m$$

Definition 4. *The* Diffie-Hellman decision *is the predicate* $\mathsf{DHd} : \mathbb{G}^3 \longrightarrow \{0, 1\}$ *defined by*

$$\mathsf{DHd}(x, y, z) \iff \exists a, b \in \mathbb{Z}_n. \; x = g^a \wedge y = g^b \wedge z = g^{ab}$$

where we abbreviate $\mathsf{DHd}(x, y, z) = 1$ *to* $\mathsf{DHd}(x, y, z)$, *and write* $\neg\mathsf{DHd}(x, y, z)$ *when* $\mathsf{DHd}(x, y, z) = 0$. *The* Decision Diffie-Hellman problem *concerns the guessing algorithms for the Diffie-Hellman decision, i.e. the feasible algorithms with random seeds. The problem is that an algorithm should do better than a coin flip, and output more than half true decisions for a given length of the seeds. Formally, this means that for all* $a, b \in \mathbb{Z}_n$ *a* DHd *algorithm should satisfy*[5]

$$\Pr\left(\mathsf{DHd}\left(g^a, g^b, g^{ab}\right)\right) > \frac{1}{2}$$

The Decision Diffie-Hellman (DDH) assumption *is that the Diffie-Hellman problem has no solution, i.e. that no feasible algorithm for guessing the Diffie-Hellman decision can do better than the coin flip.*

Proposition 3. *The El-Gamal cryptosystem is semantically secure if and only if the Decision Diffie-Hellman assumption is true.*

Proof. To model the (IND-CPA)-testing of the El-Gamal cryptosystem, i.e. choosing the plaintexts that will yield distinguishable ciphertexts, we use as the states in $\mathcal{S}$ the substrings of the tuples

$$\langle\langle k, \overline{k}\rangle, r, m_0, m_1, b, c\rangle \in \mathcal{K} \times \mathcal{R} \times \mathcal{M}^2 \times \{0, 1\} \times \mathcal{C}$$

where $k = g^{\overline{k}}$ and $c = \langle g^r, k^r \cdot m_b \rangle$. Each state can be construed as the record of a testing session, where the keys $\overline{k}$ and k are generated, the first one is sent from Gen to Enc, the second one is announced publicly; the messages m_0, m_1 are chosen and sent from Att to Enc, the bit b and the ciphertext c are generated and sent from Enc to Att and Dec.

---

[5] It is required that the chance of $\mathsf{DHd}\left(g^a, g^b, g^{ab}\right) = 1$ is feasibly distinguishable from $\frac{1}{2}$, i.e. greater by a feasible function. It follows that the chance of $\mathsf{DHd}\left(g^a, g^b, g^d\right) = 1$ for $d \neq ab$ is also significantly smaller than $\frac{1}{2}$ by a feasible function.

For each agent $X \in \{\mathsf{Gen}, \mathsf{Enc}, \mathsf{Dec}, \mathsf{Att}\}$ we define the view function $\mathcal{S} \xrightarrow{(-)x} \mathcal{S}$ to be

$$\langle k, \overline{k}, r, m_0, m_1, b, c \rangle_{\mathsf{Gen}} = \langle k, \overline{k} \rangle$$
$$\langle k, \overline{k}, r, m_0, m_1, b, c \rangle_{\mathsf{Enc}} = \langle k, r, m_b, c \rangle$$
$$\langle k, \overline{k}, r, m_0, m_1, b, c \rangle_{\mathsf{Dec}} = \langle \overline{k}, m_b, c \rangle$$
$$\langle k, \overline{k}, r, m_0, m_1, b, c \rangle_{\mathsf{Att}} = \langle k, m_0, m_1, c \rangle$$

Suppose that for the El-Gamal El-Gamal cryptosystem holds

$$C \models \mathsf{W}_\iota \, (b = 1) \qquad \not\Longleftrightarrow \qquad O \models \mathsf{W}_\iota \, (b = 1) \qquad (\neg \text{ IND-CPA})$$

Since for a fair coin (i.e. uniformly distributed) $b \in \{0, 1\}$ it is certainly true that $O \models \mathsf{W}_{\frac{1}{2}} \, (b = 1)$. The assumption $(\neg \text{ IND-CPA})$ thus means that there is an attack that makes $C \models \mathsf{W}_{\frac{1}{2}} \, (b = 1)$ false. There are thus algorithms

$$\mathsf{Att}_0 : \mathcal{M}^2 \qquad \text{and} \qquad \mathsf{Att}_1 : \mathbb{G} \times \mathcal{M}^2 \times \mathcal{C} \longrightarrow \{0, 1\}$$

such that for $\mathsf{Att}_0 = \langle m_0, m_1 \rangle$ and any $b \in \{0, 1\}$ holds

$$\Pr\left(\mathsf{Att}_1 \, (k, m_0, m_1, \langle g^r, k^r \cdot m_b \rangle) = b\right) > \frac{1}{2}$$

The Diffie-Hellman decision $\mathsf{DHd}(x, y, z)$ can now be computed for any given x, y and z from $\mathbb{G}$ as follows:

- Set and announce the public key to be $k = x$.
- Let Att_0 generate and send the messages m_0, and m_1.
- Pick any $b \in \{0, 1\}$ and announce $c = \langle y, z \cdot m_b \rangle$.
- Set $\mathsf{DHd}(x, y, z) = 1$ if and only if Att_1 correctly guesses b.

In summary,

$$\mathsf{DHd}(x, y, z) = \begin{cases} 1 & \text{if} \quad \mathsf{Att}_1 \, (k, m_0, m_1, \langle y, z \cdot m_0 \rangle) = 0 \\ & \text{and } \mathsf{Att}_1 \, (k, m_0, m_1, \langle y, z \cdot m_1 \rangle) = 1 \\ 0 & \text{otherwise} \end{cases} \qquad (\neg \text{ DDH})$$

The other way around, assuming $(\neg \text{ DDH})$ with a Diffie-Hellman decision algorithm DHd significantly better than a coin flip, the attacker Att_0 may generate m_0 and m_1 randomly, since Att_1 can always use DHd to decide which of the messages has been encrypted

$$\mathsf{Att}_1 \, (k, m_0, m_1, \langle c_0, c_1 \rangle) = \begin{cases} b & \text{if } \mathsf{DHd}\left(k, c_0, \frac{c_1}{m_b}\right) \\ \bot & \text{otherwise} \end{cases}$$

Checking that this yields $(\neg \text{ IND-CPA})$ is straightforward. $\qquad \square$

Proposition 4. *The El-Gamal cryptosystem is not adaptively secure, i.e. it can be broken by a chosen ciphertext attack.*

Proof. To model the (IND-CCA) (chosen ciphertext) testing of the El-Gamal cryptosystem, we use as the states in $\mathcal{S}$ the substrings of the tuples

$$\langle\langle k, \overline{k}\rangle, r, m_0, m_1, b, q, c, c', d\rangle \in \mathcal{K} \times \mathcal{R} \times \mathcal{M}^2 \times \{0,1\} \times \mathcal{R} \times \mathcal{C}^2 \times \mathcal{M}$$

where $k = g^{\overline{k}}$ and $c = \langle g^r, k^r \cdot m_b\rangle$, $c' \neq c$, and $d = D(\overline{k}, c')$. The projections can be

$$\langle k, \overline{k}, r, m_0, m_1, b, q, c, c', d\rangle_{\mathsf{Gen}} = \langle k, \overline{k}\rangle$$
$$\langle k, \overline{k}, r, m_0, m_1, b, q, c, c', d\rangle_{\mathsf{Enc}} = \langle k, r, m_b, c\rangle$$
$$\langle k, \overline{k}, r, m_0, m_1, b, q, c, c', d\rangle_{\mathsf{Dec}} = \langle \overline{k}, c', d\rangle$$
$$\langle k, \overline{k}, r, m_0, m_1, b, q, c, c', d\rangle_{\mathsf{Att}} = \langle k, m_0, m_1, q, c, c', d\rangle$$

In order to gain advantage in determining b, the Attacker just needs to generate $q \neq 1$, and for $c = \langle c_1, c_2\rangle$ set $c' = \langle c_1, q \cdot c_2\rangle$. Then $d = q \cdot m_b$, and b can be determined with certainty, by comparing $m_b = \frac{d}{q}$ with m_0 and m_1. □

4.3 Towards Protocols for Noisy Muddy Mistrustful Children

In some cryptanalytic attacks, the Attacker is a distributed system, consisting of several processes which locally make different observations, and send messages to each other. The Muddy Children Puzzle can be viewed as a rudimentary example of such a situation. An unknown bitstring $m \in \mathcal{M} = \{0,1\}^\ell$ can be thought of as denoting which members of a group of ℓ children have a muddy forehead. The fact that each child only sees other children's foreheads, but not its own, corresponds to the fact that an Attacker may consist of ℓ observers Att_i, $i = 1, \ldots, \ell$, and each Att_i sees the bits m_k for $k \neq i$ but does not see m_i.

In the usual version of the puzzle, the father tells the children that at least one of them has a muddy forehead, and asks each child whether it knows if its forehead is dirty. He asks them in rounds: after they all say "No", he asks them all again, and so on. Using their view of other childrens' foreheads, and hearing their answers, each child can at some point tell whether its forehead is dirty. It is assumed that each child is a perfect reasoner: it will prove everything that can be proved at that point in time. At each point in time, each child either knows with certainty whether his forehead is muddy or does not know it at all.

In the probabilistic version, each child is trying to estimate the probability that his forehead is muddy. Initially, having finished playing together, the children have an estimate of the distribution $p : n \longrightarrow [0,1]$, where p_k is the probability that exactly k of them have a dirty forehead. If a child sees k dirty foreheads, then it knows for sure that there are either k or $k+1$ dirty foreheads altogether. So the initial probability that its own forehead is dirty is $\frac{p_{k+1}}{p_k + p_{k+1}}$.

Like in the usual version, each child then proceeds to announce, in rounds, whether it knows the state of its forehead. Knowing each other, they all also have an estimate of the probability that the statement that each of them is making is false (for one reason or another).

In other words, the Attackers initially know the probability p_k that there are exactly k 1s in m. Then each Att_i is allowed to broadcast to all Atts a message, telling whether he knows m_i or not. These broadcasts continue in rounds. After a finite number of such broadcasts, all Atts can compute all of the bitstring m.

The reasoning that allows this is one of the motivating examples behind knowledge logic. Generalizing the knowledge modality into the probability modality allows refined reasoning, where unreliability of the Attacker's communications can be taken into account: their broadcast bits can be flipped, with a given probability. This probability can be thought of as a measure of noise, or of mistrust among the children.

To Be Continued

While gathering the references, in particular those that I missed during the years of missed Protocol eXchanges, I encountered reports about the extensions of strand spaces, bundles, and shapes that support quantitative and hybrid forms or reasoning about security [9,14,18]. The tradition of Joshua explaining to me how what I presented could be done using the strand space model is hoped to be continued in the future.

References

1. Barthe, G., Dupressoir, F., Grégoire, B., Kunz, C., Schmidt, B., Strub, P.-Y.: EasyCrypt: a tutorial. In: Aldini, A., Lopez, J., Martinelli, F. (eds.) FOSAD 2012-2013. LNCS, vol. 8604, pp. 146–166. Springer, Cham (2014). https://doi.org/10.1007/978-3-319-10082-1_6

2. Cervesato, I., Meadows, C., Pavlovic, D.: An encapsulated authentication logic for reasoning about key distribution protocols. In: Guttman, J. (ed.) Proceedings of CSFW 2005, pp. 48–61. IEEE (2005)

3. Daston, L.: How probabilities came to be objective and subjective. Hist. Math. **21**(3), 330–344 (1994)

4. Datta, A., Derek, A., Mitchell, J., Pavlovic, D.: A derivation system and compositional logic for security protocols. J. Comput. Secur. **13**, 423–482 (2005)

5. Dolev, D., Yao, A.: On the security of public key protocols. IEEE Trans. Inf. Theor. **29**(2), 198–208 (1983)

6. Durgin, N., Mitchell, J., Pavlovic, D.: A compositional logic for proving security properties of protocols. J. Comput. Secur. **11**(4), 677–721 (2004)

7. Durgin, N., Mitchell, J.C., Pavlovic, D.: A compositional logic for protocol correctness. In: Schneider, S. (ed.) Proceedings of CSFW 2001, pp. 241–255. IEEE (2001)

8. Goldreich, O., Micali, S., Wigderson, A.: How to play any mental game, or: a completeness theorem for protocols with honest majority. In: Proceedings of STOC, New York, NY, USA. Association for Computing Machinery (1987)

9. Guttman, J.D.: Shapes: surveying crypto protocol runs. In: Cortier, V., Kremer, S. (eds.) Formal Models and Techniques for Analyzing Security Protocols, Volume 5 of Cryptology and Information Security Series, pp. 222–257. IOS Press (2011)

10. Guttman, J.D.: State and progress in strand spaces: proving fair exchange. J. Autom. Reason. **48**(2), 159–195 (2012)
11. Guttman, J.D.: Establishing and preserving protocol security goals. J. Comput. Secur. **22**(2), 203–267 (2014)
12. Meadows, C., Pavlovic, D.: Deriving, attacking and defending the GDOI protocol. In: Samarati, P., Ryan, P., Gollmann, D., Molva, R. (eds.) ESORICS 2004. LNCS, vol. 3193, pp. 53–72. Springer, Heidelberg (2004). https://doi.org/10.1007/978-3-540-30108-0_4
13. Pavlovic, D., Meadows, C.: Actor-network procedures. In: Ramanujam, R., Ramaswamy, S. (eds.) ICDCIT 2012. LNCS, vol. 7154, pp. 7–26. Springer, Heidelberg (2012). https://doi.org/10.1007/978-3-642-28073-3_2 arxiv.org:1106.0706
14. Ramsdell, J.D., Dougherty, D.J., Guttman, J.D., Rowe, P.D.: A hybrid analysis for security protocols with state. In: Albert, E., Sekerinski, E. (eds.) IFM 2014. LNCS, vol. 8739, pp. 272–287. Springer, Cham (2014). https://doi.org/10.1007/978-3-319-10181-1_17
15. Thayer, F.J., Herzog, J.C., Guttman, J.D.: Honest ideals on strand spaces. In: Proceedings of the 11th CSFW, pp. 66–77. IEEE Computer Society (1998)
16. Thayer, F.J., Herzog, J.C., Guttman, J.D.: Mixed strand spaces. In: Proceedings of the 12th CSFW, pp. 72–82. IEEE Computer Society (1999)
17. Thayer, F.J., Herzog, J.C., Guttman, J.D.: Strand spaces: proving security protocols correct. J. Comput. Secur. **7**(1), 191–230 (1999)
18. Thayer, F.J., Swarup, V., Guttman, J.D.: Metric strand spaces for locale authentication protocols. In: Nishigaki, M., Jøsang, A., Murayama, Y., Marsh, S. (eds.) IFIPTM 2010. IAICT, vol. 321, pp. 79–94. Springer, Heidelberg (2010). https://doi.org/10.1007/978-3-642-13446-3_6

Joshua Guttman: Pioneering Strand Spaces

Sylvan Pinsky$^{(\boxtimes)}$

SRI International, Menlo Park, CA 94025, USA
`sylpinsky@aol.com`

Abstract. Joshua Guttman has made numerous contributions to formal methods and has played a leadership role in the formal analysis of cryptographic protocols. He is predominantly known for his pioneering work in developing the strand space approach to protocol analysis and his efforts to bring researchers together to form a unified, cohesive, and effective community to design and evaluate cryptographic protocols. Another of Joshua's contributions is the Interactive Mathematical Proof System (IMPS), developed jointly with colleagues at the MITRE Corporation, to provide computational support for mathematical reasoning.

1 Introduction

A cryptographic protocol represents an exchange of messages between two or more parties where a security property is provided by encryption. Authentication using encryption goes back to 1978 with the Needham and Schroeder paper [1]. Three years later, Dolev and Yao [2] published their intruder model, which quickly became the standard for analyzing the capabilities of the intruder and played a significant role in the early automated tools for protocol analysis; specifically Jonathan Millen's Interrogator [3] and Cathy Meadow's NRL Protocol Analyzer [15,17]. Dick Kemmerer [5] introduced the application of formal methods to protocol analysis in 1989.

Protocol analysis established itself, in the ensuing decade, as a vibrant research area of formal methods both in the United States and Europe. Panel discussions and conference sessions on this topic became standard at the Symposium on Security and Privacy and at the Computer Security Foundations Workshop. In 1992, Cathy Meadows wrote a paper on protocol analysis for the initial volume of the Journal of Computer Security [15]. Dick Kemmerer subsequently co-authored a paper with Jonathan Millen and Cathy Meadows [16], comparing their tools to Inatest, the verification system tool that Dick used. A logic for authentication was developed by Michael Burrows, Martín Abadi, and Roger Needham [6] and a semantics for this logic was provided by Martín Abadi and Mark Tutle [8]. Additional research on logics and reasoning about beliefs in cryptographic protocols were provided by (a) Paul Syverson and Paul van Oorschot [13,14], (b) Li Gong, Roger Needham, and Raphael Yahalom [7], and

© Springer Nature Switzerland AG 2021
D. Dougherty et al. (Eds.): Guttman Festschrift, LNCS 13066, pp. 348–354, 2021.
https://doi.org/10.1007/978-3-030-91631-2_19

(c) Illiano Cervesato, Nancy Durgin, Patrick Lincoln, John Mitchell, and Andre Scedrov [37].

In 1995, Gavin Lowe discovered a flaw in the Needham-Schroeder protocol [19] and fixed it using the Failures Divergent Refinement (FDR) verification tool for the process algebra CSP [20] (Communicating Sequential Processes introduced by Tony Hoare [4]). Gavin used Casper (Compiler for Analysis of Security Protocols) [22] to automatically produce the CSP description of the protocol. The modeling checking approach was carried forward by Ed Clarke, Somesha Jha, Will Marrero [26], Martín Abadi and Andrew Gordon [10], Riccardo Focardi and Roberto Gorrieri [25], Dawn Song [36], and John Mitchell, Mark Mitchell, and Ulrich Stern [27]. Verification techniques for authentication protocols using CSP were developed by Steve Schneider [31] and Lawrence Paulson introduced induction principles [28,30] and their use in mechanized proofs [29]. Steve Brackin [23] used HOL (the higher order logic theorem proving environment developed by Michael Gordon [11]) to analyze cryptographic protocols. Grit Denker, José Meseguer, Peter Ölvezky, Carolyn Talcott, and their colleagues specified and analyzed protocols [32,33] using the Maude environment developed by José Meseguer [43].

2   Strand Spaces

Strand spaces were developed by Joshua Guttman and his colleagues Javier Thayer Fábrega and Jonathan Herzog at the MITRE Corporation. A strand is a sequence of events that a participant may engage in. It represents the actions of that party only. A strand space is a collection of strands with a graph structure generated by the exchanged messages. A bundle consists of a number of strands (legitimate or penetrator) hooked together where one strand sends a message and another strand receives the same message. A bundle is viewed as a finite subgraph with the edges expressing the causal dependencies of the nodes. Correctness in this framework is expressed in terms of the connections between strands of different kinds. The strand space model is used to state and prove both secrecy and authentication properties. For example, one of Gavin Lowe's agreement properties [21] expressed in strand space terminology states that a protocol guarantees a participant B (as a responder) agreement for certain data items $\vec{x}$ if:

- each time a principal B completes a run of the protocol as a responder using $\vec{x}$, apparently with A, then there is a unique run of the protocol with the principal A as initiator using $\vec{x}$, apparently with B.

Strand spaces view protocol executions as bundles and security goals as the properties: (a) authentication: some regular strand exists, (b) secrecy: no node discloses a secret, and (c) recency: non-repudiation, fairness, etc.

Peter Ryan, Steve Schneider, Michael Goldsmith, Gavin Lowe, and Bill Roscoe authored a book on security protocols, how they work, and how to design and analyze them [40]. It has an excellent chapter on strand spaces that is well worth reading.

Ed Zieglar and I were the leaders of the Advanced Protocol Analysis Group at NSA where we sponsored the MITRE research effort in strand spaces. We invited Cathy and her NRL colleagues to join us when Joshua and his team visited us to discuss protocol analysis. These meetings were so productive that we scheduled future gatherings when other researchers, such as Carolyn Talcott and George Dinolt, were in the area. Ed arranged to have the University of Maryland Baltimore County (UMBC) host our meetings. In 2003, the meetings were held quarterly and the group expanded to include Mark-Oliver Stehr, José Meseguer, Santiago Escobar, Grit Denker, Andre Scedrov, John Mitchell, Dusko Pavlovic, and other researchers active in protocol analysis. That year we hosted meetings at UMBC and Illiano Cervesato initiated the first Protocol eXchange website which is now hosted by George Dinolt at the Naval Postgraduate School (NPS).

The maturing of strand space theory and multiset rewriting for protocol analysis [38] and the introduction of the Protocol Derivation Assistant (PDA) by Dusko Pavlovic [49] prompted a unified approach to protocol analysis. The Protocol eXchange Seminars provided an excellent forum to get a common framework and methodology for developing and enhancing automated tools. Cathy Meadows, Carolyn Talcott [52,53], and José Meseguer played key roles in defining how to use the best features of PVS [50] and Maude [43] as an underlying framework for the MITRE Cryptographic Protocol Shape Analyzer (CPSA), the Kestrel Protocol Derivation Assistant (PDA), and the NRL Protocol Analyzer written in Maude (Maude-NPA). Sam Owre [51] and Carolyn Talcott [55,56] further explored the PVS-Maude connection and the semantics and algebra for the interoperation of protocol analysis tools and the simulation and analysis of protocol specifications.

3   Concluding Remarks

Joshua Guttman has played a leading role in protocol analysis through his continuing research contributions and leadership in maturing and nurturing a successful research community. His pioneering work in strand spaces has been at the center of the effort to formulate a unified approach to protocol analysis. The impact of strand spaces is shown in the following figures presented at the Protocol eXchange meetings from September 2004 to June 2005. Figure 1a depicts the connection between strand spaces and the unified framework [52]. A further connection between strand spaces, the CPSA and PDA tools, and the Maude and PVS environments is shown in Fig. 1b [53]. This research was presented by Carolyn Talcott and Sam Owre with help from Shaddin Dughmi (MITRE) and Dusko Pavlovic and Matthias Anlauff (Kestrel).

Joshua has been a mentor to many young researchers and inspired my colleague Al Maneki to investigate strand space concepts [44] resulting in Al's presentation of honest functions [35] at the 12th Computer Security Foundations Workshop.

Vision

A formally based, formally verified tool for design and
analysis of strand space protocol specifications.

Idea -- use formal mappings between PVS and Maude in
order to provide the best of both worlds for a wide
range of formal modeling and analysis problems.

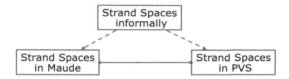

(a) A Maude-PVS Tool for Strand Spaces

Plan

- Viewing CPSA skeletons

- PVS formalization

- Execution of PDA
  processes

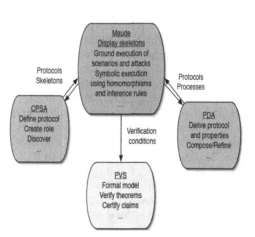

(b) CPS + Maude + PDA + PVS

Fig. 1. Protocol eXchange meetings 2004–2005

Joshua has made many contributions to formal methods and computer science in the areas of security, programming languages, and formal reasoning. I will only highlight the Interactive Mathematical Proof System (IMPS), developed jointly with Bill Farmer and Javier Thayer Fábrega at the MITRE Corporation. IMPS is an interactive mathematical proof system based on simple type theory with partial functions and subtypes [12]. It has an initial theory library containing over a thousand proofs for logic, algebra, and analysis. Bill Farmer maintains the IMPS home page at McMaster University, Canada.

It has been a pleasure, honor, and privilege to know and work with Joshua. This symposium is a well deserved tribute to his many significant contributions to protocol analysis, formal methods, and computer science.

References

1. Needham, R., Schroeder, M.: Using encryption for authentication in large networks of computers. Commun. ACM **21**, 993–999 (1978)
2. Dolev, D., Yao, A.C.: On the Security of Public Key Protocols, STAN-CS-81-854 (1981)
3. Millen, J.: The interrogator: a tool for cryptographic protocol security. In: Proceedings 1984 Symposium on Security and Privacy. IEEE Computer Security Society (1984)
4. Hoare, C.A.R.: Communicating Sequential Processes. Prentice-Hall International, Englewood Cliffs (1985)
5. Kemmerer, R.: Analyzing encryption protocols using formal verification techniques. IEEE J. Sel. Areas Commun. **7**(4), 448–457 (1989)
6. Burrows, M., Abadi, M., Needham, R.: A logic of authentication. ACM Trans. Comput. Syst. **8**(1), 18–36 (1990)
7. Gong, L., Needham, R., Yahalom, R.: Reasoning about belief in cryptographic protocols. In: Proceedings 1990 Symposium on Security and Privacy, pp. 234–248. IEEE Computer Security Society (1990)
8. Abadi, M., Tuttle, M.: A semantics for a logic of authentication. In: Proceedings of the 10th ACM Symposium on Principles of Distributed Computing, pp. 201–216 (1991)
9. Abadi, M., Needham, R.: Prudent engineering practice for cryptographic protocols. IEEE Trans. Softw. Eng. **22**(1), 6–15 (1996)
10. Abadi, M., Gordon, A.D.: Reasoning about cryptographic protocols in the spi calculus. In: Mazurkiewicz, A., Winkowski, J. (eds.) CONCUR 1997. LNCS, vol. 1243, pp. 59–73. Springer, Heidelberg (1997). https://doi.org/10.1007/3-540-63141-0_5
11. Gordon, M., Melham, T.: Introduction to HOL: A Theorem Proving Environment for Higher Order Logic. Cambridge University Press, Cambridge (1993)
12. Farmer, W., Guttman, J., Fábrega, J.T.: IMPS: an interactive mathematical proof system. J. Autom. Reason. **11**, 213–248 (1993)
13. Syverson, P.: The use of logic in the analysis of cryptographic protocols. In: Proceedings 1991 Symposium on Security and Privacy, pp. 156–170 (1991)
14. Syverson, P., van Oorschot, P.: On unifying some cryptographic protocol logics. In: Proceedings 1994 Symposium on Security and Privacy, pp. 14–28 (1994)
15. Meadows, C.: Applying formal methods to the analysis of a key management protocol. J. Comput. Secur. **1**(1), 5–35 (1992)

16. Kemmerer, R., Meadows, C., Millen, J.: Three systems for cryptographic protocol analysis. J. Cryptol. **7**(2), 79–130 (1994). https://doi.org/10.1007/BF00197942
17. Meadows, C.: The NRL protocol analyzer: an overview. J. Logic Program. **26**, 113–131 (1996)
18. Carlsen, U.: Cryptographic protocol flaws. In: Proceedings 7th IEEE Computer Security Foundations Workshop, pp. 192–200 (1994)
19. Lowe, G.: An attack on the Needham-Schroeder public-key authentication protocol. Inf. Process. Lett. **56**(3), 131–136 (1995)
20. Lowe, G.: Breaking and fixing the Needham-Schroeder Public-Key Protocol using FDR. In: Margaria, T., Steffen, B. (eds.) TACAS 1996. LNCS, vol. 1055, pp. 147–166. Springer, Heidelberg (1996). https://doi.org/10.1007/3-540-61042-1_43
21. Lowe, G.: A hierarchy of authentication specifications. In: Proceedings 10th IEEE Computer Security Foundations Workshop, pp. 31–43 (1997)
22. Lowe, G.: Casper: a compiler for the analysis of security protocols. In: 10th Computer Security Foundations Workshop, pp. 18–30. IEEE Computer Security Press (1997)
23. Brackin, S.: A HOL extension of GNY for automatically analyzing cryptographic protocols. In: 9th Computer Security Foundations Workshop. IEEE Computer Security Press (1996)
24. Roscoe, A.W.: Intensional specifications of security protocols. In: Proceedings of the 9th Computer Security Foundations Workshop, pp. 28–38 (1996)
25. Focardi, R., Gorrieri, R.: The compositional security checker: a tool for the verification of information flow security properties. IEEE Trans. Softw. Eng. **23**(9), 58–72 (1997)
26. Marrero, W., Clarke, E., Jha, S.: A Model checker for authentication protocols. In: Meadows, C., Orman, H. (eds.) Proceedings of the DIMACS Workshop on Design and Verification of Security Protocols, DIMACS, Rutgers University (1997)
27. Mitchell, J., Mitchell, M., Stern, U.: Automated analysis of cryptographic protocols using murϕ. In: Proceedings 1997 Symposium on Security and Privacy, pp. 141–153 (1997)
28. Paulson, L.: Proving properties of security protocols by induction. In: Proceedings of the 10th Computer Security Foundations Workshop, pp. 70–83 (1997)
29. Paulson, L.: Mechanized proofs of a recursive authentication protocol. In: Proceedings of the 10th Computer Security Foundations Workshop, pp. 84–94 (1997)
30. Paulson, L.: The inductive approach to verifying cryptographic protocols. J. Comput. Secur. **6**, 85–128 (1998)
31. Schneider, S.: Verifying authentication protocols with CSP. In: Proceedings of the 10th Computer Security Foundations Workshop, pp. 3–17 (1997)
32. Denker, G., Meseguer, J., Talcott, C.: Protocol specification and analysis in Maude. In: Workshop on Formal Methods and Security Protocols (1998)
33. Denker, G., et al.: Specifying a reliable broadcasting protocol in Maude. In: Workshop on Formal Methods and Security Protocols (1998)
34. Denker, G., Meseguer, J., Talcott, C.: Formal specification and analysis of active networks and communication protocols: the Maude experience. In: DARPA Information Survivability Conference and Exposition (2000)
35. Maneki, A.: Honest functions and their application to the analysis of cryptographic protocols. In: Proceedings of the 12th Computer Security Foundations Workshop (1999)
36. Song, D.: Athena: a new efficient automatic checker for security protocol analysis. In: Proceedings of the 12th Computer Security Foundations Workshop (1999)

37. Cervesato, I., Durgin, N., Lincoln, P., Mitchell, J., Scedrov, A.: A meta-notation for protocol analysis. In: Proceedings of the 12th Computer Security Foundations Workshop (1999)
38. Cervesato, I., Durgin, N., Lincoln, P., Mitchell, J., Scedrov, A.: Relating strands and multiset rewriting for security protocol analysis. In: Proceedings of the 13th Computer Security Foundations Workshop (2000)
39. Cervesato, I., Durgin, N., Lincoln, P., Mitchell, J., Scedrov, A.: A comparison between strand spaces and multiset rewriting for security protocol analysis. In: Software Security - Theories and Systems - ISSS (2002)
40. Ryan, P., Schneider, S., Goldsmith, M., Lowe, G., Roscoe, B.: Modelling and Analysis of Security Protocols. Addison-Wesley, Boston (2001)
41. Mason, I., Talcott, C.: Simple network protocol simulation within Maude. Electron. Notes Theor. Comput. Sci. **36**, 274–291 (2000). Third International Workshop in Rewriting Logic and Its Applications
42. Ölvezky, P., Meseguer, J., Talcott, C.: Specification and analysis of the AER/NCA active network protocol suite in Real-Time Maude. Formal Methods Syst. Des. **29**, 253–293 (2006). https://doi.org/10.1007/s10703-006-0015-0
43. Clavel, M., et al.: All About Maude - A High-Performance Logical Framework. LNCS, vol. 4350. Springer, Heidelberg (2007). https://doi.org/10.1007/978-3-540-71999-1
44. Fábrega, J.T., Herzog, J., Guttman, J.: Honest ideals on strand spaces. In: Proceedings of the 11th Computer Security Foundations Workshop (1998)
45. Fábrega, J.T., Herzog, J., Guttman, J.: Strand spaces: proving security protocols correct. J. Comput. Secur. **7**, 191–230 (1999)
46. Guttman, J., Fábrega, J.T.: Authentication tests and the structure of bundles. Theor. Comput. Sci. **283**, 333–380 (2001)
47. Guttman, J., Fábrega, J.T.: The sizes of skeletons: security goals are decidable. MITRE Technical Report 05B09 (2005)
48. Rushby, J.: The Needham-Schroeder Protocol in SAL. Computer Science Laboratory, SRI International (2005)
49. Anlauff, M., Pavlovic, D., Waldinger, R., Westfold, S.: Proving Authentication Properties in the Protocol Derivation Assistant, Kestrel Institute (2006)
50. Owre, S., Shankar, N., Rushby, J.: PVS: A Prototype Verification System, CADE 11 (1992)
51. Owre, S.: Maude2PVS, Protocol eXchange (2007)
52. Talcott, C.: A Maude-PVS tool for Strand Spaces, Protocol eXchange (2004)
53. Talcott, C., Owre, S.: CPSA + Maude + PDA + PVS, Protocol eXchange (2005)
54. Talcott, C.: S-expressions & Maude + PVS, Protocol eXchange (2006)
55. Talcott, C.: TOOLIP Semantics & TOOLIP - Maude NPA, Protocol eXchange (2007)
56. Talcott, C.: TOOLIP Semantics & Interoperation, Protocol eXchange (2008)

Cryptographic Protocol Analysis and Compilation Using CPSA and Roletran

John D. Ramsdell[(✉)][iD]

The MITRE Corporation, Bedford, MA 01730, USA
ramsdell@mitre.org

Abstract. The Cryptographic Protocol Shapes Analyzer CPSA determines if a cryptographic protocol achieves authentication and secrecy goals. It can be difficult to ensure that an implementation of a protocol matches up with what CPSA analyzed, and therefore be sure the implementation achieves the security goals determined by CPSA.

Roletran is a program distributed with CPSA that translates a role in a protocol into a language independent description of a procedure that is easily translated into an existing computer language. This paper shows how we ensure the procedure produced by Roletran is faithful to strand space semantics and therefore achieves the security goals determined by CPSA.

Real implementations of cryptographic functions make use of probabilistic encryption, but CPSA will conclude that two encryptions are the same if they are constructed with the same plaintext and key. The paper concludes by showing how we ensure that executions of generated code that make use of probabilistic encryption achieve the goals determined by CPSA.

1 Introduction

The Cryptographic Protocol Shapes Analyzer (CPSA) [8] attempts to enumerate all essentially different executions possible for a cryptographic protocol. We call them the shapes of the protocol. Naturally occurring protocols have only finitely many, indeed very few shapes. Authentication and secrecy properties are easy to determine from them, as are attacks and anomalies.

For each input problem, the CPSA program is given some initial behavior, and it discovers what shapes are compatible with it. Normally, the initial behavior is from the point of view of one participant. The analysis reveals what the other participants must have done, given the participant's view. The search is complete, i.e. we proved every shape can in fact be found in a finite number of steps, relative to a procedural semantics of protocol roles [7].

This paper is dedicated to Joshua Guttman in gratitude for all the wonderful collaborations we shared throughout our careers. From the first rigorous verification of the implementation of a programming language in actual use (Scheme via the VLISP project [6]), to cryptographic protocol analysis (CPSA), it has been a joy to work with you.

© The Author(s) 2021
D. Dougherty et al. (Eds.): Guttman Festschrift, LNCS 13066, pp. 355–369, 2021.
https://doi.org/10.1007/978-3-030-91631-2_20

When we say a role has procedural semantics, we mean that there exists a program that implements the intent of the specified role. Until now, establishing the correspondence between a CPSA role and its implementation has been informal. It requires a programmer that is well versed in the semantics of CPSA. As the messages used in roles become more complex, the likelihood of errors in the correspondence increases, even when employing the best programmer/CPSA expert. The Roletran compiler automates the translation of a CPSA role into a procedure that is easily translated into the source for an existing programming language, in our case, Rust. It uses the same algorithms implemented in CPSA to ensure a faithful translation. But how do we know its translations are correct?

Section 4 presents the abstract semantics of procedures used to guide our implementation of a runtime system for Roletran generated programs. It includes a definition of correctness, Definition 8, that precisely defines whether the output of Roletran correctly implements the role it is given.

The semantics presented in Sect. 4 has been specified in Coq [1]. An attempt was made to specify the Roletran compiler as a function in Coq and prove that every output of Roletran correctly implements the role it is given. However, the proofs turned out to be too complex and challenging, and the attempt was abandoned.

As a fallback, one can present Coq with the runtime semantics, a role, and procedure, and when the procedure is the output of Roletran, Coq will automatically prove it correctly implements the role. The Coq automation succeeds on protocols of substantial size. Thus for high-assurance applications, we provide a means to validate compiler input/output pairs in lieu of verifying the compiler algorithm.

There is one loose end in what might seem to be a tidy story at this point. Real implementations of cryptographic functions make use of probabilistic encryption. This means that there may be several bit patterns that correspond to one encryption term in CPSA. If the compiler generates code that asserts that two encryptions are equal, the assertion might fail at runtime if the two encryptions differ only because of the randomness used to generate them. To explore these issues, a more concrete semantics has been defined that models randomness in encryptions. The paper concludes by showing that

1. the concrete semantics is faithful to the abstract semantics, in that for every run of the concrete semantics, there is a corresponding run of the abstract semantics, and
2. the concrete semantics is adequate with respect to the abstract semantics, in that for every run of the abstract semantics and choice of random values, there is a corresponding run of the concrete semantics.

Therefore, probabilistic encryption is handled correctly.

$$* * *$$

The Roletran compiler and supporting Coq proofs were written by the author and the sources are available on GitHub [8]. The sources contain about 5800 lines of Coq scripts and the Intro module presents an overview of the work.

There have been a variety of systems that compile high-level descriptions of protocols into executable code [2,5]. To our knowledge, this is the first example of a compiler that uses the input of a cryptographic protocol analyzer as its sole input and honors its semantics.

Notation. A finite sequence f is a function from an initial segment of the natural numbers. The length of f is $|f|$, and $f = \langle f(0), \ldots, f(n-1) \rangle$ for $n = |f|$. The sequence $x :: f$ is $\langle x, f(0), \ldots, f(n-1) \rangle$. The concatenation of sequences f_1 and f_2 is $f_1 \frown f_2$.

If S is a set, then S^* is the set of finite sequences over S, and S^+ is the non-empty finite sequences over S. If S is a finite set, then $\overrightarrow{S}$ is some injective sequence that is onto S. That is, it is a sequence that contains every element in S without duplicates.

Suppose $g : X \rightharpoonup Y$ is a finite partial function.

$$g[x \mapsto y](z) = \begin{cases} y & \text{if } z = x, \\ g(z) & \text{otherwise.} \end{cases}$$

We use $\emptyset$ to denote the finite partial function that has an empty domain.

2   Message Algebras

This section describes the formalism on which CPSA message algebras are based. The parameters to an algebra are:

1. a set of messages Alg. The set of messages Alg is the carrier set (or domain) of a term algebra.
2. a set of basic values BV $\subset$ Alg. Keys and nonces are examples of basic values.
3. a *carried by* relation $\sqsubseteq \subseteq$ Alg $\times$ Alg. Intuitively, a message t_0 is carried by t_1 if it is possible to extract t_0 from t_1 by someone who knows the relevant decryption keys.

Example Message Algebra. The signature of one possible order-sorted [4] message algebra is in Fig. 1. The algebra is the simplification of the CPSA message algebra used by the examples in this paper.

In an order-sorted algebra, each variable x has a unique sort S. The *declaration* of x is $x : S$.

The algebra of interest is the order-sorted quotient term algebra generated by a set of declarations X. The message algebra Alg_X is the carrier set for sort M. The set of basic values BV_X is the union of the carrier sets for sorts A, S, and D. The carrier set for sort A contains the algebra's asymmetric key pairs. We write $t : S$ to say that term t is in the carrier set of sort S.

A variable has no intrinsic sort associated with it. The declarations that generate an algebra determine the sort of variables that occur within terms of the algebra. A variable declared to be of sort M is called a *message variable*.

Sorts: M, A, S, D
Subsorts: A < M, S < M, D < M
Operations: $(\cdot, \cdot)$: M × M → M   Pairing
             $\{\!|\cdot|\!\}_{(\cdot)}$: M × M → M   Encryption
             $\#$: M → M   Hash
             $(\cdot)^{-1}$: M → M   Key inverse
             $\tau_0, \tau_1, \ldots$: M   Tag constants
Equations: $(x^{-1})^{-1} = x$ for x : A; $x^{-1} = x$ otherwise

Fig. 1. Simple crypto algebra signature

The Simple Crypto Algebra is interesting because like CPSA's message algebra, any message can be used as a key when constructing an encryption, with the exception of a message variable. The reason for the exception is that message variable x could be unified with any basic value, and so what equation applies to x^{-1}?

Each element of the message algebra is a set of terms. The canonical representative of each element is the term with the fewest number of occurrences of the inverse operation $(\cdot)^{-1}$. Thus when x is a variable, the canonical representative of the algebra element that contains

$$((x^{-1})^{-1})^{-1}$$

is x^{-1} if x : A, and x otherwise. Message t_0 *occurs* in t_1 iff the canonical representative of t_0 is a subterm of the canonical representative of t_1. In what follows, we conflate each algebra element with its canonical representative.

Definition 1 (Encryption free terms). *Term t is* encryption free, *written* enc_free t, *iff no encryption term occurs in t.*

A message t_0 is *carried by* t_1, written $t_0 \sqsubseteq t_1$, if t_0 can be derived from t_1 given the right set of keys. That is: $\sqsubseteq$ is the smallest reflexive, transitive relation such that

$$t_0 \sqsubseteq (t_0, t_1), \quad t_1 \sqsubseteq (t_0, t_1), \quad \text{and} \quad t_0 \sqsubseteq \{\!|t_0|\!\}_{t_1}.$$

3   Strand Spaces with Channels

The foundation of this work is a version of strand spaces in which messages are transmitted over channels. This change facilitates the translation of a role into code by adding a natural handle for performing input and output in generated code.

Recall that a strand space [9] is a finite map from a local session of a protocol, called a strand, to its behavior, called a trace. The addition of channels changes the standard definition of a trace, but otherwise leaves the basic definitions of strand space theory unchanged.

A channel is a variable of sort C. For $h : \mathsf{C}$ and $t : \mathsf{M}$, $[h, t]$ associates message t with channel h, and is called a *channeled message*. The additions to a message signature required to support channels follow.

> Extra Sorts: C, CM
> Operation: $[\cdot, \cdot] : \mathsf{C} \times \mathsf{M} \to \mathsf{CM}$ Channeled messages

The sort associated with a channeled message is CM. The carrier set for that sort is $\overline{\mathsf{Alg}}_X$. Variables of sort CM are not allowed in X. The carrier set for sort C is Chn_X. Let $\widehat{\mathsf{Alg}}_X = \mathsf{Alg}_X \cup \mathsf{Chn}_X$.

Traces and Roles. The behavior of a strand, its *trace*, is a finite non-empty sequence of *events*. An *event* is either a *channeled message transmission* or a *channeled message reception*. An event transmitting $m \in \overline{\mathsf{Alg}}_X$ is written as $+m$; and an event receiving channeled message m is written as $-m$. If $e = \pm[h, t]$ is an event, then $msg(e) = t$. The set of traces over $\overline{\mathsf{Alg}}_X$ is $(\pm\overline{\mathsf{Alg}}_X)^+$.

A message t *originates* in trace c at index i iff $c(i) = +[h, t_1]$, $t \sqsubseteq t_1$, and for all $j < i$, $t \not\sqsubseteq msg(c(j))$. A message t *uniquely originates* in strand space Θ iff it originates in exactly one trace in Θ. A message t is *non-originating* in strand space Θ iff it originates in no trace in Θ.

Structure $r_X(c, i, o, u)$ is a *role* when

1. c is a trace in $(\pm\overline{\mathsf{Alg}}_X)^+$,
2. each variable declared in X occurs in c,
3. $i \in (\mathsf{BV}_X \cup \mathsf{Chn}_X)^*$ is a sequence of basic values and channels that specify the inputs to the role,
4. $o \in \mathsf{Alg}_X^*$ is a sequence of terms that specify the outputs of the role, and
5. $u \subseteq \mathsf{BV}_X$ is a set of basic values that originate in c.

The elements of i and o are a sequence because the order matters when generating a procedure from the role. Elements of u are freshly generated when the compiled role executes.

Executions. An execution $e_Y(c, i, o, u)$ is similar to a role except that its uniquely originating values are a sequence, not a set. The semantics of an execution requires that the fresh values be presented in the order in which they are consumed. Otherwise, the components of an execution must satisfy the same constraints. Let $\phi : \widehat{\mathsf{Alg}}_X \to \widehat{\mathsf{Alg}}_Y$ be a homomorphism, and $\bar{\phi}$ be the extension of ϕ to traces and sequences of terms in the obvious way.

Definition 2 (Run of a role). *Execution $e_Y(c', i', o', u')$ is a run of role $r_X(c, i, o, u)$ iff there exists a homomorphism ϕ such that $\bar{\phi}(c) = c'$, $\bar{\phi}(i) = i'$, $\bar{\phi}(o) = o'$, $\bar{\phi}(\boldsymbol{u}) = u'$, and $\boldsymbol{u}$ is some sequence that contains the elements in u.*

The strand spaces model of a protocol execution is a bundle. A bundle adds a communication relation to a strand space, and constraints that ensure that causality is respected in that every received message is transmitted previously in the bundle. In strand spaces, a Dolev-Yao adversary [3] is modeled by strands in a bundle along with the strands derived from the protocol being analyzed.

CPSA does not represent executions using bundles or adversarial behavior using strands. Instead, it uses a skeleton to represent a collection of bundles. A skeleton has a strand space, an ordering relation between events, and some origination assumptions that must be satisfied by the strand space of the skeleton. A bundle is modeled by a skeleton if it contains all of the structure specified by the skeleton, in other words, there is a homomorphism from the skeleton into the bundle.

For each input problem, CPSA is given some initial behavior, and it discovers what shapes are compatible with it. A shape is a special kind of skeleton in that it contains enough protocol behavior to explain all message receptions in the presence of adversarial behavior, and it is minimal in that if there is a homomorphism from another skeleton to the shape, then there is a homomorphism from the shape to the other skeleton.

To describe the executions of a protocol, each strand in a skeleton must be an instance of some role in the protocol, which is defined to mean there is a homomorphism from the role to the strand. The definition of a run of a role codifies that link for procedure execution semantics.

3.1   Unilateral Protocol Example

The Unilateral Protocol is a very simple authentication protocol. It consists of two roles, an initiator and a responder. The initiator encrypts a freshly chosen nonce using the public key of the responder and sends it. The responder decrypts the encryption it receives using its private key, and transmits the plaintext. If the initiator receives the nonce it sent unencrypted, it concludes it is communicating with a responder that possesses the corresponding private key, assuming the private key has not been compromised. In the notation presented above, the protocol is specified as follows.

Example 3 (Unilateral Protocol)

$$\mathsf{init} = \mathsf{r}_{h:\mathsf{C},n:\mathsf{D},k:\mathsf{A}}(\langle +[h, \{\!|n|\!\}_k], -[h, n]\rangle, \langle h, k\rangle, \langle n\rangle, \{n\})$$
$$\mathsf{resp} = \mathsf{r}_{h:\mathsf{C},n:\mathsf{D},k:\mathsf{A}}(\langle -[h, \{\!|n|\!\}_k], +[h, n]\rangle, \langle h, k^{-1}\rangle, \langle n\rangle, \{\})$$

Both the initiator and the responder use a message algebra generated by a channel h, a datum n, and an asymmetric key k. The trace of the initiator contains two events, a channeled message transmission followed by a channeled message reception. The inputs to the initiator are a channel and the public part of a key pair. The inputs to the responder are a channel and the private part of a key pair. The outputs produced by both roles is the single nonce n. The initiator freshly generates nonce n, and the responder freshly generates nothing.

CPSA determines that if an instance of an initiator role runs to completion, and the private part of the key pair is not compromised, i.e. is non-originating, then there must have been a corresponding run of the responder role that agrees with the initiator on the values of the nonce and the public key.

3.2   Channel Assumptions

With the addition of channels to CPSA, skeletons now include additional kinds of assumptions besides origination assumptions. A channel can be assumed to be authenticated and/or confidential. In a bundle, when a channel is authenticated, the adversary is not allowed to transmit a message on the channel, and when it is confidential, the adversary is not allowed to received a message on the channel. The addition of channel assumptions allows interesting new analyses of protocols, but does not impact Roletran, so it will not be further discussed.

4   Abstract Execution Semantics

Roletran generates a procedure for each role in a protocol. To build an executable program, the procedure is trivially translated into source code for an existing programming language, in our case Rust. The code is compiled and linked with a runtime system. The implementer of the program provides a main routine that invokes the procedure with inputs that must be compatible with inputs of the translated role. We trust the implementor to do so.

When the program executes, it goes through state changes associated with each statement generated by Roletran. The abstract execution semantics specifies an abstract view of properties of the states that must be preserved in order to be in compliance with the execution semantics stated in the previous section.

When the compiled translation of a role is executing, the runtime system for the source language maintains a binding between program variables and binary objects that represent message fragments. The abstract execution semantics models these bindings with a map from program variables to terms in the message algebra. This map is called an *environment*. The implementor of the runtime library must ensure that each binary object naturally abstracts into the corresponding term in the message algebra as specified by the current environment.

A runtime system for a program provides two more capabilities, support for sending and receiving messages on channels, and freshly generating random values. To model freshly generating random values, the abstract execution semantics maintains a sequence of basic values that is the source of randomness. Initially it is the sequence of uniquely originating values in an execution. The implementor of the runtime library must ensure each binary object it creates naturally abstracts into the corresponding term in the message algebra as specified by the abstract execution semantics.

To model messaging on channels, the abstract execution semantics maintains a trace that initially is the trace in the execution. The implementor of the runtime library must ensure each binary object transmitted or received naturally abstracts into the corresponding event over the message algebra as specified by the abstract execution semantics.

$$ae \ : \ V \rightharpoonup \widehat{\mathsf{Alg}_Y} \quad \text{environment}$$
$$\times \ (\pm \overline{\mathsf{Alg}_Y})^* \quad \text{input trace}$$
$$\times \ \mathsf{Alg}_Y^* \quad \text{input fresh values}$$
$$\times \ \mathcal{E} \quad \text{expression}$$
$$\times \ \mathsf{Alg}_Y \quad \text{value}$$
$$\times \ (\pm \overline{\mathsf{Alg}_Y})^* \quad \text{output trace}$$
$$\times \ \mathsf{Alg}_Y^* \quad \text{output fresh values}$$

$$ae(E, c, u, \ulcorner \mathsf{quot}(\tau) \urcorner, \tau, c, u) \tag{1}$$

$$\frac{E(v_1) = t_1 \qquad E(v_2) = t_2}{ae(E, c, u, \ulcorner \mathsf{pair}(v_1, v_2) \urcorner, (t_1, t_2), c, u)} \tag{2}$$

$$\frac{E(v_1) = t_1 \qquad E(v_2) = t_2}{ae(E, c, u, \ulcorner \mathsf{encr}(v_1, v_2) \urcorner, \{\!|t_1|\!\}_{t_2}, c, u)} \tag{3}$$

$$\frac{E(v_1) = t_1}{ae(E, c, u, \ulcorner \mathsf{hash}(v_1) \urcorner, \# t_1, c, u)} \tag{4}$$

$$\frac{E(v_1) = (t_1, t_2)}{ae(E, c, u, \ulcorner \mathsf{frst}(v_1) \urcorner, t_1, c, u)} \tag{5}$$

$$\frac{E(v_1) = (t_1, t_2)}{ae(E, c, u, \ulcorner \mathsf{scnd}(v_1) \urcorner, t_2, c, u)} \tag{6}$$

$$\frac{E(v_1) = \{\!|t_1|\!\}_{t_2} \qquad E(v_2) = t_2^{-1} \qquad enc\_free \ t_2^{-1}}{ae(E, c, u, \ulcorner \mathsf{decr}(v_1, v_2) \urcorner, t_1, c, u)} \tag{7}$$

$$\frac{E(v_1) = h}{ae(E, -[h, t] :: c, u, \ulcorner \mathsf{recv}(v_1) \urcorner, t, c, u)} \tag{8}$$

$$ae(E, c, t :: u, \ulcorner \mathsf{frsh} \urcorner, t, c, u) \tag{9}$$

Fig. 2. Abstract execution expression semantics

The output of the compiler is an executable procedure $\mathsf{x}(p, s)$, where p is a sequence of parameters and s is a sequence of statements. Each parameter is a program variable and its type, and is associated with an input when the procedure is invoked. A type is one of $\mathbb{M}$, $\mathbb{A}$, $\mathbb{I}$, $\mathbb{S}$, $\mathbb{D}$, and $\mathbb{C}$.

The code generated by the compiler is a sequence of statements. Let $\mathcal{V}$ be the syntactic category for program variables. The syntax of a statement is

$$\mathcal{S} :: = \mathcal{V} : \mathcal{T} \leftarrow \mathcal{E} \mid \mathcal{V} \approx \mathcal{V} \mid \mathsf{invp}(\mathcal{V}, \mathcal{V}) \mid \mathsf{send}(\mathcal{V}, \mathcal{V}) \mid \mathsf{return}(\mathcal{V}^*)$$
$$\mathcal{T} :: = \mathbb{M} \mid \mathbb{A} \mid \mathbb{I} \mid \mathbb{S} \mid \mathbb{D} \mid \mathbb{C}$$
$$\mathcal{E} :: = \mathsf{quot}(\tau) \mid \mathsf{pair}(\mathcal{V}, \mathcal{V}) \mid \mathsf{encr}(\mathcal{V}, \mathcal{V}) \mid \mathsf{hash}(\mathcal{V})$$
$$\mid \ \mathsf{frst}(\mathcal{V}) \mid \mathsf{scnd}(\mathcal{V}) \mid \mathsf{decr}(\mathcal{V}, \mathcal{V}) \mid \mathsf{recv}(\mathcal{V}) \mid \mathsf{frsh}$$

$$as \ : \ V \rightharpoonup \widehat{\mathsf{Alg}_Y} \quad \text{input environment}$$
$$\times \ (\pm\overline{\mathsf{Alg}_Y})^* \quad \text{input trace}$$
$$\times \ \mathsf{Alg}_Y^* \quad \text{input fresh values}$$
$$\times \ \mathcal{S} \quad \text{statement}$$
$$\times \ V \rightharpoonup \widehat{\mathsf{Alg}_Y} \quad \text{output environment}$$
$$\times \ (\pm\overline{\mathsf{Alg}_Y})^* \quad \text{output trace}$$
$$\times \ \mathsf{Alg}_Y^* \quad \text{output fresh values}$$

$$\frac{ae(E, c_1, u_1, x, t, c_2, u_2) \quad chk(t, k)}{as(E, c_1, u_1, \ulcorner v : k \leftarrow x \urcorner, E[v \mapsto t], c_2, u_2)} \tag{10}$$

$$chk(t, \mathbb{M}) \quad \text{always true}$$
$$chk(t, \mathbb{A}) \quad \text{iff } t \text{ is a variable of sort A}$$
$$chk(t, \mathbb{I}) \quad \text{iff } t^{-1} \text{ is a variable of sort A}$$
$$chk(t, \mathbb{S}) \quad \text{iff } t \text{ is a variable of sort S} \tag{11}$$
$$chk(t, \mathbb{D}) \quad \text{iff } t \text{ is a variable of sort D}$$
$$chk(t, \mathbb{C}) \quad \text{iff } t \text{ is a variable of sort C}$$

$$\frac{E(v_1) = E(v_2) \quad enc\_free \ E(v_1)}{as(E, c, u, \ulcorner v_1 \approx v_2 \urcorner, E, c, u)} \tag{12}$$

$$\frac{E(v_1) = E(v_2)^{-1} \quad enc\_free \ E(v_1)}{as(E, c, u, \ulcorner \mathsf{invp}(v_1, v_2) \urcorner, E, c, u)} \tag{13}$$

$$\frac{E(v_1) = h \quad E(v_2) = t}{as(E, +[h, t] :: c, u, \ulcorner \mathsf{send}(v_1, v_2) \urcorner, E, c, u)} \tag{14}$$

$$as*(E, \langle\rangle, \langle\rangle, \langle\rangle, E) \tag{15}$$

$$\frac{as(E_1, c_1, u_1, x, E_2, c_2, u_2) \quad as*(E_2, c_2, u_2, s, E_3)}{as*(E_1, c_1, u_1, x :: s, E_3)} \tag{16}$$

Fig. 3. Abstract execution statement semantics

At runtime, a program variable is associated with an element of a message algebra. This association is represented by an environment $E : V \rightharpoonup \widehat{\mathsf{Alg}_Y}$, a finite partial function. The semantics of a sequence of statements is specified using the relation $asret(E, c, u, s, o)$, where E is an environment, c is a trace in $(\pm\overline{\mathsf{Alg}_Y})^*$, u is a sequence of fresh terms in Alg_Y^*, s is a sequence of statements, and o is a sequence of outputs in Alg_Y^*.

$$\frac{as*(E, c, u, s, E') \quad E' \circ \langle v_0, v_1, \ldots \rangle = \langle t_0, t_1, \ldots \rangle}{asret(E, c, u, s \frown \langle \ulcorner \mathsf{return}(v_0, v_1, \ldots) \urcorner \rangle, \langle t_0, t_1, \ldots \rangle)} \tag{17}$$

The semantics of the remaining statements are given in Fig. 3. The semantics of expressions are given in Fig. 2. Note that Eq. 7, 12, and 13 make assertions that some terms must be free of encryptions. The purpose of these restrictions has to

Statement	Trace	Fresh	Environment
initial	$\langle +[h, \{n\}_k], -[h, n]\rangle$	$\langle n\rangle$	$E_0 = \emptyset[v_0 \mapsto h][v_1 \mapsto k]$
$v_2 : \mathbb{D} \leftarrow \mathsf{frsh}$	$\langle +[h, \{n\}_k], -[h, n]\rangle$	$\langle\rangle$	$E_1 = E_0[v_2 \mapsto n]$
$v_3 : \mathbb{M} \leftarrow \mathsf{encr}(v_2, v_1)$	$\langle +[h, \{n\}_k], -[h, n]\rangle$	$\langle\rangle$	$E_2 = E_1[v_3 \mapsto \{n\}_k]$
$\mathsf{send}(v_0, v_3)$	$\langle -[h, n]\rangle$	$\langle\rangle$	$E_3 = E_2$
$v_4 : \mathbb{D} \leftarrow \mathsf{recv}(v_0)$	$\langle\rangle$	$\langle\rangle$	$E_4 = E_3[v_4 \mapsto n]$
$v_2 \approx v_4$	$\langle\rangle$	$\langle\rangle$	$E_5 = E_4$
$\mathsf{return}(v_2)$	$\langle\rangle$	$\langle\rangle$	$E_6 = E_5$

Fig. 4. Initiator procedure execution

do with the correct handling of probabilistic encryption and will be explained in Sect. 7.

The intuition behind the semantics can be gleaned from the statement semantics *as* in Fig. 3. Think of an environment, trace, fresh values triple (E, c, u) as a state, and a statement as a label. Figure 3 specifies a labeled transition system. It defines how the states evolve during the course of an execution. For a sameness test $\ulcorner v_1 \approx v_2 \urcorner$ (Eq. 12), the state does not change. Execution halts if the test fails. For a send statement $\ulcorner \mathsf{send}(v_1, v_2) \urcorner$ (Eq. 14), only the trace is updated. For a bind statement $\ulcorner v : k \leftarrow x \urcorner$ (Eq. 10), all three components of the state are updated as determined by the expression semantics *ae*. The trace is changed only in response to a $\ulcorner \mathsf{recv}(v_1) \urcorner$ expression (Eq. 8), and a fresh value is consumed only in response to a $\ulcorner \mathsf{frsh} \urcorner$ expression (Eq. 9). Sequences of state transitions are tied together in the natural way by *as*∗ (Eqs. 15 and 16). The *asret* predicate (Eq. 17) ensures that the final statement in a procedure is a return statement, and that the outputs of the procedure are correctly retrieved from the final environment.

Definition 4 (Procedure execution). *Let* $p = \langle (v_0, k_0), \ldots, (v_{n-1}, k_{n-1})\rangle$ *and* $i = \langle i_0, \ldots, i_{n-1}\rangle$. *Execution* $e = \mathsf{e}_Y(c, i, o, u)$ *is an execution of procedure* $x = \mathsf{x}(p, s)$, *written* $exec(x, e)$, *iff*

1. *for all* $j < n$, $chk(i_j, k_j)$, *and*
2. $asret(E, c, u, s, o)$, *where* $E = \emptyset[v_0 \mapsto i_0] \cdots [v_{n-1} \mapsto i_{n-1}]$.

See Eq. 11 for the definition of chk.

Roletran generates the following procedures for the Unilateral Protocol.

Example 5 (Unilateral Protocol Procedures)

$\mathsf{initp} = \mathsf{x}(\langle (v_0, \mathbb{C}), (v_1, \mathbb{A})\rangle,$ $\mathsf{respp} = \mathsf{x}(\langle (v_0, \mathbb{C}), (v_1, \mathbb{I})\rangle,$
　　　$v_2 : \mathbb{D} \leftarrow \mathsf{frsh}$ 　　　　$v_2 : \mathbb{M} \leftarrow \mathsf{recv}(v_0)$
　　　$v_3 : \mathbb{M} \leftarrow \mathsf{encr}(v_2, v_1)$ 　　$v_3 : \mathbb{D} \leftarrow \mathsf{decr}(v_2, v_1)$
　　　$\mathsf{send}(v_0, v_3)$ 　　　　　$\mathsf{send}(v_0, v_3)$
　　　$v_4 : \mathbb{D} \leftarrow \mathsf{recv}(v_0)$ 　　　$\mathsf{return}(v_3))$
　　　$v_2 \approx v_4$
　　　$\mathsf{return}(v_2))$

The execution $\mathsf{inite} = \mathsf{e}_{h:\mathsf{C},n:\mathsf{D},k:\mathsf{A}}(\langle +[h, \{|n|\}_k], -[h, n]\rangle, \langle h, k\rangle, \langle n\rangle, \langle n\rangle)$ is an execution of procedure initp. The state transitions caused by this execution of procedure initp are shown in Fig. 4.

4.1   Correctness

Definition 6 (Liveness). *Procedure x is* live *for role r, iff there exists an execution e such that*

1. *e is a run of r, and*
2. *e is an execution of x.*

Definition 7 (Safety). *Procedure x is* safe *for role r, iff when*

1. *e is an execution of x, then*
2. *e is a run of r.*

Definition 8 (Correctness). *Procedure x* correctly implements *role r, iff x is live and safe for r.*

The Coq scripts that come with Roletran automatically prove that the Unilateral Protocol procedures it generates correctly implement their respective roles.

Consider the case in which Roletran mistakenly omitted the sameness test $(v_2 \approx v_4)$ in the initiator procedure. The Coq scripts would determine that $\mathsf{e}_{c:\mathsf{C},n,n':\mathsf{D},k:\mathsf{A}}(\langle +[h, \{|n|\}_k], -[h, n']\rangle, \langle h, k\rangle, \langle n\rangle, \langle n\rangle)$ is an execution of procedure initp', but note that this execution violates the safety condition. The safety condition ensures that runs of a collection of procedures that correctly implement the roles of a protocol achieve the security goals of the protocol.

5   A Runtime with Probabilistic Encryption

This section presents message algebras, called concrete message algebras, that are very similar to the ones used by the abstract execution semantics. The only difference is the way in which they model encryption. The signature used by the previous algebras has one operation for encryption, $\{|(\cdot)|\}_{(\cdot)}$ (See Fig. 1), which suggests that two encryptions are the same if the plaintext and the key used to construct them are the same. This is not true for implementations of encryption in actual use. Instead, some randomness is added to an encryption during its construction in such a way that knowledge of the randomness is not needed to recover the plaintext by someone in possession of the decryption key.

Sorts: M, A, S, D
Subsorts: A < M, S < M, D < M
Operations: $(\cdot, \cdot)$: M × M → M   Pairing
             $\{\!|\cdot|\!\}^i_{(\cdot)}$: M × M → M   Encryption
             #   : M → M   Hash
             $(\cdot)^{-1}$: M → M   Key inverse
             $\tau_0, \tau_1, \ldots$: M   Tag constants
Equations: $(x^{-1})^{-1} = x$ for $x : $ A; $x^{-1} = x$ otherwise

Fig. 5. Concrete crypto algebra signature

Figure 5 shows the signature used for concrete algebras that model probabilistic encryption. This signature features a family of encryption operations,
$\{\!|(\cdot)|\!\}^i_{(\cdot)}$, one for each natural number i. The natural number is meant to represent the randomness used while creating the encryption. In concrete algebras,
two encryptions created with the same plaintext and key are equal only if they
were created using the same random value.

The algebra of interest is the order-sorted quotient term algebra generated by
a set of declarations Y. The message algebra CAlg_Y is the carrier set for sort M.
The definitions of traces, roles, and executions, extend to concrete algebras in
the obvious ways.

Definition 9 (Forgetful function). *Let* $\mathcal{F} : \mathsf{CAlg}_Y \to \mathsf{Alg}_Y$ *be the obvious
function that forgets the randomness used to create encryptions.*

Lemma 10. *For* $x \in \mathsf{Alg}_Y$, *if* x *is encryption free (enc_free* x*), then there
exists a unique* $y \in \mathsf{Alg}_Y$ *such that* $\mathcal{F}(y) = x$.

Proof. By induction on the structure of y.

The lemma used in proofs follows.

Lemma 11. *For* $x, y \in \mathsf{CAlg}_Y$, *if* enc_free$(\mathcal{F}(x))$ *and* $\mathcal{F}(x) = \mathcal{F}(y)$, *then* $x = y$.

6   Concrete Execution Semantics

The concrete execution semantics is analogous to the abstract execution semantics except that references to message algebras are replaced with references to
concrete message algebras. There is one big exception. When executing an encr
expression, there must be a source of randomness for use in creating an encryption. To provide a source of fresh basic values, the abstract execution semantics threads a sequence of values through state changes. In the concrete execution semantics, a sequence of natural numbers γ is also threaded through state
changes and used to create encryptions.

$$\frac{E(v_1) = t_1 \qquad E(v_2) = t_2}{ce(E, c, u, \iota :: \gamma, \ulcorner \mathsf{encr}(v_1, v_2)\urcorner, \{\!|t_1|\!\}^{\iota}_{t_2}, c, u, \gamma)} \tag{18}$$

$$\frac{E(v_1) = t_1 \qquad E(v_2) = t_2}{ce(E, c, u, \langle\rangle, \ulcorner \mathsf{encr}(v_1, v_2) \urcorner, \{\!|\,t_1\,\|\}_{t_2}^{0}, c, u, \langle\rangle)} \tag{19}$$

Equation 19 handles the case in which the source of randomness has been exhausted.

Other than the case for the encr expression, the definition of the concrete execution semantics follows that of the abstract execution semantics in the obvious ways.

Definition 12 (Concrete procedure execution)
Assume $p = \langle(v_0, k_0), \ldots, (v_{n-1}, k_{n-1})\rangle$ and $i = \langle i_0, \ldots, i_{n-1}\rangle$. Execution $e = \mathsf{e}_Y(c', i', o', u')$ is a concrete execution of procedure $x = \mathsf{x}(p, s)$ with randomness γ, written $cexec(x, e, \gamma)$, iff

1. *for all $j < n$, $chk(\mathcal{F}(i_j), k_j)$;*
2. *$csret(E, c, u, \gamma, s, o)$, where $E = \emptyset[v_0 \mapsto i_0] \cdots [v_{n-1} \mapsto i_{n-1}]$;*
3. *c' is the result of mapping c using $\mathcal{F}$;*
4. *$i' = \mathcal{F} \circ i$;*
5. *$o' = \mathcal{F} \circ o$; and*
6. *$u' = \mathcal{F} \circ u$.*

7   Relating Execution Semantics

The proofs of the theorems stated in this section were performed using Coq and the proof scripts are available in the distribution of CPSA [8].

Theorem 13 (Faithfulness). *$cexec(x, e, \gamma)$ implies $exec(x, e)$.*

The proof of faithfulness is tedious but straightforward. The forgetful function in Definition 9 is used to map items in the concrete semantics to items in the abstract semantics, and then the proofs go through as expected.

Theorem 14 (Adequacy). *$exec(x, e)$ implies $cexec(x, e, \gamma)$.*

The proof of adequacy is tricky. Where there is a sequence of state transitions in the abstract execution semantics, one must find a corresponding sequence in the concrete execution semantics. During both sequences, an event in the trace is consumed when a send statement or a receive expression is encountered. The case of a receive expression is the easy situation. The received term in the complex algebra can be any term as long as applying the forgetful function to it produces the received term in the abstract algebra. However, the case of a send statement is quite different. The transmitted term in the complex algebra must agree with what is in the environment associated with the send statement's message variable. And the term in the environment depends on the particular sequence of random values consumed up to this point in the execution. Engineering a proof that maintains this property is what makes the proof tricky.

The proof of adequacy makes demands on both the abstract and concrete execution semantics. The proof depends on the fact that the following terms must not contain an encryption,

- the key used during a decryption (see Eq. 7),
- the terms compared with a sameness test (see Eq. 12), and
- the terms compared with an inverse key predicate test (see Eq. 13).

The lack of encryptions allow the use of Lemma 11.

With these checks in place, the means we use to validate compiler input/output pairs correctly handles probabilistic encryption.

8 Epilogue

The development of the Roletran compiler is part of a project aimed at addressing the fact that there are systems built on aging software components with questionable security. An approach to protecting such systems is to isolate each component, and mediate communication between the components using trusted software that achieves desired security goals. Verified implementations of protocols is a key component to our approach. Members of this project include Ian D. Kretz and Dan J. Dougherty. The project is led by Joshua D. Guttman.

The project has developed a runtime system in Rust for code generated by Roletran, and several test protocols have been analyzed and then translated into running code, the simplest of which is the Unilateral Protocol. The project has another compiler that compiles protocols that make use of state. Future work might include the construction of a verified runtime system for Roletran generated code.

The addition of channels to CPSA was due to yet another successful collaboration between Joshua and the author.

Acknowledgement. Paul D. Rowe provided valuable comments that improved this paper.

References

1. The Coq proof assistant reference manual (2021). http://coq.inria.fr
2. Bhargavan, K., Corin, R., Deniélou, P., Fournet, C., Leifer, J.J.: Cryptographic protocol synthesis and verification for multiparty sessions. In: Proceedings of the 22nd IEEE Computer Security Foundations Symposium, CSF 2009, Port Jefferson, New York, USA, 8–10 July 2009, pp. 124–140. IEEE Computer Society (2009). https://doi.org/10.1109/CSF.2009.26
3. Dolev, D., Yao, A.C.: On the security of public key protocols. IEEE Trans. Inf. Theory **29**(2), 198–207 (1983). https://doi.org/10.1109/TIT.1983.1056650
4. Goguen, J.A., Meseguer, J.: Order-sorted algebra I: equational deduction for multiple inheritance, overloading, exceptions and partial operations. Theor. Comput. Sci. **105**(2), 217–273 (1992). https://citeseer.ist.psu.edu/goguen92ordersorted.html
5. Guttman, J.D., Herzog, J.C., Ramsdell, J.D., Sniffen, B.T.: Programming cryptographic protocols. In: De Nicola, R., Sangiorgi, D. (eds.) TGC 2005. LNCS, vol. 3705, pp. 116–145. Springer, Heidelberg (2005). https://doi.org/10.1007/11580850_8
6. Guttman, J.D., Wand, M.: VLISP: a verified implementation of scheme. Lisp Symbolic Comput. **8**, 5–32 (1995). https://doi.org/10.1007/BF01128406

7. Liskov, M.D., Rowe, P.D., Thayer, F.J.: Completeness of CPSA. Technical report, MTR110479, The MITRE Corporation (2011). https://www.mitre.org/publications/technical-papers/completeness-of-cpsa
8. Ramsdell, J.D., Guttman, J.D.: CPSA4: A cryptographic protocol shapes analyzer. The MITRE Corporation (2018). https://github.com/mitre/cpsaexp
9. Thayer, F.J., Herzog, J.C., Guttman, J.D.: Strand spaces: proving security protocols correct. J. Comput. Secur. **7**(1), 191–230 (1999). http://content.iospress.com/articles/journal-of-computer-security/jcs117

On Orderings in Security Models

Paul D. Rowe$^{(\boxtimes)}$

The MITRE Corporation, Bedford, MA, USA
prowe@mitre.org

Abstract. Security decisions are often made on the basis of a comparison of two or more alternatives. Is it better go with design A or design B? Which security policy is best for my needs? What combination of defensive mitigations provide the best protection from attack? Implicit in such comparisons are ordering relations $\preceq$ among the alternatives. Such ordering relations crop up in numerous security formalisms. This paper studies preorders that arise in three formalisms for very different domains of security: attack trees, Copland specifications of layered attestations, and cryptographic protocols. While these three areas of study appear to be very different in subject matter and form, we identify a common construction for defining preorders that arise in them. This new perspective unlocks novel connections that should allow insights in one domain to bear fruit in the others as well.

Keywords: Attack trees · Layered attestation · Cryptographic protocols · Security orderings

1 Introduction

When applying formal methods to the security of systems, we often want to know if one solution is "better" than another along some dimension of interest. For example, when designing a cryptographic protocol, we may wonder whether design D_1 is better than D_2 in the sense that any security goals achieved by D_2 can also be achieved by D_1 [13]. Similarly, we might want to compare strategies for distributing firewall policies to various network routers and endpoints against their ability to enforce certain prohibitions on patterns of network traffic [1]. In such cases, what we seek is an ordering relation $\preceq$ that captures some aspect of the security characterisitics of the objects it orders.

It is too much to expect to find a total order. The multidimensional nature of security means that tradeoffs exist between alternatives that generally prevent two arbitrary objects from necessarily being ordered. We thus often content ourselves with preorders, or sometimes partial orders, along various dimensions

---

This paper is dedicated to Joshua Guttman in gratitude for what he has taught me. He has helped me to become a better researcher and to search out the essence of an idea. He has also taught me the importance of non-total orderings! This paper is presented in that spirit.

© Springer Nature Switzerland AG 2021
D. Dougherty et al. (Eds.): Guttman Festschrift, LNCS 13066, pp. 370–393, 2021.
https://doi.org/10.1007/978-3-030-91631-2_21

of security. Recall that a preorder is a relation $\leqslant$ that is reflexive and transitive, while a partial order is also anti-symmetric ($a \leqslant b$ and $b \leqslant a$ implies $a = b$).

In this work we explore preorders that have been defined for numerous security formalisms and begin to develop a unifying lens through which to view them. This line of investigation began when we identified some surprising parallels between the syntax and semantics of two formalisms. Sequential attack trees [6,7] allow researchers to formally express ways in which an adversary might attack a system, accounting for disjunction, conjunction, and sequencing of atomic actions. Copland [11] is a specification language for layered attestation defining how to orchestrate integrity measurements of a target system. In developing Copland, we were faced with the following research question: How can we devise an order on Copland expressions that reflects their strength or trustworthiness in the presence of an active attacker? The similarity between attack trees and Copland suggested that we might be able to directly translate prior work on ordering attack trees [6] to the domain of Copland. As we will see below, such a direct translation, while possible, does not produce an order that reflects the trustworthiness of Copland expressions. It does, however, define orders that capture potentially useful performance characteristics of executing Copland expressions.

Since the direct translation does not shed light on trust properties of Copland expressions, we ultimately took a different approach for Copland trust analysis [14]. We eventually understood this approach to defining a preorder to be an instance of a general construction. The original preorder on attack [6] and its direct translation to Copland expressions are also instances of this general construction. In working through the details of these connections, we realized that yet another security-related preorder—one in the domain of cryptographic protocols, and developed by the author with Guttman and Liskov [13]—might also be viewed as an instance of this general construction.

Summary and Contributions. The fundamental observation of this paper is that preorders arise naturally out of considering homomorphisms between semantic sets. While this observation is not new in itself, it provides a common vocabulary with which to describe preorders in three domains with drastically different semantics. When the semantics of some formal object (e.g. attack tree, Copland phrase, cryptographic protocol) is given as a set of structures that come equipped with a notion of a homomorphism, we can define preorders on the objects *without reference to the details of the semantics*. That is, we can treat a semantic operator $[\![\cdot]\!]$ as a black box that produces sets of structures. We can then define preorders on objects according to what homomorphisms exist between their semantic sets.

In defining a preorder for sequential attack trees, Horne et al. [6] give a "white-box" treatment of their semantics, and intersperse upward and downward closures under homomorphisms to build preorders. Our first contribution is to reformulate their ideas so we can treat the semantics as a black box that produces sets of graphs. We can then take downward and upward closures of the results without worrying about how the sets of graphs are generated (Theorems 1 and 2). We then show how to reinterpret the relationships that emerge after taking downward and upward closures in terms of the homomorphisms that exist between the sets produced by the semantics (Theorem 3). This is an alternate way of deriving the attack tree semantics of [6] (Corollary 1) that gives us a general construction for defining preorders from a black-box, base semantics.

Copland phrases bear striking syntactic similarities with attack trees that manifest as structural similarities in their semantics. The general construction suggested by Corollary 1 leads to a direct translation of the preorder on attack trees to a preorder on Copland expressions. The structural similarities in their semantics allows us to translate results from the analysis of attack trees to the analysis of Copland expressions (Theorem 4, Corollary 2) telling us what kind of properties are reflected by the translated preorder. Unfortunately, this translated preorder doesn't capture trust properties of Copland expressions. However, by modifying the Copland base semantics to account for possible adversary actions, our general preorder construction yields an order that *does* capture important aspects of trustworthiness (Theorem 5).

Finally, we demonstrate the generality of our construction of preorders by shifting our focus to the domain of cryptographic protocols. We summarize the strength order of cryptographic protocols that the author defined with Guttman and Liskov [13] and argue that it coincides with our general construction for preorders given the base semantics defined by the protocol analyzer CPSA. Numerous details prevent us from rigorously proving this correspondence, so we record it as Conjecture 1.

The paper is structured as follows. We first present some preliminary definitions and lemmas in Sect. 2. We then treat attack trees in Sect. 3, showing how to turn the white-box semantics into a black-box one that allows us to define a general construction of preorders. We introduce Copland in Sect. 4, and demonstrate the syntactic and semantic similarities with sequential attack trees. In Sect. 5 we show to leverage that connection to extract useful performance attributes along which to compare Copland phrases. We then alter the Copland base semantics to obtain a trust ordering in Sect. 6. Finally, in Sect. 7, we argue that the protocol strength ordering in an instance of our general construction.

2   Preliminaries

The common thread among all the formalisms we consider here is that they pertain to graphs. While some of the structures are graphs with extra information, the core of the structure is still a graph. We therefore focus the types of graphs and homomorphisms between them that will interest us in the current study.

Definition 1 (Graph). *A directed, labeled, acyclic graph $G = (N, E, \ell)$ is a triple in which N is a finite set of nodes, $E \subseteq N \times N$ is a finite set of edges (represented as ordered pairs of nodes from N), and $\ell : N \to L$ is a labeling function from nodes to some set L of labels. Furthermore, the edge relation is* *acyclic. When we use the unqualified term* graph, *the qualifiers "directed, labeled, and acyclic" are implied unless otherwise stated.*

Definition 2 (Homomorphism). *A* (graph) homomorphism $\eta : G \rightarrow H$ *between graphs* $G = (N_G, E_G, \ell_G)$ *and* $H = (N_H, E_H, \ell_H)$ *is a function* $\eta : N_G \rightarrow N_H$ *on the nodes such that for every edge* $(n_1, n_2) \in E_G$, $(\eta(n_1), \eta(n_2)) \in E_H$, *and for every node* $n \in N_G$, $\ell_G(n) = \ell_H(n)$.

A homomorphism is injective *iff the underlying map on nodes is injective. A* smoothing homomorphism *is one which is bijective on nodes.*

Homomorphisms between graphs bestow a preorder on graphs as follows: $G \leqslant H$ if and only if there is some homomorphism $\eta : G \rightarrow H$. In fact, any class of structures that admit homomorphisms will bestow a preorder in the natural way. We will rely on this later when we consider graphs with "extra structure". If we only allow injective homomorphisms, then the preorder is actually a partial order (up to isomorphism) because injective homomorphisms in both directions between (finite) graphs G and H imply that G and H are isomorphic.

The homomorphism preorder on graphs admits the standard notions of up-sets (or order filters) and down-sets (or order ideals) [2].

Definition 3 (Up-/down-sets). *Given a preorder* $(\mathcal{P}, \leqslant)$, *a set* $\mathcal{S} \subseteq \mathcal{P}$ *is an* up-set *(or* order filter*) iff for all structures* G *and* H, *whenever* $G \in \mathcal{S}$ *and* $G \leqslant H$, *then* $H \in \mathcal{S}$. $\mathcal{S}$ *is a* down-set *(or* order ideal*) iff for all structures* G *and* H, *whenever* $H \in \mathcal{S}$ *and* $G \leqslant H$, *then* $G \in \mathcal{S}$.

The upward closure *of a set* $\mathcal{S}$ *is* $\phi(\mathcal{S}) = \{H \in \mathcal{P} \mid \exists G \in \mathcal{S} \wedge G \leqslant H\}$. *Similarly the* downward closure *of a set* $\mathcal{S}$ *is* $\iota(\mathcal{S}) = \{G \in \mathcal{P} \mid \exists H \in \mathcal{S} \wedge G \leqslant H\}$.

The symbols ϕ and ι reflect the terminology of order filters and order ideals. Since an important aspect of the present work is to connect with Horne et al.'s work [6], it is important to note that they use an order that is dual to the homomorphism preorder. The result is that their notions of "up" and "down" are reversed from the use in this paper; so their order filters are our order ideals, etc. Readers familiar with [6] will have to swap ϕ and ι when translating between the papers. Of course, the duality principle for ordered sets ensures such translations are possible and meaningful. Despite these challenges of translation, we prefer to work in the homomorphism preorder because homomorphisms are a central, unifying theme across all the formalisms we study here.

We are now ready to define a few operations on graphs that allow us to build new graphs from old ones. They are not new and can already be found in [6].

Definition 4 ($\uplus, *$). *Let* $G = (N_G, E_G, \ell_G)$ *and* $H = (N_H, E_H, \ell_H)$ *be graphs. Then we can define*

- $N = N_G \times \{0\} \cup N_H \times \{1\}$
- $E = \{((x, 0), (y, 0)) \mid (x, y) \in E_G\} \cup \{((x, 1), (y, 1)) \mid (x, y) \in E_H\}$
- $\ell(n, 0) = \ell_G(n)$ *and* $\ell(n, 1) = \ell_H(n)$.

N is the disjoint union of the nodes of G and H, E is the disjoint union of the edges of G and H, and ℓ is the natural labeling of the nodes in N inherited from ℓ_G and ℓ_H.

We call the graph (N, E, ℓ) the disjoint union *of G and H, denoted $G \uplus H$.*

If we additionally define $E' = E \cup ((N_G \times \{0\}) \times (N_H \times \{1\}))$, then we call the graph (N, E', ℓ) the sequential composition *of G and H, denoted $G * H$.*

We can easily lift these two operations on graphs into two corresponding operations on *sets* of graphs in the following way.

Definition 5 ($\bowtie, \leadsto$)**.** *If S_1 and S_2 are sets of graphs, then the* distributive product *$S_1 \bowtie S_2$ is defined by $\{G_1 \uplus G_2 \mid G_1 \in S_1 \wedge G_2 \in S_2\}$. The* pointwise sequential composition *of two sets of graphs $S_1 \leadsto S_2$ is defined by $\{G_1 * G_2 \mid G_1 \in S_1 \wedge G_2 \in S_2\}$.*

We now prove a few properties about how upward and downward closures distribute over the above graph operations.

Lemma 1. *For any sets of labeled digraphs S and T, the following equalities hold.*

$$\iota(S \cup T) = \iota(S) \cup \iota(T)$$
$$\iota(S \bowtie T) = \iota(S) \bowtie \iota(T)$$
$$\iota(S \leadsto T) = \iota(\iota(S) \leadsto \iota(T))$$

Proof. We only prove here the most interesting of the equations. The other two proofs are quite similar.

$$\begin{aligned}
\iota(S \leadsto T) &= \{G \mid \exists S \in S, T \in T, G \leqslant S * T\} \\
&= \{G \mid \exists G_1, G_2, G_1 \leqslant S, G_2 \leqslant T, G \leqslant G_1 * G_2\} \\
&= \{G \mid \exists G_1 \in \iota(S), \exists G_2 \in \iota(T), G \leqslant G_1 * G_2\} \\
&= \iota(\iota(S) \leadsto \iota(T))
\end{aligned}$$

$\square$

Lemma 2. *For any sets of graphs S and T, the following equalities hold.*

$$\phi(S \cup T) = \phi(S) \cup \phi(T)$$
$$\phi(S \bowtie T) = \phi(\phi(S) \bowtie \phi(T))$$
$$\phi(S \leadsto T) = \phi(\phi(S) \leadsto \phi(T))$$

Proof. The proof is similar to the proof of Lemma 1 and so is omitted. $\square$

3   Attack Trees

Attack trees [15] are a popular way for security experts to formalize their thought process about how an adversary might attack a system. They allow an analyst to express combinations of activities an adversary may or must perform in order to successfully attack a system. In their original formulation, the leaves of attack trees were labeled with adversary activities, and the internal nodes were labeled with attacker sub-goals. Two types of branching were defined: disjunctive branching in which satisfying any of the child nodes is sufficient to satisfy the parent, and conjunctive nodes in which all children must be satisfied in order for the parent node to be satisfied. More recently, Jhawar et al. [7] have introduced a sequence node to attack trees in which all the children must be satisfied *in the given order* for the parent node to be satisfied. This allows attack trees to capture causal or dependency relationships among the actions. Such *sequential attack trees* are the object of study in this section.

A full treatment of attack trees in general, and sequential attack trees in particular, is out of scope for this work. For a more comprehensive introduction to all types of attack trees, we direct the reader to a useful survey by Widel et al. [17].

A key observation is that the structure of attack trees allows them to be expressed as terms in a grammar in which internal nodes of the tree are represented by an operator corresponding to the intended semantics of satisfaction as described above. That is, we can build up attack trees out of internal nodes labeled by one of the following three operators: $\triangledown, \vartriangle, \triangleright$ representing disjunction, conjunction, and sequence, respectively. They satisfy the following grammar:

$$T :: A \mid T \triangledown T \mid T \vartriangle T \mid T \triangleright T \tag{1}$$

where A represents a set of atomic actions. In practice we can allow the operators to have arity greater than 2, as is done in [7], however it is more convenient for our purposes (and without loss of generality) to use this more restricted syntax.

Numerous semantic interpretations have been given to this syntax, but we focus on the series-parallel graph semantics in which the meaning of an attack tree is given as a set of series-parallel graphs. The original semantics for sequential attack trees given in [7] uses graphs with labeled edges instead of labeled nodes. We follow the presentation in [6] and consider a dual notion of series-parallel. As discussed in [16], series parallel graphs as defined below are precisely the line graphs of so-called two-terminal series-parallel graphs as used in [7].

Definition 6 (Series-parallel). *A series-parallel graph over a set of possible nodes N is defined inductively as follows.*

- *A single labeled node is a series-parallel graph.*
- *If G and H are series-parallel graphs then $G \uplus H$ is a series-parallel graph.*
- *If G and H are series-parallel graphs then $G * H$ are both series parallel graphs*

The original semantics of [7] associates to any sequential attack tree a *set* of series-parallel graphs. The transitive closure of a series-parallel graph defines a partially ordered set. The idea of the semantics is that node represent atomic events which are ordered in the induced partially ordered set if one event depends on the results of another. Disjunction in attack trees results in several possibilities requiring a set of graphs. Thus the union in the following definition is a union of sets of graphs (not the disjoint union $\uplus$ of graphs).

Definition 7 (Base semantics). *The* base semantics *for attack trees is defined inductively as follows, where N_a denotes the graph with a single node whose label is a.*

$$\llbracket a \rrbracket_\mathcal{B} = \{N_a\} \qquad\qquad \llbracket t_1 \triangledown t_2 \rrbracket_\mathcal{B} = \llbracket t_1 \rrbracket_\mathcal{B} \cup \llbracket t_2 \rrbracket_\mathcal{B}$$

$$\llbracket t_1 \triangle t_2 \rrbracket_\mathcal{B} = \llbracket t_1 \rrbracket_\mathcal{B} \bowtie \llbracket t_2 \rrbracket_\mathcal{B} \qquad \llbracket t_1 \triangleright t_2 \rrbracket_\mathcal{B} = \llbracket t_1 \rrbracket_\mathcal{B} \rightsquigarrow \llbracket t_2 \rrbracket_\mathcal{B}$$

The base semantics in Definition 7 was designed to determine *equivalence* of attack trees. That is, two trees are equivalent precisely when they have the same semantics. But when this semantics was introduced in [7], no attention was paid to distinguishing the strength of attack trees.

To address this questions of relative strength, Horne et al. [6] introduced two additional semantics for sequential attack trees that create a "specialization" preorder on them. These preorders correspond closely to two variations on the base semantics, one involving *down-sets* and the other involving *up-sets* of graphs.[1]

Definition 8 (Down-set semantics). *The* down-set semantics *for attack trees is given by the following.*

$$\llbracket a \rrbracket_\mathcal{I} = \{N_a\} \qquad\qquad \llbracket t_1 \triangledown t_2 \rrbracket_\mathcal{I} = \llbracket t_1 \rrbracket_\mathcal{I} \cup \llbracket t_2 \rrbracket_\mathcal{I}$$

$$\llbracket t_1 \triangle t_2 \rrbracket_\mathcal{I} = \llbracket t_1 \rrbracket_\mathcal{I} \bowtie \llbracket t_2 \rrbracket_\mathcal{I} \qquad \llbracket t_1 \triangleright t_2 \rrbracket_\mathcal{I} = \iota(\llbracket t_1 \rrbracket_\mathcal{I} \rightsquigarrow \llbracket t_2 \rrbracket_\mathcal{I})$$

Definition 9 (Up-set semantics). *The* up-set semantics *is given by the following:*

$$\llbracket a \rrbracket_\mathcal{F} = \phi(\{N_a\}) \qquad\qquad \llbracket t_1 \triangledown t_2 \rrbracket_\mathcal{F} = \llbracket t_1 \rrbracket_\mathcal{F} \cup \llbracket t_2 \rrbracket_\mathcal{F}$$

$$\llbracket t_1 \triangle t_2 \rrbracket_\mathcal{F} = \phi(\llbracket t_1 \rrbracket_\mathcal{F} \bowtie \llbracket t_2 \rrbracket_\mathcal{F}) \qquad \llbracket t_1 \triangleright t_2 \rrbracket_\mathcal{F} = \phi(\llbracket t_1 \rrbracket_\mathcal{F} \rightsquigarrow \llbracket t_2 \rrbracket_\mathcal{F})$$

In these definitions, we only apply the downward (respectively upward) closures whenever the combining operator does not produce an down-set (respectively up-set). Applying them in the other cases would be redundant. Since we do not restrict ourselves to smoothing homomorphisms, we must close under ϕ in more cases than is needed for the corresponding semantics in [6]. It is interesting that this difference resulted in no change for our down-set semantics.

These two semantics generate two natural preorders on attack trees:

$$t_1 \leq_\mathcal{I} t_2 \text{ iff } \llbracket t_1 \rrbracket_\mathcal{I} \subseteq \llbracket t_2 \rrbracket_\mathcal{I}$$
$$t_1 \leq_\mathcal{F} t_2 \text{ iff } \llbracket t_1 \rrbracket_\mathcal{F} \subseteq \llbracket t_2 \rrbracket_\mathcal{F} \tag{2}$$

---

[1] Recall that we are working in an order that is dual to the one used in [6]. In comparing with that work, the reader must substitute ι with ϕ (and vice versa) and similarly for $\mathcal{I}$ and $\mathcal{F}$.

The purpose of these preorders is to enable quantitative comparisons among attack trees. It is possible to make assertions about quantitative comparisons using only the two preorders used above, provided the quantitative measures are sound with respect to the preorders. The details of such comparisons (including a definition of soundness) are given in Sect. 5. In the meantime, we proceed with an alternative derivation of the preorders in Eq. 2.

Specialization Using $[\![\cdot]\!]_{\mathcal{B}}$. Definitions 8 and 9 interleave the graph operations with the downward and upward closure operations. Our first novel insight regarding these two semantics is that they are equivalent to first applying the base semantics of Definition 7, then applying either the downward or the upward closure.

Theorem 1. *For any attack tree t, $[\![t]\!]_{\mathcal{I}} = \iota([\![t]\!]_{\mathcal{B}})$.*

Proof. We proceed by induction on the structure of t. We start with the case in which the tree is an atom a. $[\![a]\!]_{\mathcal{I}} = \{N_a\}$. And $[\![a]\!]_{\mathcal{B}} = \{N_a\} = \iota(\{N_a\})$. When $t = t_1 \triangleright t_2$ we have

$$
\begin{aligned}
[\![t_1 \triangleright t_2]\!]_{\mathcal{I}} &= \iota([\![t_1]\!]_{\mathcal{I}} \rightsquigarrow [\![t_2]\!]_{\mathcal{I}}) \\
&= \iota(\iota([\![t_1]\!]_{\mathcal{B}}) \rightsquigarrow \iota([\![t_2]\!]_{\mathcal{B}})) \\
&= \iota([\![t_1]\!]_{\mathcal{B}} \rightsquigarrow [\![t_2]\!]_{\mathcal{B}}) \\
&= \iota([\![t_1 \triangleright t_2]\!]_{\mathcal{B}})
\end{aligned}
$$

where the second equality is the inductive hypothesis and the third equality is by Lemma 1. The other inductive cases follow analogously from Lemma 1.   □

The analogous result holds for the up-set semantics.

Theorem 2. *For any attack tree t, $[\![t]\!]_{\mathcal{F}} = \phi([\![t]\!]_{\mathcal{B}})$.*

Proof. The proof uses the same ideas as that of Theorem 1 and so is omitted.□

In a sense, Theorems 1 and 2 show that the downward and upward closures in Definitions 8 and 9 are needlessly entangled with aspects of the syntax of attack trees. The base semantics of Definition 7 provides a natural and clear interpretation for attack trees. Instead of messing with the internal structure of that semantics to extract information about specialization, we can first compute the base semantics $[\![t]\!]_{\mathcal{B}}$ and then compute either the downward or upward closure.

While the semantics of [6] generate finite sets because they restrict themselves to smoothing homomorphisms that do not add any new nodes to graphs, we have chosen to consider arbitrary homomorphisms which means that the upward closure is an infinite set. This introduces a new challenge not faced in [6]. Namely, to determine if $t_1 \leq_{\mathcal{F}} t_2$ we must devise a procedure for deciding whether $\phi([\![t_1]\!]_{\mathcal{B}}) \subseteq \phi([\![t_2]\!]_{\mathcal{B}})$ that does not require us to compute either set. It turns out we can easily do this by considering the homomorphisms that exist between $[\![t_1]\!]_{\mathcal{B}}$ and $[\![t_2]\!]_{\mathcal{B}}$. This allows us to reduce an infinite question of set membership to a finite questions about what homomorphisms exists among two finite sets of graphs.

Definition 10 (Supports, Covers). *Given two sets of graphs S and T, we say that S supports T iff for every $H \in T$, there is some $G \in S$, such that $G \leqslant H$. We say that T covers S iff for every $G \in S$ there is some $H \in T$ such that $G \leqslant H$.*

Intuitively, S supports T if S is big enough to contain sources of homomorphisms to everything in T. Similarly, T covers S if T is big enough to contain targets of homomorphism from everything in S.

Theorem 3. *For any two sets of graphs S and T, $\iota(S) \subseteq \iota(T)$ if and only if T covers S. Similarly, $\phi(S) \subseteq \phi(T)$ if and only if T supports S.*

Proof. Suppose $\iota(S) \subseteq \iota(T)$. We have $S \subseteq \iota(S) \subseteq \iota(T) = \{G \mid \exists H \in T, G \leqslant H\}$. So, for every $G \in S$, there is some $H \in T$ such that $G \leqslant H$. But that's precisely the definition of T covers S.

Now suppose that T covers S. Then, for every $G \in S$, there is some $H \in T$ such that $G \leqslant H$. Now let $K \in \iota(S)$, so that there is some $G \in S$ such that $K \leqslant G$. But from above, there is some $H \in T$ such that $G \leqslant H$. Transitivity of $\leqslant$ gives us $K \leqslant H$, and hence $K \in \iota(T)$. Since K was chosen arbitrarily from $\iota(S)$ we conclude that $\iota(S) \subseteq \iota(T)$ as required.

Now suppose that $\phi(S) \subseteq \phi(T)$. We have $S \subseteq \phi(S) \subseteq \phi(T) = \{H \mid \exists G \in T, G \leqslant H\}$. So for all $H \in S$ there is some $G \in T$ such that $G \leqslant H$. But this is the definition of T supports S as required.

Finally, suppose that T supports S. So, for every $H \in S$, there is some $G \in T$ such that $G \leqslant H$. Now consider $K \in \phi(S)$. By definition, there is some $H \in S$ such that $H \leqslant K$. But from above, there is some $G \in T$ such that $G \leqslant H$. Using the transitivity of $\leqslant$ we find $G \leqslant K$, showing that $K \in \phi(T)$. Since K was chosen arbitrarily from $\phi(S)$, we conclude $\phi(S) \subseteq \phi(T)$ as required.   □

Theorem 3 gives us an effective procedure for resolving any question of the form $t_1 \leqslant_{\mathcal{F}} t_2$ or $t_1 \leqslant_{\mathcal{I}} t_2$. We simply compute $[\![t_1]\!]_{\mathcal{B}}$ and $[\![t_2]\!]_{\mathcal{B}}$ and enumerate the homomorphisms that exists between elements of those finite sets to determine if one of them covers or supports the other.

Interestingly, while Horne et al. were not faced with this challenge, they nevertheless devised a procedure for resolving such questions that does not amount to a direct check of set inclusion between finite sets. Instead, they develop two additional semantics into an extension of a fragment of linear logic (called MAV [5]) and proving that two trees can be ordered precisely when the linear logic interpretation of one implies the interpretation of the other. Since MAV is decidable, they can extract a decision procedure. This logical encoding is reminiscent of prior work by the author with Guttman and Liskov [13]. In that work, we developed a method for comparing the strength of cryptographic protocols by assigning them formulas in first order logic (expressing the security goals they satisfy) and ordering them according to implication. We will say more about this connection in Sect. 7.

An immediate corollary of Theorem 3 is the following theorem that says we can recover the intended preorders on attack trees without explicit reference to the downward and upward closures.

Corollary 1. *For any two attack trees t_1 and t_2 we have the following.*

$$t_1 \leq_{\mathcal{I}} t_2 \text{ iff } [\![\, t_2 \,]\!]_{\mathcal{B}} \text{ covers } [\![\, t_1 \,]\!]_{\mathcal{B}}$$
$$t_1 \leq_{\mathcal{F}} t_2 \text{ iff } [\![\, t_2 \,]\!]_{\mathcal{B}} \text{ supports } [\![\, t_1 \,]\!]_{\mathcal{B}}$$

This corollary gives us a reusable recipe for generating preorders. If we are given a class of objects, and some semantic operator $[\![\, \cdot \,]\!]$ on those objects yielding sets of graphs, we can *define* two preorders $\leq_{\mathcal{I}}$ and $\leq_{\mathcal{F}}$ in terms of which semantic sets cover or support which others. In fact, since the notions of covering and supporting are well defined for any structures that admit homomorphisms, this construction is quite general.

Throughout the rest of the paper, we repeatedly take inspiration from Corollary 1 to define new orders. For structures other than attack trees, we identify a "base" semantics playing the same role as Definition 7, and then define preorders according to which sets in those semantics cover or support which others. When the base semantics has a structural connection with $[\![\, \cdot \,]\!]_{\mathcal{B}}$ (such as Copland, presented in the next section) we will see that we can transport some results from attack trees to the new setting. However, it is important to note that this construction works even when the base semantics bears no resemblance to $[\![\, \cdot \,]\!]_{\mathcal{B}}$, and we will explore two such instances in Sects. 6 and 7.

4   Copland

In this section we turn our attention to Copland, a domain-specific language for specifying layered attestations [11]. On the surface, Copland has little to do with attack trees. However, we will describe a surprisingly deep connection between the two formalisms that allows some results about the preorders on attack trees to be applied directly to Copland specifications. We also believe research into attack trees can benefit from insights established about Copland.

Remote attestation is a technique for establishing trust in the integrity of a remote system. This is done by having agents local to the target system measure various aspects of the target. This typically involves hashing portions of a component's memory with predictable values that are likely to be changed as a result of an attack to the component. The measurement evidence gathered from various subcomponents is then bundled together both to reflect the way in which it was collected (who measured what, and in what order), and to provide integrity protection to the evidence itself so it cannot be tampered with in transit. Layered attestations leverage hierarchical dependencies built into many modern systems to ensure trust in the measurement apparatus can be established before relying on it to establish trust in the target. Copland was designed to support flexible specifications of layered attestations, and connect to a trust analysis framework [12] (about which more will be said below).

What follows is a very brief overview of the syntax and semantics of Copland. The reader should consult [4,11] for more in-depth descriptions and motivations. An expression in Copland is called a *phrase*. The syntax of Copland phrases is given by the following grammar:

$$
\begin{array}{ll}
C :: A(V) & \text{Atomic action with arguments} \\
\mid C \ \rightarrow \ C & \text{Linear sequence} \\
\mid C \ \overset{\pi}{\prec} \ C & \text{Sequential branching} \\
\mid C \ \overset{\pi}{\sim} \ C & \text{Parallel branching} \\
\mid @_P \ [\ C\ ] & \text{At place} \\
\mid (\ C\ ) & \text{Grouping}
\end{array}
$$

Copland is parameterized by the set of atomic actions available to use. The syntax is designed to specify both the control flow of actions as well as the data flow of evidence among them. The control flow operators are similar to the operators used in attack trees. Copland contains two sequential operators $(\rightarrow, \prec)$, and one conjunction operator $(\sim)$. The purpose of having two distinct sequential operators is to define distinct data flow patterns for the sequential control flow. This will manifest in the semantics given below. Copland does not contain any disjunction operators. There is no fundamental barrier to including disjunction; it simply was not immediately relevant for the intended use of Copland phrases. Copland also contains a new type of operator $@_P$. It indicates the transfer of data and control from one entity to another. The decorators π above $\overset{\pi}{\prec}$ and $\overset{\pi}{\sim}$ specify fine grained aspects of data flow that do not affect the results of this paper, so we will say no more about them.

The semantics of Copland is reminiscent of the base semantics of Definition 7 for sequential attack trees from [7], but it is significantly complicated by the need to carefully track data flow. As with attack trees, Copland semantics is also given in terms of series-parallel graphs, but it relies on an auxiliary *evidence-type semantics* that defines how the type of evidence is transformed throughout the execution of a phrase. In addition to a Copland phrase c, this evidence-type semantics, denoted $\mathcal{E}(c, p, e)$, is sensitive to the place p currently in control of the execution and to the evidence type e built up so far. The details of this semantics is not relevant to our current study, so we treat it as a black box that returns a given type of evidence. The semantics associated with some of the operators includes some "extra" events (req, rpy, split, and join) that serve to coordinate the evidence-type semantics with the data flow. In contrast with Definition 7, the Copland semantics results in a single graph, not a set of graphs, so it uses the graph constructors from Definition 4, and not Definition 5.

Definition 11 (Copland semantics). *The* Copland semantics *for a Copland phrase is a graph defined by the following.*

$$
\begin{aligned}
[\![\, a(\bar{v}) \,]\!]_p^e &= N_a(\bar{v}, p, e) \\
[\![\, @_q\, c \,]\!]_p^e &= \mathsf{req}(p, q) * [\![\, c \,]\!]_q^e * \mathsf{rpy}(p, q) \\
[\![\, c_1 \rightarrow c_2 \,]\!]_p^e &= [\![\, c_1 \,]\!]_p^e * [\![\, c_2 \,]\!]_p^{\mathcal{E}(c_1, p, e)} \\
[\![\, c_1 \overset{\pi}{\prec} c_2 \,]\!]_p^e &= \mathsf{split}(p, \pi) * [\![\, c_1 \,]\!]_p^{\pi_1(e)} * [\![\, c_2 \,]\!]_p^{\pi_2(e)} * \mathsf{joins}(p) \\
[\![\, c_1 \overset{\pi}{\sim} c_2 \,]\!]_p^e &= \mathsf{split}(p, \pi) * ([\![\, c_1 \,]\!]_p^{\pi_1(e)} \uplus [\![\, c_2 \,]\!]_p^{\pi_2(e)}) * \mathsf{joinp}(p)
\end{aligned}
$$

There is enough detail in Definition 11 to warrant a more detailed comparison with attack tree base semantics from Definition 7. Notice first that, since the event semantics relies on the evidence-type semantics it is also parameterized by the current entity in control p and the input evidence type e denoted by sub- and superscripts on the semantics operator. The semantics carefully transforms these values in recursively evaluating the semantics of sub-phrases. Nothing of this sort exists in the attack tree semantics because data flow is not accounted for. As mentioned above, the data flow is the key differentiator between Copland's two sequential operators. With $c_1 \to c_2$, c_2 is evaluated with the evidence produced by c_1. By contrast, in $c_1 \overset{\pi}{<} c_2$, c_2 is evaluated with $\pi_2(e)$ which is derived from the evidence type built up before c_1 and c_2 are sequenced.

The "extra" events, such as $\mathsf{req}(p, q)$, $\mathsf{split}(p, \pi)$ etc., are essential for keeping the series-parallel graph semantics in sync with the evidence-type semantics. However, these events to not alter the fundamental way in which the semantics of the sub-phrases are connected. Namely, sequential operators use the sequential composition of graphs, and the conjunction operator uses the disjoint union of graphs. The primary difference in these connections is that Copland does not use the corresponding $\bowtie$ and $\rightsquigarrow$ operators which work on sets of graphs. This is entirely due to the absence of a disjunctive operator in Copland. The result is that the semantics of a given phrase is a single graph instead of a set of graphs. In fact, we could easily re-write the Copland semantics to work on sets of graphs using $\bowtie$ and $\rightsquigarrow$, but as the resulting sets would be singletons, there is no advantage to doing so beyond clarifying the connection to attack tree semantics.

Based on these observations, the following table depicts a rough correspondence between Copland operators and attack tree operators. As each side has features not captured by the other, it is not a simple bijection. Furthermore, details regarding data flow mean there is not an exact equivalence in the semantics of corresponding operators. Nevertheless, this table represents a surprisingly deep connection between the two formalisms, especially considering they were developed independently.

The correspondence is strong enough to suggest leveraging the results from Sect. 3 to obtain two preorders on Copland phrases. After all, the Copland semantics was not designed with strength comparison in mind, just as was the case with the original semantics for sequential attack trees. A naive approach would be to attempt to replicate the semantics from Definition 8 and 9. But it is not immediately obvious how to interleave the upward and downward closures with the series-parallel graph operations. Taking inspiration from Corollary 1, we can avoid taking upward and downward closures altogether and define two preorders on Copland phrases as follows:

Table 1. Correspondence between Copland and Attack Tree operators.

Copland	Attack Trees		Copland	Attack Trees
$a(\bar{v})$	a		$c_1 \overset{\pi}{<} c_2$	$t_1 \rhd t_2$
qc			$c_1 \overset{\pi}{\sim} c_2$	$t_1 \vartriangle t_2$
$c_1 \to c_2$	$t_1 \rhd t_2$			$t_1 \triangledown t_2$

Definition 12 (Copland preorders). *The two preorders $\leq_{\mathcal{I}}^{C}$ and $\leq_{\mathcal{F}}^{C}$ on Copland phrases are defined as follows.*

$$c_1 \leq_{\mathcal{I}}^{C} c_2 \text{ iff } \{[\![c_2]\!]_p^e\} \text{ covers } \{[\![c_1]\!]_p^e\}$$
$$c_1 \leq_{\mathcal{F}}^{C} c_2 \text{ iff } \{[\![c_2]\!]_p^e\} \text{ supports } \{[\![c_1]\!]_p^e\}$$

Since the Copland semantics produces a single series-parallel graph, this is equivalent to:

$$c_1 \leq_{\mathcal{I}}^{C} c_2 \text{ iff } [\![c_1]\!]_p^e \leq [\![c_2]\!]_p^e$$
$$c_1 \leq_{\mathcal{F}}^{C} c_2 \text{ iff } [\![c_2]\!]_p^e \leq [\![c_1]\!]_p^e \tag{3}$$

Notice that, since the Copland semantics produces a single series-parallel graph, $c_1 \leq_{\mathcal{I}}^{C} c_2$ iff $c_2 \leq_{\mathcal{F}}^{C} c_1$. This is not true in general for semantics that result in sets of graphs.

5   Attribute Domains

In this section we demonstrate that the connection between attack trees and Copland is not a superficial similarity. The syntactic correspondence identified in the previous section allows us to transport results about attack trees to results about Copland phrases. In particular, we focus on how the preorders of Corollary 1 and Definition 12 relate to quantitative comparisons using attribute domains.

Definition 13 (Attribute domain). *An attribute domain is a tuple $D = (V, f_1, \ldots, f_n)$ where V is a set of values ordered by $\leq$, and $f_1, \ldots, f_n$ are functions associated with a set of operators $o_1, \ldots, o_n$. An attribute is a pair (D, ν) where D is an attribute domain and $\nu : A \to V$ is a function from the set of basic actions to the set of values.*

When applied to attack trees or Copland phrases, attribute domains provide a way of giving them quantitative values, assuming a base function $\nu : A \to V$ is given. The value $\mathcal{V}$ for an attack tree or a Copland phrase is defined inductively as follows:

$$\mathcal{V}_\nu(a) = \nu(a) \qquad\qquad \mathcal{V}_\nu(t_1 \ o_i \ t_2) = f_i(\mathcal{V}_\nu(t_1), \mathcal{V}_\nu(t_2))$$

where o_i is an operator, and f_i is its associated function.

Since the order of functions matters in the definition of an attribute domain, we fix an order for the operators of attack trees and Copland phrases respectively. For attack tree attribute domains, the list of functions (f_1, f_2, f_3) will correspond to the list $(\triangledown, \triangle, \triangleright)$, in that order. For Copland attribute domains, the list of functions (f_1, f_2, f_3, f_4) will correspond to the list $(\overset{\pi}{\sim}, \rightarrow, \overset{\pi}{<}, @_q)$, in that order.

Definition 14 (Soundness). *An attribute domain D is* sound *with respect to a given preorder $\preceq$ if and only if either*

- *for all t_1, t_2, ν, $t_1 \preceq t_2$ implies $\mathcal{V}_\nu(t_1) \leqslant \mathcal{V}_\nu(t_2)$, or*
- *for all t_1, t_2, ν, $t_1 \preceq t_2$ implies $\mathcal{V}_\nu(t_2) \leqslant \mathcal{V}_\nu(t_1)$.*

In the former case we call it co-variantly *sound, in the latter case it is* contra-variantly *sound.*

Notice that soundness is not a bi-conditional. Completeness would involve the reverse implication. But since many examples of interest involve using sets of values V that are totally ordered, and since the preorders on attack trees and Copland phrases are only preorders, we should not expect completeness in most cases.

Horne et al. [6] identify four attribute domains that are sound with respect to $\preceq_\mathcal{I}$ and $\preceq_\mathcal{F}$. These are presented in Table 2.

Table 2. Some sound attribute domains for attack trees.

Attribute domain	Preorder	Soundness direction	Interpretation
$(\mathbb{N}, \min, +, \max)$	$\preceq_\mathcal{I}$	Contra-variant	Minimum experts required
$(\mathbb{R}, \min, \max, +)$	$\preceq_\mathcal{F}$	Contra-variant	Minimum attack time
$(\mathbb{N}, \max, +, \max)$	$\preceq_\mathcal{F}$	Co-variant	Guards needed to counter attack
$(\mathbb{R}, \max, \max, +)$	$\preceq_\mathcal{I}$	Co-variant	Time required for all attacks

The first attribute domain can represent the minimum number of experts required to attack the system. This is like a measure of parallelism. If two actions can be done in parallel, then two distinct experts will be required to take advantage of this parallelism. So this is a measure of the minimal parallelism allowed by any attack. The second row can represent the minimum time required to perform an attack. The third row is sort of dual to the first row in that it essentially measures the maximal amount of parallelism of any attack. This could correspond to the number of guards required to be on duty to thwart an attack. Finally, the last row can represent the time required to make all attacks possible.

The correspondence from Table 1 suggests corresponding attribute domains for Copland. By assigning the same functions to corresponding operators, and by interpreting $@_q$ in such a way that it contributes nothing to the attribute, we immediately get a few attribute domains that are sound for the Copland semantics.

Table 3. Sound attribute domains for Copland phrases.

Attribute domain	Preorder	Soundness direction
$(\mathbb{N}, +, \max, \max, 0)$	$\preceq_{\mathcal{I}}^{C}$	Contra-variant
$(\mathbb{R}, \max, +, +, 0)$	$\preceq_{\mathcal{F}}^{C}$	Contra-variant
$(\mathbb{N}, +, \max, \max, 0)$	$\preceq_{\mathcal{F}}^{C}$	Co-variant
$(\mathbb{R}, \max, +, +, 0)$	$\preceq_{\mathcal{I}}^{C}$	Co-variant

Theorem 4. *The attribute domains in each row of Table 3 are each sound with respect to the corresponding preorder in the indicated direction.*

Theorem 4 can be proved directly, but it is also a consequence of the soundness results shown in Table 2 and the structural semantic connection between attack trees and Copland phrases.

Notice that the four attribute domains for attack trees are collapsed down to two attribute domains for Copland. This is because the attack tree attribute domains differ in pairs only in how disjunction is interpreted. As Copland has no disjunction, the correspondence collapses each pair. In the context of layered attestation, rows 1 and 3 can be interpreted as identifying the number of CPU cores required to take advantage of parallelism. As there is only one graph, the maximum is the same as the minimum, so these collapse to the same attribute domain. Rows 2 and 4 correspond to the time it takes to execute a Copland phrase. This could be interpreted as either the minimum time or the maximum time, depending on the interpretation of the function ν used.

These attribute domains are slightly contrived in the context of Copland because they essentially ignore the extra events that get added in the Copland semantics. We can easily account for these by incorporating values for these extra events into the functions corresponding to the operators that add them. For example, if the events req, rpy, split, and join took at least $q, p, s,$ and j time units to complete, then we would want to consider the attribute domain specified as $(\mathbb{R}, \max_{s+j}, +, +_{s+j}, q + p)$ where $a +_{s+j} b$ is defined to be $s + a + b + j$ and $\max_{s+j}(a, b)$ is defined to be $\max(s + a + j, s + b + j)$. This attribute domain builds in the time for the added events in the natural way. We then easily get two more soundness results.

Corollary 2. *The attribute domain $(\mathbb{R}, \max_{s+j}, +, +_{s+j}, q + p)$ is co-variantly sound with respect to $\preceq_{\mathcal{I}}^{C}$ and contra-variantly sound with respect to $\preceq_{\mathcal{F}}^{C}$.*

Proof. It is a simple exercise to verify that the consistent addition of $s, j, q,$ and p to the values does not affect the relative order of the resulting functions. Soundness thus follows immediately from Theorem 4.   □

The connection between attack trees and Copland thus provides a way for us to preorder phrases according to certain performance aspects. This is potentially very useful in designing selection policies for layered attestations. There are potentially numerous reasons to prefer one phrase over another, many of which concern the performance profiles. Some of these performance profiles are well captured by attribute domains sound with respect to $\preceq_{\mathcal{I}}^C$ and $\preceq_{\mathcal{F}}^C$. However, the direct translation of Table 2 to attribute domains for Copland only yields two attribute domains from the original four. This suggests an opportunity to research other attribute domains that might be relevant to the performance profile in executing a Copland phrase. Are there other dimensions along which we would like to compare Copland phrases that are not captured by attribute domains sound with respect to either ordering?

6   Copland Trust Ordering

Our primary interest in Copland phrases is not their performance aspects such as how quickly they can be executed, i.e., those attributes that correspond to the preorders defined in Sect. 4. We are more interested in ordering phrases based on how well they convey system trust in the presence of an active adversary.

In this section we apply the recipe for defining preorders suggested by Corollary 1 to a base semantics that incorporates adversary events into the graphs of actions. Since Copland phrases have no syntactic elements corresponding to adversarial actions, this semantics has a much looser connection to the syntactic structure of a phrase. As a consequence, we must contend with the fact that there is no straightforward way to leverage attribute domains as in the previous section.

The base adversarial semantics for Copland phrases derives from our prior work on layered attestations [12] in which we established a suitable adversary model. Concretely, we assume that adversaries can corrupt and repair components at will. Corrupted measurers will fail to detect any corruption in their targets. If the target of a measurement is corrupt before it is measured, then to avoid detection the adversary must either repair the target or corrupt the measurer (or some component the measurer depends on to correctly measure). In this model it is always possible for the adversary to undetectably corrupt a given component. But we can ask, "assuming that some given target was corrupt at the time it was measured, and that the attestation detects no corruptions, what else must the adversary have done to avoid detection?"

We recently developed a tool chain to answer such questions [14]. This tool chain computes all minimal, adversarial executions consistent with the traditional Copland semantics of Definition 11, together with some initial assumptions or hypotheses H. These include assumptions of the form that some set of components are corrupt at the time they are measured, and that all corruptions go undetected.

Let us denote this minimal set computed by the tool chain as $\mathcal{A}_H(t)$, where $\mathcal{A}$ indicates it is an adversary-enriched semantics, and H denotes the particular hypotheses assumed. This is a set of graphs with extra structure to encode assumptions about which components are corrupt at which events. Taking this as our new "base" semantics, we again define new two preorders on Copland phrases. This time they are parameterized by the hypotheses H used in the computation of the semantics.

Definition 15 (Copland trust ordering).

$$c_1 \preceq_{\mathcal{I}}^{H} c_2 \text{ iff } \mathcal{A}_H(c_2) \text{ covers } \mathcal{A}_H(c_1)$$

$$c_1 \preceq_{\mathcal{F}}^{H} c_2 \text{ iff } \mathcal{A}_H(c_2) \text{ supports } \mathcal{A}_H(c_1)$$

Definition 15 is a mechanical application of the recipe suggested by Corollary 1. A key question is whether these preorders correspond to the strength of a Copland phrase, i.e., its ability to accurately convey trust information in the presence of an active adversary. Do either of the preorders in Definition 15 capture a useful notion of trustworthiness? If so, which one?

To better understand the situation, consider the notion of trustworthiness developed in [12]. As mentioned above, the underlying adversary model always admits ways for the adversary to corrupt components without being detected. It can simply corrupt components between the time they are measured and the time they take a measurement. Alternatively, it can corrupt components deep enough in the system to undermine measurements at higher layers. We refer to these two strategies as *recent* or *deep* corruptions, respectively. Thus, recent or deep strategies allow an adversary to go undetected by an attestation. The primary question becomes whether or not the adversary has any other strategies that might be easier to perform. A rough measure of the strength of a Copland phrase is to say that it is strong (or strong enough) if the recent or deep corruption strategies are the only ones that will succeed.

Since the new base semantics $\mathcal{A}_H(\cdot)$ is not inductively defined according to the syntactic structure of a Copland term, we cannot meaningly define attribute domains in the same way as Sect. 5. However, we can still define natural maps into other ordered sets that clearly correspond to the notion of trust described above. In particular, we can define a mapping RD (for recent or deep) of Copland phrases into the 2-point lattice $\{\bot, \top\}$. $RD(c) = \top$ if the only way for an adversary to avoid detection is by employing recent or deep strategies. $RD(c) = \bot$ if there is some strategy that is neither recent nor deep that still allows the adversary to avoid detection. In fact, this mapping will depend on the set of hypotheses H as described above. Thus, we really have a family of maps $RD_H :$ Copland $\rightarrow \{\bot, \top\}$ and a corresponding family of induced orders $\preceq_{RD}^{H}$. At a coarse level, then, we consider a Copland phrase c to be sufficiently trustworthy relative to hypotheses H if $RD_H(c) = \top$, and untrustworthy otherwise.

We can now ask whether either of the preorders of Definition 15 capture the notion of trust described above. That is, we can ask if either of $c_1 \preceq_{\mathcal{I}}^{H} c_2$ or $c_1 \preceq_{\mathcal{F}}^{H} c_2$ implies the same (or possibly opposite) order on $RD_H(c_1)$ and $RD_H(c_2)$. This would be a type of soundness of RD_H with respect to the preorders.

To investigate this question, consider a simple attestation scenario involving two measurements. Atomic Copland phrase $m_1(x, y)$ represents the measurement of some component y by a well-protected component x. Atomic phrase $m_2(y, z)$ represents the measurement of component z by component y. Thus, x represents a "deep" component of the system. There are (at least) three natural ways to order these measurements.

$$c_1 = m_1(x, y) \overset{\pi}{\sim} m_2(y, z) \tag{4}$$

$$c_2 = m_2(y, z) \overset{\pi}{<} m_1(x, y) \tag{5}$$

$$c_3 = m_1(x, y) \overset{\pi}{<} m_2(y, z) \tag{6}$$

Using the tool chain we developed in [14] we can compute $\mathcal{A}_H(c_i)$ for $1 \leqslant i \leqslant 3$, where H is the hypothesis that z is corrupt when it is measured. The details of how they are computed are well beyond the scope of this work, but the results are shown in Figs. 1, 2 and 3. The figures show the transitive reduction of the edge relations which are all transitive. This semantics also "forgets" non-measurement events. The events labeled $c(\cdot)$ (respectively $r(\cdot)$) represent an event in which the adversary corrupts (respectively repairs) the given component.

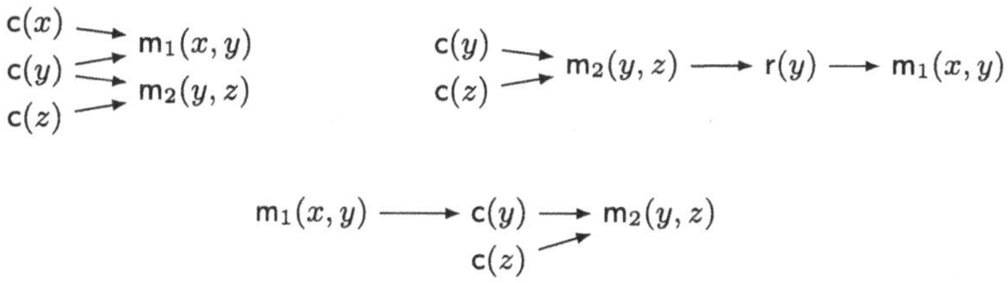

Fig. 1. The three graphs in $\mathcal{A}_H(c_1)$.

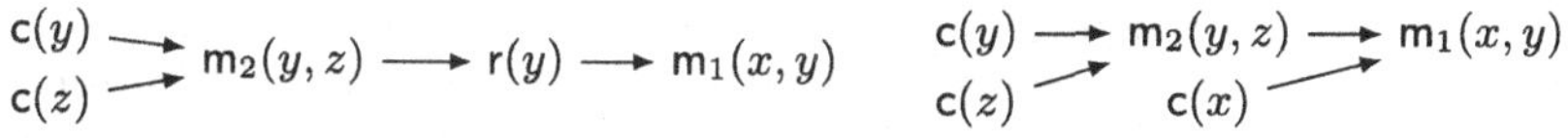

Fig. 2. The two graphs in $\mathcal{A}_H(c_2)$.

Fig. 3. The two graphs in $\mathcal{A}_H(c_3)$.

Phrases c_1 and c_2 each admit executions in which the deep component x is not corrupted, and the corruptions of y and z need not occur recently (e.g. after the start of the attestation). Thus $RD_H(c_1) = RD_H(c_2) = \bot$. In the executions admitted by c_3, there is either a deep corruption of x, or there is a recent corruption of y. Thus $RD_H(c_3) = \top$.

We can similarly determine which of the sets $\mathcal{A}_H(c_i)$ cover or support which others. It is a simple exercise to check that $\mathcal{A}_H(c_1)$ supports both $\mathcal{A}_H(c_2)$ and $\mathcal{A}_H(c_3)$, and that neither of the latter two support each other. Also, none of the sets covers any of the others. Thus, the only orders involving $\leqslant_\mathcal{I}^H$ and $\leqslant_\mathcal{F}^H$ that hold are $c_2 \leqslant_\mathcal{F}^H c_1$ and $c_3 \leqslant_\mathcal{F}^H c_1$.

This small investigation suggests that $\leq_{RD}^H$ is not related to $\leq_{\mathcal{I}}^H$, but that it might be related (contravariantly) to $\leq_{\mathcal{F}}^H$. Indeed, we can prove that $\leq_{RD}^H$ is contravariantly sound with respect to $\leq_{\mathcal{F}}^H$.

Theorem 5. *If $c_1 \leq_{\mathcal{F}}^H c_2$ then $c_2 \leq_{RD}^H c_1$.*

Proof. Since $c_2 \leq_{RD}^H c_1$ holds for all values of $RD_H(c_1)$ and $RD_H(c_2)$ *except* $RD_H(c_2) = \bot$ and $RD_H(c_1) = \top$, it suffices to show that whenever $c_1 \leq_{\mathcal{F}}^H c_2$ and $RD_H(c_1) = \top$ then $RD_H(c_2) = \top$ as well.

First note that $RD_H(c_1) = \top$ means that for every $G \in \mathcal{A}_H(c_1)$, G contains a recent corruption or a deep corruption. Also, recent and deep corruptions are both preserved under homomorphisms. Since $c_1 \leq_{\mathcal{F}}^H c_2$, we know that for every $G_2 \in \mathcal{A}_H(c_2)$, there is some $G_1 \in \mathcal{A}_H(c_1)$ such that $G_1 \leq G_2$. But since G_1 has a recent or deep corruption, this is preserved by the homomorphism to G_2. Thus every element of $\mathcal{A}_H(c_2)$ has a recent or deep corruption. So $RD_H(c_2) = \top$. $\square$

Theorem 5 is encouraging. It shows that the generalized up-set (adversary-enriched) semantics for Copland captures an intuitive, and independently defined notion of trust. This works out despite the fact that we are in a setting where the "base" semantics is given as an arbitrary set of structures not explicitly tied to the syntax. In fact, it is encouraging enough to suggest that research in attack trees might benefit from applying such a generalization. For example, attack-defense trees have been proposed as a richer formalism to discuss offensive and defensive strategies for system security. Could there be a semantics in the spirit of the adversary-enriched semantics for Copland that could be leveraged in this way to order attack(-defense) trees? Copland's tracking of dataflow could also be replicated to enrich the semantics of attack trees along that dimension.

Nevertheless, the soundness of Theorem 5 is a little unsatisfying. For one thing, the same soundness does not hold for the strict preorders. This is evident from the fact that $c_2 <_{\mathcal{F}}^H c_1$ but $c_1 \not<_{RD}^H c_2$. It is, in some sense, too sensitive to differences in Copland phrases. Just because two phrases are strictly ordered, we cannot conclude that one must force the adversary into recent or deep corruptions. Thus, we can only leverage $c_1 \leq_{\mathcal{F}}^H c_2$ for our purposes if we know $RD_H(c_2) = \top$ or $RD_H(c_1) = \bot$. The fact that c_2 and c_3 are $\leq_{\mathcal{F}}^H$-incomparable is also worrisome. Knowing that one phrase forces the adversary into recent or deep corruptions and the other doesn't is not enough to guarantee they will be ordered by $\leq_{\mathcal{F}}^H$. This indicates that $\leq_{\mathcal{F}}^H$ is, in some sense, not sensitive enough.

Theorem 5 encourages us to push forward with new ideas for ordering Copland phrases (or other formalisms), but it raises at least as many questions as it answers. What security aspects is $\leq_{\mathcal{F}}^H$ really capturing beyond the notion of recent or deep adversary strategies? Is soundness enough to view it as a generalization of the 2-point lattice ordering, or do the issues in the previous paragraph undermine that viewpoint? Is there a logical characterization of the content of models found in $\mathcal{A}_H(c)$ that enables soundness with respect to logical implication? We hope the investigation of this paper will spur research along these lines. The generality of the approach enables progress to be made by those working in diverse subfields of formal methods for security.

7 Cryptographic Protocols

While we were spurred to investigate the connection between attack trees and Copland due to the similarities in their underlying syntax and semantics, the results of Sect. 6 show that the general construction can yield interesting results even in cases with semantics that are utterly unrelated to that of attack trees. Therefore, before concluding, we make a brief detour into the world of cryptographic protocols to demonstrate the generality of the recipe for constructing preorders suggested by Corollary 1.

In 2016, Guttman, together with the author and our colleague Moses Liskov established a methodology for determining a strength order on cryptographic protocols [13]. As we outline below, the preorder generated in this way seems to correspond to the preorder that would arise from the construction we have used repeatedly throughout this paper. Due to space limitations, we can only give a very high-level overview, and the correspondence, while highly suggestive, is still technically conjectural.

The general idea from [13] is to derive a logical formula

$$\mathcal{L}(\Phi, P) = \forall X.(\Phi \Longrightarrow_{1 \leqslant i \leqslant n} \exists Y.\Psi_i)$$

that expresses the strongest conclusion achievable by protocol P from hypothesis Φ. For those familiar with CPSA, Φ represents the input to a search, and each Ψ_i represents one of the shapes of protocol P, while X and Y range over events and the variables used in messages. In general, protocols need their own set of predicates to describe their possible executions. That is, a predicate saying that some role of protocol P_1 has executed some number of steps with a given set of parameters will not, in general, have an interpretation in the executions of protocol P_2. However, when the protocols are sufficiently similar, the same logical language can easily apply to both protocols. This allows us to create a preorder on protocols parameterized by the hypothesis Φ: $P_1 \leqslant_\Phi P_2$ iff $\mathcal{L}(\Phi, P_2) \Longrightarrow \mathcal{L}(\Phi, P_1)$. This says that P_2 is stronger than P_1 (with respect to Φ) if any goal achieved by P_1 is also achieved by P_2.

It has been shown in [9] that $\mathcal{L}(\Phi, P)$ corresponds to a run of the protocol analyzer CPSA [10] when provided an input $\mathbb{A}$ that corresponds to Φ. CPSA works in the strand spaces model of cryptographic protocols (pioneered by Guttman), and produces the minimal, essentially different executions of a protocol consistent with some initial assumptions. Concretely, given a skeleton (i.e. partial execution) $\mathbb{A}$ of protocol P, it produces a finite set $\mathcal{S}_{\mathbb{A}}(P)$ of realized skeletons (i.e. full executions) $\mathbb{B}$ for which $\mathbb{A} \leqslant \mathbb{B}$.[2] Furthermore, $\mathcal{S}_{\mathbb{A}}(P)$ supports the set of all realized skeletons $\mathbb{C}$ satisfying $\mathbb{A} \leqslant \mathbb{C}$. That is, for all realized skeletons $\mathbb{C}$ such that $\mathbb{A} \leqslant \mathbb{C}$, there is an element $\mathbb{B} \in \mathcal{S}_{\mathbb{A}}(P)$ such that $\mathbb{B} \leqslant \mathbb{C}$.

The correspondence between $\mathcal{L}(\Phi, P)$ and CPSA's search arises from the ability to associate to every skeleton $\mathbb{A}$ a characteristic formula $\chi(\mathbb{A})$. For certain syntactic classes of formulas Φ we can revert the process to get a characteristic

---

[2] For technical reasons, we must restrict ourselves to injective homomorphisms only.

skeleton $\sigma_P(\Phi)$. (The inverse σ_P depends on the protocol because different protocols admit different structures.) For our purposes we may assume these two processes are inverses. Thus, in the previous paragraph, we choose $\mathbb{A}$ to be $\sigma_P(\Phi)$. The correspondence is completed by the fact that $\Psi_i = \chi(\mathbb{B}_i)$ for $\mathbb{B}_i \in \mathcal{S}_P(\mathbb{A})$ [9].

When comparing the strength of two protocols, we start with a common hypothesis Φ. We then translate that hypothesis into (possibly distinct) skeletons $\mathbb{A}_1 = \sigma_{P_1}(\Phi)$ and $\mathbb{A}_2 = \sigma_{P_2}(\Phi)$ of P_1 and P_2 respectively. Applying CPSA, we obtain the two sets of shapes $\mathcal{S}_{\mathbb{A}_1}(P_1)$ and $\mathcal{S}_{\mathbb{A}_2}(P_2)$. We then recover $\mathcal{L}(\Phi, P_i)$ by applying χ to the sets of shapes. This now gives us access to the preorder $\leq_\Phi$.

One key advantage of converting CPSA's analysis back into logical form is that it allows direct comparison between the results. Due to the detailed message structure that is purposefully not represented in the logical formulas, we typically can't talk about homomorphisms between skeletons of two different protocols. This prevents us from directly applying our recipe for defining preorders that requires us to determine whether $\mathcal{S}_{\mathbb{A}_1}(P_1)$ covers or supports $\mathcal{S}_{\mathbb{A}_2}(P_2)$, or vice versa. The translation into logic acts as a substitute in much the same way that Horne et al. [6] define a translation into linear logic to help them compute the comparisons. However, Guttman has developed a way to convert skeletons of P_1 into skeletons of P_2, provided there is a well-defined protocol transformation $\mathcal{T} : P_1 \to P_2$ [3]. So if $\mathbb{A}_1$ is a skeleton of P_1, then $\mathcal{T}(\mathbb{A}_1)$ is a skeleton of P_2. Furthermore, for sufficiently close protocols, $\chi(\mathbb{A}_1) = \chi(\mathcal{T}(\mathbb{A}_1))$. (For more distantly related protocols, the equality must be downgraded to an equivalence.) Using this theory of protocol transformation we conjecture that the $\leq_\Phi$ preorder corresponds to one of the preorders generated using Theorem 3.

Conjecture 1. *Suppose that* $\sigma_{P_1}(\Phi) = \mathbb{A}_1$ *and* $\sigma_{P_2}(\Phi) = \mathbb{A}_2$. *Let* $\mathcal{T} : P_1 \to P_2$ *be a well-defined protocol transformation. Then*

$$P_1 \leq_\Phi P_2 \text{ iff } \mathcal{S}_{\mathbb{A}_2}(P_2) \text{ covers } \mathcal{T}(\mathcal{S}_{\mathbb{A}_1}(P_1)), \text{ and}$$
$$P_2 \leq_\Phi P_1 \text{ iff } \mathcal{T}(\mathcal{S}_{\mathbb{A}_1}(P_1)) \text{ covers } \mathcal{S}_{\mathbb{A}_2}(P_2).$$

We leave it as a conjecture for now because a treatment that attends to all the details about protocol transformations and conversions to and from logical formulas would require considerable care and is beyond the aims of this paper. Indeed, it is not entirely clear that the bi-implication is correct. Perhaps it only follows that if the semantic sets are in the right covering relationship, then the corresponding order holds. Our main purpose is to highlight similarities and differences with the preorders from earlier sections to gain insights into how we might fruitfully generalize the approach to generating preorders.

We conclude with a few remarks about this conjecture that speak to the generality of our construction. Firstly, although, skeletons of a protocol are graph-like, they actually contain more information than is contained in the structures for attack trees or Copland phrases. This demonstrates that the approach is not tied to semantics that use sets of graphs, but can apply to other structures that admit a homomorphism ordering. Additionally, the conjecture would not hold if we restricted attention to smoothing homomorphisms only as is done in [6].

$P_1 \leq_\Phi P_2$ will hold when the shapes of P_2 can infer the existence of more activity (more nodes of the graph), not just more orderings among events. This was one of the principal drivers for our choice not to restrict ourselves to smoothing homomorphisms in Sect. 3 which resulted in an alteration to the up-set semantics compared to it counterpart in [6].

Just as in Sect. 6, the base CPSA semantics is not tightly tied to the syntax of protocols. So, although we cannot easily define attribute domains for protocols, the translation into logic can be viewed as serving a similar purpose. Indeed, because the logical content captures all the needed details, the corresponding order is not only sound, but the conjecture is that it is also complete with respect to the order defined through our construction. If true, this would mean that the preorder constructed according to the methods of this paper precisely capture the intended content of security goals. The connection between $\leq_{RD}^H$ and $\leq_{\mathcal{F}}^H$ in Sect. 6 was much weaker. Perhaps we could identify a sound and complete logical characterization of $\leq_{\mathcal{F}}^H$ that comes with a clear interpretation in terms of trust.

Finally, notice that the conjecture only uses the notion of "covers" and not the notion of "supports". Thus, $\leq_\Phi$ is a kind of down-set semantics. That is, it shares the same form as the $\leq_\mathcal{I}$ order on attack trees. If we write it as $\leq_\mathcal{I}^\Phi$, this suggests the natural alternative $\leq_\mathcal{F}^\Phi$ defined according to an up-set semantics. That is, which $P_1 \leq_\mathcal{F}^\Phi P_2$ when $\mathcal{T}(\mathcal{S}_{\mathbb{A}_1}(P_2))$ supports $\mathcal{S}_{\mathbb{A}_2}(P_1)$. It is not immediately clear what this preorder captures. We consider it an open problem to provide a preorder with a natural interpretation that corresponds to (or at least is sound with respect to) $\leq_\mathcal{F}^\Phi$.

8   Conclusion

In this paper we explored numerous security-related preorders from the literature. We developed a way to generalize specialization preorders of attack trees [6] to essentially any formalism which has a set-based denotational semantics for which there exists a notion of homomorphism on elements of the sets. In particular, we defined the two notions of *covers* and *supports*, and showed how these generate a preorder on the semantic sets that corresponds to the up- and down-set semantics of attack trees respectively. We applied this general construction to Copland phrases for layered attestation in two settings. The first is an adversary-free setting in which the preorders correspond to certain performance aspects of the intended executions. The second is an adversary-enriched setting in which the semantics no longer closely reflects algebraic properties of the syntax. Along the way we identified a similarity to preorders defined on cryptographic protocols. While the details are beyond this paper, we conjectured that the protocol preorders can be viewed as an instance of the general construction used here.

While our focus has been on three formalisms, the results obtained are suggestive that the construction may have a much greater reach. But the current study also raises some questions. The protocol preorder is constructed using the *covers* relation, while the corresponding construction for Copland adversarial semantics requires the *supports* relation. It is not clear when to expect the use of one versus the other. In fact, the *covers* and *supports* notions have been previously identified as providing a basis for constructing powerdomains for programs with non-deterministic execution [8,18]. A more thorough investigation into the relation of the current study with that past work may shed light on our questions and suggest a more abstract standpoint from which to view security orderings.

Acknowledgments. I would like to thank Ian Kretz and John Ramsdell for our continued collaboration on the topic of layered attestation. This paper arose out of our earlier shared attempt to leverage attack trees to help order Copland phrases.

References

1. Adão, P., Focardi, R., Guttman, J.D., Luccio, F.L.: Localizing firewall security policies. In: 2016 IEEE 29th Computer Security Foundations Symposium (CSF), pp. 194–209 (2016). https://doi.org/10.1109/CSF.2016.21
2. Davey, B.A., Priestley, H.A.: Introduction to Lattices and Order, 2 edn. Cambridge University Press (2002). https://doi.org/10.1017/CBO9780511809088
3. Guttman, J.D.: Establishing and preserving protocol security goals. J. Comput. Secur. **22**(2), 203–267 (2014). https://doi.org/10.3233/JCS-140499
4. Helble, S.C., Kretz, I.D., Loscocco, P.A., Ramsdell, J.D., Rowe, P.D., Alexander, P.: Flexible mechanisms for remote attestation. ACM Trans. Priv. Secur. **24**(4) (2021). https://doi.org/10.1145/3470535
5. Horne, R.: The consistency and complexity of multiplicative additive system virtual. Sci. Ann. Comput. Sci. **25**(2), 245–316 (2015). https://doi.org/10.7561/SACS.2015.2.245
6. Horne, R., Mauw, S., Tiu, A.: Semantics for specialising attack trees based on linear logic. Fundam. Informaticae **153**(1–2), 57–86 (2017). https://doi.org/10.3233/FI-2017-1531
7. Jhawar, R., Kordy, B., Mauw, S., Radomirović, S., Trujillo-Rasua, R.: Attack trees with sequential conjunction. In: Federrath, H., Gollmann, D. (eds.) SEC 2015. IAICT, vol. 455, pp. 339–353. Springer, Cham (2015). https://doi.org/10.1007/978-3-319-18467-8_23
8. Plotkin, G.D.: A power domain construction. SIAM J. Comput. **5**(3), 452–487 (1976). https://doi.org/10.1137/0205035
9. Ramsdell, J.D.: Deducing security goals from shape analysis sentences. CoRR abs/1204.0480 (2012)
10. Ramsdell, J.D., Guttman, J.D., Liskov, M.D., Rowe, P.D.: The CPSA specification: A reduction system for searching for shapes in cryptographic protocols (2012)
11. Ramsdell, J.D., et al.: Orchestrating layered attestations. In: Nielson, F., Sands, D. (eds.) POST 2019. LNCS, vol. 11426, pp. 197–221. Springer, Cham (2019). https://doi.org/10.1007/978-3-030-17138-4_9
12. Rowe, P.D.: Confining adversary actions via measurement. In: Kordy, B., Ekstedt, M., Kim, D.S. (eds.) GraMSec 2016. LNCS, vol. 9987, pp. 150–166. Springer, Cham (2016). https://doi.org/10.1007/978-3-319-46263-9_10
13. Rowe, P.D., Guttman, J.D., Liskov, M.D.: Measuring protocol strength with security goals. Int. J. Inf. Secur. **15**(6), 575–596 (2016). https://doi.org/10.1007/s10207-016-0319-z

14. Rowe, P.D., Ramsdell, J.D., Kretz, I.D.: Automated trust analysis of Copland specifications for layered attestation. In: Proceedings of the 23rd International Symposium on Principles and Practice of Declarative Programming. PPDP 2021. Association for Computing Machinery, New York (2021). https://doi.org/10.1145/3479394.3479418

15. Schneier, B.: Attack trees. Dr. Dobb's J. **24**(12), 21–29 (1999)

16. Valdes, J., Tarjan, R.E., Lawler, E.L.: The recognition of series parallel digraphs. In: Proceedings of the Eleventh Annual ACM Symposium on Theory of Computing, STOC 1979, pp. 1–12. Association for Computing Machinery, New York (1979). https://doi.org/10.1145/800135.804393

17. Wideł, W., Audinot, M., Fila, B., Pinchinat, S.: Beyond 2014: formal methods for attack tree-based security modeling. ACM Comput. Surv. **52**(4) (2019). https://doi.org/10.1145/3331524

18. Winskel, G.: On power domains and modality. Theoret. Comput. Sci. **36**, 127–137 (1985). https://doi.org/10.1016/0304-3975(85)90037-4

Prototyping Formal Methods Tools: A Protocol Analysis Case Study

Abigail Siegel, Mia Santomauro, Tristan Dyer, Tim Nelson[✉],
and Shriram Krishnamurthi

Computer Science Department, Brown University, Providence, RI, USA
tbn@cs.brown.edu

Abstract. Modern-day formal methods tools are more than just a core solver: they also need convenient languages, useful editors, usable visualizations, and often also scriptability. These are required to attract a community of users, to put ideas to work in practice, and to conduct evaluations of the formalisms and core technical ideas. Off-the-shelf solvers address one of these issues but not the others. How can full prototype environments be obtained quickly?

We have built Forge, a system for prototyping such environments. In this paper, we present a case-study to assess the utility of Forge. Concretely, we use Forge to build a basic protocol analyzer, inspired by the Cryptographic Protocol Shape Analyzer (CPSA). We show that we can obtain editing, basic visualization, and scriptability at no extra cost beyond embedding in Forge, and a modern, domain-specific visualization for relatively little extra effort.

1 Introduction

Formal methods are (finally) surging in popularity, including numerous domain-specific tools, even of industrial origin [2, 7–9, 18, 41, 46]. This suggests that there are many new tools that people might want to build; as exposure grows, so will the number of tools. But there's a long road from a formalism to a tool. Researchers need to quickly build prototypes that can be experimented with and refined (and perhaps even turned into a bespoke tool).

Many tools [5, 28, 29, 32, 33, 36, 38, 44] already layer a domain atop a model-finder like Alloy [23], Alloy's core engine Kodkod [54], SMT, or SAT. While these are wonderful as embedded solvers, they are only the beginning, not the end, to building a *useful* tool. Some additional concerns include:

- the development environment (IDE) experience;
- translating the domain-specific surface input language;
- visualization of the output;
- perhaps even domain-specific and interactive output visualization; and
- extensibility and scriptability.

These concerns are not academic. Tools benefit from user communities. While early adopters will use almost any interface, as communities grow, they expect all the standard modern conveniences.

D. Dougherty et al. (Eds.): Guttman Festschrift, LNCS 13066, pp. 394–413, 2021.
https://doi.org/10.1007/978-3-030-91631-2_22

Independent of community growth, our formalisms benefit from (and need) evaluations with users, especially because these can cough up unpleasant surprises [11]. But to perform such evaluations, we must equip them with at least minimal usable interfaces. Otherwise, our studies will be studying the (poverty of the) interface, not the formalism and its consequences.

Our response to this problem is a new framework, Forge[1] (the name is a tribute to Alloy), that enables researchers to quickly prototype tools. Forge is based on the *language-oriented programming* (LOP) principle [16] of the Racket programming system. That is, Racket is a system (and language) designed for building (programming) languages. The resulting languages can be used from the DrRacket programming environment [17] or with external environments (such as Visual Studio Code) using the Common Language Interface. Forge provides the Kodkod [54] and Pardinus [10] solvers. It also incorporates the Sterling [15] visualizer, which enables domain-specific visualizations. Finally, domain-specific programs can be scripted using the Racket language.

This paper presents a case study that exercises these aspects of Forge. Concretely, we will use Forge to build a prototype analyzer for cryptographic protocols, inspired by Joshua Guttman's Cryptographic Protocol Shapes Analyzer (CPSA) [12]. This prototype was largely executed by a pair of undergraduates (the first two authors) as part of a *course project* (while taking a regular course load). We believe that this demonstrates the potential utility of frameworks like Forge, and hope that this work prompts further development to support *end-to-end* prototyping of formal tools.

2   End-To-End Language-Oriented Modeling

The key philosophy of Forge lies in extending the idea of LOP to language-oriented *modeling*. We illustrate this process in Fig. 1, which is organized by tiers according to the different user perspectives involved. For concreteness, we specialize the presentation to our specific crypto-analysis case study.

Atop the pre-existing Forge engine, *Tool Authors* (in this case study, the undergraduate lead authors) model their domain (the "Base spec"), define domain-specific languages (DSLs) in Racket, the translation of those languages to Forge constraints (`#lang`), and—if needed—a domain-specific visualizer ("Custom Visualization"). These enable other user perspectives: domain experts, such as *Protocol Creators*, use DSLs (like CPSA's `defprotocol` syntax) to specify artifacts of interest in their domain without needing expertise in relational logic. *Analysts* can then phrase queries about protocol behavior. They may use Forge's query language, a DSL (such as CPSA's `defskeleton` syntax), or both, and benefit from domain-customized output. Others, such as students, might even bypass the DSLs entirely and only interact with visualizations produced by others. While a specific user may naturally belong to multiple tiers (e.g., a protocol creator may wish to double-check their specification by viewing example executions), we find this separation a useful way to think about different tool perspectives.

---

[1] Available at: www.forge-fm.org.

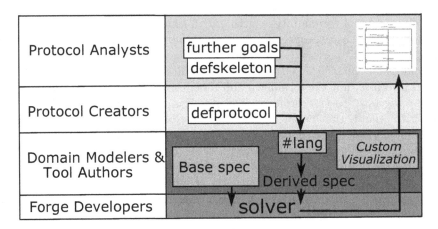

Fig. 1. Tiered organization of Domain-Specific Modeling in Forge. Components that must be implemented for each new domain (e.g., our case-study prototype) are shaded in grey. A base specification for the domain is enriched with additional constraints generated from the domain-specific input. Results from the solver are relayed to a custom visualizer. As the process is embedded in Racket, additional structure can be added via scripting (not shown) from outside the core workflow.

Crucially, this process is not specific to cryptographic protocols. Any domain that can be modeled in the relational logic of Forge (which it shares with Alloy) is a potential target of this approach.

We now briefly step through the perspective of each user, and address corresponding system-design concerns raised in Sect. 1. As a running example throughout, we use the Needham-Schroeder [35] asymmetric protocol with the known (Lowe [26]) vulnerability, taken verbatim from the CPSA example repository (https://github.com/mitre/cpsa). Concretely, this protocol describes a three-step secret exchange between two principals (**initi**ator and **resp**onder) facilitated by a public-key cryptosystem.

2.1 Protocol Analysts: Custom Visualization and Queries

A concrete example of Needham-Schroeder in action might look like Fig. 2, where horizontal arrows denote the flow of messages between principals. Our case-study prototype's model and visualization are based on the strand-space formalism [51], just as is CPSA. We discuss differences in logic (Sect. 4) and visualization (Sect. 6) later, but note that our visual layout concretizes the Dolev-Yao [13] perspective: the attacker is synonymous with the medium of communication. Our visualizer is also interactive: users can click at any point on the diagram to see the state of agents' knowledge at that time. Figure 3 shows one such report: the initiator's knowledge before the first message is sent.

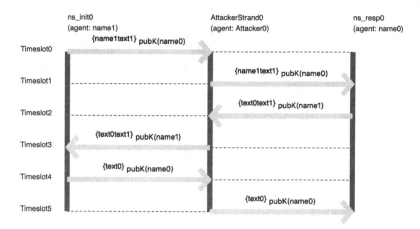

Fig. 2. A good execution of Needham-Schroeder. The "Attacker" strand represents the medium of communication. As the secrets (text0 and text1) are encrypted, they are learned (in this execution) by only the initiator and responder. The "agent:" annotations denote which agent owns each strand.

Visual Design Considerations. There are many different visualizations that a tool author might create. The lowest-cost approach would be to use the standard Alloy-style directed graphs that Forge provides by default. However,

text1
name1
{name1text1} pubK(name0)

Fig. 3. Detail of initiator's knowledge in the first timestep.

these fail to communicate domain-specific intuitions, expose unnecessary modeling details, and can become overwhelming after a certain level of complexity is reached. Instead, Forge leverages the Sterling [15] visualizer, which allows tool authors to build their own custom visualizations in JavaScript. These then execute in the browser, and benefit from the many advantages of a modern web interface.

Figure 4 shows three points in the design space of visualizing an *attack on,* rather than a good run of, Needham-Schroeder:

1. the default Alloy-style visualization, projected by timeslot and with unused atoms removed;
2. a lightweight (roughly 100 lines of JavaScript) custom visualization; and
3. the full interactive visualizer (900 lines of JavaScript).

Note that even with some effort to clean up the display, the default visualization is cluttered with modeling details and can be difficult to break down. While Alloy and Sterling do provide an alternative table-based modality, these same issues apply (with, e.g., 38 rows in the learned_times relation alone). In contrast, the custom visualizations at least communicate some pertinent information at a brief glance, and the full visualization provides more (e.g., agent knowledge) on click events. Section 6 presents the visualizer in greater detail.

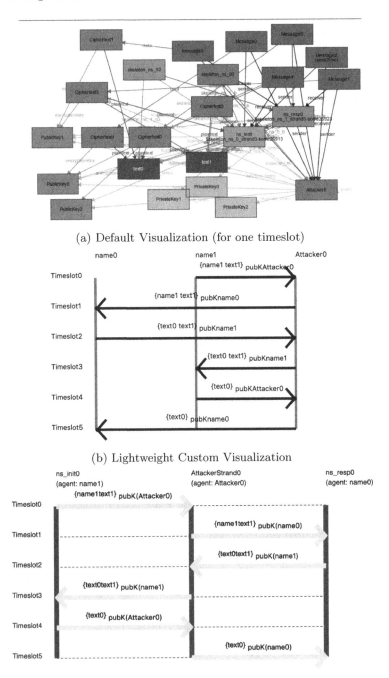

(a) Default Visualization (for one timeslot)

(b) Lightweight Custom Visualization

(c) Full Custom Visualization

Fig. 4. Three different visualizations of a concrete attack on Needham-Schroeder. Here, the man-in-the-middle attack is realized by the initiator starting a session with the attacker or an agent whose private key is known to the attacker.

Development Environment. Building atop Racket gives us immediate recourse to the DrRacket IDE, which comes with useful features such as error highlighting, a Read-Eval-Print-Loop (REPL), debugging features, etc. Moreover, many other mature editors (such as Visual Studio Code) are readily usable via a language server interface.

Query Language. Forge exposes a parenthetical query language based on the first-order relational logic of Kodkod [54]. Generating the known *attack* on Needham-Schroeder (instead of a good execution) requires only asking for scenarios where both of the initiator's nonce values are eventually learned by the attacker:

```
1  (in (+ (join ns_init ns_init_n1)
2          (join ns_init ns_init_n2))
3     (join Attacker learned_times Timeslot)))
```

Section 5 gives more detailed background for the identifiers used here. For now, we observe that `ns_init` represents an initiator strand and that `ns_init_n1` and `ns_init_n2` are relations that contain the values of each nonce variable for each initiator. The `learned_times` relation represents the state of each agent's knowledge at each point in time. The values for specific strands are obtained via relational `join` (i.e., lookup), as is the attacker's knowledge across all timeslots (the `Timeslot` relation). `+` denotes union, and `in` the (possibly improper) subset relationship.

2.2   The Protocol Creator: Translating Domain-Specific Input

In CPSA's input language, the Needham-Schroeder protocol is represented by:

```
1  (defprotocol ns basic
2     (defrole init
3        (vars (a b name) (n1 n2 text))
4        (trace
5           (send (enc n1 a (pubk b)))
6           (recv (enc n1 n2 (pubk a)))
7           (send (enc n2 (pubk b)))))
8     (defrole resp
9        (vars (b a name) (n2 n1 text))
10       (trace
11          (recv (enc n1 a (pubk b)))
12          (send (enc n1 n2 (pubk a)))
13          (recv (enc n2 (pubk b)))))
14    (comment "Needham-Schroeder"))
```

The `defprotocol` construct specifies the behaviors corresponding to well-behaved protocol participants, and is the way a protocol author would describe their protocol in CPSA's domain perspective.

CPSA also provides a `defskeleton` construct, which describes fragments of execution that analysts use to search for specific protocol behaviors. For example, the Needham-Schroeder file from CPSA's example suite contains this skeleton:

```
1  (defskeleton ns
2    (vars (a b name) (n2 text))
3    (defstrand resp 3 (a a) (b b) (n2 n2))
4    (non-orig (privk a) (privk b))
5    (uniq-orig n2)
6    (comment "Responder point-of-view"))
```

which defines a particular search in the space of executions. Each `defstrand` defines a single process executing the appropriate protocol role. The 2-tuples (e.g. `(n1 n1)`) are called *maplets* in CPSA parlance, and bind values (skeleton variables) to role variables in the protocol. The `non-orig` and `uniq-orig` annotations give constraints on how principals may behave. They enforce that these values are freshly chosen and either never sent by a principal in decryptable form (`non-orig`), or that their appearance originates on a single strand (`uniq-orig`).

One advantage of CPSA's parenthetical language is that no parser is required to process it; Racket macros can expand protocol and skeleton definitions directly into Forge formulas. While Racket permits non-parenthetical syntaxes [16], this underlying parenthetical layer saves domain modelers of having to construct source by unwieldy and bug-inducing string concatenation, as often happens when mapping to other tools. We trust that the Verified LISP [21] instantiation of Joshua Guttman would especially appreciate this.

2.3   Scripting and Extensibility

Users at any level may wish to script analysis in Forge for their own purposes. They might wish to numerate protocol runs for pattern mining, generate "ensembles" of differing runs, work with the solver iteratively [33], etc.

The core of Forge is implemented as a library in Racket. Users may work with the logic language directly (akin to what Alloy's UI provides), or use Forge as a library in a larger program. While Forge is meant to be used for prototyping "solver-aided" languages, it differs from tools like Rosette [52] by sharply separating the logic language from Racket. Thus, the engine need not be able to reason about (e.g.) recursion or other programming constructs, although computation over the logic language can still be scripted. The formula derived from a CPSA `defprotocol` s-expression can be used either as a helper predicate in the logic language or as a programmatic object in Racket. Likewise, the custom visualization applies to both naive scenario enumeration and custom exploration strategies [27,37,45].

Roadmap. After some brief background (Sect. 3), this paper covers the technical heart of the prototype: the core model (Sect. 4), the translation from CPSA inputs to supplemental constraints (Sect. 5), and custom visualization (Sect. 6), which includes graphical demonstrations on further example protocols. We then examine performance (Sect. 7), summarize related work (Sect. 8) and conclude with a discussion of lessons learned (Sect. 9).

3   Relational Model Finding

Model-finding tools find concrete solutions that satisfy a given set of declarative constraints. *Relational* model-finders, of which Alloy [23] is an especially popular example, take input in a relational constraint language and produce relational structures as output. Alloy's core engine, Kodkod [54], translates input constraints into boolean logic and then invokes an off-the-shelf SAT-solver. There are various enhancements to Kodkod, such as Pardinus [10], which Forge uses directly. However, since all these derive from Kodkod, we will disambiguate by using it as our exemplar when we speak of Forge's solver engine.

We borrow from Milicevic [33] and others by calling the input to Kodkod a *specification*, rather than the broader Alloy community's use of "model". Using "model" in this way would conflict with the fact that, in a mathematical context, the term describes an interpretation for a (relational) language—which is the type of a model-finder's *output*, not its input.

4   Modeling Protocol Executions

Our base specification provides a generic framework into which individual protocols and skeletons may be instantiated. This common framework defines the notion of message passing between strands, the knowledge of various agents involved in protocol execution, the construction of ciphertext terms, and many other ideas central to approximating the strand-space perspective.

The sorts and subsorting relationships in our specification largely echo the basic CPSA algebra: a top-level `mesg` sort for arbitrary values, `skey` and `akey` sorts for symmetric and asymmetric keys, `text` for plain values like nonces, etc. An ordered `Timeslot` sort serves as an index for message events. Relations on these sorts track key ownership (`owners`, `pairs`), long-term keys (`ltks`), message contents (`data`), the state of each agent's knowledge at any given time (`learned_times`), ciphertext contents (`plaintext`), and other essential properties of a protocol run.

Using this relational signature, the specification imposes well-formedness criteria that should hold regardless of the specific protocol being examined. Briefly, these constraints include:

- standard type constraints (e.g., that every `Ciphertext` has exactly one encryption key);
- every `mesg` is a `key`, `name`, `text`, or `Ciphertext`;
- all messages are either sent to, or received from, the attacker strand;
- sent messages only include values known to the sender;
- the plaintext relation is acyclic;
- the `pairs` relation defines one unique key pair per `name`;
- the `ltks` relation defines a partial function on ordered pairs of `names`; and
- a characterization of when an agent learns a value (the contents of a message they can encrypt, a value they have just generated, their own name, etc.)

This specification approximates the strand space formalism, but in the spirit of CPSA itself, it is worth examining the explicit and implicit assumptions made and briefly discussing their consequences. Indeed, it is worth noting that Forge's bounded relational logic was not always the most natural idiom to express our goals—we return to this in Sect. 9.

Concrete Agents. One of our goals was to explicitly represent the state of each agent's knowledge throughout a protocol execution. However, in general an agent may run multiple strands of the same protocol, and so our specification separates the notion of **strand** (and its variable bindings) from the corresponding agent (and its pool of knowledge at any given time). We make this explicit in our visualization (Sect. 6) by naming every strand's corresponding principal.

An Explicit Attacker. The **Attacker** strand is synonymous with an untrusted communication medium and is thus an explicit version of the Dolev-Yao [13] adversary. We found this to be useful, both for debugging the prototype and for visualization, since it makes it easy to track exactly which messages are delayed or rewritten and what knowledge has been exposed.

Strands and Messages. A satisfying model for our specification contains a set of strands, along with information about message send and receive events. Messages may involve an arbitrary (user-bounded) number of nested encryptions. We make two simplifying assumptions. First, we do not view strands as having a length, but rather a specific pattern of send and receive events over the duration of the run. No model can contain a partial strand. Second, message components are implicitly unordered. These choices are a semantic mismatch versus CPSA—and indeed prevent detection of some attacks!—but eased first-cut development, sufficed for the examples in Sect. 7, and could be corrected via standard techniques with some engineering effort.

Origination and Pre-existing Knowledge. In CPSA, a strand *originates* a term if (broadly) that strand sends the term, and all other strands that send the term must first receive it. CPSA uses this idea to speak of a nonce being freshly created or a key never being sent by any honest participant. We echo this idea as:

```
1  pred originates[s: strand, d: mesg] { -- d originates on
       s
2    some m: sender.s | { -- m sent by strand s
3      d in subterm[m.data] -- contains d as a sub-term
4      all m2: (sender.s + receiver.s) - m | { -- all else
5        {m2 in m.^(~(next))} -- if m2 occurred before m
6        implies
7        {d not in subterm[m2.data]} -- d is not in m2
8      }
9    }
10 }
```

Moreover, since our specification explicitly represents knowledge, certain terms must originally come to be in an agent's knowledge-base. We enforce the existence of a public-private key pair for every principal, and assert that it is known in advance, along with the identities of all participants, their public keys, and any long-term keys the principal is party to.

The Evolution of Knowledge. The `learned_times` relation indicates how an agent's knowledge grows over time. For every tuple (n, v, t), where n is a name, v is a term, and t is a timeslot, (n, v, t) is in `learned_times` if and only if n can derive v at time t from prior knowledge and any message received at t. Some caution is needed: naively, this can lead to self-justifying knowledge. We use an analogy to defining the transitive closure (TC) of a relation R in first-order logic. One might be tempted (especially after seeing the idea in Datalog) to write TC as:

$$\forall x, y \mid TC(x, y) \iff (R(x, y) \lor \exists z \mid TC(x, z) \land R(z, y))$$

Unfortunately, this sentence fails to encode that TC must be the *least* such relation. Similarly, suppose we state that (1) a ciphertext term may be known if an agent knows its contents and the appropriate public key; and (2) a term within a ciphertext may be known if an agent knows the ciphertext and the matching private key. Now it is consistent for any agent to know any value, provided they also know a ciphertext wrapping both the value and its own decryption key.

We might prevent this spurious knowledge by allowing only one such action per timeslot, but that solution would prevent fully learning from messages that contain decryption keys. Any agent receiving the two values k_1 and $\{k_2, \{k_3\}_{k_2}\}_{k_1}$ must be able to learn the innermost value k_3: the key k_1 can be used to decrypt the outermost ciphertext, which itself contains a new ciphertext and key k_2 to decrypt it, and so on.

Instead, we impose a *microtick* discipline, inspired by simulation tools like Ptolemy [43]. Microticks subdivide every timeslot, providing a frame that helps ensure that knowledge is well-founded. In any microtick, knowledge may be derived only if it was just received, was known in a previous timeslot, or has been decomposed from more complex terms in a *previous* microtick. Then (n, v, t) is in `learned_times` if and only if n has just received a message and v is in the current `workspace` for some microtick.

The Challenge of Bounds. Since Kodkod, and thus Forge, uses a bounded relational logic (Sect. 3), there is an inherent incompleteness to its analysis. This includes not merely how many nonces may be generated, but also more subtle factors like the maximum term depth. Bounds also pose a user-facing challenge: at the moment, queries must provide bounds, which can require much effort and mental arithmetic to produce. Some of these issues could be ameliorated by taking advantage [39] of sorting information on terms, and others, such as the inherent bound on the number of timesteps, cannot.

5   Processing CPSA Declarations

Our prototype uses Racket macros to expand `defprotocols` and `defskeletons` to:

1. sort definitions (e.g., every `role` induces a new sub-sort of `strand`);
2. relation definitions (e.g., every role variable becomes a new relation that maps strands of that role to the variable's sort); and
3. relational formula sets (called *predicates* in Forge) that define the meaning of the protocol or skeleton.

The predicates for each protocol, skeleton, etc. can be invoked in queries, giving the user control over which aspects of the CPSA input to include in the analysis.

Because Forge builds atop Kodkod's formalism, it has only a notion of *relations*, atop which *functions* must be defined via constraints. This means that function application must be expressed via relational algebra—most commonly by using the join operator. For instance, constraints ensure that, if s is a member of the `strand` sort, then the expression (`join s agent`) evaluates to the agent running strand s. Likewise, in the Needham-Schroeder example, strands s of role `init` have a field a. This field is represented by a relation named `ns_init_a` and the value of variable a in s can be found via (`join s ns_init_a`).

5.1   Deriving Relational Constraints

For every role R in protocol P, the translator produces a Forge formula (named `exec_P_R`) that constrains the behavior of every strand of that role. In the case of roles, the main bulk of the work lies in enforcing that all strands with that role obey the provided trace declaration. E.g., in the Needham-Schroeder initiator strand, the first event must send the term (`enc n1 a (pubk b)`), and so on. One subtlety here is that Forge's constraint language has no notion of a *term* in the sense of CPSA's algebra; it has only relations. The translator cannot speak of (`enc n1 a (pubk b)`) directly to mean *the* result of encrypting n1 and a with b's public key. Consequently, we use existentially quantified variables to stand in for non-ground terms, and recursively traverse every event to ensure the proper ordering and nesting between events and terms.

For skeletons, the main challenge is in encoding the *maplets* that equate variables in the skeleton with terms over variables in strands that the skeleton contains. A responder point-of-view skeleton for Needham-Schroeder (Sect. 2.2) contains the variables a and b (names) and a text value n2. These are bound in the strand definition (`defstrand resp 3 (a a) (b b) (n2 n2)`), which says that the skeleton's a is the same as the responder strand's a, and so on. We enforce these via equality constraints on the field relations for the corresponding strand and skeleton variables.

Declarations within a skeleton, such as a unique-origination requirements, as well as listener-strand definitions, become quantified formulas as follows:

(uniq-orig v): $\exists! s : Strand \mid originates[s, v]$

(non-orig v): $\forall s : Strand \mid \neg originates[s, v]$

(listener v): $\exists t : Timeslot \mid$ (Attacker, $v, t) \in$ learned_times

That is, respectively, there is a unique strand that originates the value, no strand originates the value, and the value is compromised at some point. Should a uniq-orig declaration appears in a role R, rather than a skeleton, it applies locally to all strands r with that role:

(uniq-orig v): $(\exists! s : Strand \mid originates[s, v]) \land originates[r, v]$

5.2   Queries and Predicates

Users write queries in terms of the base and derived specifications combined. Since every role and skeleton formula is a Racket value, queries can build on, deconstruct, or otherwise manipulate these formulas. A full query formula might then look something like the following parenthetical Racket expression:

```
1  (and wellformed              ; base constraints
2       exec_reflect_init       ; initiator strand
3       exec_reflect_resp       ; responder strand
4       constrain_skeleton_ns_1) ; responder point-of-view
```

where wellformed enforces the base specification, the two exec_ predicates add strand roles, and constrain_skeleton_ns_1 asserts that only protocol runs containing skeleton 1 and its declarations should be included.

Breaking the overall query into multiple predicates has several virtues. Not only does it ease debugging, experimentation, etc. but it is also how our prototype supports CPSA-style input files with many skeletons: queries reference the pertinent skeleton(s) and no others.

6   Visualizing Strands

Alloy comes with a directed-graph-based model visualizer that has not altered much over its lifetime. In Forge, we have instead integrated the Sterling visualizer [15]. While Sterling reproduces (a slightly more modern and attractive version of) Alloy's visualizer, it also enables scripting using JavaScript and React. Thus, anyone familiar with these widely-used systems can create custom visualizations for their domain. In spite of the theoretical literature on reasoning from diagrams [3,47], we are largely unaware of other general model-finding tools that deliberately provide scaffolding for domain-specific visualization. (A notable exception is the GUPU pedagogic Prolog system [40], which lets users define visualizations over answer substitutions returned by the engine.)

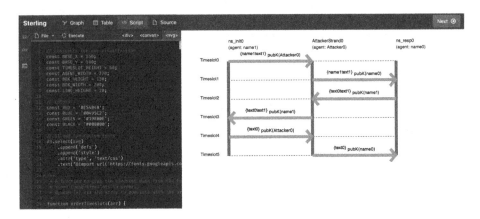

Fig. 5. The Sterling visualizer, with a Needham-Schroeder execution loaded.

Many protocol-analysis tools implement custom visualizations. Two of the most idiosyncratic are VerifPal [24] and CPSA [12], with VerifPal's more concrete display of (e.g.) agent knowledge contrasting against CPSA's minimal abstraction. We opted for a more concrete approach in order to showcase the power of custom visualizations. Figure 5 shows a full Sterling window containing a custom visualization. The left-hand pane shows the visualizer script being run—enabling changes without restarting either Sterling or Forge. The "Next" button advances to a different execution. Other key design choices include:

A Concrete Attacker. Our visualizer shows the medium of communication explicitly as an attacker who, like others, can gain knowledge over time. One downside of this approach is that, depending on strand positioning, messages may be shown "crossing over" uninvolved strands. The attacker could be factored out in alternative visualizations (perhaps replaced with a terse "..."), but we found that an explicit attacker reinforces the Dolev-Yao adversary model.

Disambiguating Key Ownership. Nonces, keys, agent names, and other data are represented in the visualizer by concrete atoms: text0 might be a nonce or secret, skey2 a symmetric key, name1 the identity of an agent, and so on. Crucially, *atoms are not the same as* CPSA-*algebra terms*: while the terms a and b may denote the same value, the atoms name0 and name1 are necessarily different. This difference is especially important for key atoms. It would be baffling to see only that a ciphertext is encrypted with akey3—an asymmetric key, but whose? Because of this, our visualizer converts key atoms to equivalent CPSA-style terms whenever possible: e.g., akey3 to pubk(name0) when akey3 is name0's public key.

Telescoping Knowledge State. If a user is trying to understand *how* a certain attack occurs, information about agents' knowledge can be vital. Yet, showing *all* knowledge quickly becomes overwhelming. To mitigate this issue, we made the visualization *interactive*: users may click to expand (or hide) agent knowledge at

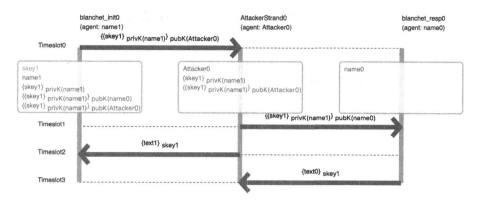

Fig. 6. A good execution of Blanchet's protocol with initial knowledge fully expanded. Freshly generated values are colored blue, and derived values (some unused) are colored red. Note also the nested ciphertexts, enabled by Sect. 4. (Color figure online)

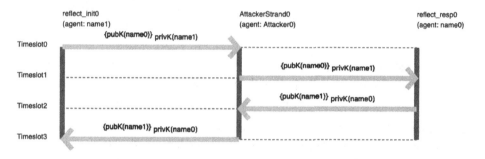

Fig. 7. A reflection attack from CPSA's example suite.

any point in time. In Sect. 2, Fig. 3 gave a magnified view of this feature; Fig. 6 shows it in the context of a full visualization of Blanchet's [4] simple example protocol. While agent knowledge is not always pertinent to understanding an attack (as in the simple reflection shown in Fig. 7), telescoping knowledge display makes it far easier to see how a value may be compromised.

7   Prototype Performance

Our goal is not to produce an optimized analysis tool, but rather a prototype that is "good enough" to iterate on. New language constructs, enrichments to the spec, or improved visualizations are all possible within the Forge framework. While some improvements such as custom search algorithms are not yet possible, many parts (especially the visualization) are portable. In addition, the prototype may be useful for validating a new, optimized engine via model-based testing.

Despite these disclaimers, honesty compels us to report performance for all examples in this paper—extreme runtimes would undermine our stated goals.

Protocol	run	sat?	Runtime (sec)
Needham-Schroeder	validation	✓	5
Needham-Schroeder	attack	✓	6
Needham-Schroeder	non-attack	✓	5
Needham-Schroeder (fixed)	validation	✓	6
Needham-Schroeder (fixed)	attack		6
Reflection	validation	✓	4
Blanchet	validation	✓	4
Blanchet	init atk		5
Blanchet	resp atk	✓	4
Blanchet (revised)	validation	✓	4
Blanchet (revised)	resp atk		5

Fig. 8. Runtime performance (rounded to nearest second).

All examples were taken from CPSA's repository (Sect. 2) and run on a 2017 MacBook Pro (i5 2.3 GHz, 8 GB RAM). Concretely, we ran on:

- the original Needham-Schroeder [35] public-key protocol;
- Lowe's [26] modification to Needham-Schroeder;
- Blanchet's simple example protocol (from the CPSA manual [25]); and
- the "reflection" protocol demo (from the CPSA example suite).

These protocols exercise a number of core ideas in the basic CPSA algebra: asymmetric key pairs, short- and long-term symmetric keys, and nested ciphertexts.

For each protocol, we first ran a *validation* check to ensure the prototype found concrete executions. All validation checks were satisfiable. For Needham-Schroeder, we demonstrated the well-known attack and verified that the attack is no longer possible in the revised version. For Blanchet's simple-example protocol, we confirmed that the secret cannot be compromised from the initiator's perspective, but that it can be from the responder's perspective. We also confirmed that this vulnerability does not exist in the revised version.

Figure 8 reports results. The **Protocol** and **run** columns indicate which analysis was being performed. The **sat?** column denotes whether the analysis was satisfiable—i.e., whether any models were produced, or if the solver completed its search empty-handed. Finally, the **Time (sec)** column reports the runtime in seconds for the analysis.

Interpretation. We find that runtime is largely uniform, in the single-digit seconds, across these simple protocols. This suggests that our (unoptimized) prototype scales reasonably to small examples. The CPSA analyzer is over an order of magnitude faster. However, roughly 2 s of Forge's time is spent on expanding the protocol and skeleton definitions and then compiling them to Racket bytecode. There may be strategies for reducing this overhead.

8   Related Work

Our end-to-end concept is partly inspired by Rosette [53], but differs significantly because of our focus on a direct encoding of domains in Forge, as well as our cultivation of domain-specific visualizations. Forge itself uses a heavily modified version of Rosette's Ocelot [6] interface to access the Kodkod [54] and Pardinus [10] relational solvers.

Our case-study prototype draws broadly from the strand-space formalism [51] and specifically from CPSA [12]. Strand spaces have been used to reason about a variety of protocols and related topics; a representative sample of which would include Guttman's work on fair exchange [20] and trust management [22]. Strand spaces also provide an interesting domain to ask foundational questions about model finding, chiefly *which* [14] models ought to be presented—a question that our prototype largely sidesteps in its present form.

There are of course several cryptographic analysis tools, such as VerifPal [24] and Proverif [4]. As our current effort focuses largely on strand spaces and CPSA's input language, from a specification perspective these other tools are largely unrelated. However, we note that Proverif's use of Horn clauses could potentially lend itself to similar prototyping in Forge. Even more, we drew inspiration from visualizations in other tools, especially Proverif, in building our prototype.

9   Discussion

We have presented the Forge system for prototyping solver-based DSLs atop Racket, and demonstrated its use in a prototype crypto-analysis tool in the vein of CPSA. The vast majority of the specification and visualization work was done by a pair of undergraduates over a (somewhat less than) one-semester course project. While we believe this work shows the viability of the approach, we would be remiss to close without first addressing a few limitations and sharing lessons learned beyond the trivial specification tricks seen in Sect. 4.

Fidelity w.r.t. CPSA. We focused our effort here on sketching Forge's language-oriented prototyping process, rather than completely conforming to the semantics of CPSA. Further refinement along these lines (such as resolving limitations mentioned in Sect. 4, automated bounds inference, support for other algebras, etc.) would have been a matter of added engineering effort for little benefit: we have no desire to actually reproduce the already-excellent CPSA in Forge, but rather make an experiment in prototyping.

Which Models? The question of *which* output model is beginning to be well studied: some works focus on minimality [37,45], or closeness to a target [10,27]. Other tools, like AUnit [48,49] and CompoSAT [42] have prioritized models based on ideas from software-testing like *coverage* and *mutation*. Works like Bordeaux [34] have even argued for producing *non-models* to ease comprehension and debugging. We largely sidestep this question here, providing the user with an Alloy-style "Next" button, but no further control. This can be frustrating, especially when compared against CPSA's sparse enumeration. We often found ourselves refining our queries and restarting the solver from scratch, rather than continuing manually. Thus, although we believe that CPSA's supreme abstractness can be a barrier to entry, especially for non-experts, we freely admit that its parsimonious output is more readily explorable at a high level than ours.

A Downside of Concreteness: Equality. Since Forge produces models in terms of concrete atoms, it is free to have one atom serve multiple purposes unless prevented by the constraints it is given. Concretely, it might return first a run of Needham-Schroeder where the initiator and responder strands are hosted by the same agent, and then another run where the agents differ. This can lead to a plethora of seemingly spurious protocol runs, unless the user adds additional constraints to their query. In contrast, CPSA does not suffer from this issue: it will not equate two terms unless it can justify doing so. It would be informative to try this prototype using a different solver, perhaps one that is more amenable to an "enrich-by-need" analysis [14].

Forge and Solvers. Forge currently uses only the Kodkod toolchain. Although it has recourse to weighted Max-SAT and other algorithmic extensions, it currently lacks a Satisfiability Modulo Theories engine. Forge is thus limited at present in its ability to reason about mathematical integers, strings, and other mainstays of SMT. Moreover, as we observed in Sect. 4, we needed non-trivial technical effort to even approximate CPSA's term algebras in Forge. However, we are encouraged by efforts to both translate relational specifications into SMT [1,19,30,50] and encode a theory of relations directly in SMT [31]. As Forge's algorithmic capabilities evolve, so too will its capacity to be used as a prototyping framework; improvements to Forge would be immediately available to domain modelers and tool authors (Fig. 1) via configuration options.

Acknowledgments. We are grateful to Joshua Guttman for many enjoyable and productive conversations. We thank the creators of CPSA for their vision, the anonymous reviewers for their feedback, and the editors for putting together this much-deserved Festschrift. This work was partly supported by the US National Science Foundation. This research was also developed with funding from the Defense Advanced Research Projects Agency (DARPA) and the Air Force Research Laboratory (AFRL). The views, opinions and/or findings expressed are those of the author and should not be interpreted as representing the official views or policies of the Department of Defense or the U.S. Government.

References

1. Abbassi, A., Day, N.A., Rayside, D.: Astra version 1.0: evaluating translations from Alloy to SMT-LIB. CoRR abs/1906.05881 (2019). http://arxiv.org/abs/1906.05881
2. Ball, T., Bounimova, E., Levin, V., Kumar, R., Lichtenberg, J.: The static driver verifier research platform. In: Touili, T., Cook, B., Jackson, P. (eds.) CAV 2010. LNCS, vol. 6174, pp. 119–122. Springer, Heidelberg (2010). https://doi.org/10.1007/978-3-642-14295-6_11

3. Barwise, K.J., Allwein, G. (eds.): Logical Reasoning with Diagrams. Oxford University Press (1996)
4. Blanchet, B.: Modeling and verifying security protocols with the applied Pi calculus and ProVerif. Found. Trends Priv. Secur. 1(1–2), 1–135 (2016)
5. Blanchette, J.C., Nipkow, T.: Nitpick: a counterexample generator for higher-order logic based on a relational model finder. In: Kaufmann, M., Paulson, L.C. (eds.) ITP 2010. LNCS, vol. 6172, pp. 131–146. Springer, Heidelberg (2010). https://doi.org/10.1007/978-3-642-14052-5_11
6. Bornholt, J., Torlak, E.: Synthesizing memory models from framework sketches and litmus tests. In: Programming Language Design and Implementation (PLDI) (2017)
7. Chudnov, A., et al.: Continuous formal verification of Amazon s2n. In: Chockler, H., Weissenbacher, G. (eds.) CAV 2018. LNCS, vol. 10982, pp. 430–446. Springer, Cham (2018). https://doi.org/10.1007/978-3-319-96142-2_26
8. Cook, B., Khazem, K., Kroening, D., Tasiran, S., Tautschnig, M., Tuttle, M.R.: Model checking boot code from AWS data centers. In: Chockler, H., Weissenbacher, G. (eds.) CAV 2018. LNCS, vol. 10982, pp. 467–486. Springer, Cham (2018). https://doi.org/10.1007/978-3-319-96142-2_28
9. Cook, B., Podelski, A., Rybalchenko, A.: TERMINATOR: beyond safety. In: Ball, T., Jones, R.B. (eds.) CAV 2006. LNCS, vol. 4144, pp. 415–418. Springer, Heidelberg (2006). https://doi.org/10.1007/11817963_37
10. Cunha, A., Macedo, N., Guimarães, T.: Target oriented relational model finding. In: Gnesi, S., Rensink, A. (eds.) FASE 2014. LNCS, vol. 8411, pp. 17–31. Springer, Heidelberg (2014). https://doi.org/10.1007/978-3-642-54804-8_2
11. Danas, N., Nelson, T., Harrison, L., Krishnamurthi, S., Dougherty, D.J.: User studies of principled model finder output. In: Cimatti, A., Sirjani, M. (eds.) SEFM 2017. LNCS, vol. 10469, pp. 168–184. Springer, Cham (2017). https://doi.org/10.1007/978-3-319-66197-1_11
12. Doghmi, S.F., Guttman, J.D., Thayer, F.J.: Searching for shapes in cryptographic protocols. In: Grumberg, O., Huth, M. (eds.) TACAS 2007. LNCS, vol. 4424, pp. 523–537. Springer, Heidelberg (2007). https://doi.org/10.1007/978-3-540-71209-1_41
13. Dolev, D., Yao, A.C.: On the security of public key protocols. IEEE Trans. Inf. Theor. 29(2), 198–207 (1983). https://doi.org/10.1109/TIT.1983.1056650
14. Dougherty, D.J., Guttman, J.D., Ramsdell, J.D.: Security protocol analysis in context: computing minimal executions using SMT and CPSA. In: Furia, C.A., Winter, K. (eds.) IFM 2018. LNCS, vol. 11023, pp. 130–150. Springer, Cham (2018). https://doi.org/10.1007/978-3-319-98938-9_8
15. Dyer, T., Baugh, J.: Sterling: a web-based visualizer for relational modeling languages. In: Raschke, A., Méry, D. (eds.) ABZ 2021. LNCS, vol. 12709, pp. 99–104. Springer, Cham (2021). https://doi.org/10.1007/978-3-030-77543-8_7
16. Felleisen, M., et al.: A programmable programming language. In: Communications of the ACM (2018)
17. Findler, R.B., et al.: DrScheme: a programming environment for Scheme. J. Funct. Program. 12(2), 159–182 (2002)
18. Fogel, A., et al.: A general approach to network configuration analysis. In: Networked Systems Design and Implementation, pp. 469–483 (2015). https://doi.org/10.5555/2789770.2789803
19. Ghazi, A.A.E., Taghdiri, M.: Analyzing Alloy formulas using an SMT solver: a case study. CoRR abs/1505.00672 (2015). http://arxiv.org/abs/1505.00672

20. Guttman, J.D.: Fair exchange in strand spaces. In: International Workshop on Security Issues in Concurrency, EPTCS, vol. 7, pp. 46–60 (2009). https://doi.org/10.4204/EPTCS.7.4
21. Guttman, J.D., Ramsdell, J.D., Wand, M.: VLISP: a verified implementation of Scheme. LISP Symb. Comput. **8**(1–2), 5–32 (1995)
22. Guttman, J.D., Thayer, F.J., Carlson, J.A., Herzog, J.C., Ramsdell, J.D., Sniffen, B.T.: Trust management in strand spaces: a rely-guarantee method. In: Schmidt, D. (ed.) ESOP 2004. LNCS, vol. 2986, pp. 325–339. Springer, Heidelberg (2004). https://doi.org/10.1007/978-3-540-24725-8_23
23. Jackson, D.: Software Abstractions: Logic, Language, and Analysis, 2nd edn. MIT Press (2012). https://doi.org/10.5555/2141100
24. Kobeissi, N., Nicolas, G., Tiwari, M.: Verifpal: cryptographic protocol analysis for the real world. In: Bhargavan, K., Oswald, E., Prabhakaran, M. (eds.) INDOCRYPT 2020. LNCS, vol. 12578, pp. 151–202. Springer, Cham (2020). https://doi.org/10.1007/978-3-030-65277-7_8
25. Liskov, M.D., Ramsdell, J.D., Guttman, J.D., Rowe, P.D.: The cryptographic protocol shapes analyzer: a manual. https://github.com/mitre/cpsa/blob/master/doc/cpsamanual.pdf. Accessed 6 Jun 2021
26. Lowe, G.: An attack on the Needham-Schroeder public-key authentication protocol. Inf. Process. Lett. **56**(3), 131–133 (1995). https://doi.org/10.1016/0020-0190(95)00144-2
27. Macedo, N., Cunha, A., Guimarães, T.: Exploring scenario exploration. In: Egyed, A., Schaefer, I. (eds.) FASE 2015. LNCS, vol. 9033, pp. 301–315. Springer, Heidelberg (2015). https://doi.org/10.1007/978-3-662-46675-9_20
28. Macedo, N., Guimarães, T., Cunha, A.: Model repair and transformation with Echo. In: Automated Software Engineering (2013). https://doi.org/10.1109/ASE.2013.6693135
29. Marinov, D., Khurshid, S.: TestEra: a novel framework for automated testing of Java programs. In: Automated Software Engineering (2001). https://doi.org/10.1109/ASE.2001.989787
30. McCormick, K.D., Cinelli, F.C.: Translating Alloy to SMT-LIB. Major qualifying project (b.s. thesis), Worcester Polytechnic Institute (2018)
31. Meng, B., Reynolds, A., Tinelli, C., Barrett, C.: Relational constraint solving in SMT. In: de Moura, L. (ed.) CADE 2017. LNCS (LNAI), vol. 10395, pp. 148–165. Springer, Cham (2017). https://doi.org/10.1007/978-3-319-63046-5_10
32. Milicevic, A., Misailovic, S., Marinov, D., Khurshid, S.: Korat: a tool for generating structurally complex test inputs. In: International Conference on Software Engineering (2007)
33. Milicevic, A., Near, J.P., Kang, E., Jackson, D.: Alloy*: a general-purpose higher-order relational constraint solver. In: International Conference on Software Engineering (2015)
34. Montaghami, V., Rayside, D.: Bordeaux: a tool for thinking outside the box. In: Huisman, M., Rubin, J. (eds.) FASE 2017. LNCS, vol. 10202, pp. 22–39. Springer, Heidelberg (2017). https://doi.org/10.1007/978-3-662-54494-5_2
35. Needham, R.M., Schroeder, M.D.: Using encryption for authentication in large networks of computers. Commun. ACM **21**(12), 993–999 (1978). https://doi.org/10.1145/359657.359659
36. Nelson, T., Ferguson, A.D., Scheer, M.J.G., Krishnamurthi, S.: Tierless programming and reasoning for software-defined networks. In: Networked Systems Design and Implementation (2014)

37. Nelson, T., Saghafi, S., Dougherty, D.J., Fisler, K., Krishnamurthi, S.: Aluminum: principled scenario exploration through minimality. In: International Conference on Software Engineering (2013)
38. Nelson, T., Barratt, C., Dougherty, D.J., Fisler, K., Krishnamurthi, S.: The Margrave tool for firewall analysis. In: USENIX Large Installation System Administration Conference (2010)
39. Nelson, T., Dougherty, D.J., Fisler, K., Krishnamurthi, S.: Toward a more complete Alloy. In: Derrick, J., et al. (eds.) ABZ 2012. LNCS, vol. 7316, pp. 136–149. Springer, Heidelberg (2012). https://doi.org/10.1007/978-3-642-30885-7_10
40. Neumerkel, U., Kral, S.: Declarative program development in prolog with GUPU. In: International Workshop on Logic Programming Environments, pp. 77–86 (2002)
41. Newcombe, C., Rath, T., Zhang, F., Munteanu, B., Brooker, M., Deardeuff, M.: How AWS uses formal methods. Commun. ACM **58**(4), 66–73 (2015). https://doi.org/10.1145/2699417
42. Porncharoenwase, S., Nelson, T., Krishnamurthi, S.: CompoSAT: specification-guided coverage for model finding. In: International Symposium on Formal Methods (FM) (2018)
43. Ptolemaeus, C. (ed.): System design, modeling, and simulation using Ptolemy II. Ptolemy.org (2014). http://ptolemy.org/books/Systems
44. Rupakheti, C.R., Hou, D.: An abstraction-oriented, path-based approach for analyzing object equality in Java. In: Working Conference on Reverse Engineering (2010). https://doi.org/10.1109/WCRE.2010.30
45. Saghafi, S., Danas, N., Dougherty, D.J.: Exploring theories with a model-finding assistant. In: Felty, A.P., Middeldorp, A. (eds.) CADE 2015. LNCS (LNAI), vol. 9195, pp. 434–449. Springer, Cham (2015). https://doi.org/10.1007/978-3-319-21401-6_30
46. Sergey Bronnikov: Practical FM. https://github.com/ligurio/practical-fm. Accessed 23 Jan 2021
47. Shimojima, A.: On the Efficacy of Representation. Ph.D. thesis. The Department of Philosophy, Indiana University (1996)
48. Sullivan, A., Wang, K., Zaeem, R.N., Khurshid, S.: Automated test generation and mutation testing for Alloy. In: Software Testing, Verification and Validation (ICST) (2017). https://doi.org/10.1109/ICST.2017.31
49. Sullivan, A., Zaeem, R.N., Khurshid, S., Marinov, D.: Towards a test automation framework for Alloy. In: Symposium on Model Checking of Software (SPIN). pp. 113–116 (2014). https://doi.org/10.1145/2632362.2632369
50. Tariq, Khadija: Linking Alloy with SMT-based Finite Model Finding. Master's thesis, University of Waterloo (2021). http://hdl.handle.net/10012/16756
51. Thayer, F.J., Herzog, J.C., Guttman, J.D.: Strand spaces: Proving security protocols correct. J. Comput. Secur. **7**(1), 191–230 (1999)
52. Torlak, E., Bodik, R.: Growing solver-aided languages with Rosette. In: Proceedings of the 2013 ACM International Symposium on New Ideas, New Paradigms, and Reflections on Programming & Software. SPLASH Onward! (2013)
53. Torlak, E., Bodik, R.: A lightweight symbolic virtual machine for solver-aided host languages. In: Programming Language Design and Implementation (PLDI) (2014)
54. Torlak, E., Jackson, D.: Kodkod: a relational model finder. In: Grumberg, O., Huth, M. (eds.) TACAS 2007. LNCS, vol. 4424, pp. 632–647. Springer, Heidelberg (2007). https://doi.org/10.1007/978-3-540-71209-1_49

Principles of Remote Sattestation

Paul Syverson[(✉)]

U.S. Naval Research Laboratory, Washington, D.C., USA
`paul.syverson@nrl.navy.mil`

Abstract. Joshua Guttman has collaborated with others to set out principles for attestation of trust in the setting of trusted computing. I describe herein attestation of trust in authentication of web addresses via a means of binding security into the addresses themselves, and I discuss the analogues of such attestation principles in this setting.

1 Introduction

Remote attestation and trust were explored by Joshua Guttman and co-authors in a pair of papers about a decade ago. The authors were primarily focused on trusted computing, in which a remote principal can form beliefs about computation by a trusted platform module (TPM) [9,10].

As such their roots of trust were devices that could reliably measure hardware or software behavior and devices that could reliably store information in a secrecy preserving way and, most relevant to our present concerns, attest to the results of a measurement. The work described below concerns trust on the web. (Or more accurately, trust within the web: one of our goals is to embed trust into the fabric of the web rather than derive it entirely from security mechanisms that have merely been ubolted onto its structure.) We do not build directly from the work of Joshua and his colleagues. We are looking at attesting to different phenomena, and I will consider out-of-scope the justification for grounding the roots of trust chosen. Nonetheless, the assumptions about what trust is and in-scope analogues to their principles are instructive. First, however, I should explain a bit more about the means by which trust can be built into the nodes (URLs) and arcs (hyperlinks) that comprise the web.

2 Overview of Self-authenticating Traditional Addresses

Trust for us is established through SATAs (self-authenticating traditional addresses) [18–20]. These are internet addresses based on traditional, typically human-meaningful, domain names like `apple.com`, `nrl.navy.mil`, or `wpi.edu`. But they also include a self-authenticating element that encodes a public key used in its authentication. This element is the same as an onion address.

Tor's onion addresses are self-authenticating: the address encodes a public key used to authenticate the address. Though onion addresses are an IETF standard [2] used by many Fortune 500 companies, government agencies, and

D. Dougherty et al. (Eds.): Guttman Festschrift, LNCS 13066, pp. 414–424, 2021.
https://doi.org/10.1007/978-3-030-91631-2_23

major media and news organizations, they are generally only reachable via the Tor network, typically via Tor Browser. The Tor Project's overview of onion services [1] provides a basic description, a list of some notable onionsites, and links to further documentation. Though self-authenticating, onion addresses are comprised only of an encoding of a public key. They thus generally appear to be meaningless, random-looking strings, though some large sites commit significant computational resources to make a portion of the address meaningful, e.g., `facebookwkhpilnemxj7asaniu7vnjjbiltxjqhye3mhbshg7kx5tfyd.onion`.

Thus a SATA for the base domain `example.com` can be given as `[onion-address].example.com`, where `[onion-address]` is a 56 character string comprising a base-32 encoding of an ed25519 key, and a checksum and a few other things [16]. This subdomain format of SATA was described in [20]. Usability improvements for both client users and service operators are made possible via the query-string format introduced in [19], in which the URL-bar display for this example would be `https://example.com/?onion=[onion-address]`.

Another advantage of SATAs is that they support discovery of the SATA simply by redirection from a given domain, while still maintaining that same domain in the URL bar and using the same TLS certificate. SATAs and sattestation thus counter attacks that are possible when redirection is to an ordinary onion address [19]. And the query-string format additionally counters the problem noted by Reynolds et al. [17] that "when examining confusing URL transforms, we found that users were least able to understand URLs with long subdomains/FQDNs."

Unlike plain onion addresses, visiting a SATA also does not require routing over Tor. Indeed, browsers that know nothing about Tor or onion addresses will process a SATA the same as any domain visited via HTTPS. Browsers that understand SATAs gain additional authentication protections, which we will explain presently. And, if Tor Browser is used, the additional routing and address lookup protections of an onion address are provided, but with the bonus of a displayed URL for a meaningful domain name rather than just a random-looking encoding of a public key. SATAs do not abandon the traditional web root of trust in certificate authorities (CAs), but they do supplement it so that, for example, CAs cannot simply usurp a website's autonomy over its own authentication by fraudulently or mistakenly issuing a TLS certificate. To be explicit, these are not alternative roots sufficient to provide the same trust. Rather they are additional roots that must occur in appropriate combination with existing roots (CAs) in order for trust to be established in the authentication of the address in question.

Connecting to a SATA is authenticated by the traditional mechanisms of TLS and TLS certificates, but to support autonomy of site owners, it is also authenticated by a credential, sent as an HTTP header, that attests to the binding of the domain name, the onion address, and optionally contextual labels about the type of site, e.g., that it is a news media site, or is a domain owned by Microsoft. We call such an attestation a *sattestation*. Such sattestations are made by a SATA, either a third-party SATA, or by a SATA about itself, in which case it also includes a fingerprint of the TLS certificate. We will return to third-party sattestations below.

After the TLS handshake, SATA-aware services send an HTTP header signed by the private key corresponding to [onion-address], i.e., the self-sattestation credential. The header data includes a timestamp, the domain name, the onion address, and a fingerprint of a TLS certificate. A self-sattestation for our running example in JSON format is given in Fig. 1. The TLS certificate should itself be for example.com and should contain [onion-address].example.com as an subject alternative name (SAN). In this way the TLS certificate and the signed HTTP header authenticate each other: by including this alternative name the TLS certificate indicates that the domain name example.com is bound to the onion address, [onion-address], and the signed HTTP header also authenticates that the TLS certificate, the domain name, and the onion address are all bound together. (The figure reflects that we have the flexibility to handle the case that a site might use multiple different TLS certificates and the self-sattestation will work for a connection using any of them as long as the fingerprint is given.)

```
{ "sattestation":  {
   "sattestation_version":1,
   "sattestor_domain":"example.com",
   "sattestor_onion":"..." // sattestor's onion addr.
   "sattestor_refresh_rate":"7 days",
   "sattestees": [
   {
   // bind domain to a self auth. address
     "domain": "example.com",
     "onion": "...",   // same as sattestor
     "cert_fingerprint": ["632B119944 ...",
                          "23964A1368 ..."],
     "issued": "2021-06-01",
     "refreshed_on": "2021-10-25"  } ]
   },
   // signature by sattestor
   "signature": "..." }
```

Fig. 1. An example sattestation in JSON format

A SATA-aware browser, such as one incorporating the Firefox WebExtension we have implemented for this, will verify the onion signature, and verify that the signed information matches the TLS certificate and its contents, and that the header timestamp is within a validity window (default of one week). A connection by client Alice to https://example.com/?onion=[onion-address] cannot be validated by a TLS certificate that does not match the SATA header and signature. Thus, a CA cannot issue a fraudulent certificate that Alice will accept for this SATA because an attacker's service attempting to authenticate a connection to it will not have the private key corresponding to that address.

2.1   Third-Party Sattestation

A CA could still issue a fraudulent certificate for [onion-address2].example.com, where the adversary holds the private key corresponding to [onion-address2]. How is Alice to know which address to trust with any greater assurance than that already provided by the TLS PKI? This is where an additional root of trust is needed. Unlike [9], the attestation statements that principals make regarding SATAs are of a single simple kind, specifically that the components of a SATA are properly bound together. In particular that the traditional domain name and the self-authenticating onion address belong to the same entity. Suppose Alice trusts Tom to make assertions about the binding of [onion-address] to example.com and Alice receives [onion-address].example.com on a channel she trusts to be authenticated to Tom. For example, this could be on a business card he hands her, in a GPG signed message, in a link to https://example.com/?onion=[onion-address] sent via Signal, etc. Tom could be the owner of example.com or it could be that Alice trusts him to only make such an assertion if he has verified that the entity who manages example.com also possesses the private key associated with [onion-address]. We are only concerned with attestations about the binding of SATAs. They are not meant to, e.g., indicate anything about the veracity of content found at the SATA, reliability of services or goods offered there, etc. We have chosen to call such attestations, 'sattestations' to reinforce the narrow scope of these attestations and avoid confusions with any other type of attestations.

An important property that such sattestations support is *dirt-simple trust*. Ordinarily for Alice to trust that she has been directed in a hijack-resistant way to a domain, she would need to receive additional statements from Tom at least about the current TLS key. Such are already provided by verification of a TLS handshake. But that is rooted in trust of statements by CAs, and we are seeking trust that site owners can control in a way that CAs cannot usurp or be tricked into granting through certificate hijack, a recognized significant problem [3,4]. With SATAs, if Alice has a properly configured browser (and other software and hardware is all proper), then she can simply be given an address from someone she trusts and that is sufficient. The address is all she needs. And if that address is, e.g., in a Signal message, then she only needs to follow the link and she is done. If Tom wanted to sattest to the binding of [onion-address].example.com he could also do so by posting that sattestation on his web page that itself has a SATA. If Alice trusted the binding of the SATA for his page (e.g. by one of the above methods) and trusted its association with Tom, that posting could serve as a sattestation.

Of course to learn about these sattestations, Alice must either request or receive a message from Tom or visit his SATA. The sattestation credential format introduced in [19] not only provides a standardized way for Tom to make sattestations, it also allows a sattestee site to send to clients third-party sattestations it has been granted without the client needing to directly contact the sattestor. These third-party sattestations have essentially the same format as the self-sattestation illustrated in Fig. 1, just without the limitation that the sattestor be the same as the sattestee. They also do not need to include certificate fingerprints: Tom is not making an assertion about binding of a TLS certificate to [onion-address] or example.com, only that these are bound to each other. Continuing with the above personal trust scenario, most sites would not be inclined to provide sattestations from Alice's friend Tom. So retrievals of sattestations directly from Tom might still be needed unless the site is specifically associated with Tom in some way or some other means of discovering them is devised.

But the same structures scale up nicely so that, e.g., if Alice trusts a base Microsoft SATA for sattestations about Microsoft, then this could support sattestations from that SATA about SATAs for live.com, office.com, office.net, microsoftonline.com, msn.com, etc. Note that even at the enterprise level, the trust we establish remains contextual. If Microsoft were trusted to provide sattestations for any site, e.g. apple.com, or nrl.navy.mil, then this would effectively be the same sort of purely structural trust already afforded CAs. To support contextual trust, our JSON sattestation credentials also support contextual labels. The above sites would likely have a *microsoft* or similar label, while, nrl.navy.mil might have a label for the U.S. Government or the Department of Defense. And clients are likely to have preloaded trusted sattestors for at least the largest, most significant entities. For government agencies, this could help obviate very real large-scale DNS attacks against them [13,14].

Likewise, even companies that are not huge can create sattestations for their domains and preconfigure employee and contractor browsers to require sattestations for these and trust a corporate SATA to sign them. This can help resist leaking login credentials or sensitive data to a hijacker site. And, a web-based VPN could be hosted at a SATA to make it hijack-resistant. Man in the Middle attacks have occurred against domains not intended to be reachable—much less accessed—by the public [7]. Making SAT versions of these domains can provide defense in depth against attacks on these internal namespaces.

2.2 Trust Yourself..., But Verify

Joshua has also explored body area networks (BANs) where "no central trusted parties can be the root of trust except that the user trusts herself" [15]. One of the virtues of sattestation is that the same mechanisms that support centralized trust at the scale of all of .gov will also support decentralized trust from individuals, small organizations, etc. In other words these mechanisms scale both up and down. Similarly, Alice can include amongst those SATAs she trusts, a list of SATAs that she has validated herself.

Many notions called 'trust' are transitive [12], though this is also sometimes criticised [8]. Like [9] our notion is not inherently transitive. Suppose Alice trusts Tom's sattestation of a SATA for Freedom of the Press Foundation (FPF). And suppose Alice sees a sattestation by that FPF SATA of a SATA for CNN. Even if she thus justifiably believes that this sattesation was made by FPF, she should not trust this sattestation unless she additionally trusts the FPF SATA to make such sattestations [20].

Nonetheless, if Alice trusts Tom to evaluate the trustworthiness of some principals to provide sattestations, then he could indicate to her that he thinks FPF is to be trusted as a sattestor (of, e.g., SAT addresses labeled *news*). As a more broadly applicable example, if Alice trusts the General Services Administration to evaluate the trustworthiness of U.S. government and military SATAs to provide appropriate sattestations, then a trusted GSA SATA could indicate to her, e.g., that it thinks that a given SATA for `navy.mil` is to be trusted as a sattestor of SAT addresses labeled *navy*. It is practical to be able to reason about such cases with formal statements. [20] simply disallows such iterated trust, and though it mentions the possibility of contextual labels, it provides no means to express or reason about them. An implementation supporting such labeled sattestations and ability to express explicitly transitive trust is described in [19]. And we are in the process of producing a formal language and logic of sattestations to support reasoning about these that will be presented in future work.

Further, if sattestations were implicitly transitive in the usual sense, notions of autonomy from centralized trust authorities would become more problematic, even with general max-flow, min-cut or similar limitations on trust propagation. Limiting iteration of trust to cases where specific iterations or contextual classes of iterations are explicitly assumed permits greater flexibility without letting go of independence from third-party authorities.

3   Principles of (S)attestation

The above is a quick overview of SATAs and sattestation, and the reader is encouraged to consult the cited papers and search for ones published since this was written for more details and developments. This overview is hopefully sufficient to revisit the principles of remote attestation set out in [9,10], and see how they apply to sattestations.

Before stating the principles, we note that the meaning we attach to "trust" is the same as given in [9].

Principal B trusts principal A with regard to the statement φ if and only if, from the fact that A has said φ, B infers that φ was true at a given time.

The first principle is,

Principle 1 (Fresh information): *Assertions about the target should reflect the running system, rather than just disk images. While some measurement tools may provide start-up time information about the target, others will inspect the current state of an active target. An attestation architecture should ensure access to the live state of the target.*

I have stated the principle in its entirety. Obviously much of it is about attesting to the state of running software. I have presented it in its entirety to underscore that. While sattestations do not need to be made about the current state of software running on a web server, they do include a timeliness window that provides a freshness guarantee. The default is set to a week to allow for clock skew at the browser of up to 3.5 days in the past or the future of the sattestation, but other windows are possible. A self-sattestation that is not fresh (within the window) will not be accepted by the WebExtension, which will produce an error message, and the connection will not be allowed to continue.

SATAs thus also support timeliness guarantees for certificate revocation without the overhead or problems associated with revocation lists or OCSP (or OCSP stapling or OCSP must-staple). This is a side benefit to their primary purpose of strengthening authentication and requires no additional overhead. A site wanting to revoke a TLS certificate simply stops providing SATA headers attesting to that certificate. A browser aware of that SATA (or once SATAs are widespread enough, configured to expect SATAs for any site) will not complete the connection and will instead raise a warning. Until SATAs and sattestation checks are widespread, however, it is necessary to continue relying on existing mechanisms. But SATAs have the ultimate potential to greatly reduce the costs of supporting revocation, and they already support a form of revocation that does not force a site owner to depend on CAs.

Finally, the TLS handshake will still have its freshness guarantees limiting decency to initiation of the handshake—provided the TLS key is still valid. Thus, sattestation decency is limited to the window provided in the self-sattestation header, which is still within the current decency requirements for OCSP if set to default values. But, absent TLS problems that sattestation is designed to counter, the overall decency guarantee for the connection is since the session was established. (I will not discuss freshness issues or other concerns stemming from permitting TLS session resumption in this paper.)

Principle 2 (Comprehensive information): *Attestation mechanisms should be capable of delivering comprehensive information about the target, and its full internal state should be accessible to local measurement tools.*

SATA headers and sattestations are only about the (timely) binding of the elements of a SATA. So, this principle can either be viewed as having no sattestation analogue or as having one that is always trivial to satisfy.

Principle 3 (Constrained disclosure): *A target should be able to enforce policies governing which measurements are sent to each appraiser.*

In general this is another principle without *direct* analogue. Sattestation does not imply any approval or attestation by the sattestee of the sattestor. In principle, it should not matter to the owner of a SATA if an entirely unfriendly or disreputable entity wants to provide a sattestation for that SATA. A SATA can, however, specify the labels under which it considers itself classifiable, e.g. *government.* Then unless a client trusts a sattestor to issue sattestations with that label, it will not trust sattestations from that sattestor for that sattestee.

SATAs do, nonetheless, support a number of disclosure protections. First, signing of headers is implemented so that signing with onion keys can be done offline (e.g., each week). This means that the key to authenticate the SATA header is less vulnerable to exposure than the key certified for TLS handshakes.

Second, SATAs are in general ordinary domains with DNS records. If desired, however, e.g., for domains not intended to be used by the public, lookup information can be given only to the Tor onion service directory system under its onion address. We briefly describe this, but readers not familiar with onion services and their protocols may wish to consult [1]. The onion service directory system is comprised of a regularly rotating distributed hash table of Tor relays where even the Tor relay holding lookup information for a specific onion service cannot in general discover for which onion addresses it has lookup information: the lookup record is stored under a hash of the onion address. So the relevant directory relays must know the onion address in order to determine the record, which is similarly cryptographically protected. And the authentication of lookup and access for connecting via onion service protocols uses a key delegation system permitting offline signatures even for realtime authenticating of the connection, separate from authenticating the TLS handshake or SATA header [16].

Third, as noted, which onion addresses a relay holds cannot be discovered without knowing the onion address already. In addition, the records can be stored so that, without an authentication key known to trusted clients, it will not be possible to know for which onion address a lookup record was recovered or to decrypt the information in that record—which is needed to know where and how to connect to the onion service [16].

Principle 4 (Semantic explicitness): *The semantic content of attestations should be explicitly presented in logical form.*

Coker et al. go on to state, "The identity of the target should be determined by this semantics, so an appraiser can collect attestations about it. The appraiser should be able to infer consequences from several attestations, e.g., when different measurements of the target jointly imply a prediction about its behavior. Hence, attestations should have uniform semantics and be composable using valid logical inferences" [9].

As already noted, a logic for sattestations is in development including a soundness result that effectively says that a principal trusts a sattestation for a SATA only if there is a chain of sattestations from a trusted root sattestation to that one. The logic is still being developed at the time of writing, and setting it out in full is, in any case, beyond the intended scope of this paper.

Principle 5 (Trustworthy mechanism): *Appraisers should receive evidence of the trustworthiness of the attestation mechanisms on which they rely. In particular, the attestation architecture in use should be identified to both appraiser and target.*

The last principle is one that sattestations, at least as currently conceived, do not support down to the root level. While the structure above the root level is identified, the reason that a client trusts a sattestor for a particular SATA or class of SATAs is not standardized in some equivalent of an architecture of measurement attestors, reporting attestors, storage attestors, etc. It is generally outside of our scope to say why Alice trust Tom to sattest to some SATA. This is not an accident. Sattestations are meant to support contextual, not merely structural trust.

It may be that Alice's trust in Tom reflects a human personal trust relationship on which this is based. Or, as already noted, it may be institutional: Alice may trust a particular Microsoft SATA to sattest to any SATA that declares itself as belonging to Microsoft, or some U.S. Government sattestor for any .gov or .mil SATAs, etc.

Nonetheless, it is possible to have general and standardized evidence of trustworthiness of sattestation. For example, a CA supporting sattestations could set out both the standard criteria for issuance of, e.g., a Domain Validation (DV) certificate as given in CA/Browser Forum Guidelines [5] coupled with a simultaneous check of control over an onion key included in a SATA that is a SAN in a certificate and that is used to sign the domain(s) checked by existing means. No CA currently does this for subdomain SATAs per se. But the CA/Browser Forum Guidelines stipulate checking possession of the private onion key for a certificate in which a corresponding .onion address is either the subject or an alternative name. And HARICA has recently begun issuing DV certificates for .onion addresses. Others have been issuing EV certificates for these for several years. Since for any certificate containing both a domain name and an onion address, issuance involves both the usual checks for control of the registered domain and possession of the private onion key, this amounts to an implicit structural sattestation from the CA. Of course it is limited to the checks that a CA performs during issuance, and as noted, strengthening authentication beyond the hijack-resistance of such issuance is a primary motivation for SATAs and sattestation.

Evidence of such checks and issuance would be included in Certificate Transparency (CT) logs [6]. CT logs are independently-operated and publicly-accessible append-only ledgers of certificates issued by CAs. Major browsers include checks during a TLS handshake for a signed certificate timestamps (SCT), a commitment by a CT log to include the certificate in its ledger. Tor Browser currently does not natively support such checks, though the steps needed to do so have been investigated [11]. Further, Tor Browser still currently benefits from the public availability and general support for checking of them, e.g., at https://crt.sh. Because of the availability of CT logs and the rules regarding issuance of certificates, it is thus possible to have architectural evidence of the trustworthiness of structural sattestations from CAs, but ultimately rooted in the limited authentication assurances of certificate issuance.

This leads to a related advantage of such evidence being contained in CT logs: it would separate cases of fraudulent issuance by CAs from DNS hijack or other attack occurring during issuance. (The CA would not be able to show that someone possessing the private onion key had participated in the issuance unless it can produce a signature using that key that it received during issuance.) That plausible deniability of such an attack is removed could thus serve as an incentive for a CA to market itself as an inherently more trustworthy (because verifiable) issuer of certificates. Thus, it is not without any advantages. Nonetheless, what such sattestations gain in scalability they lose in context. There is no contextual reason to trust the CA's sattestations for such bindings because there is no contextual reason to trust the CA's check of control over a domain. Trust becomes merely structural. For contextual trust, contextual sattestations would still be needed.

In this paper we have looked at attestation principles as set out by Joshua Guttman and his collaborators. In particular, we have explored how such principles apply beyond their original intended setting of trusted computing. We have found them to have illuminating analogues in the setting of what might be called *trusted webbing*, building security into the web itself (via SATAs and sattestation). Of course this depends on the correctness of the security protocols that establish and validate this built-in security. Establishing correctness of security protocols is the topic of other work by Joshua, perhaps the work for which he is best known, but alas, a topic for another paper.

References

1. Onion services. https://community.torproject.org/onion-services/
2. Appelbaum, J., Muffett, A.: The .onion special-use domain name (2015). https://tools.ietf.org/html/rfc7686
3. Birge-Lee, H., Sun, Y., Edmundson, A., Rexford, J., Mittal, P.: Bamboozling certificate authorities with BGP. In: 27th USENIX Security Symposium, pp. 833–849. USENIX Association (2018)
4. Birge-Lee, H., Sun, Y., Edmundson, A., Rexford, J., Mittal, P.: Using BGP to acquire bogus TLS certificates. In: Hot Topics in Privacy Enhancing Technologies (HotPETs) (2017)
5. CA/Browser Forum Baseline Requirements Certificate Policy for the Issuance and Management of Publicly-Trusted Certificates, Version 1.6.9. https://cabforum.org/wp-content/uploads/CA-Browser-Forum-BR-1.6.9.pdf (27 March 2020)
6. Certificate Transparency. https://certificate.transparency.dev/
7. Chen, Q.A., Osterweil, E., Thomas, M., Mao, Z.M.: MitM attack by name collision: cause analysis and vulnerability assessment in the new gTLD era. In: 2016 IEEE Symposium on Security and Privacy (SP), pp. 675–690. IEEE (2016)
8. Christianson, B., Harbison, W.S.: Why isn't trust transitive? In: Lomas, M. (ed.) Security Protocols 1996. LNCS, vol. 1189, pp. 171–176. Springer, Heidelberg (1997). https://doi.org/10.1007/3-540-62494-5_16
9. Coker, G., et al.: Principles of remote attestation. Int. J. Inf. Secur. **10**(2), 63–81 (2011)
10. Coker, G., Guttman, J., Loscocco, P., Sheehy, J., Sniffen, B.: Attestation: evidence and trust. In: Chen, L., Ryan, M.D., Wang, G. (eds.) ICICS 2008. LNCS, vol. 5308, pp. 1–18. Springer, Heidelberg (2008). https://doi.org/10.1007/978-3-540-88625-9_1
11. Dahlberg, R., Pulls, T., Ritter, T., Syverson, P.: Privacy-preserving & incrementally-deployable support for Certificate Transparency in Tor. Proc. Priv. Enhancing Technol. **2021**(2), 194–213 (2021)
12. Fagin, R., Halpern, J.Y.: I'm OK if you're OK: on the notion of trusting communication. J. Philos. Logic **17**, 329–354 (1998)
13. Hirani, M., Jones, S., Read, B.: Global DNS hijacking campaign: DNS record manipulation at scale, 9 January 2019. https://www.fireeye.com/blog/threat-research/2019/01/global-dns-hijacking-campaign-dns-record-manipulation-at-scale.html

14. Krebs, C.C.: Emergency directive 19-01: mitigate DNS infrastructure tampering, 22 January 2019. https://cyber.dhs.gov/assets/report/ed-19-01.pdf
15. Li, M., Yu, S., Guttman, J.D., Lou, W., Ren, K.: Secure ad hoc trust initialization and key management in wireless body area networks. ACM Trans. Sens. Netw. **9**(2), 1–35 (2013)
16. Mathewson, N.: Next-generation hidden services in Tor (Tor proposal 224). https://gitweb.torproject.org/torspec.git/tree/proposals/224-rend-spec-ng.txt
17. Reynolds, J., et al.: Measuring identity confusion with uniform resource locators. In: Proceedings of the 2020 CHI Conference on Human Factors in Computing Systems, pp. 1–12. ACM (2020). https://doi.org/10.1145/3313831.3376298
18. Syverson, P.: The once and future Onion. In: Foley, S.N., Gollmann, D., Snekkenes, E. (eds.) ESORICS 2017. LNCS, vol. 10492, pp. 18–28. Springer, Cham (2017). https://doi.org/10.1007/978-3-319-66402-6_3
19. Syverson, P., Finkel, M., Eskandarian, S., Boneh, D.: Attacks on onion discovery and remedies via self-authenticating traditional addresses. In: Livraga, G., Park, N. (eds.) ACM Workshop on Privacy in the Electronic Society, WPES 2021. ACM Press (November 2021)
20. Syverson, P., Traudt, M.: Self-authenticating traditional domain names. In: 2019 IEEE Secure Development (SecDev), pp. 147–160. IEEE (September 2019)

Author Index

Printed in the United States
by Baker & Taylor Publisher Services